# THE EVOLUTION OF NATIONAL WILDLIFE LAW

## Revised & Expanded Edition

## Michael J. Bean

Environmental Defense Fund

PRAEGER SPECIAL STUDIES • PRAEGER SCIENTIFIC

Library of Congress Cataloging in Publication Data

Bean, Michael J., 1949-
    The evolution of national wildlife law.

    Includes index.
    1. Wildlife conservation—Law and legislation—United
States.   I. Title.
KF5640.B4    1983        346.7304′695          83-11138
ISBN 0-03-063503-9        347.3064695
ISBN 0-03-063502-0 (pbk.)

Published in 1983 by Praeger Publishers
CBS Educational and Professional Publishing
a division of CBS Inc.
521 Fifth Avenue, New York, NY 10175 USA

Printed in the United States of America
on acid-free paper

*to*
*Amanda Starr Bean*

# FOREWORD

It has been suggested that there are irreconcilable differences between the study of the environment and the practice of law. Proponents of this alleged conflict cite as evidence John Muir's observation on ecology that "when we try to pick out one thing by itself, we find it hitched to everything else in the universe" and, in contrast, the description of legal reasoning proposed by the late Thomas Reed Powell of Harvard Law School: "If you can think of a thing that is inextricably linked to a second thing, without thinking of that second thing, then you have a good legal mind."

Since 1977 those who disagree with this dichotomy have had a powerful counterargument, for in that year *The Evolution of Natural Wildlife Law* first appeared. To ecologists and the ordinary layman as well as to other lawyers it provided a comprehensible and engaging account of the development of wildlife conservation law in this country with all its unexpected links and hitches. Michael Bean, its author, managed to bridge these two disciplines in order to produce a ready and reliable reference for understanding the many conservation laws now in force and the major court decisions construing them.

Since its initial publication by the President's Council on Environmental Quality, *The Evolution of National Wildlife Law* has come to be widely regarded as the single authoritative text on the subject of wildlife conservation law. It is used as a standard teaching text in law school classes and in natural resource management graduate programs. In the Justice and Interior Departments, there is scarcely a natural resources lawyer's office without it. In the private conservation sector, copies are dog-eared and well worn.

Because *The Evolution of National Wildlife Law* has been so valuable to so many, this second edition will doubtless be welcomed enthusiastically. It encompasses all the material in the original edition plus analyses of the many new conservation laws and court decisions in the six years since that original edition. Like its predecessor, this work is an essential addition to the library of anyone interested in, and committed to, the cause of wildlife conservation. It is thorough, incisive, and altogether readable. I applaud it, recommend it to conservationists everywhere, and take particular pride that the support of World Wildlife Fund–U.S. has helped make this worthy contribution possible.

> Russell E. Train
> President, World Wildlife Fund–
>     U.S.
> former Administrator, Environ-
>     mental Protection Agency, and
> Chairman, President's Council on
>     Environmental Quality

# ACKNOWLEDGEMENTS

One of the satisfactions that writing a second edition of anything provides is the oppportunity to express gratitude to those who were insufficiently acknowledged in the original edition. Two people in particular deserve my special thanks in that regard because of the trust they placed in me to carry out an assignment for which I had little proven reputation. They are Frederick Anderson, then the Executive Director of the Environmental Law Institute, and Gary Widman, then the General Counsel of the President's Council on Environmental Quality. The confidence that both of them placed in me bolstered my own resolve not to disappoint them.

Gary Widman deserves credit as well for persuading me to prepare this second edition. As Associate Solicitor for Fish, Wildlife and Parks in the Department of the Interior, he saw the need to keep current the analysis that the first edition provided.

I owe special thanks to World Wildlife Fund–United States and its President, Russell Train, whose support of my efforts over the years has made this project and other endeavors possible. In part, the material in this second edition is derived from a report done for the Department of the Interior in 1981 with support from the Department, the National Oceanic and Atmospheric Administration, and the Council on Environmental Quality. The principal research assistance for the preparation of that report was provided by James Rathvon. Others who contributed research assistance were George Utting and Michelle Wiseman. Much of the cite checking was done by volunteer paralegal Leslie Nickel. The preparation of the final manuscript required long hours of typing and consumed many weekends and evenings. To Ken Walsh and Joan Dolby, who cheerfully endured that ordeal, I am deeply indebted.

Finally, to Amanda Bean, who saw a little less of her father, and to Sandy Bean, who saw a lot less of her husband, during the writing of this book, I am most indebted. As before, Sandy pitched in with helpful proofreading and editing. Amanda did as much as any two-year-old could do—she gave me added reason to want to save some of the wild places and wild creatures that I have been fortunate to enjoy.

Michael Bean

# CONTENTS

## PART II
## THE MAJOR THEMES OF FEDERAL WILDLIFE LAW

**PART III**
**TOWARD COMPREHENSIVE FEDERAL WILDLIFE PROGRAMS**

# Chapter 1

# INTRODUCTION

> It is interesting to contemplate a tangled bank, clothed with many plants of many kinds, with birds singing on the bushes, with various insects flitting about, and with worms crawling through the damp earth, and to reflect that these elaborately constructed forms, so different from each other, and dependent upon each other in so complex a manner, have all been produced by laws acting around us.
>
> Charles Darwin
> *The Origin of Species*

The laws to which Darwin referred in the quoted passage were the laws of nature, not man. Yet it can hardly be doubted that the laws of man have also had a major impact on the tangled bank of life that Darwin described. Many of those laws have served to disentangle and destroy it; others have been intended to protect and conserve it. This book examines some of these latter laws, the federal laws to protect and conserve wildlife.

Although major federal wildlife legislation was enacted as early as 1900, and although the body of federal wildlife law is now quite voluminous and complex, until recently it had largely escaped the notice of legal commentators. Thus, prior to publication of the first edition of this work in 1977, there was no single text comprehensively analyzing wildlife law as a distinct component of federal environmental law. Nor was there much critical scrutiny of federal wildlife law in the periodical legal literature.

At the time the initial edition of this work was published, the very term "wildlife law" was novel, for few had seen fit to distinguish such a body of law from the broader categories of "environmental law" or "natural resources law." That has now clearly changed. A number of law schools now offer courses in wildlife law, for many of which the initial edition of

1

this book has been used as a basic text. In 1979, the United States Department of Justice established, within its Land and Natural Resource Division, a new Wildlife Section for the purpose of giving greater attention to the enforcement of federal wildlife conservation legislation. That Section, since expanded and renamed the Wildlife and Marine Resources Section, represents the United States in all litigation concerning the numerous federal wildlife statutes described in this text.

The original work clearly played a role in stimulating the above developments. It probably also contributed significantly to what one scholar has described as "an efflorescence of scholarship" on wildlife law.[1] Moreover, to a surprising degree, the original work proved immensely popular. It exhausted several printings and apparently reached an audience that included lawyers and nonlawyers alike.

The intense interest in the subject of wildlife law since publication of the initial edition has been matched by a greatly increased level of litigation on that subject. In the six years since publication of the initial text, the Supreme Court has decided at least ten cases presenting important questions of wildlife law. The issues addressed in these cases have included such fundamental matters as the very nature of federal and state interests in wildlife. In the lower federal courts there has been a similar intensity of activity not only by environmental, but often by commercial, interests as well.

Finally, the Congress also has not been dormant since publication of the original edition. It has enacted wholly new wildlife legislation and has made major amendments to existing statutes. All of these developments have served to render portions of the initial text increasingly outdated and less useful. The recognition of this fact was the stimulus for preparing this second edition.

Part of the difficulty of providing a focused analysis of federal wildlife law is the very fundamental fact that its boundaries are so uncertain. This uncertainty is well illustrated by reference to the now well-recognized fact that a major threat to wildlife in parts of the United States and elsewhere is posed by "acid rain," a product of high levels of atmospheric pollution. In light of that fact, the laws designed to curb air pollution would seem to be of vital importance to wildlife and therefore ought to be included in any book about "wildlife law." In this book, however, these laws will be scarcely mentioned. Similarly, zoning laws and other legal mechanisms designed to control or direct land development are critical to the preservation of wildlife habitat. Yet they too are mostly outside the scope of this work. Ultimately, the "law" of human population control may be the final

---

[1] T. Lund, American Wildlife Law 2 (1980).

determinant of the fate of much of the world's wildlife. Yet that law, to the extent that it exists,[2] is not discussed.

Quite simply, if all federal laws that have or might have some direct or indirect impact on the tangled bank of life are included under the umbrella of "wildlife law," then one can hardly exclude any law. There is no pretention that this book is that comprehensive. Rather, the laws and legal doctrines analyzed here are those that have as their express and direct purpose the regulation of wildlife or, more properly, the regulation of human utilization of wildlife. Scrupulous adherence even to that limited definition is not altogether possible, however, for there are many federal laws designed to advance a wide range of designated interests, of which wildlife conservation is but one. The most important of these laws are examined here.

If it is difficult to state precisely what constitutes federal wildlife law, some comfort can be found in the fact that it has apparently also been difficult for federal lawmakers to state precisely what constitutes wildlife. In the chapters that follow, it should become apparent that the term "wildlife" has never had a fixed and unvarying content in federal law. Indeed, its steady evolution and expansion over time is one of the important trends in the development of federal wildlife law. For purposes of this book, the term "wildlife" will be given the broadest meaning thus far recognized in federal law, encompassing all forms of nonhuman and nondomesticated animal life. In places, this edition also includes discussion of unique aspects of plant conservation under federal wildlife law. Although no compelling biological reason exists for the exclusion of plants from a definition of wildlife, plants have nonetheless occupied a conceptual status in law different from that of animals.[3]

The general question of what may be encompassed within the term "wildlife" has become even more complex as a result of the Supreme Court's 1980 decision in *Diamond v. Chakrabarty* that microorganisms produced by genetic engineering may be subject to patent protection.[4] Patentability, in the Court's view, depends not on whether the object in question is living or inanimate, but on whether it occurs in nature or is "the result of human ingenuity and research."[5] That latter distinction may be useful when considering microbes produced in a sterile laboratory but is

---

[2]*See* Elliott, Federal Law and Population Control, in Federal Environmental Law 1518–1600 (E. Dolgin & T. Guilbert eds. 1974).

[3]A very useful discussion of these differing legal concepts, as well as the bases for state and federal protection of rare plants, is found in McMahan, Legal Protection for Rare Plants, 29 Am. U.L. Rev. 515 (1980).

[4]447 U.S. 303 (1980).

[5]*Id.* at 313.

likely to be less so when applied to the myriad accomplishments of "human ingenuity and research" resulting not only from animal husbandry but from wildlife management generally.[6] Certainly, the notion that new breeds and varieties of "wild" animals might be subject to the form of ownership represented by a patent would introduce a new complexity into the questions of what wildlife is[7] and who owns it.

The discussion of federal wildlife law presented here is organized in three parts. The first Part examines the legal framework within which the development of federal wildlife law has occurred. The ancient origins of that law, including the law of feudal Europe and of England prior to the American Revolution are considered briefly as background to the nineteenth-century development of the doctrine of state ownership of wildlife. The steady erosion of that doctrine in the current century as a result of the exercise of long latent federal powers is the major focus of this first Part.

In the second Part of the book, certain major themes of federal wildlife law are considered. Among the subjects analyzed here are the principal legal mechanisms for wildlife protection and conservation, including the regulation of taking, the regulation of commerce in wildlife or wildlife products, the acquisition of wildlife habitat, and the indirect protection of wildlife and its habitat through mandatory consideration of impacts on wildlife of various development activities. Also considered in this second Part are the subjects of funding wildlife programs, the unique problem of animal damage control and the international aspects of federal wildlife law.

In the final Part of the book, three recent federal laws that attempt to provide comprehensive programs for the conservation of certain types of wildlife will be examined. These statutes include the Marine Mammal Protection Act of 1972, the Endangered Species Act of 1973, and the Fishery Conservation and Management Act of 1976.

---

[6]The Court rejected the argument that the 1930 Plant Patent Act, 35 U.S.C. §§161–164 (1976), and the 1970 Plant Variety Protection Act, Pub. L. No. 91-577, 84 Stat, 1542 (codified in scattered sections of 7, 28 U.S.C.), which provide for patent protection of new varieties of plants reproduced by asexual or sexual means respectively, reflected a recognition that artificially bred animate things were outside the compass of the general patent statute, which dates to 1793. A possible effect of this rejection is to allow the patenting of new varieties of hitherto wild animal species without enactment of any new legislative authority for that purpose.

[7]To illustrate the bizarre results that can sometimes happen when courts consider such questions, see the Canadian case of Regina v. Ojibway, 8 Criminal Law Quarterly 137 (1965–66) (Op. Blue, J.), described in United States v. Byrnes, 644 F.2d 107 (2d Cir. 1981). Allegedly, the Canadian court concluded that a pony saddled with a down pillow was a "bird" within the meaning of a statute defining the term as a "two legged animal covered with feathers." The court reasoned that two legs were the statutory minimum and that the feather covering need not be natural.

The concluding chapter of this book attempts to pull together the various strands of federal wildlife law and to describe the principal trends that have characterized its recent development. One of these important trends has already been noted, the expansion of the meaning of the very term "wildlife" as used in federal law. Related trends that will be considered include the expansion of the values recognized in law as being served by wildlife, the enlargement of the role played by the public in the development and implementation of wildlife policy, the mandating of new goals in the management of wildlife, and the changing role of science in the administration of wildlife law.

A final introductory comment to be made here is that federal wildlife law, unlike many other areas of law, is largely statutory. Apart from the nineteenth-century development of the doctrine of state ownership of wildlife and some very recent cases testing the strength of that doctrine as a basis for civil damage actions, the common law has played a minor role in the development of federal wildlife law. One consequence of this fact is that the legislative programs established by federal laws require vast administrative bureaucracies to implement them. The manner in which those bureaucracies, the names and responsibilities of which have changed repeatedly over the decades, have implemented those programs is the major subject of this book.

# Part I

# THE LEGAL FRAMEWORK

The tradition of wildlife regulation is firmly rooted in Anglo-American law. Notwithstanding that long history, disputes about the proper scope of such regulation and in particular about which governmental body is responsible for it have been frequent and recurring. In the two chapters that comprise this first Part, the constitutional foundations for state and federal wildlife regulation will be analyzed, as will certain special limitations that circumscribe that authority.

**Chapter 2**

# THE LEGAL FRAMEWORK FOR THE DEVELOPMENT OF FEDERAL WILDLIFE LAW

The ultimate source of authority for all governmental regulation in the United States is its Constitution. That document sets forth the respective powers and duties of the three branches of the federal government. It also expressly prohibits the states and the federal government from the exercise of certain powers. All powers not delegated to the federal government nor prohibited to the states, however, are "reserved to the States respectively, or to the people" by virtue of the tenth amendment to the Constitution. Thus it is often said that the federal government is a government of enumerated powers, or a "limited" government. That saying, however, is not particularly useful analytically because the Constitution's enumeration of federal powers is often couched in the most general language. By virtue of the very generality of constitutional language, the courts, and especially the United States Supreme Court, play a pivotal role in the process of constitutional interpretation, the process by which the respective legal authorities of the state and federal governments are demarcated.

This chapter examines the constitutional bases for federal authority over wildlife. It also examines the rise and fall of the very important doctrine of state ownership of wildlife, a judicially created doctrine that furnished the basis for repeated challenges to the exercise of federal authority. Before those topics are addressed, however, the ancient origins of both state and federal wildlife regulation will be explored.

## HISTORICAL ANTECEDENTS

In the history of Western thought, there is an almost unbroken tradition, starting at least as early as the Roman Empire, in which wild animals, or animals *ferae naturae,* as they were called, were regarded as occupying a nearly unique status. While in their natural state, wild animals were considered to be like the air and the oceans in that they were the property of no one. Yet unlike the air and the oceans, wild animals could become the property of anyone who captured or killed them. Apparently the only legal restriction in Rome on the right thus to acquire property in wildlife was that a private landowner had the exclusive right to reduce to possession the wildlife on his property. This restriction, however, was apparently more "a recognition of the right of ownership in land than an exercise by the State of its undoubted authority to control the taking and use of that which belonged to no one in particular but was common to all."[1]

Affirmative governmental regulation of the right to take wildlife was soon evident in feudal Europe. According to Sir William Blackstone, the eighteenth-century English legal scholar whose writings influenced Anglo-American law more than those of any other individual, the origins of game regulation in Europe were the very same as those of the feudal system itself. That is, to retain the fruits of their conquest, the feudal kings and barons of Europe sought to keep weapons out of the hands of those whom they had conquered. According to Blackstone:

> Nothing could do this more effectually than a prohibition of hunting and sporting; and therefore it was the policy of the conqueror to reserve this right to himself and such on whom he should bestow it; which were only his capital feudatories, or greater barons. And accordingly we find, in the feudal constitutions, one and the same law prohibiting the *rustici* in general from carrying arms, and also proscribing the use of nets, snares, or others engines for destroying the game.[2]

---

[1] Geer v. Connecticut, 161 U.S. 519, 523 (1896).

[2] 3 W. Blackstone, Commentaries *413. Blackstone's intense animosity toward royal privilege is quite evident in his discussion of feudal game laws. Consider the following passage, which immediately follows the passage quoted in the text:

> This exclusive privilege well suited the martial genius of the conquering troops, who delighted in a sport which in its pursuit and slaughter bore some resemblance to war....And indeed, like some of their modern successors, they had no other amusement to entertain their vacant hours; despising all arts as effeminate, and having no other learning, than was couched in such rude ditties, as were sung at the solemn carousels which succeeded these antient huntings....

Id. *414.

So too in England restrictions on hunting were very early imposed and for similar reasons. With the Saxon invasion of England around 450 A.D., land began to be parcelled out to the nobility. Such lands as were not parcelled out became known as "royal forests" in which the king alone had the right to hunt. The Norman Conquest in 1066 brought with it a great expansion of the royal forests. William Nelson, a contemporary of Blackstone, wrote that "William the Conqueror laid waste thirty-six Towns in Hampshire to make a Forest."[3] As the royal forests expanded, so too did an elaborate system of royal forest laws, together with special courts and officials charged with administering them.[4]

The Norman Conquest also witnessed an expansion beyond the Forests of the king's claimed exclusive authority to hunt. Indeed, the king soon claimed the sole right to pursue game or to take fish anywhere in the kingdom, though he frequently bestowed limited parts of that prerogative upon the favored nobility by means of various royal franchises. These included the franchises of "park" and "chase," which granted to the holder thereof the right to pursue such "superior" beasts as deer, fox, and martin across his own land, in the case of the former, or across the lands of others, in the case of the latter. Yet another franchise was that of "free-warren," which authorized its holder to kill "inferior" beasts, such as fowl and hares, in a particular area, as long as he prevented others from doing so. Similar franchises applied to fishing. A right of "free fishery" gave its holder an exclusive right of fishing in a particular river. A right of "several fishery" was essentially the same, except that it applied only in those waters adjoining the lands of the franchise holder. A "common of piscary" was a nonexclusive right to fish in particular waters.[5]

As the political system of England gradually evolved, so too did the system of wildlife regulation just described. By the thirteenth century, so many franchises of free fishery and several fishery had been granted that navigability of England's rivers was substantially impeded by the great numbers of private weirs placed in them. So great was this problem that in 1215 the Magna Charta directed their removal throughout England, a

---

[3] W. Nelson, The Laws Concerning Game (1762), quoted in W. Sigler, Wildlife Law Enforcement 3 (3d ed. 1980).

[4] Lund, British Wildlife Law before the American Revolution: Lessons from the Past, 74 Mich. L. Rev. 49, 60–61 (1975). This article appears as Chapter 2 in T. Lund, American Wildlife Law (1980); subsequent chapters provide an interesting discussion of the adaptation of English legal principles regarding wildlife by the new American states.

[5] The descriptions of the various royal franchises discussed in the text are all taken from 3 W. Blackstone, Commentaries *38–40. It should be noted that even Blackstone conceded that the distinctions between some of the franchises were "very much confounded in our law books." Id. *40.

directive which was later "judicially expanded to bar the king from granting private fisheries in tidal waters...."[6]

Royal power over wildlife also gradually gave way to Parliament. That slow transition of authority did not signal any great democratization of rights to wildlife, however. Rather, the principal mechanism of parliamentary control was enactment of the so-called "qualification statutes." These statutes prohibited the taking of game by anyone not "qualified," in the sense of having the requisite amount of wealth or land prescribed in the statute. Thus the qualification statues merely perpetuated a pervasive system of class discrimination and at the same time kept weapons out of the hands of those considered unfriendly, or potentially so, to those in power.[7]

All of these features of English wildlife law were still current at the time of the first settlement of the New World, although the Forest Jurisdiction had virtually fallen into desuetude. The qualification statutes, on the other hand, were very much alive and would continue to be so until several decades after American Independence. Stripped of its many formalities, the essential core of English wildlife law on the eve of the American Revolution was the complete authority of the king and Parliament to determine what rights others might have with respect to the taking of wildlife. What became of that central doctrine in the United States after it severed its ties with the mother country will be considered next.

## THE DEVELOPMENT OF THE STATE OWNERSHIP DOCTRINE

The first case to come before the United States Supreme Court concerning the relationships of government and citizen with respect to wildlife was that of *Martin v. Waddell* in 1842.[8] The facts of that case were ideally suited for an examination of the extent to which British wildlife law carried over to the newly independent United States.

At issue in *Martin v. Waddell* was the right of a riparian landowner to exclude all others from taking oysters from certain mudflats in New Jersey's Raritan River. The landowner claimed to own both the riparian and

---

[6]MacGrady, The Navigability Concept in the Civil and Common Law: Historical Development, Current Importance, and Some Doctrines That Don't Hold Water, 3 Fla. St. U. L. Rev. 513, 555 (1975).

[7]Lund, *supra* note 4 at 52–60. The precise relationship of the qualification statutes to the royal franchises previously discussed is not altogether clear. Blackstone asserts that the qualification statutes did not affirmatively authorize anyone to take game, that right remaining dependent upon the grant of a royal franchise, but suggests that the statutes were not commonly so understood. *See* 3 W. Blackstone, Commentaries *417–18.

[8]41 U.S. (16 Pet.) 367 (1842).

submerged lands of the river, tracing his title to a grant in 1664 from King Charles II to the Duke of York which purported to convey "all the lands, islands, soils, rivers, harbours, mines, minerals, quarries, woods, marshes, waters, lakes, fishings, hawkings, huntings and fowlings" within certain described metes and bounds.

In the view of the inventive Chief Justice, Roger Taney, the legal question presented was more than the interpretation of a mere deed of title, for the original deed from the King to the Duke "was an instrument upon which was to be founded the institutions of a great political community."[9] Accordingly, Taney deemed it necessary to consider first "the character of the right claimed by the British crown"[10] and second whether that character changed when title to the lands passed from the King to the Duke and ultimately to the plaintiff. Addressing those fundamental issues, Taney declared that "dominion and property in navigable waters, and in the lands under them [were] held by the King as a public trust" and that it "must be regarded as settled in England against the right of the king since Magna Charta," to make a private grant of such lands and waters.[11] That is, by virtue of his public trust responsibilities, the king was without power to abridge "the public common of piscary."[12]

If the public trust character of navigable waters and their submerged lands survived a grant by the king of his proprietary interest in them, there was still the question whether it also survived the American Revolution. Taney declared that it did in the following terms:

> [W]hen the people of New Jersey took possession of the reins of government, and took into their own hands the powers of sovereignty, the prerogatives and regalities which before belonged either to the crown or the parliament, became immediately and rightfully vested in the state.[13]

In so declaring, Taney seemed to place the states in the role of successors to Parliament and the crown, thus laying the groundwork for the subsequent

---

[9]*Id.* at 412.

[10]*Id.* at 409.

[11]*Id.* at 420.

[12]*Id.* at 412. One recent commentator, in a provocative article, has argued persuasively that Taney's decision vastly expanded the Magna Charta's limited prohibition against the creation of private fishing rights into a much broader prohibition against the creation of any sort of private rights in the submerged lands of navigable waters. *See* MacGrady, *supra* note 6 at 554–555 and 589–591. Nonetheless, that "public trust doctrine," as it has come to be called, is now well established in American law. *See* Sax, The Public Trust Doctrine in Natural Resource Law: Effective Judicial Intervention, 68 Mich. L. Rev. 471 (1970).

[13] 41 U.S. at 416.

development of the doctrine of state ownership of wildlife. As will become apparent in this chapter, however, that development largely ignored Taney's important qualifier that the powers assumed by the states were "subject...to the rights since surrendered by the Constitution to the general government."[14]

Until the turn of the century, there were few occasions to consider the scope of the rights surrendered by the states, because prior to 1900 the only federal wildlife legislation was limited in scope and relatively insignificant in impact.[15] There was, however, a steady growth in the regulation of wildlife at the state and territorial level. The few Supreme Court cases that considered the validity of that legislation uniformly upheld it.

In *Smith v. Maryland*, for example, the Supreme Court considered the validity of a Maryland law that prohibited the taking of oysters from the state's waters by means of scoop or drag.[16] The defendant shipowner, whose vessel was licensed by the United States to engage in the coasting trade, contended that the state law interfered with the exclusive federal power to regulate interstate commerce.[17] The Supreme Court rejected the defendant's argument and held that the state's ownership of the soil conferred upon it the authority to regulate the taking of oysters from that soil.[18] The court was at pains to emphasize the very limited scope of its holding, however, as the following passage indicates:

> The law now in question...does not touch the subject of the common liberty of taking oysters, save for the purpose of guarding it from injury,

---

[14]*Id.* at 410. Technically, the holding in Martin v. Waddell applied only to the original thirteen states. It was soon held to apply as well to all subsequently admitted states in Pollard v. Hagan, 44 U.S. (3 How) 212 (1845). Legislation admitting new states to the nation has traditionally included an "equal footing" clause, which grants to each new state the same rights and powers held by existing states. For an application of the equal footing doctrine to the question of state authority over wildlife, *see* Ward v. Race Horse, 163 U.S. 504 (1896), discussed in Chapter 3 *infra* at text accompanying notes 1–5.

[15]*See, e.g.*, Act of July 27, 1868, ch. 273, 15 Stat. 240 (repealed 1944), prohibiting the killing of certain fur-bearing animals in the territory and waters of Alaska; Act of February 9, 1871, 16 Stat. 593 (repealed 1964), creating the Office of the United States Commissioner of Fish and Fisheries "for the protection and the preservation of the food fishes of the coast of the United States"; Act of February 28, 1887, ch. 288, 24 Stat. 434, regulating the importation of mackerel into the United States; and Act of May 7, 1894, ch. 72, 28 Stat. 73, prohibiting hunting in Yellowstone National Park.

[16]59 U.S. (18 How.) 71 (1855).

[17]"The Congress shall have power... To regulate Commerce with foreign Nations, and among the several States, and with the Indian Tribes...." U.S. Const. art. I, §8, cl. 2.

[18]59 U.S. at 75.

to whomsoever it may belong, and by whomsoever it may be enjoyed. Whether this liberty belongs exclusively to the citizens of the State of Maryland, or may lawfully be enjoyed in common by all citizens of the United States; whether this public use may be restricted by the States to its own citizens, or a part of them, or by force of the Constitution must remain common to all citizens of the United States; whether the national government, by a treaty or act of congress, can grant to foreigners the right to participate therein; or what, in general, are the limits of the trust upon which the State holds this soil, or its power to define and control that trust, are matters wholly without the scope of this case, and upon which we give no opinion.[19]

Some of the many questions left unanswered by the Court's *Smith* opinion were answered relatively soon thereafter. Others remained unanswered for more than a century.[20]

*McCready v. Virginia* gave the Court its first opportunity to answer one of the questions left open in *Smith*.[21] There, the Court upheld a Virginia statute prohibiting citizens of other states from planting oysters in Virginia's tidewaters. In so doing, however, it substantially expanded the narrow holdings of *Martin v. Waddell* and *Smith v. Maryland* by declaring that the state owned not only the tidewaters, but also "the fish in them, so far as they are capable of ownership while running."[22] Accordingly, Virginia could regulate the planting or taking of oysters in those tidewaters, even to the point of excluding altogether the citizens of other states, because such a regulation "is in effect nothing more than a regulation of the use by the people of their common property."[23]

Fifteen years later, in *Manchester v. Massachusetts*, the Court upheld a Massachusetts statute prohibiting the use of purse seines for the taking of menhaden in Buzzards Bay.[24] The Court's opinion signalled a more cautious approach to the question of ultimate authority for the state's regulation. Rather than fasten that authority on any concept of "ownership" of the fish, the Court emphasized that inasmuch as the Bay was a body of navigable water within the state's territorial jurisdiction, "the subject is one which the state may well be permitted to regulate within its territory, in the absence of any regulation by the United States."[25] Moreover, the Court

---

[19]*Id.*

[20]*See* text accompanying notes 114–146 *infra.*

[21]94 U.S. 391 (1876).

[22]*Id.* at 394.

[23]*Id.* at 395.

[24]139 U.S. 240 (1891).

[25]*Id.* at 265.

felt compelled to point out that the regulation in question served a valid public purpose, the preservation of menhaden, which, "although they are not used as food for human beings, but as food for other fish which are so used, is for the common benefit."[26] The quoted language is significant because it reflects a fundamental nineteenth-century conception of the purpose of wildlife law, the preservation of a food supply.

In still other respects the *Manchester* decision reflected some uncertainty about the breadth of the principles previously announced in *McCready*. Thus the Court observed that, since the Massachusetts statute did not discriminate in favor of the citizens of that state, there was no need to consider whether there existed "a liberty of fishing for swimming fish in the navigable waters of the United States common to the inhabitants or the citizens of the United States."[27] The Court's implication that a state's powers with respect to "swimming fish" may be less than those with respect to sedentary shellfish was later to become the basis for virtually eliminating the vitality of the *McCready* decision.[28]

It was against this background of developing principles regarding state ownership of submerged land and state control over fisheries that the Supreme Court in 1896 decided the case which eloquently articulated a general theory of state "ownership" of wildlife, *Geer v. Connecticut.*[29] In that case, the defendant Geer appealed his conviction under state law for possessing game birds with the intent to ship them out of Connecticut. The birds had been lawfully killed there; only Geer's intent to transport them outside the state was unlawful. The legal question thus presented was the same as that considered in *Smith*, namely, whether the statute improperly interfered with the power of Congress to regulate interstate commerce.

In the view of Justice Edward White, writing for the majority, the answer required a thorough examination "of the nature of the property in game and the authority which the State had a right lawfully to exercise in relation thereto."[30] Tracing the history of governmental control over the taking of wildlife from Greek and Roman law through the civil law of the European continent and the common law of England, White concluded that the states had the right "to control and regulate the common property in game," which right was to be exercised "as a trust for the benefit of the people."[31] As an incident of this right of control, the states could affix

---

[26]*Id.*

[27]*Id.*

[28]*See* text accompanying notes 106–109 *infra.*

[29]161 U.S. 519 (1896).

[30]*Id.* at 522.

[31]*Id.* at 528–529.

conditions on the taking of game, and, most importantly, those conditions would remain with the game even after being killed.

Addressing the narrow legal question of whether the conditions affixed by Connecticut improperly impeded interstate commerce, White offered three alternative grounds on which to uphold the state law. First, without deciding the question, he asserted that in view of the "peculiar nature" of the state's ownership of game, "it may well be doubted whether commerce is created" by the killing and subsequent sale of such game.[32] Second, even if it did constitute commerce, it was at most only intrastate commerce.[33] Finally, even if interstate commerce were impeded, the "duty of the State to preserve for its people a valuable food supply" authorized the exercise of the state's police power to that end so long as interstate commerce was only "remotely and indirectly affected."[34]

The *Geer* opinion, because of the broad generality of its language, soon came to be regarded, and was long regarded, as the bulwark of the state ownership doctrine. Yet it is clear that the precise legal issue decided in *Geer* was quite narrow. Moreover, *Geer* itself recognized that the power that it found in the states could continue to exist only "in so far as its exercise may not be incompatible with, or restrained by, the rights conveyed to the Federal government by the Constitution."[35] Nevertheless, by intermixing questions of state authority to regulate the taking and disposition of wildlife with such technical property concepts as "ownership," *Geer* sparked a long and continuing debate about the respective powers of the state and federal governments over wildlife. Taken to its extreme, as some of its proponents would try to take it, the state ownership doctrine would render impossible the development of a body of federal wildlife law. Yet only four year after *Geer*, federal wildlife law took its first major step with passage of the Lacey Act of 1900.[36]

## THE CONSTITUTION AS AN AFFIRMATIVE SOURCE OF FEDERAL AUTHORITY FOR WILDLIFE REGULATION

The Lacey Act was a very cautious first step in the field of federal wildlife regulation. Relying upon the grant of power by the Constitution to the

---

[32]*Id.* at 530.

[33]*Id.* at 530–531. This second argument was obviously of a "bootstrap" nature, because it was the state's own prohibition of export, the very matter under dispute, that confined the commerce in game to intrastate commerce.

[34]*Id.* at 534.

[35]*Id.* at 528.

[36]Ch. 553, 31 Stat. 187 (current version at 16 U.S.C. §§701, 3371–3378 and 18 U.S.C. §42 (1976 & Supp. V 1981)).

Congress to regulate commerce between the states,[37] the Act, in its central provision, prohibited the interstate transportation of "any wild animals or birds" killed in violation of state law.[38] Thus the principal thrust of the Act was to enlist the aid of the federal government, through its powers over interstate commerce, in the enforcement of state game laws.

But the Lacey Act went even further in bolstering the states' regulatory authority over wildlife, for it included a provision taken almost verbatim from legislation designed to permit "dry" states to block the importation of alcohol, which stated that whenever any dead wildlife were imported into a state, they were subject to its laws as if they were killed there.[39] Thus, whereas *Geer* had upheld the authority of a state to prohibit the export of game lawfully killed within the state, the Lacey Act sanctioned a state's prohibition of the import of game lawfully killed in other states. Accordingly, in the view of some early courts, the Act was tantamount to an abdication of federal powers affirmatively to regulate interstate commerce.[40]

Other provisions of the Lacey Act had implications for the scope of federal power, though their importance was not much noted at the time. One such provision prohibited the importation of certain named animals, including starlings and English sparrows, and "such other birds or animals as the Secretary of Agriculture may ... declare injurious to the interest of agriculture or horticulture."[41] The source of this exercise of federal authority, the congressional power over foreign commerce, has never been seriously challenged.[42]

Finally, in direct response to the decimation of the passenger pigeon and the depletion of a number of other birds, the Lacey Act authorized the Secretary of Agriculture to adopt all measures necessary for the "preservation, distribution, introduction, and restoration of game birds and other wild birds," subject, however, to the laws of the various states and territories.[43] In this manner, the federal government began to inch slowly toward affirmative wildlife management.

The cautious approach embodied in the Lacey Act appeared to be eminently justified when, twelve years later, the Supreme Court decided

---

[37] *See* note 17 *supra.*

[38] Ch. 553, 3, 31 Stat. 188 (1900) (current version at 16 U.S.C. §3372(a) (Supp. V 1981)).

[39] Ch. 553, §5, 31 Stat. 188 (1900) (repealed 1981).

[40] *See, e.g.,* State v. Shattuck, 96 Minn. 45, 104 N.W. 719 (1905); People v. Bootman, 180 N.Y. 1, 72 N.E. 505 (1904). Cf. New York *ex rel.* Silz v. Hesterberg, 211 U.S. 31 (1908).

[41] Ch. 553, §2, 31 Stat. 188, (1900) (current version at 18 U.S.C. §42 (1976)).

[42] "The Congress shall have power ... To regulate Commerce with Foreign Nations...." U.S. Const. art. I, §8, cl. 3.

[43] Ch. 553, §1, 31 Stat. 187 (1900) (current version at 16 U.S.C. §701 (1976)).

*The Abby Dodge.*[44] In that action, the United States brought suit against a vessel for its alleged violation of a federal statute prohibiting the taking of sponges from the Gulf of Mexico or the Straits of Florida by means of diving apparatus.[45] The vessel owner contended that the sponges were taken in Florida's territorial waters and that, if the federal statute applied to such waters, it was unconstitutional because the taking of sponges there was a matter "exclusively within the authority of the states." Chief Justice White, the author of the *Geer* opinion sixteen years earlier, agreed. Although he upheld the validity of the federal statute, he did so by construing it to apply only beyond Florida's territorial waters. In explanation, he offered the following rationale:

> In view of the clear distinction between state and national power on the subject, long settled at the time the act was passed...we are of opinion that its provisions must be construed as alone applicable to the subject within the authority of Congress to regulate, and, therefore, be held not to embrace that which was not within such power.[46]

Thus Justice White's *Abby Dodge* decision was the first (and last) statement of the Supreme Court that the state ownership doctrine actually precluded federal wildlife regulation. Since then the Court's decisions have made clear that there are at least three separate sources of constitutional authority for federal wildlife regulation. Each of those is examined in detail in the discussion that follows.

## The Federal Treaty-Making Power

With the *Abby Dodge* decision only a year old, the outlook was hardly auspicious when Congress enacted the Migratory Bird Act of 1913.[47] Actually a part of the Appropriations Act for the Department of Agriculture, it declared all migratory game and insectivorous birds "to be within the custody and protection of the government of the United States" and prohibited their hunting except pursuant to federal regulations. The constitutionality of the 1913 Act was considered in two cases in the federal district courts, *United States v. Shauver*[48] and *United States v. McCullagh*,[49] and in each case it was found wanting. It appears that the government made a rather feeble effort to support its law on the basis that the migratory

---

[44]223 U.S. 166 (1912).

[45]Act of June 20, 1906, ch. 3442, 34 Stat. 313 (repealed 1914).

[46]223 U.S. at 175.

[47]Act of March 4, 1913, ch. 145, 37 Stat. 828 (repealed 1918).

[48]214 F. 154 (E.D. Ark. 1914), *appeal dismissed*, 248 U.S. 594 (1919).

[49]221 F. 288 (D. Kan. 1915).

character of the birds made them subject to its power to regulate interstate commerce. Both courts rejected the government's argument as foreclosed by *Geer*. The government made a somewhat more vigorous claim that the law was supported by the property clause of the Constitution, which authorized the Congress to make all "needful Rules and Regulations" concerning the property of the United States.[50] That argument was likewise rejected on the basis that *Geer* had placed "property" in game in the states.

The *Shauver* case was appealed to the Supreme Court and argued twice, initially before a bench of only six Justices. Apparently fearful of an adverse decision, the Department of Agriculture urged the Department of State to conclude a treaty with Great Britain (on behalf of Canada) for the protection of migratory birds.[51] The treaty was signed on August 16, 1916.[52] After passage in 1918 of implementing legislation, the Migratory Bird Treaty Act,[53] the Supreme Court dismissed the government's appeal in *Shauver* and thus never decided the constitutionality of the 1913 Act.

The constitutionality of the 1918 Act was very soon before the Supreme Court when the state of Missouri filed a bill in equity seeking to restrain one Ray Holland, a United States Game Warden, from enforcing the Act within the state. The United States contended that the Treaty and its implementing legislation took precedence over any conflicting state power of regulation by virtue of the Constitution's supremacy clause.[54] The Court's landmark decision in *Missouri v. Holland* dealt a stunning blow to those who had felt the state ownership doctrine was a bar to federal wildlife regulation.[55] Justice Oliver Wendell Holmes, writing for a seven-member majority that included Justice Louis Brandeis and even Chief Justice White, disposed of Missouri's ownership argument in the following terms:

> The State...founds its claim of exclusive authority upon an assertion of title.... No doubt it is true that as between a State and its inhabitants the

---

[50] "The Congress shall have power to dispose of and make all needful Rules and Regulations respecting the Territory or other Property belonging to the United States...." U.S. Const. art. IV, §3.

[51] Comment, Treaty-Making Power as Support for Federal Legislation, 29 Yale L.J. 445 (1920).

[52] Convention for the Protection of Migratory Birds, Aug. 16, 1916, United States–Great Britain (on behalf of Canada), 39 Stat. 1702, T.S. No. 628.

[53] Ch. 128, 40 Stat. 755 (1918) (current version at 16 U.S.C. §§703–711 (1976 & Supp. V 1981)).

[54] "This Constitution, and the Laws of the United States which shall be made in Pursuance thereof; and all Treaties made, or which shall be made, under the Authority of the United States, shall be the Supreme Law of the Land...." U.S. Const. art. VI.

[55] 252 U.S. 416 (1920).

State may regulate the killing and sale of such birds, but it does not follow that its authority is exclusive of paramount powers. To put the claim of the State upon title is to lean upon a slender reed. Wild birds are not in the possession of anyone, and possession is the beginning of ownership....

....

...But for the treaty and the statute there soon might be no birds for any powers to deal with. We see nothing in the Constitution that compels the Government to sit by while a food supply is cut off and the protectors of our forests and our crops are destroyed. It is not sufficient to rely upon the States. The reliance is vain....[56]

*Missouri v. Holland* established beyond question the supremacy of the federal treaty-making power as a source of authority for federal wildlife regulation.[57] More importantly, it forcefully rejected the contention that the doctrine of state ownership of wildlife functioned to bar federal wildlife regulation and invited the question of what further sources of federal power might be utilized in the development of a body of federal wildlife law.

## The Federal Property Power

Only eight years after *Missouri v. Holland,* the scope of the property clause, rejected by lower federal courts as a source of authority for federal wildlife regulation in *Shauver* and *McCullagh,* was to be considered by the Supreme Court. In fact, the federal government had been exercising this power for a considerable time, for it had in 1894 prohibited all hunting in Yellowstone National Park.[58] In addition, in 1906 it prohibited the hunting of birds "on all lands of the United States which have been set apart or reserved as breeding grounds for birds by any law, proclamation, or Executive order," except under regulations of the Secretary of Agriculture, thus asserting regulatory authority over the taking of wildlife on the then newly

---

[56]*Id.* at 434–435.

[57]Coggins & Hensley, Constitutional Limits on Federal Power to Protect and Manage Wildlife: Is the Endangered Species Act Endangered?, 61 Iowa L. Rev. 1099, 1124–1125 (1976), discusses various asserted limitations on the authority of the federal government to regulate wildlife through the treaty-making power, and concludes that they are illusory. Palila v. Hawaii Dep't of Land and Natural Resources, 471 F. Supp. 985 (D. Ha. 1979), *aff'd,* 639 F.2d 495 (9th Cir. 1981), might have furnished the basis for an interesting inquiry into the limits of the treaty-making power. In that action the state contested the constitutionality of the Endangered Species Act as applied to a nonmigratory bird found only on state-owned lands within a single state. With only cursory discussion of the treaty issue, the district court upheld the law under both the treaty and commerce powers of the federal government. 471 F. Supp. at 993–994.

[58]Act of May 7, 1894, ch. 72, 28 Stat. 73.

created federal wildlife refuges.[59] There are no reported cases challenging these assertions of authority, probably because the federal government was assumed to have the same right as any other landowner to prohibit hunting on its land. When the government sought to remove wildlife from such lands without complying with state law, however, several states challenged that action as being outside the scope of the powers conferred by the property clause.

The first of several cases to consider the issue was the 1928 decision of the Supreme Court in *Hunt v. United States*.[60] In that case the Secretary of Agriculture directed the removal of excess deer in Kaibab National Forest because of their threatened harm to the forest through overbrowsing. State officials arrested certain persons carrying out the Secretary's directive, whereupon the United States brought suit to enjoin the state from enforcing its game laws with respect to the removal program. The state relied upon *Geer* and the other ownership cases. Without even mentioning those cases, however, the Supreme Court ruled that "the power of the United States to thus protect its lands and property does not admit of doubt,...the game laws or any other statute of the state...notwithstanding."[61] Twelve years later, the *Hunt* holding was extended to acquired national forest lands in *Chalk v. United States*.[62]

Despite the decisions of *Hunt* and *Chalk*, disagreement concerning the authority of the federal government to regulate wildlife on its own lands remained. On December 1, 1964, the Office of the Solicitor for the Department of the Interior issued a memorandum opinion in response to a request from the Fish and Wildlife Service for a determination of the Secretary's authority to promulgate hunting and fishing regulations for lands within the National Wildlife Refuge System. The Solicitor's opinion went beyond the narrow question put to him and declared that the United States "has constitutional power to enact laws and regulations controlling and protec-

---

[59] Act of June 28, 1906, ch. 3565, 34 Stat. 536 (current version at 18 U.S.C. §41 (1976)). Pelican Island refuge, established in 1903, is often regarded as the first federal wildlife refuge. *See, e.g.,* Department of the Interior, United States Fish and Wildlife Service, Final Environmental Statement, Operation of the National Wildlife Refuge System, app. F (Nov. 1976). President Harrison's proclamation some 11 years earlier reserving Alaska's Afognak Island may in fact deserve that distinction. Harrison's proclamation reserved the island "in order that salmon fisheries in the waters of the Island, and salmon and other fish and sea animals, and other animals and birds...may be protected and preserved unimpaired." Proclamation No. 39, 27 Stat. 1052 (1892).

[60] 278 U.S. 96 (1928).

[61] *Id.* at 100.

[62] 114 F.2d 207 (4th Cir. 1940).

ting...[its] lands, including the...resident species of wildlife situated on such lands, and that this authority is superior to that of a State."[63]

The Solicitor's opinion touched off a storm of controversy. Even the comprehensive study of fish and wildlife resources on the public lands undertaken for the Public Land Law Review Commission concluded that the Solicitor had been overzealous and that at the very least the cases required a "clear showing of damage to Federal property before action in violation of State Law is sanctioned."[64]

The asserted distinction relied upon in the Commission's study was promptly rejected in *New Mexico State Game Commission v. Udall,* in which the Secretary of the Interior directed the killing of a number of deer in Carlsbad Caverns National Park solely for research purposes, without compliance with state game laws and without any showing of existing depredation by the deer.[65] The concerns of many of the state game agencies, expressed through the amicus brief of the International Association of Game, Fish, and Conservation Commissioners, were as follows:

> [T]his occurrence is but one in a series of recent endeavors by the Department of the Interior to enter the field of game management, a role which has been historically and competently fulfilled by the States.... Interior Department administrators increasingly claim that, on federally owned lands, the federal government has the right to manage and control wildlife, including the right to take and dispose of such game as the Department deems appropriate, and the State may not interfere.[66]

Similarly, the state of Michigan in its amicus brief, argued that the federal government's "next logical step will be to use this new power for the purpose of regulating hunting and fishing on these lands and charging a license for such privilege."[67] Notwithstanding these fears of the states, the court upheld the Secretary's research program because of his necessary power to determine which animals *"may be detrimental* to the use of the park."[68]

---

[63]Quoted in G. Swanson, Fish and Wildlife Resources on the Public Lands 15 (1969).

[64]*Id.* at 32.

[65]410 F.2d 1197 (10th Cir.), *cert. denied sub nom.* New Mexico State Game Comm'n. v. Hickel, 396 U.S. 961 (1969).

[66]*Id.* at 1201 n. 6.

[67]*Id.* Coggins & Hensley, *supra* note 57 at 1150, argue that the states' fear of federal wildlife regulation is probably "founded less on loss of sovereignty...than on loss of revenue."

[68]410 F.2d at 1201 (emphasis in original).

Although the *Udall* decision obviated the need for a "clear showing of damage" to federal land before wildlife removal would be permitted, there nevertheless appeared to remain some sort of required nexus between protecting the land and regulating the wildlife. Indeed, it was on such a basis that a three-judge federal court in 1975 struck down the Wild Free-Roaming Horses and Burros Act, thus setting the state for the Supreme Court's most recent, and probably definitive, pronouncement on the federal authority to regulate wildlife conferred by the property clause, *Kleppe v. New Mexico.*[69]

The Wild Free-Roaming Horses and Burros Act[70] was enacted in 1971 to protect all unbranded and unclaimed horses and burros on the public lands of the United States as "living symbols of the historic and pioneer spirit of the West."[71] The Act declared such animals to be "an integral part of the natural system of public lands" and directed the Secretaries of the Interior and Agriculture "to protect and manage [them] as components of the public lands."[72] The *Kleppe* case began when, at the request of a federal grazing permittee, New Mexico authorities removed certain of the protected burros from federal land and sold them at auction. The federal Bureau of Land Management then demanded that New Mexico recover and return them. Instead, the state sued the Secretary of the Interior to have the federal act declared unconstitutional. The lower court agreed with the state, distinguishing *Hunt, Chalk,* and *Udall* on the grounds that in those cases the federal efforts were lawful only because they served to protect the federal lands, whereas here the Act was designed solely to protect the animals.[73]

The Supreme Court unanimously reversed the lower court on the grounds that protection of federal land is only a sufficient, and not a necessary, basis for action under the property clause. While noting that the "furthest reaches of the power granted by the property clause have not yet been definitively resolved," the Court declared that the power "necessarily includes the power to regulate and protect the wildlife living there."[74] The Court's holding was a firm ratification of the controversial view expressed by Interior's Office of the Solicitor twelve years earlier. Moreover, adverting

---

[69] 426 U.S. 529 (1976).

[70] 16 U.S.C. §§ 1331–1340 (1976 & Supp. V 1981). For more extensive discussions of the Wild Free-Roaming Horses and Burros Act, see Chapter 4 *infra* at text accompanying notes 167–198, and Chapter 6 *infra* at text accompanying notes 233–267.

[71] 16 U.S.C. §1331 (1976).

[72] *Id.* §1333(a).

[73] New Mexico v. Morton, 406 F. Supp. 1237 (D. N.M. 1975).

[74] 426 U.S. at 539, 541.

to issues raised but not definitively resolved 50 years earlier in *Shauver* and *McCullagh*, the Court observed that "it is far from clear...that Congress cannot assert a property interest in the regulated horses and burros superior to that of the State."[75]

While the Supreme Court has not had further occasion to consider the scope of federal authority over wildlife under the property clause, several lower courts have addressed the interstitial questions left unresolved by the Court's decision in *Kleppe*. In particular, *United States v. Brown*, a case involving a challenge to a National Park Service prohibition against hunting on state waters within (but not a part of) the National Park System, purported to answer affirmatively the question "whether the property clause empowers the United States to enact regulatory legislation protecting federal lands from interference occurring on non-federal public lands, or, in this instance, waters."[76] Finding that the prohibition was needed to protect wildlife and visitors on the federal lands, the court upheld it as a proper exercise of property clause powers.[77]

In *Palila v. Hawaii Department of Land and Natural Resources*, the district court carried *Kleppe*'s suggestion of a federal ownership interest in wildlife a step farther.[78] Though that case upheld the Endangered Species Act, as applied to nonmigratory species found on state lands, on the basis of the treaty power and commerce clause, it nonetheless suggested that the "importance of preserving such a national resource [as an endangered species] may be of such magnitude as to rise to the level of a federal property interest."[79] Given the Supreme Court's nearly contemporaneous disposition of the state ownership theory in *Hughes v. Oklahoma*[80] and the expansive reading of the commerce clause in *Hughes* and *Douglas v. Seacoast Products, Inc.*,[81] it is doubtful that there is any necessity for courts to pursue the *Palila* inquiry further.

---

[75]*Id.* at 537. It is puzzling that after seemingly freeing itself from the decades of confusion occasioned by the use of property concepts that typified its nineteenth-century decisions, the Court was unwilling to drop any reference to "property" interests in wildlife altogether.

[76]552 F.2d 817, 822 (8th Cir. 1977).

[77]The court's alternative holding was that the waters on which hunting was prohibited were in fact a part of the National Park System. *Id.* at 821. Among recent nonwildlife cases exploring the limits of property clause authority over nonfederal lands are Leo Sheep Co. v. United States, 440 U.S. 668 (1979), United States v. Lindsey, 595 F.2d 5 (9th Cir. 1979), and Minnesota v. Bergland, 499 F. Supp. 1253 (D. Minn. 1980).

[78]*See* note 57, *supra*.

[79]471 F. Supp. at 995 n. 40.

[80]441 U.S. 322 (1979) (discussed at text accompanying notes 136–141, *infra*).

[81]431 U.S. 265 (1977) (discussed at text accompanying notes 114–121, *infra*).

## The Federal Commerce Power

The *Kleppe* decision and *Missouri v. Holland* clearly establish the property clause and the treaty-making power as sound sources of authority for the development of a body of federal wildlife law, notwithstanding the state ownership doctrine. A third source of federal authority, the power to regulate interstate commerce, has had a more uncertain relationship to the state ownership doctrine. This uncertainty stemmed largely from *Geer*, which cast considerable doubt on the federal power under the commerce clause. However, *Geer* involved a question of the validity of state action rather than federal action. Moreover, the holding in *Geer* was narrowed considerably in *Foster-Fountain Packing Company v. Haydel*, which held that a state terminates its absolute control over the utilization of wildlife once it permits part or all of such wildlife to enter the stream of commerce.[82] Nevertheless, until 1977 there was no Supreme Court decision spelling out the scope of the federal wildlife regulatory power conferred by the commerce clause.

In *Douglas v. Seacoast Products, Inc.*, the Supreme Court held that federal licenses granted to vessels pursuant to the Enrollment and Licensing Act conferred upon licensees a right to fish in coastal waters.[83] Rejecting arguments that such authority was beyond the power of Congress, the Court declared that, while "at earlier times in our history there was some doubt whether Congress had power under the commerce clause to regulate the taking of fish in state waters, there can be no question today that such power exists where there is some effect on interstate commerce."[84] Although the fish involved in *Douglas* were migratory, the Court did not fix that as the basis for federal authority. Rather, "[t]he movement of vessels from one State to another in search of fish, and back again to processing plants, is certainly activity which Congress could conclude affects interstate commerce."[85]

Two decisions in 1979 further reinforced the *Douglas* conclusion. *Hughes v. Oklahoma*, though it considered the validity of a state statute discriminating against interstate commerce rather than the validity of a federal statute enacted pursuant to the commerce clause, held that "[t]he

---

[82] 278 U.S. 1 (1928).

[83] 431 U.S. 265 (1977).

[84] *Id.* at 281–282.

[85] *Id.* at 282. *Cf.* Brown v. Anderson, 202 F. Supp. 96 (D. Alas. 1962) (Alaska fishing law an unlawful burden on interstate commerce because many of the fishermen it affected were from other states and moved in interstate commerce). *See also* Thornton v. United States, 271 U.S. 414 (1926) (grazing cattle that wander freely across state lines are subject to federal regulation).

definition of 'commerce' is the same when relied on to strike down or restrict state legislation as when relied on to support some exertion of federal control or regulation."[86] Citing *Hughes* as its authority, the Supreme Court later that same year in *Andrus v. Allard*[87] held that the Migratory Bird Treaty Act, the constitutionality of which under the treaty power had been upheld in *Missouri v. Holland,* was equally valid as an exercise of federal power under the commerce clause.[88]

Whether the commerce clause furnished an adequate basis for federal regulation of a nonmigratory species that did not itself move from state to state as part of any commercial activity was answered affirmatively in *Palila v. Hawaii Department of Land and Natural Resources.*[89] The *Palila* court reasoned that "a national program to protect and improve the natural habitats of endangered species preserves the possibilities of interstate commerce in these species and of interstate movement of persons, such as amateur students of nature or professional scientists who come to a state to observe and study these species."[90] Perhaps an even more sweeping statement of federal authority under the commerce clause is found in *United States v. Helsley,*[91] a case upholding the constitutionality of the Airborne Hunting Act.[92] Although the court was prepared to sustain the act simply on the basis of federal authority over air space, it went on to assert, *arguendo,* that even if the dominant purpose of the statute had been the regulation of game management,

> congressional regulation is not thwarted by arguments that the incidental connection between commerce and the regulation is used merely as an expedient to justify the law.... Congress may find that a class of activities affects interstate commerce and thus regulate or prohibit all such activities without the necessity of demonstrating that the particular transaction in question has an impact which is more than local.[93]

---

[86]441 U.S. 322, 326 n. 2 (1979). This issue was expressly left open in *Douglas,* 431 U.S. at 282 n. 17, but resolved the following year in Philadelphia v. New Jersey, 437 U.S. 617, 621–623 (1978).

[87]444 U.S. 51 (1979).

[88]444 U.S. at 63, note 19. In so declaring, the Court implicitly confirmed the correctness of the views expressed in the early cases of Cochrane v. United States, 92 F.2d 623 (7th Cir. 1937) and Cerritos Gun Club v. Hall, 96 F.2d 620 (9th Cir. 1938), and in the initial edition of this work at pages 31–33.

[89]471 F. Supp. 985 (D. Ha. 1979), *aff'd on other grounds,* 639 F.2d 495 (9th Cir. 1981).

[90]471 F. Supp. at 995. The court relied upon the analysis in the initial text at pages 32–33 in support of this conclusion. *Id.,* note 39.

[91]615 F.2d 784 (9th Cir. 1979).

[92]16 U.S.C. §742j–1 (1976).

[93]615 F.2d at 787.

In light of the above decisions, it is clear that the federal authority to regulate wildlife under the commerce clause is of equal stature to that conferred by the property clause. Accordingly, federal regulation of wildlife pursuant to the commerce clause is unrestrained by the state ownership doctrine. In fact, if the assertion that the state ownership doctrine is a bar to federal wildlife regulation has any validity at all, it has received no authoritative judicial support since the 1912 decision in *The Abbey Dodge,* a decision that, though never overruled, has been given a quiet interment.[94]

From the foregoing, it is clear that the Constitution, in its treaty, property, and commerce clauses, contains ample support for the development of a comprehensive body of federal wildlife law and that, to the extent such law conflicts with state law, it takes precedence over the latter. That narrow conclusion, however, does not automatically divest the states of any role in the regulation of wildlife or imply any preference for a particular allocation of responsibilities between the states and the federal government. It does affirm, however, that such an allocation can be designed without serious fear of constitutional hindrance. In designing such a system, for reasons of policy, pragmatism, and political comity, it is clear that the states will continue to play an important role either as a result of federal forbearance or through the creation of opportunities to share in the implementation of federal wildlife programs.[95]

## THE CONSTITUTION AS A SOURCE OF LIMITATIONS ON STATE AND FEDERAL REGULATION OF WILDLIFE

It will be recalled from the earlier discussion in this chapter that in the year of the nation's centennial, the Supreme Court in *McCready v. Virginia* upheld the validity of a state statute totally excluding noncitizens of the state from planting oysters in its tidewaters.[96] Despite the suggestion a few years later in *Manchester v. Massachusetts* that the Court had some doubts

---

[94]Coggins & Hensley, *supra* note 57 at 1139–1143, suggest a fourth, implied basis for federal regulation of wildlife, that being the inherent federal power to protect those wildlife species having "symbolic" value to the nation. Although this source of federal authority has not yet been tested in the courts, it has clearly been relied upon by Congress in enacting such wildlife legislation as the Wild Free-Roaming Horses and Burros Act (*see* text accompanying note 71 *supra*) and the Bald Eagle Protection Act (*see* discussion in Chapter 4 *infra*).

[95]*Compare* the respective roles of the state and federal governments in implementation of the Federal Aid in Wildlife Restoration Act (*see* Chapter 8 *infra*), the Sikes Act Extension (*see* Chapter 6 *infra*) and the Marine Mammal Protection Act (*see* Chapter 11 *infra*).

[96]*See* text accompanying notes 21–23 *supra*.

about the breadth of its *McCready* holding, it went on in the early decades of the twentieth century to uphold two other plainly discriminatory statutes. In the first of these, *Patsone v. Pennsylvania,* the Court upheld a Pennsylvania statute prohibiting unnaturalized foreign-born residents from killing wild game, and, in furtherance thereof, making the possession by such persons of shotguns and rifles unlawful.[97] A convicted defendant challenged the constitutionality of the statute under the equal protection clause of the fourteenth amendment.[98] In an opinion noteworthy by today's standards for its reluctance to probe the motivation of the legislature, the Court simply considered whether "the protection of wild life... warrants the discrimination" and concluded that it could not deem the assumption "that resident unnaturalized aliens were the peculiar source of the evil that it desired to prevent" to be "manifestly wrong."[99]

Ten years later, in *Haavik v. Alaska Packers Association,* an enactment of the Alaskan territorial legislature imposed a $5 tax on each nonresident fisherman in the state.[100] The Court found the tax not to be prohibited by the privileges and immunities clause of the Constitution,[101] because it was uniformly applied to all nonresidents and did not discriminate as against noncitizens.

In two decisions in 1948, the Supreme Court dramatically changed its course and held that the privileges and immunities clause and the equal protection clause of the fourteenth amendment, imposed strict limits on the nature of the states' wildlife regulation. In *Takahashi v. Fish and Game Commission* the Court had before it a California statute which, when originally passed during the period of Japanese evacuation, denied commercial fishing licenses to alien Japanese.[102] After the war, the law was amended so as to apply to all persons ineligible for United States citizenship, a classification that still impacted most heavily on the Japanese.

Mr. Takahashi, who had fished the waters of California pursuant to state license from 1915 to 1942, sued in the California state courts to compel the state to issue him another license. Although successful initially, Takahashi failed in the Supreme Court of California, which upheld the law on

[97]232 U.S. 138 (1914).

[98]"No state shall... deny to any person within its jurisdiction the equal protection of the laws." U.S. Const. amend. XIV, §1.

[99]232 U.S. at 144–145.

[100]263 U.S. 510 (1924).

[101]"The Citizens of each State shall be entitled to all Privileges and Immunities of Citizens of the several States." U.S. Const. art. IV, §2. In 1952, the Supreme Court characterized the *Haavik* decision as premised on the erroneous assumption that Congress had intended to relieve the Alaskan territorial legislature from constitutional restrictions applicable to the states. *See* Mullaney v. Anderson, 342 U.S. 415, 419–420 (1952).

[102]334 U.S. 410 (1948).

the basis of California's "proprietary interest in fish in the ocean waters within three miles of the shore."[103] When Takahashi sought review in the Supreme Court of the United States, he was supported by some of the best legal talent in the country. Amicus briefs on his behalf were filed by the Attorney General and the Solicitor General of the United States, Thurgood Marshall for the National Lawyers Guild, and numerous others; his case was argued before the Court by Dean Acheson. In reversing the California court, the Supreme Court, through Justice Black, quoted the "slender reed" passage of Justice Holmes's opinion in *Missouri v. Holland*,[104] and then stated the following:

> We think the same statement is equally applicable here. To whatever extent the fish in the three-mile belt off California may be "capable of ownership" by California we think that "ownership" is inadequate to justify California in excluding any or all aliens who are lawful residents of the State from making a living by fishing in the ocean off its shores while permitting all others to do so.[105]

Only Justices Reed and Jackson dissented.

At issue in the Court's other 1948 decision, *Toomer v. Witsell,* were several South Carolina statutes governing commercial fishing in the three-mile zone off its coast.[106] Principal among these was a provision imposing on nonresident commercial shrimp harvesters a license fee of $2,500, which was one hundred times greater than the fee charged residents. A group of Georgia citizens brought suit, charging that the fee differential, which the Court found to be "so great that its practical effect is virtually exclusionary," contravened the guarantees of the privileges and immunities clause.[107]

In upholding the claim of the Georgians, the Court distinguished many of its prior precedents enunciating or relying upon the state ownership doctrine. Thus *McCready* was distinguished on the basis that it concerned sedentary shellfish in inland waters, *Haavik* on the basis that it concerned the power of Congress rather than the power of a state, and *Patsone* on the basis (hardly believable) that "persuasive independent reasons justifying the discrimination" were advanced there.[108] The Court summed up its view of the ownership doctrine in the following terms:

---

[103]*Id.* at 414.

[104]252 U.S. 416, 434–435 (1920). The passage is quoted in full at text accompanying note 56 *supra*.

[105]334 U.S. at 421.

[106]334 U.S. 385 (1948).

[107]*Id.* at 396–397.

[108]*Id.* at 400.

The whole ownership theory, in fact, is now generally regarded as but a fiction expressive in legal shorthand of the importance to its people that a state have power to preserve and regulate the exploitation of an important resource. And there is no necessary conflict between that vital policy consideration and the constitutional command that the State exercise that power...so as not to discriminate without reason against citizens of other states.[109]

The Court also struck down in *Toomer* a statute requiring owners of shrimp boats fishing within three miles of South Carolina to dock at a South Carolina port, unload, pack, and stamp their catch before shipping it to another state. The state argued that if *Geer* permitted a state to prohibit altogether the shipment of its wildlife to other states, then surely it could impose lesser restrictions on export. The Court rejected the state's contention on authority of *Foster-Fountain Packing Company v. Haydel.*[110] Significantly, Justices Frankfurter and Rutledge, who in a separate opinion expressed the view that the state's "technical ownership" of its wildlife resources exempted its regulation thereof from the privileges and immunities clause, nevertheless concurred with the majority on the basis that the state statutes were offensive to the commerce clause.

*Toomer* and *Takahashi* thus enunciated broad limitations on the scope of state regulatory authority over wildlife. Nevertheless, significant opportunities for distinguishing either decision on factual grounds remained. *Toomer* itself carefully noted that a differential fee structure that "merely compensate[d] the State for any added enforcement burden [nonresidents] may impose or for any conservation expenditures from taxes which only residents pay," would be permissible.[111] Despite a myriad of state efforts to avoid their essential holdings, the courts were largely unsympathetic.[112]

In recent years, however, the Supreme Court gave some indication that it might be inclined to narrow the scope of its earlier rulings. In *Reetz v. Bozanich,* for example, the Court abstained from ruling on a challenge to

---

[109]*Id.* at 402.

[110]278 U.S. 1 (1928). The *Haydel* case is described briefly at text accompanying note 82 *supra.*

[111]334 U.S. at 399.

[112]*See, e.g.,* Mullaney v. Anderson, *supra* note 101; Massey v. Apollonio, 387 F. Supp. 373 (D. Me. 1974) (three-year residency requirement for a Maine lobster license), discussed in Note, Massey v. Apollonio: Is Residency an Impermissible Conservation Device?, 6 Envtl. L. 543 (1976); Brown v. Anderson, 202 F. Supp. 96 (D. Alas. 1962) (Alaska law permitting the emergency closure of certain salmon fishing areas to nonresidents); Edwards v. Leaver, 102 F. Supp. 698 (D.R.I. 1952) (Rhode Island Law restricting commercial menhaden licenses to residents). *Cf.* Lynden Transport, Inc. v. Alaska, 532 P.2d 700, 710 (Alas. 1975).

an Alaska statute limiting commercial net gear salmon-fishing licenses to persons who previously held such a license for specific salmon registration areas or who held any other commercial fishing license for a period of three years in a particular registration area.[113] Because the action alleged a violation of a provision of the Alaska constitution that had never been construed by an Alaskan court, the Supreme Court determined that the matter should first be considered by the state courts.

Then, in 1976, it appeared that the Supreme Court might be ready to reconsider its holdings in *Toomer* and *Takahashi* when it agreed to review a lower court decision striking down Virginia laws restricting the rights of aliens and nonresidents to engage in certain commercial fisheries within the state's coastal waters. However, the Court's decision in *Douglas v. Seacoast Products, Inc.* avoided the constitutional issues and focused instead on the narrower question whether the Virginia laws conflicted with federal legislation.[114] The precise legal question was whether Virginia's laws were preempted by the federal Enrollment and Licensing Act, a statute of 1793 vintage under which the plaintiffs' vessels had been licensed to engage in coastal fisheries.

The state sought to escape the Court's conclusion that its laws were void because they conflicted with the federal law by arguing that it could exclude federal licensees from taking resources that the state owned.[115] The Court replied that "it is pure fantasy to talk of 'owning' wild fish, birds, or animals.... The 'ownership' language of cases such as [*Geer* and its predecessors] must be understood as no more than a 19th century legal fiction expressing 'the importance to its people that a State have power to preserve and regulate the exploitation of an important resource.'"[116] Thus, while conceding the importance of state power to preserve and regulate the exploitation of wildlife, the Court flatly rejected any claim that such power derived from a state's "ownership" of wildlife.

Two members of the *Douglas* court filed a separate opinion concurring with the judgment of the majority but differing with part of its reasoning. In particular, they thought "that the States' substantial regulatory interests" had not been "given adequate shrift" by the majority.[117] While conceding that states do not "own" wildlife "in any conventional sense of that term," they nonetheless contended that "the States have a

---

[113]397 U.S. 82 (1970).

[114]431 U.S. 265 (1977).

[115]The state's argument rested not only upon *Geer* and its predecessors, but also section 3(a) of the Submerged Lands Act, 43 U.S.C. §1311(a) (1976). *See* 431 U.S. at 283–284.

[116]*Id.* at 284, quoting Toomer v. Witsell, 334 U.S. 385, 402 (1948).

[117]431 U.S. at 288 (Rehnquist, J., concurring).

substantial property interest...in the fish and game within their boundaries."[118] The states' regulatory interests, according to the two Justices,
"are of substantial legal moment, whether or not they rise to the level of a
traditional property right."[119] Indeed, in their view, the states' regulatory
interests in wildlife were so substantial that "only a direct conflict with the
operation of federal law...will bar the state regulatory action...no matter
how 'peripatetic' the objects of the regulation or however 'Balkanized' the
resulting pattern of commercial activity."[120] Two years later, however, in
*Hughes v. Oklahoma*, the Supreme Court explicitly rejected precisely that
characterization of the states' interest.[121]

Before *Hughes*, however, the Court was presented with yet another
challenge to a discriminatory state wildlife statute, a Montana law imposing upon out-of-state hunters a substantially higher fee for hunting elk
than that imposed upon state residents. Unlike *Douglas*, this case involved
no conflicting federal statute to preempt the state law. Thus the only issue
before the Court in *Baldwin v. Fish and Game Commission of Montana*[122]
was whether the state statute conflicted with the privileges and immunities
clause of article IV, §2, or the equal protection clause of the fourteenth
amendment to the Constitution. In a five-member majority opinion, the
Court held that it did not.

On the privileges and immunities claim, the plaintiffs contended that
the case was controlled by *Toomer v. Witsell*. The Court disagreed, however, distinguishing *Toomer* on the basis that it involved the licensing of
an activity for a "commercial livelihood." Recreational sport hunting, on
the other hand, was not a "fundamental" right, and therefore not protected
by the privileges and immunities clause.[123]

In determining whether recreational hunting was a "fundamental
right" and thus one that a state could not abridge for nonresidents, the
Court considered *Geer* and the other early cases concerning the right of
states to restrict wildlife resources to their own borders or for their own
citizens. The plaintiffs argued that these cases had no remaining vitality.

---

[118]*Id.* at 287–288.

[119]*Id.* at 288.

[120]*Id.*

[121]441 U.S. 322 (1979).

[122]436 U.S. 371 (1978).

[123]436 U.S. at 386, 388. The three dissenting Justices, while arguing that the fact of
discrimination against nonresidents, and not the nature of the right restricted, was
the controlling consideration, did not dispute the majority's characterization of
recreational sport hunting as a nonfundamental right. Thus it appears that no
member of the Supreme Court regards recreational sport hunting as a "fundamental" right.

The Court disagreed. While acknowledging the numerous recent cases that have chipped away at the old state ownership cases, the Court was unwilling to "completely reject" those decisions because "[t]he fact that the State's control over wildlife is not exclusive and absolute in the face of federal regulation and certain federally protected interests does not compel the conclusion that it is meaningless in their absence."[124]

The relationship of the *Baldwin* court's discussion of the ownership cases to its conclusion that recreational sport hunting is not protected by the privileges and immunities clause is very obscure. The Court seemed to be saying that the early cases that recognize the authority of states "to preserve this bounty [*i.e.,* wildlife] for their citizens alone" reflect an understanding early in our nation's history that access to that bounty was not considered a fundamental right.[125] Notwithstanding that the "ownership" theory upon which those cases rested has since been discredited, they are still instructive in determining whether a "federally protected interest," *i.e.,* a constitutionally protected privilege or immunity, is at stake.[126]

Much clearer is the relationship of the discussion of the ownership cases in the opinion of the three dissenting Justices to the rationale of that opinion. In the view of the dissenting Justices, the characterization of sport hunting as a fundamental or nonfundamental right is irrelevant. The appropriate inquiry is whether the state has a proper justification for discriminating against citizens of other states.[127] In the view of the dissenters, there were only three possible justifications: conservation, cost, or the right of a state to do what it wants with that which it owns. The dissenters concluded that the record before them failed to reveal that the discrimination was necessary for any conservation purpose.[128] As to the second possible justification, the dissenters accepted the finding of the district court that the fee differential was not justified on the basis of cost allocation.[129] The third possible justification was dismissed in the following vivid terms:

> The lingering death of the [state ownership] doctrine as applied to a State's wildlife, begun with the thrust of Mr. Justice Holmes' blade in *Missouri v. Holland* ... and aided by increasingly deep twists of the knife in [*Toomer* and other cases], finally became a reality in *Douglas v. Seacoast Products, Inc.*[130]

---

[124]436 U.S. at 386–387.

[125]*Id.* at 384.

[126]*Id.* at 386.

[127]*Id.* at 402 (Brennan, J., dissenting).

[128]*Id.* at 403–404.

[129]*Id.* at 404.

[130]*Id.* at 405.

The Chief Justice, in a separate, concurring opinion, implicitly agreed with the dissenters that the characterization of the right at stake was not the relevant inquiry. Thus, in his view, it was "the special interest of Montana citizens in its elk," rather than the nonfundamental character of the right to hunt those elk, "that permits Montana to charge nonresident hunters higher license fees without offending the Privileges and Immunities Clause."[131] Admitting that the characterization of the state's "special interest" in wildlife as ownership was a "legal anachronism of sorts," the Chief Justice maintained that "[w]hether we describe this interest as proprietary or otherwise is not significant."[132] He then recounted the many recent decisions limiting state authority over wildlife and concluded that "[n]one of those cases hold that the Privileges and Immunities Clause prevents a State from preferring its own citizens in allocating access to wildlife within that State."[133] Had the Chief Justice not omitted *Toomer* from that catalog of cases, he would not have been able to make that patently wrong assertion.[134] Had he recognized that error, he would have been compelled either to join the dissenters or disagree with them on the basis of the conservation or cost justification for the discrimination. His only alternative was to embrace the anachronistic "fundamental rights" formulation of the privileges and immunities test used by the majority.[135]

The breath of air given the state ownership doctrine by *Baldwin* proved to be its last gasp. Less than a year later, concluding "that time has revealed the error" of *Geer,* the Supreme Court expressly overruled it in *Hughes v. Oklahoma.*[136] The facts in *Hughes* were nearly identical to those in *Geer.* An Oklahoma law prohibited the shipment out of the state, for purposes of sale, of minnows seined or otherwise procured from the state's waters.[137] The defendant was a Texas minnow dealer arrested for transport-

---

[131]*Id.* at 393–394 (Burger J., concurring).

[132]*Id.* at 392.

[133]*Id.* at 393.

[134]The Chief Justice may have felt that it was appropriate to exclude *Toomer* from his list of cases restricting state authority over wildlife because elsewhere in his opinion he noted that *Toomer* held "that the doctrine [of state ownership] does not apply to migratory shrimp located in the three-mile belt of the marginal sea." He distinguished those shrimp from "the elk involved in this case [which] are found within Montana and remain primarily within the State. As such they are natural resources of the State." 436 U.S. at 392. Those shrimp, however, cannot be distinguished on that basis from the menhaden involved in *Douglas,* a case the Chief Justice included in his list.

[135]*See* L. Tribe, American Constitutional Law 34–40 (Supp. 1979).

[136]441 U.S. 322 (1979).

[137]The prohibition did not apply to hatchery minnows or to persons leaving the state with no more than three dozen minnows in their possession. *See* 441 U.S. at 323–324 n. 1.

ing out of the state minnows purchased from a licensed Oklahoma dealer. The defendant challenged the constitutionality of the Oklahoma statute on the grounds that it unreasonably interfered with interstate commerce, notwithstanding that no federal law preempted the state from regulating in this area. Seven members of the Supreme Court agreed and thus erected what may be the most formidable barrier yet to discriminatory state regulation of wildlife.

In the opinion of the Court, the *Geer* ownership analysis had "been eroded to the point of virtual extinction" in subsequent decisions.[138] While recognizing "the legitimate state concerns for conservation and protection of wild animals underlying the 19th century legal fiction of state ownership,"[139] the Court was unwilling to continue to regard wildlife as conceptually different from other natural resources in a state. Therefore, the Court expressly overruled *Geer* by concluding that "challenges under the Commerce Clause to state regulations of wild animals should be considered according to the same general rule applied to state regulations of their natural resources."[140] Applying this general rule, the Court found that, although the conservation of its minnows may be a legitimate local purpose justifying some discrimination, less discriminatory means of achieving that purpose were available.[141] Thus the state's choice of means was unconstitutional.

The most serious question to follow from *Hughes* is whether the *Baldwin* result would have been the same had the plaintiffs there based their challenge on the commerce clause rather than the privileges and immunities clause. Several commentators have opined that it might not.[142] That view has considerable force. The Oklahoma law struck down in *Hughes* could hardly have affected interstate commerce more substantially than the Montana law upheld in *Baldwin*. As the *Hughes* dissent pointed out, Oklahoma permitted the export of as many minnows as anyone would want, so long as those minnows came from hatcheries and not from natural

---

[138]*Id.* at 331.

[139]*Id.* at 336.

[140]*Id.* at 335.

[141]*Id.* at 337–338.

[142]*See, e.g.,* Coggins, Wildlife and the Constitution: the Walls Come Tumbling Down, 55 Wash. L. Rev. 295, 318 (1980) ("Oddly enough, the *Baldwin* plaintiffs seem not to have raised objections under the commerce clause. Perhaps bedazzled by the similarities with *Toomer,* they may have forfeited a better argument."); Note, Hughes v. Oklahoma and Baldwin v. Fish and Game Commission: The Commerce Clause and State Control of Natural Resources, 66 Va. L. Rev. 1145, 1155 (1980) ("[A] commerce clause challenge might better protect nonresidents' individual rights than the privileges and immunities clause").

[143]441 U.S. at 345 (Rehnquist, J., dissenting).

streams.[143] Though *Baldwin* held that recreation is not a fundamental right, there is no shortage of precedent for the proposition that recreation is commerce.[144] Indeed, Mr. Baldwin was an outfitter and licensed hunting guide whose livelihood depended in substantial part on out-of-state big game hunters.[145]

Had the *Hughes* commerce test been applied to the Montana differential license fee scheme, the Court would have had to examine whether the degree of burden placed upon interstate commerce was justified by a legitimate local public interest and whether that interest could be promoted with a lesser impact on interstate activities.[146] That, in effect, would have obliged the Court to make the same inquiry into the relationship between the fee differential and the difference in cost to the state of servicing residents and nonresidents as it made in *Toomer*. Though the *Baldwin* majority refrained from expressing any view on that question, it is clear that the three dissenters believed the Montana statute failed the test.

## NEW DIRECTIONS FOR STATE REGULATION: AN AFFIRMATIVE DUTY TO PROTECT THE PUBLIC TRUST

### Common Law Developments Prior to *Hughes v. Oklahoma*

What the doctrine of state ownership of wildlife has traditionally been thought to authorize, in the absence of affirmative federal regulation or express constitutional restraint, is state regulation of private activity directly pertaining to wildlife within state borders. A smattering of cases within the last two decades led to the emergence of a wholly new use of the doctrine. These cases have explored the question of what rights the states

---

[143]441 U.S. at 345 (Rehnquist, J., dissenting).

[144]*See, e.g.*, United States v. International Boxing Club, 348 U.S. 236, 241 (1955). *Cf.* Flood v. Kuhn, 407 U.S. 258 (1972).

[145]436 U.S. at 372. Other evidence in the case indicated that as many as half of the nonresident elk hunters used outfitters, that certain outfitters were dependent almost entirely upon business from nonresidents, and that a typical nonresident elk hunter expended $1,250 plus license fee and outfitter's fee for a week-long hunt. *Id.* at 374 n. 9, and 376.

[146]*Id.* at 331. This test derives from Pike v. Bruce Church, Inc., 397 U.S. 137, 142 (1970), and was described by the Court as applying to challenges to state regulation of exports of natural resources. If hunting license fees are analogized to state severance taxes on natural resources, the test applied in Commonwealth Edison Co. v. Montana, 453 U.S. 609 (1981), might be applicable. That test requires that the tax be "fairly related to services provided by the State" as well as not discriminate against interstate commerce. *Id.* at 617.

may have as a consequence of both the state ownership and public trust doctrines, with respect to activities that, though not directly pertaining to the taking or utilization of wildlife, nonetheless have a substantial and adverse effect upon wildlife. Principally, these cases have considered whether states may recover monetary damages for losses to wildlife resulting from pollution of the environment.[147]

One of the first such cases of this variety was a Pennsylvania state court decision, *Commonwealth v. Agway, Inc.*[148] In that action, the state sued an allegedly negligent polluter of a stream to recover the commercial value of some 72,000 fish whose deaths were attributed to the defendant's pollution. In the view of the Pennsylvania court, the controlling question was whether the state's "property interest" in the fish was sufficient to support an action for monetary damages. In answering that question in the negative, the court emphasized the state's lack of "possession" of the fish and drew a distinction between the state's powers as a "sovereign" and as an "owner" of wildlife, a distinction that it attributed to *Missouri v. Holland* and *Toomer v. Witsell*. Since, in its view, possession was a prerequisite of ownership, and ownership was necessary to support an action for damages, the state, having neither, could not maintain the action.[149]

---

[147]The rights considered here were initially asserted as common law rights. Most states have since enacted legislation specifically authorizing recovery by the state for destruction of its fish and wildlife resources. *See* Halter and Thomas, Recovery of Damages by States for Fish and Wildlife Losses Caused by Pollution, 10 Ecol. L. Q. 5 (1982). One such law, the Florida Oil-Spill Prevention and Pollution Control Act, which imposes strict liability for "all costs of cleanup or other damage" resulting from oil spills, Fla. Stat. Ann. §376.12, was upheld by the Supreme Court in Askew v. American Waterways Operators, Inc., 411 U.S. 325 (1973). Such general legislation, however, frequently fails to describe with particularity the sort of "property" for which damage recovery is authorized or spell out how its value is to be measured, thus leaving open the very questions that are most important in the common law actions.

The rights considered here do not include the rights of private parties to sue for injuries to wildlife in which they may have a "property" interest. For a discussion of that problem, see Commentary, Oil and Oysters Don't Mix: Private Remedies for Pollution Damage to Shellfish, 23 Ala. L. Rev. 100 (1970).

[148]210 Pa. Super. 150, 232 A. 2d 69 (1967).

[149]In direct response to the *Agway* decision, the Pennsylvania legislature passed a law in 1968 that expressly declared the state to have a "proprietary ownership, jurisdiction over and control of fish ... achieved through the continued expenditure of commonwealth funds and efforts to protect, perpetuate, propagate and maintain populations of fish" and authorized civil suits in trespass against "persons who unlawfully or negligently kill or destroy" the same. 30 Purdon's Statutes §202.1 (repealed 1980; current version at 30 Pa. C.S.A. §2506). To date, there have been no reported decisions construing the 1968 law or its sequel, and thus the question

The *Agway* decision was criticized for its emphasis on possession, a "judicial tool used to settle disputes between individuals of equal stature" that need not be used to circumscribe the powers of a state in its sovereign capacity.[150] More fundamentally, the *Agway* decision offered only a perfunctory analysis of the *Toomer* and *Missouri v. Holland* decisions on which it relied so heavily. It is certainly true, as has already been demonstrated here, that *Missouri v. Holland* substantially qualified the state ownership doctrine. However, it did so in the context of delineating the states' authority vis-à-vis the federal government, and did not consider the wholly different question of state authority vis-à-vis private activity.[151]

The *Agway* decision was accepted uncritically by the North Dakota Supreme Court in *State v. Dickinson Cheese Co.*, a factually similar case.[152] However, in *California v. S.S. Bournemouth*, a case brought in federal court, the possibility of a different outcome was strongly suggested.[153] In that action, the California Department of Fish and Game sought to recover monetary damages resulting from an oil spill in the state's waters. In ruling on a pretrial motion, the court stated that "[w]hile here the alleged injury was to the water itself, and possibly the marine life also, the efforts to distinguish between various types of property would serve no useful purpose."[154] Despite the court's suggestion that recovery for damage to marine life would be appropriate, however, the damages ultimately awarded were described as being equivalent to the cost of "cleanup." Whether "cleanup" included any wildlife restoration efforts is not revealed in the reported decisions.

In *Maryland v. Amerada Hess Corp.*[155] and *Maine v. M/V Tamano*,[156] the courts went a step further in recognizing the right of states to seek

---

whether the state may legislate for itself the type of "ownership" found lacking in *Agway* has not been presented.

[150]Comment, Animals Ferae Naturae—Commonwealth not Permitted to Recover Damages in Trespass for Negligent Killing of Fish by Pollution, 72 Dick. L. Rev. 200 (1967).

[151]Similarly, although *Toomer* considered the question of state authority to regulate private activity pertaining to wildlife, the limitation that it imposed on state regulation derived not from the state's lack of possession of the wildlife, but rather from express constitutional command.

[152]200 N.W. 2d 59 (N.D. 1972).

[153]307 F. Supp. 922 (D.C. Cal. 1969), *judgment granted* 318 F. Supp. 839 (C.D. Cal. 1970).

[154]307 F. Supp. at 928.

[155]350 F. Supp. 1060 (D. Md. 1972), *motion for relief denied*, 356 F. Supp. 975 (D. Md. 1973).

[156]357 F. Supp. 1097 (D. Me. 1973).

monetary damages for injuries to wildlife. The states' complaints charged that oil spills had irreparably damaged their waters and the life therein. The defendants sought to have the complaints dismissed because the state did not have a "property interest" in such waters or aquatic life. Both courts rejected the contention on the basis that the states' public trust responsibilities gave them "technical ownership."[157] The Maryland court declared that "if the State is deemed to be the trustee of the waters, then, as trustee, the State must be empowered to bring suit to protect the corpus of the trust— i.e., the waters—for the beneficiaries of the trust—i.e., the public."[158]

Both the *Amerada Hess* and *Tamano* cases were finally settled out of court. Accordingly, the courts never faced the question of what damages, if any, could be recovered or how they were to be measured. That, of course, is the next major hurdle to be cleared once it is established that a state has authority to sue for monetary damages for loss of its wildlife. One of the first cases to consider that issue is an unreported Tennessee decision, *State of Tennessee* ex. rel. *Goodrich v. Riggan.*[159]

In the *Riggan* case, Tennessee brought suit against an individual whose negligent application of a herbicide caused the death of at least eleven deer. On instructions from the trial judge to consider only the cost of replacing the deer with deer trapped elsewhere and relocated, the jury awarded a verdict in the amount of $1,119. The state appealed, claiming error in the trial judge's instructions on the damage issue. The state claimed that it was entitled to recover damages that would fully compensate it for the loss of the "aesthetic, ecological and recreational worth"[160] of the deer, a value that the state's expert witnesses estimate to be $2,500 per deer. The court of appeals, however, refused to overrule the trial judge because "a white-tailed deer is not an endangered specie in Tennessee" and is not irreplaceable.[161]

While the preceding cases represented a significant development, they also created some rather substantial legal and conceptual difficulties. For example, even if one assumes that a state is entitled to sue for injuries done to its wildlife and that the amount of those injuries can be quantified in dollar terms, there is still the fundamental question of what standard of care is to be required of persons whose actions cause those injuries. Because the common law concepts of "negligence" and "strict liability" have evolved with reference to the reasonableness of risks posed to humans or their private property, it is very difficult to translate those concepts in

---

[157]The concept of "technical ownership" was taken from Justice Frankfurter's concurring opinion in *Toomer.*

[158]350 F. Supp. at 1067.

[159]Tenn. Ct. of Appeals, Western Section (Aug. 31, 1976).

[160]Assignments of Error and Brief of Appellant, at 28.

[161]Memorandum Opinion at 5.

situations involving risks to wildlife.[162] No case illustrates the problem better than *State v. Jersey Central Power & Light Co.*[163]

In *Jersey Central,* the state brought an action as *parens patriae* for the death of about 500,000 menhaden resulting from the operation of defendant's nuclear power plant. For purposes of cooling its condensers, the plant drew water from a nearby river through an intake canal, circulated it, and then discharged it through a canal into another river. The discharged water was, of course, substantially warmer than the water taken in. As a result, menhaden remained in the discharge area throughout the year, rather than migrate to southern waters in the winter. In midwinter, the plant was forced to shut down its generators for a few days. It continued, however, to pump water through the plant, although the discharged water was no longer being warmed. The result was a precipitous drop in the water temperature in the discharge area, causing the massive die-off of menhaden there.

The trial court, citing *Amerada Hess,* but in fact going considerably beyond it, declared that "[t]he State has not only the right but also the *affirmative fiduciary obligation* to ensure that the rights of the public to a viable marine environment are protected and to seek compensation for any diminution in that trust corpus."[164] On the issue of damages, however, the trial court was less forceful:

> Although it appears generally that the environment may well have been adversely affected in many ways...the court cannot speculate as to the monetary value of these damages. It awards plaintiff a judgment of $935...or the market value attributed by the State's witness to the fish killed....[165]

Defendant sought a rehearing on the ground that there had been no proof of negligence. The trial court agreed on the evidentiary point but nonetheless upheld its judgment on the basis that the defendant was strictly liable for creating "an ultra-hazardous situation." The Appellate Division agreed with the trial court that the state had an affirmative duty to seek recovery and affirmed the lower court's decision, although it rejected strict

---

[162]The issue raised here is related to those raised by Christopher Stone in his provocative article, Should Trees Have Standing—Toward Legal Rights for Natural Objects, 45 S. Cal. L. Rev. 450 (1972). Stone's central thesis, that certain natural objects and living things should have certain legally cognizable rights, has been given an inventive, and possibly very practical extension in Reed, Should Rivers Have Running? Toward Extension of the Reserved Rights Doctrine to Include Minimum Stream Flows, 12 Idaho L. Rev. 153 (1976).

[163]69 N.J. 102, 351 A.2d 337 (1976).

[164]125 N.J. Super. 103, 308 A.2d 671, 674 (Super. Ct., N.J. Ocean Country, 1973) (emphasis added).

[165]*Id.*

liability as the basis of liability because "the pumping of cold water...cannot be considered an ultra-hazardous activity." Rather, the Appellate Division rested defendant's liability on negligence because it should have known that a "sharp reduction in water temperature would have damaged aquatic life."[166]

The New Jersey Supreme Court reversed the judgment on the grounds that defendant's actions had not caused the death of the fish.[167] The court reasoned that the fish would have died whether or not the plant continued to pump cold water through its closed plant. At most, the continued pumping merely accelerated the fatal temperature drop. In perhaps the most significant passage in the opinion, the court stated the following:

> It might be argued that defendant caused the death of the fish by attract-
> ing them to the Creek through the warming of the water therein incident
> to operation of the plant; and then, having brought them there, killed
> them by discontinuing the plant operation, thus cooling the water. But
> this thesis cannot constitute a theory of culpable causation of the killing
> as it is undenied that the operation of the plant in the manner described
> was perfectly lawful....[168]

Since the mere fact that an activity is performed lawfully does not serve to exempt that activity from liability for harm resulting therefrom if the activity is, in contemplation of law, an "ultrahazardous" activity, the above passage must mean that defendant's *operation of the plant* did not constitute an ultrahazardous activity. That represents a considerable broadening of the Appellate Division's holding that the mere pumping of water could not constitute an ultrahazardous activity and invites the question of just what is, for purposes of parens patriae suits to recover for wildlife losses, an ultrahazardous activity.

The doctrine of strict liability for ultrahazardous activities is a comparatively recent development in Anglo-American jurisprudence. Its origins can be traced to the 1868 decision of the House of Lords in *Rylands v. Fletcher*.[169] As originally understood, the doctrine applied to any activity which necessarily imposed an extreme danger to others, and which constituted a "nonnatural" use of land. As adopted into modern American law, the doctrine applies to any activity that "necessarily involves a risk of serious harm to the person, land or chattels of others which cannot be eliminated by the exercise of the utmost care" and "is not a matter of common usage."[170] Since there can be little doubt that the operation of a

---

[166]133 N.J. Super. 375, 389, 336 A.2d 750, 757 (1975).

[167]69 N.J. 102, 351 A.2d 337 (1976). The court also held that federal regulation of nuclear energy plants exempted them from state control.

[168]69 N.J. at 111, 351 A.2d at 342.

[169]L.R. 3 H.L. 330 (1868).

[170]Restatement of Torts, §§519, 520.

nuclear power plant "necessarily imposes a risk of serious harm" to wildlife "which cannot be eliminated by the exercise of the utmost care," the New Jersey Supreme Court may have felt that wildlife cannot be considered the "person, land or chattels of others." On the other hand, the court expressly stated that it was not deciding whether the doctrine of strict liability could apply in an action by the state as a public trustee.

Alternatively, the court may have felt that the operation of a nuclear power plant was a "common usage" or at least not a "nonnatural" use of land. That explanation would better serve the Appellate Division, which viewed the relevant activity merely as the pumping of water. The leading American authority on tort law "predicted with a good deal of confidence" in 1971 that the use of nuclear energy was "an area in which no court will...refuse to recognize and apply the principal of strict liability found in the cases which follow *Rylands v. Fletcher.*"[171] Perhaps five years later the New Jersey court was simply unable to regard nuclear energy plants as unnatural.[172] Perhaps it was simply unwilling to impose any sort of liability for acts harmful to wildlife.

*Jersey Central* thus makes clear that the extension of the state ownership doctrine represented by the common law cases described here will be faced with many pitfalls. To the extent that that small body of case law can be summarized, it would appear that, in at least some states, the state may sue in its capacity as public trustee for injuries to wildlife resulting from negligent private activity. Suits for injuries resulting from nonnegligent activity, however, will probably be allowed, if at all, only when the causative activity meets the classic test of being an ultrahazardous activity. There is, moreover, at least a hint that the courts will be more restrictive in defining what activities are ultrahazardous for wildlife than they have been for defining activities ultrahazardous for humans. Finally, where recovery is allowed, the measure of damages should be at least the demonstrable market value of the wildlife destroyed and perhaps even greater.

---

[171] W. Prosser, Law of Torts 516 (4th ed. 1971).

[172] There is little in law that is more mind boggling than determining what is a "nonnatural" use for purposes of the doctrine of strict liability. In *Rylands* itself, the nonnatural use was merely the construction of a reservoir in coal mining country. Of course, the problem can be avoided by legislatively imposing strict liability on a particular activity, as in the Florida Oil Spill Prevention and Pollution Control Act, discussed *supra* at note 147, which in effect declares the handling and transportation of oil to be a "nonnatural" and "ultrahazardous" activity. *Cf.* Just v. Marinette County, 56 Wis. 2d 7, 201 N.W. 2d 761 (1972), where, for purposes of ascertaining the scope of the state's authority to protect wetlands, the Wisconsin Supreme Court declared that the development of certain lake-front property by its owner was contrary to "the essential natural character of his land...for which it was unsuited in its natural state." 201 N.W. 2d at 768.

### Developments Since *Hughes v. Oklahoma*

The right of the states to recover at least some monetary damages at common law for injury to wildlife had thus become fairly well established by the late 1970s. Whether that right survives the death of the state ownership doctrine in *Hughes* has been addressed in two subsequent lower court decisions.

In *In re Steuart Transportation Co.*, the defendant challenged the right of either the Commonwealth of Virginia or the federal government to recover monetary damages for the loss of migratory waterfowl from an oil spill, on the grounds that neither government "owned" the birds.[173] The court responded that the cases on which the defendant relied, including *Hughes*, "turned upon principles of federalism and pre-emption by federal legislation of state control measures. Neither of these principles is applicable to the current issues before this court."[174] The court concluded that both governments have a "sovereign interest in preserving wildlife resources" and that therefore they could seek damages under either *parens patriae* or public trust doctrines.[175]

*Commonwealth of Puerto Rico v. SS Zoe Colocotroni* also considered whether a state could assert a recoverable interest in wildlife at common law.[176] The court declined to rule on this question because Puerto Rico also sought recovery on the basis of a state statute expressly authorizing it. In the court's view, neither *Hughes* nor the Constitution prohibited Puerto Rico from enacting such a statute. However, "where the Commonwealth of Puerto Rico has thus legislatively authorized the bringing of suits for environmental damages . . . such an action must be construed as taking the place of any implied common law action the Commonwealth as trustee, might have brought."[177]

---

[173]495 F. Supp. 38 (E.D. Va. 1980).

[174]*Id.* at 39–40.

[175]According to the court, these doctrines constitute separate theories for the same cause of action.

> Under the public trust doctrine, the State of Virginia and the United States have the right and the duty to protect and preserve the public's interest in natural wildlife resources. . . . Likewise, under the doctrine of *parens patriae* the state acts to protect a quasi-sovereign interest where no individual cause of action would lie.

*Id.* at 40. Although the differences between these doctrines are subtle, it would seem that the public trust doctrine is the more broadly applicable. *See* Hayes *et al.*, State Recovery for Wildlife Destruction: New Life for an Old Doctrine, 2 ISL L. Rev. 13, 29–30 (1977).

[176]628 F.2d 652 (1st Cir. 1980), *cert. denied,* 450 U.S. 912 (1981).

[177]*Id.* at 672.

The holding in *Zoe,* that enactment of a state statute authorizing suits by the state to recover damages for injury to its natural resources is permissible under *Hughes* and displaces common law remedies, is likely to stimulate the enactment of similar laws in other states and diminish the significance of the common law cases discussed previously. The future of common law actions is also clouded as a result of the Supreme Court's recent decision in *City of Milwaukee v. Illinois,* holding that enactment of the Federal Water Pollution Control Act Amendments of 1972 displaced the federal common law of nuisance as a basis for state actions against neighboring states or their citizens.[178]

At the federal level, a number of statutes have authorized suits to recover damages for injury to natural resources since publication of the initial text. For example, the Clean Water Act Amendments of 1977 expanded the scope of recovery against one who causes a spill of oil or other hazardous substance in navigable waters to include not only the costs of removal but also the cost to the state or federal governments of restoring or replacing natural resources damaged by such a spill.[179] Recovery for injury resulting from an oil spill was also provided by the Outer Continental Shelf Lands Act Amendments of 1978.[180] Most significant, however, is the Comprehensive Environmental Response, Compensation and Liability Act of 1980, commonly known as the "Superfund" legislation.[181] It authorizes the President or the authorized representative of any state to recover from anyone who causes the release of any of a broad range of hazardous substances such sums as are necessary to restore, rehabilitate, or acquire the equivalent of, damaged natural resources.[182] Though very comprehensive in scope, the Superfund legislation expressly preserves the right of the states to impose additional liability or requirements on persons releasing hazardous substances within the state.[183]

Actions for recovery of damages to natural resources, whether brought under common law theories or pursuant to statute, will share certain problems, the most notable of which is ascertaining the proper amount of monetary damages. This issue was extensively explored in *Zoe.* The evi-

---

[178]451 U.S. 304 (1981). Although the decision did not address whether the federal legislation displaced state common law actions, the rationale of the Court suggested that such actions may be more secure. *Id.* at 316–317.

[179]33 U.S.C. §1321(f)(4) (1976 & Supp. V 1981).

[180]43 U.S.C. §1813(a)(2)(C) and (D) (Supp. IV 1980).

[181]42 U.S.C. §§9601–9657 (Supp. IV 1980).

[182]*Id.* §9607(f).

[183]*Id.* §9614(a). This clearly preserves state authority to enact more restrictive legislation or regulations on the subject. Whether it also preserves state common law remedies against such polluters is less clear in light of *City of Milwaukee,* 451 U.S. at 327–328.

dence in that action indicated that the defendants were responsible for a release of oil that contaminated approximately 20 acres of coastal mangrove forest in a virtually uninhabited area of Puerto Rico. The defendants claimed that damages should be limited to the diminution of market value of the affected lands, the traditional measure of liability. Puerto Rico argued, however, that the mangrove area had no significant commercial or market value but considerable ecological value. The court reasoned that because the Puerto Rico statute authorized recovery of the total value "of damages to the environment," to use the traditional "diminution of value" measure of damages would frustrate the apparent intent of Puerto Rico to preserve natural areas like the one despoiled.[184] The search for an appropriate alternative measure of damages led the district and appellate courts to two different conclusions.

The major element of damages in the decision of the district court was determined by calculating the "replacement cost" of individual organisms affected by the spill.[185] The evidence presented to the court indicated that some 92 million invertebrate organisms had been affected and that the cost of acquiring similar organisms from biological supply houses was in excess of 5 million dollars. The court of appeals, however, rejected this as a proper measure of damages. Taking its guidance from the various federal statutes mentioned above, the court reasoned that the cost of "replacement" was an appropriate component of damages only when such replacement was in fact to be carried out as part of a larger restoration program.[186] The proper measure of damages, in the opinion of the court of appeals, was

> the cost reasonably to be incurred by the sovereign or its designated agency to restore or rehabilitate the environment in the affected area to is [sic] pre-existing condition, or as close thereto as is feasible without grossly disproportionate expenditures. The focus in determining such a remedy should be on the steps a reasonable and prudent sovereign or agency would take to mitigate the harm done by the pollution, with attention to such factors as technical feasibility, harmful side effects, compatibility with or duplication of such regeneration as is naturally to be expected, and the extent to which efforts beyond a certain point would become either redundant or disproportionately expensive.[187]

---

[184]628 F.2d at 673.

[185]456 F. Supp. 1327 (D.P.R. 1978).

[186]628 F.2d at 676–677. In City of Murray v. Kentucky, 13 Env't Rep. Cas. (BNA) 1558 (Ct. App. Ky. June 29, 1979), however, a Kentucky court, pursuant to a state statute providing that polluters shall be assessed an amount reasonably necessary to restock fish or wildlife that have been destroyed, awarded damages equivalent to the cost of restocking the fish killed, even though Kentucky acknowledged that it did not intend to restock.

[187]628 F.2d at 675.

The *Zoe* standard leaves a court with considerable discretion in determining what amount of restoration costs are reasonable. Moreover, as the *Zoe* court itself recognized, its standard may be inappropriate in certain situations, such as when restoration is impossible.[188] In these situations, replacement costs, off-site compensation costs, or still other measures might be appropriate alternatives. It is likely, however, that under any of these alternatives the court will also exercise a similarly broad discretion in determining reasonableness.

The scope of judicial discretion can, however, be narrowed by statute. The Superfund legislation attempts to do this by directing the President to develop regulations "for the assessment of damages for injury to, destruction of, or loss of natural resources resulting from a release of oil or a hazardous substance."[189] The assessment of damages carried out by federal officials pursuant to these regulations is presumed to be the proper measure of damages in any judicial proceeding pertaining to the spill in question, although the presumption can be rebutted.[190] As a result, in Superfund litigation the discretion of the courts will be narrowed substantially by this grant of administrative authority to the President.[191]

---

[188]Examples might include situations in which an endangered species is eliminated or in which the assault on the environment occurs suddenly but does not persist. The fish kill resulting from a sudden change in water temperature involved in State v. Jersey Central Power & Light Co., discussed at text accompanying notes 163–172, *supra,* is an example of the latter.

[189]42 U.S.C. §9651(c)(1) (Supp. IV 1980).

[190]*Id.* §9611(h)(2).

[191]The President has assigned his responsibilities to the Secretary of the Interior. *See* Exec. Order 12316, 46 Fed. Reg. 42237 (Aug. 20, 1981). Although the statute directs that these regulations be promulgated within two years (*i.e.,* by December 11, 1982), that deadline passed without any regulations even having been proposed. For a useful summary of the natural resource recovery provisions of the Superfund legislation, see Bleicher, The Impact of Superfund on Government Claims for Damages to Natural Resources, Envtl. Protection Rep. (Aug. 1981).

Chapter **3**

# INDIAN TREATY RIGHTS, A SPECIAL LIMITATION ON STATE AND FEDERAL WILDLIFE REGULATION

It has been clear, at least since *Missouri v. Holland*, that the treaties of the United States not only impose obligations upon the federal government, but also supersede conflicting state laws. In a sense, treaties between the United States and the various Indian tribes are no different from other types of treaties. However, because of certain special aspects of Indian treaties, and most particularly because of the very substantial limitations which recent federal court decisions construing such treaties have imposed on state wildlife efforts, they deserve special attention as a unique qualification on both state and federal regulation of wildlife.

## THE REGULATION OF INDIAN HUNTING AND FISHING

Generalizations about the nature of Indian treaty rights pertaining to wildlife must be made with caution because they are likely to vary from tribe to tribe, depending upon the language and historical context of the treaties involved. Nonetheless, the decisions of the Supreme Court in particular Indian treaty rights cases are often read as enunciating principles that apply more broadly than to the narrow factual contexts of those cases. This chapter focuses primarily on that Court's many recent Indian treaty cases.

One of the first occasions for the Supreme Court to consider the relationship between a state's authority to regulate wildlife and the rights of hunting and fishing reserved by Indians in their treaties was in 1896 in

*Ward v. Race Horse.*[1] The author of the Court's opinion was Justice White, who had written the majority opinion in *Geer v. Connecticut* earlier in the same year.[2] Not unexpectedly, Justice White was extremely solicitous of the claims of the state to exclusive regulation of the wildlife within its borders.

Race Horse was a Bannock Indian convicted of killing elk in violation of Wyoming law. In a habeas corpus proceeding, he contended that his conviction contravened rights guaranteed him by an 1869 treaty reserving to the Bannocks "the rights to hunt on the unoccupied land of the United States, so long as game may be found thereon." In 1890, however, the state of Wyoming was admitted to the Union, and soon thereafter it enacted game laws that it claimed to be applicable even on federal land within the state. Since Race Horse's offense was committed on such federal lands, the issue of treaty rights versus state law was squarely presented.

In Justice White's view, there was no need to decide the constitutional issue (later resolved in *Missouri v. Holland*) because nothing in the treaty evidenced a congressional intent to supersede state law. In thus discerning the congressional intent, however, Justice White assumed the conclusion of the very constitutional issue he purported not to decide (much as he was to do again later in *The Abby Dodge*).[3] That is, his reasoning that the treaty could not have been intended to create a perpetual right of hunting on federal land in derogation of state law was based on the following rough syllogism: First, whatever treaty rights were retained could be extinguished by conveying the federal lands within the state to private owners even though such private owners would thereby acquire no authority over the game on such lands; second, when the United States "called into being a sovereign State, a necessary incident of whose authority was the complete power to regulate the killing of game within its borders,"[4] the treaty rights retained could certainly not be any greater; therefore, the creation of the state of Wyoming extinguished the treaty rights of the Bannocks to hunt on federal lands. It can readily be seen that the crucial premise of Justice White's syllogism was the second, which assumed that the federal government lacked authority to regulate wildlife on federal land within the state, an assumption finally rejected definitively in 1976 in *Kleppe v. New Mexico.*[5]

The chary interpretation given by Justice White to the Indian treaty in *Race Horse* was soon to be abandoned by the Supreme Court in favor of

---

[1] 163 U.S. 504 (1896).

[2] 161 U.S. 519 (1896).

[3] 223 U.S. 166 (1912). For a discussion of The Abby Dodge, *see* Chapter 2 at text accompanying notes 44–46.

[4] 163 U.S. at 510.

[5] 426 U.S. 529 (1976). For a discussion of Kleppe v. New Mexico, *see* Chapter 2 at text accompanying notes 69–75.

rules of construction that attempted to give Indian treaties the meaning that was the probable understanding of them by the Indians at the time they were signed.[6] In 1905 in *United States v. Winans*,[7] for example, the Court for the first time considered one of the so-called "Stevens treaties"[8] and held that its reservation to the Yakima Indians of "the right of taking fish at all usual and accustomed places, in common with the citizens of the Territory" entitled the Indians to the use of privately owned land for fishing at such usual places even though the landowner had been granted a license by the state to use a fish wheel there, the practical effect of which was to exclude all others from fishing at that place. Only Justice White dissented.

The *Winans* decision was extended in 1919 in *Seufert Brothers Co. v. United States* to apply to customary Indian fishing grounds located outside the area ceded by them.[9] Thus *Winans* and *Seufert* established the supremacy of Indian off-reservation treaty rights in relationship to the rights of private landholders, while *Race Horse* seemed to make such treaty rights subordinate to the authority of the states to regulate wildlife.

The first major break in the *Race Horse* rule came in 1942 in *Tulee v. Washington* in which the Supreme Court held contrary to yet another Stevens treaty a requirement of the state that Indians purchase fishing licenses.[10] The state had argued that since the only right guaranteed by the treaty was the right of Indians to fish "in common with" other citizens, the state had only to insure that its regulations not discriminate against Indians. In rejecting that argument and requiring that the state's regulation also be "necessary for the conservation of fish," the Supreme Court planted the seed of a storm of controversy that would long rage in the Pacific Northwest.[11]

The Court's next opportunity to refine its "necessary for the conservation of fish" standard came in 1968 in *Puyallup Tribe v. Department of Game*.[12] In that action, the state of Washington sued in state court to enjoin

---

[6]These rules of interpretation actually predate the *Race Horse* decisions. *See* Choctaw Nation v. United States, 119 U.S. 1, 28 (1886).

[7]198 U.S. 371 (1905).

[8]The Stevens treaties include six treaties negotiated with the Indian tribes of the Pacific Northwest by Oregon Territorial Governor Isaac Stevens in 1854 and 1855. Each of these treaties contains language similar to that involved in the *Winans* case. Citations to the six treaties appear in Washington v. Washington State Commercial Passenger Fishing Vessel Ass'n, 443 U.S. 658, 662 n.2 (1979).

[9]249 U.S. 194 (1919).

[10]315 U.S. 681 (1942).

[11]*Id.* at 684. *See* text accompanying notes 32–51 *infra*.

[12]391 U.S. 392 (1968).

certain Indians from violating state regulations restricting the use of nets for salmon and steelhead fishing. The injunction entered by the trial court, which required the Indians to abide by all state fishing regulations, was modified by the state supreme court to require adherence only to those regulations that were "reasonable and necessary." The state supreme court remanded the case to the trial court for a determination of which regulations met that test. Before the remand, however, the United States Supreme Court reviewed and affirmed the decision of the state supreme court, announcing that, although "[t]he right to fish 'at all usual and accustomed' places may...not be qualified," nevertheless, the "manner of fishing, the size of the take, the restriction of commercial fishing, and the like may be regulated by the State in the interest of conservation, provided the regulation meets appropriate standards and does not discriminate against the Indians."[13] The "appropriate standards" referred to in the Court's *"Puyallup I"* decision were presumably the standards of reasonableness and necessity established by the state court.

The Supreme Court's efforts to articulate the permissible standards for state regulation of off-reservation treaty rights fishing thus failed to result in very clear guidance to affected states. With the legal situation in this rather confused posture, Charles A. Hobbs, a former chairman of the Indian Affairs Committee of the American Bar Association, wrote an article in which he proposed a simple but, in retrospect, shattering suggestion.[14] Hobbs argued that the heart of the problem was the guaranteeing of a "fair share" of the fishery resource to the Indians and that, since the state fishery departments had failed to resolve the problem in such terms, it became the duty of the courts to "consider the question of 'necessity' from the perspective of what is a fair share of the fish for the Indians."[15]

The Supreme Court was forced to come face to face with Hobbs's suggestion when the *Puyallup* case came back before it in 1973.[16] After the Court's first decision in the case, the Washington Department of Fisheries relaxed its restrictions on net fishing for salmon. However, the Department of Game continued its total prohibition of net fishing for steelhead trout, and the state supreme court upheld the ban because "the catch of the steelhead sports fishery alone in the Puyallup River leaves no more than a sufficient number of steelhead for escapement necessary for the conservation of the steelhead fishery in that river."[17] The effect of state regulation,

---

[13]*Id.* at 398.
[14]Hobbs, Indian Hunting and Fishing Rights II, 37 Geo. Wash. L. Rev. 1251 (1969).
[15]*Id.* at 1260.
[16]414 U.S. 44 (1973).
[17]*Id.* at 46.

therefore, was to allocate the entire harvestable run of steelhead to the non-Indian sports fishery, leaving none available to the Indians. The Supreme Court, through Justice Douglas, held that the state regulation discriminated unlawfully against the Indians and declared that the harvestable run of steelhead "must in some manner be fairly apportioned between Indian net fishing and non-Indian sports fishing...."[18] The Court's *"Puyallup II"* decision did not prescribe the manner of apportionment but left that critical question for the lower courts to decide.

In neither of its *Puyallup* decisions nor in any of its other decisions had the Supreme Court ever directly considered whether Indian hunting or fishing on reservations was, by the inherent nature of such reservations, necessarily exempt from state or federal regulatory authority. Nonetheless, the states had long been assumed to be without such authority, though definitive support for that assumption was lacking.[19] The apparent origins of this assumption can be traced to the early case of *Worcester v. Georgia,* in which Chief Justice Marshall held that the laws of the states have no force within Indian reservations because they are "distinct political communities, having territorial boundaries, within which their authority is exclusive."[20] The assumption was further reinforced by the enactment of subsequent federal legislation giving states the authority to assume general criminal or civil jurisdiction over on-reservation Indian activities but withholding from the grant of criminal jurisdiction any authority over Indian "hunting, trapping, or fishing or the control, licensing, or regulation thereof."[21]

On remand from the *Puyallup II* decision, Washington state courts allocated 45 percent of the annual natural steelhead run available for taking to the treaty fishermen's net fishing but included in the Indian share all fish taken by treaty fishermen on the Puyallup reservation.[22] When the case came before the Supreme Court a third time, the Indians maintained

---

[18]*Id.* at 48.

[19]*See* Hobbs, *supra* note 14, at 1253.

[20]31 U.S. (6 Pet.) 515, 557 (1832). For an indication of the extent to which this early notion of inherent tribal sovereignty has since been eroded, see text accompanying notes 50–51 *infra.*

[21]18 U.S.C. §1162(b) (1976). The quoted language is from the Act of Aug. 15, 1953, ch. 505, Pub. L. No. 83-280, §2,67 Stat. 588, 589, often referred to simply as "Public Law 280." Though its provisions relating to state civil jurisdiction over on-reservation Indian activities, 28 U.S.C. §1360 (1976 & Supp. V 1981), do not expressly exempt hunting and fishing, this difference between its civil and criminal provisions has not yet been deemed significant. *See, e.g.,* Menominee Tribe v. United States, 391 U.S. 404 (1968).

[22]Department of Game v. Puyallup Tribe, Inc., 86 Wash. 2d 664, 548 P.2d 1058 (1976).

that, since the state had no authority to regulate Indian fishing on the reservation, fish caught there should not be counted against the Indian share. In *Puyallup III*, the Supreme Court disagreed.[23]

The rationale of the Court's holding in *Puyallup III* was couched in terms that appeared to limit its precedential significance. The Court paid great attention to the fact that virtually all of the reservation, including all that abutted the Puyallup River, had since been alienated.[24] Indeed, though noting that whether the reservation even continued to exist was a matter of dispute, the Court declined to resolve it.[25] What the Court did say, however, was that the very treaty language that assured the Indians a share of the fishery resource also necessarily assured a share to non-Indian fishermen and that totally unregulated Indian harvest on the reservation could deprive the latter of their share.[26] Thus, invoking Justice Douglas's admonition in *Puyallup II* that "the Treaty does not give the Indians a federal right to pursue the last living steelhead until it enters their nets,"[27] the Court ruled that fish taken by treaty Indians while on their reservation must be counted against the overall share allocated to them.[28]

The reasoning of the *Puyallup III* decision was harshly attacked by some commentators,[29] while even those who agreed with its result expressed doubt whether the same result would obtain for certain of the Stevens treaties having slightly different language.[30] The two dissenting Justices likewise characterized the majority's opinion as "so narrowly fact-specific that it will probably have no significant impact on the Puget Sound Indian fishing rights case still pending in the District Court."[31] That reference was to the still boiling dispute that followed in the wake of the so-called "Boldt decision" of the Western District of Washington in

---

[23] Puyallup Tribe, Inc. v. Department of Game of Washington, 433 U.S. 165 (1977).

[24] *Id.* at 174. In Montana v. United States, 450 U.S. 544, 561 (1981), the Court again emphasized this aspect of its *Puyallup III* decision. *See* note 67 *infra*.

[25] 443 U.S. at 173 n. 11.

[26] *Id.* at 175–176.

[27] 414 U.S. at 49.

[28] 433 U.S. at 177.

[29] *See, e.g.,* Dein, State Jurisdiction and On-Reservation Affairs: Puyallup Tribe v. Department of Game, 6 Envtl. Aff. 535, 561 (1978) ("The Court in *Puyallup III* ignored the fact that treaties are the supreme law of the land").

[30] *See, e.g.,* Comment, State Regulation of Indian Treaty Fishing Rights: Putting Puyallup III Into Perspective, 13 Gonzaga L. Rev. 140, 148 n. 62 (1977) (noting that because the Treaty with the Yakimas, June 9, 1855, 12 Stat. 951, 953, guarantees "the exclusive right of taking fish in all the streams, where running through or bordering said reservation," the Yakima tribe arguably enjoys greater on-reservation fishing rights than does the Puyallup tribe, whose treaty contains no similar provision).

[31] 433 U.S. at 185 (Brennan, J., dissenting).

1974. As it developed, the Supreme Court would itself soon be called upon to resolve that even larger controversy.

One year after the *Puyallup II* decision, Senior District Judge Boldt, in the Western District of Washington, took the bold step of translating the vague and general admonitions of the Supreme Court into concrete terms. His decision in *United States v. Washington,* which soon became known widely as "the Boldt decision," attempted for the first time ever to assure to the Indians their "fair share" of the fishery resource which Charles Hobbs had argued five years earlier that the courts must ultimately determine.[32] The result was to send shock waves throughout the Pacific Northwest.

The Boldt decision concerned the rights of a number of tribes under various of the Stevens treaties to fish in the Puget Sound and Olympic Peninsula watersheds and the offshore waters adjacent to those areas. Undoubtedly aware of the enormity of his decision, Judge Boldt took great pains to document in detail its legal and factual bases. The opinion, more than a hundred pages in length, contains a detailed analysis of the major state ownership cases and of the major Indian treaty rights cases. As to the factual underpinning of the decision, Judge Boldt relied heavily upon a "joint Biological Statement" agreed to by the parties and utilized reports and testimony of professional anthropologists.

Thus armed, Judge Boldt declared that

> [e]very regulation of treaty right fishing must be strictly limited to specific measures which before becoming effective have been established by the state, either to the satisfaction of all affected tribes or...of this court, to be reasonable and necessary to prevent demonstrable harm to the actual conservation of fish.[33]

Further, he defined "reasonable and necessary" measures to include those which are appropriate to their purpose and "essential to conservation" and limited "conservation" to the "perpetuation of a particular run or species of fish,"[34] thus excluding such purposes as assuring a maximum sustained harvest and providing for an orderly fishery.[35] Moreover, he prohibited the state from any regulation whatever of the treaty rights fishing of those tribes determined to be qualified for self-regulation according to criteria set forth in the opinion.

The most far-reaching aspect of the Boldt decision, however, was the determination that the treaty language "in common with" meant *"sharing*

---

[32]384 F. Supp. 312 (W.D. Wash. 1974), *aff'd,* 520 F.2d 676 (9th Cir. 1975), *cert. denied,* 423 U.S. 1086 (1976).

[33]384 F. Supp. at 342.

[34]*Id.*

[35]*See* 520 F.2d at 686.

*equally* the opportunity to take fish at 'usual and accustomed grounds and stations.'"[36] Accordingly, Judge Boldt declared that the Indians must be given the opportunity to harvest 50 percent of the fish (not counting those necessary for the minimum conservation purpose of assuring adequate escapement) that "absent harvest en route, would be available for harvest at the treaty tribes' usual and accustomed fishing places."[37] Finally, Judge Boldt appointed a "fishmaster" to oversee implementation of the court's decision and retained continuing jurisdiction to make such modifications in the decree as might be necessary.

Only a few months after the Boldt decision, Judge Belloni in Oregon modified a decree entered five years earlier in *Sohappy v. Smith* so as to apply the same 50 percent apportionment to the treaty Indians fishing in the Columbia River system.[38] Judge Belloni's decision applied both to Oregon and Washington.

For a time, it appeared that the Supreme Court would not disturb the result in the Boldt case because in 1976 it denied Washington's petition for a writ of certiorari to review the decision of the court of appeals substantially affirming Judge Boldt's initial decision. However, compliance with the Boldt decision was not to be readily attained. When the Washington Department of Fisheries promulgated regulations to implement the Boldt decision, private interests sued in state court to invalidate them. The Supreme Court of Washington upheld the challenge, reasoning that Judge Boldt's interpretation of the treaties was erroneous and that compliance with his ruling would violate the equal protection clause of the fourteenth amendment to the Constitution and exceed the authority of state agencies under state law.[39] In response, the federal district court, which had

---

[36]384 F. Supp. at 343 (emphasis in original).

[37]*Id.* at 344. The Indians' share of the fish was exclusive of those taken on reservation or for ceremonial or subsistence purposes.

[38]302 F. Supp. 899 (D. Ore. 1969), *aff'd as modified*, 529 F.2d 570 (9th Cir. 1976).

[39]Puget Sound Gillnetters Ass'n v. Moos, 88 Wash. 2d 677, 565 P.2d 1151 (1977); Washington State Commercial Passenger Fishing Vessel Ass'n v. Tollefson, 89 Wash. 2d 276, 571 P.2d 1373 (1977). Other organs of government accommodated more easily to the Boldt decision. Since 1978, the Pacific Regional Fisheries Management Council, responsible for developing management plans for off-shore Pacific fisheries under the Fisheries Conservation and Management Act (FCMA), has reduced the optimum yield for salmon taken by ocean trollers to increase the availability of salmon inland. (For a discussion of the role of Indian fishing rights in FCMA plans see Isherwood, Indian Fishing Rights in the Pacific Northwest: Impact of the Fishery Conservation and Management Act of 1976, 8 Envtl. L. 101 (1977)). Moreover, the United States, in response to the Boldt decision, altered its policy toward the International Pacific Salmon Fisheries Commission (IPSFC), established under a convention between the United States and Canada to foster cooperative management of the Fraser River salmon fisheries. The United States, since 1977, has exempted treaty Indians in its approval of regulations issued by the

retained jurisdiction following its initial order, entered a series of orders by which it directly undertook the regulation of the fisheries at issue, thus displacing the state from any authority.[40] The court of appeals affirmed that action, emphasizing with acerbic comments that state intransigence was largely responsible for the enormous controversy.[41] With matters in this posture, the Supreme Court agreed to review the decision of the Washington Supreme Court and the federal court actions they spawned.

The Supreme Court began its analysis in *Washington v. Washington State Commercial Passenger Fishing Vessel Association* by observing that, although at the time the Stevens treaties were entered into "the Indians were vitally interested in protecting their right to take fish at their usual and accustomed places, whether on or off the reservations,"[42] neither they nor Governor Stevens "realized or intended that their agreement would determine whether, and if so how, a resource that had always been thought inexhaustible would be allocated between the native Indians and the incoming settlers when it later became scarce."[43] Two basic choices were before the Court. One, urged by the state, would interpret the treaties merely to allow the Indians the same opportunity to catch fish "at all usual and accustomed grounds and stations" as non-Indians enjoy. The other

---

IPSFC and the Department of the Interior under its authority over Indian affairs, 25 U.S.C. §§2, 9 (1976), has issued regulations giving treaty Indians more time to fish in the Fraser River than other fishermen. This new policy of selective approval of IPSFC regulations, and the Interior regulations, were upheld in United States v. Decker, 600 F.2d 733 (9th Cir.), *cert. denied,* 444 U.S. 855 (1979). *See also,* Comment, Accommodation of Indian Treaty Rights in an International Fishery: An International Problem Begging for an International Solution, 54 Wash. L. Rev. 403 (1979). Also deserving mention is the Columbia River Fisheries Council, composed of tribal, state, and federal members who have completed a detailed report for managing the Columbia River basin fisheries according to the "fair share" approach mandated in Sohappy v. Smith, 529 F.2d 570 (9th Cir. 1976).

[40] Various of the orders of the district court over the period 1974–78 are reported at 459 F. Supp. 1020 (W.D. Wash. 1974–78).

[41]    The state's extraordinary machinations in resisting the decree have forced the district court to take over a large share of the management of the state's fishery in order to enforce its decrees. Except for some desegregation cases...the district court has faced the most concerted official and private efforts to frustrate a decree of a federal court witnessed in this century. The challenged orders in this appeal must be reviewed by this court in the context of events forced by litigants who offered the court no reasonable choice.

Puget Sound Gillnetters Ass'n v. United States Dist. Court, 573 F.2d 1123, 1126 (9th Cir. 1978). For Judge Burns's similar comments three years earlier, see 520 F.2d at 693.

[42] 443 U.S. 658, 667.

[43] *Id.* at 669.

choice was to interpret the treaties to allow the Indians a quantifiable share of the fish available for taking at such places. To a considerable extent, the Court in its earlier decisions had already signalled that the latter choice would necessarily prevail. For example, in *Puyallup III* the Court had stated that the allocation by the state of 45 percent of the available steelhead run to the Indians was "precisely what we mandated in *Puyallup II*."[44]

While acknowledging that the issue before it was "virtually a 'matter decided' by our previous holdings,"[45] the Court undertook an extensive analysis of the treaty language and its historic context. Two considerations, one pragmatic and one formalistic, seemed dominant in the Court's analysis. The pragmatic consideration was that the "equal opportunity" interpretation urged by the state was likely, "in light of the far superior numbers, capital resources, and technology of the non-Indians," to "net [the Indians] virtually no catch at all."[46] The more formalistic consideration emphasized the treaty language guaranteeing a right of *taking* fish, as opposed to a right to try to take fish.[47] The right thus to *take* fish implied, in the Court's view, a right to take a share of the available fish in a time of shortage.

To determine that treaty Indians are entitled to a share of available fish does not, however, determine what that share should be. Relying upon reserved water rights cases, the Court reasoned that the treaties guaranteed "so much as, but no more than, is necessary to provide the Indians with a livelihood—that is to say, a moderate living."[48] If that amount were less than 50 percent of the available fish, then an appropriate lower figure should be determined by the district court. However, the Court concluded that the Indian share could never exceed 50 percent of the available fish because the Indians' right to take fish "in common with" non-Indian settlers implied an equal division.[49]

In the above respects, the Supreme Court substantially affirmed Judge Boldt's initial decision. It did, however, adopt a different formula in determining which fish should be counted against the respective Indian and non-Indian shares. Most significantly, it insisted that fish taken by Indian treaty fishermen on reservations be counted toward the Indian share. Quietly breaking new ground, the Court declared that "although it is clear that the Tribe may exclude non-Indians from access to fishing within the reservation," *Puyallup III* had "unequivocally rejected the

---

[44]433 U.S. at 177.

[45]443 U.S. at 679.

[46]*Id.* at 677 n. 22.

[47]*Id.* at 678.

[48]*Id.* at 686.

[49]*Id.*, note 27.

Tribe's claim to an untrammeled right to take as many of the steelhead running through its reservation as it chose."[50] Even Justices Brennan and Marshall, who as dissenters in *Puyallup III* found that decision to be anything but unequivocal,[51] joined in this sweeping characterization of the *Puyallup III* decision.

To what extent the Supreme Court's decisions in *Puyallup III* and *Washington State Commercial Passenger Fishing Vessel Association* will influence the interpretation of treaties other than the Stevens treaties remains largely conjectural. Since those decisions, the Court has refused to review a case in which the Supreme Court of Minnesota upheld the right of White Earth Indians to fish on their reservation completely free of state regulation.[52] Going still further, the district court for the western district of Michigan recently found the state of Michigan to be without any authority to regulate even off-reservation gill-net fishing in Lake Michigan by Chippewa and Ottawa Indians.[53] The Court of Appeals for the Sixth Circuit, while strongly intimating its belief that the state could regulate such fishing if necessary to prevent extinction or irreparable damage to fisheries, remanded to the district court to determine whether subsequently enacted federal regulations had a preemptive effect upon state authority or jurisdiction.[54] When Secretary of the Interior Watt allowed those regulations to expire in 1981, however, the state again urged the court of appeals to review the district court's ruling.[55] This time, the court of appeals held that "[t]he state bears the burden of persuasion to show by clear and convincing evidence that it is highly probable that irreparable harm will occur and that the need for regulation exists."[56] Otherwise, the state may

---

[50]*Id.* at 683–684.

[51]*See* text accompanying note 31 *supra*.

[52]State v. Clark, 282 N.W.2d 902 (Minn. 1979), *cert. denied*, 445 U.S. 904 (1980).

[53]United States v. Michigan, 471 F. Supp. 192 (W.D. Mich. 1979), *remanded*, 623 F.2d 448 (6th Cir. 1980).

[54]United States v. Michigan, 623 F.2d 448 (6th Cir. 1980). The federal regulations were adopted pursuant to 25 U.S.C. §§2 and 9 (1976), provisions that confer, in broad terms, general authority upon the President and the Secretary of the Interior to manage Indian affairs. However, it seems doubtful whether such general authority enables the federal government to act in a manner barred to the states, since state obligations to Indians are derivative from treaties between Indian tribes and the federal government. For a discussion of the derivative nature of state duties under Indian treaties, see United States v. Washington, 506 F. Supp. 187, 206 (W.D. Wash. 1980). Although the affected tribes participated closely in the development of the regulations here in issue, they did not agree with all of their particulars. *See* 44 Fed. Reg. 65747 (Nov. 15, 1979).

[55]United States v. Michigan 653 F.2d 277 (6th Cir. 1981).

[56]*Id.* at 279.

not restrict Indian treaty fishing. The state ultimately abandoned its effort to show that its regulations could meet that stringent standard.[57]

While all of the above cases concern state wildlife regulation, there has also been some litigation concerning federal regulation. Although Congress has the power unilaterally to abrogate or modify existing treaty rights,[58] the courts have generally been unwilling to infer an intent to do so, absent an explicit expression from Congress.[59] Thus, in *United States v. Cutler*, the Migratory Bird Treaty Act was held inapplicable to on-reservation hunting by Shoshone Indians.[60] Case law under the Bald Eagle Protection Act, however, is split as to whether it was intended to abrogate existing Indian treaty rights.[61] A keener awareness of the existence of Indian treaty rights as a result of these and related decisions involving state regulations has led to the creation of special, often complex, exemptions for certain Indians in recent federal wildlife legislation.[62] Whether those exemptions supplant or merely supplement preexisting rights is seldom explicitly stated.

## CONGRESSIONAL RESPONSE TO THE PACIFIC NORTHWEST FISHERIES DISPUTE: THE SALMON AND STEELHEAD CONSERVATION AND ENHANCEMENT ACT OF 1980

Desirous of consolidating and improving management authority over the Pacific fisheries and of quieting the contentious political divisions that arose after the Boldt decision, as well as of rectifying the overcapitalized fishing capacity of commercial fishermen, Congress passed the Salmon and Steelhead Conservation and Enhancement Act of 1980.[63] The principal feature of the Act is the creation of a Salmon and Steelhead Advisory Committee, composed of tribal, state, and federal representatives, charged with developing, within fifteen months, a comprehensive report outlining the establishment of a fisheries management structure for the Washington and Columbia River management areas. The Act also sets forth procedures by which tribes and states may procure federal grants to implement the

---

[57]*Id.* 520 F.Supp. 207, 211 (W.D. Mich. 1981).

[58]*See* Lone Wolf v. Hitchcock, 187 U.S. 553, 564–567 (1903).

[59]*See* Pigeon River Co. v. Cox, Ltd., 291 U.S. 138, 160 (1934); Menominee Tribe of Indians v. United States, 391 U.S. 404, 412–413 (1968).

[60]37 F. Supp. 724 (D. Idaho 1941).

[61]*See* Chapter 4 at text accompanying notes 149–160.

[62]*See* Chapter 11 at text accompanying notes 35–39 and Chapter 12 at text accompanying notes 153–154.

[63]16 U.S.C. §§3301–3345 (Supp. V 1981).

comprehensive report and undertake enhancement projects. Finally, the Act creates a "Fleet Adjustment Program" by which the state of Washington may receive federal funds for the purchase of commercial fishing and charter vessels and licenses, to reduce the excessive ocean fishing capacity in that state.[64]

## THE REGULATION OF NON-INDIAN HUNTING AND FISHING ON INDIAN RESERVATIONS

Just two years after the Supreme Court stated in *Washington State Commercial Passenger Fishing Vessel Association* that it was "clear that the Tribe may exclude non-Indians from access to fishing within the reservation,"[65] the Court carved out an exception to that broad statement in *Montana v. United States.*[66] In that action, the Crow tribe of Montana sought to prohibit all hunting and fishing within its reservation by nonmembers of the tribe, even though more than a quarter of the reservation was owned by such nonmembers. Addressing first the specific treaty by which the reservation had been created, the Court found that insofar as it conferred upon the tribe the authority to control hunting and fishing on the reservation, that authority did not extend to lands alienated pursuant to subsequent allotment acts.[67]

The Court also considered to what extent tribal authority over reservation hunting and fishing was an incident of inherent tribal sovereignty. The test, in the Court's view, was whether such authority was "necessary to protect tribal self-government or to control internal rela-tions."[68] As applied to nonmembers hunting or fishing on lands no longer

---

[64]Subsequent to enactment of the federal statute, the United States Court of Appeals affirmed a 1976 ruling of Judge Boldt that Indians who buy fishing vessels that the state of Washington had purchased to reduce the fishing capacity of commercial fishermen may not be prevented from using those vessels in their own fishing operations, even though non-Indian repurchasers may be so prevented. United States v. Washington, 645 F.2d 749 (9th Cir. 1981).

[65]*See* text accompanying note 50 *supra.*

[66]450 U.S. 544 (1981).

[67]The Court cited its decision in *Puyallup III* for the proposition that "treaty rights with respect to reservation lands must be read in light of the subsequent alienation of those lands." *Id.* at 561. That the Court would emphasize this factual aspect of its *Puyallup III* decision seems remarkable in light of the way the Court characterized that decision in Washington v. Washington State Commercial Passenger Fishing Vessel Ass'n. *See* text accompanying note 50 *supra.*

[68]450 U.S. at 564.

owned by the tribe, the Court concluded that such authority was not necessary to those purposes.[69]

Implicitly, the Court found that the exercise of such authority over nonmembers on tribal lands was necessary to tribal self-government, for it agreed with the court of appeals that the tribe could prohibit nonmembers from hunting or fishing on such lands or condition their entry by charging a fee or establishing bag and creel limits.[70] If, however, the authority to prohibit or condition hunting and fishing by nonmembers is an inherent aspect of tribal sovereignty, then it can fairly be asked whether the state may exercise its regulatory authority over such nonmembers. The Supreme Court did not address this issue, though it noted that the court of appeals had "held that non-members permitted by the Tribe to hunt or fish within the reservation remained subject to Montana's fish and game laws."[71] A different result, however, was reached by the Court of Appeals for the Fourth Circuit in *Eastern Band of Cherokee Indians v. North Carolina Wildlife Resources Commission*.[72] That decision prevented North Carolina from enforcing its licensing requirements against non-Indian fishermen on the Cherokee reservation but in doing so declared that "[e]ach case of state regulation of on-reservation hunting and fishing is unique," thus refusing to articulate any general rules.[73]

## PHASE II OF *UNITED STATES v. WASHINGTON* AND THE RIGHT AGAINST ENVIRONMENTAL DESTRUCTION OF TREATY FISHERIES

Remarkable as it may seem, Judge Boldt only disposed of one of three key questions originally presented in the *United States v. Washington* litigation—whether treaty Indians have a right to a fair share of fish

---

[69]*Id.* at 566. In White Earth Band of Chippewa Indians v. Alexander, 518 F. Supp. 527, 534 (D. Minn. 1981), this authority was said to be based in part upon 18 U.S.C. §1165 (1976), which makes it a federal offense to trespass upon an Indian reservation for the purpose of hunting, fishing, or trapping. The court went on to say, however, that a tribe's authority to prohibit or condition hunting and fishing by nonmembers does not authorize it to arrest or fine violators but only to suspend or revoke its permission, evict violators, or refer violators to federal authorities for prosecution under the above provision. *Id.* at 535. For a discussion of 18 U.S.C. §1165 in relation to the Lacey Act, see Chapter 5 at note 38.

[70]*Id.* at 557.

[71]*Id.* at 550.

[72]588 F.2d 75 (4th Cir. 1978), *cert. denied,* 446 U.S. 960 (1980).

[73]*Id.* at 79 n. 3. In this way, the court reached a different result from, but did not disagree with, United States v. Sanford, 547 F.2d 1085 (9th Cir. 1976). In *White*

passing their tribal fishing grounds. In "Phase II" of that litigation, Judge Orrick, replacing the retired Judge Boldt, disposed of the remaining two questions: whether the Indians' share includes hatchery-reared fish and whether treaty Indians have enforceable rights against destruction of their treaty fisheries.[74] The judge answered both affirmatively.

In concluding that hatchery-reared fish were "fish" under the Stevens treaties and therefore to be included in the Indians' allocation, Judge Orrick noted that hatchery fish have been introduced in the Pacific Northwest to counter the decline of natural fish adversely affected by recent non-Indian activities and that hatchery fish have become an increasingly significant portion of the annual harvest. Under these circumstances, the court concluded that it would be unfair to exclude these fish from the Indians' allocation. Moreover, the court rejected the state of Washington's claim of ownership over these fish. The court reasoned that "[w]hatever merit the State's argument might have when applied to fish confined within hatchery facilities, it has no logical application to harvestable fish that have been released from such facilities and are freely swimming alongside naturally-bred fish in the State's rivers, streams, and bays."[75]

Of greater importance, however, was the court's second holding. Considering that "[t]he most fundamental prerequisite to exercising the right to take fish is the existence of fish to be taken," the court held that "implicitly incorporated in the treaties' fishing clause is the right to have the fishery habitat protected from man-made despoliation."[76] This holding drew support from a line of federal cases, beginning with *Winters v. United States*,[77] finding an implied reservation of water for lands reserved by the federal government. Here, Judge Orrick agreed that the treaties reserved water "of sufficient *quality* to sustain the salmon and steelhead trout which [the Indians] have the expressly-reserved right to take."[78]

---

*Earth Band of Chippewa Indians, supra* note 64, the court was "not persuaded that the imposition of a dual license requirement on non-members would result in any economic hardship to the Band because of non-member reluctance to utilize Indian-owned and trust resources." 518 F. Supp. at 537. It reached this decision without citing either *Sanford* or *Eastern Band of Cherokee Indians*.

[74]United States v. Washington, 506 F. Supp. 187 (W.D. Wash. 1980), *aff'd in part, rev'd in part*, 694 F.2d 1374 (9th Cir. 1983).

[75]*Id.* at 201.

[76]*Id.* at 203.

[77]207 U.S. 564 (1908). Earlier cases implying reserved water rights for fishing by Pacific Northwest Indians include United States v. Anderson, No. 3643 (E.D. Wash. July 23, 1979), and United States v. Adair, 478 F. Supp. 336 (D. Ore. 1979). For a discussion of these cases in the context of hydropower operations in the Pacific Northwest see Blumm, Hydropower v. Salmon: The Struggle of the Pacific Northwest's Anadromous Fish Resources for a Peaceful Coexistence with the Federal Columbia River Power System, 11 Envtl. L. 211, 286–290 (1981).

[78]506 F. Supp. at 205 (emphasis in original). Since the plaintiffs sought only

The court did not define the scope of this new environmental right, deferring that determination until an actual controversy arose.[79] However, it indicated that once the Indians make a *prima facie* case that a proposed action will harm their fisheries, the burden shifts to the acting party to show that the Indians' treaty rights will not be violated. Moreover, the court perceived that the state, the federal government, and any third parties, were under a "correlative duty" to "refrain from degrading the fish habitat to an extent that would deprive the tribes of their moderate living needs."[80] Although the court rejected a "no significant deterioration" standard as inappropriate for protection of implied treaty rights, the court added:

> The tribes' treaty allocation is currently set at 50 percent.... That the ceiling has been applied creates the presumption that the tribes' moderate living needs exceed 50 percent and are not being fully satisfied under the treaties. As the burden is upon the State to demonstrate to the Phase I court that the tribes' needs may be satisfied by a lesser allocation, the State must also bear the burden in Phase II to demonstrate that any environmental degradation of the fish habitat proximately caused by the State's actions...will not impair the tribes' ability to satisfy their moderate living needs.[81]

In January 1983, the Court of Appeals for the Ninth Circuit affirmed that hatchery fish were encompassed within the Indians' treaty rights, but, on the issue of treaty-derived environmental rights, it substantially narrowed Judge Orrick's ruling.[82] It held that the Indians did not have a guaranteed right to an adequate supply of fish but that they and the state "must each take reasonable steps commensurate with their respective resources and abilities to preserve and enhance the fishery."[83] For the state, that obligation pertains both to projects that it undertakes directly and to those which it permits others to undertake.[84] The appeals court ruling leaves uncertain, however, what such "reasonable steps" must include.[85]

---

prospective relief, the court did not have to consider whether past degradation of water quality violated any rights or imposed any liabilities. *See id.* at 202 n. 57.

[79] Recently the Phase II decision saw its first application when the watermaster of the Sunnyside Valley Irrigation District was instructed to maintain sufficient water flows in the Yakima River to prevent destruction of chinook salmon nests. Kittitas Reclamation Dist. v. Sunnyside Irrigation Dist., Civ. No. 21 (E.D. Wash., Nov. 28, 1980).

[80] 506 F. Supp. at 208.

[81] *Id.*

[82] 694 F.2d 1374 (9th Cir. 1983).

[83] *Id.* at 1381.

[84] *Id.* at 1381 n. 15.

[85] Judge Reinhardt's concurring opinion suggests that the state's obligation

Determining the scope and substance of those "reasonable steps" may ultimately be the most significant decisions that the court will ever make in the context of Indian treaty rights. A multitude of cases in the state and federal court have heretofore examined Indian treaties from the limited perspective of whether they serve to free treaty Indians from the regulatory authority of state and federal governments. Now, "Phase II" of the Boldt litigation raises the possibility that Indian treaties will impose upon those same units of government new, affirmative duties to protect the underlying fish and wildlife resources. If that is to be their legacy, then Indian treaties may yet be among the most powerful weapons for conservation in the entire legal arsenal.

---

requires to consider the necessity of a project in light of its probable adverse impact on treaty fisheries, the feasibility of alternative measures, and reasonable mitigating measures. *Id.* at 1391.

# Part II

# THE MAJOR THEMES OF FEDERAL WILDLIFE LAW

In the chapters that comprise this second Part, the great diversity of problems confronting federal wildlife law and the variety of approaches designed to solve them will be examined. The initial chapters focus on the four basic tools of federal wildlife regulation: the regulation of taking, the regulation of commerce in wildlife and wildlife products, the acquisition and management of wildlife habitat, and the mandating of consideration of the impacts on wildlife of various forms of development. Succeeding chapters consider certain special aspects of federal wildlife law, including methods of funding, predator control, pesticide usage, and international agreements.

The bureaucratization of federal wildlife law that was previously described will be readily apparent in the following chapters. The many federal wildlife programs described here have been administered by numerous agencies bearing various names over the last several decades. A brief summary of the names and responsibilities of those agencies is provided here to assist the reader in following the shifts in bureaucratic responsibility. Most wildlife responsibilities for resources other than marine fisheries were originally assigned to the Bureau of Biological Survey in the Department of Agriculture. The Bureau of Fisheries in the Department of Commerce had responsibility generally over marine fishery matters. Both bureaus were transferred to the Department of the Interior in 1939 and there consolidated in 1940 into one agency known as the Fish and Wildlife Service. That consolidation was undone by the Fish and Wildlife Act of 1956, which created within the Fish and Wildlife Service a Bureau of Sports Fisheries and Wildlife and a Bureau of Commercial Fisheries, between which authority was divided pretty much as it had been between the two pre-1939 bureaus. A further executive reorganization in 1970 transferred the Bureau of Commercial Fisheries to the newly created National Oceanic and Atmospheric Administration within the Commerce Department, where it became known as the National Marine Fisheries Service. Meanwhile, the Bureau of Sports Fisheries and Wildlife, which remained in the Interior Department, was renamed the Fish and Wildlife Service in 1974. By virtue of the 1970 reorganization, administration of several major wildlife laws has been divided between the Fish and Wildlife Service and the National Marine Fisheries Service.

# Chapter 4

# REGULATING THE TAKING OF WILDLIFE

The earliest and simplest form of wildlife regulation is the prohibition or limitation of the killing of wildlife. Because that form of regulation was well established at the state level during the nineteenth century, the initial federal foray into wildlife regulation at the beginning of the next century was designed simply to buttress that system of state regulation.[1] It was not long, however, before the federal government itself became directly involved in limiting the "taking" of wildlife. This chapter examines certain statutes that rely either exclusively or predominantly on this form of wildlife regulation. The most important of these are the Migratory Bird Treaty Act, the Bald Eagle Protection Act, and the Wild Free-Roaming Horses and Burros Act. More recent federal laws that attempt to integrate restrictions on taking into comprehensive programs for the protection of marine mammals and endangered species are examined in later chapters,[2] as is the subject of restrictions on taking in connection with the management of federal lands.[3]

---

[1]*See* the discussion of the Lacey Act in Chapter 2 at text accompanying notes 36–43 and in Chapter 5 at text accompanying notes 8–12. For a discussion of the great variety of early state restrictions on wildlife taking and the many difficulties of enforcing them, see T. Lund, American Wildlife Law 28-31 (1980).

[2]*See* Chapters 11 and 12.

[3]*See* Chapter 6.

## LIMITATIONS ON THE TAKING OF MIGRATORY BIRDS

The events leading to the signing in 1916 of the Convention with Great Britain for the Protection of Migratory Birds,[4] passage in 1918 of the Migratory Bird Treaty Act,[5] and the Supreme Court's landmark decision in *Missouri v. Holland*,[6] upholding the constitutionality of both the Convention and the Act, were described in Chapter 2.[7] This chapter focuses on the terms of the Convention and the Act that implements it, as well as upon subsequent treaties with Mexico, Japan, and the Soviet Union providing similar protection for migratory birds.

### The Treaties

The Convention with Great Britain is a brief and rather simple document. In general terms, it establishes three separate groups of migratory birds: (1) migratory game birds, (2) migratory insectivorous birds, and (3) other migratory nongame birds. For each group, a "close season" is established by article II, during which "no hunting shall be done except for scientific or propagating purposes under permits." The close season for migratory insectivorous and other migratory nongame birds is year round, except that certain enumerated types of birds in the latter grouping may be taken by Eskimos and Indians for food and clothing but may not be sold or offered for sale. With respect to migratory game birds, article II of the Convention provides that the close season shall be between March 10 and September 1[8] and that the "season for hunting shall be further restricted to such period not exceeding three and one-half months as the High Contracting Powers may severally deem appropriate and define by law or regulation."[9] In addition, article V prohibits the taking of nests or eggs of migratory birds, except for scientific or propagating purposes. Finally, article VII authorizes the issuance of permits to kill any migratory birds that, "under extraordinary conditions, may become seriously injurious to agricultural or other interests in any particular community."

---

[4]Aug. 16, 1916, 39 Stat. 1702, T.S. No. 628 (hereinafter referred to as Canadian Convention).

[5]Ch. 128, 40 Stat. 755 (1918) (current version at 16 U.S.C. §§703–711 (1976 & Supp. V 1981)).

[6]252 U.S. 416 (1920).

[7]*See* Chapter 2 at text accompanying notes 47–57.

[8]Canadian Convention, art. II, §1. For Atlantic coast shorebirds, a special close season between February 1 and August 15 is prescribed.

[9]For a discussion of recent litigation concerning the meaning of the quoted language, see text accompanying notes 93–97 *infra*.

Subsequent treaties pertaining to the conservation of migratory birds, closely patterned after the 1916 Convention, were signed with Mexico in 1936,[10] Japan in 1972,[11] and the Soviet Union in 1976.[12] Each of these treaties, however, is slightly different in its particulars from the original Convention. The Mexican treaty, for example, limits the length of the hunting season for migratory birds to a maximum of four months and requires that such hunting be conducted "under permits issued by the respective authorities in each case."[13] In addition, it calls for the establishment of "refuge zones in which the taking of such birds will be prohibited,"[14] and the prohibition of hunting from aircraft.[15] The Japanese Convention specifies no dates or lengths for hunting seasons but requires that whatever seasons are set by each party "avoid their principal nesting seasons and...maintain their populations in optimum numbers."[16] In addition, it directs the parties to "endeavor to establish sanctuaries and

---

[10] Convention for the Protection of Migratory Birds and Game Mammals, Feb. 7, 1936, United States–Mexico, 50 Stat. 1311, T.S. No. 912 (hereinafter referred to as Mexican Convention).

[11] Convention for the Protection of Migratory Birds and Birds in Danger of Extinction, and their Environment, March 4, 1972, United States–Japan, 25 U.S.T. 3329 (hereinafter referred to as Japanese Convention).

[12] Convention Concerning the Conservation of Migratory Birds and Their Environment, Nov. 19, 1976, United States–U.S.S.R., 29 U.S.T. 4647, T.I.A.S. No. 9073 (hereinafter referred to as Russian Convention).

[13] Mexican Convention, art. II(C). The Mexican Convention is quite inartfully drafted insofar as the establishment of close seasons is concerned. Article II(A) provides generally for their establishment but does not specify their length; article II(C) then limits the permissible hunting period to no more than four months in each year; article II(D) prescribes a close season of from March 10 to September 1 for wild ducks; and article II(E) prescribes a year round close season for "migratory insectivorous birds." The ambiguity arises from article IV, however, which lumps all migratory birds into only two categories: migratory game birds and migratory nongame birds. If the latter grouping was intended to include any birds other than "migratory insectivorous birds," then the Convention fails to indicate what close or open seasons are to apply to such other birds. The matter was further confused when, by exchange of notes on March 20, 1972, the governments of Mexico and the United States supplemented the 1936 Treaty by agreeing to a lengthy list of additional birds to be protected. These birds are described as "additions...to the list of birds set forth in Article IV," without specifying whether the same are to be considered "migratory game birds" or "migratory nongame birds." By administrative regulation, however, they are all treated as nongame birds, and protected from hunting. See 50 C.F.R. §§10.13, 20.11 (1981).

[14] Mexican Convention, art. II(B).

[15] Id. art. II(F).

[16] Japanese Convention, art. III, §2. For a discussion of recent litigation concerning the requirement to maintain optimum numbers, see text accompanying notes 93–99 infra.

other facilities for the protection or management of migratory birds."[17] The Russian Convention prohibits not only the taking of migratory birds, but also the "collection" of their nests or eggs and the "disturbance of nesting colonies."[18] Without specifying any dates or overall durations, it authorizes the parties to establish hunting seasons, so long as they assure "the preservation and maintenance of stocks of migratory birds."[19] It also directs each party, to the maximum extent possible, to establish preserves, protected areas, and facilities for the conservation of migratory birds and to "manage such areas so as to preserve and restore the natural ecosystems."[20]

The authorization of hunting seasons is not the only exception from the basic prohibition against taking common to each treaty. Other exceptions are authorized as well, and these too vary from treaty to treaty. Like the 1916 Convention, the Mexican Convention creates an exception for the taking of migrating birds for scientific and propagating purposes but also adds a new exception for museums.[21] The Japanese and Russian Conventions add educational and "other specific purposes not inconsistent with" the objectives of the Conventions to the list of taking exceptions.[22] Both the Mexican and Japanese Conventions also contain specific exemptions for "private game farms."[23]

The four conventions differ as well in the degree to which they authorize otherwise prohibited takings to control bird-caused problems. Whereas the 1916 Convention authorized, under "extraordinary conditions," the taking of birds that "may become seriously injurious to the agricultural or other interests in any particular community,"[24] the Mexican Convention has a more limited authorization for taking of birds only "when they become injurious to agriculture and constitute plagues."[25] The Japanese and Russian Conventions, on the other hand,

---

[17] Japanese Convention, art. III, §3.

[18] Russian Convention, art. II, §1. The prohibition of disturbance of nesting colonies is a new feature not found in any of the earlier treaties, or in the Migratory Bird Treaty Act, although it is arguably subsumed in the prohibition against "taking," a term undefined in the treaties and the Treaty Act. Implementing regulations of the Fish and Wildlife Service, however, define taking in a restrictive fashion that would not seem to include nesting colony disturbance. See 50 C.F.R. §10.12 (1981).

[19] Russian Convention, art. II, §2.

[20] Id. art. VII.

[21] Mexican Convention, art. II(A).

[22] Japanese Convention, art. III, §1(a).

[23] Id. art. III, §1(d); Mexican Convention, art. II(A).

[24] Canadian Convention, art. VII.

[25] Mexican Convention, art. II(E).

contain a very expansive authorization for takings to protect "persons or property."[26]

The many differences among the four treaties are of more than academic interest. One illustration of the potential importance of such differences concerns the controversial issue of the taking of migratory birds by Eskimos and other Native Americans. The original 1916 Convention made no special provision for such taking with respect to game birds but did authorize taking of nongame birds by Eskimos and Indians for food and clothing.[27] The comparable exception in the Japanese Convention applies to all migratory birds, not just nongame birds.[28] The Russian Convention introduces yet another variation, authorizing each party to prescribe seasons for the taking of migratory birds and the collection of their eggs by indigenous inhabitants of certain designated areas, including Alaska, for their own nutritional and other essential needs.[29] Significantly, however, and perhaps because indigenous peoples comprise such a large portion of the Mexican population, the Mexican Convention admits of no special exception for native peoples from its taking prohibition. Notwithstanding the failure of the Mexican Convention to authorize it, the Secretary of the Interior has long permitted subsistence taking of nongame birds in Alaska.[30] Recognizing the legal vulnerability of that practice, however, he has recently proposed that the original three treaties be amended to bring them into conformity with the Russian Convention.[31]

The considerable overlap among species protected by the four treaties thus results in differing substantive standards applicable to the protection of the same bird. Indeed, there has even been controversy over what species are protected by the various conventions. The 1916 Convention describes the birds it protects by the common names of certain general groups, such

---

[26] Japanese Convention, art. III, §1(b); Russian Convention, art. II, §1(d).

[27] Canadian Convention, art. III, §3.

[28] Japanese Convention, art. III, §1(e).

[29] Russian Convention, art. II, §1(c).

[30] Current administrative regulations permit year round subsistence taking of auks, auklets, guillemots, murres, and puffins by Eskimos and Indians in Alaska as well as of snowy owls and cormorants by any person in Alaska. See 50 C.F.R. §20.132 (1981). The addition of snowy owls and cormorants was effectuated in 1973 without ever having been the subject of a proposed rulemaking open for public comments. At the time it was done, the Fish and Wildlife Service explained that its action was authorized by article I of the Mexican Treaty. See 38 Fed. Reg. 17841 (July 5, 1973). In fact, not only did article I not authorize the action taken, but article II specifically prohibited it. For a case discussing the relationship of the Migratory Bird Treaty Act to Indian rights, see note 47 infra.

[31] See U.S. Fish and Wildlife Service, Final Environmental Assessment, Subsistence Hunting of Migratory Birds in Alaska and Canada (1980).

as "woodpeckers," "gulls," and so forth.[32] The Mexican Convention, on the other hand, identifies the birds subject to its protection solely in terms of their scientific family names. The Japanese Convention, following still a third approach, gives the full scientific name for each species of bird that it protects and further defines the term "migratory bird" to include only those species "for which there is positive evidence of migration" between the United States and Japan or which have subspecies or populations "common to both countries."[33] The Russian Convention takes a similar, though still different, approach.[34] After many years of using a more liberal interpretation, the Fish and Wildlife Service proposed in 1976 to apply retroactively the definition of the Japanese Convention to the earlier conventions. Had this proposal been adopted, it would have removed from the list of federally protected migratory birds certain species not known to be migratory between or common to the United States and Mexico, notwithstanding that they are included in the families designated in the Mexican Convention or the groupings designated in the 1916 Convention.[35]

While the prohibition against taking migratory birds is the major focus of all of these treaties, the more recent treaties with Japan and the Soviet Union contain important measures aimed at protecting migratory bird habitat. For example, the Japanese Convention directs the parties to "endeavor to take appropriate measures to preserve and enhance the environment of birds protected under" the Convention, such as by

---

[32] Migratory game birds are identified in the Canadian Convention not only by their common names, but also by their scientific family names. See Canadian Convention, art. I, §1. Migratory insectivorous birds under that Convention include not only those specifically listed by common name, but also "all other perching birds which feed entirely or chiefly on insects." Id. art. I, §2.

[33] Japanese Convention, art. II, §1.

[34] The Russian Convention applies to all species and subspecies that migrate between the two countries and to those with separate populations sharing common breeding, wintering, feeding, or moulting areas. Russian Convention, art. I, §1. The list of migratory birds may in effect be expanded unilaterally by either party, at least as to areas under, or persons subject to, its own jurisdiction, by virtue of authority conferred by article VIII. That article authorizes either party, in its discretion, to treat any species or subspecies of bird as though it were a protected migratory bird under the Convention, as long as it belongs to the same family as any bird that is so protected.

[35] See 41 Fed. Reg. 50010 (Nov. 12, 1976). See also United States v. Lumpkin, 276 F. 580 (N.D. Ga. 1921), in which the trial court refused to consider a criminal defendant's contention that the birds he was charged with taking unlawfully had never in fact been anywhere other than in the state in which they were taken. The trial court had instructed the jury not to "consider the question whether or not they actually went out of Georgia, or were raised in Georgia, or whether they came from Canada or anywhere else at all." Id. at 584.

preventing "damage resulting from the pollution of the seas" and by controlling the importation and introduction of live animals and plants that are "hazardous to the preservation of such birds" or that "could disturb the ecological balance of unique island environments."[36]

The Russian Convention articulates a similar, though more detailed, set of duties with respect to habitat protection. Article IV of the Russian Convention includes a broadly worded exhortation to take measures necessary to "protect and enhance the environment and to prevent and abate the pollution or detrimental alteration of that environment,"[37] and a number of more specific directives aimed at accomplishing that goal.[38] The latter include the establishment of a warning system whereby each party can promptly advise the other of impending or existing environmental damage and take steps to avert or minimize it; the control of the importation, exportation, and establishment of injurious wild animals and plants; and the designation of areas of special importance to migratory birds, both within and without the two signatory nations, for special protection.

Of potentially great importance is the requirement in article IV that each party identify "areas of breeding, wintering, feeding, and moulting which are of special importance to the conservation of migratory birds within the areas under its jurisdiction."[39] These areas are to be included in a list to be appended to the Convention, and, to the maximum extent possible, the parties are to "undertake measures necessary to protect [their] ecosystems...against pollution, detrimental alteration and other environmental degradation."[40] A closely related provision in article IV authorizes the parties, by mutual agreement, to designate areas not under the jurisdiction of either of them as areas of special importance to the conservation of migratory birds.[41] These areas are to be included on a second list to be appended to the Convention. The parties have two duties with respect to these areas. The simplest is merely to disseminate information about their significance. More important is the obligation that each party "to the maximum extent possible, undertake measures necessary to ensure that any citizen or person subject to its jurisdiction will act in accordance with the principles of this Convention in relation to such areas." What acting "in accordance with the principles of" the Convention means is not altogether clear. Presumably, it is intended to give such areas

---

[36] Japanese Convention, art. VI.
[37] Russian Convention, art. IV, §1.
[38] *Id.* §§2, 3.
[39] *Id.* §2(c).
[40] *Id.*
[41] *Id.* §3.

the same or a similar degree of protection as the areas of special importance within the jurisdiction of the parties. To date, however, no areas of special importance have yet been designated by the United States.

The mutual warning system mandated by article IV requires each party to establish procedures for warning the other of "substantial anticipated or existing damage to significant numbers of migratory birds or the pollution or destruction of their environment."[42] Once warned, the parties are to cooperate "in preventing, reducing or eliminating such damage" and in rehabilitating the environment. Apparently, this provision was intended to facilitate early detection of and cooperative action in combatting major disasters, such as oil spills.

Article V of the Russian Convention provides for special protection measures for migratory birds in danger of extinction. Whenever either party decides that any species, subspecies, or "distinct segment of a population" is endangered and establishes special measures for its protection, it is to inform the other party of its action. The other party is then directed to "take into account such protective measures in the development of its management plans." This is a broader mandate than that of a similar provision in the Japanese treaty that merely directs each party to control the exportation or importation of any species or subspecies found by the other party to be endangered.[43]

### The Migratory Bird Treaty Act

#### The Structure of the Act

All four of the conventions just described are implemented by the Migratory Bird Treaty Act. That Act reads very much today as it did when originally passed in 1918. Notwithstanding the many differences among them, the ratification of each new convention did not result in a major overhaul of the Act but only in technical amendments that merely added appropriate references to each subsequent convention. Thus, to the extent that the new features of the later conventions cannot be subsumed within the general language of the Act, those features remain unimplemented by domestic legislation.[44]

That concern, however, is alleviated by virtue of the broad and general language that the Act employs. In fact, as originally passed in 1918, the

---

[42]*Id.* §2(a).

[43]Japanese Treaty, art. IV, §3.

[44]For a discussion of the extent to which international treaties are self-executing, without the need for implementing legislation, see Comment, The Migratory Bird Treaty: Another Feather in the Environmentalist's Cap, 19 S.D.L. Rev. 307, 311–316 (1974).

Migratory Bird Treaty Act amplified in a number of respects the narrow terms of the 1916 Convention.[45] Thus, whereas the Convention prohibited the "hunting" of migratory birds during their close seasons, the Act made it unlawful, inter alia, "to hunt, take, capture, kill,...[or] possess" any bird protected by the Convention, except as permitted by regulation of the Secretary of Agriculture.[46] In promulgating such regulations, the Secretary is charged with determining not only when, which the Convention clearly authorizes, but also "to what extent, if at all, and by what means" to permit the above activities.[47] In making these determinations, he is directed to give "due regard to the zones of temperature and to the distribution, abundance, economic value, breeding habits, and times and lines of migratory flight of such birds."[48] Moreover, all such determinations are expressly made "subject to the provisions... of the conventions."[49] Finally, very important to its administration, the Act provides that nothing therein prevents the states from making or enforcing laws or regulations that are consistent with the conventions or the Act or that give further protection to migratory birds, their nests or eggs.[50]

---

[45]The amplification was obviously intentional, for the Act's caption described it as being "An Act to give effect to the convention...and for other purposes." 40 Stat. 755.

[46]Migratory Bird Treaty Act, ch. 128, §2, 40 Stat. 755 (1918) (current version at 16 U.S.C. §703 (1976 & Supp. V 1981)). The authority of the Secretary of Agriculture was transferred to the Secretary of the Interior in 1939 pursuant to Reorganization Plan No. II, §4(f), 4 Fed. Reg. 2731, 53 Stat. 1433. Hereafter in this chapter, the term "Secretary" refers either to the Secretary of Agriculture or the Secretary of the Interior, as appropriate. The Canadian Convention and the Treaty Act also prohibit certain forms of commerce in migratory birds. Those aspects of the Convention and the Act will be considered in Chapter 5.

[47]16 U.S.C. §704 (1976). As originally passed in 1918, the Act clearly contemplated that the Secretary could rely upon this general source of authority to promulgate regulations governing the taking of birds for scientific or propagating purposes. Migratory Bird Treaty Act, ch. 128, §8, 40 Stat. 756 (1918). The Act said nothing, however, about the exception in the Canadian Convention for taking by Indians and Eskimos. Notwithstanding that omission and the fact that no similar exception is found in the Mexican Convention, existing regulations authorize taking for certain limited purposes by Indians and Eskimos but limit it to those in Alaska. See note 30 supra. The scope of Indian taking rights may in fact be considerably greater than these regulations suggest. United States v. Cutler, 37 F. Supp. 724 (D. Idaho 1941), held that existing Indian treaty rights were not affected by passage of the Migratory Bird Treaty Act.

[48]16 U.S.C. §704 (1976).

[49]Id.

[50]16 U.S.C. §708 (1976). To implement the Treaty Act, two types of federal regulations are promulgated. The first is of a general and continuing nature and governs such subjects as hunting methods, tagging and identification requirements, scientific and other permit requirements, and other similar matters. These

### Litigation Under the Act

The Supreme Court's 1920 decision in *Missouri v. Holland,* upholding the constitutionality of the Treaty Act against a broad and generalized attack, was not to be the last of the legal assaults upon it. In the years since Justice Holmes's decision, the Act and its implementation have been attacked on a number of more narrowly defined grounds. The most far reaching of these is the contention that the Treaty Act, by prohibiting private landowners from hunting on their own lands, deprives them of a valuable property right without just compensation.

### THE TAKING PROHIBITION AS AN INFRINGEMENT OF PROPERTY RIGHTS

There is, of course, nothing unique about the Treaty Act that subjects it to a "confiscation of private property" attack; any governmental prohibition of hunting is equally vulnerable to such a claim. Nonetheless, and despite the holding of *Geer v. Connecticut* that individual property rights in wildlife can only be acquired in such manner as the sovereign may allow,[51] a number of cases have been brought to nullify hunting prohibitions under the Treaty Act on the grounds that those prohibitions constitute unlawful "takings" of private property.

The first case to address the issue in detail was *Bailey v. Holland,* which concerned the designation of certain private lands adjacent to Back Bay Migratory Waterfowl Refuge as a closed area in which no hunting of migratory birds was to be permitted.[52] The plaintiff landowner alleged that

---

are found at 50 C.F.R. Part 20, subparts A–J and L, and Part 21 (1981). The second type fixes season lengths, shooting hours, bag limits, and so forth, and is revised annually on the basis of bird population data, and the recommendations of affected states, "Flyway Councils," and various advisory committees. These are found at 50 C.F.R. Part 20, subpart K (1981). The end-product of these formalized proceedings is the promulgation of so-called "framework regulations," which offer individual states a range of choices regarding season lengths, shooting hours, bag limits, and so forth. Individual states select from among the choices offered in the framework regulations, and their selections are then published as final federal regulations. The annual process of formulating these regulations is described·in more detail in Department of the Interior, Fish and Wildlife Service, Final Environmental Statement for the Issuance of Annual Regulations Permitting the Sport Hunting of Migratory Birds, FES 75–54, app. VIII (June 1975).

[51] 161 U.S. 519 (1896).

[52] 126 F.2d 317 (4th Cir. 1942). The Secretary has, since 1931, designated several areas adjacent to federal wildlife refuges as closed areas. *See* 126 F.2d at 323. Although his authority for such designations arguably derives from the power conferred by the Treaty Act to determine the "extent" and "manner" of migratory bird hunting, it was nowhere made express until the 1936 Convention with Mexico, which provided in article II for the establishment of "refuge zones in which the taking of such birds will be prohibited." The Treaty Act has never been amended to incorporate the "refuge zone" concept of the Mexican Convention. Nonetheless, the Secretary has continued to designate areas adjacent to national wildlife refuges as closed areas in

the Secretary's designation had in effect extended the boundaries of the refuge so as to encompass his land and argued that the only lawful way for the Secretary to do that was to purchase the land pursuant to the Migratory Bird Conservation Act.[53] The court disposed of the plaintiff's contentions in the following terms:

> If the Government wishes to do more in the way of protecting migratory birds than prohibiting their slaughter, e.g., erect improvements to lessen the dangers resulting from the drainage of marshy areas, it must acquire some proprietary interest in the areas suitable for such uses. It was to meet this need that Congress enacted the Migratory Bird Conservation Act.... The 1929 Act does not deprive the Secretary of his regulatory authority under the 1918 statute. Merely because the Government purchases certain land in order to do more than prohibit hunting, it does not follow that compensation must be made for all land closed to hunting.[54]

Despite the unequivocal nature of the *Bailey* holding, the same issue was litigated ad infinitum in connection with the Secretary's designation of a closed area adjacent to Horseshoe Lake Preserve in Illinois. Certain of the affected landowners brought suit initially in federal district court to enjoin the Secretary's action. The district court's denial of an injunction was affirmed by the court of appeals because no property right of the plaintiffs had been invaded, and the Supreme Court refused to review the decision.[55] The district court's subsequent dismissal of the suit was likewise affirmed by the court of appeals, which declared it irrelevant "that plaintiffs have devoted real estate to, and developed other valuable facilities for, the hunting of migratory wild fowl."[56] Again, the Supreme Court declined to review. Undeterred, some of the same plaintiffs brought yet another action in federal court, based on the Federal Tort Claims Act, in which they sought to recover for damages allegedly resulting to their agricultural crops as a consequence of the hunting prohibition. Again, the district court dismissed the action, the court of appeals affirmed, and the Supreme Court declined to review.[57] Finally, yet another action was commenced, this time

---

which migratory bird hunting is prohibited. The codification of such areas appearing at 50 C.F.R. §32.4 (1981), on its face, places such areas off limits to all types of hunting. Individual designations, however, make clear that only migratory bird hunting is to be prohibited. *See, e.g.,* 41 Fed. Reg. 31539 (July 29, 1976).

[53] The Migratory Bird Conservation Act is discussed in Chapter 6 *infra* at text accompany notes 5–15.

[54] 126 F.2d at 324.

[55] Lansden v. Hart, 168 F.2d 409 (7th Cir.), *cert. denied,* 335 U.S. 858 (1948).

[56] Lansden v. Hart, 180 F.2d 679, 684 (7th Cir.), *cert. denied,* 340 U.S. 824 (1951).

[57] Sickman v. United States, 184 F.2d 616 (7th Cir. 1950), *cert. denied,* 341 U.S. 939 (1951).

in the Court of Claims. Plaintiffs claimed an unconstitutional taking, both of their hunting facilities and of their crops. Holding that the plaintiffs' claim that the right to hunt is a property right "can not be taken seriously," the Court of Claims dismissed the action and finally put an end to the long litigation.[58]

Thus the Treaty Act has uniformly been upheld against claims that it constitutes confiscation of private property. Nonetheless, on the broader issue of whether hunting rights constitute property rights, a few recent state court decisions have reached results contrary to those of the decisions described above.[59] Although those recent decisions have been criticized,[60] the Interior Department has, on at least some occasions, treated hunting rights as property rights by bringing condemnation proceedings against them when acquiring lands pursuant to the Migratory Bird Conservation Act.[61]

RESTRICTIONS ON THE "MANNER" OF TAKING BIRDS:
THE QUESTION OF SCIENTER

Less far reaching in scope, but more persistent in frequency, have been the attacks leveled at the Secretary's authority under section 3 of the Treaty Act to regulate the manner of migratory bird hunting. The most fundamental of these attacks asserts that, insofar as the Act permits the Secretary to determine both the extent and the means by which migratory birds may be taken, it exceeds the powers conferred by the conventions, which only authorize the determination of close seasons.

In *Cochrane v. United States*[62] and *Cerritos Gun Club v. Hall*,[63] the Secretary's authority to limit the means of taking was challenged on this ground. In each case the court stated that the Treaty Act could, if necessary, be sustained solely on the basis of the congressional power to regulate interstate commerce. The reason they reached this issue was that the

---

[58]Bishop v. United States, 126 F. Supp. 449 (Ct. Cl. 1954).

[59]*See, e.g.,* Alford v. Finch, 155 So. 2d 790 (Fla. 1963), and Allen v. McClellan, 75 N.M. 400, 405 P.2d 405 (1965). For a discussion of litigation related to the *Allen* case, see *infra* at text accompanying notes 73–76. For decisions contra, see Platt v. Philbrick, 8 Cal. App. 2d 27, 47 P.2d 302 (1935), Maitland v. People, 93 Colo. 59, 23 P.2d 116 (1933), State v. McKinnon, 153 Me. 15, 133 A.2d 885 (1957), Bauer v. Game, Forestation & Parks Comm'n., 138 Neb. 436, 293 N.W. 282 (1940), and Cook v. State, 192 Wash. 602, 74 P.2d 199 (1937).

[60]*See, e.g.,* Plimpton, Power of State to Designate Game Preserves, 6 Nat. Res. J. 361 (1966).

[61]*See, e.g.,* Swan Lake Hunting Club v. United States, 381 F.2d 238 (5th Cir. 1967), in which the "owner" of the hunting rights was a party other than the owner of the land.

[62]92 F.2d 623 (7th Cir. 1937).

[63]96 F.2d 620 (9th Cir. 1938).

question whether the 1916 Convention authorized restrictions on the manner of taking birds was, in the words of the *Cerritos* court, "not in the realm of obvious certitude."[64] Nonetheless, both courts upheld the Act and the Secretary's implementing regulations as a valid exercise of power conferred both by the Convention and by the commerce clause. The *Cochrane* court so concluded by reasoning, with respect to the Convention, that "the authority to deprive the hunters of *any* open season carries with it the power to provide for a limited open season *for limited purposes only*,"[65] and, with respect to the Act as an exercise of the commerce power, that "the asserted limitations of the treaty may well be ignored for they offer no bar to the legislation as an act whose object is to regulate interstate commerce."[66]

The authority of the Secretary to require that migratory waterfowl be hunted in designated areas with steel, rather than lead, shot was challenged unsuccessfully in *National Rifle Association of America v. Kleppe*.[67] Without focusing at all on the scope of the Secretary's authority with respect to the regulation of activities, the adverse effect of which on migratory birds is indirect and unintentional, the court upheld the challenged regulations on the ground that they had an adequate factual basis.[68] Though unsuccessful in court, opponents of lead shot restrictions have succeeded in Congress. Riders to the annual Interior Department appropriations legislation have prevented the enforcement of those restrictions except in states that agree to them.

The one restriction on the manner of taking migratory birds that has generated more controversy than any other is that which prohibits hunting "[b]y the aid of baiting, or on or over any baited area."[69] The controversy

---

[64]*Id.* at 629.

[65]92 F.2d at 626 (emphasis in original). Similar reasoning has not always been found persuasive. *See, e.g.*, Foster-Fountain Packing Co. v. Haydel, discussed in Chapter 2 at text accompanying note 82.

[66]92 F.2d at 627.

[67]425 F.Supp. 1101 (D.D.C. 1976).

[68]Apparently, the Secretary has taken a narrow view of his own regulations. In commenting upon the draft environmental impact statement that accompanied the proposed lead shot regulations, the Arkansas Game and Fish Commission urged that consideration be given to the "appreciable amount of lead shot [that] is deposited" as a result of "squirrel hunting or hunting other forms of wildlife in timbered overflow bottomlands." The Secretary merely responded that "[a]uthority to regulate the hunting of squirrels and other types of resident game...is vested in the States rather than with the Federal government." Department of the Interior, Fish and Wildlife Service, Final Environmental Statement, Proposed Use of Steel Shot for Hunting Waterfowl in the United States 90–91 (Jan. 1976). Despite the Secretary's response, it is far from clear that he would be without such authority if the manner of hunting resident game were demonstrably harmful to migratory birds.

[69]50 C.F.R. §20.21 (i) (1981).

has arisen from the fact that no scienter, or guilty knowledge that an area has been baited, is required to prove a violation. This principle was established as early as 1939 in *United States v. Reese,* a decision that relied heavily upon the following purely pragmatic considerations:

> There appears no sound basis here for an interpretation that the Congress intended to place upon the Government the extreme difficulty of proving guilty knowledge of bird baiting on the part of persons violating the express language of the applicable regulations...but it is more reasonable to presume that Congress intended to require that hunters shall investigate at their peril conditions surrounding the fields in which they seek their quarry.[70]

Almost without exception, the *Reese* holding has been followed in circuit after circuit,[71] even in one case in which the defendant relied upon a written communication from an Assistant Secretary of the Interior that attempted to clarify the meaning of the baiting regulation.[72]

Interestingly, one of the few cases to reject the *Reese* holding, *Allen v. Merovka,* arose out of a successful effort by certain private landowners to establish that their hunting rights were property rights under state law.[73] Plaintiffs' land was surrounded on three sides by a state waterfowl refuge. In state court proceedings, the plaintiffs obtained an order restraining state officials from prohibiting hunting on their land.[74] Thereafter, federal officials sought to post plaintiffs' land as a "baited area" because corn grown on the adjoining refuge had been knocked down to feed migrating waterfowl. The landowners again went to court, although this time to federal court, to restrain the federal authorities from trespassing on their land and from "conspiring" with state authorities to prevent hunting thereon.

Had the court accepted the *Reese* doctrine that scienter is not required for a baiting violation, a substantial constitutional question, pitting federal regulatory authority against private property rights under state law, would have been presented. Instead, the court skirted the constitutional issue by rejecting the *Reese* doctrine outright. The following rationale was offered by the court:

---

[70]27 F.Supp. 833, 835 (W.D. Tenn. 1939).

[71]*See, e.g.,* United States v. Green, 571 F.2d 1 (6th Cir. 1977); United States v. Bullock, 579 F.2d 1116 (8th Cir. 1978); Rogers v. United States, 367 F.2d 998 (8th Cir. 1966); and cases cited in note 76 *infra.*

[72]Clemons v. United States, 245 F.2d 298 (6th Cir. 1957).

[73]382 F.2d 589 (10th Cir. 1967).

[74]Allen v. McClellan, 75 N.M. 400, 405 P.2d 405 (1965).

The prohibited "hunting method"... contemplates that the hunting and the feeding are in some way related, and that the hunters are performing or have some part directly or indirectly in the baiting or it is done for their benefit as a part of a "hunting method." The acts of third parties totally independent of the acts of hunting should not be used to make illegal what otherwise is proper. The prohibited acts refer to those of the hunter, not to the independent and unrelated acts of others. The regulations formerly attempted to expressly cover situations regardless of who may have placed the feed, but were changed to the present wording. This change is significant in deciding the problem before us.[75]

Notwithstanding the plausibility of the above reasoning, it is clearly contrary to the holding of *Reese* and numerous subsequent decisions. Moreover, the change in the wording of the regulations, referred to in the last two quoted sentences, has not been deemed significant in baiting cases that have followed the *Allen* decision.[76]

No circuit has yet elected to follow the lead of the Tenth Circuit in *Allen*, though that decision was followed in part by the district court for Delaware in *United States v. Bryson*.[77] The Fifth Circuit found in *United States v. Delahoussaye* "that a minimum form of scienter—the 'should have known' form—is a necessary element of the offense."[78] Under this test, if the presence of bait "could reasonably have been ascertained," then liability may be imposed.[79]

Although elimination of the scienter requirement has substantially eased the burden of law enforcement against baiting violators, there has been a considerable clamor for change because of the arrest and conviction of many allegedly unwitting violators. Accordingly, in recent years bills have been introduced in nearly every Congress to redefine the baiting offense so as to apply only to those who actually place the bait or who hunt

---

[75]382 F.2d at 591.

[76]*See, e.g.*, United States v. Ireland, 493 F.2d 1208 (4th Cir. 1973) and United States v. Jarman, 491 F.2d 764 (4th Cir. 1974). The baiting regulations were in fact amended after the *Allen* decision to exclude the taking of migratory game birds other than waterfowl over areas where feed has been distributed as a result of manipulation of a crop on the land where grown for wildlife management purposes. *See* 38 Fed. Reg. 22021 (Aug. 15, 1973).

[77]414 F.Supp. 1068 (D. Del. 1976). The *Bryson* court found two separate duties in the regulation. It followed *Allen* insofar as the prohibition on taking "by the aid of baiting" is concerned but held that strict liability could be imposed for taking "on or over any baited area." The significance of the latter holding is diminished, however, by the court's literal reading that the birds taken must be directly on or over the bait itself. *Id.* at 1073.

[78]573 F.2d 910, 912 (5th Cir. 1978).

[79]*Id.*

over a baited area with knowledge that it is baited. Such proposed legislation has also typically included an express grant of authority to the Secretary to close hunting areas found to be baited, although it is far from clear that such authority does not already exist.[80]

The premise of the baiting cases that scienter is not required to establish a violation of the Treaty Act, together with the ambiguity of the undefined term "take" that appears in both the Convention and the Treaty Act,[81] raises the question of whether the logic of those cases might be applied to other activities that result in the killing of migratory birds as an unintended consequence. Two recent cases answer that question in the affirmative.[82]

---

[80]It would certainly appear that the Secretary's statutory authority to determine the extent and means of hunting migratory birds, when combined with his often-exercised authority to establish refuge zones, is broad enough to encompass closure of baited areas. Because of the emergency nature of such closures, good cause would appear to be present for noncompliance with the procedures of informal rule-making. Indeed, an emergency system for closure or temporary suspension of migratory bird hunting seasons when continuation thereof could pose an imminent threat to endangered or threatened species of wildlife was recently established in just such a fashion. See 50 C.F.R. §20.26 (1981).

[81]The ambiguity of the term "take" is well illustrated by recent press reports of the prosecution of a University of Florida agronomy professor who, to protect seeds being used in his research, put out poison that killed as many as 300 migratory birds. See The Miami Herald, July 28, 1976, at 4-B, col. 1. Though the term "take" is not defined in the Treaty Act, general regulations of the Fish and Wildlife Service define it to mean "to pursue, hunt, shoot, wound, kill, trap, capture, or collect, or attempt" any of the foregoing. 50 C.F.R. §10.12 (1981). This language would appear to be broad enough to include poisoning. On the other hand, the definition of "take" that appeared in the Bald Eagle Act prior to 1972 included "pursue, shoot, shoot at, wound, kill, capture, collect", etc. Despite the breadth of this latter definition, it was amended in 1972 so as expressly to include "poison." See 16 U.S.C. §668c (1976). Note also that prior to 1977 the Fish and Wildlife Service required a permit to "scare" or "herd" migratory birds for depredation control purposes. See 50 C.F.R. §21.41 (1976). Query: How could a permit be required for such activities unless they also constitute "takings"?

[82]For a discussion of similar unreported, and ultimately inconclusive, cases, see Coggins & Patti, The Resurrection and Expansion of the Migratory Bird Treaty Act, 50 U. Colo. L. Rev. 165, 183–85 (1979). The seminal discussion of the issue addressed in the text is found in the comment cited in note 44 supra. All of these cases raise interesting additional questions. For example, if the federal government recovers fines or civil penalties for such "takings" of migratory birds, are the states thereby precluded from seeking damages for the loss of such wildlife? Does the federal government have an analogous right to recover damages for loss of other types of wildlife on federal lands? Note especially Justice Marshall's admonition in Kleppe v. New Mexico that "it is far from clear...that Congress cannot assert a property interest in the regulated [wildlife] superior to that of the State." 426 U.S. 529, 537 (1976). If the federal or state governments have such rights to sue but fail to exercise them, what remedies does the private citizen have? Answers to these and

In *United States v. FMC Corp.*, the Second Circuit upheld the conviction of a pesticide manufacturer whose waste discharges into a storage pond caused the deaths of a number of migratory birds attracted to the pond.[83] The court found that the discharge of the toxic wastes was unintentional and that the defendant undertook remedial measures to keep birds from the pond once it learned of the problem. Nonetheless, the court imposed liability by analogizing the situation to those in which strict liability has been imposed on those who engage in "extrahazardous activities."[84]

A slightly different rationale was employed in *United States v. Corbin Farm Service.*[85] There an employee of a pesticide distributor, the owner of an alfalfa field, and an aerial pesticide applicator were charged with violating the Migratory Bird Treaty Act as a result of the spraying of the field with a registered pesticide that caused the deaths of a number of birds. The defendants sought to dismiss the charges on the ground that it was undisputed that they had no intent to kill any birds. The court denied their pretrial motions on the basis that the relevant inquiry was not whether the defendants intended to kill birds but whether they acted with "reasonable care under the circumstances."[86] This standard is essentially that adopted by the Fifth Circuit in the *Delahoussaye* baiting case.

Both of the above cases labor with the question of how to avoid carrying the potential logical conclusions of their holdings to the point of logical absurdity. Both courts suggest that such hypothetical examples as bird deaths caused by collisions with automobiles, glass windows, etc., should not form the basis for prosecutions under the Act. The *FMC* court said that a "construction that would bring every killing within the statute...would offend reason and common sense" and that "the sound discretion of prosecutors and the courts" was an adequate safeguard against such possibilities.[87] By resting this conclusion upon prosecutorial

---

many similar questions do not exist as yet because no cases have directly presented them, yet such cases are doubtless not far distant.

[83]572 F.2d 902 (2d Cir. 1978).

[84]*Id.* at 907–908. The court suggested that the production of pesticides was an extrahazardous activity for both humans and wildlife. The difficulty of utilizing extrahazardous activity concepts in other contexts is discussed in Chapter 2 at text accompanying notes 163–172.

[85]444 F.Supp. 510 (E.D. Cal.) *aff'd*, 578 F.2d 259 (9th Cir. 1978).

[86]*Id.* at 536. Two other issues were decided in this case. Relying upon the initial text, the court concluded that "poisoning" of birds is encompassed within the Act's prohibition of killing. *Id.* at 532. The court also ruled that a single act resulting in bird deaths can support only a single count, regardless of the number of birds killed by that act. *Id.* at 526–531. The latter ruling was upheld on appeal in United States v. Corbin Farm Service, 578 F.2d 259 (9th Cir. 1978).

[87]572 F.2d at 905.

discretion, however, the court implicitly acknowledged the great difficulty of determining what, for birds at least, should be deemed an extrahazardous activity.[88]

The *Corbin Farm Service* court dismissed the hypothetical extreme examples in a manner that was at least consistent with its rationale for imposing liability. "The hypothetical car driver," the court reasoned, "is not reasonably in a position to prevent the bird's death whereas a person applying pesticides might be able to foresee the danger and prevent it."[89] The reason that the latter person is presumed to be able to foresee a danger is apparently that, in the court's view, "[w]hen dealing with pesticides, the public is put on notice that it should exercise care to prevent injury to the environment and to other persons."[90] Whether the "notice" to which the court referred is a presumed general notice that pesticides may be hazardous to the environment rather than a specific notice embodied in a particular pesticide label is unclear. If the former, the court seems to be saying that the public at large, when engaged in certain types of activities, will be deemed to owe a duty of care to the environment. If the latter, then the court would seem to be requiring an element of culpability not present in the baiting and *FMC* cases.[91]

## CHALLENGES TO THE AUTHORITY OF THE SECRETARY TO PERMIT HUNTING

There have been in recent years a number of challenges to the administration of the federal migratory bird program, which, unlike earlier challenges, allege that such administration is too lax rather than too restrictive. In *Fund for Animals, Inc. v. Morton*, for example, plaintiffs sought an injunction against the 1974–75 migratory bird hunting regulations because of the Secretary's failure to prepare an environmental impact statement with respect thereto as required by the National Environmental Policy Act.[92] The case was ultimately settled out of court upon the Secretary's

---

[88]*See* note 84 *supra.*

[89]444 F.Supp. at 535.

[90]*Id.* at 536.

[91]Coggins & Patti, *supra* note 82, at 192, attempt to devise a test to guide future decisions of this character and include a requirement that there be "some degree of 'culpability' in the action." Though they say their test is consistent with the baiting and nonbaiting cases discussed above, culpability has not been a requirement either of most of the baiting or of the *FMC* cases. The *FMC* and *Corgin Farm Service* cases are also analyzed in Margolin, Liability under the Migratory Bird Treaty Act, 7 Ecol. L. Q. 989 (1979); Comment, The Courts Take Flight: Scienter and the Migratory Bird Treaty Act, 36 Wash. & Lee L. Rev. 241 (1979); and Comment, Courts Hold Scienter Not Required for Conviction Under Migratory Bird Treaty Act, 8 Envtl. L. Rep. (Envtl. L. Inst.) 10092 (1978).

[92]Civil No. 74-1581 (D. N.J. 1974). The National Environmental Policy Act is discussed in Chapter 7 *infra.*

agreement to prepare a programmatic impact statement. The following year, many of the same plaintiffs returned to court in *Fund for Animals, Inc. v. Frizzell.*[93] In the latter action, a number of claims were made, the most vigorously pressed of which was that a new environmental impact statement was required with respect to the proposed hunting of certain species that had not been hunted in immediately preceding years and that had not been fully discussed in the programmatic statement. More fundamental were the contentions that the Convention with Great Britain required either a single 3½-month season for all birds or separate 3½-month seasons for each of the five families of migratory game birds designated in the Convention, and that the Japanese Convention required a determination of "optimum numbers" for each of the protected species prior to permitting their hunting.

The district court denied plaintiffs' motion for a preliminary injunction because of their failure to demonstrate either a substantial likelihood of success on the merits or that they would suffer irreparable harm from a denial of the injunction.[94] The court of appeals affirmed the decision of the lower court, but in so doing it addressed only the impact statement claim and limited itself to a consideration of the plaintiffs' likelihood of sustaining irreparable harm.[95] Before the case could come to trial back in the district court, the hunting season had ended. On plaintiffs' motion, the district court subsequently dismissed the action without prejudice. Thus the district court never made more than a preliminary inquiry into the merits of the two most fundamental claims, and the court of appeals did not examine them at all. Accordingly, their merits will be briefly considered here.

With respect to the claim that the Convention with Great Britain requires a single 3½-month migratory bird hunting season, the basic contention is that the Secretary's practice of so limiting the hunting season within each state, while prescribing successively later seasons for more southern states, results in a hunting season that exceeds six months when all states are lumped together. Literally, the Convention refers only to a "season for hunting" migratory game birds. Despite this literal reading of the Convention, it has apparently been the continuous practice of both the United States and Canada to prescribe separate seasons for each state or province. It was this consistent administrative practice, together with the absence of any relevant negotiating history, that persuaded the district court to find that plaintiffs did not have a substantial chance of success on the merits of the claim in the *Frizzell* case.[96] The court was also persuaded

---

[93] 530 F.2d 982 (D.C. Cir. 1975), *aff'g* 402 F. Supp. 35 (D.D.C. 1975).

[94] 402 F. Supp. at 39-40.

[95] 530 F.2d at 984-986.

[96] While courts typically give great deference to a long-established administrative

by Interior's assertion that its interpretation of the 3½-month provision was appropriate because it gave greater flexibility in the management of migratory birds than would a uniform 3½-month season.[97]

Even more problematical is the meaning of the requirement in the Japanese Convention that bird-hunting seasons be set so as "to maintain their populations in optimum numbers." Just as the negotiating history of the Canadian Convention failed to illuminate the meaning of the 3½-month provision, so too the negotiating history of the Japanese Convention sheds no light on the meaning of the term "optimum numbers." Plaintiffs in the *Frizzell* case argued that the term should have the same meaning as the term "optimum sustainable population" as used in the Marine Mammal Protection Act, because the Treaty and the Act were drafted at approximately the same time. The government, on the other hand, argued that the Treaty's failure to include a definition of the term indicated an intent not to borrow the Marine Mammal Protection Act's definition. Instead, the government urged that the term imposed no different duty on the Secretary than what he had always done in promulgating hunting regulations under the Treaty Act. The district court again concluded that the plaintiffs had failed to demonstrate a substantial likelihood of disproving the government's interpretation.[98]

In evaluating the meaning of the term "optimum numbers" in the Japanese Treaty, neither the parties nor the court adequately addressed one

---

interpretation of a statute, they are not bound thereby. For an interesting example of how courts respond when a long-established administrative practice abruptly changes, see the discussion of Udall v. Wisconsin, in Chapter 8 at text accompanying notes 32–36.

[97] It is doubtless true that Interior's position offers more flexibility. On the other hand, it would be possible to achieve still greater flexibility by subdividing individual states into multiple zones and prescribing separate hunting seasons for each. In this manner, each state could have a migratory bird hunting season that exceeds six months in length. While zoning of individual states has not been used much in migratory bird management, its use necessarily sharpens the question of what meaning, if any, the Convention's reference to a 3½-month hunting season has.

[98] In fact, neither party offered a convincing explanation of the relationship between the language of the Convention and that of the Marine Mammal Protection Act. At the time of the signing of the Japanese Convention, the Act had not yet been enacted. Moreover, the term "optimum sustainable population" did not even come into being until the Senate Commerce Committee reported out a marked-up bill three months after the signing of the Japanese Treaty. S. Rep. No. 863, 92d Cong., 2d Session (1972). At the time of the signing of the Treaty, the House bill, H.R. 10420, 92d Cong., 1st Sess. (1971), contained the term "optimum sustainable yield." Accordingly, if there is any nexus between the terms used in the Japanese Convention and the Marine Mammal Protection Act, the latter would seem to

apparently relevant consideration. That is, since the term is not found in either of the preceding migratory bird conventions, its meaning may be linked to the Japanese Treaty. Examining the preambles to each of the conventions, one finds the following statement of purpose in the 1916 Convention:

> Many of these species are of great value as a source of food or in destroying insects which are injurious to forests and forage plants on the public domain....

In a similar vein, the Mexican Convention states its purpose as being to "permit a rational utilization of migratory birds for the purpose of sport as well as for food, commerce and industry." In a strikingly dissimilar manner, the preamble to the Japanese Treaty notes that the birds subject to its protection "constitute a natural resource of great value for recreational, aesthetic, scientific, and economic purposes, and that this value can be increased with proper management." Because this articulation of values is broader and more diverse than comparable articulations in the earlier treaties, it seems not unreasonable to suggest that the term "optimum numbers" is really a direction to optimize the values served.

Because the Secretary's authority to issue hunting regulations under the Treaty Act is "[s]ubject to the provisions and in order to carry out the purposes of the conventions," the Act implicitly incorporates the diverse purposes of the Japanese Convention, at least insofar as the birds protected by it are concerned. Thus, to the extent that those purposes are broader than, or otherwise different from, the purposes to be served by the earlier treaties, the Secretary's regulations should reflect them.[99]

*Humane Society of the United States v. Watt* presented a narrower challenge to the Secretary's decision to continue sport hunting of black ducks in the face of at least some evidence suggesting a steady, long-term decline in the black duck population.[100] The case was factually complex and hinged ultimately on the adequacy of the evidence available to support

---

constitute a refinement and clarification of a term, the meaning of which was still uncertain at the time of the signing of the Convention. For a discussion of the concept of "optimum sustainable population" in the Marine Mammal Protection Act, see Chapter 11 at text accompanying notes 48–69.

[99]It is interesting to note that in *Frizzell* the government emphasized as a "key factor" in the promulgation of the Secretary's regulations the economic value of the waterfowl resource. Significantly, economic value appears last in the listing of purposes to be served by the Japanese Treaty, just as it does in the Marine Mammal Protection Act. *See* 16 U.S.C. §1361(6) (Supp. V 1981).

[100]551 F. Supp. 1310 (D.D.C. 1982).

the Secretary's decision. In the court's view, evidence of such a decline was contradictory as to its cause and its gravity. Under such circumstances, the court was unwilling to disturb the Secretary's judgment. One of the few clear propositions of law asserted in the opinion was that the Migratory Bird Treaty Act "does not impose upon the [Fish and Wildlife] Service a mandatory duty to prohibit the hunting of any species whose population, for whatever reason, is declining."[101] The court suggested that such a mandatory duty would exist only if the duck declined to such an extent that it became eligible for protection under the Endangered Species Act.[102]

Thus, in no case have the standards of the Migratory Bird Treaty Act or the treaties that it implements been held to circumscribe the authority of the Secretary to permit migratory bird hunting. However, the Secretary's authority may be limited by other laws when his authorization of hunting affects interests protected by such other laws. At least one case, *Defenders of Wildlife v. Andrus,* holds that the Endangered Species Act limits the Secretary's authority under the Migratory Bird Treaty Act.[103] That case and the related case of *Connor v. Andrus*[104] are discussed in detail in Chapter 12.

OTHER LITIGATION

The remaining litigation under the Migratory Bird Treaty Act has concerned the question whether birds raised in captivity or acquired before the Act became applicable to them are subject to regulation under the Act. The Tenth Circuit has twice considered the question of the Act's applicability to captive-reared birds. In 1978, in *United States v. Richards,* the Tenth Circuit concluded that captive-reared falcons are subject to the Act.[105] A year later, in *United States v. Conners,* the same circuit concluded that captive-reared ducks are not.[106] The principal asserted basis for this different result is that two of the original three treaties refer to "wild" ducks whereas none of those treaties makes a similarly limited reference to falcons. That explanation is not only unpersuasive but, in light of the Supreme Court's subsequent decision in *Andrus v. Allard,*[107] clearly wrong as a basis for the result in *Conners.*

*Andrus v. Allard* involved a challenge to the authority of the Secretary of the Interior to prohibit the sale of artifacts containing parts of birds

---

[101]*Id.* at 1319.

[102]*Id.*

[103]428 F.Supp. 167 (D.D.C. 1977).

[104]453 F.Supp. 1037 (W.D. Tex. 1978).

[105]583 F.2d 491 (10th Cir. 1978).

[106]606 F.2d 269 (10th Cir. 1979). For a case discussing the applicability of the Endangered Species Act to captive-reared wildlife, see Cayman Turtle Farm, Ltd. v. Andrus, 478 F.Supp. 125 (D.D.C. 1979), *aff'd without opinion* (D.C. Cir. Dec. 12, 1980), discussed in Chapter 12.

[107]444 U.S. 51 (1979).

lawfully acquired before the Migratory Bird Treaty Act applied to them. The Court upheld that authority on the basis that since "a flat proscription on the sale of wildlife, without regard to the legality of the taking" is "a traditional legislative tool for enforcing conservation policy," an explicit statutory exception was necessary to overcome the presumption that the act was intended to be all encompassing.[108] The Court was also clearly mindful of the practical enforcement difficulties that would result from an exception for certain products identical in appearance to those clearly covered by the Act.[109]

While not explicitly disapproving of the result in *Conners,* the Court rejected arguments based upon a literal reading of one of the treaties.[110] Instead, the Court held that the various treaties "establish *minimum* protections for wildlife; Congress could and did go further in developing domestic conservation measures."[111] Further, the Court cited the *Richards* decision approvingly.[112] Thus it can with confidence be asserted on the basis of the *Allard* decision, from which no member of the Court dissented,[113] that *Conners* was wrongly decided.

The Court addressed the question of whether its interpretation of the Act constituted an unconstitutional taking of private property. Though the Court found it "undeniable" that a prohibition against the sale of the artifacts would "prevent the most profitable use of appellees' property," it refused to treat that as an unconstitutional taking.[114] On another constitutional issue the Court rejected the conclusion of at least one early decision that congressional authority for the regulation of migratory birds must rest upon the treaty power rather than the federal commerce power.[115] Thus the Court effectively concluded that the Constitution's commerce clause confers ample authority for federal regulation of migratory wildlife.

## LIMITATIONS ON THE TAKING OF BALD AND GOLDEN EAGLES

### The Structure of the Bald Eagle Protection Act

In 1940 Congress, believing that the bald eagle was threatened with extinction, and desirous of preserving it as the nation's symbol, enacted

---

[108]*Id.* at 61.

[109]*Id.* at 58.

[110]*Id.* at 62–63 n. 18.

[111]*Id.* (emphasis in original). The Court relied upon the discussion at pages 74–76 of the initial text in support of this proposition.

[112]444 U.S. at 63 n. 19.

[113]Chief Justice Burger concurred without a separate opinion.

[114]444 U.S. at 66.

[115]The decision rejected was United States v. Marks, 4 F.2d 420 (S.D. Tex. 1925).

legislation to protect it. The Bald Eagle Protection Act, as that legislation was known, made it a criminal offense, with certain exceptions, for any person to take or possess any bald eagle or any part, egg, or nest thereof.[116] For violations, the Act prescribed penalties identical to those prescribed by the Migratory Bird Treaty Act, six months' imprisonment and $500 in fines, or both.[117]

As originally enacted, the Act contained a number of important exceptions. Among these were that the Secretary of the Interior could permit the taking and possession of bald eagles "for the scientific or exhibition purposes of public museums, scientific societies, and zoological parks," as well as "for the protection of wildlife or of agricultural or other interests in any particular locality."[118] The Secretary could permit such activities only "after investigation" and upon his determination "that it is compatible with the preservation of the bald eagle" to do so.[119] A further exception contained in the original Act was that it did not prohibit the possession of any bald eagle, or part, nest, or egg thereof, which was lawfully taken prior to passage of the Act.[120] All of the foregoing exceptions continue in the Act today. The only other original exception, eliminated by amendment in 1959, provided that the terms of the Act did not apply in Alaska.[121]

Since its original enactment, the Act has twice been substantially amended. As a result of these amendments, it has been made more stringent in some respects and less so in others. The first such amendment occurred in 1962, and was designed to enhance the protection of immature bald eagles, which are difficult to distinguish from golden eagles, by extending to the latter the same protection that applied to bald eagles.[122] The 1962 amendment also created two new exceptions. First, it permitted the taking and possession of eagles "for the religious purposes of Indian tribes."[123] Second, it provided that the Secretary, on request of the governor of any state, "shall authorize" the taking of golden eagles "for the purpose of seasonally protecting domesticated flocks and herds in such State,... in

---

[116]16 U.S.C. §§668–668d (1976 & Supp. V 1981).

[117]Ch. 278, §1, 54 Stat. 250 (1940) (current version at 16 U.S.C. §668(a) (Supp. V 1981)).

[118]16 U.S.C. §668a (1981).

[119]*Id.* The Secretary's regulations pertaining to the issuance of permits for scientific or exhibition purposes, found at 50 C.F.R. §22.21 (1981), purport to apply to parts, eggs, and nests of eagles, as well as to the eagles themselves, whereas the statutory exception extends only to "specimens" of eagles. 16 U.S.C. §668a (Supp. V 1981).

[120]16 U.S.C. §668(a) (1976).

[121]Act of June 25, 1959, Pub. L. No. 86-70, §14, 73 Stat. 143.

[122]Act of Oct. 24, 1962, Pub. L. No. 87-884, 76 Stat. 1246.

[123]16 U.S.C. §§668a (Sup. V 1981).

such part or parts of such State and for such periods as the Secretary determines to be necessary to protect such interests."[124] Although a number of such "blanket permits" for taking depredating golden eagles were issued prior to 1969, and despite the statutory authority to continue to do so, the Secretary established as a matter of administrative policy in March, 1970, that no further blanket permits would be issued.[125]

The second time that the Act was substantially amended was in 1972.[126] The impetus for amendment was provided by the widely publicized death of several dozen bald and golden eagles in 1971 as a result of the indiscriminate use by certain Wyoming ranchers of thallium sulfate, apparently as a means of coyote control, and the equally well-publicized deliberate shooting of several hundred eagles from helicopters, likewise at the behest of ranchers. With respect to the poisonings, the Interior Department took the view that under the Act as it then existed, no prosecutions could be brought unless it were shown that the person who placed the poison actually intended to kill eagles.[127] Accordingly, to lessen the degree of intent required to establish a violation, Congress amended the Act to provide that whoever "shall knowingly, or with wanton disregard for the consequences of his act," take any eagle, shall be subject to penalties prescribed.[128] At the same time, through an abundance of caution, Congress amended the Act's definition of the term "take" to include poisoning, though it is far from clear that this amendment was necessary.[129]

---

[124]*Id.* The statute is unclear as to whether, with respect to this exception, the Secretary must determine that any permitted taking "is compatible with the preservation of" the golden eagle. However, *see* note 138 *infra*.

[125]The new policy, set forth in a memorandum dated March 5, 1970, from Secretary of the Interior Walter J. Hickel to the Director of the Bureau of Sports Fisheries and Wildlife, is reprinted at 41 Fed. Reg. 50355 (Nov. 15, 1976). Despite the change in policy, administrative regulations continue to provide for issuance of blanket depredation control orders. *See* 50 C.F.R. §22.31 (1981). These regulations provide for publication in the Federal Register and notice to the requesting governor, *after* the Director's decision. With respect to other types of permits for taking bald or golden eagles, no public notice is required at any time.

[126]Act of Oct. 23, 1972, Pub. L. No. 92-535, §1, 86 Stat. 1064.

[127]*See* Hearings Before the Subcommittee on Agriculture, Environmental, and Consumer Protection of the Senate Committee on Appropriations on Predator Control and Related Problems, 92d Cong., 1st Sess. 44 (1971).

[128]16 U.S.C. §668(a) (1976).

[129]Poisoning was apparently thought to be comprehended by the definition of "take" that appeared in the Act prior to 1972, for the eagle regulations that were promulgated in 1963 provided that takings authorized pursuant to permit or depredation control order must be "by firearms, traps, or other suitable means *except by poison*." 50 C.F.R. §11.4 (1964) (emphasis added). Further, the undefined term "take" that appears in the Migratory Bird Treaty Act is apparently thought to include poisoning. *See* note 81 *supra*.

The 1972 amendments also substantially increased the penalties for violations of the Act. For first violations, maximum penalties were set at $5,000, one year's imprisonment, or both; for subsequent violations, the applicable maxima were $10,000 and two years' imprisonment.[130] In addition to increasing the existing criminal penalties, the 1972 amendments also authorized two additional types of sanctions. First, civil penalties of up to $5,000 per violation could be assessed against any person taking or possessing any eagle, part, nest, or egg thereof.[131] Second, the federal grazing privileges of any person convicted of a violation of the Act were made subject to immediate cancellation.[132] Finally, the 1972 amendments introduced a "citizen bounty" by providing that one-half of any fine, up to $2,500, was to be paid to any person giving information that leads to a conviction under the Act.[133]

Like the amendments a decade earlier, the 1972 amendments were not exclusively designed to strengthen the prohibitions of the Act. They also created a new exemption for the taking and possession of golden eagles for the purposes of falconry. However, the only golden eagles that may be taken for such purposes are those initially taken "because of depredations on livestock or wildlife."[134] Probably because no "blanket" depredation permits have been issued since 1969, the Secretary has never adopted regulations to implement the falconry exemption.[135]

The Bald Eagle Protection Act's prohibition on the taking of eagles extends to the taking of their nests. Perceiving a significant and increasing

---

[130]Though the maximum fine prior to 1972 was $500, actual fines levied were substantially less. According to the Senate report that accompanied the 1972 amendments, the average fine imposed for the 32 convictions under the Act during the preceding five years was less than $50. S. Rep. No. 1159, 92d Cong., 2d Sess. 4 (1972).

[131]The civil penalty provision, 16 U.S.C. §668(b) (1976), is essentially identical to the criminal sanction provision as it existed before the 1972 amendment added the words "knowingly, or with wanton disregard for the consequences." Accordingly, since the criminal sanction was thought to apply only to "willful" violations prior to 1972, the civil penalty provision arguably applies only to "willful" violations now. If so, the rather unusual result is that the Act requires a lesser standard of culpability for imposition of criminal sanctions than it requires for imposition of civil sanctions.

[132]16 U.S.C. §668(c) (1976).

[133]*Id.* §668(a).

[134]*Id.* §668a (Supp. V 1981).

[135]General falconry regulations under the Migratory Bird Treaty Act were promulgated in 1976. 50 C.F.R. §§21, 22 (1981). Those regulations, however, apply to golden eagles only if a special permit has been issued under the Bald Eagle Protection Act. *Id.* §21.28(e)(1).

potential conflict between this prohibition and future coal-mining activities in the West, Congress in 1978 added yet another exception to the Act's prohibitions. That exception authorizes the Secretary of the Interior to permit, by regulation, "the taking of golden eagle nests which interfere with resource development or recovery operations."[136] Although the legislative history indicates that Western coal development was the exclusive focus of congressional concern,[137] the Act neither defines "resource development or recovery" nor limits the exception to any geographic region. Similarly, the Act is unclear as to what, if any, standards govern the exercise of Secretarial discretion, though the legislative history suggests that compatibility with the preservation of the species was intended.[138]

### Litigation Under the Act

Most of the legal issues that have arisen in the reported cases under the Bald Eagle Protection Act have also arisen under the Migratory Bird Treaty Act. Indeed, in *Andrus v. Allard* the Supreme Court simultaneously addressed the question of the application of the restrictions on commerce in both the Bald Eagle Protection Act and the Migratory Bird Treaty Act to eagle parts acquired prior to the enactment of either law.[139] The Court found that the restrictions of both Acts did so apply. With respect to the Bald Eagle Act, its holding was facilitated by a limited exception in that Act for the possession or transportation (but not the sale) of eagles taken prior to its enactment. From this narrow exception the Court drew the negative inference that no exception for sale of such eagles was intended.

Not all issues common to the Bald Eagle and Migratory Bird Treaty Acts have been resolved in a consistent fashion, however. The 1965 decision of *United States v. Martinelli*,[140] for example, held that a defendant charged with violating the Bald Eagle Protection Act had a right to a jury trial even though the maximum penalties prescribed make the offense a "petty"

---

[136]Fish and Wildlife Improvement Act of 1978, Pub. L. No. 95-616, §9, 92 Stat. 3114 (codified at 16 U.S.C. §668a (Supp. V 1981)).

[137]S. Rep. No. 1175, 95th Cong., 2d Sess. 6–7, *reprinted in* 1978 U.S. Code Cong. & Ad. News 7641, 7645.

[138]*Id.* at 7646. This legislative history suggests that the compatibility standard applies to all of the exceptions contained in 16 U.S.C. §668a (Supp. V 1981). If that is the appropriate reading of the provision, the language is rather inartfully designed to achieve it.

[139]444 U.S. 51 (1979).

[140]240 F.Supp. 365 (N.D. Cal. 1965).

offense[141] and although the clear weight of authority under the Migratory Bird Treaty Act is to the contrary.[142] This difference, however, is no longer important, for the 1972 amendment, by increasing the penalties under the Bald Eagle Act, removed violations of that Act from the category of petty offenses.

A more significant difference in the interpretation of the two acts concerns the requirement of intent. Under the Migratory Bird Treaty Act, scienter, or guilty knowledge, is not an element of a violation.[143] In *United States v. Hetzel,* however, the court insisted on a showing of criminal intent, holding that "[r]ules of decision developed under the Migratory Bird Treaty Act may not automatically be applied to a prosecution under the Bald Eagle Protection Act."[144] The *Hetzel* decision is a good example of the axiom that bad cases make bad law. In that action, the defendant was charged with a violation of the Bald Eagle Act because of his possession of a pair of bald eagle talons. He apparently removed them from a dead bald eagle that he found while hunting on a national wildlife refuge, intending to give them to a Boy Scout organization. The defendant was convicted before a United States Magistrate and fined one dollar. Despite the nominal fine, the defendant appealed.

On appeal, the court emphasized the change in the degree of intent required for a violation as a result of the 1972 amendments. The court reasoned that since prior to 1972 only "willful" violations were punishable, the defendant's act, which occurred prior to the 1972 amendments, could not be punished, lest "thousands of Boy Scouts who have innocently obtained and now possess eagle feathers would also be subject to criminal prosecution by the government."[145] Thus the court seemed to hold that the requirement of "willfullness" was met only if it could be shown that the defendant knew that what he was doing violated the law.

A different, and more convincing, result was reached a year later in *United States v. Allard,* in which an Indian was charged with selling a bonnet containing golden eagle feathers.[146] The defendant sought to show that he was unaware that such sale was unlawful by introducing evidence

---

[141]*See* 18 U.S.C. §1(3) (1976).

[142]The *Martinelli* decision was based on Smith v. United States, 128 F.2d 990 (5th Cir. 1942), a case arising under the Migratory Bird Treaty Act. The *Smith* decision has not been followed, however, in subsequent Treaty Act cases. *See, e.g.,* United States v. Ireland, 493 F.2d 1208 (4th Cir. 1973), United States v. Jarman, 491 F.2d 764 (4th Cir. 1974), and United States v. Cain, 454 F.2d 1285 (7th Cir. 1972).

[143]*See* text accompanying notes 69–91 *supra.*

[144]385 F. Supp. 1311, 1314 (W.D. Mo. 1974).

[145]*Id.* at 1316.

[146]397 F. Supp. 429 (D. Mont. 1975).

that the sale of eagle feather bonnets was commonplace among Indians. In rejecting this effort, the court drew a distinction that had eluded the *Hetzel* court:

> The effect of the word "knowingly" is to require that...the defendant [know] that the feathers were golden eagle feathers, and I think it clear that a conviction would not be had were a person to sell golden eagle feathers thinking them to be turkey feathers.... The Act does not, and no statute that I recall seeing, makes the defendant's knowledge of the law an element of the crime.[147]

In thus distinguishing between knowledge of the law and knowledge of the facts, the court's holding seems consistent with the purpose behind the 1972 amendments, which, as has already been shown, were directed at practices that, though not done with the purpose of violating the law, necessarily resulted in the deaths of large numbers of eagles.[148]

*United States v. Allard* also raised some interesting questions concerning the relationship of the Bald Eagle Protection Act to Indian treaty hunting rights. That issue was first raised in *United States v. White,* which involved the prosecution of a Chippewa Indian for shooting at a bald eagle while on a reservation.[149] The Indian claimed a treaty right to hunt eagles. The question thus presented was whether Congress, in passing the Bald Eagle Act, had clearly expressed its intention to abrogate existing Indian treaty rights. The district court dismissed the action on the basis of an earlier case that held that Indian treaty rights were not affected by passage of the Migratory Bird Treaty Act.[150] In the court of appeals, attention focused on the 1962 amendment creating a special exemption "for the religious purposes of Indian tribes." The Indian defendant's purpose in attempting to shoot the eagle was unrelated to any religious purpose. The government argued that in the 1962 amendment Congress created the *only* exception applicable to Indians and thus any other treaty rights were abrogated. Unfortunately, however, the legislative history of the 1962 amendment was silent as to its purpose. The court therefore rejected the government's argument, pointing out that the exception was

---

[147]*Id.* at 432.

[148]Both the *Hetzel* and *Allard* decisions rely upon Morissette v. United States, 342 U.S. 246 (1952), in support of their opposite conclusions. *Morissette* considered the difference in criminal intent between crimes "malum in se" and crimes "malum prohibitum." *Allard* concluded that the distinction drawn in *Morissette* supported its findings that no criminal intent was required because wildlife laws are designed to achieve "social betterment" and because "the taking of wildlife is traditionally regulated by laws not requiring specific intent." 397 F. Supp. at 432–33.

[149]508 F.2d 453 (8th Cir. 1974).

[150]United States v. Cutler, 37 F. Supp. 724 (D. Idaho 1941).

not limited to the taking of eagles by Indians or to the taking of eagles on Indian reservations....Theoretically non-Indians could be thus permitted by the Secretary to take the eagles, on or off a reservation, as long as it was for the "religious purposes of Indian tribes."[151]

The court also pointed to an internal Interior memorandum, predating the 1962 amendments, which stated that Indian treaty rights under the Bald Eagle Act were analogous to those under the Migratory Bird Treaty Act.[152]

Judge Lay wrote a strong dissent to the majority's opinion in *White*. He argued that the majority's insistence upon finding some clear and unequivocal expression of congressional intent overlooked "the broad wording and the pervasive purpose which the Act is intended to fulfill."[153] Going still a step further, he argued that "a conservation statute will achieve its purpose only if it applies to everyone."[154] In *United States v. Fryberg*, a factually similar case, the Ninth Circuit expressly declined to follow the holding of the Eighth Circuit in *White*.[155] The *Fryberg* court agreed with the *White* court that the 1962 amendment to the Bald Eagle Protection Act did not on its face show "an unambiguous express intent to abrogate Indian treaty hunting rights."[156] Nonetheless, the *Fryberg* court found an implicit congressional intent to abrogate treaty rights because of three considerations. First was the biological consideration that "[t]he life of the bald eagle has become so precarious that all threats, including takings pursuant to Indian treaty, should be banned to assure the species' survival."[157] A second statutory consideration was the "comprehensive structure of the Act,"[158] consisting of sweeping prohibitions limited only by narrow exceptions, as reflected in the Supreme Court's *Allard* decision. A final cultural consideration was that the abrogation was "relatively insignificant" in light of the absence of any "evidence that the bald eagle historically provided the Indian with any commercial benefit or had any subsistence value."[159]

---

[151]508 F.2d at 458.

[152]Memorandum from the Office of the Solicitor, U.S. Department of the Interior, to the Director, Bureau of Sports Fisheries and Wildlife, dated April 26, 1962.

[153]508 F.2d at 459.

[154]*Id.* at 461.

[155]622 F.2d 1010 (9th Cir. 1980). Earlier, the district court in United States v. Allard, *supra* note 146, endorsed Judge Lay's dissent in *White*. Technically, that endorsement was dictum, since *Allard* involved the sale of eagles rather than their taking. 622 F.2d at 1012 n. 6.

[156]622 F.2d at 1013.

[157]*Id.* at 1015.

[158]*Id.* at 1016.

[159]*Id.* at 1014.

The conflict between the Eighth and Ninth Circuits on the treaty abrogation issue may eventually invite Supreme Court resolution. In the author's view, the *Fryberg* decision and the strong dissent by Judge Lay in *White* present the better-reasoned arguments, particularly in light of the Supreme Court's *Allard* opinion narrowly construing the pre-Act exception of the Bald Eagle Act.[160]

An as yet unlitigated question under the Bald Eagle Protection Act is its application to federal agencies. Prior to 1982, the practice of the Interior Department had consistently been to require of federal agencies the same permits required of private persons when taking eagles for scientific, exhibition, or other authorized purposes. However, in 1982, Interior Secretary Watt's Solicitor issued an opinion concluding that the Act is inapplicable to the federal government.[161] Remarkably, however, the opinion never mentions *Andrus v. Allard*, the only case in which the Supreme Court has interpreted the Act. Whereas that decision is premised upon the view that conservation legislation is to be broadly construed and its exceptions narrowly limited, the Solicitor's opinion proceeds from precisely the opposite assumption, arguing that unless the Act contains specific mention of its application to federal agencies, an exception for such agencies should be implied. The Solicitor's opinion is poorly reasoned and, in this author's opinion, wrong.

One final legal uncertainty regarding the Bald Eagle Protection Act, which has never been raised in any reported litigation, is its very constitutionality. As was pointed out at the outset of this chapter, the purpose behind the original legislation was the protection of a symbol of the nation. Some commentators have argued that there is no apparent treaty or commerce power justification for such legislation.[162] Nonetheless,

---

[160]It is possible to distinguish most of the Indian treaty rights cases discussed in Chapter 3 from the issue under consideration here. The former cases concern the relationship of Indian treaty rights to state authority. Federal authority was involved only to the extent of the applicable statehood acts admitting the respective states to the Union. The instant issue, however, concerns the conflict between Indian treaty rights and an express federal conservation measure. The admonition against finding an implied repeal of Indian treaty rights in the various statehood acts is less forceful in the context of federal conservation measures. Moreover, as Judge Lay pointed out, United States v. Cutler, the decision that set the precedent under the Migratory Bird Treaty Act, is based upon the faulty premise that an Indian treaty can preclude subsequent amendment by Congress. *See* 508 F.2d at 459 n. 1.

[161]Memorandum from William H. Coldiron, Solicitor of the Department of the Interior, to the Director of the U.S. Fish and Wildlife Service, June 30, 1982.

[162]*See* Guilbert, Wildlife Preservation Under Federal Law, in Federal Environmental Law 588 n. 267 (E. Dolgin & T. Guilbert, eds. 1974). *But see* the discussion of the federal commerce power in Chapter 2.

it will probably be more difficult to have the Bald Eagle Protection Act declared unconstitutional than it was to sustain the conviction of a Boy Scout leader in the *Hetzel* case.[163]

### Conclusion

Perhaps the best measure of the effectiveness of the Bald Eagle Protection Act was the decision of the Secretary in 1978 to list the bald eagle as an endangered species under the Endangered Species Act in all but five of the 48 conterminous states and to list it as a threatened species in the remaining five states.[164] That step indicates that, despite some 38 years in which the taking of bald eagles had been prohibited,[165] their survival remains very much in jeopardy and cannot be assured without the habitat protection measures afforded by the Endangered Species Act. How effective that protection is likely to be is discussed in Chapter 12.[166]

### RESTRICTIONS ON THE TAKING OF WILD HORSES AND BURROS

The culmination of many years of effort to protect the dwindling herds of wild horses and burros on the Western range came with passage in 1971 of the Wild Free-Roaming Horses and Burros Act.[167] Like the Bald Eagle

---

[163] It has been argued that the federal government has an inherent power to protect wildlife having "symbolic" value to the nation, wholly without regard to whether there exists any express constitutional basis for such protection. *See* Coggins & Hensley, Constitutional Limits on Federal Power to Protect and Manage Wildlife: Is the Endangered Species Act Endangered? 61 Iowa L. Rev. 1099, 1139–1143 (1976).

[164] 50 C.F.R. §17.11 (h) (1981). A subspecies, commonly known as the Southern bald eagle, had been listed as an endangered species since 1967. The 1978 listing eliminated any distinction between the two subspecies.

[165] In fairness, it must be pointed out that the prohibition against taking has not in fact stopped the intentional killing of bald eagles. The 1971 massacre of several hundred eagles from helicopters, described previously, is a shocking example. Even today, according to the Fish and Wildlife Service, shooting remains the major cause of bald eagle mortality. *See* 43 Fed. Reg. 6232 (Feb. 14, 1978).

[166] Some interesting, but probably only theoretical, problems arise from the listing of the bald eagle. For example, permits for otherwise unauthorized activities are available for a much narrower range of activities under the Endangered Species Act than under the Bald Eagle Protection Act. Presumably the more restrictive provisions of the later act take precedence over the earlier act, but the matter is not entirely free from doubt. One must also question whether the Endangered Species Act's limited exception for subsistence taking by Alaskan natives can be read as eliminating the special Indian exemption in the Bald Eagle Act.

[167] 16 U.S.C. §§1331–1340 (1976 & Supp. V 1981).

Protection Act, its object was to protect the symbolic value of a vanishing type of animal life. Just as the bald eagle has long been the symbol of the nation, Congress declared wild horses and burros to be "living symbols of the historic and pioneer spirit of the West."[168] Unlike the Bald Eagle Protection Act, however, humanitarian concerns figured prominently in the passage of the Horses and Burros Act and are evident in many of its provisions.[169] Also, unlike the Bald Eagle Protection Act, the Horses and Burros Act does not rely principally on a prohibition of taking but seeks to afford horses and burros an additional measure of protection by requiring that they be treated "as an integral part of the natural system of the public lands."[170] That important aspect of the Act is considered in detail in Chapter 6.

Before turning to an examination of the various provisions of the Act, its background deserves some mention. The 1971 Act was not the first federal effort aimed at protection of wild horses and burros. A 1959 law made it a crime to use an aircraft or motor vehicle to hunt wild horses or burros on the public lands or to pollute any watering hole on such lands "for the purposes of trapping, killing, wounding or maiming" the same.[171] Violations of that law were punishable by a fine of up to $500 and imprisonment for up to six months, or both.

The limited scope of the 1959 Act meant that wild horses and burros remained vulnerable to harassment or death from a wide range of other causes. They had no protection under state law because they were not considered "game" animals, and they received no protection from federal land managers until the Bureau of Land Management initiated a "wild horse policy" in 1967.[172] Congress was soon persuaded that without some more far-reaching remedial measure the last wild horse populations would likely disapppear. The result was the 1971 Wild Free-Roaming Horses and Burros Act, in which, relying upon the property clause of the Constitution,

---

[168]*Id.* §1331 (1976).

[169]The Senate Report that accompanied the bill that was to become the Horses and Burros Act emphasized the humane impetus for the legislation in the following terms:

> They have been cruelly captured and slain and their carcasses used in the production of pet food and fertilizer. They have been used for target practice and harassed for "sport" and profit. In spite of public outrage, this bloody traffic continues unabated, and it is the firm belief of the committee that this senseless slaughter must be brought to an end.

S. Rep. No. 242, 92d Cong., 1st Sess. 1 (1971).

[170]16 U.S.C. §1331 (1976).

[171]18 U.S.C. §47(b) (1976).

[172]*See* the discussion in Chapter 6 *infra* at text accompanying notes 234–236.

Congress boldly preempted the states from any jurisdiction over wild horses and burros on federal lands under the jurisdiction of the Forest Service or the Bureau of Land Management. The constitutional challenge to that exercise of authority has already been described in Chapter 2 and will not be repeated here.[173] Suffice it to say here that the Act declared all wild free-roaming horses and burros "to be under the jurisdiction of the Secretary [of the Interior or Agriculture, as appropriate] for the purpose of management and protection."[174]

The 1971 Act confronted a problem nearly unique among wildlife laws. The animals it aimed to protect could not always be readily distinguished from other animals not subject to its protection. That is, the Act's provisions extended only to "unbranded and unclaimed horses and burros on public lands of the United States."[175] Branded or otherwise claimed animals are not protected even though they may intermingle freely with animals that are. The Act permits owners of such unprotected animals to recover them "if recovery is permissible under the branding and estray laws of the State in which the animal is found."[176] The physical task of capturing recoverable animals presents obvious difficulties;[177] establishing legal ownership of such animals entails certain difficulties as well.

*American Horse Protection Association v. United States Department of the Interior* presented the question of whether ownership of a particular horse or burro is to be determined by state or federal officials.[178] Because section 5 of the Act makes recovery contingent upon satisfaction of branding and estray[179] laws of the states, the most likely reading of this provision would place that responsibility upon state officials. Moreover, the relevant legislative history summarized by the court seemed to reinforce that reading.[180] However, the facts of the case were perhaps the most inauspicious possible for that result. The plaintiffs sought damages and other relief from the government for the latter's alleged acquiescence in a private horse roundup that, because of the abuse inflicted on the horses,

---

[173]*See* Chapter 2 at text accompanying notes 69–75.

[174]16 U.S.C. §1333(a) (1976).

[175]*Id.* §1332(b).

[176]*Id.* §1335 (1976).

[177]The difficulty in effecting recovery has been attributable in part to the restrictions of the 1959 Act prohibiting the use of aircraft or motor vehicles in capturing wild horses. The Federal Land Policy and Management Act of 1976 amended the Horses and Burros Act to permit the Secretary to use helicopters, under specified conditions, in administering the Act. 16 U.S.C. §1338a (1976).

[178]551 F.2d 432 (D.C. Cir. 1977).

[179]"Estray" laws govern the recovery of stray domestic animals.

[180]551 F.2d at 438–439.

was aptly characterized by the court as "sordid."[181] Subsequent to the filing of that suit, the Idaho Brand Inspector was asked to determine the ownership of the horses in question and he found none of them to be wild and free-roaming after a procedure that was grossly perfunctory.[182] The plaintiffs contended on appeal that a final determination of ownerships was the responsibility of federal, not state, officials. The court of appeals, citing certain implementing regulations of the Bureau of Land Management and the general concern of Congress about "the ability and the willingness of the states to promote the survival of wild free-roaming horses and burros," concluded that to allow state officials the final authority to determine ownership would "risk the possibility of rendering the Act more or less nugatory."[183]

The result in *American Horse Protection Association* might well have been different had the case not involved such an egregious abuse of the horses at issue and such a perfunctory ownership determination by the state official. Nonetheless, that result was reaffirmed in *Sheridan v. Andrus*, a case in which plaintiffs asserted ownership of certain horses being rounded up by the federal defendants.[184] Their complaint was dismissed for their failure to have exhausted the procedure for determining ownership of the horses in question.

A final variation on the question of the interplay between state estray laws and the federal Act was addressed in *United States v. Christiansen*.[185] The question considered was whether the Act's prohibition against removal of wild horses from public lands[186] could be applied to one whose act of removal was in accordance with procedures for establishing ownership under state law. The court stated, in *dictum*, that if the "claim of ownership of the horses has a substantial basis, and the procedures of State law have been followed, the Act does not make [such] activities criminal."[187] The court went on to add, however, that "if state law conflicts with the Act, the state law must give way."[188] Put differently, one seeking to establish ownership of unbranded horses on federal lands should be careful to follow not only the procedures of state law but also the requirements contained in the regulations of the federal land-managing agencies.

---

[181]*Id.* at 434.

[182]The Brand Inspector's decision and the process by which it was made are described at 551 F.2d 435–436.

[183]*Id.* at 440.

[184]465 F. Supp. 662 (D. Colo. 1979).

[185]504 F. Supp. 364 (D. Nev. 1980).

[186]16 U.S.C. §1338(a)(1) (1976).

[187]504 F. Supp. at 367.

[188]*Id.*

Further complicating the issue of the Act's coverage is the question of what protection is afforded to horses and burros on private lands. By the Act's definition, such animals are not "wild free-roaming horses and burros." However, if they have strayed from public lands onto private lands, the protection for which they were eligible while on public lands remains with them.[189] The private landowner onto whose lands such animals have strayed may maintain them "if he does so in a manner that protects them from harassment, and if the animals were not willfully removed or enticed from the public lands."[190] Alternatively, he may "inform the nearest Federal marshall or agent of the Secretary, who shall arrange to have the animals removed."[191] In *Roaring Springs Associates v. Andrus*, this latter provision was found to impose a nondiscretionary duty upon the Secretary, enforceable by mandamus.[192] In reaching this conclusion, the court voided regulations of the Secretary of the Interior requiring removal only from fenced private lands in states where landowners are required to fence their property to protect against trespassing livestock. Thus, in these so-called "fence-out" or "open range" areas, federal land managers will be held to a special duty to remove roaming wild horses from unfenced areas where private livestock owners have no similar duty to remove their cattle.[193]

Putting aside the definitional ambiguities, the Act's prohibitions on taking are reasonably straightforward. They provide that any person who "maliciously causes the death or harassment"[194] of a protected horse or burro, or who "processes or permits to be processed into commercial products the remains"[195] of same, may be fined up to $2,000 or imprisoned for up to one year, or both. Identical penalties may be imposed on anyone

---

[189]Whether this aspect of the Act is constitutional was expressly left undecided in Kleppe v. New Mexico, 426 U.S. 529, 546–547 (1976).

[190]16 U.S.C. §1334 (1976).

[191]*Id.*

[192]471 F.Supp. 522 (D. Ore. 1978).

[193]The Interior Department sought legislative relief from the Roaring Springs decision as part of the Public Rangelands Improvement Act of 1978, Pub. L. No. 95-514, 92 Stat. 1803, but was unsuccessful. *See* S. Rep. No. 1267, 95th Cong. 2d Sess. 24, *reprinted in* 1978 U.S. Code Cong. & Ad. News 4065, 4088.

[194]16 U.S.C. §1338(a)(3) (1976). The bill passed by the House, H.R. 9890, 92d Cong., 1st Sess. (1971), used the term "substantial harm" rather than "harassment." The Conference Committee agreed to the Senate terminology "in order to widen the scope of prohibited activities," explaining that "[c]oncern was expressed by the conferees for activities which although not immediately causing substantial harm, would have a cumulatively detrimental effect on the health and welfare of the animals." H. Rep. No. 681, 92d Cong., 1st Sess. at 6 (1971).

[195]16 U.S.C. §1338(a)(4) (1976).

who, without permission from the appropriate Secretary, "willfully removes or attempts to remove a wild free-roaming horse or burro from the public lands."[196]

Under standards to be explored in more detail in Chapter 6, the Secretaries may remove "excess" horses and burros from public lands. Prior to 1978, such animals could be "adopted" by private individuals. Under the applicable regulations, however, adopted animals remained the property of the federal government. By amendment in 1978, Congress largely codified the adoption program and authorized the Secretary, under appropriate conditions, to grant title to the adopted animals after a year of humane care.[197] To prevent this provision from becoming a loophole through which large numbers of adopted animals can be converted to commercial use, the Secretary can transfer title to no more than four animals annually to any transferee.[198]

---

[196]*Id.* §1338(a)(1), (2).

[197]16 U.S.C. §1333(c) (Supp. V 1981).

[198]United States v. Hughes, 626 F.2d 619 (9th Cir. 1980) involved an individual who, prior to the 1978 amendments, adopted 109 horses in slightly more than a year and sold a large number of them to a slaughterhouse. The most significant aspect of the case was the court's holding that the sale of the adopted horses could be prosecuted as a violation of the general prohibition against conversion of government property to private use found in 18 U.S.C. §641 (1976) as well as a violation of the specific prohibition against unauthorized conversion of a wild free-roaming horse or burro found in section 8(a)(2) of the Act, 16 U.S.C. §1338(a)(2) (1976). Maximum penalties are higher under the former provision than under the latter.

Chapter **5**

# REGULATING COMMERCE IN WILDLIFE

No federal wildlife statute relies exclusively on the regulation of taking to achieve its goals. In fact all federal statutes which restrict the taking of wildlife also restrict at least some aspects of commerce in wildlife or wildlife products. Thus, for example, the Migratory Bird Treaty Act, in addition to restricting the hunting, taking, killing and capturing of migratory birds, as discussed in the preceding chapter, also makes it unlawful for any person to "possess, offer for sale, sell, offer to barter, barter, offer to purchase, purchase, deliver for shipment, ship, export, import, cause to be shipped, exported, or imported, deliver for transportation, transport or cause to be transported, carry or cause to be carried, or receive for shipment, transportation, carriage, or export" them except as permitted under regulations of the Secretary of the Interior.[1] These prohibitions are considerably more expansive than the limited proscriptions contained in the 1916 Convention with Great Britain against the

---

[1] 16 U.S.C. §703 (1976). It is noteworthy that the Act does not require that these activities be conducted in interstate commerce to be unlawful. The Act does, however, prohibit the transportation in interstate commerce of "any bird, or any part, nest, or egg thereof, captured, killed, taken, shipped, transported, or carried... contrary to the laws of the State, Territory, or district in which it was captured, killed, or taken, or from which it was shipped, transported, or carried." *Id.* §705. The latter prohibition is not entirely redundant of the former because the latter applies to *all* birds, not just migratory birds, protected under the treaties. *See* Bogle v. White, 61 F.2d 930 (5th Cir. 1932). It is, however, with the possible exception of its application to nests, redundant of the Lacey Act. *See* text accompanying note 37 *infra.*

"shipment or export" of migratory birds from any state during its close season and against the "international traffic" in unlawfully taken migratory birds.[2]

The Bald Eagle Protection Act likewise prohibits not only the taking of bald and golden eagles, but also their possession, sale, purchase, barter, transportation, exportation, or importation.[3] Finally, the Wild Free-Roaming Horses and Burros Act prohibits the processing of wild horse or burro remains into commercial products and the sale of any wild horse or burro maintained on private land.[4] In each of these examples, the restrictions relating to commerce serve in part to supplement and buttress federal prohibitions on taking. While federal authority for the underlying prohibition has frequently been challenged, there has seldom been any serious doubt concerning the constitutional authority for federal regulation of interstate and foreign commerce in wildlife and wildlife products.

In fact, as has been shown in Chapter 2, the first major federal wildlife statute enacted was aimed solely at regulating interstate commerce in wildlife and scrupulously refrained from asserting any federal authority over its taking.[5] That Act, the Lacey Act of 1900,[6] supplemented until 1981 by the Black Bass Act of 1926,[7] is the cornerstone of federal efforts to conserve wildlife through the regulation of commerce.

The Lacey Act, as originally passed, had two principal purposes. The first was to strengthen and supplement state wildlife conservation laws. The second was to promote the interests of agriculture and horticulture by prohibiting the importation of certain types of wildlife determined to be injurious to those interests. Both of these original purposes have been expanded considerably in the more than eighty years of the Act's existence. That steady process of expansion is described in detail in this chapter.

---

[2] Convention for the Protection of Migratory Birds, United States–Great Britain (on behalf of Canada), Aug. 16, 1916, 30 Stat. 1702, T.S. No. 628, art. VI. For a discussion of cases upholding the validity of the Migratory Bird Treaty Act insofar as it authorizes greater restrictions on taking of migratory birds than those imposed by the Convention, see Chapter 4 at text accompanying notes 62–66.

[3] 16 U.S.C. §668(a)(1976 & Supp. V 1981).

[4] 16 U.S.C. §1338(a)(1976).

[5] In the debate that preceded passage of that statute, Congressman Lacey explained that his bill would not itself prohibit the taking of any wildlife because "to do that it would become necessary to enact a national game law, which...would be unconstitutional." 33 Cong. Rec. 4873 (1900). As described in Chapter 2, Lacey's comments reflected the thinking of the day that the federal role in wildlife regulation was extremely narrow because of the state "ownership" of wildlife.

[6] Ch. 553, 31 Stat. 187 (current version at 16 U.S.C. §§701, 3371–3378 and 18 U.S.C. §42 (1976 and Supp. V 1981).

[7] Ch. 346, 44 Stat. 576 (codified at 16 U.S.C. §§851–856) (1976) (repealed 1981).

## THE PROHIBITION OF COMMERCE IN
## UNLAWFULLY TAKEN WILDLIFE

According to the House committee report that accompanied the Lacey Act, its "most important purpose" was "to supplement the State laws for the protection of game and birds,"[8] by making it unlawful for any person to deliver to a common carrier, or for any common carrier to transport from one state or territory to another, wild animals or birds killed in violation of state or territorial law.[9] To facilitate enforcement of this prohibition, the Act also required that all packages containing dead animals, birds, or parts thereof be clearly marked when shipped in interstate commerce.[10] For violations of its various provisions, the Lacey Act prescribed maximum fines of $200 for shippers and for consignees "knowingly receiving such articles," and $500 for carriers "knowingly carrying or transporting the same."[11]

To bolster the effectiveness of state wildlife laws even further, the Lacey Act also sought to prevent game from being shipped into a state in order to circumvent prohibitions on the sale of local game killed in violation of a state's laws. Thus, section 5 of the Act, recently repealed, provided that "the dead bodies, or parts thereof, of any wild game animals, or game or song birds transported into any State or Territory . . . shall . . . be subject to the operation and effect of the laws of such State or Territory . . . as though such animals or birds had been produced in such State or Territory."[12]

The issue of the constitutionality of the Lacey Act has never been presented to the Supreme Court. The very few lower courts that have considered its constitutionality have uniformly upheld it.[13] Indeed, most of the early litigation relating to the Lacey Act concerned its effect on state power to regulate the possession or sale of wildlife imported from other states. Illustrative is the New York case of *People v. Bootman,* involving the state's Forest, Fish and Game Law of 1900.[14] That law, which prohibited

---

[8]H.R. Rep. No. 474, 56th Cong., 1st Sess. 2 (1900).

[9]Lacey Act, §3 (current version at 16 U.S.C. §3372(a)(Supp. V 1981)).

[10]*Id.* §3372(b).

[11]Lacey Act, §4 (current version at 16 U.S.C. §3373 (Supp. V 1981).

[12]Lacey Act, §5 (codified at 16 U.S.C. §667e (1976)(repealed 1981)). The unusual wording of the provision came almost verbatim from the Wilson Original Package Act of 1890, 27 U.S.C. §121 (1976), which permitted states to regulate or prohibit the importation of alcoholic beverages. *See* H.R. Rep. No. 474, 56th Cong., 1st Sess. 3 (1900).

[13]*See, e.g.,* Rupert v. United States, 181 F. 87 (8th Cir. 1910), and Eager v. Jonesboro, Lake City and Eastern Express Co., 103 Ark. 288, 147 S.W. 60 (1912).

[14]180 N.Y. 1, 72 N.E. 505 (1904).

the possession of certain birds during the state's close season, was sought to be applied to persons who had lawfully acquired birds in another state, brought them into New York during its open season, and continued to possess them after its close. The New York court, which, prior to passage of the Lacey Act, had held a nearly identical statute to be inapplicable in such circumstances,[15] reached the same result again, while offering the following comment on the effect of the Lacey Act:

> If the federal statute had been passed first it would not be unreasonable to believe that the legislature intended to so expand the meaning of our game laws as to forbid the possession of imported game during the close season. It was not passed, however, until after the enactment of the state law, and hence can have no effect upon its meaning.[16]

*State v. Shattuck* was a similar case in which the Lacey Act was held to have removed all doubt as to the authority of a state to prohibit the possession of game lawfully acquired in another state.[17]

The issue addressed in *Bootman* and *Shattuck* was rendered moot by the 1908 decision of the Supreme Court in *New York ex rel. Silz v. Hesterberg*, upholding the power of a state to apply its game laws to wildlife brought in from outside the state, wholly without regard to the Lacey Act.[18] The extreme reach of state law was well illustrated in the *Silz* case, where the state law in question, which prohibited the possession of all grouse and plover during the close season, was applied to birds not even found in the United States but imported from England and Russia.

Although the Lacey Act, as originally passed, applied literally to "wild animals or birds" without limitation, in actual practice that terminology was apparently construed to apply only to game birds and fur-bearing mammals.[19] It was for this reason that in 1926 Congress enacted wholly new legislation to provide essentially identical protection for two species of fish known commonly as black bass. The Black Bass Act, like the Lacey Act, prohibited the interstate shipment of such fish when taken contrary to state law, required the clear marking of all packages containing such fish, and authorized states to treat such fish, when brought in from other states, as though they had been produced in the receiving state.[20] Maximum

---

[15]People v. Buffalo Fish Co., 164 N.Y. 93, 58 N.E. 34 (1900).

[16]180 N.Y. at 7, 72 N.E. at 506–507.

[17]96 Minn. 45, 104 N.W. 719 (1905).

[18]211 U.S. 31 (1908). As a result of this holding, the repeal of section 5 of the original Lacey Act in 1981 had no practical consequence.

[19]*See* 67 Cong. Rec. 9385 (1926) (Remarks of Congressman Hawes).

[20]The Black Bass Act, which was codified at 16 U.S.C. §§851–856 (1976), was repealed and its provisions consolidated with those of the Lacey Act as a result of the Lacey Act Amendments of 1981, Pub. L. No. 97-79, 95 Stat. 1073.

penalties for violations of the Act were fixed at $200, or three months imprisonment, or both.[21]

Both the Lacey and Black Bass Acts have been amended on several occasions. A 1935 amendment extended the former's prohibition on interstate commerce to include wild animals, birds, and parts or eggs thereof, captured or killed contrary to federal law or the laws of any foreign country.[22] The Black Bass Act was likewise amended so as to apply to any fish taken contrary to the laws of a foreign country, though this amendment was not enacted until 1969.[23]

In fact, a significant step toward aiding the enforcement of foreign conservation laws was taken prior to the 1935 Lacey Act amendment with the passage of the Tariff Act of 1930. Section 527 of the Tariff Act provides that if the laws of any foreign country or political subdivision thereof restrict the taking or exportation of any wild mammal, bird, or part or product thereof, no such bird or mammal may be imported, directly or indirectly, into the United States without a certification from the United States consul at the place of export that it was not acquired or exported in violation of those laws.[24] Animals or products imported in violation of the foregoing are subject to seizure and forfeiture, regardless of any culpability on the part of the importer.[25]

Though the Tariff Act was a progressive measure in 1930, substantially enhancing the effectiveness of the Lacey Act, its narrow scope has reduced its importance today. Most notably, it is limited solely to birds and mammals, whereas the Lacey Act now prohibits importation and interstate commerce in any type of unlawfully acquired foreign fish or wildlife.[26]

---

[21]26 U.S.C. §853 (1976)(repealed 1981). Earlier, the Black Bass Act had been expanded to encompass all "game" fish in 1947, Act of July 30, 1947, ch. 348, 61 Stat. 517, and then to all United States fish in 1952, Act of July 16, 1952, ch. 911, §2, 66 Stat. 736.

[22]Act of June 15, 1935, ch. 261, tit. II, §201, 49 Stat. 380 (current version at 16 U.S.C. §3372(a)(2)(A)(Supp. V 1981)).

[23]Endangered Species Conservation Act of 1969, Pub. L. No. 91-135, §9(a), 83 Stat. 275 (repealed 1981). Earlier, the Black Bass Act had been amended to encompass all "game" fish in 1947, Act of July 30, 1947, ch. 348, 61 Stat. 517, and then to all United States fish in 1952, Act of July 16, 1952, ch. 911, §2, 66 Stat. 736.

[24]19 U.S.C. §1527(a)(1976).

[25]Id. §1527(b). This was the holding in United States v. Fifty-three (53) Eclectus Parrots, 685 F.2d 1131, 1133–1134 (9th Cir. 1982). Until amended in 1981, the Lacey Act authorized forfeitures of illegally traded wildlife only in connection with "knowing and willful" violations of that Act. Compare 16 U.S.C. §3374(a)(Supp. V 1981) with 18 U.S.C. §43(e)(1976)(repealed 1981).

[26]In addition to the Lacey Act's prohibition on importation of unlawfully taken foreign wildlife, the Tariff Act of 1962, 19 U.S.C. §1202, schedule a, part 15, subpart D, headnote 2 (1976), prohibits the importation of the "feathers or skin" of any bird. Certain named types of birds are expressly excepted from this prohibition, as are

Accordingly, whereas under the Tariff Act consular certification is required for certain imported birds and mammals, for other types of foreign wildlife whose importation is prohibited by the Lacey Act, no consular certification is required and effective enforcement therefore depends heavily upon the knowledge by customs agents of foreign wildlife laws.[27]

The Tariff Act also presents some anomalies in terms of its exceptions. For example, animals imported for scientific or educational purposes are exempt from its requirements.[28] This exemption may have reflected a policy judgment in 1930 that for the purposes specified the United States would not assist in the enforcement of foreign wildlife laws; nevertheless, that policy was reversed when the Lacey Act was amended in 1935 to prohibit the importation of *all* wildlife taken contrary to foreign law, without exception for scientific, educational, or other purposes. Accordingly, the exemption in the Tariff Act is an anachronism serving no current policy.

Until recently, it has been unclear whether the Tariff Act is adequate to protect against the practice of exporting to the United States from one country wildlife unlawfully taken in a third country. The Act purports to bar the importation, "directly or indirectly," of wildlife taken contrary to the laws of the country of origin. The only certification it requires, however, is that of the United States consul "for the consular district in which is located the port or place from which such [animal] was exported." The Court of Appeals for the Ninth Circuit recently interpreted the latter provision "to require proper documentation from the animal's country of

---

skins or feathers imported for scientific or educational purposes and fully manufactured artificial flies used for fishing. In addition, the importation of skins bearing feathers of eight named species of birds may be imported up to specified quotas under permit of the Secretary of the Interior. By administrative determination, however, the Secretary has eliminated the quotas on two such species. *See* 50 C.F.R. §15.11 (1981).

[27]Administrative regulations of the Fish and Wildlife Service provide that when foreign law restricts the taking or exportation of a species sought to be imported, "the owner, importer, or consignee *may* be required to produce foreign documentation showing that such laws or regulations have not been violated." 50 C.F.R. §14.41 (1981)(emphasis added). When such foreign documentation is required, it can be satisfied by producing either official permits from the countries of origin and export or consular certification. 50 C.F.R. §14.42(a), (b)(1981). As a result of the Convention on International Trade in Endangered Species of Wild Fauna and Flora (hereinafter CITES), official export permits *must* accompany all specimens listed on any of its three appendices. *See* Chapter 12 at text accompanying notes 30–46. Although any country that is a party to that Convention may list on Appendix III those species within its jurisdiction whose protection requires the cooperation of other parties, the failure to list any protected species does not diminish the requirement of the Lacey Act that only lawfully taken animals from that species may be imported.

[28]19 U.S.C. §1527(c)(2)(1976).

origin, whether or not the United States importer was involved in the initial export from that country."[29]

A second major amendment to the Lacey Act occurred in 1949. It prohibited the importation of "wild animals or birds" under conditions known to be "inhumane or unhealthful" and authorized the Secretary of the Treasury to prescribe requirements for transportation of such animals under humane and healthful conditions.[30] The amendment further provided that "the presence ... of a substantial ratio of dead, crippled, diseased, or starving wild animals or birds shall be deemed prima facie evidence" of a violation. The ambiguity inherent in the terms used in the statute (including the very term "wild animals or birds") perhaps explains why there have been virtually no reported cases under this provision in the nearly three decades of its existence.[31]

Responsibility for administration of the Lacey and Black Bass Acts was originally vested in the Secretaries of Agriculture and Commerce, respectively. After three decades of consolidated responsibility in the Secretary of the Interior, administration was once again divided between the Secretaries of Commerce and the Interior in 1970.[32] The justification for that division of authority seems questionable, since the only administrative responsibility under the Acts is of a purely law enforcement nature.[33]

The first truly comprehensive amendments to the Lacey Act came in 1981, nearly a century after its enactment. The Lacey Act Amendments of 1981 repeal the entirety of the Black Bass Act and most of the Lacey Act, substituting provisions that, in effect, consolidate these two closely related

---

[29]United States v. Fifty-three (53) Eclectus Parrots, 685 F.2d 1131, 1134 (9th Cir. 1982). This decision is consistent with the administrative regulations of the United States Customs Service, which incorporate by reference the foreign documentation requirements of the Fish and Wildlife Service extending to both the country of origin and the country of export. *See* 19 C.F.R. §12.28 (1981). Under CITES, "re-export" certificates are required whenever importation of listed species is from a country other than its country of origin. *See* Chapter 12 at text accompanying note 41.

[30]Act of May 24, 1949, ch. 139, §2, 63 Stat. The responsibilities of the Secretary of the Treasury were transferred to the Secretary of the Interior by amendment in 1981. *See* 18 U.S.C. §42(c)(Supp. V 1981).

[31]In United States v. States Marine Lines, Inc., 334 F. Supp. 84, 89 (S.D.N.Y. 1971), the court declined to rule that 15 percent mortality among shipped animals at the time of arrival or 30 percent mortality within a few days thereafter constituted the required "substantial ratio" for a prima facie violation of the statute.

[32]Reorg. Plan No. 4 of 1970, 35 Fed. Reg. 15627, 84 Stat. 2090.

[33]Indicative of the fact that transition to shared responsibility has not been particularly smooth is the Secretary of Commerce's failure to publish final regulations concerning procedures for assessment of civil penalties for violations of the Lacey Act until July 30, 1976. *See* 42 Fed. Reg. 31825. *See also* note 61 *infra*.

statutes.[34] The amendments also substantially expand the scope of the laws they consolidated, revise somewhat the duties they impose, and generally strengthen the enforcement handles they make available. The only significant part of either law left untouched is the provision of the Lacey Act governing the importation of injurious wildlife.[35]

The major changes worked by the 1981 amendments pertain to the provisions prohibiting certain dealings in specimens taken, transported, or sold in violation of underlying state, federal, or foreign laws. As formerly written, these provisions pertained only to wild vertebrates other than migratory birds, mollusks, and crustaceans;[36] they now apply to all wild animals, including those bred in captivity, and to certain wild plants.[37] The underlying laws, violation of which can lead to a Lacey Act violation, now include Indian tribal laws and federal treaties, in addition to the previous state, federal, and foreign laws.[38] Finally, whereas formerly the law prohibited most interstate or foreign trafficking in specimens "taken, transported, or sold" contrary to underlying laws, it now also prohibits such trafficking in specimens "possessed" contrary to any underlying state or foreign law.[39]

In addition to the foregoing changes in scope, the 1981 amendments also substantially increase the penalties that may be assessed for Lacey Act violations. The maximum criminal fine that may be assessed is doubled to $20,000; the maximum jail sentence is increased from one to five years. Penalties of this magnitude can be assessed against importers, exporters, or

[34]Pub. L. No. 97-79, 95 Stat. 1073.

[35]18 U.S.C. §42(a) and (b) (1976). See text accompanying notes 61–79 *infra*.

[36]18 U.S.C. §43 (1976) (repealed 1981).

[37]16 U.S.C. §3372(a)(Supp. V 1981). Plants now subject to the Lacey Act include only those that are indigenous to any state and that are either listed on any appendix of CITES or pursuant to any state law providing for the conservation of species threatened with extinction. *Id.* §3371(f). Plant conservation laws of foreign countries are not among the underlying laws, violation of which can lead to a Lacey Act violation. *Cf. Id.* §3372(a)(2), (b)(2).

[38]*Id.* §3372(a)(1). 18 U.S.C. §1165 (1976) prohibits trespass upon Indian reservation for the purpose of hunting, trapping, or fishing. United States v. Sanford, 547 F.2d 1085, 1088 (9th Cir. 1976), held that transport of wildlife taken after such an unlawful trespass is not a violation of the Lacey Act since it is not the taking, but rather the trespass, that is prohibited by federal law. That distinction is eliminated by the 1981 amendments since any taking after such trespass will violate Indian tribal law.

[39]Treaties and Indian tribal laws are treated differently from underlying state and foreign laws in that specimens "taken or possessed" contrary to the former are subject to the Lacey Act, whereas specimens "taken, possessed, transported, or sold" contrary to state laws are so subject. *Compare* 16 U.S.C. §3372(a)(1)(Supp. V 1981) *with id.* §3372(a)(2).

those engaged in the purchase or sale of protected specimens if they knew that such specimens were taken, possessed, transported, or sold in violation of an underlying law.[40] With the exception of importers and exporters, however, these severe criminal penalties apply only when the market value of the specimens involved exceed $350.[41] Under the law prior to these amendments, criminal penalties could be assessed only against those who "knowingly and willfully" violated the Lacey Act.[42] By abandoning this standard, the law no longer requires the government to prove that a violator knew of the Lacey Act's prohibitions and intended to violate them.

Offenses that fit within the above categories are, by virtue of the maximum penalties that may be imposed, considered felonies. Misdemeanor offenses include any violation of the Act in which the violator knowingly engaged in conduct prohibited by the Act and, in the exercise of due care, should have known that the specimens involved were taken, possessed, transported, or sold contrary to an underlying law.[43] For these, maximum criminal penalties of a $10,000 fine and a year in prison may be imposed. The same due care standard governs the imposition of civil penalties. However, to be assessed a civil penalty, one need not knowingly engage in conduct prohibited by the Act. Maximum civil penalties are $10,000 per violation.[44]

Several other enforcement related changes deserve mention. The law as amended contains a strict liability forfeiture provision for the specimens

---

[40]*Id.* §3373(d)(1). Criminal penalties are inapplicable to violations of the Act's container-marking requirements. *See* text accompanying note 50 *infra.* At least one case, United States v. Plott, 345 F. Sup. 1229 (S.C.N.Y. 1972), holds that violations of the Lacey Act may also constitute violations of 18 U.S.C. §2314 (1976), which makes it a crime to "transport in interstate or foreign commerce any goods...of the value of $5,000, or more, knowing the same to have been stolen, converted or taken by fraud." In that action, the defendant contended that poached alligator hides could not be considered "stolen" goods because the peculiar nature of a state's "ownership" of alligators was not the type of ownership contemplated by the use of the term "stolen." The court disagreed on the ground that "taking from an owner in trust constitutes stealing or converting within the meaning of §2314 just as much as taking from any other owner." 345 F. Supp. at 1232. The practical significance of the *Plott* decision is that violations of §2314 are subject to stiffer penalties, including imprisonment of up to 10 years, than are violations of the Lacey Act.

[41]16 U.S.C. §3373(d)(1)(B)(Supp. V 1981). Query: How will market value be ascertained for species having no legal markets?

[42]18 U.S.C. §43(d) (1976) (repealed 1981).

[43]16 U.S.C. §3373(d)(2)(Supp. V 1981).

[44]*Id.* §3373(a)(1). The civil penalty may not exceed the maximum imposable under the underlying law when the violation pertains to specimens valued at less than $350 and does not involve importation, exportation, or sale of such specimens. *Id.* In the case of violations of the Act's container-marking requirements, the maximum civil penalty is $250. *Id.* §1373(a)(2).

involved in any violation.[45] Forfeiture of equipment used in a violation may result when a felony conviction is obtained.[46] Beginning in fiscal year 1983, the Secretary of the Treasury is authorized to pay rewards to persons furnishing information that leads to conviction or certain other enforcement actions.[47] The amounts of such rewards may be determined by the Secretary of the Treasury or by the Secretaries of the Interior or Commerce.[48] Finally, a variety of federal licenses or permits may be suspended or cancelled as an additional sanction against criminal violators.[49]

The one part of the Lacey Act significantly relaxed by the 1981 amendments is the provision requiring the marking of packages containing fish or wildlife. As amended, the law merely requires the Secretaries of Commerce and the Interior to promulgate jointly container-marking regulations that are "in accordance with existing commercial practices."[50] Only civil penalties in a maximum amount of $250 may be assessed for violations of those regulations.

Taken together, the 1981 amendments represent a significant broadening and strengthening of the Lacey Act and the former Black Bass Act. They are likely to lead to much more effective enforcement of state, federal, foreign, and tribal conservation laws.

Prior to the 1981 amendments, very few Lacey Act decisions were reported. Indeed, students of the Lacey Act owe thanks primarily to one Henry Molt for what little case law construing the Lacey Act has recently been reported. Molt was a Philadelphia reptile dealer whose reptile dealings aroused the interest of federal law enforcement agents in 1974. His subsequent prosecution produced a total of five reported decisions by the United States Court of Appeals for the Third Circuit, all bearing the name *United States v. Molt*.[51] Some of those decisions settled some important interpretational questions under the Lacey Act.

The Lacey Act, prior to the 1981 amendments, made it unlawful for any person to transport or sell in interstate or foreign commerce "any wildlife taken, transported, or sold in any manner in violation of any law or regulation of any State or foreign country."[52] In the second of its *Molt*

---

[45]*Id.* §3374(a)(1).

[46]*Id.* §3374(a)(2).

[47]*Id.* §3375(d).

[48]*Id.*

[49]*Id.* §3373(e).

[50]*Id.* §3372(b).

[51]589 F.2d 1247 (3d Cir. 1978); 599 F.2d 1217 (3d Cir. 1979); 615 F.2d 141 (3d Cir. 1980); 10 Envtl. L. Rep. (Envtl. L. Inst.) 20777 (3d Cir. July 17, 1980); and 631 F.2d 258 (3d Cir. 1980).

[52]18 U.S.C. §43(a)(2)(1976)(current version at 16 U.S.C. §3372(a)(Supp. V 1981)).

decisions, the Third Circuit decided that the words "any law or regulation" of a foreign country did not in fact mean "any," but only those "laws and regulations designed and intended for the protection of wildlife in those countries."[53]

Thus Molt argued successfully that his violation of a general customs law, applicable to all exports, was outside the scope of the Lacey Act because its purpose was merely the raising of revenue, not the protection of wildlife.[54] On the one hand, that was not an unreasonable result because wildlife protection is the purpose of the Lacey Act itself, and it is therefore reasonable that the foreign laws from which it derives its force should also serve that purpose. On the other hand, this result arguably placed on federal prosecutors the burden of proving the purpose of allegedly violated foreign laws.

It is unclear whether the 1981 amendments would produce a different result in the same case today. The House Report disapproved the "designed and intended for the conservation of wildlife" standard, finding it "too restrictive."[55] On the other hand, that Report also indicated that "[t]he Act's reference to 'any law, treaty or regulations' is not intended to include laws, treaties or regulations that are plainly and solely revenue laws with no specific reference to wildlife," an apparent endorsement of the *Molt* result, if not its reasoning.[56] In many cases, however, as in *Molt* itself, the purpose of a law may not be readily apparent from its face. Indeed, Molt subsequently argued that the Lacey Act was unconstitutionally vague in that it made criminal the violation of a foreign law that "an ordinary person would have no way of knowing…was of a kind that Congress indicated should not be violated."[57] The Third Circuit summarily rejected this argument.[58]

The only other significant reported Lacey Act decision of recent vintage is *United States v. Sylvester*.[59] The Ninth Circuit there upheld a conviction for violation of the Act's prohibition on commerce in wildlife sold in violation of state law even though, under state law, the defendant's transactions did not constitute a "sale." The defendant's argument was

---

[53]599 F.2d at 1218–1219.

[54]*Id.* at 1219. *Compare* United States v. Sanford, *supra* note 38.

[55]H.R. Rep. No. 276, 97th Cong. 1st Sess. 14 (1981).

[56]*Id.*

[57]631 F.2d at 263.

[58]*Id.* It is difficult to reconcile the court's summary rejection of this claim with its earlier *Molt* holding that section 9 of the Endangered Species Act was unconstitutionally vague. *See* United States v. Molt, 10 Envt. L. Rep. (Envtl. L Inst.) 20777 (3d Cir. July 17, 1980) discussed in Chapter 12.

[59]605 F.2d 474 (9th Cir. 1979).

that, under Alaska law, the transaction in question did not constitute a completed "sale" until after the delivery of the goods to a purchaser in another state. The court rejected that argument, holding that, where the sale is an integral part of the transfer of wildlife products, the Lacey Act reaches it.[60]

## THE IMPORTATION OF INJURIOUS WILDLIFE

Beyond supplementing state wildlife conservation laws, the Lacey Act sought to protect domestic agricultural interests by prohibiting the importation of certain kinds of wildlife thought to be injurious to those interests. Thus, as originally enacted, the Lacey Act prohibited, except for "natural history specimens for museums or scientific collections," the importation of mongooses, fruit bats, English sparrows, starlings, and "such other birds or animals as the Secretary of Agriculture may from time to time declare injurious to the interest of agriculture or horticulture" and authorized the Secretary of the Treasury to make regulations for implementing the section.[61] For 70 years, however, this latter authority remained largely unexercised.[62]

During that 70-year period, the authority to prohibit the importation of injurious wildlife was expanded significantly. In 1960, the Department of the Interior persuaded Congress to amend the Act to clarify its authority over the importation of injurious "birds or animals" by changing those words to become "wild mammals, wild birds, fish (including mollusks and

---

[60]*Id.* at 475.

[61]Lacey Act, §2 (current version at 18 U.S.C. §42(1976 & Supp. V 1981). The duty originally vested in the Secretary of Agriculture is now shared by the Secretaries of Commerce and the Interior. The two Secretaries were unable to finalize a memorandum of understanding concerning their respective authorities to regulate importation of injurious wildlife until January, 1975. *See* Department of the Interior, Fish and Wildlife Service, Draft Environmental Statement on Proposed Injurious Wildlife Regulations 71 (DES 75-6, Feb. 1975). The Secretary of the Treasury shares with the two Secretaries the duty of enforcing the injurious wildlife importation restrictions. 18 U.S.C. §42(a)(5)(1976).

[62]Current injurious wildlife regulations are found at 50 C.F.R. part 16 (1981). Importation of certain foreign wildlife is also subject to regulation by the Public Health Service under the Public Health Service Act, 42 U.S.C. §264 (1976). The purpose of such regulation is to prevent the spread of communicable diseases. Current Public Health Service regulations regulating the importation of psittacine birds, turtles, tortoises, terrapins, and primates are found at 42 C.F.R. §§71.161–71.189 (1981). The Department of Agriculture, in order to protect domestic livestock from foreign-borne disease, also regulates the importation of wild ruminants and swine under section 306 of the Tariff Classification Act, 19 U.S.C. §1306 (1976).

crustacea), amphibians, reptiles, or the offspring or eggs of any of the foregoing."[63] Moreover the interests to be protected from the importation of injurious wildlife were expanded by the same amendment from the original "agriculture or horticulture" to "human beings,...agriculture, horticulture, forestry,...wildlife or the wildlife resources of the United States."[64]

Notwithstanding that clarification of its authority, the Department of the Interior never sought to implement the authority in a comprehensive fashion until 1973. In that year, it proposed to treat all foreign wildlife as injurious to one or more of the interests specified in the statute.[65] However, if the importation of a particular species could be shown to present a "low risk" of injury to the specified interests, its importation would not be restricted. A relatively short list of wildlife already determined to present a low risk was included in the original Interior proposal.

The original proposal, because it threatened to prohibit certain interests (most notably the pet trade) from importation of much foreign wildlife, and because it threatened to complicate the task of others (particularly the zoological and scientific communities) in importing foreign wildlife by requiring importation permits, caused a storm of protest. A special congressional hearing was called just to review the proposed action of the Department.[66] The Department came under heavy pressure to back off its proposal[67] as affected interests claimed economic

---

[63] Act of Sept. 2, 1960, Pub. L. No. 86-702, §1, 72 Stat. 753 (current version at 18 U.S.C. §42(a)(1)(1976)). Even this change, however, did not entirely accomplish the stated objective of the Department of the Interior to clarify its authority to regulate "without question, the importation of fish, including mollusks and crustacea, *or any type of animal found to be injurious.*" (emphasis added). Department of the Interior letter transmitting the proposed bill, reprinted in S. Rep. No. 1883, 86th Cong., 2d Sess. 4 (1960).

[64] The 1970 amendment also added a definition of the terms "wildlife" and "wildlife resources," as used in the quoted passage, which included "wild mammals, wild birds, fish (including mollusks and crustacea), and all other classes of wild creatures whatsoever, and all types of aquatic and land vegetation upon which such wildlife resources are dependent." Thus the wildlife resources sought to be protected by the importation restrictions are substantially broader than the range of wildlife that may be kept out of the country through such restrictions.

[65] *See* 38 Fed. Reg. 34970 (Dec. 20, 1973).

[66] Hearings on Proposed Injurious Wildlife Regulations Before the Subcomm. on Fisheries and Wildlife Conservation and the Environment of the House Comm. on Merchant Marine and Fisheries, 93d Cong., 2d Sess. (1974).

[67] The sort of pressure placed on Interior is well illustrated by the following exchange between C.J. Lankford, Program Coordinator for Mammals and Non-Migratory Birds, Fish and Wildlife Service, and Congressman Biaggi (D–N.Y.):

Mr. Lankford: [T]here are those that feel that their privileges, and in essence, I think they even use the term civil rights, were being usurped

ruin and contended that it had no authority to proceed in the manner proposed.[68]

Two months after the Congressional hearings, Interior issued a revised proposal that, while expanding the predetermined list of low risk wildlife and modifying slightly the proposed procedures for issuance of permits, still adhered to the same basic approach.[69] However, no further action was taken on either proposal until August 1976, more than two and one-half years after the original proposal, when Interior announced that it was abandoning altogether its proposed approach in favor of seeking a legislative "clarification" of its authority to proceed in that manner. Its stated justification for this reversal was its inability to persuade Congress to appropriate the extra funds needed to undertake the program and its apprehension of a legal challenge if it adopted its earlier proposals.[70]

The legislative clarification that Interior was to seek has yet to occur. Nonetheless, an Executive Order issued in 1977 gave added force to the effort to protect natural ecosystems from the adverse effects of introduced organisms. Executive Order 11987, issued on May 24, 1977, did not confer any new authority upon federal agencies, but it did purport to direct those agencies to use their existing authority so as to restrict the introduction of exotic species into natural ecosystems on lands or waters that they administer.[71] The export of native species for the purpose of introducing them into natural ecosystems of foreign countries was also required to be restricted to the extent permitted by law.[72] Exceptions to the foregoing restrictions could be made upon a finding of no adverse effect on natural

---

when they are told they cannot go anywhere in the world and find a new species and introduce it in the environment of the United States.
    Mr. Biaggi: I agree with that.

*Id.* at 149.

[68]*See, e.g.,* the comments of the American Association of Zoological Parks and Aquariums in response to the original Notice of Proposed Rulemaking, on file with the Fish and Wildlife Service.

[69]*See* 40 Fed. Reg. 7935 (Feb. 24, 1975).

[70]Interior had earlier advised Congress that it saw no merit to the assertion that the legislative history of the Lacey Act precluded its adoption of a low-risk approach. Hearings, *supra* note 66 at 137 (statement of John Oberheu). In fact, the legislative history is silent regarding whether the Secretary's determinations must be made on an individual species basis or whether they may be made in more general terms. The arguments of certain affected organizations that the Lacey Act requires species by species determinations are based on doubtful inference rather than clear legislative history.

[71]Exec. Order No. 11987, §2(a), 3 C.F.R. 116 (1977 Comp.), *reprinted in* 42 U.S.C. §4321 note (Supp. IV 1980).

[72]*Id.* §2(c).

ecosystems by the Secretary of Agriculture or the Interior.[73] The latter Secretary was directed to promulgate regulations for the implementation of the Executive Order but has yet to do so.[74]

One of the significant features of the Executive Order is that the "exotic species" whose introduction it seeks to restrict can include not only animals, but also plants.[75] Existing authority to regulate the importation of plants, vested in the Department of Agriculture under the Plant Pest Act[76] and the Plant Quarantine Act,[77] is designed primarily to protect against introduction of diseases or pests harmful to other plants. The Federal Noxious Weed Act of 1974 provides authority for restricting not only the importation, but also the interstate movement, of foreign plants that "can directly or indirectly injure crops, other useful plants, livestock or poultry or other interests of agriculture, including irrigation, or navigation or the fish and wildlife resources of the United States or the public health."[78] Although it is unclear whether the designation of fish and wildlife as an "other interest of agriculture" was intended to limit the scope of protection available to wildlife, it would appear that the measure offers at least some basis for addressing the growing problem of native habitat disruption caused by foreign plant introductions.[79]

---

[73]*Id.* §2(d).

[74]*Id.* §3.

[75]*Id.* §1(c).

[76]7 U.S.C. §§147a, 149, and 150aa–150jj (1976).

[77]7 U.S.C. §§151–167 (1976).

[78]7 U.S.C. §2802 (1976).

[79]Not surprisingly, the "noxious weeds" designated in existing regulations at 7 C.F.R. §360.200 (1981) reflect a concern with restricting importation of plant pests directly harmful to crop plant production. A limited authority to control the importation of plants that "could disturb the ecological balance of unique island environments" is contained in the Convention for the Protection of Migratory Birds and Birds in Danger of Extinction, and Their Environment, March 4, 1972, United States–Japan, art. VII, [1974] 25 U.S.T. 3329, T.I.A.S. No. 7990.

# Chapter 6

# ACQUISITION AND MANAGEMENT OF WILDLIFE HABITAT

The well being of wildlife is vitally dependent upon the health of its habitat. It is therefore abundantly clear that the management of federally owned lands, which comprise nearly one third of the total land area of the United States, is of great significance for much of the nation's wildlife. Without some mechanism for assuring that the management of those lands protects their habitat values, the regulation of direct taking and the regulation of commerce in wildlife necessarily constitute an incomplete federal program of wildlife conservation.

This chapter examines the laws pertaining to the conservation of wildlife on federal lands. The initial part of the chapter treats those federal lands that were acquired or reserved expressly for wildlife conservation purposes. It examines both the laws providing for their acquisition and those providing for their administration. The second part of the chapter concerns the national forests and national resource lands, federal lands required to be managed under the principle of "multiple use," in which wildlife conservation is but one of several purposes to be served. The final part examines the wildlife aspects of the management of lands devoted to special purposes other than wildlife conservation, including the national parks and monuments, wilderness areas, marine sanctuaries, and military reservations.

## THE NATIONAL WILDLIFE REFUGE SYSTEM

### The Origins of the Refuge System and Federal Authority to Acquire Refuges

The National Wildlife Refuge System is the only extensive system of federally owned lands managed chiefly for the conservation of wildlife. Its

119

origins can be traced to the turn of the century, when the first federal wildlife refuges were established by presidential proclamation.[1] Soon thereafter, Congress also became directly involved in the creation of wildlife refuges, first by authorizing the President in 1905[2] and 1906[3] to designate areas within Witchita National Forest and Grand Canyon National Forest, respectively, as wildlife ranges, and then by itself establishing a National Bison Range in Montana in 1908.[4]

The stimulus for establishing a systematic program of refuge acquisition was provided by the Migratory Bird Treaty Act. The failure of the Act to authorize the acquisition of migratory bird habitat came to be recognized as a serious shortcoming. To provide the needed acquisition authority, Congress passed the Migratory Bird Conservation Act in 1929.[5] The Conservation Act established a Migratory Bird Conservation Commission to review and approve proposals of the Secretary of the Interior for the purchase or rental of areas under the Act.[6] As originally enacted, the Conservation Act provided that all refuges acquired pursuant to its authority be operated as "inviolate sanctuaries."[7] That terminology has been rendered largely meaningless as subsequent enactments have authorized the Secretary to permit public hunting on an ever-increasing proportion of the total area of any such refuge, if "compatible with the major purposes for which such areas were established."[8] One final noteworthy feature of the Conservation Act is that it, unlike most other statutes authorizing federal acquisition of land, requires that the Secretary

---

[1]*See* Chapter 2 at note 59.

[2]Act of Jan. 24, 1905, ch. 137, 33 Stat. 614, (current version at 16 U.S.C. §§684–686 (1976).

[3]Act of June 29, 1906, ch. 3593, 34 Stat. 607, (current version at 16. U.S.C. §§684–686 (1976)).

[4]Act of May 23, 1908, ch. 192, 35 Stat. 267, (current version at 16 U.S.C. §671 (1976)).

[5]16 U.S.C. §§715–715d, 715e, 715f–715k, and 715n–715r (1976).

[6]The authority of the Secretary of the Interior to initiate acquisition proposals was originally vested in the Secretary of Agriculture. Both Secretaries serve on the Migratory Bird Conservation Commission, as does the Secretary of Transportation and two members each from the Senate and the House of Representatives. For purposes of considering the acquisition of areas within a particular state, the ranking officer of the game agency of that state is an *ex officio* member of the commission. 16 U.S.C. §715a (1976).

[7]16 U.S.C. §715d (1976).

[8]The Act of Aug. 12, 1949, ch. 421, §2, 63 Stat. 600, authorized the Secretary to permit public hunting on up to 25 percent of the area of any theretofore "inviolate" sanctuary. That proportion was increased to 40 percent by the Act of Aug. 1, 1958, Pub. L. No. 85–585, §2, 72 Stat. 486. The National Wildlife Refuge System Administration Act of 1966, Pub. L. No. 89–669, §4, 80 Stat. 927, authorized the Secretary to permit "compatible" hunting on any unit of the National Wildlife Refuge System, retaining the 40 percent limitation only with respect to the hunting

first obtain the legislative consent of the state in which the lands to be acquired are located before acquisition can be carried out.[9]

Enactment of the Migratory Bird Hunting Stamp Act in 1934 assured a steady source of funding for refuge acquisition under the Conservation Act but in a way that almost assured the development of a refuge system keyed principally to the production of migratory waterfowl.[10] Although acquisition authority was contained in a number of subsequent statutes, including the Fish and Wildlife Coordination Act,[11] the Fish and Wildlife Act of 1956,[12] the Land and Water Conservation Fund Act,[13] and the Endangered Species Acts of 1966, 1969, and 1973,[14] the Conservation Act continues to be a major source of authority for wildlife refuge acquisition.[15]

---

of migratory waterfowl. The Fish and Wildlife Improvement Act of 1978, Pub. L. No. 95–616, §6, 91 Stat. 3114 (codified at 16 U.S.C. §668dd(d)(1)(A)(Supp. V 1981)), authorized the Secretary to permit migratory waterfowl hunting on more than 40 percent of any given refuge if the Secretary finds that to do so would be beneficial to the species. The principal purpose of this amendment was to reduce the occasion for waterfowl mortality from communicable diseases by controlling bird concentrations in refuges. See S. Rep. No. 1175, 95th Cong., 2d Sess. 5, reprinted at 1978 U.S. Code Cong. & Ad. News 7641, 7644.

[9] 16 U.S.C. §715f (1976).

[10] For a discussion of the Migratory Bird Hunting Stamp Act, 16 U.S.C. §§718–718b and 718c–718h (1976 & Supp. V 1981), see Chapter 8 at text accompanying notes 4–13. A 1958 amendment authorized the expeditures of funds derived from the Hunting Stamp Act for the acquisition of "waterfowl production areas," which are small wetland or pothole areas. The acquisition of such areas is expressly exempted from the legislative consent requirement of the Conservation Act, and such areas are likewise exempt from its "inviolate sanctuary" provision. 16 U.S.C. §718d(c)(1976). However, the Wetlands Loan Act of 1961 required that the consent of the governor or the head of the appropriate state agency be obtained prior to any acquisition of such areas. 16 U.S.C. §715k-5 (1976). This added requirement apparently only formalized prior administrative practice under the Conservation Act. See 74 Cong. Reg. 17172 (1961) (remarks of Senator Hruska). For the Supreme Court's interpretation of this requirement, see text accompanying notes 28–33 infra.

[11] The Fish and Wildlife Coordination Act provides that lands acquired or administered by a federal agency pursuant to its authority may be made available to the Secretary of the Interior for administration by him "where the particular properties have value in carrying out the national migratory bird management program." 16 U.S.C. §663(b)(1976). It is discussed in detail in Chapter 7.

[12] 16 U.S.C. §742f(a)(1976).

[13] 16 U.S.C. §460l-4 through 460l-11 (1976). The Land and Water Conservation Fund Act is discussed in detail in Chapter 8.

[14] The acquisition authority of the various Endangered Species Acts is discussed in Chapter 12.

[15] Despite the many sources of acquisition authority, the Advisory Committee on Wildlife Management reported to Secretary of the Interior Udall in 1968 that "there is not support nor clear authority for the Bureau of Sport Fisheries and Wildlife to

Before turning to a consideration of some of the litigation concerning the scope of federal acquisition authority under the Conservation Act, méntion should be made of the Department of Agriculture's Water Bank Program for Wetlands Preservation, carried out under authority of the Water Bank Act of 1970.[16] Under that program, the Secretary of Agriculture may enter into 10-year renewable agreements with private landowners and operators in important migratory waterfowl nesting and breeding areas.[17] In return for payment of an agreed upon annual fee, the participating landowner or operator agrees "not to drain, burn, fill, or otherwise destroy the wetland character" of areas included in the program, or "to use such areas for agricultural purposes."[18] If a private party violates the agreement and his violation "is of such a nature as to warrant termination of the agreement," he must forfeit all rights to receive future payments and refund past payments under the agreement.[19] The total payments that the Secretary is authorized to make in any one year under the program may not exceed $10 million.[20] Thus the Water Bank Program offers a significant alternative to outright acquisition for the protection of migratory bird habitat.

The scope of the authority of the federal government to acquire lands for wildlife refuge purposes has been tested in only a very few cases. *Swan Lake Hunting Club v. United States* was one of the most significant of these.[21] It involved a challenge to the authority of the Secretary of the Interior to acquire lands by condemnation under the Migratory Bird

---

extend the refuge system in relation to wildlife needs other than for migratory birds." The Committee's report, commonly known as the Leopold Report, is reprinted in Department of the Interior, Fish and Wildlife Service, Final Environmental Statement, Operation of the National Wildlife Refuge System, app. W (1976).

[16]16 U.S.C. §§1301–1311 (1976).

[17]*Id.* §1302.

[18]*Id.* §1303. The annual payment is greater if the participating owner or operator permits public access for hunting, trapping, fishing, and hiking on his program lands. *Id.* §1304.

[19]*Id.* §1303. The administrative regulations of the Department of Agriculture provide for withholding of payment for any year during which a violation of a lesser character occurs. *See* 7 C.F.R. §752.15(a)(1981). Considerable controversy occurred in the summer of 1976 when, to alleviate drought conditions in the North Central states, the Agricultural Stabilization and Conservation Service, which administers the Water Bank Program, announced that it would permit, under certain conditions, limited grazing and haying on Water Bank lands, subject only to a forfeiture of the annual payment otherwise due. *See* N.D. Wildlife Federation, Flickertales, vol. 19, no. 4 at 5 (Sept. 1976).

[20]16 U.S.C. §1310 (1976).

[21]381 F.2d 238 (5th Cir. 1967).

Conservation Act. The defendants contended unsuccessfully that the statutory authorization to "purchase or rent" lands did not include acquisition by condemnation. The *Swan Lake* decision also rejected efforts to construe narrowly the terms of legislative and gubernatorial consents to federal acquisition under the Conservation Act.

The United States Supreme Court first considered the scope of federal refuge acquisition authority in *United States v. Little Lake Misere Land Co.*[22] In *Little Lake*, the United States had acquired under the Conservation Act certain parcels of land in Cameron Parish, Louisiana, for Lacassine National Wildlife Refuge, the sellers retaining mineral rights for 10 years thereafter. Shortly after the acquisition, Louisiana passed a law providing that in any sale of land to the United States, retained mineral rights were imprescriptable. Some 30 years after its purchase, the United States brought suit to quiet title to the land. The Supreme Court, while acknowledging that state law ordinarily governs land transactions to which the United States is a party, held that it did not govern in this case because the instant acquisitions were ones "arising from and bearing heavily upon a federal regulatory program."[23] Further, in fashioning a federal rule of law to govern the acquisition, the Court rejected the customary route of "borrowing" state law because the state law in question was "plainly hostile to the interests of the United States."[24]

The *Little Lake* rule has been extended substantially in two decisions of the United States Court of Appeals for the Eighth Circuit. In *United States v. Albrecht*, the government sought to enforce an "easement" against the drainage of a pothole area in North Dakota.[25] The defendant argued that the purported "easement" was not a recognized property interest under North Dakota law. Following *Little Lake*, the Court held that the question was one to be decided by federal law because it bore heavily upon a federal regulatory program, acquisition of pothole areas under the Migratory Bird Hunting Stamp Act. The Court likewise refused to "borrow" North Dakota law on the following grounds:

> We fully recognize that laws of real property are usually governed by the particular states; yet the reasonable property right conveyed to the United States in this case effectuates an important national concern...and should not be defeated by any possible North Dakota law barring the conveyance of this property right.... We, therefore, specifically hold that

---

[22] 412 U.S. 580 (1973).

[23] *Id.* at 592.

[24] *Id.* at 596.

[25] 496 F.2d 906 (8th Cir. 1974).

the property right conveyed to the United States in this case, whether or
not deemed a valid easement or other property right under North Dakota
law, was a valid conveyance under federal law and vested in the United
States the rights as stated therein.[26]

The *Albrecht* decision demonstrated an extraordinary solicitousness
toward federal land acquisition in furtherance of wildlife conservation
programs. In effect, the *Albrecht* court was prepared to recognize any
"reasonable" federal property right, wholly without regard to state law.[27]

Another opportunity to examine the clash between state and federal
interests came only a few years later. In 1977 North Dakota passed laws
placing strict limitations on the acquisition of easements by the federal
government and the Governor, piqued by the controversy over the Garrison
Diversion project, purported to revoke the authority granted by predecessors for easement acquisition pursuant to the Wetlands Loan Act of
1961.[28] The United States sued to declare invalid the North Dakota law and
the purported gubernatorial revocation.

The Supreme Court upheld the federal government's claims in *North
Dakota v. United States*.[29] The Court held that gubernatorial consent to
easement acquisition required by the Wetlands Loan Act, once given,
cannot be revoked, at least not so long as the United States did not
unreasonably delay in carrying out its acquisitions.[30] The two dissenting
Justices would have remanded to determine whether the federal government had in fact delayed unreasonably.[31]

As to the legislative restrictions enacted by North Dakota, the Court
held that they could not be applied to land acquisitions carried out
pursuant to previously given gubernatorial consents.[32] The Court expressly refrained from deciding whether any of the state's restrictions, requiring
concurrence by county commissions, limiting the duration of easements

---

[26]*Id.* at 911.

[27]*Compare* the Supreme Court's decision in Cappaert v. United States, 426 U.S. 128
(1976), holding that the United States need not comply with state law to reserve
unappropriated groundwater when setting aside lands under the Act for the
Preservation of American Antiquities for the purpose of preserving the endangered
Devil's Hole pupfish.

[28]*See* note 10 *supra.*

[29]103 S.Ct. 1095 (1983).

[30]*Id.* at 1103–1104.

[31]*Id.* at 1107 (O'Connor, J. dissenting).

[32]*Id.* at 1105–1106.

and prohibiting certain types of easements, might be valid as applied to easements acquired pursuant to subsequent gubernatorial consents.[33]

## The Administration of the National Wildlife Refuge System

Until 1966, there was no single law governing the administration of the many federal wildlife refuges. In fact, there were numerous administrative units, known variously as "game ranges," "wildlife ranges," "wildlife management areas," "waterfowl production areas," and "wildlife refuges," all under the jurisdiction of the Fish and Wildlife Service, or, in a few cases, under the joint jurisdiction of the Fish and Wildlife Service and Bureau of Land Management (hereinafter referred to as "BLM"). A measure of rationalization was introduced into this system by passage of the "National Wildlife Refuge System Administration Act of 1966."[34] That Act consolidated these various units into a single "National Wildlife Refuge System." Beyond that fact of consolidation, however, the Act did little to spell out standards to guide the administration of the System. Basically, it (1) placed restrictions on the transfer, exchange, or other disposal of lands within the system; (2) clarified the Secretary's authority to accept donations of money to be used for land acquisition; and (3) most importantly, authorized the Secretary, under regulations, to "permit the use of any area within the System for any purpose, including but not limited to hunting, fishing, public recreation and accommodations, and access whenever he determines that such uses are compatible with the major purposes for which such areas were established."[35] This authorization of "compatible" uses thus made clear that the national wildlife refuges were not necessarily to be managed as "single-use" lands, but more properly as "dominant use" lands.[36]

The 1966 Act did not affect two earlier statutes relating to the management of wildlife refuges. The first of these was the Refuge Recreation Act of 1962.[37] It authorizes the Secretary to administer areas of

---

[33]*Id.*

[34]16 U.S.C. §§668dd, and 668ee (1976 & Supp. V 1981). The National Wildlife Refuge System Administration Act was the name given in 1969 to sections 4 and 5 of the Endangered Species Preservation Act of 1966, Pub. L. No. 69–669, 80 Stat. 926.

[35]16 U.S.C. §668dd(d)(1)(1976).

[36]*See* the discussion of the Public Land Law Review Commission's "dominant use" recommendation at text accompanying notes 139–141 *infra*.

[37]16 U.S.C. §§460k–460k-4 (1976 & Supp. V 1981).

the System "for public recreation when in his judgment public recreation can be an appropriate incidental or secondary use; *Provided*, that such public recreation use shall be permitted only to the extent that it is practicable and not inconsistent with...the primary objectives for which each particular area is established."[38] Recreational uses "not directly related to the primary purposes and functions of the individual areas" of the System may also be permitted, but only upon an express determination by the Secretary that they "will not interfere with the primary purposes," of the refuges and that funds are available for their development, operation, and maintenance.[39] The Refuge Recreation Act also authorizes the Secretary to acquire lands for various specified purposes, including the conservation of threatened and endangered species.[40]

The second statute unaffected by the 1966 Act was the Refuge Revenue Sharing Act of 1964.[41] That Act provides that the net receipts from the "sale or other disposition of animals, timber, hay, grass, or other products of the soil, minerals, shells, sand, or gravel, from other privileges, or from leases for public accommodations or facilities...in connection with the operation and management" of areas of the National Wildlife Refuge System shall be paid into a special fund. The monies from the fund are then to be used to make payments for public schools and roads to the counties in which refuges having such revenue producing activities are located.[42]

The three statutes just described constitute the basic authority within which the National Wildlife Refuge System operates. In recent years, a number of varied controversies have arisen regarding various aspects of the administration of that System. These controversies have concerned such issues as the Secretary's authority to permit or prohibit particular uses under the compatibility standard; his authority to transfer lands from the System; the application of the National Environmental Policy Act[43] to decisions affecting the refuges; and, most fundamentally, the placement of

---

[38]*Id.* §460k.

[39]*Id.*

[40]*Id.* §460k-1. The long-standing controversy concerning the availability of Land and Water Conservation Fund monies for refuge acquisition under the Refuge Recreation Act is described in Chapter 8 at text accompanying notes 107–112.

[41]16 U.S.C. §715s (1976 & Supp. V 1981).

[42]The only reported litigation concerning the Refuge Revenue Sharing Act is Cameron Parish Police Jury v. Hickel, 302 F. Supp. 689 (W.D. La. 1969), discussed in Chapter 8 at text accompanying notes 37–38 and Watt v. Alaska, 451 U.S. 259 (1981), discussed at text accompanying notes 77–80 *infra*.

[43]42 U.S.C. §§4321–4347 (1976). The National Environmental Policy Act (hereinafter referred to as NEPA) is considered in detail in Chapter 7 at text accompanying notes 90–128.

ultimate responsibility for their management with the appropriate governmental agency.

The consolidation of so many disparate units effectuated by the National Wildlife Refuge System Administration Act could not, by itself, change the fact that some of those units were established for purposes somewhat different from those for which others were established. In particular, the System included some units expressly established both for the protection of wildlife *and* for grazing of domestic livestock. Reflecting that duality of purpose, certain of these units, known as "game ranges," were jointly administered until 1975 by the Fish and Wildlife Service and BLM. In that year, however, the Secretary of the Interior directed that sole management of three such game ranges be vested in BLM.[44] The prospect that the Fish and Wildlife Service, whose paramount mission is wildlife conservation, would be divested of its authority in favor of the multiple-use–oriented BLM so alarmed wildlife proponents that a lawsuit to reverse the Secretary's action was filed almost as proposed legislation to achieve the same end was introduced.

Both the litigative and legislative efforts were successful. In *Wilderness Society v. Hathaway*, the District Court for the District of Columbia enjoined the transfer on the ground that "the Secretary is required to exercise his discretion and authority with respect to the administration of game ranges and wildlife refuges through the Fish and Wildlife Service."[45] One month later, that result was confirmed by the passage of an amendment to the National Wildlife Refuge System Administration Act specifically directing that all units of the System be administered through the Fish and Wildlife Service and that all units then within the System remain so except under certain limited conditions.[46]

The requirement of the 1976 Act that the Refuge System be administered by the Fish and Wildlife Service has been given two dramatically different interpretations by the courts. In one, *Schwenke v. Secretary of the Interior*,[47] the federal district court in Montana regarded the 1976 Act as a mere "shuffling of administration from one agency to another"[48] that did nothing to alter the fact that public grazing has "a co-equal priority with

---

[44]Memorandum from the Under Secretary of the Interior to the Directors of BLM and the Fish and Wildlife Service, dated Feb. 5, 1975.

[45]Civil No. 75–1004 (D.D.C. Jan. 26, 1976).

[46]Act of Feb. 27, 1976, Pub. L. No. 94–223, 90 Stat. 199 (codified at 16 U.S.C. §§668dd (1976)). The game range controversy is described at greater length in Comment, National Game Ranges: The Orphans of the National Wildlife Refuge System, 6 Envtl. L. 515 (1976).

[47]Civil Act. 79–133–BLG (D. Mont. Jan. 14, 1982).

[48]*Id.* slip op. at 9.

wildlife conservation"[49] on the Charles M. Russell National Wildlife Refuge, one of the refuges previously managed jointly by BLM and the Fish and Wildlife Service. The narrow basis for the court's dubious holding was that neither the 1976 Act nor prior administrative actions had expressly revoked the original withdrawal for grazing purposes of lands that were later to compose the Russell Refuge. Without any express revocation of that withdrawal, the court reasoned, subsequently established uses for those lands could at most be given an equal priority with the original grazing use.

The effect of the court's ruling in *Schwenke* is unclear because the court declined to enter either declaratory or injunctive relief. In addition, although the court stated in the initial paragraph of its opinion that the plaintiff "ranchers grazing permits cannot be revoked,"[50] it went on to say later that "we are not calling in doubt [the Fish and Wildlife Service's] or the Secretary's authority to revoke any or all existing grazing permits, so long as the Taylor Grazing Act is followed."[51] While reconciling these directly conflicting statements is impossible, the court apparently meant that the Fish and Wildlife Service may exercise whatever rights to revoke existing grazing permits that the Taylor Grazing Act confers upon the Secretary of the Interior; it may not, however, terminate them on the basis that grazing is incompatible with the Refuge's wildlife conservation purposes under the National Wildlife Administration Act.

The federal district court for Alaska gave a quite different interpretation to the Administration Act in *Trustees for Alaska v. Watt*.[52] At issue in that case was the delegation by the Secretary of the Interior of certain responsibilities pertaining to oil and gas exploration and development in the Arctic National Wildlife Refuge to the United States Geological Survey (USGS). These responsibilities were to develop by regulation certain initial guidelines for exploration, to review and approve exploration plans, and, after a period of five years, to recommend whether additional exploration or development was warranted.[53] The USGS had the exclusive responsibility for the first and last of these; with respect to the approval of exploration plans, its approval was subject to the requirement of concurrence by the Fish and Wildlife Service.

The court concluded that this arrangement violated the requirement of the Administration Act that all units of the Refuge System be

---

[49]*Id.* at 1.

[50]*Id.*

[51]*Id.* at 13. The Taylor Grazing Act is discussed at text accompanying notes 178–181 *infra.*

[52]524 F. Supp. 1303 (D. Alas. 1981), *aff'd*, 690 F.2d 1279 (9th Cir. 1982).

[53]These responsibilities were imposed by the Alaska National Interest Lands Conservation Act of 1980, 16 U.S.C. §3142(d), (e), (h)(Supp. V 1981) (ANILCA). ANILCA is discussed further at text accompanying notes 81–92 *infra.*

administered by the Fish and Wildlife Service. To "administer" a refuge is to "manage" it, the court reasoned, and the Service's duty to manage required it "to control and direct the Refuge by regulating human access in order to conserve the entire spectrum of wildlife found in the Refuge."[54] Even the preparation of a report to Congress that "supplies information essential to determining whether development activity will be permitted within the Refuge" was, in the court's view, "a Refuge Administration function."[55] As to the requirement of Fish and Wildlife concurrence in the approval of any exploration plan, the court concluded that this constituted the very sort of "joint administration" of a refuge that the 1976 Act had been designed to prohibit.[56] The district court's decision was subsequently affirmed and its opinion expressly embraced by the United States Court of Appeals for the Ninth Circuit.

More frequent than controversies of the above character are those concerning the Secretary's authority to limit the uses of refuges to those that are "compatible with the major purposes" thereof. One of the first of these concerned the Secretary's authority to restrict public access to refuges. In *Coupland v. Morton* certain North Carolina property owners sued to invalidate regulations severely restricting their ability to drive over the beaches of Virginia's Back Bay National Wildlife Refuge in order to reach their properties.[57] The landowners claimed that the regulations were unauthorized and that the environmental impact statement that accompanied them was inadequate because it failed to consider the environmental effects of requiring an alternate and substantially longer means of access outside the refuge.

As to the NEPA claim, the court not only found the impact statement adequate, but stated in *dictum* its belief "that the United States, as the owner of the Back Bay National Wildlife Refuge, should be able to exclude a trespasser without filing an environmental impact statement."[58] As to the validity of the regulations, the court found "that the continued and rapidly escalating use of the Refuge beach as a traffic corridor for land developers and land owners... is inimical to the use of the property as a wildlife refuge and is a depredation of the purpose of the property as a wildlife refuge."[59]

---

[54] 524 F. Supp. at 1309.

[55] *Id.* at 1310.

[56] *Id.* at 1309–1310.

[57] 5 Envtl. L. Rep. (Envtl. L. Inst.) 20504 (E.D. Va.), *aff'd,* 5 Envtl. L. Rep. (Envtl. L. Inst.) 20507 (4th Cir. 1975).

[58] 5 Envtl. L. Rep. (Envtl. L. Inst.) at 20506. For a similar case reaching the same conclusion with respect to National Park Service limitations on private vehicle use of Fire Island National Seashore, see Biderman v. Secretary of Interior. 7 Env't Rep. Cas. (BNA) 1279 (E.D.N.Y.), *aff'd sub nom.* Biderman v. Morton, 5 Envtl. L. Rep. (Envtl. L. Inst.) 20027 (2d Cir. 1974).

[59] 5 Envtl. L. Rep. (Envtl. L. Inst.) at 20506. Although the court's reasoning would

Thus the court affirmed a potentially far-reaching power of the Secretary to protect the national wildlife refuges.[60]

While the *Coupland* case affirms the authority of the Secretary under the Refuge Administration Act to prohibit uses incompatible with the primary purpose of a refuge, more recent cases explore the question whether the standards of that and the related Refuge Recreation Act impose judicially enforceable limitations upon the authority of the Secretary to permit such uses. In *Defenders of Wildlife v. Andrus,* the plaintiff challenged certain regulations of the Fish and Wildlife Service governing motor boating and water skiing within Ruby Lake National Wildlife Refuge, a refuge providing "one of the most important habitats and nesting areas for over-water nesting waterfowl in the United States."[61] The regulations permitted boats of unlimited horsepower to use the waters of the refuge, subject to certain speed limitations.

The court focused on three requirements of the Refuge Recreation Act: (1) that any authorized recreational use be "an appropriate incidental or secondary use"; (2) that any such use be compatible with the primary purposes of the refuge; and (3) that before he may permit any recreational use that "is not directly related to the primary purposes and functions" of a refuge, the Secretary must determine "that such recreational use will not interfere with the primary purposes for which the areas were established."[62] With respect to each of these three requirements, the court held that the Secretary bore the burden of proof to demonstrate compliance.[63] In its initial decision, the court held that the last of these requirements had been violated, because the Secretary had failed to make the expressly required determination, and further held that inasmuch as the challenged regulations represented a balancing of economic, political, and recreational

---

seem to be based on the "compatibility" requirement of the Administration Act, in fact the court never mentioned that Act but upheld the regulations as a proper exercise of authority under the Migratory Bird Conservation Act.

[60] After having the validity of its initial regulations confirmed, the Fish and Wildlife Service revised them so as to permit greater usage by the North Carolina property owners. 41 Fed. Reg. 22361 (June 3, 1976) and 41 Fed. Reg. 31537 (July 29, 1976). The political pressures for a relaxation of the original rules were apparently so enormous that Interior was forced to yield much of the authority it had just won. *See* Comment, The Back Bay Wildlife Refuge "Sand Freeway" Case: A Legal Victory in Danger of Political Emasculation, 5 Envtl. L. Rep. (Envtl. L. Inst.) 10148 (1975). In 1980 Congress passed a law permitting certain full time residents of the area south of the refuge to commute across it daily. *See* Act of July 25, 1980, Pub. L. No. 96–315, §3, 94 Stat. 958.

[61] 11 Env't Rep. Cas. (BNA) 2098, 2100 (D.D.C. July 14, 1978).

[62] 16 U.S.C. §460k (1976).

[63] 11 Env't. Rep. Cas. (BNA) at 2101.

interests against the primary purpose of the refuge, they were beyond the authority of the Secretary.[64]

Five days after this decision, the Secretary repromulgated substantially identical regulations accompanied, however, by an express determination that the permitted uses would not interfere with the primary purposes of the refuge. The original plaintiff sued again, and the court found the Secretary's determination to be arbitrary and capricious.[65] The court also found that "the degree and manner of boating use" permitted by the regulations violated each of the three requirements of the Refuge Recreation Act identified in the earlier decision, *i.e.*, that such use is "not incidental or secondary use, is inconsistent, and would interfere with the Refuge's primary purpose."[66] The court reached these conclusions after finding that proposed speed limitations were "obviously unenforceable" and that the Secretary's failure to rely instead upon horsepower limitations was "completely contrary to all reason and the facts of the record."[67] Though these two related cases are obviously limited by their particular facts, they are nonetheless significant because they place judicially enforceable limits upon the exercise of the Secretary's discretion with respect to recreational uses of wildlife refuges.

The general subject of what uses should be permitted within the national wildlife refuges and under what conditions continues to be a source of controversy; it was also the principal focus of a 1979 report from a secretarial advisory committee on the administration of the National Wildlife Refuge System.[68] The report, though evidencing a diversity of views on this subject, gave generally restrictive advice to the Secretary. For the most part, that advice was accepted by Secretary Andrus. However, Secretary Watt subsequently disregarded one of the recommendations Andrus had accepted restricting the use of chemical pesticides on refuges. The suit that was filed to challenge Watt's action resulted in a settlement binding the new Secretary to his predecessor's decision. In ruling that the plaintiffs had prevailed by virtue of the settlement and were therefore entitled to attorney's fees, the court stated that "the record reveals that before this action was initiated, federal defendants made no attempt to

---

[64]*Id.* at 2101–2102.

[65]Defenders of Wildlife v. Andrus, 455 F. Supp. 446, 449 (D.D.C. 1978).

[66]*Id.* By limiting this finding to the "degree and manner of boating" permitted by these regulations, the court backed away from the suggestion in its initial opinion that motor boating *per se* might be inconsistent with refuge purposes under the Refuge Recreation Act. 11 Env't Rep. Cas. (BNA) at 2102.

[67]455 F. Supp. at 449.

[68]U.S. Dept. of the Interior, Final Recommendations on the Management of the National Wildlife Refuge System (1979).

'obey the law'" and that "one beneficial aspect of the settlement...has been to clarify the uncertain status of the policies in the final Recommendation, which had previously been disregarded." [69]

One other facet of the Administration Act that has been litigated concerns the Secretary's authority to exchange refuge lands for other lands. In *Sierra Club v. Hickel,* plaintiffs challenged a land exchange between the Secretary and two public utility companies, the effect of which was to allow the construction of a nuclear power plant immediately adjacent to a national wildlife refuge. [70] In the court of appeals, the three judges who decided the case were unable to agree on a single rationale. Two judges believed the challenge was barred by the doctrine of sovereign immunity, emphasizing that the land exchange had already been completed. One of them also believed exchange of the lands was so committed to the discretion of the Secretary that no judicial review thereof could be had. The third, in a dissenting opinion, believed that the exchange was reviewable and that the proper standard of review was the compatibility of the resulting arrangement with the purposes of the refuge. Had the challenge been initiated prior to completion of the exchange, Judge McCree, who rested his opinion solely on sovereign immunity grounds, would have had to face the issue of reviewability. In the author's opinion, the dissenting judge was correct, both as to the reviewability of the exchange and as to the standard of review.

Although the issue of the compatibility of various uses with the purposes of refuges was, and remains, controversial, there have been two recent Supreme Court decisions affecting other aspects of the National Wildlife Refuge System. One of these concerned the question whether the National Environment Policy Act (NEPA) [71] required the preparation of an environmental impact statement in connection with the annual budget proposals for financing the National Wildlife Refuge System. At the time of the initial edition of this text, a federal district court had concluded that such a statement was required. [72] The skepticism expressed in that initial edition about whether the decision would be sustained on appeal proved correct; in 1979, the Supreme Court ruled that no environmental impact statement was required. [73] The Court reasoned that requests for appropriations were neither "proposals for legislation" nor "proposals for...other major federal actions" within the meaning of NEPA. The Court relied upon the traditional distinction that Congress has drawn

---

[69] Environmental Defense Fund v. Watt, 18 Env't Rep. Cas. (BNA) 1336, (E.D.N.Y. Oct. 22, 1982).

[70] 467 F.2d 1048 (6th Cir. 1972).

[71] 42 U.S.C. §§4321–4347 (1976).

[72] Sierra Club v. Morton, 395 F. Supp. 1187 (D.D.C. 1975).

[73] Sierra Club v. Andrus, 442 U.S. 347 (1979).

between "legislation" and "appropriations" and concluded that preparation of an environmental impact statement was ill suited to the budget preparation process.[74] In reaching this conclusion, the Supreme Court rejected the rationale used by the District of Columbia Court of Appeals that requests for appropriations might require environmental impact statements when such requests would bring about a significant change in the status quo.[75] Importantly, however, the Court did conclude that if, in response to budget cuts, the Fish and Wildlife Service were to revise its ongoing programs in ways that significantly affected the quality of the environment, impact statements would be required for such revisions.[76]

The only other Supreme Court opinion concerning the National Wildlife Refuge System addressed the relationship between the Refuge Revenue Sharing Act and the Mineral Leasing Act of 1920[77] for refuges reserved from the public domain. In *Watt v. Alaska,* the issue at stake was the distribution of revenues from oil and gas leases on the Kenai National Moose Range (now known as the Kenai National Wildlife Refuge).[78] These receipts had since 1954 been distributed on the basis of section 5 of the Mineral Leasing Act of 1920 so as to provide 90 percent of lease revenues to the State of Alaska and 10 percent to the United States Treasury. However, the Refuge Revenue Sharing Act of 1935 provides for a payment of 25 percent of the net receipts from the sale of various resources to the counties in which reserved refuge lands are located and the remainder to the U.S. Treasury.[79] In 1964 the Refuge Revenue Sharing Act was amended so as to include "minerals" in the list of resources subject to such payments. The issue confronted by the Court was thus whether that amendment superseded the revenue distribution formula of the 1920 Act. The Supreme Court held that it did not. Instead, the Court reasoned that the addition of the term "minerals" in 1964 constituted a mere "perfecting" amendment, which brought the Refuge Revenue Sharing Act into conformity with the 1947

---

[74]*Id.* at 361–364.

[75]Andrus v. Sierra Club, 581 F.2d 895, 903 (D.C. Cir. 1978).

[76]442 U.S. at 363. For a case involving the application of NEPA to a transfer of federal land owned by the General Services Administration into the National Wildlife Refuge System, see New England Power Co. v. Goulding, 486 F. Supp. 18 (D.D.C. 1979).

[77]30 U.S.C. §§181–287 (1976 & Supp. V 1981) (Mineral Leasing Act); 16 U.S.C. §715s (1976 & Supp. V 1981) (Refuge Revenue Sharing Act).

[78]451 U.S. 259 (1981).

[79]A different, optional formula, revised by amendments in 1978, governs payments to counties in which refuges comprised of acquired lands are located. The 1978 amendments also added "salmonoid carcasses" to the list of refuge resources subject to shared payments. See 16 U.S.C. §715s(a) and (c) (1976 & Supp. V 1981).

Mineral Leasing Act for Acquired Lands.[80] The effect of the Court's holding is to require that net receipts from mineral leases on refuges comprised of reserved lands be distributed according to the Mineral Leasing Act, whereas the same receipts from leases on refuges comprised of acquired lands must be distributed according to the Refuge Revenue Sharing Act.

### The Refuge System and the Alaska National Interest Lands Conservation Act

One final major development affecting the National Wildlife Refuge System was enactment in 1980 of the Alaska National Interest Lands Conservation Act.[81] In addition to more than doubling the total acreage within the system, that Act enunciated major new management standards for units of the System within Alaska. It requires, for the first time, that comprehensive management plans be drawn up for each Alaskan unit and establishes a timetable within which such plans are to be completed.[82] It also sets forth a succinct statement of the purposes for which each unit is established and, in part, establishes priorities among such purposes. These purposes include, for each refuge:

1. to conserve fish and wildlife populations and habitats in their natural diversity;
2. to fulfill the international treaty obligations of the United States with respect to fish and wildlife and their habitats; and
3. to ensure, to the maximum extent practicable and in a manner consistent with the first purpose set forth above, water quality and necessary water quantity within the refuge.[83]

A further express purpose of each refuge unit other than Kenai National Wildlife Refuge is "to provide...the opportunity for continued subsistence uses by local residents."[84] However, this purpose is to be fulfilled "in a manner consistent with" the first two purposes identified in the preceding paragraph.[85] Thus, in the event of inconsistency, the purpose of continuing subsistence uses by local residents is subservient to the

---

[80]30 U.S.C. §§351–359 (1976).

[81]Pub. L. No. 96–487; 94 Stat. 2371 (1980) (partially codified in scattered sections of 16, 43 U.S.C.).

[82]*Id.* §304(g); 94 Stat. 2394–2395 (uncodified).

[83]*Id.* §§302, 303; 94 Stat. 2385–2393.

[84]*Id.*

[85]*Id.*

purposes of conserving the "natural diversity" of fish and wildlife populations and habitats and fulfilling international treaty obligations.

Overlaying this express statement of purposes for each refuge unit is title VIII of the Act, governing subsistence uses in general on all public lands in Alaska. That title declares a qualified policy that the utilization of the public lands is to cause the least adverse impact possible on rural residents who depend upon subsistence uses of the resources of such lands, and a further policy that nonwasteful subsistence uses of fish and wildlife and other renewable resources shall be the priority consumptive uses of all such resources.[86] The substantive provisions that effectuate these policies, however, give rise to a number of ambiguities and potential inconsistencies.

Section 815(4) sets forth a general disclaimer against anything in title VIII "modifying or repealing the provisions of any Federal law governing the conservation or protection of fish and wildlife, including the National Wildlife Refuge System Administration Act of 1966."[87] That presumably leaves unaffected the duty of the Secretary to determine that particular uses, including hunting, are compatible with the purposes of a refuge before he may allow them. Despite that disclaimer, section 816(b) provides that "[n]otwithstanding any other provision of the Act or other law, the Secretary...may temporarily close any public lands...to subsistence uses of a particular fish or wildlife population only if necessary for reasons of public safety, administration, or to assure the continued viability of such population."[88] Read alone, this provision would seem to override the Refuge Administration Act. Read in conjunction with section 815(4), it leaves the Secretary's closure authority in considerable confusion.

The Secretary's authority to restrict subsistence taking on refuges short of total closure is similarly clouded. Section 804 provides that "[w]henever it is necessary to restrict the taking of populations of fish and wildlife on [federal] lands for subsistence uses in order to protect the continued viability of such populations, or to continue such uses," the Secretary shall do so through the application of specified criteria.[89] Arguably, the Secretary's authority thus to restrict subsistence taking is limited by this section to those instances in which such restrictions are necessary to protect the "continued viability" of fish or wildlife populations, the same standard that governs closure authority. However, sections 302 and 303 clearly make subsistence uses of refuges secondary to conserving fish and wildlife populations in their natural diversity and fulfilling the international treaty obligations of the United States. Moreover, to the extent that sections 302

---

[86] 16 U.S.C. §3112 (Supp. V 1981).

[87] *Id.* §3125 (4).

[88] *Id.* §3126 (b).

[89] *Id.* §3114.

and 303 make subsistence uses even a secondary purpose of Alaskan refuges, such purpose is limited to subsistence uses by "local residents," whereas title VIII defines "subsistence uses" more broadly to refer to uses by "rural Alaska residents."[90] Thus the Secretary's authority to restrict subsistence uses on Alaskan refuges may in fact be greater than what section 804 implies.

While the detailed provisions of the subsistence title represent a major novel aspect of legislatively mandated management of the National Wildlife Refuges, other provisions of the Alaska Act are similarly unique. For example, section 304(d) obliges the Secretary to continue to permit the exercise of preexisting commercial fishing rights or privileges and various uses of refuge lands incidental to those rights and privileges.[91] He is not obliged, however, to permit a "significant expansion" of commercial fishing activities within refuges. Finally, section 304(f) authorizes the Secretary to enter into cooperative management agreements with nearby landowners for management of lands outside the refuges in ways compatible with the major purposes of such refuges.[92]

The refuge management provisions of the Alaskan National Interest Lands Conservation Act of 1980 are likely to be the focus of much attention in the years immediately ahead, especially as the management plans for particular refuges are developed. Reconciling, or adjusting, the requirements of that Act to preexisting general legislation governing the management of wildlife refuges will present a number of potentially difficult problems as well as the opportunity for rethinking how the more general legislation might be restructured.

## FEDERAL LANDS MANAGED UNDER THE PRINCIPLE OF "MULTIPLE USE"

### The National Forest System

During the nineteenth century, the United States pursued an affirmative policy of disposing of the vast quantities of land that it obtained from other sovereigns as a result of its westward expansion. A variety of disposal laws encouraged homesteaders, miners, and others to convert useful areas of the public domain into private ownership.[93] Toward the end of that century,

---

[90]*Id.* §3113.

[91]Pub. L. No. 96–487, §304(d); 94 Stat. 2393.

[92]*Id.* §304(f); 94 Stat. 2394.

[93]The term "public domain," in its most technical meaning, refers solely to those federal lands originally acquired by the United States from another sovereign and

however, largely in reaction to widespread abuse of lands transferred to private owners, there grew the recognition that the policy of wholesale disposal ought to be curbed.[94] The mechanism to accomplish this was the reservation or withdrawal of certain specially valuable lands from the operation of some or all of the disposal laws.

Authority for the first systematic withdrawal of federal lands was provided by the Forest Reserve Act of 1891, which authorized the President to "set apart and reserve...public lands wholly or in part covered with timber or undergrowth, whether of commercial value or not, as public reservations."[95] These public reservations, initially managed by the Interior Department's General Land Office,[96] were the country's first national forests.

The political pendulum soon began to swing the other way, however, as Western interests became angered by the magnitude of presidential withdrawals and chafed at the restrictions imposed by the Forest Reserve Act[97] against timber cutting, trespassing, and mining. The result was the Forest Service Organic Administration Act of 1897, which restricted the President's authority under the earlier act by providing that "[n]o public forest reservation shall be established except to improve and protect the forest within the reservation, or for the purpose of securing favorable conditions of waterflows, and to furnish a continuous supply of timber for the use and necessities of citizens of the United States."[98] This Act, which became known simply as the Organic Act, prescribed the standards that were to govern the management of the national forests. It said not a word about wildlife.

Literally, the language of the Organic Act appeared to limit the purposes for which national forests could be established to three: (1) protection of the forest; (2) securing favorable waterflows; and (3) furnishing a supply of timber. It did not necessarily limit the purposes for which such forests, once established, could be managed. Nor did it amplify the

---

continuously so held since the time of their acquisition. All other federal lands are referred to technically as "acquired lands." Although, for some purposes, substantive consequences sometimes attach to these distinctions, they rarely do for any purpose relating to wildlife. Accordingly, except where expressly so noted, the terms "public lands" and "federal lands" are used to refer both to public domain and acquired lands.

[94]M. Clawson, America's Land & Its Uses 25 (1972).

[95]Act of March 3, 1891, ch. 561, §24, 26 Stat. 1103 (repealed 1976).

[96]Authority to manage the national forests was transferred to the Department of Agriculture by the Forest Reserve Transfer Act of 1905, 16 U.S.C. §472 (1976).

[97]See Note, The Multiple Use–Sustained Yield Act of 1960, 41 Ore. L. Rev. 49, 57 (1961).

[98]Act of June 4, 1897, ch. 2, 30 Stat. 34, (current version at 16 U.S.C. §475 (1976)).

meaning of the directive to "protect the forest," which could arguably have referred to more than just the trees.[99] Whatever the justification, it is clear that the Forest Service, almost from the outset, managed the forests for a number of uses in addition to those specified in the Organic Act. The Agriculture Appropriation Act of 1907, for example, included money for the care of fish stocks in waters of the national forests.[100] Other uses, such as grazing and general recreation, became well established in the early decades of Forest Service management.[101] Thus, without any express statutory authority, the Forest Service began what was in effect a policy of "multiple use" of the national forests, permitting as many varied uses of the forests as were compatible with the three statutorily expressed purposes.

Within this framework of discretionary multiple use, the management of wildlife soon became a controversial issue, not so much because of its conflict with the statutory purposes of timber, waterflow, and forest protection, but because of jurisdictional disputes between the federal government and the states over their respective authorities within national forests. That dispute, described in greater length in Chapter 2, resulted in a 1928 decision of the Supreme Court, *Hunt v. United States*, upholding the power of the Secretary of Agriculture to order the removal of deer threatening harm to Kaibab National Forest through overbrowsing.[102]

Six years later, buoyed by the *Hunt* decision, the Forest Service issued a regulation by which it took upon itself the authority to establish "hunting and fishing seasons . . . , fix bag and creel limits, specify sex of animals to be killed, [and] fix the fees to be paid" for hunting and fishing in designated national forests.[103] In the same month, Congress authorized the President to establish within national forests "fish and game sanctuaries or refuges . . . devoted to the increase of game birds, game animals, and fish of all kinds naturally adapted thereto."[104] Within such sanctuaries, all "hunting, pursuing, poisoning, angling for, killing, or capturing by trapping,

---

[99] In 1901, the Attorney General apparently took the view that protection of forests did not include protection of forest wildlife, for he advised the Secretary of the Interior that the Organic Act "declared the objects of forest reservations to be the protection of forests and . . . conferred specific powers upon the Secretary with reference to their control and management, but not including the power" to regulate the killing of big game. 23 Op. Att'y Gen. 589, 593 (1901). *But see* note 119 *infra*.

[100] 34 Stat. 1269.

[101] *See* Note, The Multiple Use–Sustained Yield Act of 1960, 41 Ore. L. Rev. 49, 66–71 (1961).

[102] 278 U.S. 96 (1928).

[103] Regulation G-20-A, 1 Fed. Reg. 1259, 1266 (Aug. 15, 1936) (originally promulgated March 29, 1934).

[104] 16 U.S.C. §694 (1976). In 1916, Congress had given the President similar authority with respect only to those national forests acquired rather than reserved from the

netting, or any other means" was prohibited,[105] except for "predatory animals...destructive to livestock or wild life or agriculture."[106] Most importantly, although such sanctuaries were to remain as parts of the national forests, other uses could be made of them but only "so far as such uses may be consistent with the purposes for which such fish and game sanctuaries or refuges are authorized to be established."[107]

Thus bold administrative and legislative strokes taken in a single month established federal authority to preempt states from wildlife regulation in the national forests and to designate within those forests areas where wildlife conservation was to be the *dominant* use. Little came of either authority, however. The authority to create sanctuaries within national forests, despite periodic calls for action, has been essentially unutilized.[108] The administrative assertion of authority to regulate the taking of wildlife in national forests evoked such strong opposition from the states that it was never implemented but was replaced in 1941 with new regulations providing for cooperative agreements between the Forest Service and the states under which state law governs the taking of all game.[109] Those regulations have continued in effect unchanged since their promulgation more than three and a half decades ago.[110]

---

public domain. *See* Act of Aug. 11, 1916, ch. 313, 39 Stat. 476 (current version at 16 U.S.C. §683 (1976)).

[105] 16 U.S.C. §694a (1976).

[106] *Id.* §694b.

[107] *Id.* §694.

[108] *See* Guilbert, Wildlife Preservation Under Federal Law, in Federal Environmental Law 594 (E. Dolgin & T. Guilbert eds. 1974). The failure may be attributable in part to the complex and, since 1939, confused division of responsibilities. Although the President retains ultimate authority for designation of sanctuaries, it could only be exercised, under the Act as originally passed, "upon the recommendation of the Secretary of Agriculture and Secretary of Commerce and with the approval of the State legislatures of the respective States in which said national forests are situated." In 1939, however, Reorganization Plan No. II, §4(f), 53 Stat. 1431, transferred the functions of the Secretary of Agriculture relating to the conservation of wildlife to the Secretary of the Interior. Accordingly, when the 1934 Act was codified, the Secretary of the Interior was substituted for the Secretary of Agriculture each time reference to the latter was made in the Act. Under the language of the statute as thus codified, the Secretary of the Interior is responsible (with the Secretary of Commerce) for recommending to the President the designation of wildlife sanctuaries within national forests. Because such sanctuaries remain a part of the national forests, however, they continue to be under the jurisdiction of the Department of Agriculture. For consistency, the codified statute gives the Secretary of the Interior authority to permit other compatible uses in all designated sanctuaries. It is hard to imagine a situation better calculated to provoke interagency conflicts.

[109] *See* Gottschalk, A Sovereign Union of Sovereign States, in Council on Environmental Quality, Wildlife and America (1978).

[110] 36 C.F.R. §241.1 *et seq.* (1981).

The controversy concerning authority over wildlife in the national forests was of a unique character. So long as both public and private forests were abundant, there were few occasions for serious conflict among the various uses to which the national forests could be put. In the period following World War II, however, vastly increased demand for forest products and a similar dramatic increase in the demand for outdoor recreation created a great potential for conflict.[111] Necessarily, the question arose whether the Forest Service had discretion to permit forest uses other than those prescribed in the Organic Act. Congress answered that question in 1960 by passing the Multiple Use–Sustained Yield Act.[112]

The Multiple Use–Sustained Yield Act declares it to be "the policy of Congress that the national forests are established and shall be administered for outdoor recreation, range, timber, watershed, and wildlife and fish purposes."[113] It further directs the Secretary of Agriculture "to develop and administer the renewable surface resources of the national forests for multiple use and sustained yield of the several products and services obtained therefrom," giving "due consideration... to the relative values of the various resources in the particular areas."[114] While the Act includes a definition of "multiple use,"[115] it does not define "due consideration." Thus, while it is clear that "wildlife and fish purposes" are among the purposes for which the national forests are to be administered, it is far from clear how the Forest Service in any particular instance is to reconcile the potentially competing purposes spelled out in the statute.

In fact, there is at least a suggestion that the purposes expressed in the Organic Act are, in case of conflict, to be preferred over purposes added by the 1960 Act, for the latter declares its enumeration of purposes to be "supplemental to, but not in derogation of, the purposes for which the

---

[111] G. Robinson, The Forest Service: A Study in Public Land Management 14 (1975).

[112] 16 U.S.C. §§528–531 (1976).

[113] *Id.* §528.

[114] *Id.* §529.

[115]    The management of all the various renewable surface resources of the [lands] so that they are utilized in the combination that will best meet the needs of the American people; making the most judicious use of the land for some or all of these resources or related services over areas large enough to provide sufficient latitude for periodic adjustments in use to conform to changing needs and conditions; that some land will be used for less than all of the resources, each with the other, without impairment of the productivity of the land, with consideration being given to the relative values of the various resources, and not necessarily the combination of uses that will give the greatest dollar return or the greatest unit output.

*Id.* §531.

national forests were established" under the Organic Act.[116] This language was apparently inserted to appease the timber interests, who had objected strenuously to the Agriculture Department's assertion that the Organic Act had not established any priorities for the purposes it expressed.[117] On the other hand, both the House and Senate committees that considered the legislation emphasized that "no resource would be given a statutory priority over the others."[118] Thus the language of the 1960 Act is not only vague because of its generality, but also compounds preexisting interpretational difficulties.[119]

Before turning to an examination of how the multiple use standard for forest management has been interpreted and implemented, mention should be made of the Supreme Court's one opportunity to explore the purposes of the Organic Act and the subsequent expansion of those purposes in the Multiple Use–Sustained Yield Act. In *United States v. New Mexico* the Supreme Court, by a vote of 5–4, concluded that the 1897 Act authorized the reservation of National Forests for only two purposes, timber and waterflow, and not for "aesthetic, environmental, recreational, or wildlife-preservation purposes."[120] At issue in the *New Mexico* case was whether the 1899 reservation of Gila National Forest in New Mexico implicitly reserved federal water rights in the Rio Mimbres sufficient to preserve a minimum instream flow for fish and wildlife conservation purposes. Had the Court been willing to conclude that the 1897 Act's first stated purpose to "improve and protect the forest" was independent of its purposes to conserve water flows and furnish a supply of timber, it would have been obliged to consider whether "the forest" referred solely to the trees therein or some broader assemblage of life. Justice Powell's dissent took strong exception to the majority's refusal so to hold and concluded that "[i]t is inconceivable that Congress envisioned the forests it sought to preserve as including only inanimate components such

---

[116]*Id.* §528.

[117]*See* H. R. Rep. No. 1551, 86th Cong., 2d Sess. 2 (1960).

[118]*Id.* at 3.

[119]Though the legislative history of the 1960 Act is pretty clear that the "not in derogation of" language was inserted as a political compromise rather than a logical elucidation, it seems possible to offer a logical explanation of this otherwise confusing language. That is, the 1960 Act's directive to serve outdoor recreation, range, and fish and other wildlife purposes may be construed as amplifying the Organic Act's directive to "improve and protect the forest," a directive not otherwise expressly carried over into the 1960 Act. *Compare* the language of the 1960 Act providing that "[t]he establishment and maintenance of areas of wilderness are consistent with the purposes and provisions" of the Act. 16 U.S.C. §529 (1976).

[120]438 U.S. 696, 707–708 (1978).

as the timber and flora. Insofar as the Court holds otherwise, the 55th Congress is maligned and the Nation is poorer, and I dissent."[121]

Less clear was the Court's resolution of the question whether passage of the Multiple Use–Sustained Yield Act had the effect of reserving additional water rights for a broader array of uses, including fish and wildlife, for previously reserved national forests. The majority appeared to say that it did not have this effect,[122] although the dissent treats this as dicta.[123] The majority expressly declined to say whether the 1960 Act authorized the subsequent reservation of National Forests for which a broader array of reserved water rights would be implied.[124]

Turning now to the multiple use standard embodied in the 1960 Act, it was at least a standard against which one might have hoped to measure the propriety of particular decisions by the Forest Service in resolving the many user conflicts that were then beginning to arise. That hope, however, has been largely unfulfilled, at least insofar as judicial review of Forest Service decisions is concerned.

*Parker v. United States,* a case in which certain plaintiffs sought to enjoin a proposed timber sale in White River National Forest, offered a promising beginning.[125] It held that the Secretary's duty to give "due consideration to the relative values of the various resources" under the Multiple Use Act was mandatory and reviewable. The *Parker* case was ultimately successful on other grounds,[126] however, and subsequent decisions under the Multiple Use Act have failed to amplify much the nature of the duty it imposes.

*Dorothy Thomas Foundation v. Hardin,* for example, involved a similar challenge to a proposed timber sale in Nantahala National Forest.[127] Because the Forest Service could show that it had given at least some consideration to each of the purposes specified by the 1960 Act, however, plaintiffs were unable to demonstrate that the resulting decision

---

[121]438 U.S. at 723–724 (Powell, J., dissenting). Justice Rehnquist, who wrote the majority opinion argued in a footnote that although the 1897 Act authorized the establishment of National Forests to improve and protect the forest *or* for timber and water supply, the word "or" really meant "or, in other words." *Id.* at 707 n. 14. Justice Powell retorted by quoting Justice Rehnquist's own dissent in an earlier opinion to the effect that "the Court not surprisingly attempts to keep this provision in the background, addressing it only…in a footnote." *Id.* at 720.

[122]438 U.S. at 713–715.

[123]*Id.* at 718–719 n. 1.

[124]*Id.* 715 n. 22.

[125]307 F. Supp. 685 (D. Colo. 1969).

[126]448 F.2d 793 (10th Cir. 1971), *aff'g* 309 F. Supp. 593 (D. Colo. 1970).

[127]317 F. Supp. 1072 (W.D.N.C. 1970).

to sell the timber was arbitrary, capricious, and an abuse of discretion.[128] Much the same result was reached in *Sierra Club v. Hardin*, which challenged a proposed timber sale of over one million acres, then the largest such sale in Forest Service history.[129] Although the district court was persuaded by plaintiff's evidence of the

> overwhelming commitment of the Tongass National Forest to timber harvest objectives in preference to other multiple use values, Congress has given no indication as to the weight to be assigned each value and it must be assumed that the decision as the proper mix of uses within any particular area is left to the sound discretion and expertise of the Forest Service.[130]

Further emphasizing the degree of discretion to be exercised by the Forest Service, the court rejected the plaintiffs' contention that "due" consideration meant "equal" consideration, because the Act's definition of multiple use "clearly contemplates that some areas may be unsuited to utilization of all resources."[131] In fact, the court stated that the requirement of due consideration was "impossible to define" and not an "objective standard." Accordingly, the court "considered that evidence in the record of 'some' consideration was sufficient to satisfy the Act absent a showing that no *actual* consideration was given to other uses."[132]

More than a year after entry of the district court's judgment in *Sierra Club*, the plaintiffs discovered a highly critical report prepared by a team of independent environmental experts for the company to which the timber sale was to be made. The plaintiffs persuaded the court of appeals to order the trial court to consider their motion for a new trial on the basis of that evidence because it was relevant to the question whether the Forest Service had in fact been aware of the ecological consequences of its proposed sale. In its "memorandum" decision,[133] the court of appeals stated that it would, for purposes of its order, accept the district court's interpretation that "due consideration" required only "some consideration," but

---

[128]*Accord*, Gandt v. Hardin, Civil No. 1334 (W.D. Mich., Dec. 11, 1969).

[129]325 F. Supp. 99 (D. Alas. 1971).

[130]*Id.* at 123.

[131]*Id.* at n. 48.

[132]*Id.* (emphasis in original).

[133]Sierra Club v. Butz, 3 Envtl. L. Rep. (Envtl. L. Inst.) 20292 (9th Cir. March 16, 1973). The Ninth Circuit distinguishes between "memoranda" and "opinions." The former "will not be regarded as precedent in this court and shall not be cited in this Court in briefs or oral argument." 9th Cir. R. 21(c). Thus the *Sierra Club* decision occupies an uncertain status of legal limbo.

with the caution that "due consideration" to us requires that the values in question be informedly and rationally taken into balance. The requirement can hardly be satisfied by a showing of knowledge of the consequences and a decision to ignore them.[134]

Despite the qualified promise that such language offered, subsequent litigation challenging Forest Service decisions has not elucidated the "due consideration" standard of the Multiple Use Act but has instead been based primarily on the National Environmental Policy Act, the Wilderness Act and, recently, the "rediscovered" 1897 Organic Act.[135]

The many attempts to assert judicial control over Forest Service discretion under the multiple use standard were complemented by legislative efforts to circumscribe that authority. The Wilderness Act of 1964 was the first successful result of those efforts.[136] Although the Multiple Use–Sustained Yield Act expressly recognized the establishment of wilderness areas as consistent with its multiple use mandate, nothing compelled the Secretary of Agriculture to establish such areas or, once having established them, to keep them as wilderness areas. One of the major purposes of the Wilderness Act was to eliminate this discretion on the part of the Secretary and to place the ultimate responsibility for wilderness classifications on the Congress.[137] While the importance of the Wilderness Act for Wildlife interests will be discussed later in this chapter, it is noteworthy here because it represents a direct and unequivocal limitation on Forest Service discretion.

---

[134]*Id.* at 20293.

[135]Cases challenging Forest Service discretion under the Wilderness Act include Minnesota Public Interest Research Group v. Butz, 541 F.2d 1292 (8th Cir. 1976), Izaak Walton League of America v. St. Clair, 353 F. Supp. 698 (D. Minn. 1973), *rev'd on other grounds,* 497 F.2d 849 (8th Cir. 1974), and Parker v. United States, 448 F.2d 793 (10th Cir. 1971); similar cases under NEPA include Minnesota Public Interest Research Group v. Butz, 498 F.2d 1314 (8th Cir. 1974), Wyoming Outdoor Coordinating Council v. Butz, 484 F.2d 1244 (10th Cir. 1973), and Kisner v. Butz, 350 F. Supp. 310 (N.D.W.Va. 1972); similar cases under the Organic Act include West Virginia Div. of Izaak Walton League of America, Inc. v. Butz, 522 F.2d 945 (4th Cir. 1975), Zieske v. Butz, 406 F. Supp. 258 (D. Alas. 1975), and Texas Committee on Natural Resources v. Butz, 433 F. Supp. 1235 (E.D. Tex. 1977), *rev'd sub nom.* Texas Committee on Natural Resources v. Bergland, 573 F.2d 201 (5th Cir. 1978).

[136]16 U.S.C. §§1131–1136 (1976 & Supp. V 1981). For a discussion of the Wilderness Act and its origins, *see* McCloskey, The Wilderness Act of 1964: Its Background and Meaning, 45 Ore. L. Rev. 228 (1966).

[137]The Wilderness Act declares that nothing therein "shall be deemed to be in interference with the purpose for which national forests are established as set forth in the [Organic Act] and the Multiple Use–Sustained Yield Act." 16 U.S.C. §1133(a)(1). For a possible explication of this logic-defying language, see note 119 *supra.*

In the same year that Congress enacted the Wilderness Act, it also established the Public Land Law Review Commission and directed it to undertake a comprehensive study and evaluation of the nation's laws affecting the public lands.[138] The Commission's report was completed six years later.[139] One of its major and most controversial recommendations was that Congress expressly authorize the Forest Service (and the Bureau of Land Management) to adopt a "dominant use" zoning system in which the "highest and best use of particular areas of land" would be recognized as "dominant over other authorized uses."[140] The Commission argued that in fact such a system of dominant use was already employed; by giving it express legislative sanction, the endless squabbles over the authority to prefer a particular use in a particular area might be eliminated. Although those concerned with the interests of wildlife might be apprehensive that various commercial uses of the public lands would, in most circumstances, be preferred to wildlife uses,[141] the Commission apparently arrived at its ultimate dominant use recommendation after first concluding that in some circumstances the conservation of wildlife should take precedence over all incompatible uses and that the protection of rare and endangered species should always take such precedence, absent "compelling circumstances."[142]

The Commission's dominant use recommendation was never enacted into law. Certain of its more specific recommendations pertaining to wildlife were, however. Among these was its recommendation that "[f]ormal statewide cooperative agreements should be used to coordinate public land fish and wildlife programs with the states."[143] The law embodying this recommendation, known as the Sikes Act Extension, was enacted in 1974.[144] It directs the Secretaries of Agriculture and the Interior,

---

[138] 43 U.S.C. §1392 (1976).

[139] Public Land Law Review Commission, One Third of the Nation's Land (Government Printing Office, 1970) (hereafter, PLLRC Report).

[140] *Id.* at 48–50.

[141] Although the Commission argued that a dominant use system was already in existence, cases like Kisner v. Butz, 350 F. Supp. 310 (N.D.W. Va. 1972), suggest that wildlife is seldom accorded a dominant status. In *Kisner,* plaintiffs challenged the construction of a 4.3 mile connecting link between two segments of a forest road in Monongahela National Forest. The only apparent adverse effect of the construction was to endanger one of the few remaining black bear breeding habitats in the state. The Forest Supervisor decided to go ahead with construction because "to decide the road construction question solely upon consideration of the black bear habitat would in effect create a dominant or exclusive management plan for the" area in question. 350 F. Supp. at 314.

[142] Hagenstein, One Third of the Nation's Land—Evolution of a Policy Recommendation, 12 Nat. Res. J. 56, 66 (1972).

[143] PLLRC Report at 159.

[144] 16 U.S.C. §§670g–670o (1976).

in consultation with the appropriate state fish and game agencies, to develop "comprehensive plan[s] for conservation and rehabilitation programs" to be implemented on public lands under their respective jurisdictions in each state.[145] In accordance with these comprehensive plans, the respective Secretaries are directed, in cooperation with the states, to "develop, maintain, and coordinate programs for the conservation and rehabilitation of wildlife, fish, and game."[146] Such programs must include "specific habitat improvement projects and related activities and adequate protection for species considered threatened or endangered."[147] Finally, the Act provides that the state fish and game agency may enter into "cooperative agreements" with the Secretaries in connection with the programs to be implemented in that state.[148]

The Sikes Act Extension has been described as "by far the broadest and most ambitious attempt to encourage wildlife habitat management on the public lands that has ever been conceived."[149] On the other hand, the Department of Agriculture characterized the legislation as "duplicative and totally unnecessary" because it simply restated authority already conferred by the Multiple Use Act.[150] The latter authority, however, is purely discretionary, whereas the Sikes Act authority is mandatory. Beyond that difference, however, it is unclear how much impact the Sikes Act Extension will have.

In the first place, although the Act requires the development of "comprehensive plans," it does not define them or otherwise prescribe their required contents in any detail. Nor does it require public participation in the development of plans. All that it seems to require is that the plans consist of "programs," which in turn must include habitat improvement projects and "adequate protection" for threatened and endangered species.[151] When cooperative agreements are entered into to implement those programs, the

---

[145]*Id.* §670h(a)(1). The Secretary of the Interior has a similar duty with respect to lands under the jurisdiction of the National Aeronautics and Space Administration and the Energy Research and Development Administration. Comprehensive plans with respect to those lands require the prior written approval of the respective agency heads. *Id.* §670h(a)(2).

[146]*Id.* §670g(a).

[147]*Id.*

[148]*Id.* §670h(c).

[149]Swanson, Wildlife Conservation on Public Lands, in Council on Environmental Quality, Wildlife and America (1978).

[150]S. Rep. No. 934, 93d Cong., 2d Sess., reprinted in 1974 U.S. Code Cong. & Ad. News. 5790, 5802.

[151]Compare the Public Land Law Review Commission's recommendation that rare and endangered species "be given a preference over other uses of public lands." PLLRC Report at 160.

agreements must contain certain other features, such as range rehabilitation, control of off-road vehicles, and other "necessary and appropriate" terms and conditions.[152] With or without a cooperative agreement, any state may agree with the Secretaries to require "public land area management stamps" of anyone hunting, trapping, or fishing on public lands subject to a Sikes Act Extension program.[153] Revenues from the sale of such stamps go to the states and must be used for carrying out programs under the act.[154]

Overshadowing the Sikes Act Extension's failure to be very specific about what it requires is the fact that it expressly states that it is not to "be construed as limiting the authority of the Secretary of the Interior or the Secretary of Agriculture... to manage the national forests or other public lands for wildlife and fish and other purposes in accordance with the Multiple Use–Sustained Yield Act of 1960 or other applicable authority."[155] Thus, while the Act may make more efficient the carrying out of such wildlife programs as are possible within the confines of multiple use management, it does nothing to change the virtually unlimited discretion that the land management agencies exercise in fulfilling their multiple use mandate.[156]

The first potentially significant legislative inroad into that discretion since the Wilderness Act is the National Forest Management Act of 1976.[157] Although, as has been chronicled here, criticism and dissatisfaction have accompanied the multiple use management concept since its inception, the impetus for the 1976 Act was a series of decisions[158] declaring clearcutting

---

[152]16 U.S.C. §670h(c)(3) (1976).

[153]*Id.* §670i.

[154]*Id.* §670i(b). Compare the PLLRC Report recommendation that a "land use fee...be charged for hunting and fishing on all public lands open for such purposes." PLLRC Report at 169. Under the Sikes Act Extension, land management area stamps cannot be required in any state in which all federal lands therein comprise 60 percent or more of the total area of such state (Alaska, Idaho, Nevada and Utah), though a substantially similar fee may be required. 16 U.S.C. §670l (1976).

[155]*Id.* §670h (c).

[156]Arguably, the formal planning requirements of the Sikes Act Extension may, through a process of bureaucratic osmosis, serve to enhance the status of wildlife in multiple use decision-making generally. *See* remarks of John E. Crawford, Chief, Division of Wildlife, Bureau of Land Management, before the Sixty-fifth Convention of the International Association of Game, Fish and Conservation Commissioners 108 (1975).

[157]Pub. L. No. 94–588, 90 Stat. 2949 (codified at 16 U.S.C. §§1601–1614 (1976 & Supp. V 1981).

[158]West Virginia Division of Izaak Walton League of America, Inc. v. Butz, 522 F.2d 945 (4th Cir. 1975), Zieske v. Butz, 406 F. Supp. 258 (D. Alas. 1975), and Texas

in national forests to violate the 1897 Organic Act's requirement that only such "dead, matured, or large growth" trees as were "marked and designated" could be cut.[159] In the process of amending these features of the Organic Act, Congress imposed a number of detailed standards governing future Forest Service management. Among these are a number of provisions with substantial potential importance for wildlife.

The most significant provisions of the 1976 Act are in the form of amendments to the Forest and Rangelands Renewable Resources Planning Act of 1974.[160] That earlier Act was designed to facilitate long range planning for the utilization of the renewable resources of the National Forest System by directing the Secretary of Agriculture to prepare and update quinquennially a Renewable Resources Program providing for the protection, management, and development of the System.[161] As a part of the Renewable Resources Program the Secretary was to develop "land and resource management plans for units of the National Forest System"[162] using "a systematic interdisciplinary approach to achieve integrated consideration of physical, biological, economic, and other sciences."[163]

Among the glaring inadequacies of the 1974 Act was its failure to specify how such individual land management plans were to be prepared and what they were to contain. The 1976 Act fills those gaps in copious detail. First, it directs the Secretary, within two years, to promulgate pursuant to informal rulemaking procedures of the Administrative Procedure Act, regulations describing the process of development and revision of land management plans.[164] To assist in the preparation of these regulations, the Secretary is required to appoint an advisory committee of non–Forest Service scientists "to assure that an effective interdisciplinary approach is proposed and adopted."[165]

As to the substance of the Secretary's regulations, the Act requires that they specify procedures that insure compliance with NEPA in the preparation of land management plans.[166] Further, the regulations must

---

Comm. on Natural Resources v. Butz, 433 F. Supp. 1235 (E.D. Tex. 1977), *rev'd sub nom.* Texas Comm. on Natural Resources v. Bergland, 573 F.2d 201 (5th Cir. 1978). Cir. 1978).

[159]16 U.S.C. §476 (1970) (repealed 1976).

[160]Pub. L. No. 93–378, 88 Stat. 476.

[161]16 U.S.C. §1602 (1976).

[162]*Id.* §1604(a).

[163]*Id.* §1604(b).

[164]*Id.* §1604(g). The regulations were promulgated at 47 Fed. Reg. 43026 (Sept. 30, 1982) and are to be codified at 36 C.F.R. part 219.

[165]16 U.S.C. §1604(h)(1) (1976).

[166]*Id.* §1604(g)(1).

specify "guidelines" that "provide for diversity of plant and animal communities based on the suitability and capability of the specific land area;"[167] which "insure consideration of the economic and environmental aspects of various systems of renewable resource management, including the related systems of silviculture and protection of forest resources, to provide for outdoor recreation (including wilderness), range, timber, watershed, wildlife and fish;"[168] and which "insure that timber will be harvested... only where... protection is provided for streams, streambanks, shorelines, lakes, wetlands, and other bodies of water from detrimental changes... where harvests are likely to seriously and adversely affect water conditions or fish habitat."[169] Finally, clearcutting or other even-aged management is to be permitted only if "the potential environmental, biological, esthetic, engineering, and economic impacts on each advertised sale area have been assessed"[170] and if "such cuts are carried out in a manner consistent with the protection of soil, watershed, fish, wildlife, recreation and esthetic resources."[171]

The regulations that the Secretary must promulgate are to form the basis for the development of land management plans applicable to individual units of the National Forest System. The Act states as a goal the incorporation of the standards and guidelines set forth in the regulations into all land management plans of the System by September 30, 1985.[172] As a part of that process of incorporation, the Secretary is directed to provide for public partipation through making plans available to the public, holding public meetings, or otherwise soliciting public comment.[173]

The new procedures required by the National Forest Management Act offer those interested in wildlife conservation important new opportunities. First, although the Act recites at numerous places that multiple use management is to remain the standard for management of the national forests, the detailed guidelines and standards that it sets forth may narrow substantially the nearly untrammeled discretion that has characterized multiple use management in the past. The new standards could furnish the basis for renewed efforts to subject forest management decisions to judicial scrutiny.

---

[167]*Id.* §1604(g)(3)(B). Texas Committee on Natural Resources v. Bergland, 573 F.2d 201, 210 (5th Cir. 1978), held that a Forest Service decision to allow clearcutting was not subject to judicial review while the required guidelines were being established.
[168]16 U.S.C. §1604(g)(3)(A) (1976).
[169]*Id.* §1604(g)(3)(E)(iii).
[170]*Id.* §1604(g)(3)(F)(ii).
[171]*Id.* §1604(g)(3)(F)(v).
[172]*Id.* §1604(c).
[173]*Id.* §1604(d).

The Act also substantially increases the opportunity for public participation in decision making. In the past, the lack of opportunity for public participation in Forest Service management decisions has been strongly criticized.[174] Now, by virtue of the Act, public participation is required at every significant stage of administrative action. The importance of this development for wildlife may be difficult to measure, but it will certainly be real, for it guarantees to the commercial and noncommercial users of the nation's forests equal access to the decision-making process.

Finally, the Act offers still other, more tangible, benefits to wildlife by amending the Knutson-Vandenburg Act[175] to provide that certain receipts from timber sales may be spent for, among other purposes, wildlife habitat management.[176] All of these changes, taken together, offer the promise of a new era in wildlife management in the nation's forests.

### The National Resource Lands

The National Resource Lands comprise those remaining areas of the public domain that have not been reserved or withdrawn for particular uses. Located almost exclusively in the far West and Alaska, these lands have, since 1946, been under the jurisdiction of the Interior's Bureau of Land Management (BLM).[177] The history of the management of the National Resource Lands is strikingly similar to that of the National Forest System. Originally managed under statutory authority that appeared to favor particular uses, actual management embraced the principles of multiple use. That administrative practice was latter confirmed legislatively by a law compelling multiple use management. Finally, as with the nation's forest resources, ever-increasing conflicts among competing users have led to recent enactment of major legislation to guide BLM discretion in the resolution of such conflicts.

This part of the chapter examines those aspects of the laws and regulations governing National Resource Land management that directly relate to wildlife. The more general analysis of "multiple use" as a legally enforceable standard will not be repeated, because the discussion of that issue in connection with the National Forest System is equally applicable here. In fact, there has been relatively little litigation in which the multiple

---

[174]See Note, Managing Federal Lands: Replacing the Multiple Use System, 82 Yale L.J. 787, 791–792 (1973).

[175]16 U.S.C. §576–576b (1976).

[176]Id. §576b.

[177]The Bureau of Land Management came into being in 1946 as a result of the consolidation of Interior's General Land Office and its Grazing Service according to section 403 of the Reorganization Act of 1945, Dec. 20, 1945, ch. 582, 59 Stat. 613.

use standard has been asserted to be a limitation on BLM management discretion; most such litigation has concerned the Forest Service.

Until 1934, there was no statutory mandate for the management of the unreserved and unappropriated public domain. In that year, the Taylor Grazing Act was passed.[178] Born of a concern for the deterioration of the range as a result of uncontrolled grazing and adverse weather, and for the imminent catastrophe facing the grazing industry as a result of the combined effects of that deterioration and the economic Depression, the Taylor Grazing Act was intended to bring about a more orderly use and regeneration of the range. It sought to accomplish this by authorizing the Secretary of the Interior to establish "grazing districts...from any part of the public domain...which in his opinion are chiefly valuable for grazing and raising forage crops."[179] In these grazing districts, the privilege of grazing livestock was to be regulated through a system of allocating grazing permits.

The Taylor Grazing Act was thus directed primarily at rescuing the Western grazing industry, just as the 1897 Organic Act was aimed principally at assuring future timber supplies. Both acts, however, had additional purposes as well. Recall that among the purposes specified in the 1897 Organic Act was the "protection" of the forests; the counterpart in the Taylor Act was the directive to the Secretary to "do any and all things necessary to...preserve the land and its resources from destruction or unnecessary injury."[180] Whereas the Organic Act made no express mention of wildlife, the Taylor Act apparently contemplated that wildlife was among the resources that the Secretary was directed to preserve, for it required him to cooperate with various parties "interested in the use of grazing districts," including "official State agencies engaged in conservation or propagation of wild life."[181]

Any doubt as to BLM's authority to manage lands under its jurisdiction for wildlife conservation purposes was laid to rest by the Classification and Multiple Use Act of 1964, which directed that all such lands be administered under principles of multiple use and sustained yield.[182] That Act enumerated the same basic purposes for management, including fish and wildlife, as had been enumerated in the Multiple Use–Sustained Yield Act four years earlier, but in addition it enumerated several other purposes, among them industrial development, mineral production, and occu-

---

[178] 43 U.S.C. §§315–315g, 315h–315m, 315n–315o, and 315p–315r (1976 & Supp. IV 1980).

[179] *Id.* §315.

[180] *Id.* §315a.

[181] *Id.* §315h.

[182] 43 U.S.C. §§1411–1418 (1976).

pancy.[183] Moreover, just as the 1960 Act had declared itself to be "not in derogation of" the 1897 Organic Act, so too the Classification and Multiple Use Act of 1964 declared itself to be "[c]onsistent with and supplemental to the Taylor Grazing Act."[184] Thus BLM's discretionary management authority was made at least as broad as, if not broader than, that of the Forest Service.[185]

In carrying out his authority the Secretary has promulgated regulations that require an "allocation of vegetation resources among livestock grazing, wild free-roaming horses and burros, wildlife, and other uses."[186] To what extent available forage will be allocated to wildlife is a question that BLM District Managers have traditionally had nearly unfettered discretion to answer. The advisory boards with which they were to consult on such questions, however, were, until 1975, composed of from five to twelve local stockmen and one wildlife representative, thus assuring a decidedly pro-grazing input from that source.[187]

Within the limits of what BLM will permit as the appropriate level of usage for wildlife on the National Resource Lands, the actual implementation of wildlife programs is carried out cooperatively by BLM and the individual states. This cooperative approach, which was in effect well before the Sikes Act Extension,[188] has traditionally allocated "species management" responsibilities to the states and "habitat management" responsibilities to BLM.[189] The Sikes Act Extension, principally directed at

---

[183]*Id.* §1411(a).

[184]*Id.*

[185]Technically, the authority conferred by the 1964 Act expired in 1970, six months after submission of the PLLRC Report. However, BLM has continued to manage lands under its jurisdiction according to multiple use principles. *See* Guilbert, *supra* note 108, at 594 n. 87.

[186]43 C.F.R. §4110.2-2 (1981).

[187]43 U.S.C. §315o-1 (1976). The Federal Advisory Committee Act, 5 U.S.C. App. I, §14(a)(1976), terminated all existing BLM advisory committees as of January 5, 1975. BLM has subsequently established a three-tiered system of advisory boards, the membership of which is to be "balanced in terms of the points of view represented and the functions to be performed." 40 Fed. Reg. 25452 (June 16, 1975).

The Federal Land Policy and Management Act of 1976, 43 U.S.C. §1753 (1976 & Supp. IV 1980), authorizes the reestablishment of "grazing advisory boards" for each BLM district office and National Forest headquarters office in the eleven Western states having jurisdiction over more than 500,000 acres of land used for commercial livestock grazing. Such boards are to be composed solely of licensees or permittees in the particular area.

[188]*See* 35 Fed. Reg. 14573 (Sept. 17, 1970).

[189]*See* remarks of Curt Berklund, Director, BLM, before the Sixty-fifth Convention of the International Association of Game, Fish and Conservation Commissioners 84 (1975).

habitat management, may assure the states a greater role in that aspect of wildlife management than they have previously enjoyed.[190]

As has already been discussed in connection with the National Forest System, the multiple use standard imposes few objective limits on management discretion. Such limits as have come about are legislative rather than judicial in origin. However, the most significant of these for the national forests, the Wilderness Act, did not initially apply to lands under the jurisdiction of BLM.[191] Thus BLM multiple use management has, until very recently, been virtually unfettered.

In recent years, the scope of BLM discretion under the Classification and Multiple Use Act of 1964 has been narrowed as a result of several federal statutes and a Presidential order. Probably the most significant of these is the National Environmental Policy Act of 1969.

In 1974, BLM prepared a draft programmatic impact statement under NEPA for its entire livestock grazing program.[192] This programmatic statement was intended to serve as the foundation for all subsequent actions implementing that program. The Natural Resources Defense Council, however, challenged the sufficiency of that statement as a basis for actual "on the ground" actions to be taken in each of BLM's 52 grazing districts. In *Natural Resources Defense Council, Inc. v. Morton* the District Court for the District of Columbia agreed and ordered BLM to prepare individual statements for each of its more than 200 planning units.[193] The preparation

---

[190]Prior to the Sikes Act Extension, BLM formalized its cooperative agreements with various states as "Memoranda of Understanding" that set forth in general terms the division of responsibilities between the states and BLM. The actual management programs were contained in individual Habitat Management Plans, or "HMPs," each applicable to a particular biological unit or ecotype. Memoranda of Understanding have been signed with each of the eleven Western states; over 150 HMPs have been developed for those same states. Compliance with the Sikes Act Extension is effected by means of supplemental agreements to the existing Memoranda and HMPs.

[191]The Federal Land Policy and Management Act of 1976, 43 U.S.C. §1782 (1976), directs a study of certain BLM lands to determine their suitability for inclusion in the National Wilderness Preservation System. Even prior to that Act, BLM had authority to designate areas under its jurisdiction as "primitive areas" or "natural areas," in which only activities not interfering with the character of such areas were permitted. 43 C.F.R. §§2070 (1981). For a discussion of these areas, see Note, Bureau of Land Management Primitive Areas—Are They Counterfeit Wilderness?, 16 Nat. Res. J. 621 (1976).

[192]Department of the Interior, Bureau of Land Management, Draft Environmental Impact Statement, Livestock Grazing Management on National Resources Land (March, 1974).

[193]388 F. Supp. 829 (D.D.C. 1974), *aff'd without opinion*, 527 F.2d 1386 (D.C. Cir.), *cert. denied*, 427 U.S. 913 (1976).

of those statements will take place through 1988 and will subject BLM planning to closer scrutiny than ever before.[194]

Rivaling NEPA in its implications for BLM management of the National Resource Lands is the Wild Free-Roaming Horses and Burros Act.[195] That Act requires that BLM (and the Forest Service) treat wild horses and burros as "an integral part of the natural system of the public lands."[196] The precise nature of this directive and its implementation by BLM are discussed in detail later in this chapter.

A further source of limitation on BLM land management discretion stems from an Executive Order in 1972 regulating the use of an increasingly popular type of recreational equipment, the "off-road vehicle," on public lands. That order directed various agency heads, including the Secretary of the Interior, to establish procedures for the designation of particular areas of lands under their respective jurisdictions where such vehicles would either be permitted or prohibited.[197] Although the order applied generally to a number of federal agencies, it is worthy of discussion here because of a successful challenge to the implementing regulations promulgated by BLM in *National Wildlife Federation v. Morton*.[198]

In that action, the plaintiff persuaded the court that BLM's implementing regulations failed to comply with the terms of the Order in a number of ways, among them by providing for blanket designations rather than specific site designations and by failing to provide for adequate public participation. Of most interest for wildlife purposes, however, was the court's conclusion that the BLM regulations "significantly diluted the standards" of the Order.[199] In particular, the court pointed to the Order's requirement that "[a]reas and trails shall be located to minimize harassment of wildlife or significant disruption of wildlife habitat," whereas the regulations only provided for "[c]onsideration of the need to minimize harassment of wildlife or significant disruption of wildlife habitat."[200]

---

[194]For subsequent related litigation, see Natural Resources Defense Council v. Andrus, 11 Env't Rep. Cas. 1523 (D.D.C. April 14, 1978).

[195]16 U.S.C. §§1331–1340 (1976 & Supp. V 1981).

[196]*Id.* §1331 (1976). The Act applies both to BLM lands and lands under the jurisdiction of the Forest Service. Its significance, however, is much greater for BLM because more than 95 percent of all protected horses and burros are on its lands. See Department of the Interior, Bureau of Land Management, Second Report to Congress: Administration of the Wild Free-Roaming Horses and Burros Act 1 (1976).

[197]Exec. Order No. 11644, 3 C.F.R. 332 (1974).

[198]393 F. Supp. 1286 (D.D.C. 1975).

[199]*Id.* at 1295.

[200]39 Fed. Reg. 13612 (April 15, 1974).

While the language of the regulations might appear to be but an innocent attempt to paraphrase the Order, the court felt that it reflected a subtle change of emphasis contrary to the strict mandate of the Order. Whether subsequently promulgated regulations issued in response to the suit, which repeat verbatim the standards of the Order, will result in substantive difference is impossible to gauge.[201]

Closer public scrutiny of BLM management decisions is certain to come about as a result of the Federal Land Policy and Management Act of 1976 (hereinafter FLPMA).[202] Culminating years of efforts to give BLM an "organic act" comprehensively defining its responsibilities and authorities, FLPMA has many similarities to the National Forest Management Act of 1976, which was passed contemporaneously.

As its most basic mandate, FLPMA directs the Secretary of the Interior to develop and maintain "land use plans which provide by tracts or areas for the use of the public lands."[203] Such plans are to be based on an inventory of all public lands and their resources that the Secretary is required to prepare and maintain on a continuing basis[204] and are to be coordinated with land use plans for the National Forests.[205] Finally, the Secretary is directed, in the development of land use plans, to "use a systematic interdisciplinary approach to achieve integrated consideration of physical, biological, economic, and other sciences."[206]

While FLPMA sets no definite timetable for the development of land management plans, it does require that "regulations and plans for the protection of public land areas of critical environmental concern be promptly developed."[207] Such areas include those where "special management attention is required...to protect and prevent irreparable damage to...fish and wildlife resources or other natural systems or processes."[208] The concept of "areas of critical environmental concern" was an innovative idea offering the opportunity for environmentally sensitive land management without the severe strictures of wilderness areas. Unfortunately, however, the concept has been little used thus far.

---

[201] The regulations, appearing at 43 C.F.R. §§8340 *et seq.*, add the requirement that "[s]pecial attention...be given to protect endangered species and their habitats." For a more extended discussion of this controversy, see Rosenberg, Regulation of Off-Road Vehicles, 5 Envtl. Aff. 175 (1976).

[202] 43 U.S.C. §§1701–1784 (1976 & Supp. IV 1980).

[203] *Id.* §1712(a).

[204] *Id.* §1711(a).

[205] *Id.* §1712(b).

[206] *Id.* §1712(c)(2).

[207] *Id.* §1701(a)(11).

[208] *Id.* §1702(a).

At all stages of planning and implementation, the Act requires active public participation. Thus it declares as a statement of policy that in exercising his discretionary authority, the Secretary shall "be required to establish comprehensive rules and regulations after considering the views of the general public; and to structure adjudication procedures to assure adequate third party participation, objective administrative review of initial decisions, and expeditious decision-making."[209] More specifically, FLPMA requires "public involvement"[210] in the formulation of plans and programs relating to management of the public lands,[211] opportunity for a public hearing in connection with all land withdrawals other than emergency withdrawals,[212] and the promulgation of rules and regulations, in accordance with the Administrative Procedure Act, "to carry out the purposes of this Act and of other laws applicable to public lands."[213]

Whereas the National Forest Management Act of 1976 contains copious details limiting the scope of Forest Service management discretion, thus potentially providing a number of judicially enforceable standards, FLPMA has fewer precise standards. Instead, it substitutes Congress itself as the overseer of certain major management decisions by BLM. Thus, by concurrent resolution of the House and Senate, the Congress can veto proposed sales of tracts of the public lands exceeding 2,500 acres,[214] withdrawals of more than 5,000 acres,[215] the termination of certain preexisting withdrawals,[216] or management decisions that totally eliminate one or more of the "principal or major uses"[217] for two or more years with respect to any tract of land of 100,000 acres or more.[218]

FLPMA also contains a number of measures specifically geared to wildlife. First, it directs that half the monies received by the United States as

---

[209]*Id.* §1701(a)(5).

[210]"Public involvement" is defined as "the opportunity for participation by affected citizens in rulemaking, decisionmaking, and planning with respect to the public lands, including public meetings or hearings held at locations near the affected lands, or advisory mechanisms, or such other procedures as may be necessary to provide public comment in a particular instance." *Id.* §1702(d).

[211]*Id.* §1712(a), (f).

[212]*Id.* §1714(h).

[213]*Id.* §1740. This provision, as well as those cited in the immediately preceding two notes, may furnish the basis for opening up the process of developing "comprehensive plans" under the Sikes Act Extension.

[214]*Id.* §1713(c).

[215]*Id.* §1714(c)(1).

[216]*Id.* §1714(l).

[217]One of the six "principal or major uses" specified in the Act is "fish and wildlife development and utilization." *Id.* §1702(l).

[218]*Id.* §1712(e)(2).

fees for grazing domestic livestock be put in a special fund to be spent solely for "range betterment," including "fish and wildlife habitat enhancement."[219] Second, it permits the exchange of public lands for private lands where the Secretary determines that the public interest will be served thereby and requires him, in making such determination, to consider the fish and wildlife aspects of the proposed exchange.[220] Finally, although FLPMA declares a general policy that the United States should "receive fair market value of the use of the public lands and their resources,"[221] it specifically does not authorize requiring "[f]ederal permits to hunt and fish on public lands or on lands in the National Forest System and adjacent waters."[222] It does, however, in section 302(b) authorize the Secretaries of the Interior and Agriculture to designate areas under their jurisdiction "where, and establish periods when, no hunting or fishing will be permitted for reasons of public safety, administration, or compliance with provisions of applicable law."[223]

---

[219]*Id.* §1751(b)(1).

[220]*Id.* §1716(a).

[221]*Id.* §1701(a)(9).

[222]*Id.* §1732(b).

[223]*Id.* According to the Conference Report, "[t]he word 'administration' authorizes exclusion of hunting and fishing from an area in order to maintain supervision. It does not authorize exclusions simply because hunting and fishing would interfere with resource-management goals." H.R. Rep. No. 1724, 94th Cong., 2d Sess. 60 (1976). However, in introducing the conferee's bill to the Senate, Senator Metcalf disputed the above language of the Conference Report and offered the following explanation:

> Unfortunately, in attempting to define the term "administration," the statement of managers confuses the issue and could be wrongly interpreted to prevent the Secretary from protecting the public lands.
>
> Traditionally, the States have regulated fishing and hunting of resident species of wildlife. The BLM and the Forest Service have not attempted to manage resident species of wildlife, but have focused on management of their habitat. This bill does nothing to change that. However, as a property owner the Federal Government has certain rights, and those rights have been upheld by the Supreme Court, most recently in Kleppe against New Mexico....
>
> The conference report does not in any way surrender Congress power.
>
> The language of the statement of the managers could be interpreted as so narrowing the definition of "administration" that the agency would be unable to close an area to hunting even where the number of a species is drastically reduced. Carried further this language could be interpreted to mean that an area which was used for habitat research could not be closed to hunting and fishing "simply because hunting and fishing would interfere with resource management goals."
>
> In this legislation for the first time we are giving BLM basic statutory authority to manage the public lands on a multiple-use basis. Two of

Congressional intent with respect to the last-quoted provision of FLPMA figured prominently in a complex series of cases involving a state program of wolf reduction on federal lands in Alaska. In *Defenders of Wildlife v. Andrus*, the plaintiffs alleged that under section 302(b) of FLPMA the Secretary of the Interior had the authority to halt the state program and, having that authority, the duty under the National Environmental Policy Act to prepare an environmental impact statement before permitting it through acquiescence.[224] The district court, in ruling on plaintiffs' motion for preliminary injunction, agreed with both contentions.[225]

Subsequently, the state of Alaska, which had elected not to join the earlier litigation, instituted its own action in Alaska against the Secretary of the Interior, challenging the lawfulness of actions taken by the Secretary to carry out the former court's order.[226] The Alaska court, though it initially concluded on the basis of legislative history that the Secretary lacked authority to halt the wolf kill, ultimately decided that the statute was clear on its face that such authority existed.[227] On the question of NEPA's applicability, however, the Alaska court disagreed with the former court, reasoning that more than mere federal acquiescence in the state program was necessary to trigger NEPA's requirements.

Ultimately, these issues were presented to the Courts of Appeals for both the Ninth and the District of Columbia Circuits. Although the United States had by then reversed its position and concluded that it did, indeed, have authority to halt the wolf kill, neither court ruled on that issue. Instead, both courts agreed that whether the authority existed or not, the Secretary had no duty under NEPA to prepare an environmental impact statement in the absence of an affirmative federal action authorizing the wolf kill.[228] The Ninth Circuit based its conclusion on an analysis of NEPA

---

those uses are hunting and fishing, but they should not take precedence over all other uses. Further, it makes no sense to give an agency authority and then to tie its hands.

When this matter was discussed by the conferees, the right—indeed the responsibility—of BLM and the Forest Service to manage wildlife habitat was agreed to by all. I believe the language in the statement of managers could be interpreted differently and thus does not accurately reflect the conferees' agreement on this issue.

122 Cong. Reg. 34511 (1976).

[224]7 Envtl. L. Rep. (Envtl. L. Inst.) 20225 (D.D.C. Feb. 14, 1977).

[225]*Id.* at 20228–20229. The court relied heavily on the legislative history quoted in note 223 *supra.*

[226]Alaska v. Andrus, 429 F. Supp. 958 (D. Alas. 1977).

[227]*Id.* at 962.

[228]Alaska v. Andrus, 591 F.2d 537 (9th Cir. 1979); Defenders of Wildlife v. Andrus,

alone. The District of Columbia Circuit reasoned more broadly from the relationship of NEPA and FLPMA that the "cautious and limited permission to intervene in an area of state responsibility and authority" provided by section 302(b) of FLPMA did not impose "such supervisory duties on the Secretary that each state action he fails to prevent becomes a 'Federal action.'"[229]

In the final footnote to its opinion, the District of Columbia Circuit suggested the possibility of a violation of FLPMA independent of its relationship with NEPA.[230] Though the footnote did not elaborate upon the matter, the court appeared to refer to the wolf kill as a possible violation of FLPMA's substantive duty to "manage the public lands under principles of multiple use and sustained yield."[231] The court declined to express any view on that but clearly raised the possibility of substantive review of federal land management actions under FLPMA.

A final provision of FLPMA of substantial indirect significance for wildlife is its directive that the Secretary review all roadless areas of 5,000 acres or more for possible inclusion in the National Wilderness Preservation System. That review and the litigation it has spawned are considered in detail later in this chapter.

The effects of FLPMA on BLM land management are similar to those of the National Forest Management Act of 1976 on the Forest Service, previously described. Although both acts reaffirm the management principle of "multiple use" they circumscribe the unfettered discretion that BLM and the Forest Service had previously enjoyed under that standard.[232] Unlike the National Forest Management Act, however, that circumscription for BLM takes the form of more stringent congressional oversight rather than enumeration of detailed standards and guidelines. Beyond that,

---

627 F.2d 1238 (D.C. Cir. 1980). The latter case was the appeal from an action filed subsequent to dismissal of the earlier case by the same name cited in note 224, *supra.*

[229]627 F.2d at 1250.

[230]*Id.* at 1250 n. 10.

[231]43 U.S.C. §1732(a)(1976). *But see* note 232 *infra.*

[232]*See, e.g.,* 43 U.S.C. §§1701(a)(7), 1702(b), 1703(c) and 1732(a). However, in Utah v. Andrus, 486 F. Supp. 995, 1003 (D. Utah 1979), the court strongly implied that FLPMA provides no standards against which the validity of individual management decisions can be gauged:

> If all the competing demands reflected in FLPMA were focused on one particular piece of public land, in many instances only one set of demands could be satisfied. A parcel of land cannot both be preserved in its natural character and mined. Thus, it would be impossible for BLM to carry out the purposes of the Act if each particular management decision were evaluated separately. It is only by looking at the overall use of the public lands that one can accurately assess whether or not BLM is carrying out the broad purposes of the statute.

the two acts are similar in vastly expanding the opportunity for citizen participation in future management decisions. For wildlife interests, that may be the most important part of the Federal Land Policy and Management Act.

## The Wild Free-Roaming Horses and Burros Act and Federal Multiple Use Lands

Several important federal statutes superimpose additional duties on federal land managers responsible for the management of multiple use lands. The Wild Free-Roaming Horses and Burros Act is one.[233] The duties it imposes apply to all lands under the jurisdiction of the Forest Service and the BLM. The Supreme Court's resolution of the challenge to the constitutionality of this statute was previously considered in Chapter 2. Other aspects of the statute have been considered in Chapter 4. This chapter explores the particular aspects of the Wild Free-Roaming Horses and Burros Act as they pertain to the land management responsibilities of the federal multiple use land managers.

Prior to its enactment in 1971, the only protection that wild horses and burros received from federal land managers was the limited protection afforded by BLM's "wild horse policy" initiated in 1967.[234] Though the substantive provisions of that policy were rather meager, at least one case, *Humane Society of the United States v. Udall,* sought to utilize it as a vehicle for challenging a proposed BLM roundup of wild horses in the Pryor Mountains.[235] That action was ultimately dismissed when the BLM represented that it had no plans to undertake the proposed roundup. Prior to dismissal, however, there was an interesting exchange at oral argument between Judge Hart, who professed to know nothing about Western land law, and the plaintiff's attorney, who endeavored to persuade him that the case did not involve esoteric questions of Western land law, but familiar ones of administrative law and constitutional due process. Judge Hart was not inclined to hear such arguments, however, and dismissed them in the following fashion:

> Well, Bless me if I can define Constitutional due process for a herd of mustangs. It is a little difficult for me, but maybe eventually.[236]

---

[233] 16 U.S.C. §§1331–1340 (1976 & Supp. V 1981).

[234] BLM's "wild horse policy" was set forth in Instruction Memo 67–361 (Sept. 5, 1967). Among other things, it required that consideration "be given to reservation of forage for wild horses or burros where it is needed and is definitely in the public interest."

[235] Civil No. 2158–68 (D.D.C. 1968).

[236] Transcript of hearing on plaintiff's request for a temporary restraining order, at 16.

The initial litigation under the Act concerned its obscure and arguably conflicting management standards. To some extent, those standards have been clarified as a result of amendments in 1978.[237] On the one hand, the Act's directive that protected horses and burros "be considered...an integral part of the natural system of the public lands" suggested simply that they were to be given the same "due consideration" as other types of resources under traditional multiple use management. This interpretation was consistent with at least one reading of the Act's legislative history, which is that it was intended to give a previously lacking "status" to horses and burros.[238] On the other hand, the only time the original Act specifically referred to multiple use management was in connection with those ranges that the Secretary was authorized to designate as sanctuaries for wild horses and burros and which were to be "devoted principally but not exclusively to their welfare in keeping with the multiple-use management concept for the public lands."[239]

The suggestion that protected horses and burros were to have a "first among equals" status was at least implied in other parts of the Act as originally enacted. For example, the Act directs that "[a]ll management activities shall be at the minimal feasible level."[240] Moreover, in a provision since substantially amended, the Act authorized the destruction of protected horses and burros only when, in the Secretary's judgment, "such action is necessary to preserve and maintain the habitat in a suitable condition for continued use," or, when an area is found to be overpopulated, destruction for the latter reason may not be done unless it is "the only practical way to remove excess animals from the area."[241]

If Congress intended to afford wild horses and burros a first among equals status, it is clear that it did not contemplate that the protected animals would displace all other types of range users over a continually expanding area. The Act's directive that they be considered an integral part of the natural system of the public lands applies only "in the area where presently found." Moreover, the Act carefully prescribes that designated ranges include "the amount of land necessary to sustain an *existing herd* or herds of wild free-roaming horses and burros, *which does not exceed their*

---

[237]Pub. L. No. 95–514, §14, 92 Stat. 1810, amending 16 U.S.C. §§1332(f), 1333(b) (1976).

[238]*See* H.R. Rep. No. 480, 92d Cong., 1st Sess. at 4 (1971). The Senate report suggests, however, that the purpose of the Act, in part, was to codify the preexisting practice of considering the interests of wild horses and burros in making multiple use decisions. *See* S. Rep. No. 242, 92d Cong., 1st Sess. at 3 (1971), and note 234 *supra*.

[239]16 U.S.C. §1332(c)(1976). The authority to designate wild horse ranges has been little utilized. Only three have been designated thus far.

[240]16 U.S.C. §1333(a)(1976).

[241]*Id.* §1333(c)(1976) (current version at 16 U.S.C. §1332(b)(Supp. V 1981)).

*known territorial limits.*"[242] Finally, the Act contains an express denial of any authority "to relocate wild free-roaming horses or burros to areas of public lands where they do not presently exist."[243]

This fundamentally dichotomous nature of the original Act was reflected in the first decisions under it. In *American Horse Protection Association, Inc. v. Frizzell,* the plaintiff challenged the proposed roundup of some 400 wild horses alleged to be in excess of the grazing capacity of Stone Cabin Valley, Nevada.[244] Licensed livestock in the Valley accounted for more than 75 percent of its estimated grazing capacity. Of the remainder, nearly half had been reserved by the Bureau of Land Management for wildlife. The other half was deemed insufficient to support the 900 to 1200 wild horses living in the Valley. The plaintiff contended that the proposed roundup violated both the Horses and Burros Act and the National Environmental Policy Act. The NEPA claim was confused somewhat by the fact that as a result of the *Natural Resources Defense Council* case previously discussed, BLM was in the process of preparing an environmental impact statement with regard to the overall management of an area that encompassed Stone Cabin Valley.[245] The court assumed that when that impact statement was prepared it would contain a long term solution to the overgrazing problem, and thus it was willing to view the proposed roundup "as an interim measure to preserve the range" pending completion of the ordered impact statement.[246] Focusing narrowly on the roundup alone, the court concluded that NEPA was not applicable because it would not have a significant impact on the Stone Cabin Valley environment and suggested that it would rule otherwise only if it were satisfied that "the proposed roundup would extinguish the wild horse population" there.[247]

As to the claimed violation of the Wild Horses and Burros Act, the court emphasized the broad discretion which the Act vests in the Secretary and rejected plaintiff's assertion that under the Act "wild horses were given a higher priority on the public lands than other grazers."[248] The court, by stating that the only statutory or regulatory support for plaintiff's assertion was an administrative regulation authorizing the closure of certain areas to livestock grazing when it was necessary to allocate all available forage to horses and burros, refused to read into the Act's many special management

---

[242]*Id.* §1332(c)(1976) (emphasis added).

[243]*Id.* §1339.

[244]403 F. Supp. 1206 (D. Nev. 1975).

[245]*See* text accompanying notes 192–194 *supra.*

[246]403 F. Supp. at 1219 n. 10.

[247]*Id.* at 1219.

[248]*Id.* at 1220.

provisions for horses and burros the directive that they be given special status generally.[249] Moreover, the court was of the view that the regulation to which it referred applied only "to a situation where wild horses and burros were in danger of extinction."[250]

In short, the court held that under the principle of multiple use, "neither wild horses nor cattle possess any higher status than the other on the public lands."[251] Underscoring how little room for judicial supervision exists under that standard, the court stated that it would probably not have overturned the Secretary's decision if that decision had been to remove only cattle and no horses.[252]

The second case under the Act reached a strikingly different result. That action, *American Horse Protection Association, Inc. v. Kleppe*, involved essentially similar facts.[253] A roundup of wild horses near Challis, Idaho, was proposed because of the alleged overutilization of the range by cattle, sheep, wild horses, and other wildlife. This time, however, District Court Judge Richey was unwilling to rest his decision on broad generalizations about the extent of the discretion retained by BLM under the Act. Instead, he found that BLM's estimates of horse populations in the affected area were "unreliable" and "meaningless" and that the proposed roundup was for that reason alone arbitrary and capricious.[254] In addition, however, he found that the Act's requirement that "[a]ll management activities shall be at the minimal feasible level" meant that "careful and detailed consideration must be given to *all* alternative courses of action that would have a less severe impact on the wild horse population."[255] The only alternative involving the reduction of livestock grazing that had been considered by BLM was the elimination of all grazing in the region. Judge Richey insisted that there were other, less drastic, alternatives that required consideration, including the elimination of livestock grazing in the critical winter range of the horses.[256]

Judge Richey pointed to still other grounds on which to void the proposed roundup. One was that the failure to have "professional

---

[249]*Id.* The current version of the regulation cited by the court appears at 43 C.F.R. §4730.4 (1981).

[250]403. F. Supp. at 1220.

[251]*Id.* at 1221.

[252]*Id.* The court noted that in fact both cattle and horses were to be removed from the Valley as a result of the "voluntary" decision of the cattle ranchers using the area. *Id.* n. 12. It is impossible to tell to what extent, if at all, this factor influenced the court's decision.

[253]6 Envtl. L. Rep. (Envtl. L. Inst.) 20802 (D.D.C. Sept. 9, 1976).

[254]*Id.* at 20804.

[255]*Id.* (emphasis in original).

[256]*Id.*

veterinary assistance on-site at all times during the roundup" or "to develop contingency plans for veterinary assistance in case of unforeseen circumstances during the roundup" violated the Act's requirement that horse removals be conducted under "humane conditions and care."[257] Finally, as in the Nevada case the year before, a comprehensive environmental impact statement concerning the entire domestic livestock grazing program in the Challis areas was in preparation. Rather than permit the roundup to proceed as an "interim measure" pending completion of that statement, however, Judge Richey insisted that to do so "would eliminate one major alternative to the grazing allotments plan proposed" in the Bureau of Land Management's draft impact statement, thus violating NEPA.[258]

As a result of amendments in 1978, the Secretaries of the Interior and Agriculture now enjoy arguably clearer authority to remove and destroy excess animals. Amended section 3(b)(2) of the Act directs that the Secretary "immediately remove excess animals" whenever he makes two determinations: (1) that an overpopulation exists on a given area and (2) that action is necessary to remove excess animals.[259] Literally, this provision imposes two separate duties on the Secretary and admits of at least the possibility that he may find an overpopulation to exist, yet find that action is not necessary to remove excess animals. On the other hand, the Act now defines "excess animals" to mean those that "must be removed... in order to preserve and maintain a thriving natural ecological balance and multiple-use relationship" in a particular area.[260] Thus, if animals meet this definition, then the Secretary would seem obliged always to order their removal, notwithstanding the wording of section 3(b)(2). The definition of "excess animals" has further internal ambiguities of its own. Since wild horses and burros are nonnative, feral animals, it is unclear how a "natural" ecological balance is to be preserved and maintained; it is similarly interesting to contemplate the potential hurdles that confront any effort to maintain both a "thriving natural ecological balance" and "multiple-use relationship."[261]

Following enactment of the 1978 amendments, BLM endeavored to persuade Judge Richey to lift his injunction entered two years earlier. In an

---

[257]*Id.*

[258]*Id.*

[259]16 U.S.C. §1333(b)(2)(Supp. V 1981).

[260]*Id.* §1332(f).

[261]The Secretaries are to receive independent advice on how to determine when excess animals exist from a special report required by amended section 4(b)(3), 16 U.S.C. 1333(b)(3) (Supp. V 1981). In the meantime, the Act directs the Secretary to act "on the basis of all information currently available to him." *Id.* §1333(b)(2).

unreported opinion, he refused because BLM had failed to comply with his order to give serious consideration to protecting the horses' winter ranges by restricting cattle grazing. The court of appeals agreed that BLM's efforts to fulfill the requirements of the injunction had been "at best, half-hearted" and inadequate.[262] However, the appellate court concluded that Judge Richey had not properly interpreted the 1978 amendments, which, in the appellate court's view, reflected a congressional purpose to "cut back on the protection the Act affords wild horses"[263] by giving the Secretary broad discretion to determine when a wild horse overpopulation exists and directing him to remove excess animals promptly. Rather than lift the district court's injunction, however, the court of appeals remanded for a decision based on the following holding:

> Today we hold only that further consideration of the "winter range" alternative, on which the district court conditioned removal of horses in its 1976 injunction, is, in light of the 1978 legislation, not required. It remains open to the district court to determine on remand whether, in light of the goals of the Act as it now stands, and on the basis of the information the Secretary now has, the Agency's current plan to reduce the size of the wild horse herd well below the 340 animals the winter range can support is rationally grounded.[264]

Thus, though circumscribed, the district court was left with limited authority to continue the injunction.

None of these potential ambiguities stemming from the 1978 amendments was addressed in the only other subsequent case involving a challenge to an excess animal removal program. Instead, in *American Horse Protection Association v. Andrus,* the only question was whether the National Environmental Policy Act required that an environmental impact statement (EIS) be prepared for the challenged program.[265] The trial court held that it did not, apparently because of its view that the grazing allotment EISs being prepared pursuant to the *Natural Resources Defense Council* case totally satisfied the agency's obligation under

---

[262]American Horse Protection Ass'n, Inc. v. Watt, 694 F.2d 1310 (D.C. Cir. 1982).

[263]*Id.* at 1319.

[264]*Id.* at 1319 (footnote omitted). In a well-reasoned dissenting opinion, Judge Robinson attacked the majority's holding as creating a meaningless semantic distinction. He argued that the district court "could easily have found that the Bureau's intended course of action was not 'rationally grounded' upon the data it had because its deficient consideration of the winter range alternative represented an 'irrational' evaluation of that data," and thus have satisfied the standard articulated by the majority. *Id.* at 1322.

[265]608 F.2d 811 (9th Cir. 1979).

NEPA.[266] In reversing, the court of appeals made no determination whether an EIS was in fact required, but, implicitly at least, held that the duty to remove excess animals imposed by the 1978 amendments did not function as an exemption from NEPA.[267]

### The National Wilderness Preservation System

The Wilderness Act of 1964 scarcely mentions the word "wildlife," yet its importance for long term preservation of wildlife habitat is great. Indeed, it has been said of wilderness that "without wildlife [it] is mere scenery."[268] By singling out those remaining areas of federal land "where the earth and its community of life are untrammeled by man, where man himself is a visitor who does not remain," and by directing that they be managed for "the preservation of their wilderness character,"[269] the Act assures that substantial areas of public lands will be spared for all time from the most damaging forms of use and development.

Unlike the other federal land systems discussed in this chapter, there is no single federal agency responsible for the administration of the Wilderness Preservation System. Rather, the Forest Service, the National Park Service and the Fish and Wildlife Service retain jurisdiction over those areas of land that were under their jurisdiction at the time of passage of the Act and that were found suitable for wilderness classification and formally added to the System by Congress.[270] By virtue of the Federal Land Management and Policy Act of 1976, BLM lands will also become eligible for inclusion in the System.[271] Although the Wilderness Act is careful to state that its purposes are merely "supplemental" to the purposes for which

---

[266]460 F. Supp. 880 (D. Nev. 1978).

[267]The Court refused to address the claims of appellants that, even if no EIS were required, the challenged action would represent an abuse of the Secretary's discretion under the Wild Free-Roaming Horses and Burros Act, or of appellees that the Secretary's discretion was absolute. See 608 F.2d at 815 n. 2. In light of this refusal, little significance should be given the conclusion of the trial court that in an area that constituted a "checkerboard" of unfenced private and public lands and in which most of the private landowners had requested removal of wild horses, removal of all wild horses in the area was the only practical way in which compliance with section 4 of the Act could be achieved. But see Mountain States Legal Foundation v. Andrus, 16 Env't Rep. Cas. (BNA) 1351 (D. Wyo. April 21, 1981).

[268]C. Schoenfeld & J. Hendee, Wildlife Management in Wilderness 23 (1978) (quoting L. Crisler, Arctic Wild (1958)).

[269]16 U.S.C. §1131(a), (c)(1976).

[270]Id. §1131(b).

[271]See text accompanying notes 231–232 supra.

the forests, parks, and refuges were originally established,[272] it clearly imposes restrictions not applicable elsewhere. For example, it altogether prohibits commercial enterprises and permanent roads within wilderness areas and sharply restricts temporary roads, mechanical transport, and the construction of installations in those areas.[273] Not all economic uses of wilderness areas are prohibited, however.[274] Most significantly, the Wilderness Act authorizes the continued application of mining and mineral-leasing laws to wilderness areas for twenty years, until the end of 1983.[275]

Virtually the only thing that the Wilderness Act says expressly about wildlife is that the "jurisdiction or responsibilities of the several States with respect to wildlife and fish in the national forests" is not affected thereby.[276] There has, however, been some sentiment among state fish and game agencies that the restrictions otherwise imposed by the Wilderness Act unduly restrict their flexibility in practicing wildlife management in wilderness areas.[277] Thus far, however, no wildlife issue has yet figured directly in any reported litigation under the Wilderness Act.

Before turning to a discussion of some of the more important wilderness litigation to date, it is important first to describe the process by which wilderness areas are designated. Only Congress can designate a wilderness area. The role of the federal land–managing agencies in the designation of wilderness areas is simply that of inventorying, evaluating, and ultimately recommending to the President that particular areas be either so designated or not designated. The President, in turn, makes his own recommendation to Congress, which is free to accept or reject the President's recommendation as it pleases.

Virtually all of the Wilderness Act litigation to date has concerned either the procedures by which areas are considered and designated as

---

[272]16 U.S.C. §1133(a)(1976).

[273]*Id.* §1133(c).

[274]Grazing is permitted to continue in those wilderness areas of the national forests where it was established prior to passage of the Act. *Id.* §1133(d)(4).

[275]*Id.* §1133(d)(3). This exemption has been attacked as fundamentally inconsistent with the paramount wilderness values that the Act is intended to serve. *See* Izaak Walton League of America v. St. Clair, 353 F. Supp. 698 (D. Minn. 1973), *rev'd on other grounds*, 497 F.2d 849 (8th Cir. 1974). *See also* Comment, Closing the Mining Loophole in the 1964 Wilderness Act, 6 Envtl. L. 469 (1976); Comment, Geothermal Leasing in Wilderness Areas, 6 Envtl. L. 489 (1976); and Comment, Geothermal Energy Exploitation in Wilderness Areas: The Courts Face a Hot Issue, 4 Envtl. L. Rep. (Envtl. L. Inst.) 10119 (1974).

[276]16 U.S.C. §1133(d)(7)(Supp. V 1981).

[277]*See* Report of the Land Resources Committee of the Sixty Fifth Convention of the International Association of Game Fish and Conservation Commissioners 241–246 (1975).

wilderness or the question of what restrictions apply to potentially eligible areas prior to final decision on their inclusion in the system. The latter question stems in large part from the early decision of *Parker v. United States,* that in order to provide the President and Congress a meaningful opportunity to consider the addition of an area having wilderness value to the System, the Forest Service must refrain from authorizing activities that destroy that value prior to such final decision.[278] The *Parker* result has effectively been codified for BLM lands by section 603(c) of FLPMA.[279]

To speed the consideration of potentially eligible areas and thus to remove use restrictions on areas found ineligible, the Forest Service in 1977 initiated a comprehensive second "Roadless Area Review and Evaluation," commonly known by its acronym RARE II. The result of RARE II was to assign all remaining roadless areas in the National Forest System to one of three categories: (1) those appropriate to be recommended for wilderness designation, (2) those inappropriate for such recommendation, and (3) those requiring further study. In *California v. Bergland,* the state of California challenged successfully the adequacy of a programmatic environmental impact statement prepared for the RARE II study insofar as the statement examined the impact upon the wilderness quality of some 47 California roadless areas not recommended for wilderness designation.[280] As a result, the Forest Service was required to prepare site specific environmental impact statements for the individual California areas. The congressional response when considering the RARE II recommendations relating to other states has typically been to declare legislatively the sufficiency of the programmatic statement as applied to that state and to "release" for full multiple use the areas found inappropriate for wilderness designation.

The relationship between RARE II, the Wilderness Act, FLPMA, and the Mineral Leasing Act of 1920[281] was at issue in *Mountain States Legal Foundation v. Andrus.*[282] Under the last of these statutes, the Secretary of the Interior has authority to lease public lands containing oil and gas deposits, including lands within the National Forest System. As a matter of long-standing policy, however, the Secretary requests the recommendation of the Forest Service when lands under the latter's jurisdiction are involved and defers to its recommendations. At issue in the suit were allegedly energy rich Forest Service lands that had apparently been assigned to the "further

---

[278]448 F.2d 793 (10th Cir. 1971), *cert. denied,* 405 U.S. 989 (1972).

[279]*See* text accompanying notes 287–298 *infra.*

[280]483 F. Supp. 465 (E.D. Cal. 1980), *aff'd in part, rev'd in part sub nom.* California v. Block, 690 F.2d 753 (9th Cir. 1982).

[281]30 U.S.C. §§181–287 (1976 & Supp. V 1981).

[282]499 F. Supp. 383 (D. Wyo. 1980).

study" category by RARE II.[283] The Forest Service had, for a period of years, simply withheld any recommendations to the Secretary of the Interior on oil and gas applications relating to these lands. As a result, the Secretary had taken no final action on those applications. To force the Secretary to act on the pending applications before the expiration of the 20-year grace period for oil and gas leasing, the plaintiff, represented by the soon-to-be Secretary of the Interior James Watt, charged that Secretary Andrus's nonaction constituted a "withdrawal" within the meaning of section 103(j) of FLPMA[284] and as such required prior congressional approval.[285] The court agreed and ordered Secretary Andrus either to notify Congress of the withdrawal or to cease withholding the lands from oil and gas leasing, exploration, and development for the purpose of preserving the wilderness characteristics thereof.[286] Ultimately, when Watt changed roles with the Secretary, Congress would frustrate his aim to open the wilderness areas to extensive oil and gas leasing.

Although *Mountain States Legal Foundation* prohibited the withholding of potential wilderness areas in the National Forest System from leasing, except by means of withdrawal, it did not address whether and to what extent the activities of lessees could be regulated once the leases were issued. With respect to potential wilderness areas on BLM lands, however, FLPMA, unlike the Wilderness Act itself, provides statutory standards governing this issue. Interpretations of those standards are reflected in two recent cases, *Utah v. Andrus*[287] and *Rocky Mountain Oil & Gas Association v. Watt*.[288] *Utah* concerned the authority of the Secretary of the Interior to limit access to mining claims on state and federal lands under section 603 of FLPMA, its wilderness provision.[289] In the course of its ruling, the court considered at length a number of legal issues addressed by an opinion of the Interior Department Solicitor interpreting section 603.[290] The court

---

[283]The opinion is clear that at least one of the areas involved was assigned to this category, *id.* at 387, but is less clear as to the others.

[284]43 U.S.C. §1702(j) (1976).

[285]*Id.* §1714(c).

[286]499 F. Supp. at 397. The withdrawal issue was not addressed in Southern Appalachian Multiple Use Council, Inc. v. Bergland, 15 Env't Rep. Cas. (BNA) 2049 (W.D.N.C. April 16, 1981), which upheld the authority of the Secretary of Agriculture to manage as wilderness those areas, the suitability of which for ultimate wilderness designation he was then studying. The court stated that the Secretary had stopped timber cutting, mining, and other activities in such areas. *Id.* at 2053.

[287]486 F. Supp. 995 (D. Utah 1979).

[288]696 F.2d 734 (10th Cir. 1982).

[289]43 U.S.C. §1782 (1976).

[290]The Solicitor's opinion is dated September 5, 1978.

concurred with the opinion on nearly all the issues considered. In *Oil & Gas Association*, the Solicitor's opinion was itself the target of the suit. The plaintiff charged that it was "completely erroneous" and, although the district court discussed relatively few aspects of the opinion, it awarded the plaintiff summary judgment.[291] The court of appeals recently reversed. The following is a summary of these two cases.

Section 603(c) of FLPMA provides that areas of BLM lands potentially eligible for wilderness designation are to be managed, pending a final determination thereon, "so as not to impair the suitability of such areas for preservation as wilderness."[292] That requirement, however, is "subject... to the continuation of existing mining and grazing uses and mineral leasing in the same manner and degree in which the same was being conducted on the date of approval" of FLPMA.[293] That qualification of the nonimpairment duty is itself subject, however, to the proviso that the Secretary "shall by regulation or otherwise take any action required to prevent unnecessary or undue degradation of the lands and their resources or to afford environmental protection."[294]

*Utah* concluded that the above provisions imposed two separate management standards that depended upon the nature and date of the use in question. Uses not occurring at the time of FLPMA's enactment or not of types referred to in section 603(c) are subject to the nonimpairment standard; uses of the types referred to there and occurring at the time of FLPMA's enactment are subject to a less restrictive undue degradation and environmental protection standard.[295] *Utah* further limited the less restrictive standard to "*actual* uses, not merely a statutory right to use," such as yet unexercised rights of access to mineral leases.[296] The district court in *Oil & Gas Association*, on the other hand, concluded that mineral lessees, regardless of when they acquired their leases, were exempt from the strict nonimpairment standard.[297] The court of appeals reversed, holding that

---

[291] Rocky Mountain Oil & Gas Ass'n v. Andrus, 500 F. Supp. 1338 (D. Wyo. 1980).

[292] 43 U.S.C. §1978(c) (1976).

[293] *Id.*

[294] *Id.*

[295] 486 F. Supp. at 1003.

[296] 486 F. Supp. at 1006 (emphasis in original). However, even where the use is not an existing use, if such use flows from an existing right, the nonimpairment standard cannot be so restrictively applied as to "take" that right. *Id.* at 1011.

[297] This seems to be the result of the court's reasoning at 500 F. Supp. 1344. However, elsewhere the court suggests that although the nonimpairment standard can be applied to post-FLPMA leases, it cannot be applied so restrictively as to constitute a taking of the property rights represented by the lease. *Id.* at 1345. The latter conclusion seems highly dubious since the property interest acquired in post-FLPMA leases is clearly subject to wilderness protection restrictions incorporated in the lease.

only lessees who had acquired their leases prior to FLPMA were exempt and then only to the extent of their on-the-ground activities at the time of FLPMA's enactment.[298]

*Utah* resolved a number of other important issues not addressed in *Oil & Gas Association*. Because the lands at issue in *Utah* had not yet been formally designated a "wilderness study area," yet the court was willing to apply the nonimpairment standard to them, the court implicitly held that application of the nonimpairment standard does not first require a study area designation.[299] Second, *Utah* held that section 603 amended the Mining Law of 1872 and thus that "[r]ights under that law, including rights of ingress and egress, can be impaired by virtue of section 603."[300] Finally, *Utah* held that section 603 did not authorize restrictions on access to so-called "state school trust lands" that render such lands "incapable of their full economic development," a standard that could be violated by action short of an unconstitutional "taking" of property.[301]

The wilderness issue has been a volatile political issue during the administration of Interior Secretary James Watt. For Forest Service lands, the Wilderness Act permits oil and gas leasing in wilderness areas until midnight, December 31, 1983. To prevent Secretary Watt from issuing a host of eleventh-hour leases, Congress has prohibited him from using appropriated funds for that purpose. For BLM lands, mineral leasing may continue until the wilderness or nonwilderness status of particular areas is finally resolved. However, the nonimpairment standard of FLPMA, as interpreted in *Utah* and *Oil & Gas Association*, should provide ample interim protection for the wildlife and other wilderness values of such areas.

## SPECIAL PURPOSE LANDS

### The National Park System

The National Park System is comprised of a number of diverse units known variously as national parks, national monuments, national seashores,

---

[298] 696 F.2d at 750.

[299] 486 F. Supp. at 1001. Designation of a wilderness study area requires only a determination that the area is roadless, of the requisite size, and has wilderness characteristics. See 16 U.S.C. §1782(a) (1976). *Utah* clearly held that this designation, unlike the ultimate designation of an area as a recommended wilderness or nonwilderness area, does not require a balancing of mineral or other economic values against wilderness values.

[300] 486 F.Supp. at 1006. Similarly, *Utah* found nothing in section 201 of FLPMA, 43 U.S.C. §1711 (1976), that limited Interior's authority to restrict access to federal claims under section 603. 486 F. Supp. at 1006–1007.

[301] *Id.* at 1009.

national lakeshores, national wild rivers, national preserves, and still others.[302] All are managed by the National Park Service in the Department of the Interior. The overriding mission of the Park Service in the administration of the System is to provide recreational enjoyment for present and future generations. The National Park Service Act, passed in 1916, sets forth the general standards governing the administration of the System.[303] It explicitly recognizes the conservation of wildlife as among the purposes that the parks are to serve:

> [T]he fundamental purpose of the said parks, monuments, and reserva-
> tions...is to conserve the scenery and the natural and historic objects and
> the wild life therein and to provide for the enjoyment of the same in such
> manner and by such means as will leave them unimpaired for the
> enjoyment of future generations.[304]

Whether this statement of purpose imposes any judicially enforceable duties on the Secretary of the Interior in his administration of the System was presented in a series of court actions in which the Sierra Club challenged the adequacy of the Secretary's efforts to address threats to the resources of Redwood National Park arising from logging practices on its periphery. The legislation that initially established the Park authorized the Secretary to take certain actions to address the problems caused by peripheral logging. Those actions included modification of Park boundaries, acquisition of interests in land beyond the boundaries, and negotiation of cooperative agreements with adjoining landowners concerning their land management practices to minimize harm to Park resources. The Sierra Club contended that the Secretary's exercise of his discretion with respect to these authorities was judicially reviewable and that it had been arbitrary and capricious. An initial decision from the district court for the northern district of California found that the Secretary's actions were indeed reviewable,[305] and a second decision held them to be arbitrary and capricious.[306] Both decisions rested in part upon the court's finding that, in addition to the express statutory authorization to the Secretary, he had a further "public trust" duty to protect park resources.[307] As a result of the

---

[302]The more than a dozen types of units within the Park System are identified in 36 C.F.R. §1.2(g)–1.2(i)(1981).

[303]16 U.S.C. §§1 and 2–3 (1976). Many of the units within the System are administered under the terms of the special statutes that establish them.

[304]*Id.* §1.

[305]Sierra Club v. Department of the Interior, 376 F. Supp. 90 (N.D. Cal. 1974).

[306]398 F. Supp. 284 (N.D. Cal. 1975).

[307]376 F. Supp. at 93, 95–96.

court's second decision, the Interior Department submitted to the Office of Management and Budget (OMB) proposed legislation that would give the Department express regulatory power over peripheral timber operations, proposed timber-harvesting guidelines to timber companies managing adjoining lands, and requested that the Justice Department initiate litigation against certain timber companies to restrain timber practices imminently endangering the park. OMB disapproved Interior's request for new legislative authority, the timber companies declined to accept the harvesting guidelines, and the Justice Department had not yet decided whether to initiate litigation when the court entered a third decision.[308] This decision found that, in light of Interior's efforts, "primary responsibility for the protection of the Park rests, no longer upon Interior, but squarely upon Congress."[309] Thus Interior was in effect deemed to lack any power, in and of itself, to compel actions necessary to protect the Park from outside threats.

Congress responded in 1978 by enacting the Redwood National Park Expansion Act.[310] One feature of that legislation substantially expanded Redwood National Park and created a "Park Protection Zone" in which the Secretary could acquire additional lands under certain conditions. A second feature provided a new and very rigorous general standard governing the exercise of the Secretary's discretion in managing all park areas. That standard was embodied in a directive that

> [t]he authorization of activities shall be construed and the protection, management, and administration of [national park] areas shall be conducted in light of the high public value and integrity of the National Park System and shall not be exercised in derogation of the values and purposes for which these various areas have been established, except as may have been or shall be directly and specifically provided by Congress.[311]

The House Report accompanying this legislation described the intent of the foregoing provision to be "to afford the highest standard of protection and care to the land within Redwood National Park."[312] In fact, because the provision quoted above applies to all units of the National Park System, it reflects a directive that the "highest standard of protection and care" be given to the entire National Park System.

---

[308]Sierra Club v. Department of the Interior, 424 F. Supp. 172 (N.D. Cal. 1976).

[309]*Id.* at 175.

[310]Pub. L. No. 95–250, 92 Stat. 166.

[311]16 U.S.C. §1a-1 (Supp. V 1981).

[312]H.R. Rep. No. 581, pt. I, 95th Cong., 1st Sess. 21, *reprinted in* 1978 U.S. Code Cong. & Ad. News 463, 468.

Notwithstanding the apparent effect of the 1978 amendments, the Secretary's failure to take discretionary action in defense of park resources was upheld in *Sierra Club v. Andrus.*[313] There, the plaintiff challenged, among other things, the failure of the Secretary to join pending adjudications of water rights in the state of Utah so as to protect claimed federal reserved water rights in various Western parks. The plaintiff claimed that the 1978 amendments obligated the Secretary to participate in such pending adjudications. The court disagreed, largely because of its conclusion that the pending adjudication did not present "a real and immediate water supply threat" to the resources of the various parks. The court also expressed the view that the 1978 amendments "eliminated 'trust' notions in National Park System management," in response to the earlier Redwoods litigation.[314] The court concluded that the Secretary had "broad discretion in determining what actions are best calculated to protect park resources," although such discretion is "not unlimited."[315] This decision leaves considerable uncertainty as to the precise nature of the Secretary's authorities and duties with respect to the administration of the National Park System and the appropriate role for the courts to play in reviewing Secretarial action.[316] In contradistinction to the above cases, in which environmental plaintiffs have unsuccessfully challenged the Secretary's failure to take particular actions, the Secretary's duty to leave the parks "unimpaired for the enjoyment of future generations" has often been held to be an affirmative source of support for the actions he has taken. Thus, for example, *New Mexico State Game Commission v. Udall,*[317] held that this authority, coupled with the express authority elsewhere in the 1916 Act to destroy "such animals...as may be detrimental to the use of any of said parks, monuments or reservation,"[318] authorized the taking of deer in Carlsbad Caverns National Park solely for research purposes and without compliance with state game laws. So also in *Cappaert v. United States* the Supreme Court held that in reserving a tract of land in Nevada as part of Death Valley National Monument in order to protect a rare species of fish, the federal government also implicitly reserved the groundwater appurtenant to the land, lest the purpose of preserving the monument "unimpaired for the enjoyment of future generations" be frustrated.[319]

---

[313]487 F. Supp. 443 (D.D.C. 1980).

[314]*Id.* at 449.

[315]*Id.* at 448.

[316]Although the Sierra Club did not appeal that portion of the district court's decision refusing to order the Secretary to join the pending state water adjudications, he did in fact subsequently join such proceedings.

[317]410 F.2d 1197 (10th Cir.), *cert. denied,* 396 U.S. 961 (1969).

[318]16 U.S.C. §3 (1976).

[319]426 U.S. 128 (1976). The tract of land involved in *Cappaert* was reserved pursuant

Yet another example is *United States v. Brown,* which upheld the authority of the Secretary to prohibit hunting on waters within the boundaries of Voyageurs National Park, when such water arguably had not been ceded to the federal government but had instead remained the property of the state.[320] Although the court found, as an alternative holding, that the state had in fact ceded jurisdiction over both lands and waters within the park, it went on to hold that had the state not ceded jurisdiction over the waters, the federal government could regulate activities on those waters, including hunting, as a proper exercise of its powers under the property clause. The statutory provision implementing that authority was deemed by the court to be the general authority of the Secretary of the Interior to promulgate "such rules and regulations as he may deem necessary or proper for the use and management of the park."[321] In so ruling, the court purported to decide the question left open in *Kleppe v. New Mexico*[322] "whether the Property Clause empowers the United States to enact regulatory legislation protecting federal lands from interference occurring on non-federal public lands, or in this instance, waters."[323] Notwithstanding this decision, the significance of the case is limited both by the fact that the court's finding was an alternative holding and by the further fact that the waters at issue were within the boundaries of the National Park, albeit arguably not a part of the Park.

As these cases suggest, the broad statement of purpose contained in the National Park Service Act gives considerable discretion to the Secretary in his management of the units of the System.[324] Thus, he has generally prohibited hunting within all but the "recreational areas," while fishing is generally permitted throughout the System.[325] Beyond these matters, however, the national parks obviously have substantial importance for many types of wildlife simply because they function as one more mechanism to preserve needed habitat.

---

to the Act for the Preservation of Antiquities, 16 U.S.C. §§431–433 (1976). That Act authorizes the reservation of land containing "historic landmarks, historic and prehistoric structures, and other objects of historic or scientific interest." The *Cappaert* court rejected the contention that the Antiquities Act was intended to protect only archaeological sites and held that the "rare inhabitants" (referring to the endangered Devil's Hole pupfish) of the land in question were "objects of historic and scientific interest."

[320]552 F.2d 817 (8th Cir. 1977).

[321]16 U.S.C. §3 (1976).

[322]426 U.S. 529 (1976).

[323]552 F.2d at 822.

[324]36 C.F.R. §2.32 (1981). "Recreational areas" include national seashores, lakeshores, scenic riverways, recreation areas, wild rivers, and a few other designated areas. *Id.* §1.2(i).

[325]*Id.* §2.13.

## Military Lands

Earlier in this chapter, the Sikes Act Extension was shown to provide a mechanism for the cooperative management of wildlife on Forest Service, BLM, and certain other federal lands. The original Sikes Act, passed in 1960, provided a similar, though optional, mechanism for cooperative wildlife management on military reservations.[326] That Act authorized the Secretary of Defense, pursuant to a "cooperative plan" agreed to by the Secretary of the Interior and the appropriate state fish and game agency, to "carry out a program of planning, development, maintenance, and coordination of wildlife, fish and game conservation in military reservations."[327] Similar authority was also granted with respect to migratory game birds[328] and the development of public outdoor recreation resources.[329]

The original Sikes Act said virtually nothing about the required contents of the cooperative plans it authorized. It did provide, however, that such plans could require special state hunting and fishing permits and special migratory game bird hunting permits. For the former, only a nominal fee could be charged. Revenues from either type of permit could be expended only for carrying out the wildlife or migratory game bird cooperative plans.

In 1974, when the Sikes Act Extension was enacted, the original Sikes Act was also amended so as to impose certain minimum requirements for the cooperative wildlife plans it authorized. Those requirements were that such plans provide for "(1) fish and wildlife habitat improvements or modifications, (2) range rehabilitation where necessary for support of wildlife, and (3) control of off-road vehicle traffic."[330] Provision for the protection of endangered and threatened wildlife, required in cooperative plans under the Sikes Act Extension, is conspicuous by its absence. Like the Sikes Act Extension, however, the original Sikes Act makes no provision for public participation in the development of cooperative plans.

## The Outer Continental Shelf

If one takes an expansive meaning of the term "land," then surely the most extensive system of lands under federal control is the outer continental shelf of the United States. The outer continental shelf, comprising the submerged lands that slope gradually downward from the coasts for as much as

---

[326]16 U.S.C. §§670a–670f (1976).

[327]*Id.* §670a.

[328]*Id.* §670b.

[329]*Id.* §670c.

[330]*Id.* §670a.

200 miles or more before dropping precipitously into the deep sea, was not subject to the jurisdiction of any single nation prior to World War II. However, by presidential proclamation in 1945[331] and enactment of the Outer Continental Shelf Lands Act in 1953,[332] the United States claimed for itself the exclusive jurisdiction over the subsoil and seabed of the shelf.

The Outer Continental Shelf Lands Act served two major purposes. First, in conjunction with the Submerged Lands Act,[333] passed in the same year, it divided jurisdiction over the shelf between the states and the federal government. The states were given authority over that part of the shelf within the three-mile territorial sea; beyond that, the federal government had exclusive control.[334] The second major purpose of the Outer Continental Shelf Lands Act was to set up a system for the leasing and systematic exploitation of the mineral resources of the federal portion of the continental shelf.

While the Outer Continental Shelf Lands Act proclaimed an exclusive federal authority over exploitation of the mineral resources of most of the shelf, it expressly disclaimed any such authority over the rights of navigation and fishing in the waters above the shelf.[335] It did, however, seek to protect the living resources of the shelf by authorizing the Secretary of the Interior, in connection with the leasing of mineral rights, to promulgate "such rules and regulations as he determines to be necessary and proper in order to provide for . . . the conservation of the natural resources of the outer Continental Shelf."[336] The Secretary's exercise of this authority to suspend drilling operations in the Santa Barbara Channel after the massive blowout of 1969 was upheld in *Gulf Oil Corp. v. Morton.*[337]

Major amendments to the Act in 1978 gave further authority to the Secretary to protect living marine resources from the adverse effects of Outer Continental Shelf oil and gas leasing.[338] Prior to leasing any area, the Secretary is to conduct a study "to establish information needed for assessment and management of environmental impacts on the human, marine, and coastal environments"[339] and to "predict impacts on the

---

[331]Presidential Proclamation No. 2267, 59 Stat. 884, 10 Fed. Reg. 12303 (Sept. 28, 1945).

[332]43 U.S.C. §§1331–1356 (1976 & Supp. V 1981).

[333]*Id.* §§1301–1315 (1976).

[334]The federal authority is exercised through the Secretary of the Interior.

[335]43 U.S.C. §1332(2)(Supp. V 1981).

[336]*Id.* §1334(a)(1).

[337]493 F.2d 141 (9th Cir. 1973), *modified on rehearing,* 4 Envtl. L. Rep. (Envtl. L. Inst.) 20377 (9th Cir. March 25, 1974).

[338]Pub. L. No. 95–372, 92 Stat. 632.

[339]43 U.S.C. §1346(a)(1)(Supp. IV 1980).

marine biota which may result from chronic low level pollution of large spills."[340] After issuing a lease, the Secretary may cancel it if "continued activity pursuant to such lease...would probably cause serious harm or damage to life (including fish and other aquatic life)...or to the marine coastal, or human environment."[341] On a similar basis, the Secretary may disapprove any production plan submitted to him.[342] These and other aspects of the amended Outer Continental Shelf Lands Act are described in *North Slope Borough v. Andrus*[343] and *Conservation Law Foundation v. Andrus*,[344] cases that are discussed in more detail in Chapter 12.

What the Outer Continental Shelf Lands Act does not confer is the authority to carry out affirmative programs of wildlife conservation. Two recent federal statutes have since provided that authority. The most comprehensive of these, the Fishery Conservation and Management Act of 1976, proclaims exclusive federal conservation and management authority over all fisheries within a 197-mile-wide zone contiguous to the territorial sea of the United States, as well as over certain living resources of the Continental Shelf wherever it extends beyond that zone.[345] That Act is discussed in detail in Chapter 13.

The other federal statute conferring affirmative conservation authority over the continental shelf is the Marine Protection Research and Sanctuaries Act of 1972.[346] It authorizes the Secretary of Commerce, with the approval of the President, to designate as "marine sanctuaries" areas of the ocean out to the edge of the Continental Shelf, or the Great Lakes, "which he determines necessary for the purpose of preserving or restoring such areas for their conservation, recreational, ecological, or esthetic values."[347]

The designation of sanctuaries is accomplished through a three-step process. The first step requires consultation regarding a proposed sanctuary with all interested federal agencies and, if the sanctuary includes waters within the territorial limits of a state, with "responsible officials" of that state.[348] The second step requires public hearings in the coastal areas most directly affected.[349] The final step is the preparation of an order designating

---

[340]*Id.* §1346(a)(3).

[341]*Id.* §1334(a)(2)(A)(i).

[342]*Id.* §1351(h)(1)(D).

[343]642 F.2d 589 (D.C. Cir. 1980).

[344]623 F.2d 712 (1st Cir. 1979).

[345]16 U.S.C. §§1801–1882 (1976 & Supp. V 1981).

[346]33 U.S.C. §§1401–1444 and 16 U.S.C. §§1431–1434 (1976 & Supp. V 1981).

[347]16 U.S.C. §1432(a)(1976).

[348]*Id.* §1432(a), (b)(1976 & Supp. V 1981).

[349]*Id.* §1432(e)(1976).

the sanctuary for approval of the President and specifying the types of activities to be regulated by the Secretary.[350] A sanctuary designation becomes effective unless disapproved by both houses of Congress or, in the case of sanctuaries within the territorial waters of a state, by the governor of that state.[351]

Once having made a designation, the Secretary must, again after consultation with interested agencies, issue "necessary and reasonable regulations" to control the activities specified in the sanctuary designation.[352] If the sanctuary includes waters outside the territorial jurisdiction of the United States, the Secretary of State must "take such actions as may be appropriate to enter into negotiations with other governments for the purpose of arriving at necessary agreements with those Governments, in order to protect such sanctuary and to promote the purposes for which it was established."[353] Violations of the Secretary's regulations are punishable by civil penalties of up to $50,000.[354]

The marine sanctuaries program is still very much a fledgling program with only six sanctuaries designated thus far.[355] Nonetheless, if it lives up to the ambitions embodied in its implementing regulations, it offers substantial promise of protecting marine wildlife habitats. Those regulations stress that the primary emphasis of the program "will be the protection of natural and biological resources."[356] Thus marine sanctuaries could be established as, in effect, marine wildlife refuges. Obviously, however, the protection of such areas will necessarily entail developing a regulatory framework adequate to deal with the unique problems of protecting ocean areas. The land-based wildlife refuges will offer only limited utility as analogous areas from which to derive management principles.

---

[350]*Id.* §1432(a), (f)(1)(1976 & Supp. V 1981).

[351]The procedure for designation of marine sanctuaries can be contrasted with that for designation of wilderness areas, which requires, as its final step, approval by Congress.

[352]16 U.S.C. §1432(f)(2)(Supp. V 1981).

[353]*Id.* §1432(c)(1976). Query: What actions, if any, need be taken by the Secretary of State, now that the United States has extended its claim of exclusive fisheries jurisdiction out 200 miles from its coasts under the Fishery Conservation and Management Act of 1976?

[354]*Id.* §1433.

[355]Those sanctuaries are the U.S.S. Monitor Sanctuary off the coast of North Carolina, the Key Largo Coral Reef Sanctuary near the Florida Keys, the Looe Key Sanctuary in Florida, the Channel Islands and Point Reyes-Farallon Islands Sanctuaries in California, and the Gray's Reef Sanctuary off Georgia.

[356]15 C.F.R. §922.1(b)(1981).

# Chapter 7

# WILDLIFE CONSERVATION THROUGH MANDATING CONSIDERATION OF WILDLIFE IMPACTS

As early as the 1930s, it was apparent that the conservation of wildlife could not be assured solely by means of laws that regulated its direct utilization or set aside sanctuaries for its protection. What was needed as well were legal measures to interject into the planning of a myriad of activities taking place outside those sanctuaries some consideration of their likely impacts on wildlife. By thus requiring such consideration, it could be hoped that alternatives having less adverse impacts on wildlife could be identified.

This chapter examines a number of federal statutes utilizing that strategy to varying degrees to achieve wildlife conservation. Some, like the Fish and Wildlife Coordination Act, are narrowly drawn to mandate a consideration only of wildlife impacts. Others, like the more recent federal pollution legislation, seek to achieve a wide range of environmental goals including, but not limited to, wildlife conservation. There are also significant differences in how these statutes seek to compel consideration of wildlife and other environmental values. Some do so through requiring consideration of the impacts of individual projects; others require the development of long range comprehensive plans encompassing a broad spectrum of development activities. Still others incorporate a consideration of such impacts in the setting of regulatory standards. Finally, there is a substantial degree of overlap and interrelationship among the statutes considered there, a fact which often reinforces, but sometimes dilutes, the mission of any single statute.

## THE FISH AND WILDLIFE COORDINATION ACT

Probably the first major federal wildlife statute to employ the strategy of compelling consideration of wildlife impacts was the Fish and Wildlife Coordination Act.[1] In some respects, the Coordination Act originally passed in 1934 was a remarkably forward-looking statute. For example, it authorized "investigations...to determine the effects of domestic sewage, trade wastes, and other polluting substances on wild life,"[2] encouraged the "development of a program for the maintenance of an adequate supply of wild life" on the public domain and other federally owned lands,[3] and called for state and federal cooperation in "developing a Nation-wide program of wild life conservation and rehabilitation."[4]

The need for legislation like the Clean Water Act[5] and the Sikes Act Extension[6] some 40 years later underscores the failure of the original Coordination Act's promise. Part of that failure can be attributed to its purely hortatory nature. Only two provisions appeared to be mandatory. They required consultation with the Bureau of Fisheries prior to the construction of any dam[7] and opportunity to use the impounded waters of any dam "for fish-culture stations and migratory bird resting and nesting areas...not inconsistent with the primary use of the waters."[8] As to the consultation requirement, however, the only apparent object was to determine if fish ladders or other aids to migration were "necessary...[and] economically practicable."[9] Moreover, the mandatory nature of both these provisions was questionable, for, according to the House Report:

> [T]here is nothing but a spirit of cooperation which is insisted on in this bill. There is nothing mandatory about the bill.[10]

Not surprisingly, Congress soon concluded that the 1934 Act had "proved to be inadequate in many respects."[11] The result was a major

---

[1] 16 U.S.C. §§661–667e (1976).

[2] Act of March 10, 1934, ch. 55, §2, 48 Stat. 401.

[3] *Id.* §5.

[4] *Id.* §1.

[5] 33 U.S.C. §§1251–1376 (1976 & Supp. V 1981), discussed at text accompanying notes 166–200 *infra*.

[6] 16 U.S.C. §§670a–670o (1976 & Supp. V 1981), discussed in Chapter 6 at text accompanying notes 143–156.

[7] Act of March 10, 1934, ch. 55, §3(b), 48 Stat. 402.

[8] *Id.* §3(a), 48 Stat. 401.

[9] *Id.* §3(b), 48 Stat. 402.

[10] H.R. Rep. No. 850, 73d Cong., 2d Sess. 1 (1934).

[11] H.R. Rep. No. 1944, 79th Cong., 2d Sess. 1 (1946).

legislative overhaul in 1946.[12] In part, the revisions of 1946 represented a retreat from some of the more ambitious goals of 1934. Deleted were the goals of establishing a nationwide program of wildlife conservation and of maintaining an "adequate supply" of wildlife on the federal public lands. In part, however, the 1946 amendments also sought to expand the scope of some of the specific directives of the original Act. For example, consultation with the Fish and Wildlife Service (successor to the Bureau of Fisheries) and with the appropriate state wildlife agency was required not only in the case of dam construction, but "[w]henever the waters of any stream or other body of water are authorized to be impounded, diverted, or otherwise controlled for any purpose whatever by any department or agency of the United States, or by any public or private agency under Federal permit."[13] The recommendations of the resource agencies resulting from such consultation were required to "be made an integral part of any report submitted by any agency of the Federal Government responsible for engineering surveys and construction of such projects."[14] The object of such consultation was not merely to aid the migration of fish, but to prevent "loss of and damage to wildlife resources,"[15] an object of enormous potential scope because of the following broad (and circular) definition given to "wildlife":

> [B]irds, fishes, mammals, and all other classes of wild animals and all types of aquatic and land vegetation upon which wildlife is dependent.[16]

A further expansion of the Coordination Act by the 1946 amendments was the requirement that, whenever the duty to consult applied to any federal project, so too did the requirement of making "adequate provision consistent with the primary purposes of such impoundment, diversion, or other control...for the conservation, maintenance, and management of wildlife."[17] To this end, the Act directed that the waters and lands thus utilized be made available without cost for administration by the appropriate state wildlife agency or by the Secretary of the Interior if the area had "particular value" for migratory bird management.[18] The "adequate

---

[12]Act of August 14, 1946, ch. 965, 60 Stat. 1080.

[13]*Id.* §2.

[14]*Id.* For a discussion of the limited character of this obligation, see Sierra Club v. Sigler, 532 F. Supp. 1222, 1242–1243 (S.D. Tex 1982), *rev'd on other grounds*, 695 F.2d 957 (5th Cir. 1983).

[15]Act of August 14, 1946, ch. 965, §2, 60 Stat. 1080.

[16]*Id.* §8.

[17]*Id.* §3.

[18]*Id.*

provision" requirement would have been given further specific content by a directive in the original House bill that the Corps of Engineers consider impacts on wildlife in its operation of impoundment facilities. However, the War Department successfully lobbied against that operating restriction.[19]

In the only significant reported case to consider the 1946 amendments, *Rank v. Krug*, the court found "great cogency" in plaintiff landowners' argument that the statutorily required "adequate provision" for wildlife had not been made with respect to the Bureau of Reclamation's Friant Dam on the San Joaquin River.[20] Nonetheless, viewing the state as the proper party to insist upon compliance with the Act, the court refused to hear plaintiffs' claim. Resting on a principle now largely abandoned, the court held that:

> It is too plain to need argument that a citizen cannot compel compliance where that duty is lodged with regularly selected officials whose duties are clearly defined by statute, any more than a private citizen could step in and assume the duties of prosecuting attorney or governor....[21]

The court's reference to a "duty" of the state to compel compliance was not amplified, and the court expressly refrained from deciding whether that duty could be enforced through a private mandamus action.

Once again in 1958, Congress concluded that the results of the amended Coordination Act had "fallen far short of the results anticipated."[22] The result was another major legislative overhaul of the Act,[23] principally to require that wildlife conservation be given "equal consideration" with other features of water resource development.[24] In addition, whereas preventing wildlife losses had been the object of earlier versions of the Act, the 1958 amendments introduced the further goal of wildlife enhancement.[25] Further, the list of water-related activities to which the Act's consultation requirement applied was expanded to include channel deepenings and all modifications of any body of water.[26] Finally, in

---

[19]*See* Shipley, the Fish and Wildlife Coordination Act's Application to Wetlands, in A. Reitze, Environmental Planning: Law of Land and Resources, ch. 2 at 49 (1974).

[20]90 F. Supp. 773 (S.D. Cal. 1950).

[21]*Id.* at 801.

[22]S. Rep. No. 1981, 85th Cong., 2d Sess. 4 (1958).

[23]Act of August 12, 1958, Pub. L. No. 85–624, 72 Stat. 563.

[24]16 U.S.C. §661 (1976).

[25]*Id.* §662(a).

[26]*Id.* Federal activities exempt from the requirements are described at 16 U.S.C. §662(h)(1976).

addition to the previous requirement that the recommendations of the resource agencies be made an "integral part" of any report submitted by a federal construction agency, the 1958 amendments added the further duty that "the project plan...include such justifiable means and measures for wildlife purposes as the reporting agency finds should be adopted to obtain maximum overall project benefits."[27]

As a result of the 1946 and 1958 amendments, two distinctly different types of federal actions are now clearly subject to the Coordination Act. First, for major federal water development projects, such as dams, reclamation efforts, and channelization projects, the reports and recommendations of the Fish and Wildlife Service (or, since 1970, the National Marine Fisheries Service) and of the state wildlife agency are required to be given "full consideration" by the federal project agency and to be "made an integral part of any report prepared or submitted by" it to Congress or any other entity having authority to authorize the project.[28] The second category consists of the various water-related activities for which federal permits are required, most notably Corps of Engineers permits issued under section 404 of the Clean Water Act.[29] As to these, the wildlife agencies can recommend that the requested permit be denied, an option that is seldom available as a practical matter with respect to major federal water development projects, or conditioned in a way to reduce the adverse impacts on wildlife of the permitted activity. For this second category, the statute does not specify the degree of deference to be paid by the permitting agency to the recommendations of the wildlife agencies beyond the generally applicable goals of wildlife conservation and enhancement.[30]

Early judicial decisions construing the 1958 amendments led some legal commentators to think that the Coordination Act would finally be

---

[27]*Id.* §662(b).

[28]*Id.* Typically, the recommendations of the wildlife agencies take the form of suggested modification in project design or acquisition of land valuable as wildlife habitat to replace that which will be lost as a result of the project. By requiring that such "mitigation plans" be included in reports to Congress, that body ultimately decides how effective the Coordination Act will be with respect to any particular major water development project.

[29]33 U.S.C. §1344 (Supp. V 1981). Prior to 1972, the Corps of Engineers had the responsibility of issuing similar permits under section 10 of the River and Harbor Act of 1899, 33 U.S.C. §403 (1976). *But see* text accompanying notes 64–66 *infra.*

[30]Sierra Club v. Sigler, *supra* note 14, held the requirement of 16 U.S.C. §662(b)(1976) that the report and recommendations of the Fish and Wildlife Service be made an "integral part" of any federal agency project report inapplicable to federally licensed or permitted private development projects. Though not specifically addressed, that holding would seem to extend as well to the requirement of the same provision that "justifiable means and measures for wildlife purposes" be included in any "project plan."

elevated to a position of prominence in federal wildlife law. For example, in *Udall v. FPC*, Justice Douglas concluded that the Federal Power Commission had failed to explore and evaluate adequately the likely effects of a proposed dam on the Snake River, as required by the Coordination Act.[31] While Douglas's opinion cited a number of other grounds in reversing the Commission's decision,[32] and though his opinion was far from clear as to the nature of the duties imposed by the Coordination Act, it nonetheless clearly established that compliance with the Act could not be accomplished perfunctorily.[33]

Two years after the *Udall* decision, Congress enacted the National Environmental Policy Act.[34] Originally proposed as an amendment to the Coordination Act, NEPA became instead an independent directive to all federal agencies to consider and evaluate, through the preparation of detailed environmental impact statements, the impacts of all major actions "significantly affecting the quality of the human environment."[35] The scope of that directive will be considered in more detail later in this chapter. Its significance here, however, is in how it was to become intertwined with the duties imposed by the Coordination Act.

The first case to arise under the Coordination Act after enactment of NEPA was *Zabel v. Tabb*.[36] In that action, the Corps of Engineers refused to issue a permit under section 10 of the River and Harbor Act of 1899[37] because of the adverse ecological effects of the proposed dredging. The permit applicants sued, charging that the Corps could only consider the

---

[31] 387 U.S. 428 (1967).

[32] In particular, Douglas pointed to the Anadromous Fish Conservation Act of 1965, Pub. L. 89-304, §2, 79 Stat. 1125 (current version at 16 U.S.C. §757b (Supp. V 1981)), which merely directed the Secretary of the Interior to make studies and recommendations "for the conservation and enhancement of anadromous fishery resources," as evidencing a special congressional concern for the protection of anadromous fish.

[33] In fact, Justice Douglas's opinion directed that the FPC consider whether the dam ought to be constructed at all. On remand to the FPC, the Presiding Examiner concluded that construction should be deferred and the status quo preserved until 1976, by which time the Departments of the Interior and Agriculture and the Congress could determine the suitability of the Snake River for inclusion in the National Wild and Scenic Rivers System. Pacific Northwest Power, Project No. 2243, 1 Envtl. L. Rep. (Envtl. L. Inst.) 30017 (FPC, Feb, 23, 1971). With the creation of Hell's Canyon National Recreation area in 1975 Douglas's vision of a free-flowing river was realized. *See* 16 U.S.C. §§460gg to 460gg-13, 1274(a)(12)(1976 & Supp. V 1981).

[34] 42 U.S.C. §§4321–4361 (1976)(hereinafter referred to as NEPA).

[35] The legislative history of NEPA is described in R. Liroff, A National Policy for the Environment: NEPA and its Aftermath 10–35 (1976).

[36] 430 F.2d 199 (5th Cir. 1970), *cert. denied*, 401 U.S. 910 (1971).

[37] 33 U.S.C. §403 (1976).

effects of the proposed action on navigation, the Coordination Act notwithstanding. The district court sustained the developers, but the appellate court reversed because of "the government-wide policy of environmental conservation [that] is spectacularly revealed" by the Coordination Act and NEPA.[38] Similar reasoning was applied in *Akers v. Resor*, in which the Coordination Act, construed in light of NEPA, was held in a pretrial decision to require the preparation of a new wildlife mitigation plan both with respect to that part of an authorized Corps project for which appropriations were being sought, as well as for that part for which they had been granted several years before and for which a pre-NEPA mitigation plan had previously been prepared.[39]

On the basis of the *Zabel* and *Akers* decisions, early commentators optimistically described the relationship between the Coordination Act and NEPA as synergistic[40] or symbiotic.[41] However, even before the *Akers* decision, at least one cloud had already appeared on the horizon of NEPA–Coordination Act relations in the form of the *Gillham Dam* decision, *Environmental Defense Fund v. Corps of Engineers*.[42] In that case, which challenged a major Corps of Engineers project already two-thirds completed, the court resurrected the two-decade-old *Rank v. Krug* decision by expressing doubt whether private parties could maintain actions for noncompliance with the Coordination Act. In addition, since the court regarded it unreasonable to order the Corps to undertake the Coordination Act's required consultation procedures 13 years after the project plans had been made, it concluded that "if defendants comply with the provisions of [NEPA] in good faith, they will automatically take into consideration all of the factors required by the Fish and Wildlife Coordination Act."[43]

The court's language in the *Gillham Dam* decision raised some major conceptual questions that were further obfuscated in other parts of the opinion. For example, the quoted language can be understood as implying that the requirements of the Coordination Act are purely procedural rather than substantive. On the other hand, the court stated that plaintiffs could attempt to prove noncompliance with the Coordination Act as an element of their claim arising under NEPA, "since departures from the congressional policies set forth in [the Coordination Act] should be acknowledged

---

[38]430 F.2d at 209.

[39]339 F. Supp. 1375 (W.D. Tenn. 1972).

[40]Shipley, *supra* note 19, at 49.

[41]Guilbert, Wildlife Preservation Under Federal Law, in Federal Environmental Law 557 (E. Dolgin & T. Guilbert eds. 1974).

[42]325 F. Supp. 749 (E.D. Ark. 1971), *injunction dissolved*, 342 F. Supp. 1211, *aff'd*, 470 F.2d 289 (8th Cir. 1972).

[43]325 F. Supp. at 754.

in any" impact statement.[44] In fact, however, the *Gillham Dam* impact statement did not acknowledge any such "departures" but actually claimed benefits for enhancement of fish and wildlife resources. Nonetheless, while professing to have no power of substantive review under NEPA, the court proceeded to find the impact statement inadequate in part because "the evidence indicates that there are a number of serious possibilities for injury to fish and wildlife which might occur if the dam is constructed."[45]

Accordingly, the *Gillham Dam* decision's statement that compliance with NEPA constitutes compliance with the Coordination Act is both confused and confusing. Nonetheless, many courts have repeatedly and uncritically accepted it as a basis for dismissing Coordination Act claims when coupled with NEPA claims.[46] Unfortunately, few of the subsequent decisions attempt to elucidate the precise meaning of NEPA–Coordination Act equivalence. However, as suggested by several commentators,[47] the equating of the Coordination Act with NEPA may not bear up to critical scrutiny.

The first clear recognition of the inadequacy of the reasoning of *Gillham Dam* came in *National Wildlife Federation v. Andrus,*[48] where action was brought under both NEPA and the Coordination Act to enjoin construction by the Bureau of Reclamation of a power plant. In granting the injunction, the court held that the Bureau had failed to provide Congress with the Fish and Wildlife Service's consultation report regarding the project, as required under the Coordination Act. Significantly, the court refused to follow defendant's urging that *Gillham Dam* controlled, ruling that "plaintiffs have identified a FWCA policy, that of informing Congress of environmental effects, which may not be duplicated by NEPA. In such circumstances, strict compliance with FWCA should be required."[49]

---

[44]*Id.*

[45]*Id.* at 760.

[46]*See, e.g.,* Environmental Defense Fund v. Froehlke, 473 F.2d 346 (8th Cir. 1972); Environmental Defense Fund v. Alexander, 501 F. Supp. 742, 766–767 (N.D. Miss. 1980), *aff'd in part and rev'd in part on other grounds sub nom.* Environmental Defense Fund v. Marsh, 651 F.2d 983 (5th Cir. 1981); County of Trinity v. Andrus, 438 F. Supp. 1368, 1383 (E.D. Cal. 1977); Save Our Sound Fisheries Ass'n v. Callaway, 387 F. Supp. 292 (D.R.I. 1974); and Cape Henry Bird Club v. Laird, 359 F. Supp. 404 (W.D. Va.), *aff'd,* 484 F.2d 453 (4th Cir. 1973).

[47]*See* Parenteau, Unfulfilled Mitigation Requirements of the Fish and Wildlife Coordination Act, 42 N. Am. Wildlife Conf. Proc. 179 (1977), and Blumm, Hydropower vs. Salmon: The Struggle of the Pacific Northwest's Anadromous Fish Resources for a Peaceful Coexistence with the Federal Columbia River Power System, 11 Envtl. L. 211, 268–276 (1981).

[48]440 F. Supp. 1245 (D.D.C. 1977).

[49]*Id.* at 1255. The court believed this result was "especially true in view of the

One year later, in *Texas Committee on Natural Resources v. Alexander*,[50] other distinctive features of the Coordination Act were recognized. Here, the court held that the Army Corps of Engineers was obliged under the Coordination Act to continue to consult with the Fish and Wildlife Service, even after its Cooper Lake and Channels Project was authorized and after the Service had submitted an initial mitigation report, so as to be able to include in its Environmental Impact Statement (EIS) a current mitigation plan for wildlife affected by the project. The court was presented with evidence that the methodology for evaluating habitat impacts had changed substantially in the 10 years between the initial Service report and the preparation of the EIS. In enjoining the project because, *inter alia*, the EIS failed to include a mitigation plan based on such changed methodology, the court succinctly stated that, "[w]hen a project involves the impoundment of water, compliance with the FWCA is a *sine qua non* to the validity of an EIS concerning that project."[51] With this language, the court thus appeared to turn *Gillham Dam* upside-down by insisting upon Coordination Act compliance as the first step of its NEPA review.

By giving force to the distinctive procedural obligations of development or licensing agencies under the Coordination Act, these cases breathe new life into the Act. However, unlike NEPA, it would seem that the Coordination Act's requirements are more than purely procedural.[52] For example, unless the Coordination Act's mandate that project plans "include such justifiable means and measures for wildlife purposes as the reporting agency finds should be adopted to obtain maximum overall project benefits," is intended to vest absolute discretion in such agencies, this mandate would appear to provide a substantive standard against which reviewing courts can measure an agency's compliance.[53] That absolute discretion was not intended is implied by the Act's central

---

doubtful authorization by Congress of the [challenged] project in the first place." *Id.* In Environmental Defense Fund v. Andrus, 596 F.2d 848 (9th Cir. 1979), however, the Coordination Act and NEPA were held to apply to the modification or supplementation of plans for previously authorized projects, even when such modifications were within the scope of prior congressional authorization. *But see* County of Trinity v. Andrus, 438 F. Supp. 1368 (E.D. Cal. 1977).

[50]12 Env't Rep. Cas (BNA) 1676 (E.D. Tex. Dec. 8, 1978).

[51]*Id.* at 1680.

[52]*See* text accompanying notes 126–128 *infra*.

[53]16 U.S.C. §662(b)(1976). In County of Trinity v. Andrus, *supra*, note 49, a statutory standard authorizing and directing the Secretary of the Interior "to adopt appropriate measures to insure the preservation and propagation of fish and wildlife" in connection with a water diversion project was held to constitute a judicially reviewable substantive standard.

objective, that wildlife conservation receive "equal consideration" with other features of water resource development programs.[54]

If the foregoing suggests that courts have yet to embrace any substantive obligations that the Coordination Act imposes on development and licensing agencies, it is also evident that they have not yet clearly defined the requirements the Act imposes on the "wildlife" agencies, *i.e.,* the Fish and Wildlife Service and the National Marine Fisheries Service. Only one case, *Sun Enterprises, Ltd. v. Train,* evidences an earnest attempt to discern those requirements.[55]

In *Sun Enterprises,* the Environmental Protection Agency Administrator issued a National Pollution Discharge Elimination System (hereinafter referred to as NPDES) permit pursuant to section 402 of the Federal Water Pollution Control Act.[56] At the time of his receipt of the permit application, the Administrator notified the Fish and Wildlife Service and invited its comments. Rather than respond substantively, however, the Service advised that, due to lack of personnel, no recommendation on the application would be made. The Administrator subsequently issued the permit, and plaintiffs challenged it on the grounds that the required consultation had not occurred. The district court disagreed, holding that the Service had no affirmative duty to make a substantive reply to the Administrator's consultation request.[57]

---

[54] 16 U.S.C. §661 (1976). Sierra Club v. Alexander, a case involving a challenge to the Corps of Engineers' issuance of a section 404 "dredge and fill" permit in the face of unresolved objections by the Fish and Wildlife Service, held that the Corps was obliged by the Coordination Act to give serious consideration to the Service's recommendations but need not follow them. 484 F. Supp. 455, 470 (N.D.N.Y. 1980). *See also* Sierra Club v. Sigler, *supra* note 14, at 1243, holding that "Congress intended only that the Corps consult [the Fish and Wildlife Service] before issuing a permit for private dredge and fill operations." That view finds support in the legislative history of the Coordination Act's 1958 amendments, wherein it is emphasized that the wildlife agencies are not intended to exercise a "veto power" over agencies required to consult with them. *See* Hearings on H.R. 13138 Before the Senate Comm. on Interstate and Foreign Commerce, 85th Cong., 2d Sess. 4 (1958). For an interpretation of another provision mandating consultation but disclaiming any grant of veto power to the agency consulted, see the discussion of section 7 of the Endangered Species Act in Chapter 12. *See also* the statement in Sierra Club v. Butz, 3 Envtl. L. Rep. (Envtl. L. Inst.) 20292, 20293 (9th Cir. 1973), that the requirement of "due consideration" under the Multiple Use–Sustained Yield Act "can hardly be satisfied by a showing of knowledge of the consequences and a decision to ignore them." The Coordination Act's standard of "full consideration" would seem to demand no less.

[55] 532 F.2d 280 (1st Cir. 1976).

[56] 33 U.S.C. §1342 (1976 & Supp. V 1981).

[57] 394 F. Supp. 211, 218 (S.D.N.Y. 1975).

The court of appeals held that since section 509 of the Clean Water Act conferred exclusive jurisdiction on the courts of appeal to consider challenges to the issuance of permits not involving alleged violations of effluent standards, the district court had been without jurisdiction to consider the plaintiff's suit. Moreover, the court held that the plaintiff was time barred from filing under section 509 now, since that provision limited review to petitions filed within 90 days of a permit's issuance.[58] Significantly, the court expressly refrained from deciding whether the plaintiff possessed a private right of action to enforce the Coordination Act that could confer upon the district court independent jurisdiction to consider the suit. However, the court noted that "compliance with the Coordination Act might be a consideration in connection with a §509 petition for review of an NPDES permit."[59] In explaining its ruling, the court stated:

> Certainly it would be an unsatisfactory result if the otherwise exclusive mode of review of an NPDES permit's issuance, a §509 petition to the court of appeals, could be circumvented by an action in the district court against Interior. If the failure of Interior to respond substantively to the EPA is reviewable, review must be sought by a §509 petition challenging the issuance of a permit in the absence of either any comment or exercise of discretion not to comment by Interior.[60]

What the court meant by the phrase "in the absence of either any comment or exercise of discretion not to comment by Interior" is difficult to fathom. However, the phrase may be interpreted in light of the court's subsequent pronouncements concerning Interior's consultation obligations under the FWCA. Rejecting the district court's suggestion that "the lack of any express requirement [in the Act] that Interior respond to EPA is an implicit grant of discretion to Interior allowing it to utilize its resources as it sees fit," the court reasoned that "[t]o employ a narrow construction of the word 'consult,' as urged, would be to emasculate the Coordination Act."[61] Indeed, the court asserted that "the consultation requirement of the Coordination Act [is] especially important in the context of NPDES permits."[62] Thus

---

[58]532 F.2d at 289.

[59]*Id.* at n. 10.

[60]532 F.2d at 289 (footnote omitted).

[61]*Id.* at 290.

[62]*Id.* The court thus gave an emphatic affirmative to the question whether the Coordination Act applies to NPDES permits. See 532 F.2d at 288 n. 9. The court was unwilling, however, to express a view as to whether it continued to apply once authority for issuance of NPDES permits was transferred to a state. See 532 F.2d at 289 n. 10. A fascinating history of the persistent and ultimately successful efforts of Congressmen Reuss, Dingell, and Vander Jagt to persuade EPA, the Bureau of

Interior's position that funding and personnel are inadequate to meet the burdensome demands of reviewing NPDES permits is entitled to little weight.... Whatever the reason, while we appreciate the difficulties involved in reviewing the large number of applications forwarded by EPA to Interior, we cannot condone what amounts to administrative or executive repeal of an act of Congress.[63]

Taken together, what the court appears to be saying is that the Coordination Act imposes upon Interior either a nondiscretionary duty to consult, or a duty to exercise a cognizable standard in declining to consult. In either case, Interior's failure to respond to a consultation request should, therefore, be reviewable.

The problem underscored in *Sun Enterprises,* insufficient funds and personnel within the Fish and Wildlife Service to carry out the mandate of the Coordination Act, is of relatively recent vintage, though it has quickly taken on significant proportions. The fact that the problem never emerged until recently can be attributed in large part to the practice of the Corps of Engineers prior to 1970 of not requiring permits under section 10 of the River and Harbor Act of 1899[64] for the erection of structures or the filling of wetlands shoreward of established "harbor lines," or under section 13[65] for the discharge of refuse into navigable waters of the United States. The 1970 reversal of the Corps' harbor line policy at the urging of the House Committee on Government Operations,[66] and the passage of the Federal Water Pollution Control Act amendments of 1972, which substituted the NPDES permit system for the permit requirements of section 13 of the 1899 Act, brought about a quantum leap in the number of permits subject to Coordination Act review by the Fish and Wildlife Service.[67] The

---

Sports Fisheries and Wildlife, and the National Oceanic and Atmospheric Administration that the Coordination Act did apply to section 402 permits is contained in Protecting America's Estuaries: Florida, Hearings Before the Subcomm. on Conservation and Natural Resources of the House Comm. on Government Operations, 93rd Cong., 1st Sess., app. 4, pt. C, at 1261–1342 (1973).

[63]532 F.2d at 290.

[64]33 U.S.C. §403 (1976).

[65]*Id.* §407 (1976).

[66]*See* House Comm. on Government Operations, Our Waters and Wetlands: How the Corps of Engineers Can Help Prevent Their Destruction and Pollution, H.R. Rep. No. 917, 91st Cong., 2d Sess. (1970). The Corps' current harbor line policy declares such lines to be guidelines only for determining the impact on navigation of shoreward structures or fills. *See* 47 Fed. Reg. 31793, 31806 (July 22, 1982) (to be codified at 33 C.F.R. §320.4(o)).

[67]The total number of permit applications to which the Coordination Act applied increased more than eightfold between 1970 and 1974, while the total number of federal wildlife personnel investigating and reporting on the same increased from 248 to only 411. *See* General Accounting Office, Improved Federal Efforts Needed to

workload increased still further as a result of the decision in *Natural Resources Defense Council v. Callaway* substantially expanding the jurisdiction of the Corps of Engineers to issue dredge and fill permits under section 404 of the Clean Water Act.[68]

While the practical problem posed in *Sun Enterprises* is significant, solving it will not enhance the Coordination Act's utility to environmental litigants if the legal problem presented by the first case under the Coordination Act persists. In a number of recent decisions, the courts have brought the Coordination Act back full circle to where it had been decades earlier in *Rank v. Krug* by holding that private plaintiffs cannot even assert causes of action under it.[69]

In *Sierra Club v. Morton*[70] the district court held that no private right of action could be asserted under the Coordination Act, though private plaintiffs could assert claims under sections 9 and 10 of the River and Harbor Act of 1899.[71] Ultimately, that case found its way to the Supreme Court, although by then only the River and Harbor Act questions remained. The Court ruled that no private right of action could be asserted under that statute.[72] Though the Court's opinion never mentioned the Coordination Act, it raises a very serious cloud of doubt whether any different result would apply to the latter statute.[73] However, neither does the Court's opinion address the Administrative Procedure Act (APA), which provides generally for a right of action to any "person suffering legal wrong because of agency action, or adversely affected or aggrieved by

---

Equally Consider Wildlife Conservation with Other Features of Water Resource Development, app. IV, at 57, 59 (1974), and Department of the Interior, Fish and Wildlife Service, Conserving Our Fish and Wildlife Heritage, Annual Report–FY 1975.

[68]392 F. Supp. 685 (D.D.C. 1975). The Fish and Wildlife Service estimated that in fiscal year 1976 an additional 7,000 permit applications would result from the *Callaway* decision. *See* Conserving Our Fish and Wildlife Heritage, *supra* note 67 at 74. Legislative efforts to overturn the *Callaway* decision have been made repeatedly in recent years, but without success.

[69]*See, e.g.,* Environmental Defense Fund v. Alexander, 501 F. Supp. 742, 766–767 (N.D. Miss. 1980), *aff'd in part, rev'd in part on other grounds sub nom.* Environmental Defense Fund v. Marsh, 651 F.2d 983 (5th Cir. 1981); County of Trinity v. Andrus, 438 F. Supp. 1368, 1383 (E.D. Cal. 1977); and Sierra Club v. Morton, 400 F. Supp. 610 (N.D. Cal. 1975), *aff'd in part, rev'd in part on other grounds sub nom.* Sierra Club v. Andrus, 610 F.2d 581 (9th Cir. 1979), *rev'd on other grounds sub nom.* California v. Sierra Club, 451 U.S. 287 (1981).

[70]*See* note 69 *supra.*

[71]33 U.S.C. §§401, 403 (1976).

[72]California v. Sierra Club, 451 U.S. 287 (1981).

[73]Since the Coordination Act, unlike the River and Harbor Act, contains no provision authorizing the Department of Justice to enforce it, the argument in support of a private right of action would appear stronger for the Coordination Act.

agency action within the meaning of a relevant statute."[74] The Supreme Court's opinion may, therefore, elevate form over substance since a properly framed complaint, carefully invoking the APA, would seem to permit judicial review of agency action alleged to violate the Coordination Act.[75]

Even if the Coordination Act has been an ineffective tool for environmental litigants, it does not necessarily follow that the Act has failed to achieve its purposes, for it is always possible that the affected agencies have diligently implemented the statutory policies without the stimulus of judicial intervention. What evidence there is on this, however, is discouraging.

The failure of the Corps of Engineers prior to 1970 to implement fully its permit issuance jurisdiction has already been described. In addition, a study done by the General Accounting Office during 1972 to 1974 examined 11 major development projects and 17 individual permit requests.[76] The GAO study concluded that the policies of the Coordination Act "had not been effectively carried out," because the construction and permitting agencies had not always consulted with the wildlife agencies when required to do so, because the wildlife agencies had often failed either to evaluate adequately the wildlife effects of proposed developments or to make their evaluations available in sufficient time to influence development decisions, and because the Fish and Wildlife Service and the National Marine Fisheries Service had been unable to resolve jurisdictional disputes stemming from the 1970 executive reorganization.[77]

The perceived failure of the Coordination Act to achieve its stated goals has recently resulted in two different responses. Legislatively, the response has taken the form of special measures to address the fish and wildlife conservation needs of the Columbia River system through the Pacific Northwest Electric Power Planning and Conservation Act of 1980.[78] Construction of the first of more than thirty federal and private hydroelec-

---

[74] 5 U.S.C. §702 (1976).

[75] In Chrysler Corp. v. Brown, 441 U.S. 281 (1979), the Court, per Justice Rehnquist, held that the absence of a private right of action under a specific statute is no bar to a litigant obtaining APA review of alleged agency violations of that statute. This holding follows from 5 U.S.C. §704 (1976): "[F]inal agency action *for which there is no other adequate remedy in a court* [is] subject to judicial review." (Emphasis added.) Earlier, the Ninth Circuit recognized that the APA provided a basis for reviewing claims of Coordination Act violations in Association of N.W. Steelheaders v. United States Army Corps of Engineers, 485 F.2d 67, 70 (9th Cir. 1973). For a similar case in another context subsequent to the Supreme Court's opinion, see California v. Watt, 683 F.2d 1253, 1270 (9th Cir. 1982).

[76] General Accounting Office, *supra* note 67.

[77] *Id.* at 43.

[78] 16 U.S.C. §§839–839h (Supp. V 1981).

tric dams on the Columbia River and its tributaries began in 1933, the year prior to enactment of the original Coordination Act. Despite the contemporaneous development of the Coordination Act and of the hydroelectric capacity of the Columbia River, the dams that were the tool of the latter have been the principal cause of a major decline in the anadromous salmon and steelhead trout fisheries of the Columbia.[79] That fact led Congress to conclude in 1980 that existing environmental legislation, including the Coordination Act, "is not adequate to offset the cumulative impact of the hydroelectric dams of the Columbia and its tributaries on fish and wildlife."[80]

The principal requirement of the 1980 law is the development, by a state-appointed regional planning council,[81] of a regional conservation and electric power plan and, as an element thereof, a "program to protect, mitigate, and enhance fish and wildlife, including related spawning grounds and habitat, on the Columbia River and its tributaries."[82] The purpose of the plan and program is to guide the future acquisition of power resources by the Administrator of the Bonneville Power Administration.[83] In addition, the Bonneville Administrator, as well as all other federal agencies responsible for managing, operating, or regulating hydroelectric facilities (federal or private) on the Columbia River, must take into account "to the fullest extent practicable" the regional council's fish and wildlife program "at each relevant stage of decisionmaking processes" in the operation or regulation of such facilities.[84] Thus one important consequence of the legislation may be to require, or at least authorize, modification in the operation of existing dams to reduce fish losses and otherwise promote wildlife conservation.[85]

Whether the Pacific Northwest Electric Power Planning and Conservation Act will be any more successful in bringing about fish and wildlife conservation on the Columbia River than was the Coordination Act will not be known for some time. The regional conservation and electric power plan is to be prepared within two years after the regional council is

---

[79] For a well-documented account of the history of hydroelectric development of the Columbia and of its impact upon the river's fisheries, see Blumm, *supra* note 47.

[80] H.R. Rep. No. 976, pt. I. 96th Cong. 2d Sess. 48 (1980).

[81] 16 U.S.C. §839b(a) (Supp. V 1981). The Act prescribes an alternative mechanism for appointment of council members by the Secretary of Energy in the event the state appointment mechanism fails. *Id.* §839(b).

[82] *Id.* §§839b(e)(3)(F), 839b(h)(1)(A).

[83] *Id.* §§839b(d)(3), 839d.

[84] *Id.* §839b(h)(11)(A)(ii).

[85] An extended and very useful discussion of this and other features of the Act, as well as its legislative history, can be found in 11 Natural Resources L. Inst., Anadromous Fish Law Memo 1 (1981).

established, *i.e.*, before mid-1983. The objective of the legislation is to ensure that fish and wildlife conservation is given equal consideration with the energy objectives of the regional plan. That objective is, in fact, nothing more than the objective of the Coordination Act itself. The means to secure that objective, however, are vastly different in the 1980 legislation. The creation of a new institutional structure, the detailed particularization of decision-making procedures, extensive opportunities for public participation, and express provision for judicial review together represent a major departure from the Coordination Act. If the experiment succeeds, it may serve as a model for improving fish and wildlife conservation in other river systems.

The perceived inadequacies of the Coordination Act have also recently resulted in a more general response at the administrative level. Pursuant to a presidential directive,[86] the Departments of the Interior and Commerce jointly published in 1979 proposed regulations for implementation of the Coordination Act.[87] Following the public comment period, however, they were withdrawn for reconsideration. Modified regulations implementing the Coordination Act were reproposed in 1980.[88] In the Reagan Administration, however, the proposed regulations were again reconsidered and ultimately abandoned.[89]

## THE NATIONAL ENVIRONMENTAL POLICY ACT

Although the National Environmental Policy Act has figured prominently in litigation arising under the Fish and Wildlife Coordination Act, it vastly exceeds the latter in both scope and significance. In fact, NEPA is the most comprehensive, the best known, the most written about, and surely the most litigated federal environmental statute ever enacted.[90] It may also be among the most important federal statutes for the protection of wildlife, yet it never so much as mentions the word "wildlife."

Though the drafters of NEPA omitted any express mention of wildlife, it is hardly likely that they intended to exclude wildlife from its scope. Rather, the broad environmental policies that it enunciates necessarily subsume wildlife conservation. Thus NEPA states its recognition of "the profound impact of man's activity on the interrelations of all components

---

[86] 14 Weekly Comp. of Pres. Doc. 1044 (June 6, 1978).

[87] 44 Fed. Reg. 29300 (May 18, 1979).

[88] 45 Fed. Reg. 83412 (Dec. 18, 1980).

[89] 47 Fed. Reg. 31299 (July 19, 1982).

[90] For general discussions of NEPA, see Liroff, *supra* note 35 and F. Anderson, NEPA in the Courts: A Legal Analysis of the National Environmental Policy Act (1973).

of the natural environment"[91] and declares a policy to "promote efforts which will prevent or eliminate damage to the environment and biosphere,"[92] to "create and maintain conditions under which man and nature can exist in productive harmony,"[93] to "fulfill the responsibilities of each generation as trustee of the environment for succeeding generations,"[94] to "preserve important...natural aspects of our national heritage and maintain, wherever possible, an environment which supports diversity,"[95] and to "enhance the quality of renewable resources."[96]

To accomplish these broadly stated and ambitious objectives, NEPA requires all federal agencies to do certain specific things. The most important of these is to prepare detailed environmental impact statements with respect to all "proposals for legislation and other major Federal actions significantly affecting the quality of the human environment."[97] In preparing these, the agency involved must "consult with and obtain the comments of any Federal agency which has jurisdiction by law or special expertise with respect to any environmental impact involved."[98] When prepared, the statements must be made available to the public, must be included in recommendations or reports concerning the proposal addressed in the statement, and must "accompany the proposal through the existing agency review processes."[99] Accordingly, the clear intent of the required procedure is to force the agency involved to become fully aware of the environmental impacts of the actions it proposes before it commits itself to them. In this way, NEPA's purpose is that avoidable adverse environmental effects be foreseen and avoided.

There has been a great deal of litigation under NEPA in its 14 years of existence. Much of it concerns the question whether particular proposed actions require the preparation of environmental impact statements. The answer usually turns on whether the action is "major," whether it is "federal," and whether it will "significantly" affect the quality of the human environment.[100] Relatively less attention has focused on the fact

[91]42 U.S.C. §4331(a)(1976).

[92]*Id.* §4321.

[93]*Id.* §4331(a).

[94]*Id.* §4331(b)(1).

[95]*Id.* §4331(b)(4).

[96]*Id.* §4331(b)(6).

[97]*Id.* §4332(2)(C).

[98]*Id.*

[99]*Id.*

[100]For a discussion of these issues and citations to many of the cases that have raised them, *see* Baum, Negative NEPA: The Decision Not to File, 6 Envtl. L. 309, 322–39 (1976).

that the environment that NEPA seeks to protect is described as the "human" environment, and the related question whether wildlife is to be considered a part of that environment.[101] The few cases that have touched on that question suggest an affirmative answer. Thus, in *Natural Resources Defense Council v. Grant,* the court stated:

> Any action that substantially affects, beneficially or detrimentally, the depth or course of streams, plant life, wildlife habitats, fish and wildlife, and the soil and air "significantly affects the quality of the human environment."[102]

*Minnesota Public Interest Research Group v. Butz* focused even more narrowly on the meaning of the "human environment."[103] In that action, the plaintiff challenged the Forest Service's failure to prepare an environmental impact statement with respect to the proposed cutting of timber in Minnesota's Boundary Waters Canoe Area (BWCA). The following passage illustrates well the expansive meaning that the court ascribed to the term "human environment":

> [D]efendants contend that any adverse effect on the BWCA does not "significantly affect the quality of the *human* environment" as there is no evidence showing that human users of the BWCA have even seen a timber sale. This appears to be a too restrictive view.... We think NEPA is concerned with indirect effects as well as direct effects. There has been increasing recognition that man and all other life on this earth may be significantly affected by actions which on the surface appear insignificant....Apart from what may be referred to as "existence value," the evidence indicated that there are direct effects on the human environment from logging....[104]

---

[101]There has been considerable litigation and discussion concerning whether impacts of a sociological nature constitute affects on the human environment. *See, e.g.,* Durschslag & Junger, HUD and the Human Environment: A Preliminary Analysis of the Impact of the National Environmental Policy Act of 1969 upon the Department of Housing and Urban Development, 59 Iowa L. Rev. 805 (1973), and Friesma & Culhane, Social Impacts, Politics, and the Environmental Impact Process, 16 Nat. Resources J. 339 (1976). There has also been much commentary on the extraterritorial application of NEPA. Natural Resources Defense Council v. Nuclear Regulatory Comm'n, 647 F.2d 1345 (D.C. Cir. 1981), holding that NEPA does not require the preparation of an impact statement in connection with the licensing of nuclear exports when the only significant impacts occur in a foreign country, contains the most comprehensive discussion of this issue.

[102]341 F. Supp. 356, 367 (E.D.N.C. 1972).

[103]498 F.2d 1314 (8th Cir. 1974).

[104]*Id.* at 1322 (emphasis in original).

Underscoring its concern with effects on "all other life on this earth," the court offered the following explanation of what it meant by the term "existence value":

> Existence value refers to that feeling some people have just knowing that somewhere there remains a true wilderness untouched by human hands, such as the feeling of loss people might feel upon the extinction of the whooping crane even though they had never seen one....[105]

While the foregoing seems clearly to establish that impacts on wildlife will be considered impacts on the human environment, there is some authority suggesting that actions that *only* affect wildlife may not be considered to have "significant" effects on the human environment. In *Kisner v. Butz*, for example, the completion of a 4.3-mile segment of a forest road in Monongahela National Forest was held to be neither a "major" action nor one "significantly" affecting the human environment, where the only recognized impact of the action was to endanger one of the few black bear breeding habitats in the state.[106] On the other hand, in *Action for Rational Transit v. Westside Highway Project* the court held that the Army Corps of Engineers must prepare for itself an environmental impact statement when a statement previously prepared for the same project by a related federal agency failed to assess adequately the impacts of the project on fishery resources.[107]

Once it is established that an impact statement is needed, NEPA requires that it discuss, among other things, possible adverse effects of the proposed action and alternatives thereto.[108] The Council on Environmental Quality's implementing regulations, which elaborate on NEPA's requirements, specify that impact statements are to include discussions of "[n]atural or depletable resource requirements and conservation potential of various alternatives and mitigation measures."[109] This requirement, when coupled with the further requirement to consult with and obtain the comments of other federal agencies having special expertise with respect to

---

[105]*Id.* at n. 27.

[106]350 F. Supp. 312 (N.D. W.Va. 1972). *See also* note 124 *infra.*

[107]536 F. Supp. 1225 (S.D.N.Y. 1982).

[108]42 U.S.C. § 4332(2)(C)(1976).

[109]40 C.F.R. § 1502.16(f)(1981). The Council's regulations were promulgated in 1978 pursuant to Executive Order 11, 991, 3 C.F.R. 124 (1977 Comp.). They replace earlier informal "guidelines" and they have been held by the Supreme Court to be "entitled to substantial deference." Andrus v. Sierra Club, 442 U.S. 347, 358 (1979). All federal agencies have developed their own supplemental procedures to guide their compliance with the Council's general regulations.

the environmental impact involved, guarantees for the Fish and Wildlife Service and other resource conservation agencies access to the decision-making processes of other federal agencies and creates a substantial likelihood that such access will at least result in a rational discussion of the alternatives.[110] NEPA thus forces federal agencies unaccustomed to treating environmental considerations seriously to do so. To the extent that the environmental "consciousness" of such agencies is raised thereby, wildlife is likely to be among the beneficiaries.

A related salutary impact of NEPA is that it has been interpreted to enlarge the statutory authority of federal agencies to encompass environmental protection. This aspect of NEPA is illustrated well by two related cases, *Public Service Company of New Hampshire v. U.S. Nuclear Regulatory Commission*[111] and *Detroit Edison Company v. U.S. Nuclear Regulatory Commission*.[112] Both cases involved challenges to the authority of a federal licensing agency to impose in its licenses conditions pertaining to environmental quality unrelated to the agency's specific statutory mandate. Challenged in *Public Service Company of New Hampshire* was the authority of the Nuclear Regulatory Commission to condition a license for the construction of nuclear facilities on the rerouting of certain off-site transmission lines so as to avoid a wetland area that, among other things, served as an important habitat area for migratory waterfowl. The court examined the Commission's organic statute to determine whether there was an "inevitable clash" between it and the broad duties imposed by NEPA.[113] Finding none, the court held that the challenged authority derived from NEPA, which it said obliged the Commission, in exercising its authority to condition licenses, to "minimize the adverse environmental impact flowing therefrom."[114] *Detroit Edison* involved a generic challenge

---

[110] According to an early report by the Council on Environmental Quality, the Fish and Wildlife Service invested more of its resources in commenting on the impact statements of other agencies than did any other federal agency, except the Department of Commerce. *See* Council on Environmental Quality, Environmental Impact Statements: An Analysis of Six Years' Experience by Seventy Federal Agencies 46 (March 1976). While the "returns" on such investments are obviously difficult to measure, the comments of the Fish and Wildlife Service and other wildlife organizations and agencies have sometimes apparently had major impacts in causing the modification of agency proposals. *See* Andrews, Agency Responses to NEPA: A Comparison and Implications, 16 Nat. Resources J. 301, 317 (1976).

[111] 582 F.2d 77 (1st Cir.), *cert. denied*, 439 U.S. 1046 (1978).

[112] 630 F.2d 450 (6th Cir. 1980). For yet a third case from another circuit illustrating the point made here, see Grindstone Butte Project v. Kleppe, 638 F.2d 100 (9th Cir. 1981), *cert. denied*, 454 U.S. 965 (1982).

[113] 582 F.2d at 82.

[114] *Id.* at 85.

to the same agency's conditional licensing authority. The court rejected that challenge in the following broad terms: "Under the Atomic Energy Act, the Commission can issue conditional licenses for regulatory purposes. There can be no objection to its use of the same means to achieve environmental ends as well."[115]

The resource conservation agencies have responsibilities under NEPA beyond that of commenting on the proposals of development-oriented agencies. Most fundamentally, they are subject to NEPA's requirement that an impact statement be prepared for all major actions significantly affecting the quality of the human environment. Apparently thinking that NEPA was intended to apply only to agencies that had not previously had any mandate to consider environmental factors, many resource conservation agencies initially resisted its application to themselves.[116] Such resistance was reinforced by broad statements in cases concerning the Environmental Protection Agency that NEPA might not be applicable to "environmentally protective regulatory agencies."[117] To a limited extent, that resistance has been vindicated.[118] In general, however, exemptions from NEPA's requirements have been narrowly construed, and it is now accepted that even agencies like the Fish and Wildlife Service, whose sole mission is resource conservation, are subject to NEPA's requirements.

Engrafting NEPA procedures onto the established procedures of the federal wildlife agencies has not been without its difficulties. For the first several years after NEPA's passage, most of the environmental impact statements prepared by all federal agencies were related to specific individual projects. Thus the Fish and Wildlife Service prepared individual statements for the inclusion of specific areas in the National Wildlife Refuge or National Wilderness Preservation Systems,[119] and, for certain special regulatory actions, such as the proposed injurious wildlife regula-

---

[115]630 F.2d at 454.

[116]See R. Liroff, supra note 35 at 125–126, and Wichelman, Administrative Agency Implementation of the National Environmental Policy Act of 1969: A Conceptual Framework for Explaining Differential Response, 16 Nat. Resources J. 264, 269 (1976).

[117]Portland Cement Ass'n v. Ruckelshaus, 486 F.2d 375, 381 (D.C. Cir. 1973).

[118]The listing of species as threatened or endangered under the Endangered Species Act was held not to require the preparation of an environmental impact statement in Pacific Legal Foundation v. Andrus, 657 F.2d 829 (6th Cir. 1981). Similarly, no statement has been required with respect to the acquiescence of federal agencies in state wildlife control programs carried out on federal lands. See Defenders of Wildlife v. Andrus, 627 F.2d 1328 (D.C. Cir. 1980) and Alaska v. Andrus 591 F.2d 537 (9th Cir. 1979).

[119]According to Liroff, supra note 35 at 126, the Bureau of Sports Fisheries and Wildlife prepared its first impact statement for a wilderness designation in January 1972, even though it had completed over a dozen wilderness studies in the preceding two years.

tions under the Lacey Act[120] and the migratory waterfowl lead shot regulations.[121] For many actions that were part of long established and ongoing wildlife programs, the proper scope of the required statement was uncertain. Thus, in 1974, certain plaintiffs challenged the 1974–75 migratory bird–hunting regulations because of the Department of the Interior's failure to prepare an accompanying environmental impact statement.[122] The case was settled out of court upon the Fish and Wildlife Service's agreement to prepare a "programmatic" statement applicable to the annual regulation-setting process.[123] When the Service proposed in the following year to permit the hunting of certain species that had not been hunted in immediately preceding years, the same plaintiffs went back to court claiming that a new impact statement was required. That claim was rejected, however, in part on the grounds that the programmatic statement had discussed in general terms the effects of regulated bird hunting, thus eliminating the need for more specific statements.[124]

Several conclusions emerge from the foregoing. First, it is apparent that programmatic statements applicable to certain on-going wildlife programs may in some cases take the place of more particularized statements. Second, it is clear that NEPA offers a means of limited judicial intervention in the administration of federal wildlife programs. The major limitation is that, with respect to the decision making of both development oriented and resource conservation agencies, NEPA is at bottom a procedural statute.

Early in NEPA's history, some courts and a few commentators urged that NEPA impose substantive, judicially enforceable standards of envi-

---

[120]Department of the Interior, Fish and Wildlife Service, Draft Environmental Statement on Proposed Injurious Wildlife Regulations (DES 75–6, Feb. 1976).

[121]Department of the Interior, Fish and Wildlife Service, Final Environmental Statement, Proposed Use of Steel Shot for Hunting Waterfowl in the United States (Jan. 1976).

[122]Fund for Animals, Inc. v. Morton, Civil No. 74-1581 (D.N.J. 1974).

[123]So-called "programmatic" statements are authorized, and indeed encouraged, by the Council on Environmental Quality's regulations. See 40 C.F.R. §1502.4(b) (1981). They have also been given explicit sanction by the courts. See, e.g., Scientists' Institute for Pub. Information v. AEC, 481 F.2d 1079 (D.C. Cir. 1973). For a discussion of the problem of knowing when a programmatic statement, rather than an individual statement, is appropriate, and a recommended solution to the problem, see Miller, Anderson & Liroff, The National Environmental Policy Act and Agency Policy Making: Neither Paper Tiger nor Straitjacket. 6 Envtl. L. Rep. (Envtl. L. Inst.) 50020 (1976).

[124]Fund for Animals v. Frizzell, 530 F.2d 982 (D.C. Cir. 1976). The court was not as clear on this point as one would have liked, for it also found that no new impact statement was required because the effects on the human environment of the proposed new regulations were insignificant. Id. at 989 n. 15.

ronmental quality.[125] The Supreme Court, however, has not embraced that view. In *Vermont Yankee Nuclear Power Corp. v. Natural Resources Defense Council,* the Court stated that, although NEPA established "significant goals for the Nation," its obligations were "essentially procedural."[126] Two years later, this decision was reinforced in *Stryker's Bay Neighborhood Council, Inc. v. Karlen,* in which the Court declared that NEPA required only "consider[ation of]...environmental consequences....NEPA requires no more."[127] Nonetheless, the *Stryker's* opinion clearly implies that an agency's consideration of the environmental consequences of its actions can still be struck down, pursuant to the Administrative Procedure Act,[128] if it is arbitrary and capricious. Thus, even if NEPA's obligations are purely procedural, its mandate that agencies unaccustomed to thinking about the environmental effects of their activities do so will continue to be of substantial benefit to wildlife.

## THE PROTECTION OF COASTAL AND ESTUARINE AREAS

The nation's coastal and estuarine areas are of great importance for marine life, migratory birds, and other forms of wildlife. At the same time, however, such areas offer obvious attractions for commercial, residential, recreational, and other types of development often inimical to wildlife interests. The first federal effort to assess the status of these areas with specific reference to their wildlife attributes was included in the Clean Water Restoration Act of 1966.[129] That Act directed the Secretary of the Interior to undertake a "comprehensive study of the effects of pollution, including sedimentation, in the estuaries and estuarine zones of the United States on fish and wildlife, on sport and commercial fishing, on recreation, on water supply and water power, and on other beneficial purposes."[130]

---

[125] For a sampling of some of the commentary, containing citations to the relevant cases, *see* Yarrington, Judicial Review of Substantive Agency Decisions: A Second Generation of Cases Under the National Environmental Policy Act, 19 S.D.L. Rev. 279 (1974); Kumin, Substantive Review Under the National Environmental Policy Act: EDF v. Corps of Engineers, 3 Ecology L.Q. 173 (1973): Arnold, The Substantive Right to Environmental Quality Under the National Environmental Policy Act, Envtl. L. Rep. (Envtl. L. Inst.) 50028 (1973); and Note, The Least Adverse Alternative Approach to Substantive Review Under NEPA, 88 Harv. L. Rev. 735 (1975).

[126] 435 U.S. 519, 558 (1978).

[127] 444 U.S. 223, 227 (1980).

[128] 5 U.S.C. §706(2)(A)(1976).

[129] Pub. L. No. 89-753, 80 Stat. 1246 (superseded 1972).

[130] *Id.* §201(b) (superseding version at 33 U.S.C. §1254(n)(1)(1976)).

The scope of the Secretary's study was expanded two years later by the Estuarine Areas Act,[131] which declared as its purpose

> to provide a means for considering the need to protect, conserve, and restore these estuaries in a manner that adequately and reasonably maintains a balance between the national need for such protection in the interest of conserving the natural resources and natural beauty of the Nation and the need to develop these estuaries to further the growth and development of the Nation.[132]

To accomplish that purpose, it directed the Secretary of the Interior to carry out, in conjunction with the ongoing pollution study, a "study and inventory of the Nation's estuaries," including those of the Great Lakes. In the course of this expanded study, he was further specifically directed to consider, among other things, "their wildlife and recreational potential, their ecology, their value to the marine, anadromous, and shell fisheries and their esthetic value."[133]

One of the objects of the study mandated by the Estuarine Areas Act was to identify particular areas, the protection of which required state or federal acquisition.[134] It also authorized the Secretary of the Interior, subsequent to the completion of the study, to enter into agreements with the states concerning the administration and management of estuarine areas owned by the states.[135] Finally, it directed him to "encourage states and local subdivisions to consider, in their comprehensive planning and proposals for financial assistance" under the Pittman-Robertson Act, the Dingell-Johnson Act, the Land and Water Conservation Fund Act and other federal grant programs, "the needs and opportunities for protecting and restoring estuaries."[136]

The Secretary of the Interior completed the required study in 1969.[137] Rather than serve as the stimulus for prompt legislative action, however, it had little noticeable impact, in part because the Federal Water Pollution Control Administration, which had directed the study for the Secretary of the Interior, was transferred from the Interior Department to the newly

---

[131] 16 U.S.C. §§1221–1226 (1976).

[132] *Id.* §1221.

[133] *Id.* §1222(a).

[134] *Id.* §1222(b).

[135] *Id.* §1223.

[136] *Id.* §1225.

[137] Federal Water Pollution Control Administration, The National Estuarine Pollution Study (1969), Doc. No. 58, 91st Cong., 2d Sess. (1970).

created Environmental Protection Agency in the year following its completion.[138]

In 1972, however, major federal legislation affecting the future development, not only of the nation's estuaries, but of its entire coasts and Great Lakes, was passed in the form of the Coastal Zone Management Act, administered by the Secretary of Commerce.[139] The object of the 1972 Act was "to preserve, protect, develop, and where possible, to restore or enhance, the resources of the Nation's coastal zone for this and succeeding generations."[140] It was to accomplish this by encouraging the states to develop and implement "management programs" for the protection and development of their coastal zones that would give "full consideration to ecological, cultural, historic, and esthetic values as well as to needs for economic development."[141] State management programs are to provide for nine specified objectives, the first of which is "the protection of natural resources, including wetlands, flood plains, estuaries, beaches, dunes, barrier islands, coral reefs and fish and wildlife and their habitat."[142] Two incentives were held out to the states for the development of such management programs. One was the familiar incentive of federal money, originally on a two-to-one matching basis and more recently on a four-to-one basis for the development and implementation of state programs.[143] The other was the promise that once a state management program was developed and approved, most federal activities or development projects in or affecting a state's coastal zone would have to be "consistent with" the state's management program.[144] These incentives were sufficient to induce each of the 30 eligible states to begin planning for the development of their own management programs; 28 states have now developed approved programs.

No effort will be made here to analyze in detail each of the many steps involved in the process of developing and securing federal approval for state coastal zone management programs. That sort of analysis, together

---

[138]See Power, the Federal Role in Coastal Development, in Federal Environmental Law 792, 836 (E. Dolgin & T. Guilbert eds. 1974).

[139]16 U.S.C. §§1451–1464 (1976 & Supp. V 1981).

[140]Id. §1452(1)(Supp. V 1981).

[141]Id. §1452(2).

[142]Id. §1452(2)(A).

[143]Id. §1454, 1455. The Reagan Administration has endeavored to eliminate grants for the implementation of approved state programs.

[144]Id. §1456(c), (d). The Act's consistency provisions have been described as potentially "one of the most important mechanisms for state and local governments to assert their developmental and environmental objectives against an unsympathetic federal government." Greenberg, Federal Consistency Under the Coastal Zone Management Act: An Emerging Focus of Environmental Controversy in the 1980's, 11 Envtl. L. Rep. (Envtl. L. Inst.) 50001, 50001 (1981).

with a discussion of some of the perplexing legal questions raised by the Act, can be found elsewhere.[145] Rather, the intention here is to focus narrowly on those aspects of the Coastal Zone Management Act of most significance for wildlife conservation purposes.

The Act prescribes nine features that must be included in every state management program. The most significant of these is that the program include "[a]n inventory and designation of areas of particular concern."[146] While the statute does not itself define such areas, the implementing regulations include several examples that underscore the importance of this concept for wildlife purposes. Thus the regulations offer the following factors to assist in the designation of such areas:

(A) Areas of unique, scarce, fragile, or vulnerable natural habitat...; (B) Areas of high natural productivity or essential habitat for living resources, including fish, wildlife, and the various trophic levels in the food web critical to their well-being; (C) Areas of substantial recreational value and/or opportunity;...and (G) Areas needed to protect, maintain, or replenish coastal lands or resources, such areas including coastal flood plains, aquifer recharge areas, sand dunes, coral and other reefs, beaches, offshore sand deposits, and mangrove stands.[147]

Closely related to the designation of areas of particular concern are the requirements that the management program contain "[b]road guidelines on priorities of uses in particular areas"[148] and that it identify "the means by which the state proposes to exert control over" such uses.[149] Before approving a state management program, the Secretary must find that it provides for "procedures whereby specific areas may be designated for the purpose of preserving or restoring them for their conservation, recreational, ecological, or esthetic values."[150] These requirements give substantive effect to the designation of critical areas by assuring a means of protection for them.

Apart from the Act's substantive requirements for state management programs, there are also certain procedural requirements that assure a voice

---

[145]See, e.g., Power supra note 138. See also American Petroleum Inst. v. Knecht, 609 F.2d 1306 (9th Cir. 1979), the only reported case involving a challenge to the approval of a state management plan.

[146]16 U.S.C. §1454(b)(3)(1976).

[147]15 C.F.R. §920.13(b)(1)(1981).

[148]16 U.S.C. §1454(b)(5)(1976).

[149]Id. §1454(b)(4).

[150]Id. §1455(c)(9). The Secretary may make grants to eligible states for the preservation or restoration of such areas as well as for areas containing coastal resources of national significance. Id. §1455a(b)(1)(Supp. V 1981). See note 153 infra.

for wildlife proponents in the development of such programs. Thus, before the Secretary may approve a management program, thereby making it eligible for federal "administrative grants," he must find that the state has held public hearings and given "the opportunity of full participation [to] relevant Federal agencies,... and other interested parties, public and private."[151] Further, the Secretary must find that the management program "provides for adequate consideration of the national interest involved in... the siting of facilities... which are necessary to meet requirements which are other than local in nature."[152] While this requirement was apparently directed principally at energy-related facilities, it is broad enough to encompass regional or national conservation needs.[153]

The other feature of the Act that may have substantial importance for wildlife purposes is a provision authorizing the Secretary to make available to coastal states federal grants of up to 50 percent of the cost of acquiring, developing, and operating "estuarine sanctuaries,"[154] defined in the Act as "a research area which may include any part or all of an estuary and any island, transitional area, and upland in, adjoining, or adjacent to such estuary, and which constitutes to the extent feasible a natural unit, set aside to provide scientists and students the opportunity to examine over a period of time the ecological relationships within the area."[155] This provision also authorizes similar grants for "acquiring lands to provide for the preservation of islands."[156] The estuarine sanctuary and island acquisition authority is given without regard to whether a particular state applying for a grant has established a coastal zone management program, although the implementing regulations state that among the criteria to be considered in passing on applications for estuarine sanctuary grants is "the benefit of the proposal to the development or operations of the overall coastal zone management program."[157]

From the foregoing, it is apparent that the Coastal Zone Management Act offers at least the potential for coordinated state and federal wildlife conservation in an ecological area with substantial significance for

---

[151]*Id.* §1455(c)(1)(1976).

[152]*Id.* §1455(c)(8).

[153]Section 306(i) of the Act, 16 U.S.C. §1455(i)(Supp. V 1981), encourages states to provide in their management programs for the designation and protection of "coastal resources of national significance," a term defined to include "fish or wildlife habitat... determined by a coastal state to be of substantial biological... value." *Id.* §1453(2).

[154]16 U.S.C. §1461(1)(1976 & Supp. V 1981).

[155]*Id.* §1453(8)(Supp. V 1981).

[156]*Id.* §1461(2).

[157]15 C.F.R. §921.20(a)(1981).

wildlife. Like NEPA, however, the purposes of the Coastal Zone Management Act are far broader than just wildlife conservation. Still, it provides one more mechanism for introducing into the planning of future development activities some consideration of their likely effects on our wildlife resources.

## WILDLIFE AND FEDERAL POLLUTION CONTROL LAWS

It was said at the outset of this book that there is no satisfactory way to draw a line between those federal statutes that may properly be considered within the body of "wildlife law" and those outside it. For it is true of nearly every law that, if one looks at its effects rather than its purposes, one can almost always find a significant wildlife effect. Nowhere is this more evident than in connection with the recent federal pollution statutes.

Consider the problem of air pollution. The federal laws that seek to control it are principally concerned with human health and secondarily with a broadly defined "public welfare." Yet recent evidence would indicate that one of the major threats to certain types of wildlife—indeed, whole ecosystems—in various parts of the world, including the northeastern United States, is "acid rain," a phenomenon caused by ever-increasing emissions of pollutants, especially sulfur dioxide, into the atmosphere.[158] Thus laws to control air pollution may be among the most important federal wildlife laws, yet one finds wildlife mentioned only once in the Clean Air Act.[159]

One of the principal mechanisms established by the Clean Air Act of 1970 for the control of air pollution is the promulgation of so-called "primary" and "secondary" ambient air quality standards by the Administrator of the Environmental Protection Agency (EPA) for each air pollutant found by him to be adverse to the public health or welfare. The primary standard is intended to establish that level of air purity necessary to "protect the public health," allowing for "an adequate margin of safety."[160] The secondary standard is intended "to protect the public welfare from any known or anticipated adverse effects."[161] The Act's definition of public welfare is the only place the word "wildlife" appears, and there it is lumped

---

[158]See, e.g., Ferenbaugh, Acid Rain: Biological Effects and Implications, 4 Envtl. Aff. 745 (1975), and Risebrough, The Effects of Pesticides and Other Toxicants, in Council on Environmental Quality, Wildlife and American (1978).

[159]42 U.S.C. §§7401–7642 (Supp. IV 1980).

[160]Id. §7409(b)(1).

[161]Id. §7409(b)(2).

together with "soils, water, crops, vegetation, manmade materials,...
weather, visibility, and climate" and still other factors.[162]

Thus the only time that air pollution effects on wildlife must be
considered is in connection with the promulgation of secondary ambient
air quality standards. Those standards were promulgated for certain
pollutants as early as 1971.[163] The Act requires that each state submit to the
Administrator within nine months after promulgation of the primary and
secondary standards a plan or plans for the implementation, maintenance,
and enforcement of the primary standards within three years thereafter and
of the secondary standards within "a reasonable time."[164] What constitutes
a reasonable time has not been determined.[165]

Thus, despite the apparent threat to wildlife from atmospheric
pollution, the Clean Air Act offers only very limited mechanisms for the
protection of wildlife. The secondary standards can be made more stringent
and the "reasonable time" limit might arguably require speeding up of
implementation plans in order to avert a wildlife catastrophe. In both
cases, however, the Administrator's discretion to act or not act is very broad.

Considerably more attention to the protection of wildlife is reflected in
the federal statutes regulating water pollution. Indeed, the Clean Water
Act[166] states as its fundamental objective the restoration and maintenance
of "the chemical, physical, and biological integrity of the Nation's
waters"[167] and as one of its two national goals the attainment by July 1,
1983, of a level of water quality "which provides for the protection and
propagation of fish, shellfish, and wildlife and provides for recreation in
and on the water."[168]

To meet its objectives, the Act establishes an elaborate enforcement
mechanism, the principal features of which are federally promulgated
"effluent limitations" and state-promulgated "water quality standards."
Effluent limitations prescribe for particular types of pollutant dischargers
the level of permissible discharge, generally in terms of a specified amount

---

[162]Id. §7602(h).

[163]See 40 C.F.R. §§50.5–50.12 (1981).

[164]42 U.S.C. §7410(a)(2)(A)(Supp. IV 1980).

[165]See Train v. Natural Resources Defense Council, 421 U.S. 60, 80 (1975); Ohio
Environmental Council v. EPA, 593 F.2d 24, 31 (6th Cir. 1979).

[166]33 U.S.C. §§1251–1376 (1976 & Supp. V 1981).

[167]Id. §1251(a)(1976).

[168]Id. §1251(a)(2). This goal, characterized as an "interim goal," is qualified by the
words "wherever attainable." The Act's ultimate goal is the elimination of the
discharge of all pollutants into navigable waters by 1985. Id. §1251(a)(1). Though
not expressly qualified, this goal too is subject to a number of economic and
technological constraints. See Zener, The Federal Law of Water Pollution Control,
in Federal Environmental Law 723–26 (E. Dolgin & T. Guilbert eds. 1974).

per unit of time or unit of production, or a specified concentration. Such limitations are to be attained in two stages. The first stage, to have been attained by July 1, 1977, requires certain point source discharges to reduce their discharge of pollutants to the level provided by the "best practicable control technology currently available."[169] The second stage, to be achieved by July 1, 1983, requires reduction to the level provided by the "best available technology economically achievable."[170] State-promulgated water quality standards, on the other hand, establish the permissible levels of ambient water pollution for particular water bodies and are keyed directly to the biological and other effects of particular ambient pollution levels.[171]

In the development and periodic revision of their water quality standards, the states are to be guided by certain information and criteria developed by the Administrator of EPA. Among other things, such information and criteria must specify "the kind and extent of all identifiable effects on health and welfare including, but not limited to, plankton, fish, shellfish, wildlife, plant life, shorelines, beaches, esthetics, and recreation which may be expected from the presence of pollutants in any body of water"[172] and "the factors necessary for the protection and propagation of shellfish, fish, and wildlife for classes and categories of receiving waters."[173]

There is one special category of pollutants subject to federally promulgated effluent limitations based on considerations of their effects as well as available control technology. For all "toxic pollutants," defined as those pollutants or combinations of pollutants that will "cause death, disease, behavioral abnormalities, cancer, genetic mutations, physiological malfunction (including malfunctions in reproduction) or physical deformations" in any organism,[174] effluent limitations "shall take into account the toxicity of the pollutant,...the usual or potential presence of the affected organisms in any waters, the importance of the affected organisms and the nature and extent of the effect of the toxic pollutant on such organisms."[175]

---

[169]33 U.S.C. §1311(b)(1)(A)(1976). The term "point source" means "any discernible, confined and discrete conveyance, including but not limited to any pipe, ditch, channel, tunnel, conduit, well, discrete fissure, container, rolling stock, concentrated animal feeding operation, or vessel or other floating craft, from which pollutants are or may be discharged." Id. §1362(14)(Supp. V 1981).

[170]Id. §1311(b)(2)(A).

[171]Id. §1313 (1976).

[172]Id. §1314(a)(1)(A).

[173]Id. §1314(a)(2).

[174]Id. §1362(13).

[175]Id. §1317(a)(2)(1976 & Supp. V 1981).

If the 1977 effluent limitations promulgated by the Administrator are not stringent enough to implement any water quality standard applicable to any waters of a state, the state must establish the "total maximum daily loads" for certain pollutants in those waters and an appropriate allocation system so as not to exceed such maximum loads.[176] Here a special provision is made for thermal discharges. Each state is required to identify those waters within its boundaries "for which controls on thermal discharges... are not stringent enough to assure protection and propagation of a balanced indigenous population of shellfish, fish and wildlife," and to estimate the maximum daily thermal load necessary to assure such protection.[177] If approved by the Administrator, the maximum daily thermal load must also be incorporated into the state control system.

Water quality–related effluent limitations more stringent than the technology based effluent limitations may also be imposed by the Administrator if he determines that

> discharges of pollutants from a point source or groups of point sources...
> would interfere with the attainment or maintenance of that water quality
> in a specific portion of the navigable waters which shall assure protection
> of public water supplies, agricultural and industrial uses, and the
> protection and propagation of a balanced population of shellfish, fish
> and wildlife, and allow recreational activities in and on the water....[178]

Given that even these effluent limitations must be based in part on economic and technological considerations,[179] it is unclear how the above authority will be translated into more stringent effluent limitations.[180]

The basic day-to-day mechanism for implementation of the Act is provided by two permit systems. The broader of these is the National Pollutant Discharge Elimination System or NPDES permit program, under which any person wishing to discharge any pollutant from a point source into navigable waters must first obtain a permit.[181] Permits are issued either by the Administrator or by the state if the latter has an approved NPDES program.[182]

NPDES permits are also required for the discharge of pollutants into the territorial sea or the oceans. Such permits, however, must comply with

---

[176]*Id.* §1313(d).

[177]*Id.*

[178]*Id.* §1312(a).

[179]*See* 33 U.S.C. §1312(b)(1976).

[180]*See* Zener, *supra* note 168 at 724–726.

[181]33 U.S.C. §1342 (1976 & Supp. V 1981).

[182]*See id.* §1342(b)–1342(f).

special guidelines developed by the Administrator that determine the effect of disposal of pollutants on "human health or welfare, including but not limited to plankton, fish, shellfish, wildlife, shorelines, and beaches"[183] and on "marine life including...changes in marine ecosystem diversity, productivity, and stability; and species and community population changes."[184] This permit requirement overlaps somewhat similar requirements imposed by the Marine Protection, Research, and Sanctuaries Act.[185] The latter act prohibits, except under permit, both the dumping of materials into ocean waters and the transportation of any materials from the United States or by a United States vessel for the purpose of dumping them into ocean waters.[186] Permits for the former are issued by the Administrator of EPA in accordance with guidelines essentially identical to those prescribed by the Clean Water Act.[187]

For the transportation and dumping of dredged materials into the ocean, the Corps of Engineers has permit-granting authority.[188] In issuing such permits, however, the Corps must comply with the same guidelines that govern the Administrator's permit-issuing authority. Further, the Administrator may object to the issuance of any permit if he believes it not to be in compliance with the guidelines. The Corps may overrule his objection only if there is no "economically feasible method or site available" and unless the Administrator finds that the dumping "will result in an unacceptably adverse impact on municipal water supplies, shell-fish beds, wildlife, fisheries (including spawning and breeding areas), or recreational areas."[189]

The second major permitting program under the Clean Water Act regulates the discharge of "dredged or fill" material into the nation's waters. This program, which implements section 404 of the Act, is an important tool for the protection of wetland and other wildlife habitats.[190] The United States Army Corps of Engineers, which administers the section 404 program, estimates that the program has slowed the loss of wetlands by 300,000 acres annually.[191] In *Natural Resources Defense Council v.*

---

[183]*Id.* §1343(c)(1)(A).

[184]*Id.* §1343(c)(1)(B).

[185]33 U.S.C. §§1401–1444 (1976 & Supp. V 1981) and 16 U.S.C. §§1431–1434 (1976 & Supp. V 1981).

[186]33 U.S.C. §1411(b)(1976).

[187]*Id.* §1412(a).

[188]*Id.* §1413.

[189]*Id.* §1413(d).

[190]33 U.S.C. §1344 (Supp. V 1981).

[191]U.S. Army Corps of Engineers, Draft Impact Analysis of the Corps Regulatory Program 112 (1982).

*Callaway*,[192] the District Court for the District of Columbia ruled that the "waters of the United States" to which section 404 applies were intended to include all waters that Congress may constitutionally regulate under its commerce clause authority. Prior to that decision, the Corps of Engineers had limited its jurisdiction to traditionally navigable waters. The expansion of regulatory jurisdiction that the *Callaway* decision mandated brought such ecologically significant areas as prairie potholes, playa lakes, and wet tundra under the purview of section 404.

The Corps' initial response to the *Callaway* decision was gradually to phase in nonnavigable waters.[193] However, in 1982 the Corps issued certain "nationwide general permits," which effectively provide a blanket authorization for the discharge of dredged or fill material by any person at any time and without any prior or after-the-fact notice, into most of the very waters that the *Callaway* decision had directed the Corps to begin regulating.[194] Although Congress in 1977 had given the Corps limited authority to issue general permits in lieu of individual discharger-by-discharger permits, that authority extends only to the categories of activities that are similar in nature and that have only minimal individual and cumulative adverse environmental effects.[195] Whether the 1982 general permits satisfy these requirements is a question now in litigation.[196]

Section 404 contains no express standard to govern the issuance or denial of dredge and fill permits. Both individual and general permits are to be "based on" guidelines developed by the EPA Administrator comparable to those previously described for ocean dumping permits.[197] Apart from those guidelines, which specify in considerable detail the biological and other impacts that the Corps must consider, Corps permitting decisions are based on an administratively developed "public interest" test that attempts to balance economic, environmental, social, and other factors.[198] Occasionally, application of that test results in decisions to condition permits so as to reduce adverse impacts on wildlife and their habitats or to deny permit applications altogether.[199]

---

[192]392 F. Supp. 685 (D.D.C. 1975).

[193]The Corps' approach was described in 40 Fed. Reg. 31322 (July 25, 1975).

[194]The permits described in the text were published at 47 Fed. Reg. 31793, 31832 (July 22, 1982) and are to be codified at 33 C.F.R. §4330.4.

[195]33 U.S.C. §1344(e)(Supp. V 1981).

[196]National Wildlife Federation v. Marsh, Civil Act. No. 82-3632 (D.D.C. filed Dec. 22, 1982).

[197]33 U.S.C. §1344(a), (e)(Supp. V 1981). The EPA Guidelines are published at 40 C.F.R. part 230 (1981).

[198]*See* 47 Fed. Reg. 31793, 31803–31806 (to be codified at 33 C.F.R. §320.4).

[199]*See* Deltona Corp. v. Alexander, 504 F. Supp. 1280 (M. D. Fla. 1981), *aff'd*, 682 F.2d 888 (11th Cir. 1982). The Administrator has the authority under section 404(c),

Important though section 404 may be for the protection of wetlands, it provides a means only of regulating their loss through filling activities. Some wetland areas, like the bottomland hardwood forests of the Southeast, are being reduced through clearing and conversion to agricultural land. In *Avoyelles Sportsmen's League v. Alexander,* these activities also were brought within the compass of section 404, where the mechanized clearing of vegetation resulted in incidental discharge of scraped soil and leaf litter into the wetlands.[200] If that decision, now on appeal, is sustained, it will represent a major expansion of section 404 to activities not traditionally regarded as involving the discharge of dredged or fill material.

The last subject worthy of mention here relates to the prevention and clean-up of oil spills or spills of other hazardous substances. The Clean Water Act provides for the assessment of penalties against persons responsible for such spills in the navigable waters of the United States or the waters of the contiguous zone. As part of this program, the Act directs the Administrator to promulgate regulations

> designating as hazardous substances, other than oil...such elements and compounds which, when discharged...into [such] waters...present an imminent and substantial danger to the public health or welfare, including, but not limited to, fish, shellfish, wildlife, shorelines, and beaches.[201]

The Act also directs the President to determine by regulation the quantities of the above substances that will cause the described adverse effects. This authority is subject to the qualification that

> in the case of the discharge of oil into or upon the waters of the contiguous zone, only those discharges which threaten the fishery resources of the contiguous zone or threaten to pollute or contribute to the pollution of the territory or the territorial sea of the United States may be determined to be harmful.[202]

Finally, the Intervention on the High Seas Act[203] authorizes the Coast Guard to take measures on the high seas to prevent, mitigate, or eliminate

---

13 U.S.C. §1344(c)(Supp. V 1981), to prohibit the specification of particular disposal sites under permits issued by the Corps if he determines that discharge at such sites will have unacceptable adverse effects on fishery areas, wildlife, and other specified interests.

[200]473 F. Supp. 525 (W. D. La. 1979), and 511 F. Supp. 278 (W. D. La. 1981).

[201]33 U.S.C. §1321(b)(2)(A)(Supp. V 1981).

[202]*Id.* §1321(b)(4).

[203]33 U.S.C. §§1471–1487 (1976).

the danger of harm from an oil spill on the high seas when it poses "a grave and imminent danger to the coastline or related interests of the United States."[204] The determination of whether a grave and imminent danger exists must be based in part upon consideration of the threat posed to "fish, shellfish, and other living marine resources, [and] wildlife."[205]

Less expressly solicitous of wildlife interests are recent laws governing hazardous chemical substances.[206] The Toxic Substances Control Act,[207] for example, authorizes the Administrator of EPA to regulate the manufacture, processing, or distribution in commerce of any chemical substance that "presents or will present an unreasonable risk of injury to health or the environment."[208] The term "environment" is defined in that statute to include "water, air, and land and the interrelationship which exists among and between water, air, and land and all living things."[209] Apart from that broad definition, no mention of wildlife is made anywhere else in the statute. The Resource Conservation and Recovery Act[210] has as its aim "the protection of public health and the environment" without ever defining "public health" or "environment." Despite the absence of clear focus in either of these laws on the interests of wildlife, it is undisputed that wildlife will be among the beneficiaries of the safer environment they are intended to further.

Thus, in the diverse ways here described, federal laws pertaining to the pollution of the atmosphere, inland waters, and high seas and the regulation of toxic chemicals provide at least a measure of consideration for wildlife. How effectively that consideration is translated into affirmative action benefiting wildlife is infinitely difficult to calculate, though the danger to wildlife from such sources has become increasingly apparent.

---

[204]*Id.* §1472.

[205]*Id.* §1473.

[206] Not discussed here are federal pesticide laws addressed in Chapter 9.

[207]15 U.S.C. §2601–2629 (1976 & Supp. V 1981).

[208]15 U.S.C. §2605(a)(1976).

[209]*Id.* §2602(5).

[210]42 U.S.C. §6901–6987 (1976 & Supp. IV 1980).

# Chapter 8

# FEDERAL SOURCES OF FUNDING FOR WILDLIFE PROGRAMS

Since the 1930s funds for both federal and state wildlife programs have been derived in part from specially earmarked taxes and license fees as well as from general tax revenues. This fact has afforded those programs a measure of insulation from annual appropriations battles and guaranteed them a fairly constant level of funding. This chapter examines the most significant of the federal statutes that establish special funds, the revenues from which are to be used for wildlife or other closely related purposes. These include the Migratory Bird Hunting Stamp Act, which generates approximately $15 million annually for the acquisition of national wildlife refuges[1] and two related statutes that together have generated over $1 billion in revenues for state wildlife programs,[2] the Federal Aid in Wildlife Restoration Act, and the Federal Aid in Fish Restoration Act. Also considered here is the Land and Water Conservation Fund Act, a statute that, in less than 20 years, has generated more than $2 billion for a wide variety of state and federal outdoor recreational programs[3] and the most recent federal grant-in-aid measure, the Fish and Wildlife Conservation Act of 1980.

## THE MIGRATORY BIRD HUNTING STAMP ACT

The Migratory Bird Conservation Act of 1929 provided the authority for a systematic federal program of wildlife refuge acquisition.[4] However, it

---

[1]*See* H.R. Rep. No. 335, 94th Cong., 1st Sess. 7 (1975).

[2]*See* Department of the Interior, Fish and Wildlife Service, Conserving Our Fish and Wildlife Heritage, Annual Report—FY1975 at 41.

[3]*See* H.R. Rep. No. 1021, 94th Cong., 2d Sess. 3 (1976).

[4]16 U.S.C. §§715d–715k and 715l–715r (1976 & Supp. V 1981). The Migratory Bird Conservation Act is discussed in Chapter 6 at text accompanying notes 5–9 and 21.

failed to assure a continuing availability of funds with which to implement that program. Indeed, the failure of Congress to appropriate even the limited funds that the Act authorized persuaded the Special Senate Committee on the Conservation of Wild Life of the need to establish a revenue base independent of political vagaries.[5] The resulting legislation, the Migratory Bird Hunting Stamp Act of 1934, was the first major federal statute to establish a special fund to be used exclusively for wildlife conservation purposes.[6]

The special Migratory Bird Conservation Fund created by the 1934 Act was to be comprised of proceeds from the sale of federal migratory bird hunting stamps, required of each person above 16 years of age taking migratory waterfowl. For its first two and a half decades, the fund was used principally for refuge operation, development, and administration; a relatively small percentage of the monies from the fund was spent for refuge acquisition. Because this use of the fund "was not in accord with the understanding of the sportsmen"[7] who had supported the Stamp Act, Congress amended it in 1958 to provide that such revenues could be spent *only* for the acquisition of refuges and "waterfowl production areas."[8]

While the 1958 amendments to the Stamp Act guaranteed a continuous source of income to the fund for acquisition purposes, the revenue generated by the sale of hunting stamps failed to keep pace with the rising cost of land and the ever-accelerating conversion of wetlands to other uses. Accordingly, to expedite the acquisition of some 2.5 million acres of wetlands needed to meet a long range goal of the Department of the Interior, Congress enacted the Wetlands Loan Act of 1961.[9] The Loan Act authorized an advance appropriation to the fund, without interest, of up to $105 million over a seven-year period. The repayment period for advances to the fund has since been extended in 1967[10] and 1976.[11] The 1976 amendment also increased the authorization ceiling to $200 million[12] and

---

[5]*See* S. Rep. No. 262, 73 Cong., 2d Sess. 1 (1934); 78 Cong. Rec. 1147–1148 (1934) (remarks of Senators Walcott and Pittman); 78 Cong. Rec. 2002 (remarks of Senator Dill).

[6]16 U.S.C. §§718–718h (1976 & Supp. V 1981).

[7]H.R. Rep. No. 2182, 85th Cong., 2d Sess. 1 (1958).

[8]Act of Aug. 1, 1958, Pub. L. No. 85-585, §3, 72 Stat. 486 (current version at 16 U.S.C. §718d (1976 & Supp. V 1981)).

[9]16 U.S.C. §§715k-3 to 715k-5 (1976).

[10]Act of Dec. 15, 1967, Pub. L. No. 90-205, §1(b), 81 Stat. 612.

[11]Act of Feb. 17, 1976, Pub. L. No. 94-215, §2(b), 90 Stat. 189.

[12]As of 1975, 600,000 acres of Interior's original acquisition goal remained to be acquired. Moreover, new Interior estimates recommended a federal acquisition of an additional 1.3 million acres beyond its original goal. *See* 121 Cong. Reg. H6324

sought to encourage nonhunters to contribute to the fund by changing the name of the stamp to the "migratory bird hunting and conservation stamp."[13]

Under current law, the obligation to repay the Treasury for monies advanced to the Migratory Bird Conservation Fund pursuant to the Wetlands Loan Act begins October 1, 1983.[14] Repayment is to be made by paying 75 percent of the revenues from the sale of hunting and conservation stamps to the Treasury.[15] As has happened twice before, however, it is likely that the repayment obligation will be postponed again, perhaps even forgiven altogether.

## THE FEDERAL AID IN WILDLIFE RESTORATION ACT

The Federal Aid in Wildlife Restoration Act, more commonly known as the Pittman-Robertson Act, serves as the principal mechanism for providing federal assistance to states for the acquisition, restoration, and maintenance of wildlife habitat; for the management of wildlife areas and resources; and for research into problems of wildlife management.[16] Its enactment in 1937 culminated efforts to put the funding of state wildlife programs on a secure basis and provided a model for subsequent federal legislation pertaining to state fishery programs.

The principal feature of the original Pittman-Robertson Act was the creation of a special "federal aid to wildlife restoration fund" in the Treasury of the United States.[17] The fund was comprised exclusively of revenues derived from the federal excise taxes on the sale of firearms, shells, and cartridges. From this fund, the Secretary of Agriculture[18] could utilize up to 8 percent of the annual revenues for his administration of the Pittman-Robertson Act and of the Migratory Bird Conservation Act.[19] The

---

(daily ed. July 8, 1975) (remarks of Congressman Oberstar). As of mid-1982, 1.6 million of that 1.9 million acres remained to be acquired.

[13]Act of Feb. 17, 1976, Pub. L. No. 94-215, §3a, 90 Stat. 189.

[14]16 U.S.C. §715k-5 (1976).

[15]*Id.*

[16]16 U.S.C. §669-669i (1976 & Supp. V 1981).

[17]*Id.* §669b (1976).

[18]The authority of Secretary of Agriculture was transferred to the Secretary of the Interior in 1939 pursuant to Reorganization Plan No. II, §4(f), 4 Fed. Reg. 2731, 53 Stat. 1433.

[19]16 U.S.C. §669c(a) (1976).

remainder, however, was to be apportioned among the states, one-half on the basis of geographic area and one-half on the basis of the number of paid hunting-license holders in each state.[20] Upon submission of proposals for qualified wildlife restoration projects, eligible states would be entitled to receive from the sums apportioned to them up to 75 percent of project costs.[21]

The original Pittman-Robertson Act was more than just a conduit for the funneling of federal tax revenues to the states; it also prescribed certain standards to be met before the states could receive funds.[22] Most fundamentally, through a "carrot-and-stick" approach, it forced the states to put their wildlife conservation programs on a stable financial base by providing that

> no money apportioned under this chapter to any State shall be expended therein until its legislature, or other State agency authorized by the State constitution to make laws governing the conservation of wildlife, shall have . . . passed laws for the conservation of wildlife which shall include a prohibition against the diversion of license fees paid by hunters for any other purpose than the administration of said State fish and game department.[23]

The "carrot" of 75 percent federal funding apparently outweighed any desire of the states to maintain complete flexibility in the use of their hunting license revenues, for all states adapted their laws so as to be eligible for Pittman-Robertson funds.

A second means of attaining a measure of federal control over the utilization of Pittman-Robertson monies was the requirement that only those wildlife restoration projects determined by the Secretary to be "substantial in character and design" would qualify for federal funding.[24] This standard, undefined in the statute, was long interpreted in the implementing regulations to mean that a proposed project's "benefits to hunters and fishermen" must be commensurate with its cost.[25] As indicated

---

[20]Id. §669c(a), (b). For a discussion of the meaning of the term "paid hunting-license holders," see text accompanying notes 33–36 infra.

[21]16 U.S.C. §669e(a) (1976).

[22]The standards should be compared with those that must be met by the states to receive federal funds under the Marine Mammal Protection Act and the Endangered Species Act of 1973. See Chapter 11 at text accompanying notes 110–141 and Chapter 12 at text accompanying notes 291–301.

[23]16 U.S.C. §669 (1976).

[24]Id. §669e(a).

[25]50 C.F.R. §80.1(g) (1981) (amended 1982). The reference to fishermen was found here because the regulation was applicable both to the Pittman-Robertson Act and to the Federal Aid in Fish Restoration Act. For Pittman-Robertson purposes, project substantiality was presumably measured solely with reference to hunters.

later in this chapter, the actual administrative implementation of the program suggests that, in practice, a somewhat looser standard is utilized.[26]

Finally, the original Pittman-Robertson Act limited the types of activities eligible for funds by adopting a somewhat restrictive definition of the term "wildlife-restoration project." That term was defined to include principally the acquisition and restoration of wildlife habitat, the construction of works thereon, and research into problems of wildlife management.

The opportunity for significant federal influence over state wildlife programs as a result of the above features of the Act has been steadily diminished and the corresponding flexibility of the states in their utilization of Pittman-Robertson funds increased, through a series of amendments broadening the scope of state activities eligible for federal aid. The first such broadening amendment, which came in 1946, included maintenance of completed projects within the definition of "wildlife restoration project."[27] A further amendment in 1955 permitted the expenditure of funds for management of wildlife areas and resources, exclusive of law enforcement and public relations activities.[28]

By far the most significant of these broadening amendments, however, was that of 1970, which made two important changes.[29] First, it directed that the existing federal excise tax on pistols and revolvers be paid into the wildlife restoration fund and that half the annual revenues from this source be apportioned to the states for hunting safety programs, including the construction, operation and maintenance of outdoor target ranges.[30] This special "fund within the fund," which, since fiscal year 1975, has also included half the federal tax imposed on bows and arrows, is apportioned among the states solely on the basis of their populations and may, at the discretion of the state, be used for traditional wildlife restoration projects rather than for hunter safety programs.

The second change introduced by the 1970 amendments was potentially of even greater significance. It gave the states the option of submitting a "comprehensive fish and wildlife resource management plan" in lieu of the traditional individual restoration projects. The elements of such a plan are described in very general terms in the statute. It must cover a period of at

---

[26]See text accompanying notes 51–52 infra.

[27]Act of July 24, 1946, ch. 605, §2, 60 Stat. 656, (current version at 16 U.S.C. §669g(o) (1976)).

[28]Act of Aug. 12, 1955, ch. 861, §2, 69 Stat. 698, (current version at 16 U.S.C. §669g(a) (1976)).

[29]Act of Oct. 23, 1970, Pub. L. No. 91-503, tit. I, §§101–02, 84 Stat. 1097 (current version at 16 U.S.C. §669b, c, g (1976)).

[30]In 1972, the requirement that public target ranges be "outdoor" ranges was deleted. Act of Oct. 25, 1972, Pub. L. No. 92-558, tit. I, §102(a), 86 Stat. 1173 (current version at 16 U.S.C. §669g(b) (1976)).

least five years, be "based on projections of desires and needs of the people" for a period of at least fifteen years, and include provisions for updating at least every three years. Beyond that, the only substantive standard imposed by the statute requires that comprehensive fish and wildlife management plans "insure the perpetuation of these resources for the economic, scientific, and recreational enrichment of the people."[31] No procedural requirement that the public be permitted to participate in the development of the comprehensive plan is imposed.[32]

Given the duration and magnitude of the Pittman-Robertson program and the widely divergent views of those interested in its administration, it is striking how little litigation there has been concerning it. In fact, the Secretary's discretion in approving or disapproving a particular project application has never been challenged in any reported case. That issue was touched on, however, in an action that pitted three states against the Secretary of the Interior with respect to the meaning of the term "paid hunting-license holders" as used in the Act's apportionment formula. In that action, *Udall v. Wisconsin*, the states, all of which issued multiple types of hunting licenses rather than a single general hunting license, contended that the term really meant the number of licenses rather than the number of individuals holding licenses.[33] The states were aided in their claim, despite the literal wording of the statute, by a somewhat conflicting legislative history and by the fact that, until 1959, the Secretary had in fact administered the Act as though the term "license-holders" meant "licenses."[34] The court of appeals rejected these arguments, however, and held that the Act meant what it said and that the Secretary of the Interior, albeit late, had correctly applied it.[35]

---

[31] 16 U.S.C. §§669e(a)(1) (1976). *Compare* the somewhat more detailed requirements for "comprehensive plans" pertaining to wildlife conservation on federal lands. *See* Chapter 6 at text accompanying notes 143–156. Query: What incentive is there for electing the comprehensive plan option over the traditional individual project approach? Congress apparently thought that the comprehensive plan option would be attractive to states because it would enable them to utilize their federal aid funds more efficiently. *See* S. Rep. No. 1289, 91st Cong., 2d Sess. 1970. However, the federal matching grant share is 75 percent, no matter which option is chosen. Accordingly, to date no state has elected the comprehensive planning option.

[32] One must question whether the requirement that comprehensive plans be based on the "desires and needs of the people," when coupled with the Secretary's authority to make rules and regulations to carry out the Act, 16 U.S.C. §669i (1976), authorizes (or even compels) him to require public participation in the development of such plans.

[33] 306 F.2d 790 (D.C. Cir. 1962), *cert. denied*, 371 U.S. 969 (1963).

[34] 306 F.2d at 793–794.

[35] *Id.* at 795.

In the course of its ruling, the court suggested in dictum that there may be a distinction between a court's power to review the Secretary's exercise of his initial apportionment function and of his subsequent function of approving or disapproving individual applications for funds. That is, while the court viewed the former function as "almost a purely mechanical one" involving no discretion on the part of the Secretary, for which judicial review by mandamus would be appropriate, it offered the following observation on his latter function in a footnote:

> This is not to say that the Secretary exercises no discretion at later stages of the administrative process. It may well be, for instance, that approval or disapproval of a conservation project submitted by a state...involves an administrative judgement which is not judicially reviewable by mandamus.[36]

To say that the Secretary's approval or disapproval of a particular project is not reviewable by mandamus is not, however, to say that is altogether unreviewable.

First, other federal statutes impose substantive standards that restrict the Secretary's discretion under the Pittman-Robertson Act. An illuminating case is *Cameron Parish Police Jury v. Hickel.*[37] It involved the Refuge Revenue Sharing Act, which directs that certain of the receipts from the operation of national wildlife refuges be paid to the counties in which they are located for the benefit of public schools and roads.[38] Although the Secretary's duty to apportion receipts among eligible counties is presumably nondiscretionary, the intervening Civil Rights Act of 1964, by prohibiting federal financial assistance without an assurance of nondiscrimination, imposed a further substantive duty on the Secretary's actual payment of funds to particular counties. The *Cameron Parish* case clearly recognized that further duty as the basis for judicial review of the Secretary's actions.

By a parity of reasoning, the same substantive restrictions imposed by the Civil Rights Act must serve as a basis for judicial review of the Secretary's actions under the Pittman-Robertson Act. Beyond that, however, is the question of judicial reviewability under other statutes imposing other duties, such as the National Environmental Policy Act and the Endangered Species Act of 1973. Although the Fish and Wildlife Service

---

[36]*Id.* at 793 n. 15.

[37]302 F. Supp. 689 (W.D. La. 1969).

[38]16 U.S.C. §715s (1976 & Supp. V 1981). For a discussion of the Refuge Revenue Sharing Act, *see* Chapter 6 at text accompanying notes 41–42.

recognizes the applicability of NEPA to the Pittman-Robertson program,[39] there have been few impact statements prepared with respect to individual restoration projects.[40]

The issue of the Secretary's failure to prepare an impact statement before granting Pittman-Robertson monies was raised in *Defenders of Wildlife v. Alaska Department of Fish and Game,* an action stemming from an experimental wolf control program in Alaska.[41] There the Fish and Wildlife Service suspended Pittman-Robertson payments in support of the program pending further review of whether an impact statement was required.[42] Before completion of that review, however, Alaska rescinded its request for federal financial participation, and the controversy was ultimately decided on the basis of other issues.[43]

Yet another case that never fully materialized raised the issue of potential conflict between the Secretary's administration of the Pittman-Robertson Act and the Endangered Species Act. In June 1976, the Sierra Club Legal Defense Fund gave formal notice to the Secretary of the Interior that his continued funding under the Pittman-Robertson Act of a Hawaiian program to maintain a population of feral sheep and goats on Mauna Kea jeopardized the continued existence of an endangered bird, the palila, by threatening to destroy its habitat, thus violating section 7 of the Endangered Species Act. After the Pittman-Robertson Act funding was terminated, the Hawaii program was successfully challenged on other bases.[44]

While none of the cases here discussed resulted in a final judicial decision, it would seem that the Secretary's decision to approve or disapprove a particular application for federal money cannot escape judicial review where it is alleged that his action violates a clear command of another federal statute. Not yet resolved is the reviewability of the Secretary's determination that a proposed project meets the substantive standard of the Pittman-Robertson Act itself, *i.e.,* whether it is "substantial in character and design."[45]

---

[39]*See* U.S. Fish and Wildlife Service, Environmental Statement: Operation of the Federal Aid in Sport Fish and Wildlife Restoration Program (1978).

[40]*See, e.g.,* Department of the Interior, Fish and Wildlife Service, Fishery Rehabilitation of the Rock River (FES 75-42, 1975) (involving grants under both the Pittman-Robertson and Dingell-Johnson Acts).

[41]Civil No. A76-13 (D. Alaska, March 8, 1976).

[42]Telegram from Lynn Greenwalt, Director, Fish and Wildlife Service, to James W. Brooks, Commissioner, Alaska Department of Fish and Game, dated Jan. 19, 1976.

[43]*See* Chapter 6 at text accompanying notes 224–231.

[44]*See* Chapter 12 at text accompanying notes 117–118.

[45]It is noteworthy that, when describing the identical standard employed in the Federal Aid in Fish Restoration Act, Congressman Dingell, its chief House sponsor, offered the following:

Although the Secretary's implementation of the Pittman-Robertson Act has thus far escaped any challenge, apart from the *Udall* case, there are aspects of that administration that raise substantial legal questions. For example, while the Pittman-Robertson Act contains a lengthy definition of "wildlife restoration project," it does not contain a definition of "wildlife." Until 1956, because the Fish and Wildlife Service had no special administrative definition of the term for purpose of the Pittman-Robertson Act, its general definition, which included "wild mammals, wild birds and their nests and eggs,...crustacea, mollusca, fishes, reptiles, amphibians, and their eggs," presumably applied.[46] In that year, however, administrative regulations under the Pittman-Robertson Act were revised, ostensibly to effectuate the 1955 amendment authorizing the expenditure of program funds for management of wildlife areas and resources, and "to simplify administrative procedures."[47] As part of that general revision, however, a special definition of "wildlife" was introduced that limited it to wild birds and mammals. That narrow definition, which has been carried forward to the present,[48] is nowhere compelled by the statute, though it undoubtedly reflects very closely both the principal focus of state wildlife agency activities and the major interest of those whose tax payments make up the wildlife restoration fund.[49]

---

The amount of interference so far as the Federal Government is concerned in the bill just prescribes a certain minimal standard. They are absolutely reduced to a minimum. It just prescribes certain acceptable standards and above that, everything else is strictly in the hands of the State.

Hearings Before the Subcomm. on Fisheries and Wildlife Conservation of the House Comm. on Merchant Marine and Fisheries on Miscellaneous Wildlife Bills, 81st Cong., 1st Sess. 55 (1949).

[46]50 C.F.R. §1.7 (1949).

[47]21 Fed. Reg. 9429 (Dec. 1, 1956).

[48]*See* 47 Fed. Reg. 22538, 22540 (May 25, 1982) (to be codified at 50 C.F.R. §80.5(a)(1)). This was neither the first nor the last time that the scope of a federal wildlife statute was narrowed as a result of a restrictive definition of "wildlife" imposed by the administering agency. For similar self-imposed limitations on the scope of the Lacey Act and the Endangered Species Preservation Act of 1966, *see* Chapter 5 at text accompanying note 19 and Chapter 12 at text accompanying notes 14–15.

[49]One must question whether feral animals qualify as "wild birds and wild mammals" under the Pittman-Robertson Act. If the allegations of the Sierra Club Legal Defense Fund were correct (*see* text accompanying note 44 *supra*), Pittman-Robertson monies have in fact been paid to support state programs maintaining feral animal populations where such animals are hunted. Yet the International Association of Game, Fish and Conservation Commissioners argues in an amicus brief in Kleppe v. New Mexico, 426 U.S. 529 (1976), that wild horses and burros, being feral animals, should not be considered wildlife. The Supreme Court did not address the purported distinction.

Very closely related to the restrictive definition of "wildlife" is the unique definition of "project substantiality" found in the administrative regulations until 1982. The definition, interpreting the only statutorily prescribed substantive standard for wildlife restoration projects, provided in part that "[a] substantial project is one which provides benefits to hunters and fishermen commensurate with cost."[50] Despite these restrictive definitions, actual administrative practice in recent years has been somewhat more flexible, providing limited grants for state projects involving endangered or other nonhunted species, and, in a few rare cases, for species other than birds and mammals.[51] In 1982 the Fish and Wildlife Service brought its regulations into conformity with its actual practice by eliminating the restrictive definition of project substantiality.[52]

The 1982 regulatory change seems consistent with the 1970 amendment introducing the option of "comprehensive fish and wildlife resource management plans." That amendment indicated a congressional intent that the Act not be administered with a narrow focus solely on game birds and mammals. The very term "comprehensive" seems inconsistent with such a narrow focus, as does the requirement that such plans "insure the perpetuation of [fish and other wildlife] resources for the economic, scientific, and recreational enrichment of the people."[53] Moreover, the Fish and Wildlife Service requires that a state that chooses the comprehensive plan option submit a "strategic plan" that, among other things, "[i]dentifies rare, endangered, or unique plant and animal communities for preservation and management."[54]

A final legal issue that has arisen under the Pittman-Robertson Act concerns the administrative restriction against "diversion" of federal funds. The Act, from its very beginning, has required states to assure that their hunting license revenues be used solely for the administration of their fish and game departments.[55] The Act also provides that, if federal funds are used for purposes other than those for which they were granted, "they shall be replaced by the State before it may participate in any further apportionment."[56] By administrative regulation, such a diversion is deemed to occur when real property acquired or constructed with Pittman-Robertson

---

[50]50 C.F.R. §80.1(g) (1981). The definition referred to benefits to fishermen because it was applicable to both the Pittman-Robertson and Dingell-Johnson programs.

[51]See Wildlife Management Institute, Current Investments, Projected Needs & Potential New Sources of Income for Nongame Fish & Wildlife Programs in the United States 74–78 (1975).

[52]47 Fed. Reg. 22538 (May 25, 1982).

[53]16 U.S.C. §669e(a)(1) (1976).

[54]See Department of the Interior, Fish and Wildlife Service, Federal Aid Manual §14.3 (1973).

[55]16 U.S.C. §669 (1976).

[56]Id. §669e(a).

monies passes from the control of the state fish and game department.[57] If the state fails within three years to replace such property, using nonfederal aid funds, with "property of equal value at current market prices and with commensurate benefits to fish and wildlife," it thereby becomes ineligible for further participation in the Pittman-Robertson program.[58] There are a few reported cases in which private litigants have sought to use the alleged vulnerability of a state to loss of Pittman-Robertson funds as a grounds for attacking development projects that include the disposal of state lands.

One example is *Cape Henry Bird Club v. Laird,* in which the plaintiffs sought to block a Corps of Engineers dam project that required the purchase of a state wildlife management area acquired with Pittman-Robertson monies.[59] The plaintiffs contended that the state would thereby lose its eligibility for future Pittman-Robertson funds because the area to be transferred was so unique that no other area offering "commensurate benefits to fish and wildlife" existed, or, if it did, its cost would far exceed the amount to be paid for the land transferred. The court seemingly treated these as two separate contentions, holding that the possible loss of funds through the unavailability of "commensurate land" was "mere speculation"[60] and that the need to spend a sum in excess of the transfer price for replacement land need only be considered as a cost of the project in the Corps' calculation of a benefit/cost ratio.[61] Thus the court appears to have disregarded the literal language of the Pittman-Robertson regulations, which require *both* that the replacement land be of commensurate benefit to wildlife and that it be of equal market value. Other efforts to invoke the Act's sanction for diversion of funds against major development projects have been equally unsuccessful.[62]

## THE FEDERAL AID IN FISH RESTORATION ACT

The Federal Aid in Fish Restoration Act, more commonly known as the Dingell-Johnson Act, is essentially identical to the Pittman-Robertson Act, except that it provides federal assistance to states for projects pertaining to fish.[63] The Dingell-Johnson Act was enacted in 1950 apparently because of

---

[57]50 C.F.R. §80.5(a) (1981).

[58]*Id.* §80.5(b).

[59]359 F. Supp. 404 (W.D. Va.), *aff'd,* 484 F.2d 453 (4th Cir. 1973).

[60]*Id.* at 414.

[61]*Id.*

[62]*See* Citizens Committee for the Columbia River v. Callaway, 494 F.2d 124 (9th Cir. 1974).

[63]16 U.S.C. §777–777k (1976 & Supp. V 1981).

general satisfaction with the Pittman-Robertson Act and because a special wartime tax on certain fishing equipment was likely to be terminated unless it could be earmarked for fish restoration purposes.[64]

The provisions of the Dingell-Johnson Act almost precisely parallel those of the Pittman-Robertson Act. Funds derived from the federal excise tax on fishing rods, creels, reels, and artificial lures, baits, and flies are annually apportioned among the states, 40 percent on the basis of geographical area and 60 percent on the basis of the number of persons holding paid sport fishing licenses, after first deducting up to 8 percent for administration of the Act and "for aiding in the formulation, adoption, or administration or any compact between two or more States for the conservation and management of migratory fishes in marine or fresh waters."[65]

Funds so apportioned to the states are available for use by them for "fish restoration and management projects" or, since 1970, "comprehensive fish and wildlife resource management plans."[66] The federal share in the cost of such projects or plans is not to exceed 75 percent.

The Dingell-Johnson and Pittman-Robertson Acts are in fact so much alike that the Fish and Wildlife Service utilizes a common set of administrative regulations and a common "Federal Aid Manual" for the administration of both programs. Accordingly, the legal issues that might arise with respect to the Dingell-Johnson Act are much the same as those already discussed in connection with the Pittman-Robertson Act. In fact, however, there has as yet been no reported litigation arising under the Dingell-Johnson Act.

The two acts are distinguishable in at least one respect. Whereas the Pittman-Robertson Act contains the undefined term "wildlife," which was long restricted by regulation to birds and mammals of benefit to hunters, the Dingell-Johnson Act applies expressly only to "fish which have material value in connection with sport or recreation in the marine and/or fresh waters of the United States."[67] Accordingly, there would appear to be a stronger statutory justification for the administrative practice of determining "project substantiality" in terms of benefits to fishermen. Again, however, notwithstanding the statute and regulations, there appear to have

---

[64]See Hearings Before the Comm. on Interstate and Foreign Commerce on S.1075 and S.1076, 81st Cong., 1st Sess. 61 (1949).

[65]16 U.S.C. §777c (1976).

[66]Id. §777e.

[67]Id. §777a. Although the annotation following 16 U.S.C.A. §777 indicates that the functions of the Secretary of the Interior under the Act relating to marine sports fisheries were transferred to the Secretary of Commerce by Reorganization Plan No. 4 of 1970, 35 Fed. Reg. 15627, 84 Stat. 2090, in fact the Secretary of the Interior exercises exclusive authority over all aspects of the Dingell-Johnson program.

been at least some Dingell-Johnson payments for projects involving endangered (and therefore nonfished) fish.[68]

## THE FISH AND WILDLIFE CONSERVATION ACT OF 1980

In the late 1970s the impetus grew for enactment of a new program, parallel to the Pittman-Robertson and Dingell-Johnson programs, that would be directed to the conservation of nongame wildlife. As already indicated, a very small amount of nongame funding was already occurring under the former programs despite administrative regulations of doubtful validity that appeared to prohibit it. To provide the additional $40 million annually that was estimated to be necessary to sustain comprehensive conservation programs in the states,[69] new legislation was needed.

The Fish and Wildlife Conservation Act of 1980,[70] commonly referred to as the "Non-game Act" actually serves a broader purpose than its common name implies. The impetus for the enactment of this legislation was the perception that animals not ordinarily valued for sport hunting or commercial purposes receive insufficient attention and funds from state wildlife management programs. However, the Non-game Act actually strives to encourage comprehensive conservation planning, encompassing both nongame and other wildlife.

As previously described, the idea of comprehensive conservation planning was introduced into both the Pittman-Robertson and Dingell-Johnson Acts in 1970. In both those statutes the development of a comprehensive conservation plan is an optional means for a state to secure eligibility for receipt of federal grants-in-aid. In the Non-game Act, on the other hand, comprehensive planning is clearly the preferred means of securing eligibility for federal grants-in-aid, although it is not the exclusive means.

Under section 6 of the Act, the Secretary of the Interior may reimburse a state for up to 90 percent of the cost of developing a conservation plan, except that the Secretary's reimbursement may not exceed 75 percent of such costs in any fiscal year subsequent to fiscal year 1984.[71] No reimbursement for plan development may be made after fiscal year 1991.[72] In this way, the act encourages states to initiate plan development sooner rather than later.

---

[68]*See* Wildlife Management Institute, *supra* note 51 at 74–78.
[69]*Id.* at 51–53.
[70]16 U.S.C. §§2901–2911 (Supp. V 1981).
[71]*Id.* §2905(e)(3)(A).
[72]*Id.* §2905(e)(2)(A).

The object of plan development efforts is to produce a plan having the ten elements set forth in section 4 of the Act.[73] Among these are the identification of so-called "plan species," those being the fish and wildlife of the state "valued for ecological, educational, esthetic, cultural, recreational, economic, or scientific benefits by the public."[74] With respect to such plan species, the plan must determine "the size, range, and distribution of their populations" and the status of their "significant habitats,"[75] identify problems adversely affecting them or their habitats,[76] identify needed conservation actions,[77] and establish priorities among such actions.[78]

If a plan meets the requirements of section 4 and is otherwise "substantial in character and design," it may be approved by the Secretary pursuant to section 5.[79] Once approved, up to 75 percent of the cost of implementing those conservation actions specified in the plan that pertain to nongame fish and wildlife are reimbursable by the Secretary.[80] Even without an approved plan, a state able to demonstrate need can receive such reimbursement for the implementation of particular nongame conservation actions,[81] but only through fiscal year 1986.[82] Thus the Act creates a clear financial incentive for states not only to develop conservation plans but to submit them for federal approval. This contrasts with the Pittman-Robertson and Dingell-Johnson Acts, in which there is no financial incentive for the submission of a plan once it is developed.

The relationship of the conservation plans called for by the Non-game Act to the optional comprehensive fish and wildlife resource management plans encouraged by the Pittman-Robertson and Dingell-Johnson Acts is likely to be a source of considerable confusion in the future. On the one

---

[73]*Id.* §2903.

[74]*Id.* §2903(2). Endangered or threatened species and marine mammals may not be designated nongame plan species. *Id.* §2902(6).

[75]*Id.* §2903(3). Considerable controversy accompanied the court-imposed similar requirement for reliable population estimates of species listed on Appendix II of the Convention on International Trade in Endangered Species of Wild Fauna and Flora. *See* Chapter 12 at text accompanying notes 317–329.

[76]16 U.S.C. §2903(4) (Supp. V 1981).

[77]*Id.* §2903(5).

[78]*Id.* §2903(6).

[79]*Id.* §2904(a)(3).

[80]*Id.* §2905(e)(3)(B). If the action is undertaken jointly by two or more states, the federally reimbursable share is 90 percent. After 1991, the maximum federal reimbursement for implementation of conservation actions is either 50 or 75 percent, depending on whether the plan covers only nongame species or has broader coverage. *Id.* §2905(e)(3)(D).

[81]*Id.* §2904(d).

[82]*Id.* §2905(e)(2)(B).

hand, section 5(b) of the Non-game Act says that the portion of an approved plan under that Act that pertains to wildlife "shall be deemed to be an approved plan for purposes of section 6(a)(1)" of the Pittman-Robertson Act;[83] similarly, that portion pertaining to fish "shall be deemed to be an approved plan for the purposes of section 6(a)(1)" of the Dingell-Johnson Act.[84] Under those latter two acts, however, a state may elect to avail itself of the benefits thereof *either* by submitting a comprehensive fish and wildlife resource management plan *or* by submitting individual fish or wildlife restoration projects.[85] Thus, if plans developed under the Non-game Act are to be deemed comprehensive plans for purposes of the Pittman-Robertson and Dingell-Johnson Acts, states will presumably want to include the full range of their game species in such plans so as to be able to continue to receive funding under the latter two acts for projects relating to game species. Yet the Non-game Act seems to make discretionary the inclusion of game species in the plans it requires.[86] Indeed, it seems even to contemplate the possibility that some plans might pertain solely to nongame species.[87]

Though game species clearly may be included in the conservation plans required by the Non-game Act, invertebrates may not.[88] The legislative history indicates that the reason for this exclusion was that "the potential number of invertebrate species could quickly exhaust the money and overwhelm the planning process of the proposed programs."[89] That explanation, however, is not very persuasive. The plans called for by the Act need not encompass every nongame species in a state, but only those valued for the particular purposes specified in section 4(2).[90] Thus the authority to conserve or plan for the conservation of invertebrates would tax the resources of a state only to the extent it chose to exercise that authority. By denying the authority, the statute denies states the choice.

Although earlier versions of the legislation that became the Non-game Act would have financed the program by means of special excise taxes, the Act as passed requires general appropriations from the Treasury. In what was to be the first year of the Act's operation, Congress appropriated no funds. Thus the Non-game Act has already fallen victim to the political vagaries from which excise tax–based programs such as Pittman-Robertson and Dingell-Johnson are exempt. That immediate experience should not

---

[83]*Id.* §2904(b)(1).

[84]*Id.* §2904(b)(2).

[85]16 U.S.C. §§669e(a), 777e(a) (1976).

[86]16 U.S.C. §2903(2) (Supp. V 1981).

[87]*Id.* §2905(e)(3)(D)(i).

[88]*Id.* §2902(5), (6).

[89]126 Cong. Rec. S12307 (daily ed. Sept. 9, 1980) (remarks of Senator Chafee).

[90]16 U.S.C. §2903(2) (Supp. V 1981).

be forgotten when the Director of the Fish and Wildlife Service carries out the comprehensive study mandated by section 12 "to determine the most equitable and effective mechanism for funding State conservation plans and actions under [the Non-game Act], including, but not limited to, funding by means of an excise tax on appropriate items."[91]

## THE LAND AND WATER CONSERVATION FUND ACT

It was said at the outset of this chapter that the funding of wildlife programs in the United States is highly dependent upon the utilization of specially earmarked taxes and license fees. The same has been true of outdoor recreation programs generally since 1964. In that year Congress enacted the Land and Water Conservation Fund Act for the purpose of "preserving, developing and assuring accessibility to all citizens... of outdoor recreation resources."[92] In the manner of the Pittman-Robertson and Dingell-Johnson Acts, the Land and Water Conservation Fund Act established in the Treasury a special "land and water conservation fund" comprised of certain specially earmarked revenues and available only for certain prescribed purposes. Unlike those earlier Acts, however, the Land and Water Conservation Fund Act generates funds from a wide variety of sources and applies them to a broad range of both state and federal recreational programs.

Under the Act as originally passed, the fund was to be comprised of certain user fees, proceeds from the disposal of surplus federal property, and the federal motorboat fuels tax. These sources of revenue were supplemented by later amendments that authorized sufficient unappropriated Treasury funds and miscellaneous receipts under the Outer Continental Shelf Lands Act to be appropriated to the fund so as to provide it an annual income of at least $900 million for the period 1978–84.[93]

As originally enacted, the Act authorized the President to designate land or water areas "administered primarily for scenic, scientific, historical, cultural, or recreational purposes" by various federal agencies, including the National Park Service, Bureau of Land Management, Bureau of Sport Fisheries and Wildlife, Forest Service, and others, at which "entrance, admission, and other forms of recreation user fees shall be charged."[94] In the establishment of such fees, "direct and indirect costs to the Government, benefits to the recipient, public policy or interest served, and other pertinent factors" were required to be taken into account.[95] Although the

---

[91] 16 U.S.C. §2911.

[92] 16 U.S.C. §§4601 through 4601-11 (1976 & Supp. V 1981).

[93] 16 U.S.C. §4601-5(c) (Supp. V 1981).

[94] Land and Water Conservation Fund Act, Pub. L. No. 88-578, §2(a), 78 Stat. 898 (current version at 16 U.S.C. §4601-6a (1976 & Supp. V 1981).

[95] *Id.*

President promptly implemented his authority by Executive Order, [96] Congress in 1974 sharply cut back the extent to which such fees could be charged.[97] Under existing law, entrance or admission fees may be charged only at designated units of the National Park System and National Recreation Areas administered by the Department of Agriculture; recreation user fees may be charged only for "specialized outdoor recreation sites, facilities, equipment, or services."[98]

Up to 60 percent of the annual appropriation from the fund is to be made available to the states for "planning, acquisition, and development of needed land and water areas and facilities" and the remainder to the federal government for "acquisition and development of certain lands."[99] Funds available for state use are apportioned according to a statutory formula that gives the Secretary of the Interior considerable discretion based on his perception of "need."[100] To be eligible to receive the monies apportioned to it, a state must first submit a "comprehensive statewide outdoor recreation plan,"[101] for which the Act prescribes minimal substantive requirements.[102] Once its comprehensive plan has been approved, a state may then receive, for individual projects, federal payments of up to 50 percent of the costs of such projects.[103] It is difficult to be certain how much of the money paid to the states is actually utilized for the advantage of fish and other wildlife, because most projects serve more general purposes, such as the acquisition of state parks or other recreational areas. Such areas, however, doubtless have substantial indirect benefits for wildlife.

More readily identifiable are the opportunities for benefiting wildlife provided by the federal share of the fund. The federal share may be used for

---

[96]Executive Order No. 11200, 30 Fed. Reg. 2645 (Feb. 26, 1965).

[97]Act of July 11, 1972, Pub. L. No. 92-347, 86 Stat. 459 (codified at 16 U.S.C. §4601-6(a) (1976 & Supp. V 1981). In fact, Congress had in 1968 directed the repeal, effective March 31, 1970, of that part of the Land and Water Conservation Fund Act authorizing admission and user fees on federal lands. Act of July 15, 1968, Pub. L. No. 90-401, 82 Stat. 354. In 1970, Congress postponed that repeal until December 31, 1971, and directed the Secretary of the Interior to prepare in the interim a special study of user and admission fee policies. Act of July 7, 1970, Pub. L. No. 91-308, 84 Stat. 410 (1970). In 1972, the Senate recommended that the existing user and admission fee be continued essentially unchanged. S. Rep. No. 490, 92d Cong., 1st Sess. 1971. The House, however, recommended a substantial narrowing of that authority, H.R. Rep. No. 742, 92d Cong., 1st Sess. (1971), and its view prevailed.

[98]16 U.S.C. §4601-6a (1976 & Supp. V 1981).

[99]16 U.S.C. §4601-7 (Supp. V 1981).

[100]16 U.S.C. §4601-8b (1976).

[101]Id. §4601-8(d).

[102]See Hearings on H.R. 2763 Before the Subcomm. on National Parks and Recreation of the House Comm. on Interior and Insular Affairs, 94th Cong., 1st Sess. 84 (1975).

[103]16 U.S.C. §4601-8(c) (1976).

a variety of purposes, including the acquisition of lands and waters or interests therein in the National Park System, where wildlife is generally protected, or adjacent to national forests, where wildlife is treated as a resource subject to multiple use management.[104] The federal share of the fund may also be used for the acquisition of areas needed for conserving endangered or threatened species of plants or animals.[105] This use of the fund was in fact the most substantial part of the Fish and Wildlife Service's once proposed long range acquisition program. More than half of the Service's once-planned $453.7 million of acquisitions using the fund were for endangered and threatened species.[106]

A further use to which the federal share of the fund may be put pertains to national wildlife refuges. Considerable controversy has existed with respect to this authority, however. The Act initially provided that the federal share of funds may be used for the "incidental recreation purposes" of section 2 of the Refuge Recreation Act.[107] Although section 2 of the Refuge Recreation Act authorizes the acquisition of lands "for the protection of natural resources" as well as for incidental recreational development, Congress had insisted that any refuge lands acquired with monies from the fund must have recreational facilities developed thereon, because an undeveloped refuge, by itself, was not regarded as having "recreational" value.[108] Nor, for the same reasons, had the Fish and Wildlife Service been able to acquire refuge lands with monies from the fund under that part of the Act that authorizes expenditure of the federal share for "areas... administered by the Secretary of the Interior for outdoor recreation purposes."[109]

---

[104]16 U.S.C. §460l-9(a)(1) (1976).

[105]*Id.* As originally passed, the Land and Water Conservation Fund Act, though it preceded any federal endangered species legislation, authorized the expenditure of the federal share of the fund for "any national area which may be authorized for the preservation of species...that are threatened with extinction." Land and Water Conservation Fund Act, Pub. L. No. 88-578, §6(a)(1), 78 Stat. 903. The Endangered Species Preservation Act of 1966 authorized the appropriation of up to $15 million from the fund for such purposes. No more than $5 million could be appropriated annually, however, nor could more than $750,000 be used for any one area. Act of Oct. 15, 1966, Pub. L. No. 89-669, §2, 80 Stat. 926. The Endangered Species Conservation Act of 1969 increased the maximum amount that could be used for purchase of any one area to $2.5 million. Act of Dec. 5, 1969, Pub. L. No. 91-135, §12(b), 83 Stat. 282. The Endangered Species Act of 1973 removed all limitations on the use of the fund monies for acquisition of areas for the conservation of endangered species. 16 U.S.C. §1534(b) (1976).

[106]S. Rep. No. 367, 94th Cong., 1st Sess. 10 (1975).

[107]16 U.S.C. §460k-1 (1976).

[108]S. Rep. No. 367, 94th Cong., 1st Sess. 9 (1975).

[109]*Id.*

The refuge acquisition question was finally clarified by legislation in 1976.[110] Not only has the authority of the Fish and Wildlife Service to acquire refuge lands without development thereof been made clear,[111] but the acquisition authority pertaining to national forests has also been enlarged.[112]

Beyond the provisions most directly affecting wildlife, the 1976 legislation worked other major changes in the Act. Among these were the requirement for "ample opportunity for public participation" in the development of state comprehensive outdoor recreation plans and the directive that the Secretary "develop, in consultation with others, criteria for public participation."[113] This feature of the Act has no counterpart in the development of comprehensive fish and wildlife management plans under the Pittman-Robertson and Dingell-Johnson Acts.[114]

The Land and Water Conservation Fund Act has been an important device for generating and distributing revenues for outdoor recreation purposes, including many of substantial direct or indirect benefit to wildlife. To date, the total amount given to the states in matching grants under the fund or used for federal land acquisition and development purposes exceeds $2 billion. Despite the enormity of the program, there has been no reported litigation of direct relevance to wildlife concerning it. Nor has compliance with NEPA posed an insurmountable problem. According to the Council on Environmental Quality, the Department of the Interior's Bureau of Outdoor Recreation routinely prepares environmental assessments for all grant applications, which numbered approximately 2,500 in fiscal year 1975;[115] in addition, a number of environmental impact statements have been prepared for particular grants, as has what is in effect a full programmatic statement.[116]

---

[110]Act of September 28, 1976, Pub. L. No. 94-422, 90 Stat. 1313.

[111]*Id.* §101(4) (codified at 16 U.S.C. §4601-9(a)(1) (1976)).

[112]*Id.*

[113]*Id.* §101(3) (codified at 16 U.S.C. §4601-8 (1976).

[114]*But see* note 32 *supra.*

[115]Council on Environmental Quality, Environmental Impact Statements: An Analysis of Six Years' Experience by Seventy Federal Agencies 18 (1976).

[116]*See, e.g.,* Department of the Interior, Bureau of Outdoor Recreation, Final Environmental Impact Statement, Nationwide Outdoor Recreation Plans, (FES 73-69, 1973).

# Chapter 9

# ANIMAL DAMAGE CONTROL—
# PREDATORS AND PESTICIDES

Since publication in 1962 of Rachel Carson's *Silent Spring*, considerable public controversy has attended the use of chemical toxicants to control or eradicate certain forms of wildlife thought to be injurious to agricultural or other human interests. The principal focus of the controversy has concerned the adverse effects of those efforts on man and other nontarget organisms. In response to that concern, there has emerged in recent years a substantial body of federal "pesticide law" designed to protect both man and the environment from such harm. This chapter treats those parts of that body of law having the most direct relevance to wildlife protection.

Also treated here is the related and equally controversial issue of control of predatory and depredatory wildlife. There is, admittedly, a certain artificiality in treating these issues separately, just as there is an artificiality in attempting to distinguish "pests," "predators," and "depredators." Certainly, both issues share in common the concern to avoid harm to nontarget species, a concern that basically involves the means of pest or predator control. Where they differ, however, is with respect to ends. Although there seems to be general agreement that the goal of controlling or even eradicating "pests" (by which one generally means insect pests) is appropriate, there is substantial disagreement about whether the control or eradication of higher forms of predatory and depredatory wildlife is an appropriate social goal. It is perhaps for this reason that the pesticide and the predator issues have been perceived as separate. Because the latter involves more fundamental questions and because it has a somewhat longer legal history, it will be addressed first. It is important to keep in mind, however, that this separate treatment derives as much from convenience and history as from logic.

## THE CONTROL OF PREDATORY
## AND DEPREDATORY WILDLIFE

While the controversy regarding the control of predatory wildlife may be relatively recent, the fact of such control is not. At the local level, bounty laws aimed at the eradication of certain predators were enacted more than a century before the American Revolution.[1] At the federal level, predator control began at least as early as 1909, when Congress appropriated money to the Agriculture Department for "experiments and demonstrations in destroying noxious animals."[2] The statutory authority for such undertakings was unclear,[3] however, until 1931, when Congress enacted a law authorizing and directing the Secretary of Agriculture

> to conduct such investigations, experiments, and tests as he may deem necessary in order to determine, demonstrate, and promulgate the best methods of eradication, suppression, or bringing under control on national forests and other areas of the public domain as well as on State, Territory, or privately owned lands of mountain lions, wolves, coyotes, bobcats, prairie dogs, gophers, ground squirrels, jack rabbits, and other animals injurious to agriculture, horticulture, forestry, animal husbandry, wild game animals, fur-bearing animals, and birds, and for the protection of stock and other domestic animals through the suppression of rabies and tularemia in predatory or other wild animals; and to conduct campaigns for the destruction or control of such animals: *Provided*, That in carrying out the provisions of this section the Secretary of Agriculture may cooperate with States, individuals, and public and private agencies, organizations, and institutions.[4]

Two aspects of the 1931 statute are noteworthy. First, by authorizing federal cooperation with "individuals...and private agencies, organizations, and institutions," it gave express sanction to the "partnership" between Agriculture Department officials and private landowners that had developed pursuant to the "demonstration" directive of the earlier appro-

---

[1] Wildlife Management Institute, Current Investments, Projected Needs & Potential New Sources of Income for Nongame Fish & Wildlife Programs in the United States 1 (1975).

[2] Act of March 4, 1909, ch. 301, 35 Stat. 1051.

[3] Arguably, the Forest Service Organic Administration Act of 1897, pertaining to the national forests, provided statutory authority for control of at least some types of wildlife. That Act directed the Secretary of Agriculture to "make provisions for the protection against destruction by fire and depredations upon the public forests." Whether "depredations" was intended to include the depredations of wildlife, however, is uncertain. Act of June 4, 1897, ch. 2 §1, 30 Stat. 35 (repealed 1979).

[4] 7 U.S.C. §426 (1976).

priations statutes.[5] Second, unlike the animal control activities conducted under the earlier appropriations statutes, all of which were to have taken place on federal lands,[6] the 1931 Act expressly authorized such activities on privately owned lands as well.

The federal predator control program, once firmly based on clear statutory authority, continued to operate without major objection for another three decades.[7] In the 1960s, however, voices of protest began to be raised. In response, Secretary of the Interior Udall appointed a special Advisory Board on Wildlife Management, headed by A. Starker Leopold, to investigate the issue. The Board's report, "Predator and Rodent Control in the United States," also known simply as the Leopold report, was highly critical of existing control programs.[8] It rested upon two basic tenets, the first of which forced a reexamination of the fundamental assumptions underlying existing control programs, by positing that

> all native animals are resources of inherent interest and value to the people of the United States. Basic governmental policy, therefore, should be one of husbandry of all forms of wildlife.[9]

The second tenet, however, tempered the first by recognizing the need to balance that interest against the fact that at some times and in some places certain forms of wildlife pose a threat to certain human interests. The principle recommended in striking this balance was that "[c]ontrol should be limited strictly to the troublesome species, preferably to the troublesome individuals, and in any event to the localities where substantial damage or danger exists."[10]

Guided by these basic tenets, the report recommended a number of more concrete proposals, among them the appointment of a permanent advisory board, an expansion of research, and the designing of legal controls "to regulate the distribution and use of 1080 or any other poison

---

[5]See Hearings on S.3483 Before the Senate Comm. on Agriculture, 71st Cong., 2d and 3d Sess. 50–58 (1931).

[6]Id.

[7]Aldo Leopold's famous "American Game Policy," presented at the 1930 American Game Conference, recognized predator control as a "controversial issue" but stated flatly that "there can be no reasonable objection to predator-control as such." It forecast that disagreements over methods and extent of control would lessen over time.

[8]The report is reprinted in Predatory Mammals and Endangered Species: Hearings on H.R. 689 and Related Bills Before the Subcomm. on Fisheries and Wildlife Conservation of the House Comm. on Merchant Marine and Fisheries, 92d Cong., 2d Sess. 495–506 (1972).

[9]Id. at 496.

[10]Id.

capable of having severe secondary effects on nontarget wildlife species."[11] Though many of the recommendations of the Leopold report were adopted as internal policy guidelines, they were not embodied in new legislation or even in binding administrative regulations but rather were disseminated "through conversation, speeches, memorandums, letters, and... conferences."[12]

The failure of the Leopold report to bring about any tangible change in predator control policies led to the appointment of yet another special Advisory Committee on Predator Control, whose 1971 report, known commonly as the Cain report, for its chairman, Stanley Cain, reaffirmed many of the recommendations of the Leopold report seven years earlier.[13] This time, however, implementation of the report's recommendations was more decisive. Within a matter of weeks, President Nixon issued an Executive Order that prohibited the use, on federal lands or in federal programs of mammal or bird damage control, of any chemical toxicant for the purpose of killing predatory mammals or birds and of any chemical toxicant that causes secondary poisoning effects for the purpose of killing other mammals, birds, or reptiles.[14] The only exception to the foregoing was that the head of a federal agency could authorize the "emergency use" of such toxicants on federal lands after first making written findings regarding the essentiality of that use and after consulting with the Secretaries of the Interior, Agriculture, and Health, Education and Welfare, and the Administrator of the Environmental Protection Agency.[15]

Nixon's Executive Order thus utilized one clear source of authority, the power to regulate the use of the federal lands, as a means of regulating predator control activities. As to control activities occurring elsewhere, however, some other form of federal authority was clearly required. That authority, embodied in the Federal Insecticide, Fungicide and Rodenticide Act, was likewise exercised shortly after release of the Cain report when the Environmental Protection Agency (hereinafter referred to as EPA) suspended and cancelled the registration of the three toxic chemicals most widely used for predator control purposes—strychnine, sodium cyanide, and sodium fluoroacetate (Compound 1080)—thus effectively prohibiting their use by anyone at any place.[16]

---

[11]*Id.* at 506.

[12]Hearings Before the Subcomm. on Fisheries and Wildlife Conservation of the House Comm. on Merchant Marine and Fisheries, 89th Cong., 2d Sess. 17 (1966).

[13]Predator Control—1971, Report to the Council on Environmental Quality and the Department of the Interior by the Advisory Commitee on Predator Control (1972).

[14]Exec. Order 11643, 3 C.F.R. 664 (1971–75 Comp.).

[15]*Id.* §3(b).

[16]*See* text accompanying notes 76–77 *infra.*

In the years since release of the Cain report, both the Executive Order pertaining to the use of toxicants on federal lands and the EPA action against registration of certain toxicants have been the focus of sharp political controversy. The Executive Order was first modified in 1975 so as to permit the use "on an experimental basis, of sodium cyanide to control coyote and other predatory mammal or bird damage to livestock on Federal lands or in Federal programs."[17] This action followed the decision of EPA to issue a series of experimental use permits for a particular cyanide ejector device. When EPA subsequently registered the device,[18] the Executive Order was again modified to permit the operational use of sodium cyanide ón certain federal lands or in federal programs.[19]

In 1978, Interior Secretary Andrus initiated a major study of mammal predation on Western livestock and appointed a third advisory committee to assist that study. Though this third study had a narrower substantive scope than either of the two earlier advisory committee studies, it was carried out in a far more comprehensive fashion. Public meetings and hearings were held in various parts of the country, draft and final environmental impact statements were prepared and written comments received thereon,[20] the office of the Inspector General performed a special review of the federal animal damage control program,[21] and the final results were published in a comprehensive study of exceptional quality.[22]

Based on the above record, Secretary Andrus in November 1979 announced major reforms in the federal government's policies aimed at controlling predation on livestock in the Western United States. These reforms all derived from a stated long term objective of preventing predator damage rather than controlling predators. That objective reflected the fundamental tenet of the Leopold committee, 15 years earlier, that all native wildlife "are resources of inherent interest and value."

To achieve the objective of preventing predator damage rather than controlling predators, the new policy sought to reduce the occasion for predation by encouraging livestock husbandry techniques that decrease exposure to predators. It also sought to emphasize corrective control, aimed at specific situations of documented significant predation problems rather

---

[17]Exec. Order 11870, §3(c), 3A, C.F.R. 177 (1975).

[18]See note 78 infra.

[19]Exec. Order 11917, 41 Fed. Reg. 22239 (May 28, 1976).

[20]Final Environmental Impact Statement, U.S. Fish and Wildlife Service's Mammalian Predator Damage Management for Livestock Protection in the Western States, U.S. Fish and Wildlife Service (1979).

[21]Review of the Animal Damage Control Program, U.S. Department of the Interior, Office of Audit and Investigation (No. E-FW-FWS-1-78, Nov. 1978).

[22]Predator Damage in the West: A Study of Coyote Management Alternative, U.S. Fish and Wildlife Service (Dec. 1978).

than general preventive control aimed at reducing overall predator populations. Most controversial was its directive to terminate further research or development of Compound 1080.

The Andrus policy directive took the form of a memorandum to the Assistant Secretary for Fish and Wildlife and Parks.[23] Its implementation, rather like the recommendations of the Leopold report 15 years earlier, was largely achieved through conversation, speeches, memoranda, letters, and conferences. When the Reagan Administration assumed office, the Andrus policy was quickly abandoned. Yielding to the pressure that his three predecessors had withstood, Reagan repealed the Nixon Executive Order against the use of toxic predacides on federal lands,[24] and the Environmental Protection Agency Administrator Anne Gorsuch initiated proceedings to consider the reregistration of Compound 1080 for predacidal uses.[25]

At least one of the recommendations of the Cain report was embodied in a more permanent form. That was its recommendation for controls on aerial hunting of wildlife. Actually, the Airborne Hunting Act,[26] imposing such restrictions, was enacted a few months prior to release of the report. Although that legislation imposed substantial penalties for the shooting or harassing of wildlife from aircraft, it is not principally aimed at predator control activities because it exempts from its prohibitions any person who "is employed by, or is an authorized agent of or is operating under a license or permit of, any State or the United States to administer or protect or aid in the administration or protection of land, water, wildlife, livestock, domesticated animals, human life, or crops."[27] One commentator has observed that the Act's exception is virtually big enough to "swallow up the law."[28] The constitutionality of the Airborne Hunting Act was upheld in *United States v. Helsley.*[29]

---

[23] Memorandum from the Secretary to the Assistant Secretary, Fish and Wildlife and Parks, on Animal Damage Control Program, Nov. 8, 1979.

[24] Exec. Order 12342, 47 Fed. Reg. 4223 (Jan. 29, 1982).

[25] As this book was readied for press, the EPA Administrator had yet to act on an October 1982 decision of an EPA administrative law judge that Compound 1080 should be reregistered for predacidal use.

[26] 16 U.S.C. §742j-742l (1976).

[27] *Id.* §742j-742l(b)(1). Regulations of the Fish and Wildlife Service make clear that only sport hunting is absolutely prohibited by the statute. *See* 50 C.F.R. §19.31(a)(1981). It is therefore curious that, although certain "depredating" bald and golden eagles may be taken under the authority of the Bald Eagle Protection Act, they may not be taken from aircraft. *See* 50 C.F.R. §§22.23(b)(1)(1981) and Chapter 4 *supra* at text accompanying notes 124–125.

[28] Guilbert, Wildlife Preservation Under Federal Law, in Federal Environmental Law 582 (E. Dolgin & T. Guilbert eds. 1974).

[29] 615 F.2d 784 (9th Cir. 1979).

The Cain report made a number of other recommendations that have yet to find expression in law or formal administrative policy. Among these were its recommendations for long term research on predator ecology, socioeconomic costs and benefits of predation and the epidemiology of rabies, for study of insurance as an alternative or supplement to predator control and for elimination of the financial and operational partnership between governmental and private interests in predator control programs. These recommendations represent an effort to adjust long-standing predator control policies to more recent ecosystem-oriented wildlife management philosophies without unduly impinging upon the private interests most affected by predators.

Rivalling the controversy over predator control in recent years has been that over controlling winter "blackbird" roosts. Large roosts of starlings, cowbirds, red-winged blackbirds, and related species have increasingly come into conflict with human interests by feeding on nearby agricultural crops and allegedly by increasing the risk of certain types of disease, principally histoplasmosis. Efforts to disperse or otherwise control such roosts were not very effective until the development of PA-14, an "avian stressing agent" also known as Tergitol. PA-14, when applied under the right meteorological conditions, works by reducing the natural ability of the target birds to withstand cold.

In early 1975, the United States Army planned to use PA-14 against roosts on and near certain military bases in Kentucky and Tennessee. Because of the need to act quickly, an environmental impact statement was hastily prepared and made available for public comment only seven days prior to the planned action. Attacking the adequacy of the impact statement and the substantive decision to proceed, the Society for Animal Rights and other plaintiffs sought a preliminary injunction. The district court's denial of that injunction was promptly affirmed by the court of appeals in *Society for Animal Rights v. Schlesinger,* and the attack on the birds took place.[30] In the course of its opinion, however, the court expressed concern about the need for better information by directing the Defense Department

> [p]rior to any subsequent applications of PA-14,...[to] incorporate new findings of significance into its analysis, perhaps by way of amending the existing EIS, with opportunity for comment by other agencies and members of the public. And, consistent with NEPA, it must reassess its determination to go forward in light of any changes in environmental impact analysis occasioned by its discoveries.[31]

---

[30]512 F.2d 915 (D.C. Cir. 1975).
[31]*Id.* at 918.

The following winter, when the blackbirds returned again, the threat that the still-pending litigation would block further control activities seemed more real. To avert that possibility, both houses of Congress passed, in a single day and without benefit of any hearings or committee reports, a law exempting all blackbird control activities undertaken by the states of Kentucky or Tennessee or by the federal government in those states on or before April 15, 1976, from the National Environmental Policy Act, the Federal Environmental Pesticide Control Act "or any other provision of law," as long as certain minimal certifications were made by the state governor and the Secretary of the Interior.[32]

In response to those and other similar controversies, the Fish and Wildlife Service developed a plan to kill up to 50 million blackbirds annually over an indefinite period.[33] The program, which is to be carried out in close cooperation with state and local governments, is aimed at reducing the threats posed by specific large roosts rather than at bringing about any long term population reductions. Accordingly, it offers no long range solution to the problem it seeks to combat, thus underscoring not only the limitations on our present ability to control certain types of animal damage, but also the uncertainty of what that public policy ought to be.

## WILDLIFE ASPECTS OF FEDERAL PESTICIDE LAW

As was stated at the outset of this chapter, the control or eradication of "pests" appears to be a goal about which there is little dispute. To the extent that our laws permit or encourage the attainment of that goal, they embody a policy favoring the control or eradication of certain forms of wildlife.[34] The consensus as to the appropriateness of this goal is probably attributable to the fact that pests (most often insects) are perceived as posing significant threats to certain economic and social interests, principally agriculture and public health. Moreover, the need to control pest popula-

---

[32]Act of Feb. 4, 1976, Pub. L. No. 94-207, 90 Stat. 28. Hearings on the legislation were held five days *after* its passage. *See* Hearings on H.R. 11510 Before the Subcomm. on Fisheries and Wildlife Conservation and the Environment of the House Comm. on Merchant Marine and Fisheries, 94th Cong., 2d Sess. 1–158 (1976).

[33]*See* Department of the Interior, Fish and Wildlife Service, Final Environmental Statement, The Use of Compound PA-14 Avian Stressing Agent for Control of Blackbirds and Starlings at Winter Roosts (FES 76-39, 1976). *See also* 41 Fed. Reg. 48580 (Nov. 4, 1976).

[34]Even the Endangered Species Act of 1973 exempts from its coverage certain insect pests. *See* Chapter 12 *infra* at note 63.

tions often arises from outbreaks attributable to intensive monoculture or other significant human disturbances of natural conditions.

If our laws have encouraged the control or eradication of pests, they have also, from very early in this century, imposed certain limits on those activities. The first such federal measure, the Insecticide Act of 1910, was aimed primarily at protecting the purchasers of insecticides and fungicides from fraud.[35] It prohibited the manufacture or interstate shipment of such products if they were "adulterated" or "misbranded," terms that included a product's failure to meet "the professed standard or quality under which it is sold,"[36] or to have on its labeling a correct statement of its contents.[37] The machinery to enforce the Act's limited prohibitions was clearly inadequate because it contained no provision requiring registration of insecticides and fungicides prior to sale. Thus violations could not be prevented, but only discovered and punished after the fact.

In 1947, the Insecticide Act was repealed and replaced by the Federal Insecticide, Fungicide, and Rodenticide Act (hereinafter referred to as FIFRA).[38] It substantially expanded the scope of federal regulatory authority. First, whereas the 1910 Act had only applied to "insecticides and fungicides," terms that were expressly limited to products directed at insects and fungi, FIFRA's provisions applied to all "economic poisons," a term that was defined to include all products

> intended for preventing, destroying, repelling, or mitigating any insects, rodents, nematodes, fungi, weeds, and other forms of plant or animal life... which the Secretary shall declare to be a pest...[or] intended for use as a plant regulator, defoliant or dessicant.[39]

Second, while FIFRA, like the 1910 Act, prohibited the sale of "misbranded" poisons, it substantially broadened the concept of misbranding. Thus any poison was deemed to be "misbranded" if it did not bear a label containing "a warning or caution statement which may be necessary and if

---

[35] Act of April 26, 1910, ch. 191, 36 Stat. 331 (repealed 1947).

[36] *Id.* §7.

[37] *Id.* §8.

[38] Act of June 25, 1947, ch. 125, 61 Stat. 163 (current version at 7 U.S.C. §§136–136y (1976 and Supp. V 1981)).

[39] *Id.* §2(a). The "Secretary" refers to the Secretary of Agriculture. In fact, the definition of economic poisons is even broader than the language quoted in the text would indicate. For example, the term "insect" is elsewhere defined to include not only members of the class Insecta, but also "other allied classes of arthropods whose members are wingless and usually have more than six legs, as, for example, spiders, mites, ticks, centipedes, and wood lice." *Id.* §2(h) (Current version at 7 U.S.C. §136(o)(1976)).

complied with adequate to prevent injury to living man and other vertebrate animals, vegetation, and useful invertebrate animals."[40] In addition, certain economic poisons, including insecticides, nematocides, fungicides, and herbicides were deemed misbranded if "when used as directed or in accordance with commonly recognized practice it shall be injurious to living man or other vertebrate animals."[41] An identical special misbranding provision governed plant regulators, defoliants, and dessicants, except for the omission of the words "or in accordance with commonly recognized practice."[42] Thus, through this rather curious and indirect concept of "misbranding," consideration of the effects of certain poisons on nontarget wildlife was, for the first time, compelled by federal law.

A further substantial expansion of federal regulatory authority brought about by FIFRA was its requirement that all economic poisons be registered. Although, as originally passed, FIFRA required that all registration applications, even those for poisons that in the judgment of the Secretary of Agriculture failed to meet the Act's substantive requirements (*i.e.*, were misbranded) be accepted,[43] a subsequent amendment in 1964 permitted the Secretary to refuse to register such poisons or, having previously registered them, to cancel their registration.[44] In addition, where such action was "necessary to prevent an imminent hazard to the public," the Secretary could immediately suspend the registration of a poison, thus effectively removing it from the market while the elaborate and time-consuming procedures to effectuate cancellation went forward.

The 1964 amendments to FIFRA thus, for the first time, gave the Secretary of Agriculture authority to prevent the marketing of poisons that posed a threat to nontarget wildlife. In addition, they furnished a vehicle for private persons to compel the Secretary to take action against already registered poisons. To test the effectiveness of this vehicle, the Environmental Defense Fund and others petitioned the Secretary of Agriculture on October 31, 1969, to initiate cancellation proceedings against all pesticides containing DDT and, pending completion of such proceedings, to suspend immediately the registration of all such pesticides. The Secretary responded

---

[40]*Id.* §2(u)(2)(d) (current version at 7 U.S.C. §136(q)(1976 & Supp. V 1981)).

[41]*Id.* §3(u)(2)(g).

[42]*Id.* §3(z)(2)(h).

[43]If the Secretary believed that a particular poison failed to meet FIFRA's substantive requirements, he could register it "under protest." The registrant of a protested poison was made subject to higher penalties and immediate cancellation of the registration if convicted of a violation of FIFRA. To prove a violation, however, the government had the burden of showing, beyond a reasonable doubt, that the violation had occurred. *See* S. Rep. 573, 88th Cong., 1st Sess. 8 (1963).

[44]Act of May 12, 1964, Pub. L. No. 88-305, §3.

by initating cancellation proceedings against certain limited uses of DDT, requesting further comment on action to be taken with respect to other uses and ignoring the request for suspension.[45] The Secretary's failure to take more definitive action was challenged in the court of appeals in *Environmental Defense Fund, Inc. v. Hardin*.[46] The *Hardin* decision set some extremely important precedents for federal pesticide law. First, it upheld the standing of persons alleging "biological harm to man and to other living things" to challenge the Secretary's actions (or inactions) under FIFRA.[47] Second, it clearly held that the Secretary's refusal to initiate cancellation proceedings against, or to suspend, a pesticide about which such allegations were made was judicially reviewable.[48] Because the administrative record before the court was inadequate to determine the basis on which the Secretary had made his decision, however, the court remanded for a fuller explication by the Secretary.

In subsequently setting forth his reasons for declining to issue further cancellation notices or to suspend any DDT registrations, the Secretary emphasized the need to await completion of an internal review process for each of the existing DDT uses, despite his express findings that DDT is "toxic to certain birds, bees, and fish" and "has produced cancer in test animals and various injuries in man."[49] In reviewing the Secretary's further decision not to act, the court of appeals, in *Environmental Defense Fund, Inc. v. Ruckelshaus*, established yet another important FIFRA precedent.[50] It held that, as a result of the 1964 amendments, "any substantial question of safety" compels the Secretary to initate cancellation proceedings, thereby "shifting to the manufacturer the burden of proving the safety of his product."[51] Since the Secretary's own findings clearly indicated a substantial question as to the safety of DDT, the court directed that cancellation notices be issued.

As a result of the *Ruckelshaus* decision, cancellation notices were promptly issued, the beginning of a more than year long proceeding that culminated in the cancellation of all registered uses of DDT save for public health and agricultural pest quarantine use. Industry attacked the decision as too sweeping, environmentalists as too limited. Reviewing the case for

---

[45]34 Fed. Reg. 18827 (Nov. 25, 1969).

[46]428 F.2d 1093 (D.C. Cir. 1970).

[47]*Id.* at 1096.

[48]*Id.* at 1098.

[49]Environmental Defense Fund, Inc. v. Ruckelshaus, 439 F.2d 584, 594 (D.C. Cir. 1971).

[50]*Id.*

[51]*Id.* at 593.

yet a third time, the court of appeals upheld the partial cancellation decision because it was supported by "substantial evidence" in the record that DDT posed hazards both to man and the environment.[52]

The lengthy DDT litigation thus established a number of important principles regarding federal authority to act against pesticides harmful to nontarget wildlife, and regarding citizen standing to invoke the aid of the courts to compel such federal action. During the course of that litigation, however, two further significant developments had occurred. First, in 1970, an executive reorganization had transferred the authority of the Secretary of Agriculture under FIFRA to the Administrator of the newly created Environmental Protection Agency.[53] Second, in 1972, FIFRA had been substantially amended by the Federal Environmental Pesticide Control Act (hereinafter referred to as FEPCA).[54]

FEPCA substantially expanded federal regulatory authority over pesticides by extending that authority to purely intrastate sales of pesticides. Further, it gave the federal government its first authority over the actual use of pesticides by prohibiting any person from using a pesticide "in a manner inconsistent with its labeling."[55] Finally, it set up a two-category system of registration whereby all registered pesticides were to be classified either for "general use" or for "restricted use"; the latter could be used only by applicators certified to be competent in the use of such products.[56] The touchstone for deciding which category of registration is appropriate, as well as for making determinations of cancellation or suspension, is the avoidance of "unreasonable adverse effects on the environment." How this standard suffuses the framework of FEPCA and embodies a substantial degree of protection for wildlife will now be explored.

The standard of avoiding "unreasonable adverse effects on the environment" appears in no fewer than 10 separate places in FEPCA. For example, before approving an application for registration, the Administrator must determine that the product in question "will perform its

---

[52]Environmental Defense Fund, Inc. v. EPA, 489 F.2d 1247 (D.C. Cir. 1973).

[53]Reorganization Plan No. 3 of 1970, 84 Stat. 2086.

[54]7 U.S.C. §§136–136y (1976 & Supp. V 1981). FEPCA has been analyzed in a number of publications. Among the best is Butler, Federal Pesticide Law, in Federal Environmental Law 1232–1288 (E. Dolgin & T. Guilbert eds. 1974).

[55]7 U.S.C. §136j(a)(2)(G)(1976).

[56]Id. §§136a(d), 136(b) (1976 & Supp. V 1981). The statute is ambiguous as to whether the federal government may certify applicators of restricted use pesticides or whether that is a function that only the states are to perform. For an extensive analysis of this question, see Megysey, Governmental Authority to Regulate the Use and Application of Pesticides: State vs. Federal, 21 S.D. L. Rev. 652, 659–666 (1976).

intended function without unreasonable adverse effects on the environment"[57] and that "when used in accordance with widespread and commonly recognized practice it will not generally cause unreasonable adverse effects on the environment."[58] If a product "may generally cause, without additional regulatory restrictions," such effects, it can only be registered as a restricted use pesticide.[59] After registration, if "additional factual information regarding unreasonable adverse effects on the environment" comes to the attention of the registrant, he must make that information available to the Administrator,[60] who in turn must either initiate cancellation proceedings or hold a hearing to determine whether to cancel the registration of the pesticide in question or change its classification, if, on the basis of such information or any other in his possession, "it appears to [him] that [the] pesticide . . . , when used in accordance with widespread and commonly recognized practice, generally causes unreasonable adverse effects on the environment."[61] Similarly, the Administrator may immediately suspend the registration of any pesticide if such action is "necessary to prevent an imminent hazard,"[62] a situation defined as one in which

> the continued use of a pesticide during the time required for cancellation proceeding would be likely to result in unreasonable adverse effects on the environment or will involve unreasonable hazard to the survival of a species declared endangered or threatened. . . .[63]

Finally, the standard appears as well in connection with the Administrator's authority to issue experimental use permits for pesticides prior to

---

[57] 7 U.S.C. §136a(c)(5)(C)(1976 & Supp. V 1981).

[58] *Id.* §136a(c)(5)(D).

[59] *Id.* §136a(d)(1)(C)(1976).

[60] *Id.* §136d(a)(2).

[61] *Id.* §136d(b) (Supp. V 1981). Compare this standard for cancellation with the standard for registration as a restricted use pesticide, *supra* note 58. The difficulty of distinguishing these two standards has been pointed out by others. *See* Butler *supra* note 54 at 1248. This conceptual difficulty is compounded by the fact that in making initial registration decisions, the Administrator is expressly precluded from making "any lack of essentiality a criterion for denying registration." 7 U.S.C. §136a(c)(5)(Supp. V 1981), which has generally been understood to mean that he may not consider the availability of other products that are equally safe and effective. See National Academy of Sciences, Pest Control: An Assessment of Present and Alternative Technologies 271–272 (1975). Yet, in making cancellation or suspension decisions, he is required to balance the costs and benefits of such actions, a process that has traditionally included consideration of available alternatives. *See, e.g.,* Environmental Defense Fund, Inc. v. EPA, 489 F.2d 1247 (D.C. Cir. 1973).

[62] 7 U.S.C. §136d(c)(1)(1976).

[63] *Id.* §136(1)(1976).

registration,[64] and in connection with his authority to permit the continued sale of existing stocks of any pesticide whose registration has been automatically cancelled at the end of a five-year registration period.[65]

It is obvious, if only because of its very pervasiveness, that the standard of avoiding "unreasonable adverse effects on the environment" is of crucial significance to an assessment of how useful FEPCA can be to the protection of wildlife. The statutory definition of the standard is not particularly elucidating. It provides that the standard

> means any unreasonable risk to man or the environment, taking into account the economic, social, and environmental costs and benefits of the use of any pesticide.[66]

Thus, at a minimum, the standard compels a balancing of certain costs and benefits and includes "risks to man" within the umbrella of "effects on the environment." The latter aspect is made expressly clear by a further definition of "environment" to include "water, air, land, and all plants and man and other animals living therein, and the interrelationships which exist among these."[67] Further, whereas FIFRA's protections extended only to vertebrate and useful invertebrate animals, FEPCA defines "animal" to include "all vertebrate and invertebrate species."[68]

From the foregoing, it is clear that the substantive standards of protection embodied in FEPCA extend to the protection of wildlife. It is also quite clear, however, that they also encompass the protection of man. In fact, the administrative decisions and litigated cases under both FIFRA and FEPCA suggest that the principal benefit to wildlife occurs as an incident to the protection of human health. The DDT litigation, already discussed, is a case in which the pesticide under scrutiny was believed to be harmful to both man and wildlife, though neither the administrators nor the courts made any attempt to separate the two elements of harm. Subsequent suspension decisions, however, have clearly made such a separation.

The aldrin-dieldrin case is an example. On December 3, 1970, the Environmental Defense Fund petitioned for the immediate suspension and ultimate cancellation of all registered uses of these two related pesticides. Three months later, the Administrator issued the requested cancellation notices but declined to suspend any registration because of the lack of an "imminent hazard." The Administrator's decision not to suspend the

---

[64]*Id.* §§136c(d)(e).

[65]*Id.* §136d(a)(1).

[66]*Id.* §136(bb).

[67]7 U.S.C. §136(j)(1976).

[68]*Id.* §136(d).

products in question was made notwithstanding his finding that certain studies indicated "an equivalent potential for adverse effect on non-target predatory wildlife" as that of DDT.[69] As in the DDT case, the Environmental Defense Fund sought judicial review of the Administrator's decision not to suspend, attacking it as irrational. Insofar as environmental harm was concerned, the court of appeals was willing to uphold the Administator's decision. However, the court was considerably more troubled by the petitioner's "nontrivial showing with respect to carcinogenicity."[70] The Administrator's decision had addressed this topic only cursorily. Frankly acknowledging the special status of this concern, the court stated that "candor compels us to say that when the matter involved is as sensitive and fright-laden as cancer, even a court scrupulous to the point of punctilio in deference to administrative latitude is beset with concern" by a less than full discussion of the Administrator's reasoning.[71]

On remand, the Administrator initially continued to refuse to suspend the pesticides. However, midway through the cancellation proceedings, he took that further action on the basis that evidence developed in the interim indicated an "imminent hazard." However, whereas "the cancellation hearing encompass[ed] a broad range of issues concerning the effect of aldrin-dieldrin on the environment as well as on human beings, the suspension hearing was confined to whether the pesticides present a cancer hazard to man."[72] The Administrator's final suspension order, based on that limited consideration, was upheld in *Environmental Defense Fund, Inc. v. EPA*.[73] Similarly, the suspension order issued against most uses of the pesticides heptachlor and chlordane was based on proceedings in which carcinogenicity was the sole issue.[74]

What these cases suggest, at least for suspension orders, is that human health, and particularly the concern for cancer, is the paramount issue, while wildlife and other environmental concerns are clearly secondary.[75] It

---

[69]Environmental Defense Fund v. EPA, 465 F.2d 528 (D.C. Cir. 1972).

[70]*Id.* at 537.

[71]*Id.* at 538.

[72]Environmental Defense Fund, Inc. v. EPA, 510 F.2d 1292, 1298 (D.C. Cir. 1975).

[73]*Id.*

[74]That suspension order was upheld in all but minor respects in Environmental Defense Fund, Inc. v. EPA, 548 F.2d 998 (D.C. Cir 1976), *cert. denied sub nom.* Velsicol Chemical Corp. v. EPA, 431 U.S. 925 (1977).

[75]The second decision of the court of appeals involving DDT, Environmental Defense Fund, Inc. v. Ruckelshaus, 439 F.2d 584, 597 (D.C. Cir. 1971), stated that the Secretary of Agriculture then interpreted the "public," for purposes of ascertaining the existence of an "imminent hazard to the public," to include fish and wildlife. It is noteworthy, however, that a suspension order was never issued at any time in the DDT proceedings, so the Secretary's interpretation was never put to the test.

is, however, more difficult to assess the relative weights given to each of the many values to be protected under FEPCA when registration, experimental use, cancellation, or other decisions requiring balancing of risks and benefits occur. Very interesting in this regard is the following assessment and recommendation contained in a comprehensive pest control study recently undertaken by the National Academy of Sciences.

> In an EPA risk-benefit analysis, greater weight is given to the risk that human health will be impaired than to risks that ecosystem stability will be disrupted where the impact on human health or on the future human use of the resource is not known. The weight assigned by the EPA to risks to human health compared with that assigned to risks to ecosystem stability is consistent with the Western rational tradition. A "problem" exists only where the health of human beings is threatened or a future human use of a resource might be foreclosed. It is beyond the scope of this report to challenge this view directly or to suggest radical philosophical departures from it. We merely point out, as the EPA partially recognizes, that the costs of technological advancement have historically been defined very narrowly and that recent thinking about the value of relatively undisturbed ecosystems qua ecosystems is undergoing a fundamental reevaluation. Therefore, we recommend that the EPA view the variables relevant to risk-benefit analysis as dynamic and that the concept of cost be subject to expansion as societal attitudes toward our natural resources change.[76]

The one apparent exception to the foregoing is the decision taken under FIFRA in 1972 to suspend and cancel three economic poisons then in common use for coyote control: strychnine, sodium fluoracetate (1080) and sodium cyanide.[77] The dominant, if not exclusive, issue in that decision was the effect of the poisons on nontarget wildlife. Still, it is a precedent of questionable value. The suspension and cancellation decisions seem to have been made simultaneously—indeed, as a single decision—and without objection from the registrant. Accordingly, there is neither an administrative nor a judicial decision developed in an adversarial context.[78]

---

Elsewhere, however, the court seemed to recognize the paramount position of protecting human health when it suggested that, in the process of weighing the benefits of continued registration, "greater weight should be accorded the value of a pesticide for the control of disease, and less weight should be accorded its value for the protection of a commercial crop." *Id.* at 594.

[76]National Academy of Science, Pest Control: An Assessment of Present and Alternative Technologies 277–78 (1975).

[77]37 Fed. Reg. 5718 (March 18, 1972).

[78]Some two years after the cancellation, the state of Wyoming sought to enjoin its enforcement. The state's contention that the cancellation order was invalid, because

The emphasis that the cases, other than the coyote control case, place on protecting human health should not obscure the fact that wildlife can and has also benefited greatly from the protective provisions of FEPCA. In fact, the regulations and guidelines for the registration and reregistration of pesticides suggest a significant potential utility of FEPCA for wildlife protection purposes. Those regulations specify precise "risk criteria," both for hazards to humans and domesticated animals and for hazards to wildlife that, if met or exceeded, will cause a "rebuttable presumption" to arise against registration or in favor of cancellation.[79] Moreover, the guidelines elaborate in detail the types of tests that will be required to show that a given product is acceptable under the risk criteria of the regulations.[80]

Limiting the value of the "rebuttable presumption against registration" procedure for wildlife conservation interests is the decision of the Court of Appeals for the District of Columbia Circuit in *Environmental Defense Fund v. Costle*.[81] That case held that if the Administrator issues a preliminary notice against registration but ultimately fails to cancel all uses of the pesticide, only the registrant and users of the pesticide are entitled to an administrative hearing to challenge cancelled uses. The only recourse for environmental interests is to initiate a challenge in a district court, where the Administrator's action is subject to a highly deferential "arbitrary and capricious" standard of review. If these interests had a right to a hearing before the Administrator, his decision after that hearing would be subject to the less deferential "substantial evidence" standard of review.

Wildlife also shares with humans the vulnerability to pesticide exposure occurring as a result of certain exceptions to FEPCA's coverage. Among the most controversial of these is the provision authorizing the Administrator to "exempt any Federal or State agency from any provision of this Act if he determines that emergency conditions exist which require such exemption."[82] The Administrator's implementing regulations provide for three categories of such emergency exemptions, one of which, the so-called "crisis" exemption, allows the state or federal agency to use an unregistered pesticide for a limited period without first making any request to do so.[83] Although no pesticide that has been suspended or cancelled may

---

it was not accompanied by an environmental impact statement, was rejected in Wyoming v. Hathaway, 525 F.2d 66 (10th Cir. 1975). Other issues in related litigation against EPA remain outstanding. Meanwhile, EPA has modified its 1972 order so as to permit the registration of sodium cyanide in the so-called "M-44" spring-loaded device. See 40 Fed. Reg. 44726 (Sept. 29, 1975).

[79]40 C.F.R. §162.11(1981).

[80]*Id.* §§162. 41–47 (1981).

[81]631 F.2d 922 (D.C. Cir. 1980), *cert. denied*, 449 U.S. 1112 (1981).

[82]7 U.S.C. §136p (1976).

[83]40 C.F.R. §166.2(c)(1981).

be used for any use prohibited under the terms of such suspension or cancellation pursuant to a crisis exemption, there is no similar express prohibition for the other two categories of emergency exemptions.[84]

Of more importance, probably, is the limited reach of our federal pesticide laws precisely because they are simply *pesticide* laws. It is now abundantly clear that pesticides are but one of many types of chemical substances posing a hazard to the natural environment, to the wildlife in it, and to human health as well. However, the recently enacted Toxic Substances Control Act of 1976,[85] the Resource Conservation and Recovery Act of 1976,[86] and the Comprehensive Environmental Response, Compensation and Liability Act of 1980[87] are designed to provide a measure of protection against those further hazards. All of those statutes clearly extend their protections to wildlife.[88] Based on the example of the federal pesticide laws, however, it seems likely that the major benefit to wildlife will result from actions directed principally at protecting public health.

---

[84]EPA has in fact granted so-called "specific" emergency exemptions for use of DDT against the pea leaf weavil and the Douglas fir tussock moth in the Pacific Northwest. *See* 39 Fed. Reg. 10322 (March 19, 1974) and 39 Fed. Reg. 8377 (March 5, 1974). When the state of Louisiana sought a specific emergency exemption for use of a massive quantity of DDT against the tobacco bud worm, EPA announced a new policy that it would treat similar requests involving cancelled pesticides as requests for modification of the earlier cancellation order, rather than simply as requests for emergency exemptions, for which literally no consideration of the risks of pesticide use is required. EPA explained its earlier exemptions on the grounds that they involved particular uses not expressly covered by its 1972 cancellation order. 40 Fed. Reg. 12261 (March 18, 1975).

[85]15 U.S.C. §§2601–2609 (1976 & Supp. V 1981).

[86]42 U.S.C. §§6901–6987 (1976 & Supp. IV 1980).

[87]42 U.S.C. §§9601–9657 (Supp. IV 1980).

[88]See Chapter 7 at text accompanying notes 206–210.

# Chapter 10

# INTERNATIONAL ASPECTS OF FEDERAL WILDLIFE LAW

## INTRODUCTION

It was stated at the outset of this book that the ultimate source of authority for all governmental regulation in the United States is its Constitution. That document describes the respective powers of the state and federal governments and allocates among the three branches of the federal government the authority for enacting, enforcing, and interpreting federal laws. Once properly enacted, those laws are binding on all persons subject to the jurisdiction of the United States. They are, in the words of the Constitution, "the supreme Law of the Land."[1]

In the world community, there is no constitution providing a mechanism for the development of laws to bind nations. There is no elected legislature with the authority to enact such laws, no universal executive to enforce them, and no supreme judicial tribunal to interpret them. There is instead a somewhat ill-defined system for accommodating the competing interests of nations. When that system works smoothly, accommodation takes place through formal agreements between two or more nations in which each undertakes to restrain in some manner the untrammeled pursuit of its own interests. When the system fails to work smoothly, the pursuit of individual interests is restrained ultimately by the threat of economic or military reprisal.

---

[1]U.S. Const. art. VI.

252

Wildlife is a particularly appropriate subject for international regulation. Certain forms of wildlife, such as birds, migrate between two or more countries during their life cycles. Others, like fish and most marine mammals, spend part or all of their lives in the high seas, beyond the claim of any single nation, yet subject to the exploitation of all.[2] Unless some means of restraining the pursuit of individual national objectives can be devised, each nation is capable of destroying for all nations the value of the wildlife resource it exploits.[3]

The difficulties of devising an effective means of international restraint are numerous. Most fundamentally, the conservation measures embodied in any international agreement can only bind the nations that ratify or accede to the agreement. So long as all the nations exploiting or otherwise affecting a wildlife resource are party to an agreement for its conservation, that agreement can function effectively. When other nations begin to exploit or affect the same resource but refuse to be bound by the preexisting agreement, its effectiveness is diminished or destroyed.

The ability of individual nations to thwart international regulation argues forcefully for the inclusion of as many nations as possible in conservation agreements. At the same time, however, to achieve the necessary degree of inclusivity, either the substantive conservation measures embodied in such agreements must be diluted to the lowest common denominator of acceptability, or some procedure must be established whereby individual nations can avoid the applicability of conservation measures they deem too stringent. A variety of mechanisms to accomplish the latter objective are found in existing international agreements. Some require the affirmative approval of all member nations before any new conservation measure takes effect. Others require the approval of only some specified percentage of the member nations but absolve nonconsenting nations from adhering to the measure. Perhaps the most flexibility is found in those agreements that make new conservation measures automatically binding when agreed to by some percentage of the member nations but permit those nations that affirmatively express their objection or reservation to escape its applicability.

Even when an agreement encompasses all the nations that it should, and even when they all agree to be bound by each of its conservation measures, there is still a very difficult problem of enforcement. The one

[2] In recent years, the claims of coastal nations to exclusive authority over the living resources of their adjacent waters have expanded significantly. That history is described briefly in Chapter 13 at text accompanying notes 2–23.

[3] It has been argued persuasively that each individual or nation exploiting a "common property" resource not only has the potential for destroying it for all others, but even has a rational incentive for doing so. See Hardin, The Tragedy of the Commons, 162 Science 1243 (1968).

aspect of sovereignty to which nations cling tenaciously is the exclusive right to enforce the terms of international agreements against their own nationals. Effective enforcement therefore depends not only on the ability of enforcement officials to conduct physical observations and investigations of those engaged in the regulated activity, but also upon the trust that those same officials have in their foreign counterparts to carry out their enforcement duties diligently. Where that trust is lacking, the incentive to overlook violations in order to avoid a competitive disadvantage is created.

A final general observation about international agreements concerns their unique status in United States law. On the one hand, they are like federal laws enacted by Congress in that they are declared by the Constitution to be "the supreme Law of the Land." On the other hand, they are rather like contracts between the United States and the other nations that agree to them. As such, they may or may not be automatically effective within the United States without further implementing legislation; similarly, they may or may not impose mandatory duties or confer enforceable rights on private citizens within the United States.[4] Finally, the courts are often reluctant to interject themselves into disputes arising under international agreements because such disputes necessarily involve the foreign relations of the United States, an area in which the Executive Branch has traditionally been accorded great deference.[5]

Notwithstanding these unique characteristics of international wildlife agreements, they have an important interplay with domestic federal wildlife legislation. For example, it was shown in Chapter 2 that the Convention with Great Britain for the Protection of Migratory Birds provided the legal basis for a broad exercise of federal regulatory authority and stimulated a fundamental rethinking of the meaning of the then current doctrine of state ownership of wildlife.[6] Subsequent international treaties have afforded similar bases for even more far-reaching domestic

---

[4]The self-executing nature of international treaties and the question of their creation of private rights are addressed in Guilbert, Wilderness Preservation II: Bringing the Convention into Court, 3 Envtl. L. Rep. (Envtl. L. Inst.) 50044 (1973); Comment, the Migratory Bird Treaty: Another Feather in the Environmentalist's Cap, 19 S.D.L. Rev. 307 (1974); and Comment, Criteria for Self-Executing Treaties, 1968 U. Ill. L.F. 49.

[5]In Diggs v. Dent, Civil No. 74-1292 (D.D.C. 1975), the court dismissed a challenge to the importation of seal skins from South Africa as a violation of the United Nations Charter, various United Nations Security Council resolutions, and an advisory opinion of the International Court of Justice because the action challenged was "within the foreign policy authority of the President and...nonjusticiable."

[6]Aug. 16, 1916, 39 Stat. 1702, T.S. No. 628. See Chapter 2 at text accompanying notes 47–57.

legislation, such as the Endangered Species Act of 1973.[7] At the same time, however, as the scope of federal regulatory authority over wildlife has broadened under expanded interpretations of the Constitution's commerce and property clauses, and the need to premise exercises of that authority on preexisting international treaties has correspondingly diminished, federal lawmakers have sought affirmative ways to project domestic wildlife policies into the international arena. Thus federal wildlife law has both influenced and been influenced by the international law of wildlife.

In this chapter, certain of the more noteworthy international wildlife agreements to which the United States is a party will be examined. So also will certain recent domestic laws that have sought to influence the implementation of those agreements so as to shape international wildlife policy into the mold of federal wildlife policy. The object here is not to give a comprehensive analysis of each of the many wildlife treaties to which the United States is a party;[8] rather, it is to trace the evolution of those treaties and to compare and contrast it with the evolution of the purely domestic aspect of federal wildlife law.

## TREATIES RELATING TO THE DIRECT PROTECTION OF WILDLIFE

### The Northern Fur Seal

The impetus for enactment of the Lacey Act of 1900, the first significant federal wildlife legislation, was the inability of individual states to protect wildlife resources adequately against well-organized commercial interests able to harvest excessive quantities of wildlife and promptly ship them in interstate commerce out of the reach of the state where they were harvested.[9] Similar factors underlay the first effort of the United States to conserve wildlife resources through international agreement. The focus of that effort was on the northern fur seal, a marine mammal prized for its fine fur.

In the latter part of the nineteenth century, the northern fur seal was heavily exploited by commercial sealers operating under exclusive lease from the United States on the Pribilof Islands in the Bering Sea, which the

---

[7] See Chapter 12.

[8] The more than 70 international treaties and agreements to which the United States is a party pertaining to wildlife or other environmental matters are collected in Senate Comm. on Commerce, Science, and Transportation, Treaties and Other International Agreements on Fisheries, Oceanographic Resources, and Wildlife Involving the United States (1977).

[9] See Chapter 5 at text accompanying notes 8–12.

seals used each year as a breeding ground. They were also harvested on other island rookeries then under the jurisdiction of Russia and Japan. Since the fur seal is a migratory mammal, it also became increasingly vulnerable to harvesting while swimming along its migratory routes, a notably inefficient and wasteful practice known as pelagic sealing.[10]

Despite the waste, pelagic sealing enabled each nation to harvest seals otherwise destined for rookeries under the jurisdiction of the other countries. Great Britain as well, because it claimed none of the island rookeries, had an obvious interest in pelagic sealing. Toward the end of the nineteenth century, the United States spearheaded efforts to obtain international agreement respecting the exploitation of northern fur seals and most particularly the practice of pelagic sealing.[11] Those efforts finally bore lasting fruit in 1911 when Russia, Japan, Great Britain, and the United States concluded a Treaty for the Preservation and Protection of Fur Seals.[12]

The central provisions of the 1911 Treaty were its total ban on pelagic sealing[13] and its requirement that future seal harvests on each of the island rookeries be conducted under the supervision of the nation having authority thereover.[14] The *quid pro quo* for agreeing to mutual restraint on pelagic sealing was the requirement that each nation share a specified part

---

[10]The wastefulness of pelagic sealing as it was then practiced derived from the difficulty of retrieving killed or wounded seals and from the fact that it often resulted in the killing of pregnant or nursing females.

[11]A brief history of northern fur seal exploitation and of efforts to regulate it can be found in Department of Commerce, National Marine Fisheries Service, Final Environmental Impact Statement, Renegotiation of Interim Convention on Conservation of North Pacific Fur Seals, app. E (1976). A longer and more popular account is given by Reiger, Song of the Seal, 77 Audubon 6 (Sept., 1975). A fascinating part of that history is also contained in an 1898 Supreme Court decision in a case brought by the United States against its exclusive lessee of the right to harvest seals on the Pribilof Islands for monies owed under the lease. The lessee contended unsuccessfully that restrictions on the size of the permitted harvest arising from an informal agreement between the United States and Great Britain abrogated the lease. *See* North American Commercial Company v. United States, 171 U.S. 110 (1898).

[12]July 7, 1911, 37 Stat. 1542, T.S. No. 564.

[13]A special exemption from the pelagic sealing ban was carved out for "Indians, Ainos, Aleuts, or other aborigines...in canoes...propelled entirely by oars, paddles, or sails...in the way hitherto practiced and without the use of firearms." *Id.* art. IV.

[14]This aspect of the 1911 Treaty set a precedent that, although it continues in effect today, has not been followed in other wildlife treaties. Only with respect to northern fur seals is the United States itself directly involved in the commercial harvest of wildlife.

of its rookery harvest with the other signatory nations.[15] The 1911 Treaty also prohibited the importation of any sealskins other than those officially marked and certified as having been taken under a government-supervised harvest and provided a limited means of enforcement by each signatory nation against the others. That is, each nation was authorized to seize the vessels of any other nation, except when the offending vessel was in the other's territorial waters, if such vessels were engaged in pelagic sealing. However, the seizing nation was obliged to deliver the vessel as soon as possible to the nation having authority over it.[16] Only the latter nation was empowered to try the offense for which the vessel was seized and to impose such penalties as it deemed appropriate.[17]

The 1911 Treaty did not expressly articulate any clear policy regarding the level of harvest to be carried out, nor did it establish any formal mechanism for the determination of that level. Rather, each country having control over an island rookery was free to establish its own harvest level. It is quite clear, however, that the Treaty contemplated that there would be a substantial harvest. Thus the Treaty required that the United States make lump sum advance payments of $200,000 to Japan and Great Britain, for which the United States was to reimburse itself by retaining skins from the shares otherwise owing to those nations. Further, the Treaty required that the respective shares for Great Britain and Japan be not less than 1,000 annually, thus contemplating a yearly harvest on the Pribilofs of at least 6,500 seals. Though the United States could totally prohibit the harvest in any year, it could do so only upon paying $10,000 each to Great Britain and Japan, unless the total seal population on the Pribilofs fell below 100,000.[18] Thus there were significant incentives to continue the commercial seal harvest under the Treaty, wholly apart from the obvious incentive provided by the considerable commercial value of the skins. Though the Treaty did not expressly prescribe such a standard, it was clear that the interests of the United States were best served by an annual harvest that was as high as could be sustained from year to year.

Though the 1911 Treaty has since been superseded by the Interim Convention on Conservation of North Pacific Fur Seals, the basic tenets of

---

[15] Only Japan was required to share its harvest with all other signatories. The harvests of Russia and the United States were shared with the other two signatories, but not with each other. Since World War II, the Soviet Union has held the island rookeries formerly held by Japan. Under the present agreement, the harvest from those rookeries is shared only with Canada and Japan.

[16] Treaty for the Preservation and Protection of Fur Seals, art. I, July 7, 1911, 37 Stat. 1542, T.S. No. 564.

[17] *Id.* art. VI.

[18] *Id.* art. XI.

the original treaty remain unchanged.[19] Thus, whereas the management goal of the earlier treaty could only be determined by inference, the present agreement expressly states a policy of "achieving the maximum sustainable productivity of the fur seal resources...so that the fur seal population can be brought to and maintained at the levels which will provide the greatest harvest year after year."[20] Although each signatory retains the authority to establish yearly harvest levels on the islands under its control, those levels are based at least in part on the recommendations of the North Pacific Fur Seal Commission, among whose other duties are the formulation and coordination of an extensive research program.[21]

In 1972, Congress attempted to formulate a comprehensive federal policy of marine mammal management. That policy, embodied in the Marine Mammal Protection Act, is discussed in detail in Chapter 11. Suffice it to say here, however, that the Act sought to incorporate in the

---

[19]The 1911 Treaty was terminated as a result of Japan's withdrawal in 1941. In 1957, the same four parties to the original agreement entered into a new agreement, which, because it was to last for only six years, was known as the Interim Convention, Feb. 9, 1957, [1957] 8 U.S.T. 2283, T.I.A.S. No. 3948, 314 U.N.T.S. 105. The Interim Convention was renewed in 1963, Protocol Amending the Interim Convention, Oct. 8, 1963, [1964] 15 U.S.T. 316, T.I.A.S. No. 5558, and again in 1969. Agreement Extending the Interim Convention, Sept. 3, 1969, [1969] 20 U.S.T. 2992, T.I.A.S. No. 6774. The Interim Convention was extended again for four years each in 1976, Protocol Amending the Interim Convention on Conservation of North Pacific Fur Seals, May 7, 1976, 27 U.S.T. 3371, T.I.A.S. No. 8368, and in 1980, Protocol Amending the Interim Convention on Conservation of North Pacific Fur Seals, Oct. 14, 1980, T.I.A.S. No. 10020. The Interim Convention is implemented by means of the Fur Seal Act, 16 U.S.C. §§1151–1187 (1976). The latter carries over a prohibition against the taking of sea otters on the high seas that was contained in the 1911 Treaty but not in the Interim Convention. Id. §1171. Regulations partially implementing the Fur Seal Act can be found at 50 C.F.R. part 215 (1981).

[20]Interim Convention, preamble. This policy is to be tempered by giving "due regard" to the relation of fur seal populations "to the productivity of other living marine resources of the area." Id. Elsewhere the Convention seems to restrict the range of the "other living marine resources" to which due regard is to be given by authorizing a cooperative research program to determine "the relationship... between fur seals and other living marine resources and whether fur seals have detrimental effects on other living marine resources substantially exploited by any of the Parties." Id. art. II, §1(b).

[21]The original 1911 Treaty did not provide for any commission. The North Pacific Fur Seal Commission established by the Interim Convention consists of one representative from each of the four member nations. The recommendations of the Commission must be made by unanimous vote. Id. art. V, §4. However, only those nations sharing the kill from a particular herd may vote on any recommendation for the size of that kill. Id. Thus representatives of Japan, Canada, and the United States vote with respect to the recommended level of kill on the Pribilof Islands; the United States has no vote with respect to the kills conducted on islands under the jurisdiction of the Soviet Union.

management of marine mammals consideration of the health and stability of the ecosystems of which they are a part, considerations of humaneness, and requirements for strict compliance with rigorous procedures prior to any taking. The Interim Convention contained no clear authority for any of these. Nonetheless, the Act created a special exception for the harvest of fur seals pursuant to the Interim Convention by providing that the provisions of the Act "shall be deemed to be in addition to and not in contravention of the provisions of any existing international treaty, convention or agreement, or any statute implementing the same, which may otherwise apply to the taking of marine mammals."[22]

Notwithstanding this special exemption, the Act directed a "comprehensive study" of the Interim Convention "to determine what modifications, if any, should be made...to make the Convention and [the Act] consistent with each other."[23] While directing the Secretary of State to initiate negotiations to achieve any needed modifications to the Interim Convention identified by that study, the Act also provided that if he failed in those efforts, he was "to take such steps as may be necessary to continue the existing Convention beyond its" termination date of October, 1976.[24]

The "comprehensive study" mandated by the Act was transmitted to Congress in November, 1973. It filled two-thirds of a page, half of which consisted of quotations from the Act and the Interim Convention, when subsequently published in the Federal Register.[25] It concluded that there was "no basic incompatibility" between the Act and the Interim Convention but nevertheless recommended renegotiation of the latter because of "differences of emphasis" between the two. Efforts to renegotiate, which began in 1974, met with very little success. Japan steadfastly resisted all efforts to change the Interim Convention's requirement that seals be harvested so as to achieve their "maximum sustainable productivity." The United States did persuade the other nations to accept amendments authorizing research on the effects of commercial fisheries and man-caused environmental changes on fur seal populations and requiring the use of humane methods in the capturing and killing of fur seals.[26]

When the Senate ultimately ratified the amendments to the Interim Convention, it took note of the changed circumstances resulting from the Fishery Conservation and Management Act of 1976.[27] That Act had amended the Marine Mammal Protection Act so as to make its prohibitions

---

[22] 16 U.S.C. §1383 (1976).

[23] *Id.* §1378(b)(1)(B).

[24] *Id.* §1378(b)(2).

[25] 39 Fed. Reg. 12053 (April 2, 1974).

[26] Protocol Amending the Interim Convention, May 7, 1976, arts. II, III, and X.

[27] 16 U.S.C. §§1801–1882 (1976 & Supp. V 1981). Discussed in Chapter 13.

on the taking of marine mammals applicable within a zone extending 200 miles out from the coasts of the United States. The Senate reasoned that the effect of that amendment may be to diminish the threat posed to fur seal populations by pelagic sealing and urged the Secretary of State to consider negotiating a bilateral treaty with Canada to replace the Interim Convention.[28]

Rather than negotiate a bilateral replacement for the Interim Convention, the United States opted instead to extend its life another four years in 1981.[29] This time, however, the Senate concurred in the ratification of that decision with the understanding that alternative sources of employment for Pribilof Island residents would be carefully studied prior to extending the agreement again.[30] The past history of other such understandings suggests strongly that the Interim Convention will continue to be renewed periodically without fundamental change.

### Migratory Birds

Just five years after concluding the 1911 Treaty for the Preservation and Protection of Fur Seals, the United States concluded with Great Britain, on behalf of Canada, a Convention for the Protection of Migratory Birds.[31] Similar bilateral treaties were concluded with Mexico in 1936, Japan in 1974, and the Soviet Union in 1976. Each of these treaties has been analyzed in some detail in Chapter 4, which need not be repeated here. However, certain aspects of these treaties are noteworthy for purposes of comparing them with the Fur Seal Treaty.

Like the 1911 Fur Seal Treaty and its successor, the Interim Convention, the chief feature of the various migratory bird treaties is their restriction on taking. However, unlike the Fur Seal Treaty, the migratory bird treaties, with one exception, do not prescribe any clear management standard.[32] The migratory bird treaties likewise make no attempt to allocate the harvest of birds between the signatory nations, nor do they establish any international commissions with authority to oversee their implementation.[33] The treaties' ultimate reliance on mutual self-restraint

---

[28]See S. Exec. Rep. No. 36, 94th Cong., 2d Sess. 5 (1976).

[29]Protocol Amending the Interim Convention on Conservation of North Pacific Fur Seals, Oct. 14, 1980, T.I.A.S. No. 10020.

[30]See 127 Cong. Rec. S6078-87 (daily ed. June 11, 1981).

[31]Aug. 16, 1916, 39 Stat. 1702, T.S. No. 628.

[32]The one exception is the treaty with Japan, which requires that migratory bird populations be maintained at their "optimum numbers." For a discussion of this requirement, see Chapter 4 at text accompanying notes 93–99.

[33]The idea of establishing an international body to allocate the annual migratory bird harvest surfaces from time to time. It was among the alternatives briefly considered in the Fish and Wildlife Service's programmatic impact statement on

has succeeded, at least in the case of the two oldest treaties, because of the exceptionally harmonious relations that the United States and its neighboring nations have traditionally enjoyed.

One other difference to be noted between the Fur Seal Treaty and the migratory bird treaties is the recognition in the latter of the need to protect the habitat upon which the birds depend. Neither the 1911 Fur Seal Treaty nor the 1916 Convention with Great Britain for the Protection of Migratory Birds contained any habitat protection measures. The 1936 treaty with Mexico, however, introduced the concept of "refuge zones" for migratory birds. The 1974 treaty with Japan built upon this concept by obligating the parties to "take appropriate measures to preserve and enhance the environment of birds" protected by it. The 1976 treaty with the Soviet Union obligates each nation to identify areas under its jurisdiction that are "of special importance in the conservation of migratory birds" and to "undertake measures necessary to protect the ecosystems in those special areas...against pollution, detrimental alteration and other environmental degradation."[34]

## Fish

The United States has entered into more international agreements pertaining to the commercial exploitation of fish than it has with respect to any other type of wildlife. Beginning in 1923 with an agreement with Canada relating to the Pacific halibut fishery, the United States has since concluded dozens of bilateral and multilateral fisheries agreements. Those agreements, like the Fur Seal Treaty, typically require the management of the particular fishery concerned to achieve its maximum sustainable yield.[35] The variations among the agreements, in terms of regulatory

annual migratory bird–hunting regulations. *See* Department of the Interior, Fish and Wildlife Service, Final Environmental Statement for the Issuance of Annual Regulations Permitting the Sport Hunting of Migratory Birds 222–223 (FES 75-54, 1975).

[34]Compare this obligation with the obligation imposed on federal agencies by section 7 of the Endangered Species Act of 1973. *See* Chapter 12 at text accompanying notes 178–276.

[35]The management principle of maximum sustainable yield or some minor variation thereof has a deeply established standing in the international law of fishing. It is defined in note 44 *infra*. The Convention on Fishing and Conservation of the Living Resources of the High Seas, April 29, 1958, [1966] 17 U.S.T. 138, T.I.A.S. 5969, 559 U.N.T.S. 285, one of the four international agreements to emerge from the International Conference on the Law of the Sea held in Geneva in 1958, requires the "conservation of the living resources of the high seas," which it defines as "the aggregate of the measures rendering possible the optimum sustainable yield from those resources so as to secure a maximum supply of food and other marine products." *Id.* art. 2. As used here, "optimum" refers to the aggregate yield from all

authority and enforcement apparatus, are many. Certain significant characteristics of the most important of these agreements are described in Chapter 13.

The international order of fisheries regulation has recently undergone dramatic change. As a result of the growing number of nations, including the United States, that have asserted claims of exclusive management authority over all fisheries within broad zones contiguous to their territorial seas, a new international regime has emerged. The background of that process, and the Fishery Conservation and Management Act of 1976, by which the United States became a part of it, are considered in detail in Chapter 13.

### Whales

Probably the best known of the many international wildlife agreements to which the United States is a party are those pertaining to the regulation of whaling. Efforts to bring under international control the heedless destruction of whale stocks began at least as early as the 1920s.[36] Those early efforts culminated in the conclusion in 1931 of the largely ineffectual Convention for the Regulation of Whaling.[37] This first of several international agreements to regulate whaling was limited substantively to prohibiting the most egregious forms of waste, such as "killing of calves or suckling whales, immature whales, and female whales which are accompanied by calves (or suckling whales)."[38] These specific directives were accompanied by the more general directive to make the "fullest possible use" of all whales taken.[39]

In the decade and a half after the conclusion of the Convention for the Regulation of Whaling, several attempts were made to improve upon it. The outbreak of World War II cut short those efforts, just as it interrupted most commercial whaling. In the year following the war's end, however,

---

commercially exploited species; the yield from any particular species within that aggregate may or may not correspond to the maximum sustainable yield of that species.

[36] A good source for a comprehensive treatment of historical, biological, and legal aspects of whaling and its regulation is The Whale Problem: A Status Report (W. Schevill ed. 1974).

[37] Sept. 24, 1931, 49 Stat. 3079, T.S. No. 880. While nearly 50 nations are party to the 1931 Convention, including the United States, they do not include the world's major whaling nations, Japan and the Soviet Union.

[38] Id. art. 5.

[39] Id. art. 6.

the agreement that has since governed most whaling activity was concluded, the International Convention for the Regulation of Whaling.[40]

The 1946 Convention was signed by only about one-third the number of countries that had signed the 1931 Convention. However, they included the major whaling nations of the world, Japan and the Soviet Union. The 1946 Convention retains the major substantive provisions of the 1931 agreement. In addition, it establishes an International Whaling Commission (hereinafter referred to as the IWC), comprised of one representative from each signatory, with the power to designate certain species of whales as protected species, fix open and closed seasons or areas, and specify size limits, overall catch limits, and methods of whaling.[41] This power extends to all oceans in which whales occur and is exercised through periodic amendments to that part of the Convention known as the Schedule. To amend the Schedule, however, the concurrence of three-fourths of the members is required. In addition, the Convention provides a mechanism whereby any member not wishing to be bound by a proposed amendment to the Schedule may, by registering an objection within 90 days of its adoption, escape its applicability.[42]

The policies to be achieved by periodic amendments to the Schedule are set forth in ambiguous and arguably conflicting fashion in the Convention's preamble. There it is recited that the nations of the world have an interest "in safeguarding for future generations the great natural resources represented by the whale stocks." To serve this interest, the Convention proposes, through proper regulation, to achieve "increases in the size of whale stocks," thus permitting the attainment of "the optimum level of whale stocks as rapidly as possible." On the other hand, the preamble recites an objective to "make possible the orderly development of the whaling industry."

The duality of purposes reflected in the 1946 Convention, the conservation of the living resource and the "development" of the industry that exploits it, resulted in a long history of decisions sacrificing the former objective for the attainment of the latter. For example, although the Convention preamble declares that to achieve its objectives "whaling

---

[40]December 2, 1946, 62 Stat. 1716, T.I.A.S. 1849. The Convention is implemented in the United States by the Whaling Convention Act of 1949, 16 U.S.C. §§916–916l (1976).

[41]*Id.* art. V, §1. One of the powers expressly denied the IWC is the power to allocate catch quotas among the signatory nations. Nonetheless, the practice of national allocations has arisen outside of formal IWC mechanisms.

[42]*Id.* §3. If any nation registers an objection within the prescribed 90-day period, an additional period of up to 120 days is allowed for other nations to withdraw their previously registered approval of the amendment.

operations should be confined to those species best able to sustain exploitation," the IWC in fact promptly adopted and utilized for two and a half decades the "blue whale unit" as its yardstick for annual catch limits, a regulatory measure that, by treating all species of baleen whales as, in effect, fungible commodities, rendered nugatory any effort to develop conservation measures that took into account the unique status of each species.[43] So too, although the Convention recited an undefined goal of attaining "optimum levels" of whale stocks, the actual management standard employed was that of "maximum sustainable yield."[44]

With no clear mandate for whale conservation, a directive to consider the needs of the whaling industry, and a regulatory structure that enables individual nations to frustrate coordinated conservation actions by registering objections to them, the IWC has for most of its life served as overseer of successive depletions of individual whale stocks.[45] However, in recent years, in part due to the efforts of Congress to force reforms in the international regulation of whaling, the IWC moved dramatically to fulfill its mandate of whale conservation.[46]

---

[43] The oil of baleen whales being essentially interchangeable, the blue whale unit served as a device for regulating the annual catch in terms of the gross measure of oil capable of being produced from the catch rather than in terms of the harvest of individual species. For example, in terms of blue whale units, one fin whale was equivalent to one and a fourth humpback whales or three sei whales. See Christol, Schmidhauser & Totten, Law and the Whale: Current Developments in the International Whaling Controversy 4 (work paper presented at the Seventh Conference on the Law of the World, 1975).

[44] Department of Commerce, National Oceanic and Atmospheric Administration, International Whaling Commission and Related Activities 8 (July, 1976). Maximum sustainable yield or MSY is defined in the same document as follows:

> MSY is a concept often employed by managers of living resources to provide a goal towards which exploited populations would be managed. At MSY level, the population is thought to be capable of producing on a continuing basis the largest amount (either in weight or numbers) of harvestable surplus. In its simplest application, the MSY concept is limited to a single species or stock and does not consider ecosystem relationships or external factors such as economics or esthetics.

Id. at 3. MSY and its relationship to "optimum" population levels are discussed at greater length in Chapter 11 at text accompanying notes 48–72.

[45] Thus overexploitation caused the IWC to prohibit all commercial taking of blue and humpback whales in 1966, to prohibit commercial taking of fin and sei whales in the North Pacific in 1975, and to extend those prohibitions to still other areas and other species in 1976.

[46] The change in IWC effectiveness was also influenced greatly by world opinion, which, by 1972, had turned strongly against the whaling policies of the Soviet Union and Japan. In fact, one of the specific recommendations contained in the Stockholm Declaration, infra note 99, was for a 10-year moratorium on commercial whaling.

The principal statutory levers used by the United States to influence recent IWC policy are the Marine Mammal Protection Act, the so-called Pelly Amendment to the Fisherman's Protective Act of 1967,[47] and the so-called Packwood Amendment to the Fishery Conservation and Management Act.[48] The first, as the discussion of the Fur Seal Treaty indicates, mandates a wholly new approach to the management by the United States of marine mammals. In addition, it directs the Secretaries of Commerce and the Interior, through the Secretary of State, to "initiate the amendment of any existing international treaty for the protection and conservation of any species of marine mammal to which the United States is a party in order to make such treaty consistent with the purposes and policies" of the Act.[49] This directive has given the United States delegation to the IWC authority to press vigorously for more stringent conservation measures.

The Pelly Amendment backs up the authority of the Marine Mammal Protection Act with substantial economic sanctions. Specifically, it authorizes the Secretary of Commerce, whenever the nationals of a foreign country "are conducting fishing operations in a manner or under circumstances which diminish the effectiveness of an international fishery conservation program," to certify such fact to the President.[50] The President may then direct the Secretary "to prohibit...the importation...of fish products of the offending country for such duration as he determines appropriate and to the extent that such prohibition is sanctioned by the General Agreement on Tariffs and Trade."[51] The President need not direct such prohibition. If he fails to do so, however, he must inform Congress as to his reasons.[52]

The Packwood Amendment to the Fishery Conservation and Management Act was designed to add a further sanction against nations, the trade or fishing practices of which diminish the effectiveness of the 1946 Whaling Convention. The sanction is a 50 percent reduction in the allocation of fish to which the offending nation would otherwise be entitled under the Fishery Conservation and Management Act.[53] Unlike

---

[47]22 U.S.C. 1978 (Supp. V 1981).

[48]16 U.S.C. §1821(e)(2)(Supp. V 1981).

[49]Id. §1378(a)(4)(1976).

[50]22 U.S.C. §1978(a)(Supp. V 1981). The term "international fishery conservation program," as used in the Pelly Amendment, includes not only programs for the conservation of fish, but also those pertaining to any "living resource of the sea." Id. §1978(h)(3).

[51]Id. §1978(a). Article XX(g) of the General Agreement on Tariffs and Trade recognizes the validity, under certain circumstances, of trade restrictions relating to exhaustible natural resources. See 1971 U.S. Code Cong. & Ad. News, 92d Cong. 1st Sess. 2413.

[52]22 U.S.C. §1978(b) (Supp. V 1981).

[53]The Fishery Conservation and Management Act is discussed in Chapter 13. The complex formula by which fish not harvested by American fishermen are allocated

under the Pelly Amendment, however, the imposition of this sanction is mandatory rather than discretionary.

The procedures of the Pelly Amendment were first invoked in 1974, when the Soviet Union and Japan, having objected to proposed IWC quotas for the harvest of minke whales in the Antarctic, set their own substantially higher quotas. The Secretary of Commerce made the requisite determination, but the President refused to order the embargo of fish products.[54] His explanation to Congress recited two reasons: (1) his belief that Japan and Russia would abide by future IWC quotas, and (2) the domestic economic disruption that would be caused by halting the substantial imports from the two countries. As to the first, the President's prediction proved true; as to the second, it would appear that the sanction of the Pelly Amendment can never be applied without some adverse effect within the United States. Accordingly, except in extreme circumstances, the President's second proffered reason would appear to be inappropriate for refusing to order the Pelly Amendment sanctions.[55]

The year following the President's refusal to invoke the sanctions of the Pelly Amendment, Japan and the Soviet Union agreed to the restrictions adopted at the next IWC meeting. Those restrictions, embodied in a so-called New Management Procedure, protect certain severely depleted stocks of whales from commercial harvesting. Remaining stocks are placed in one of two categories and harvested at levels that would initially achieve a maximum sustainable yield population level and then an optimum population level when the latter is determined.[56] While the New Management Procedure fell short of the standards of the Marine Mammal Protection Act, it nonetheless represented a substantial departure from past whaling practices.

In 1979 the IWC took a further major conservation step by designating most of the Indian Ocean a "whale sanctuary" in which no commercial whaling was to be allowed. The most dramatic step of all, however, came in 1982, when, by a vote of 25 to 7, the IWC voted to halt all commercial whaling by 1986. However, within months of that historic vote, four

---

to foreign fishermen fishing in the United States fishery conservation zone is contained in 16 U.S.C. §1821(d)(1976 & Supp. V 1981).

[54]President's Message to the Congress Submitting a Report on International Whaling Operations and Conservation Programs, 11 Pres. Doc. 55 (Jan. 16, 1975).

[55]For a fuller account of the President's refusal to invoke the Pelly Amendment against Japan and the Soviet Union, see Comment, Not Saving Whales: President Ford Refuses to Ban Fish Imports from Nations Which Have Violated International Whaling Quotas, 5 Envtl. L. Rep. (Envtl. L. Inst.) 10044 (1975).

[56]See Department of Commerce, National Marine Fisheries Service, Administration of the Marine Mammal Protection Act of 1972, 41 Fed. Reg. 30152, 30158 (July 22, 1976).

nations, among them Japan and the Soviet Union, filed objections. At this writing, the United States is struggling to determine whether to impose sanctions against the objecting nations. The outcome of the international discussions now underway may determine not only the future of commercial whaling but perhaps the very future of the IWC.

While achieving a moratorium on commercial whaling has been a long-pursued objective of the United States, a highly divisive issue has been that of aboriginal whaling. In 1977 the IWC voted to terminate all aboriginal harvesting of the bowhead whale, a highly endangered whale species traditionally hunted by coastal Eskimo communities in Alaska. The United States, unwilling to appear compromised in its opposition to commercial whaling, abstained from the IWC vote and elected not to object to it.[57] Ultimately, the United States was able to persuade the IWC to authorize a limited aboriginal harvest of bowheads. The United States implements and enforces the IWC restrictions through a cooperative agreement with an Eskimo-originated "Alaska Eskimo Whaling Commission."[58]

## Polar Bears

The efforts of Congress to reform the international regime for the regulation of whaling reflect a growing tendency on the part of Congress to interject itself into the formulation of international wildlife policy. Another example of that tendency was the passage of a joint resolution by both Houses of Congress in 1972 directing the executive branch to seek an international agreement for the protection of the polar bear.[59] In response, the following year, the United States, Norway, Canada, Denmark, and the Soviet Union concluded an Agreement on the Conservation of Polar Bears.[60]

Although the Agreement outlaws generally the taking of polar bears[61] and obligates each of the parties to "take appropriate action to protect the ecosystems of which polar bears are a part,"[62] the former is riddled with exceptions and the latter is nowhere translated into concrete directives. The most extensive exception to the taking prohibition authorizes each country

---

[57]For a thus-far-inconclusive challenge to the United States' failure to object, see Hopson v. Kreps, 622 F.2d 1375 (9th Cir. 1980).

[58]The cooperative agreement was published at 47 Fed. Reg. 20137 (May 11, 1982) and amended at 47 Fed. Reg. 47843 (Oct. 28, 1982).

[59]H.J. Res. 1268, 92d Cong., 2d Sess. (1972).

[60]Nov. 15, 1973, T.I.A.S. No. 8409.

[61]*Id.* art. I.

[62]*Id.* art. II.

to "allow the taking of polar bears when such taking is carried out... wherever polar bears have or might have been subject to taking by traditional means by its nationals." This exception is highly ambiguous and is susceptible to widely different interpretations, depending on whether the final six words are intended to define both the type of taking that is to be permitted in the future and the area where it may occur or only to delimit the area where taking has been done in the past. If the former, taking may be done by a country's own nationals, but only "by traditional means" and only where taking has or may have previously been done. If the latter, taking may be permitted by anyone using any means, provided that it is done only in the area where it has or might have been done in the past by traditional means. The Fish and Wildlife Service apparently takes the former view.[63] Neither view imposes any restrictions as to area or means for takings pursuant to the other exceptions set forth in the Convention.[64] Article IV's prohibition of the use of aircraft or large motorized vessels for the purpose of taking polar bears would appear to apply to any form of taking permitted under the agreement, though here again the Fish and Wildlife Service interprets the prohibition to be inapplicable to takings for scientific purposes.[65]

## Antarctic Living Resources

In 1959, Argentina, Australia, Belgium, Chile, France, Japan, New Zealand, Norway, South Africa, the Soviet Union, Great Britain, and the United States concluded the Antarctic Treaty.[66] The principal purposes of that Treaty were to bar the use of that continent for military purposes, to prohibit nuclear explosions and the disposal of radioactive waste there, and to foreclose assertions of claims to territorial sovereignty. Although Antarctica represented the world's last great wilderness, the Treaty said virtually nothing about conservation of the continent's wildlife. It merely delegated to each of its signatory nations the authority to make recommendations for the "preservation and conservation of living resources" at periodic meetings.[67]

---

[63] Department of the Interior, Fish and Wildlife Service, Environmental Assessment: Ratification of the Agreement on the Conservation of Polar Bears 6 (April 1975).

[64] These other exceptions include taking for (1) bona fide scientific purposes, (2) conservation purposes, and (3) prevention of "serious disturbance of the management of other living resources," as well as "by local people using traditional methods in the exercise of their traditional rights." What difference there is, if any, between "traditional methods" and "traditional means" is unexplained.

[65] *Supra* note 63 at 6.

[66] Dec. 1, 1959, [1961] 12 U.S.T. 784, T.I.A.S. No. 4780, 402 U.N.T.S. 71.

[67] Id. art. IX, §1(f).

Pursuant to that authority, the parties to the Treaty promulgated in 1964 a set of Agreed Measures for the Conservation of Antarctic Fauna and Flora.[68] In the same year, a Norwegian company began an exploratory sealing expedition in the Antarctic. As a result of that expedition and the fact that neither the Agreed Measures nor subsequent recommendations specifically addressed at sealing were binding, the need for a new treaty addressing the subject of sealing became evident. The result was the signing in 1972 of a Convention for the Conservation of Antarctic Seals, which was ratified by the Senate in 1976 and which came into force in 1978.[69]

Though no commercial sealing has yet begun on the Antarctic continent, this Convention would provide that yearly harvest levels not exceed "optimum sustainable yield," would prohibit pelagic sealing, and would fix other harvest restrictions, though without providing for any enforcement mechanism or any permanent commission. The State Department, which was much criticized for the secrecy that surrounded the negotiation of the Convention, frankly acknowledges that it falls short of the standards for marine mammal management set forth in the Marine Mammal Protection Act.[70] Nonetheless, to prevent the initiation of commercial sealing without any international regulation, the Senate gave its consent to the ratification of the Convention.

At their ninth Consultative Meeting, in 1977, the Antarctic parties called for the establishment of a "definitive regime" for the conservation of Antarctic marine living resources.[71] That recommendation led to the negotiation by 15 nations of a Convention on the Conservation of Antarctic Marine Living Resources[72] in 1980, which the United States has signed and ratified.

The major impetus for the Convention was the likelihood of a greatly expanded, unregulated commercial harvest of krill[73] and the possible

---

[68] Recommendations of the Third Antarctic Consultative Meeting, June 2–13, 1964, [1966] 17 U.S.T. 991; T.I.A.S. No. 6058, app. The Agreed Measures were implemented in the United States in 1978 by Pub. L. No. 95-541, 92 Stat. 2048, which prohibits the taking of mammals or birds in Antarctica and the taking of native plants in protected areas except under permit from the Director of the National Science Foundation. See 16 U.S.C. §§2401–2412 (Supp. V 1981).

[69] June 1, 1972, 29 U.S.T. 441, T.I.A.S. No. 826.

[70] See S. Exec. Rep. No. 35, 94th Cong., 2d Sess. 5 (1976).

[71] Recommendations of the Ninth Antarctic Consultative Meeting, Sept. 19–Oct. 7, 1977, Recommendation IX-2.

[72] The text of the Convention is included in a Senate document identified as "Executive X," 96th Cong., 2d Sess. (1980). The 15 nations include the 13 Antarctic Treaty powers, the Federal Republic of Germany, and the German Democratic Republic.

[73] Krill are an abundant group of crustaceans. An estimated 200–600 million tons of

effects of that harvest on numerous other species, including baleen whales, seals, penguins, and fish. The Convention represents an effort to insure that the harvest of krill will be carried out in a way that gives consideration to the impact of that harvest on these other species and thus protects the stability of the Antarctic marine ecosystem.

Although krill represent the major concern giving rise to the Convention, they are not its exclusive focus. Rather, by its terms, the Convention applies to all Antarctic living marine resources, a term defined to include all species of living organisms, including birds, found south of the Antarctic Convergence.[74] Article II of the Convention sets forth the following three "principles of conservation" to govern the harvesting of such resources and activities associated with such harvesting:

> (a) Prevention of decrease in the size of any harvested population to levels below those which ensure its stable recruitment. For this purpose its size should not be allowed to fall below a level close to that which ensures the greatest net annual increment;
> (b) Maintenance of the ecological relationships between harvested, dependent and related populations of Antarctic marine living resources and the restoration of depleted populations to the levels defined in sub-paragraph (a) above; and
> (c) Prevention of changes or minimization of the risk of changes in the marine ecosystem which are not potentially reversible over two or three decades, taking into account the state of available knowledge of the direct and indirect impact of harvesting, the effect of the introduction of alien species, the effects of associated activities on the marine ecosystem and of the effects of environmental changes, with the aim of making possible the sustained conservation of Antarctic marine living resources.[75]

Perhaps the most important and most difficult conceptual task relating to the implementation of the Convention will be the interpretation of these principles and their translation into criteria and methods for the formulation of conservation measures. Subparagraph (a) and the reference to "depleted populations" in the second clause of subparagraph (b) appear to require that harvest and associated activities not cause any population in

---

krill are present in Antarctic waters during the summer. Current harvests of krill are estimated at 120–500 thousand tons annually. National Academy of Science, An Evaluation of Antarctic Marine Ecosystem Research (1981).

[74] Art. 1, para. 2. The Antarctic Convergence is a seasonally shifting oceanographic boundary between Antarctic waters to the south and warmer, sub-Antarctic waters to the north. Article 1, para. 4, defines it arbitrarily by reference to a set of coordinates roughly approximating the actual Convergence.

[75] Art. II, para. 3.

the Antarctic ecosystem, whether or not harvested itself, to be reduced below the level of greatest net annual increment.[76] Because this requirement applies to *all* populations and not just those harvested, its effective implementation will require careful selection of vulnerable species and indicator species for research and monitoring. The third conservation principle, requiring the "[p]revention of changes or minimization of the risk of changes in the marine ecosystem which are not potentially reversible over two or three decades" is an important innovation in international conservation law because it addresses the resilience of the ecosystem to harvest and associated activities, rather than just desired states of an ecosystem, such as attainment of particular population levels.

To implement the foregoing conservation principles, the Convention establishes regulatory and scientific bodies with the authority to impose a fully panoply of conservation measures and the flexibility to adopt or to revise such measures expeditiously. The principal regulatory organ of the Convention is the Commission for the Conservation of Antarctic Marine Living Resources. All signatories and certain other parties are represented on the Commission,[77] which makes decisions by consensus on matters of substance.[78] The Commission is to hold regular annual meetings and to exercise the function of providing for the conservation of Antarctic marine living resources in accordance with the principles of article II. This objective is to be achieved through the acquisition and analysis of necessary data and the adoption of conservation measures. Such measures may include, but are not limited to, limitations on the kind, quantity, place, duration, and methods of harvest and designation of special areas for protection and for scientific study.[79] The last of these authorities is clearly intended to authorize the establishment of a system of marine reserves paralleling the heretofore terrestrial system of specially protected areas and sites of special scientific interest established by the Agreed Measures for the Conservation of Antarctica Fauna and Flora and by recommendations adopted at various meetings of the Antarctic Treaty Consultative Parties.

The designation of protected areas of sea where commercial harvest would be prohibited and where ecological relationships can be maintained would assure the maintenance of relatively pristine areas in Antarctica and would tend to buffer harvested areas against overexploitation. In light of

---

[76]The term "greatest net annual increment" is likely to be interpreted so as to equate with the term "maximum productivity" as used in the Marine Mammal Protection Act's definition of "optimum sustainable population." *See* Chapter 11 at text accompanying notes 48–69.

[77]Art. VII.

[78]Art. XII.

[79]Art. IX.

the yet primitive understanding of the Antarctic ecosystem, areas open to harvest should be the exception rather than the rule.

Whether the Convention will live up to its great potential in preserving the Antarctic through its comprehensive ecosystem approach remains to be seen. The first meeting of the Commission was held in 1982 and decided little other than minor procedural matters. When it becomes fully operational, the stage will be set for the international community to establish a precedent of prudent use and conservation of one of the world's last unspoiled natural areas.

## TREATIES RELATING TO THE INDIRECT PROTECTION OF WILDLIFE

Just as in the domestic sphere the need to protect wildlife through indirect measures became apparent soon after the enactment of legislation restricting its direct taking, so too in the international sphere the same need was early perceived. This part of the chapter discusses several of the international agreements having the most significance for indirect wildlife protection. Perhaps the most interesting of these is the 1940 Convention on Nature Protection and Wildlife Preservation in the Western Hemisphere,[80] a little-known treaty of considerable potential implications that has been largely ignored by legal commentators[81] and government officials[82] alike.

The Convention on Nature Protection and Wildlife Preservation in the Western Hemisphere contains far-reaching provisions concerning the establishment of special areas for wildlife preservation, the control of international trade in specially protected species of wildlife, and the protection of wildlife generally. As to the setting aside of special areas, the Convention directs each signatory nation to "explore at once the possi-

---

[80]Oct. 12, 1940, 56 Stat. 1354, T.S. No. 981, U.N.T.S. No. 193.

[81]The only legal commentary on this Convention appears to be in two articles by the same author: Guilbert, Wilderness Preservation I: A Recent Case and a Not-So-Recent Treaty, 3 Envtl. L. Rep. (Envtl. L. Inst.) 50023 (1973), and Guilbert, Wilderness Preservation II: Bringing the Convention into Court, 3 Envtl. L. Rep. (Envtl. L. Inst.) 50044 (1973).

[82]Thirty-one years after the Convention came into effect, the Endangered Species Act of 1973, 16 U.S.C. §1537(A)(e)(Supp. V 1981), directed the President to designate those agencies that are to represent the United States in all regards as required by the Convention. The President finally did so in 1976, naming the Secretary of the Interior, in consultation with the Secretary of State, as the representative of the United States. Exec. Order No. 11, 911, 3 C.F.R. 112 (1976 Comp.). That executive designation was effectively codified by Congress in 1982. See Endangered Species Act Amendments of 1982, Pub. L. No. 97-304, §5(3), 96 Stat. 1421 (amending 16 U.S.C. §1537A(e)).

bility of establishing in their territories" each of four types of areas, denominated "national parks," "national reserves," "nature monuments," and "strict wilderness reserves." The Convention further directs that "[i]n all cases where such establishment is feasible, the creation thereof shall be begun as soon as possible."[83]

Because several of the area types referred to in the Convention bear names identical or substantially similar to those of existing administrative units in the United States, it might be thought (and apparently has been thought) that the Convention would have little practical impact inside the United States. Closer scrutiny of the Convention's definitions, however, reveals certain discrepancies between those definitions and such existing units. For example, the Convention's "strict wilderness reserves" would not seem to include all, or even most, wilderness areas established under the Wilderness Act, for the former include only regions "wherein there is no provision for the passage of motorized transportation and all commercial developments are excluded."[84] In most wilderness areas, however, certain types of commercial activities, such as mining, are permitted.[85]

Similarly, it is unclear whether any existing administrative units in the United States precisely correspond with the Convention's definition of "national reserves." That definition is as follows:

> Regions established for conservation of natural resources under government control, on which protection of animal and plant life will be afforded in so far as this may be consistent with the primary purpose of such reserves.[86]

Arguably, publicly managed areas around water development projects may satisfy the Convention's definition, by virtue of the Fish and Wildlife Coordination Act.[87] The National Forests and National Resource Lands would not appear to qualify, however, if one adheres scrupulously to the tenet that there are no "primary purposes" of multiple use lands.

The most interesting category of the Convention is that of "nature monument," because it includes not only areas of land having aesthetic, historic, or scientific interest, but also "living species of flora or fauna" having those same characteristics.[88] By virtue of the special protection afforded it, the bald eagle would appear to come closer than any other

---

[83] Art. II.

[84] Art. I.

[85] See Chapter 6 at note 275.

[86] Art. I.

[87] 16 U.S.C. §663(a)(1976). See Chapter 7.

[88] Art. I.

living species to being this type of "nature monument." The Convention's definition, however, requires that nature monuments be "inviolate... except for duly authorized scientific investigations or government inspection." Neither the bald eagle nor any other species is that completely protected.[89] However, in *Cappaert v. United States*,[90] the Supreme Court held that the Act for the Preservation of Antiquities,[91] the basic statutory authority for the establishment of national monuments, authorized the protection not only of important archaeological sites, but also of areas inhabited by rare forms of wildlife (in that case, the endangered Devil's Hole pupfish). Thus it is possible that some national monuments may qualify as "living species" nature monuments under the Convention. So also may a few national wildlife refuges, such as the Hawaiian Islands National Refuge, home of the endangered Hawaiian monk seal and generally off-limits to all persons other than scientists conducting government-approved research projects.

In summary, it is unclear, apart from our national parks and possibly a few unique national monuments or wildlife refuges, whether the United States has yet established the four categories of areas contemplated by the Convention. If it has not, it is not alone, for most of the other signatory nations have likewise apparently ignored its requirements.[92]

The second far-reaching aspect of the Convention is its requirement that the parties adopt or at least propose

> suitable laws and regulations for the protection and preservation of flora and fauna within their national boundaries, but not included in the national parks, national reserves, nature monuments, or strict wilderness reserves.... Such regulations shall contain proper provisions for the taking of specimens of flora and fauna for scientific study and investigation by properly accredited individuals and agencies.[93]

Arguably, the above language provides a basis, wholly independent of any commerce clause or property clause power, for federal regulation of all forms of wildlife, including "resident" wildlife traditionally managed by the states. If so, the recurrent legal clashes concerning state and federal authority over wildlife have, at least since 1940, been unnecessary.[94] On the

---

[89]*See* Chapter 4 at text accompanying notes 118–138.

[90]426 U.S. 128(1976).

[91]16 U.S.C. §§431–433 (1976).

[92]Savini, Report on International and National Legislation for the Conservation of Marine Mammals, Part I: International Legislation 5 (Food and Agriculture Organization Fisheries Circular No. 326, 1974).

[93]Art. V.

[94]*See* Chapter 2.

other hand, the phrase "suitable laws and regulations" in the language quoted might be interpreted so as not to affect the otherwise applicable distribution of authority between the states and the federal government. A middle ground also seems possible. The preamble to the Convention recites a purpose "to protect and preserve in their natural habitat representatives of all species and genera...in sufficient numbers and over areas extensive enough to assure them from becoming extinct through any agency within man's control." Thus "suitable" laws and regulations might mean those designed to accomplish that limited purpose. In fact, the Endangered Species Act of 1973, which does preempt the states from their authority to regulate the taking of resident endangered and threatened species, recites the Convention as one of its sources of authority.[95] Whether the Convention would also authorize more sweeping federal regulation, not limited to wildlife in danger of extinction, is as yet untested.

The final noteworthy aspect of the Convention is its regulation of international trade in protected species. Article VIII of the Convention provides for the listing in an Annex of species whose protection "is declared to be of special urgency and importance."[96] Article IX then requires that protected species not be exported or imported without a certificate of lawful exportation from the country of origin. Although this form of regulation was substantially improved and broadened in 1973 by the Convention on International Trade in Endangered Species of Wild Fauna and Flora,[97] the authority conferred by the 1940 Convention may nonetheless still be important. Thus, for example, at least four Latin American nations that are parties to the 1940 Convention had not yet ratified the 1973 Convention as of January 1983.

After decades of scant attention, the Western Hemisphere Convention has recently attracted the interest of Congress. In 1982, as part of the Endangered Species Act Amendments of that year, Congress directed the Secretaries of State and the Interior to give greater attention to the implementation of the Convention.[98] In particular, Congress instructed the Secretaries to take steps to identify bird species that migrate between the United States and one or more of its convention partners and to pursue cooperative measures aimed at preventing such birds from becoming

---

[95] 16 U.S.C. §1531(a)(4)(C)(1976).

[96] The list of species included in the Annex can be found at T.S. No. 981, pp. 27–77. It includes some, but not all species listed as endangered pursuant to the Endangered Species Act of 1973.

[97] March 3, 1973, 27 U.S.T. 1087, T.I.A.S. No. 8249. The Convention on International Trade in Endangered Species of Wild Fauna and Flora is discussed in Chapter 12 at text accompanying notes 29–49.

[98] Endangered Species Act Amendments of 1982, Pub. L. No. 97-304, §5(3), 96 Stat. 1421 (amending 16 U.S.C. §1573A(e)(Supp. V 1981)).

threatened or endangered. In addition, Congress directed the Secretaries to pursue similar measures for the protection of wild plants, as contemplated by the Convention. Together, these directives reflect a growing congressional awareness of the need to protect New World tropical habitats if our efforts at ensuring bird and other living resources in the United States are to succeed.

In very recent years, the protection of wildlife has been subsumed under international agreements directed more broadly at a variety of environmental concerns. Here too, there exists a parallel of sorts with recent domestic environmental legislation. Principal among these are the Declaration of the United Nations Conference on the Human Environment[99] and the Convention Concerning the Protection of the World Cultural and Natural Heritage.[100] The former, also known simply as the Stockholm Declaration, is a nonbinding statement of general environmental principles subsequently approved by the United Nations General Assembly.[101] Among these principles is one recognizing a "special responsibility to safeguard and wisely manage" wildlife and its habitat. More general are principles stating the importance of preserving "representative samples of natural ecosystems" and of "preserving vital renewable resources." Imposing on nations the duty to consider the environmental impacts of their activities are further principles stating the obligation of states "to ensure that activities within their jurisdiction or control do not cause damage to the environment of other nations" and to "take all possible steps to prevent pollution of the seas by substances that are liable... to harm living resources or marine life."

The Convention Concerning the Protection of the World Cultural and Natural Heritage has as its object the preservation of both cultural monuments and natural areas having "universal value."[102] Among the natural areas included are "precisely delineated areas that constitute the habitat of threatened species of animals and plants of outstanding universal value from the point of view of science or conservation." The designation of such areas is the responsibility of the nations in which they occur, as is the promulgation of protective regulations. The Convention also establishes a World Heritage Committee, with the power to grant international assistance to countries designating such areas. While the

[99] June 16, 1972, 67 Dept. of State Bull. 116 (1972), 11 Int'l Leg. Mats 1416-69 (1972).

[100] Nov. 23, 1972, T.I.A.S. No. 8226.

[101] U.N. Doc. A/PV.2112, at 6 (Dec. 15, 1972). The Stockholm Convention is analyzed in detail in Sohn, The Stockholm Declaration on the Human Environment, 14 Harv. Int'l. L. J. 423 (1973).

[102] The Convention and its background are discussed in Meyer, *Trauvaux Préparatoires* for UNESCO World Heritage Convention, 2 Earth L. J. 45 (1976).

Convention is of limited utility for wildlife because of its failure to specify protective standards, it does offer a much-needed mechanism for providing financial assistance to the less-developed countries for wildlife protection purposes.

## THE ASSERTION OF CONGRESSIONAL AUTHORITY IN INTERNATIONAL REGULATION OF WILDLIFE

In recent years, Congress has asserted for itself an ever-larger role in the development of international wildlife conservation policies. This chapter has already considered how the Pelly Amendment to the Fishermen's Protective Act, the Packwood Amendment to the Fishery Conservation and Management Act, and the Marine Mammal Protection Act seek to achieve that. The latter Act seeks to establish a whole international program of marine mammal protection around its policies. Only two of the ways it seeks to do this have thus far been considered.

In addition to the two provisions already considered, the Marine Mammal Protection Act directs the Secretaries of Commerce and the Interior, through the Secretary of State, to initiate negotiations for new bilateral or multilateral agreements respecting three subjects: (1) marine mammal protection and conservation generally;[103] (2) commercial fishing operations that are unduly harmful to marine mammals;[104] and (3) the protection of specific ocean and land regions that are of special significance to the health and stability of marine mammals.[105] Though such efforts have begun, there have been few tangible results thus far.[106] Similarly, though the Act directed that an "international ministerial meeting on marine mammals" be convened before July 1, 1973,[107] it has yet to occur.

Restrictions on the importation of certain products appear at several places in the Act. Most fundamentally, the Act requires that no marine mammal or marine mammal product "be imported into the United States unless the Secretary certifies that the program for taking marine mammals in the country of origin is consistent with the provisions and policies" of the Act.[108] In addition, however, the Act also authorizes the Secretary of the

---

[103] 16 U.S.C. §1378(a)(1)(1976).

[104] *Id.* §1378(a)(2).

[105] *Id.* §1378(a)(3).

[106] For details as to the efforts undertaken thus far, see the annual reports of the Secretary of Commerce concerning the Administration of the Marine Mammal Protection Act of 1972.

[107] 16 U.S.C. §1378(a)(5)(1976).

[108] *Id.* §1371(a)(3)(A). This provision has been the focus of lengthy battles regarding the importation of seal skins from South Africa. For details, see Chapter 11.

Treasury to "ban the importation of commercial fish or products from fish which have been caught with commercial fishing technology which results in the incidental kill or incidental serious injury of ocean mammals in excess of United States standards."[109] Compliance with this requirement is achieved through submission of "reasonable proof" from the foreign government involved. The adequacy of these measures to protect United States fishermen from foreign competition is one of the contested issues concerning the incidental taking of porpoise while purse seining for tuna.[110] Finally, the Act prohibits the importation of any fish "caught in a manner which the Secretary has proscribed for persons subject to the jurisdiction of the United States, whether or not any marine mammals were in fact taken incident to the catching of the fish."[111] Neither this nor the immediately preceding prohibition has yet been the subject of any formal action.

In the endangered species area, Congress has recently sought to assert some control over the way in which the Executive Branch carries out its responsibilities under the Convention on International Trade in Endangered Species of Wild Fauna and Flora. Amendments to the Endangered Species Act in 1982 not only prescribe the standards under which the Secretary of the Interior must make the determinations required by that Convention, but also seek to influence how the executive casts its vote for or against the protection of particular species under that Convention. These and other aspects of this important international agreement are considered in greater detail in Chapter 12.

One of the most recent, and certainly the most far-reaching, assertions of congressional authority for international wildlife policy making is contained in the Fishery Conservation and Management Act of 1976. That very important piece of federal wildlife legislation will be considered in detail in Chapter 13.

---

[109]16 U.S.C. §1371(a)(2)(Supp. V 1981).

[110]*See* Chapter 11 at text accompanying notes 142–175.

[111]16 U.S.C. §1372(c)(3)(1976).

Part **III**

# TOWARD COMPREHENSIVE
# FEDERAL WILDLIFE PROGRAMS

In the last few years, the character of federal wildlife regulation has changed significantly. In that period there has been a conscious effort to develop comprehensive programs of wildlife regulation. Those programs in part represent efforts to combine the best features of the many diverse components of federal wildlife law that have been examined in the preceding chapters. In part, also, they represent efforts to develop wholly new institutional arrangements for the effective implementation of wildlife policy. The three chapters that comprise this Part examine the recent federal statutes that embody this significant new development in federal wildlife law.

Chapter **11**

# THE PROTECTION OF
# MARINE MAMMALS

## INTRODUCTION

### Background

Until the late 1960s, federal wildlife legislation generally made no attempt to establish comprehensive and coordinated programs for the conservation of broad classifications of wildlife. The one exception was the federal program for the protection of migratory birds, which was initiated a half-century earlier by passage of the Migratory Bird Treaty Act. Enactment of the Endangered Species Preservation Act of 1966 and the Endangered Species Conservation Act of 1969 signalled an important renewal of interest in establishing a more prominent federal presence in the regulation of wildlife. Still, the programs they initiated were relatively modest.[1]

Not long after enactment of the 1969 Act, there came to be expressed a strong sentiment that the conservation of the world's ocean mammals required a comprehensive and coordinated federal program. The well-springs for this sentiment were quite diverse. Commercial interests and some members of the scientific community felt that marine mammals represented an important commercial and food resource that, under proper management, could be utilized indefinitely through sustained harvests.[2]

---

[1] The Endangered Species Preservation Act of 1966 and the Endangered Species Conservation Act of 1969 are discussed in detail in Chapter 12 *infra* at text accompanying notes 3–28.

[2] The principal bill reflecting these interests was the so-called Anderson-Pelly bill, H.R. 10420, 92d Cong., 1st Sess. (1971).

Other members of the scientific community were of the view that marine mammals had an important ecological role to play in marine ecosystems and that the first priority of federal policy ought to be to recognize and protect that role. Still a third group of interested citizens, dubbed "protectionists," believed that marine mammals, because of their apparent intelligence and for diverse other reasons, ought to be left undisturbed and declared off-limits to human harvesting.[3]

Whatever their motivation, nearly all concerned were in agreement that the existing patchwork of laws and regulations pertaining to marine mammals was inadequate. Although the International Whaling Commission had been charged with safeguarding the world's whale stocks for future generations, its regulations were so ineffective that in 1970 eight species of whales were listed as threatened with worldwide extinction under the Endangered Species Conservation Act of 1969.[4] And, though a few other species of marine mammals were subject to some form of federal protection, including the West Indian and Amazonian manatees,[5] the Mediterranean monk seal,[6] the sea otter,[7] and the north Pacific fur seal,[8] the remainder were either protected only by state law or not at all.

For reasons that should be obvious from the descriptions of the various concerned groups, their common desire for change did not produce any unanimity as to what form that change should take. Instead, it was left to Congress to forge a compromise between the seemingly irreconcilable views of the "managers" and the "protectionists."[9] Precisely because that major compromise was necessary, the legislation that finally resulted, the Marine Mammal Protection Act of 1972, articulated policy goals of broad

---

[3] The principal bill reflecting these interests was the so-called Harris-Pryor bill, H.R. 6554, 92d Cong., 1st Sess. (1971).

[4] 35 Fed. Reg. 18319 (Dec. 2, 1970).

[5] The West Indian manatee was determined to be threatened with extinction under the Endangered Species Preservation Act of 1966. See 32 Fed. Reg. 4001 (Mar. 11, 1967). The Amazonian manatee was listed pursuant to the 1969 Act. See 35 Fed. Reg. 8491 (June 2, 1970).

[6] The Mediterranean monk seal was determined to be threatened with worldwide extinction under the Endangered Species Conservation Act of 1969. See 35 Fed. Reg. 8491 (June 2, 1970).

[7] Taking of sea otters on the high seas by persons subject to the jurisdiction of the United States was prohibited by the Fur Seal Act of 1966, 16 U.S.C. §1171 (1976).

[8] The "protection" of north Pacific fur seals consisted of their management, according to sustained-yield principles, pursuant to the Interim Convention on the Conservation of North Pacific Fur Seals, discussed in Chapter 10 supra at text accompanying notes 9–28.

[9] The legislative history is described in Gaines & Schmidt, Wildlife Population Management Under the Marine Mammal Protection Act of 1972, 6 Envtl. L. Rep. (Envtl. L. Inst.) 50096, 50103–08 (1976).

generality and implemented them with specific directions that were neither purely protectionist nor purely exploitive, but were almost always complex.[10]

## An Overview of the Marine Mammal Protection Act

Whatever its complexities and ambiguities, the Marine Mammal Protection Act clearly represented a drastic departure from the scheme of regulation that had existed previously. Most fundamentally, it completely preempted the states from any authority over marine mammals and substituted for the many state programs a single federal program intended to be comprehensive in scope and coordinated in implementation. The central feature of that federal program was a moratorium of indefinite duration during which no marine mammals could be taken by any person subject to the jurisdiction of the United States or imported into the United States. Limited exceptions were carved out for scientific and public display purposes, for taking by natives of the North Pacific and Arctic coasts, and for takings incidental to commercial fishing operations or pursuant to international treaty.

Although the Act immediately preempted state authority over marine mammals, it also established a mechanism whereby states could regain that authority, together with federal financial assistance for the carrying out of approved state programs. Similarly, although the Act established a moratorium on the taking and importation of marine mammals, it also established a detailed and highly formal procedural mechanism whereby the moratorium could be waived and taking and importation permitted for any species or population stock of marine mammal found to meet the Act's novel and complex population criteria.[11]

-------

[10]16 U.S.C. §§1361–1362, 1371–1384, and 1401–1407 (Supp. V 1981), as amended by the Commercial Fisheries Research and Development Act, Pub. L. No. 97-389, §§201–202, 96 Stat. 1949 (1982).

[11]One of the major innovations of the Act was its protection for individual population stocks as well as species of marine mammals. The Act defines a "population stock" as "a group of marine mammals of the same species or smaller taxa in a common spatial arrangement, that interbreed when mature." 16 U.S.C. §1362(10)(Supp. V 1981). This represented a significant departure from the Endangered Species Conservation Act of 1969, which applied only to species and subspecies. Pub. L. No. 91-135, §3(a), 83 Stat. 275 (repealed 1973). This broadening of the scope of protection was in response to the recognition that the health of many species or subspecies was dependent upon the continuing viability of their various population stocks. See, e.g., the following statement of Dr. Kenneth S. Norris:

It is important that we preserve not only the species but the population structure as well, since this [is] part of the way animals have evolved in

Finally, the Act attempted to establish an ambitious international program for marine mammal protection. As a component of that program, the Act directed that its policies be the official policies of the United States in the negotiation and renegotiation of international agreements concerning marine mammals. Further, the Act provided authority for restricting the importation of certain products from foreign countries whose fishing or other practices impeded the attainment of the Act's goals.

### Federal Agency Responsibilities Under the Act

Primary responsibility for implementation of the Act is shared by the Secretaries of Commerce and the Interior. The former, through the National Marine Fisheries Service, has authority with regard to all members of the order Cetacea (whales and porpoises) and all members, except walruses, of the order Pinnipedia (seals).[12] The Secretary of the Interior, through the Fish and Wildlife Service, administers the Act with respect to all other marine mammals (manatees, dugongs, polar bears, sea otters, and walruses).[13]

In carrying out their functions under the Act, both Secretaries are required to consult with the Marine Mammal Commission, a special

---

the world and have managed to meet the changes in the environment that assail [them].

Marine Mammals: Hearings on H.R. 690 and Related Bills Before the Subcomm. on Fisheries and Wildlife Conservation of the House Comm. on Merchant Marine and Fisheries, 92d Cong., 1st Sess. 410 (1971) (Norris was later to become a member of the Committee of Scientific Advisors to the Marine Mammal Commission. See text accompanying notes 14–19 infra).

[12] 16 U.S.C. §1362(11)(A)(Supp. V 1981) does not expressly refer to the Secretary of Commerce, but rather to "the department in which the National Oceanic and Atmospheric Administration is operating." That agency is presently located in the Department of Commerce as a result of Executive Reorganization Plan No. 4 of 1970, 35 Fed. Reg. 15627 (Oct. 3, 1970), 84 Stat. 2090. The Secretary of Commerce has delegated his functions under the Act to the Administrator of the National Oceanic and Atmospheric Administration, 37 Fed. Reg. 26745 (Dec. 15, 1972), who in turn has delegated them to the Director of the National Marine Fisheries Service, 38 Fed. Reg. 4793 (Feb. 22, 1973), amended by 41 Fed. Reg. 46361 (Oct. 20, 1976).

[13] 16 U.S.C. §1362(11)(B)(Supp. V 1981). This division of jurisdiction, though hotly contested at the time of the Act's passage, was premised in part on the belief that there would soon be established a Department of Natural Resources in which authority over all wildlife resources would be consolidated. See Coggins, Legal Protection for Marine Mammals: An Overview of Innovated Resource Conservation Legislation, 6 Envtl. L. 1, 26–27 (1975). That consolidation never occurred. Because the Act imposes identical duties on the Secretaries of Commerce and the Interior, the term "Secretary" shall be used in the text without distinguishing between them or their respective delegates.

independent advisory body created by the Act.[14] The Commission was intended to serve as an impartial and nonpolitical source of expert scientific advice to the Secretaries.[15] To insure the scientific integrity of the Commission, the Act requires that its three members be appointed by the President from "a list of individuals knowledgeable in the fields of marine ecology and resource management" submitted by the Chairman of the Council on Environmental Quality, the Secretary of the Smithsonian Institution, the Director of the National Science Foundation, and the Chairman of the National Academy of Sciences.[16]

Prior to the Reagan Administration, the members of the Marine Mammal Commission had been among the most highly regarded scientists in the field of mammalogy. However, the Reagan Administration, seizing upon the ambiguity in the statute as to whether only one or all four agencies had to agree on the qualifications of each individual recommended to the President, began the practice of appointing Commissioners who were recommended only by the White House–controlled Council on Environmental Quality. On the eve of the rumored appointment of another such individual in December 1982, and to prevent further deterioration of the Commission's credibility as an expert scientific agency, the lame-duck 97th Congress attached to other, unrelated legislation the additional requirement that Commission appointments be made subject to Senate confirmation.[17]

The role of the Marine Mammal Commission is broad and very important. Among other things, it must conduct a continuing review and study of all stocks of marine mammals and of all activities of the United States relating to them; it must also conduct such further studies as it deems necessary and make formal recommendations for the protection and conservation of marine mammals.[18] The Commission is supported in these duties by a statutorily created Committee of Scientific Advisors on Marine Mammals.[19]

---

[14] 16 U.S.C. §1402 (Supp. V 1981).

[15] The Commission's intended role has aptly been described as that of an "expert watchdog agency." Erdheim, The Immediate Goal Test of the Marine Mammal Protection Act and the Tuna/Porpoise Controversy, 9 Envtl. L. 283, 289 n.35 (1979).

[16] 16 U.S.C. §1401(b)(1) (1976).

[17] Commercial Fisheries Research and Development Act of 1982, Pub. L. No. 97-389, §202, 96 Stat. 1950. (amending 16 U.S.C. §1401(b)(1) (1976)).

[18] The failure of any agency head to adopt a recommendation of the Commission must be given a "detailed explanation" by such agency head. 16 U.S.C. §1402(d) (1976).

[19] Id. §1403(a). The Committee of Scientific Advisors is a nine-member body of scientists appointed by the Chairman of the Marine Mammal Commission. Its members may not include federal employees. Recommendations of the Committee

## IMPLEMENTATION OF THE MARINE MAMMAL PROTECTION ACT

### The Moratorium and the Exceptions to It

The central feature of the Marine Mammal Protection Act is its moratorium on the taking and importation of marine mammals and marine mammal products. The prohibition against taking is intentionally quite broad, for the Act defines the term "take" to mean "to harass, hunt, capture, or kill" any marine mammal.[20] By including harassment within the scope of this definition, the Act was intended to prohibit even unintentional acts adversely affecting marine mammals.[21] No previous federal wildlife law had utilized such an expansive understanding of "taking."[22] The prohibition against importation, on the other hand, is left undefined.[23]

---

that are not adopted by the Commission must be transmitted to the appropriate agency head and to Congress with the Commission's "detailed explanation" for not accepting such recommendations. *Id.* §1403(c).

[20]*Id.* §1362(13).

[21]According to the House Committee Report, "[t]he act of taking need not be intentional: the operation of motor boats in waters in which these animals are found can clearly constitute harassment." H.R. Rep. No. 707, 92d Cong., 1st Sess. 23 (1971). Congress probably had in mind the operation of pleasure boats in waters where the manatee is found, as well as "whale-watching" boats in calving areas. One must ask, however, whether the concept of harassment was intended to include ordinary commercial shipping operations that may disturb marine mammals.

[22]The Migratory Bird Treaty Act had not defined the term "take" at all. The Bald Eagle Protection Act originally defined it to include "willful" molesting and disturbing of protected eagles. Just two days after enactment of the Marine Mammal Protection Act, an amendment to the Bald Eagle Protection Act deleted the term "willfully" from its definition of "take." Act of Oct. 23, 1972, Pub. L. No. 92-535, §4, 86 Stat. 1065 (codified at 16 U.S.C. §668(c)(1976)). *See* discussion in Chapter 4 at text accompanying notes 126–129. *Compare* the definition of "take" in the Endangered Species Act of 1973, 16 U.S.C. §1532(19)(Supp. V 1981).

[23]In Marine Wonderland & Animal Park, Ltd. v. Kreps, 610 F.2d 947 (D.C. Cir. 1979), the question of the proper meaning of the term "importation" was presented, but skirted. Plaintiffs, a Canadian amusement park and certain employees, were charged with importing marine mammals without a permit when a plane, commissioned by the park to deliver dolphins captured in Mexico, was forced to land to clear customs after entering United States airspace. Plaintiffs' dolphins were thereupon discovered and seized. Claiming that the National Marine Fisheries Service (NMFS) had neither subject matter nor personal jurisdiction, plaintiffs sought to enjoin impending administrative proceedings. The district court refused. In affirming the lower court, the court of appeals held that NMFS had primary jurisdiction over the interpretation of such statutory terms as "importation." Thus the court held that NMFS itself could decide in the first instance the extent of its own jurisdiction. *Compare* the definition of "import" in the Endangered Species Act, 16 U.S.C. §1532(10)(Supp. V 1981).

Although the Act defines the term "moratorium" to mean a "complete cessation" of taking and a "complete ban" on importation,[24] there are in fact a number of important exceptions to these prohibitions. First among these is the authority of the Secretary to issue permits for the taking and importation of marine mammals "for purposes of scientific research and for public display."[25] Before such permits may be issued, however, the Secretary must seek the advice of the Marine Mammal Commission and its Committee of Scientific Advisors regarding the consistency of the proposed taking or importation with the purposes and policies of the Act. Permits may be issued for scientific research purposes, but not for public display, in the case of any marine mammal that is depleted.[26] The Act also appears to draw a distinction between scientific research and public display permits with respect to the requirement of humaneness. Section 104(b)(2)(B) requires that permits authorizing the taking or importation of marine mammals specify "the location and manner (which manner must be determined by the Secretary to be humane) in which they may be taken, or from which they may be imported."[27] Yet section 102(b), prohibiting the importation of any marine mammal that was "taken in a manner deemed inhumane by the Secretary," is expressly made inapplicable in the case of any permit for scientific research.[28]

A second set of exceptions to the moratorium applies to the incidental taking of marine mammals in the course of commercial fishing operations.[29] During the initial two-year period following enactment of the Act, such incidental taking was to be subject to regulations designed to reduce it "to the lowest practicable level."[30] Thereafter, incidental taking could

---

[24] 16 U.S.C. §1362(7)(1976).

[25] *Id.* §1371(a)(1). *Compare* the Endangered Species Act of 1973, which authorizes the taking of endangered species for scientific purposes, or "to enhance the propagation or survival of the affected species." *Id.* §1539(a). For a suggestion that the latter purpose may, at least with respect to already captive animals, include certain types of public display, see 50 C.F.R. §17.3 (1981). The public display exception in the Marine Mammal Protection Act is not limited to already captive animals.

[26] 16 U.S.C. §1371(a)(3)(B)(1976). For a discussion of "depleted" species, see text accompanying notes 70–72 *infra*.

[27] *Id.* §1374(b)(2)(1976). Elsewhere, the Act defines "humane" taking as "that method of taking which involves the least possible degree of pain and suffering practicable to the mammal involved." *Id.* §1362(4).

[28] *Id.* §1372(b).

[29] *Id.* §§1371(a)(2), (4) (Supp. V 1981).

[30] *Id.* §§1381(b) (1976). The Secretary's failure to promulgate the required regulations for nearly a year prompted the filing of a lawsuit, Project Jonah v. Dent, Civil No. 1255-73 (D.D.C., filed Sept. 12, 1973), which was dismissed when the proposed regulations were finally published soon thereafter.

continue to be permitted, despite the moratorium, though, as will be described later, only pursuant to much more rigorous regulation.[31]

Under a third exception, the Secretary may authorize the taking of marine mammals incidental to an unspecified range of nonfishing activities.[32] This authority was added by amendment in 1981. It and the authority to permit taking incidental to commercial fishing are discussed in more detail hereafter.

A special temporary exemption from the moratorium briefly existed for persons, other than commercial fishermen, who would otherwise suffer "undue economic hardship" as a result of the Act's prohibitions.[33] Unlike the similar exemption in the Endangered Species Conservation Act of 1969, on which it was based, the availability of this exemption was not limited to those who had entered into contracts prior to the date that the prohibition became effective but extended to any person who could satisfactorily demonstrate economic hardship of any kind.[34] This exemption lapsed one year after enactment of the Act.

Yet another exemption applies to the taking of marine mammals by any "Indian, Aleut, or Eskimo who dwells on the coast of the North Pacific Ocean or the Arctic Ocean."[35] However, this exemption applies to such native taking only when done for one of two purposes, "subsistence" or "creating and selling authentic native articles of handicrafts and clothing." Though this provision of the Act does not define the term "subsistence," the legislative history suggests that a narrow interpretation was not intended.[36] On the other hand, the Act attempted to prevent the handicraft

---

[31] The controversy surrounding the Secretary's action with respect to the incidental taking of marine mammals is recounted at text accompanying notes 142–175 *infra*.

[32] 16 U.S.C. §1371(a)(5) (Supp. V 1981).

[33] *Id.* §1371(c) (1976).

[34] *See* Pub. L. No. 91-135, §3(b), 83 Stat. 275 (repealed 1973). *Compare* the economic hardship exemption of the Endangered Species Act of 1973, 16 U.S.C. §1539(b) (1976), which, unlike the Marine Mammal Protection Act, gives detailed guidance to the meaning of "undue economic hardship."

[35] 16 U.S.C. §1371(b) (1976 & Supp. V 1981).

[36] The Conference Report gave the following explanation of subsistence:

> By retention of the phrase permitting 'subsistence' taking by Alaska Natives, the conferees intend to permit taking not only for food but also for clothing, shelter, transportation, and the other necessities of life.

H.R. Rep. No. 1488, 92d Cong., 2d Sess. 24 (1972). In 1981, a definition of "subsistence" was added to section 109, which governs the return of management authority to states. 16 U.S.C. §1379(f)(2)(Supp. V 1981). This definition differs in various particulars from the administrative definitions previously adopted. *See* 50 C.F.R. §§18.3, 216.3 (1981). Because the 1981 statutory definition only applies for purposes of section 109, the meaning of the term "subsistence" could vary,

and clothing exemption from becoming a gaping loophole by prohibiting the use of "mass copying devices" in the production of such items.[37] Whether taken for subsistence or handicraft purposes, the Act requires that the taking not be done "in a wasteful manner."[38] Finally, the Act authorizes the Secretary to promulgate regulations restricting otherwise exempt takings by Alaskan natives whenever he determines a species or population stock of marine mammal to be depleted.[39]

A further exemption from the Act's prohibitions applies to the taking and importation of northern fur seals harvested pursuant to the Interim Convention on Conservation of North Pacific Fur Seals.[40] Although this exemption is couched in general terms that state that the Act is "not in contravention of the provisions of any existing international treaty... which may otherwise apply to the taking of marine mammals,"[41] its practical effect, up to now, has been limited to the fur seal convention.[42]

---

depending upon whether the federal government or the state of Alaska exercises management authority.

[37] 16 U.S.C. §1371(b)(2) (1976). The 1981 statutory definition of "subsistence" for purposes of section 109 encompasses the production and sale of handicrafts but contains no prohibition against the use of mass copying devices. Despite that, however, there is no evidence that Congress intended to relax this restriction if management authority were transferred to the state of Alaska.

[38] 16 U.S.C. §1371(b)(3) (1976).

[39] The determination of species or stocks as depleted is discussed at text accompanying notes 70–72 infra.

[40] See Chapter 10.

[41] 16 U.S.C. §1383 (1976).

[42] See 50 C.F.R. §§18.21, 216.21 (1981). By virtue of section 404 of the Fishery Conservation and Management Act of 1976, Pub. L. No. 94-265, 90 Stat. 331 (codified at 16 U.S.C. §1362(14)(Supp. V 1981)), the Marine Mammal Protection Act's prohibition on taking now applies throughout the 200 mile fishery conservation zone. See Chapter 13. According to the Conference Report that accompanied the 1976 Act, section 404 was "not intended to alter U.S. obligation under any existing international agreement which applies to the taking of marine mammals, for example, those applying to whales or fur seals." S. Rep. No. 711, 94th Cong., 2d Sess. 59 (1976). It is unclear whether the exemption referred to in the text exempts the whaling activities of foreign nations pursuant to the International Convention for the Regulations of Whaling from the operation of the amended Marine Mammal Protection Act. It might be argued that under that Convention the United States has no obligation to allow any part of the whaling quotas established to be taken in its fishery conservation zone, thus rendering the Act's exemption inapplicable. This argument finds some support in the Act's prohibition against taking marine mammals in waters under the jurisdiction of the United States, including its fishery conservation zone, "except as *expressly* provided for by an international treaty." 16 U.S.C. §1372(a)(2)(A)(1976) (emphasis added). On the other hand, it can also be argued with some plausibility that, since the Marine Mammal Protection Act itself establishes renegotiation of existing treaties as the

A final limitation on the moratorium against taking has been recognized by one federal appellate court. In *United States v. Mitchell,* an indictment charging certain defendants with taking dolphins in the territorial waters of the Bahamas was initially sustained against a motion to dismiss on the grounds that section 102(a) of the Act prohibited takings only within the jurisdiction of the United States or on the high seas.[43] The district court reasoned that the Act's imposition of a general moratorium prohibited United States citizens from taking marine mammals at any locale, notwithstanding those more limited specific prohibitions. In reaching this conclusion, the court relied upon the opening sentence of the House Report[44] and an administrative regulation that interpreted the moratorium as applying to the taking of marine mammals by United States citizens at any time or place.[45]

Finding insufficient evidence of congressional intent to rebut the usual presumption against the application of United States statutes in foreign countries, the court of appeals reversed.[46] In the appellate court's view, control of the taking of marine mammals in the territorial waters of foreign sovereigns must be effected "by the usual methods of negotiation, treaty, and convention."[47]

### Standards for Marine Mammal Management

#### Optimum Sustainable Population

Just as the moratorium established by the Marine Mammal Protection Act is not in fact complete, neither is it permanent. Instead, the Act prescribes a complex procedure whereby the moratorium may be "waived" for a particular species or population stock and both taking and importation of that species or stock permitted under appropriate regulation. The waiver of a moratorium is the mechanism that shifts the focus of the Act from the protection of marine mammals to their management through regulated

---

mechanism for altering existing marine mammal harvesting policies of foreign nations, the 1976 Act should not be read to interfere with that directive. Moreover, in the exceedingly unlikely, but nonetheless theoretically possible, circumstance that the United States resumed whaling activities pursuant to the Convention, those activities would appear to qualify under the exemption discussed here.

[43] 6 Envtl. L. Rep. (Envtl. L. Inst.) 20683 (S.D. Fla. Apr. 26, 1976).

[44]    The purpose of this legislation is to prohibit the harassing, catching and killing of marine mammals by U.S. citizens or within the jurisdiction of the United States....

H.R. Rep. No. 707, 92d Cong., 2d Sess. 11 (1972).

[45] 50 C.F.R. §216.11(c)(1981). This regulation has not been changed, despite the reversal of the district court's decision, as discussed in the text.

[46] United States v. Mitchell, 553 F.2d 996, 1004 (5th Cir. 1977).

[47] *Id.* at 1005. This decision has been strongly criticized. *See, e.g.,* Comment, Marine Mammal Protection Act and U.S. v. Mitchell: Disregarding the Moratorium?, 16 Urban L. Ann. 375 (1979).

taking. It is precisely in the standards prescribed for this management that the Act is most innovative.

What the Marine Mammal Protection Act sets out to do is unlike what has been done historically in the management of commercially valuable wildlife. Most such wildlife has generally been managed under the principle of "maximum sustained yield" (commonly referred to as MSY), a standard which, in its purest form, focuses solely on the effects of a given level of harvest on the ability of the harvested species to replenish itself.[48] That narrow focus may have been appropriate where the commercial value of the wildlife harvested was its only recognized value. However, the 1972 Act declares that marine mammals have "esthetic and recreational as well as economic" value.[49] To further these and other associated values, it provides that the "primary objective" of marine mammal management "should be to maintain the health and stability of the marine habitat."[50] Thus the Act seeks to compel a broader vision in the management of marine mammals than had previously prevailed.

Having established the health and stability of the ecosystem as its primary objective, the Act further provides that "[w]henever consistent with this primary objective, it should be the goal to obtain an optimum sustainable population keeping in mind the carrying capacity of the environment."[51] Literally, the quoted language can only mean that there may be occasions when the attainment of an optimum sustainable population (commonly referred to as OSP) is not consistent with the Act's primary objective and thus must give way.[52] What those occasions might be

---

[48]For a definition of "maximum sustainable yield," see Chapter 10 *supra* at note 44. Occasionally, the management standard of "optimum sustainable yield" has been employed, particularly in fisheries management. However, that standard "means the same thing, except that [it] permits the achievement of something less than the maximum where the use of the stock is interrelated with the use of other stocks." F. Christy, Alternative Arrangements for Marine Fisheries: An Overview 23 (1973).

[49]16 U.S.C. §1361(6)(Supp. V 1981).

[50]*Id.*

[51]*Id.*

[52]The relative status of the two objectives was clearly apparent in the language of the bill passed by the House, H.R. 10420, 92d Cong., 1st Sess. In that bill, the counterpart to the language quoted in the text was as follows:

Whenever consistent with this primary objective, a secondary objective should be to obtain an optimum sustainable population.

The Senate amendment to the House-passed bill reversed these priorities and established the achievement of optimum sustainable populations as the primary objective of marine mammal management, while reducing the health and stability of the ecosystem to one of the factors to be kept in mind. The version that emerged from the Conference Committee clearly adopted the House priorities rather than those of the Senate, despite the deletion of the term "secondary" that had described the goal of obtaining OSP in the original House version.

are difficult to decipher.[53] This confusion is but one of several reasons why the Act's population policy has been described as its "most intricate and the most poorly articulated component."[54]

Whatever its intricacies, it is clear that OSP has the central role to play in the operation of the Act. Unfortunately, however, its definition is clouded in ambiguity:

> The term "optimum sustainable population" means, with respect to any population stock, the number of animals which will result in the maximum productivity of the population or the species, keeping in mind the carrying capacity of the habitat and the health of the ecosystem of which they form a constituent element.[55]

Two of the key variables in this definition are the "maximum productivity" of the species and the "health of the ecosystem." The former is to subject some degree of measurement; the latter is much less so. To the extent one places emphasis on the former, the less OSP appears to differ from traditional marine mammal management standards, which were based solely on the annual "production" of new individuals to replace those harvested the previous year.[56] To the extent one emphasizes the latter, OSP seems to compel the minimum feasible level of disturbance to the ecosystem, especially where the effects of any action are largely uncertain. Some writers have suggested that the two components of the definition can be reconciled by arguing that the former need not refer to narrow biological productivity but can be read to refer to "ecological productivity."[57] That

---

[53]In explaining the Conference bill to the House, Congressman Dingell, then Chairman of the Subcommittee on Fisheries and Wildlife Conservation of the Committee on Merchant Marine and Fisheries, was likewise unable to foresee any incompatibility in the Act's two major goals, but he recognized that in the event of conflict, ecosystem health was to be paramount:

> I will say that I cannot imagine a case in which the objectives of ecosystem stability and non-disadvantageous taking might conflict; but if they should, it is ecosystem protection which must prevail.

118 Cong. Rec. 34637 (1972).

[54]Gaines & Schmidt, *supra* note 9 at 50101.

[55]16 U.S.C. §1362(8)(Supp. V 1981). As originally enacted, the term "optimum carrying capacity" was used in lieu of "carrying capacity." The best explication of the original legislative history of the OSP standard can be found in Gaines & Schmidt, *supra* note 9 at 50103–50108.

[56]*See* Gaines & Schmidt, *supra* note 9 at 50106.

[57]*Id.* at 50107. The Marine Mammal Commission accepts this as a possible reading of the definition.

> Maximum productivity may mean maximum productivity to the ecosystem or maximum net productivity to mankind, including both consumptive and non-consumptive values. The level that provides maximum net consumptive values to mankind on a continuing basis is

interpretation, however, is based more on the "spirit" of the Act than on anything in the Act that expressly compels it.[58] More convincing is the Marine Mammal Commission's conclusion that the Act's definition of OSP "includes certain features which are potentially inconsistent and certain other features which call for subjective value judgments that are not amenable to quantification on the basis of available data."[59]

Not surprisingly, the Secretaries have sought to retain as much flexibility in the determination of OSP as they can. The National Marine Fisheries Service in 1976 promulgated the following definition:

> "Optimum sustainable population" is a population size which falls within a range from the population level of a given species or stock which is the largest supportable within the ecosystem to the population level that results in maximum net productivity. Maximum net productivity is the greatest net annual increment in population numbers or biomass resulting from additions to the population due to reproduction and/or growth less losses due to natural mortality.[60]

This definition has been endorsed by the Interior Department's Fish and Wildlife Service,[61] approved by at least one district court,[62] and in effect ratified by Congress in 1981.[63]

---

> usually considered to be the well-known maximum sustainable yield (MSY) level.

Marine Mammal Commission, The Concept of Optimum Sustainable Populations 7 (undated).

[58]There is some support in the legislative history for this view. Thus Senator Stevens, author of the bill considered by the Senate, gave the following explanation:

> It also requires a judgment, not only on the maximum population of the species, but on the maximum total productivity of the environment including all constituent elements.

118 Cong. Rec. 25258 (1972). Curiously, however, this explanation was offered in regard to the Act's original term "optimum carrying capacity" rather than "optimum sustainable population."

[59]Marine Mammal Commission, *supra* note 57 at 1.

[60]50 C.F.R. §216.3 (1981).

[61]The Fish and Wildlife Service has not promulgated a definition of OSP, but has endorsed the National Marine Fisheries Service's definition. *See* 44 Fed. Reg. 2540, 2541–2542 (January 11, 1979).

[62]Committee for Humane Legislation, Inc. v. Kreps, No. 77-0564 (D.D.C. June 30, 1977). Judge Richey found that "maximum net productivity" was a reasonable interpretation of "maximum productivity," a term included in the statutory definition of OSP.

[63]Congress actually amended the definition of OSP in 1981 by deleting from it the reference to "optimum carrying capacity," a term eliminated altogether from the Act. Act of October 9, 1981, Pub. L. No. 97-58, §§1(a), 1(b)(1), 95 Stat. 979 (1981). The legislative history indicates, however, that this change was not intended to change

While these actions confirm that OSP refers to a range of population levels, there remains the important question of precisely where to place the lower limit of that range. Administrative Law Judge Littlefield, in his 1977 recommended decision regarding Alaska's request for return of marine mammal management, concluded that the lower limit of the above definition was essentially equivalent to the level of MSY, a standard expressly rejected by Congress in enacting the Marine Mammal Protection Act. Therefore, he disapproved the regulatory definition, holding that the lower limit of OSP was "somewhere above" the level of maximum net productivity.[64] Upon review, the Administrator of the National Oceanic and Atmospheric Administration rejected Judge Littlefield's conclusion without commenting on the relationship between maximum net productivity and MSY.[65] Similarly, the Director of the Fish and Wildlife Service, in his review of Judge Littlefield's recommended decision, endorsed the regulatory definition of OSP, suggesting without explanation that maximum net productivity affords greater protection to marine mammals than does MSY.[66] Neither agency indicated whether management at the level of MSY comports with the Act.

The silence of both agencies with respect to this question perhaps reflects approval of Judge Skelly Wright's earlier disposition in *Animal Welfare Institute v. Kreps*,[67] handed down about the time of Judge Littlefield's recommended decision. In this case, to be discussed more fully later, Judge Wright considered whether South Africa's MSY-based management program for fur seals was compatible with the Act. While expressing the view that "the definitions of both OSP and optimum carrying capacity are singularly unenlightening," Judge Wright held that, "we cannot conclude that MSY is definitely inconsistent with OSP."[68] That equivocal conclusion is about as much as can be safely said.[69]

---

the meaning of OSP. Rather, while recognizing "that new scientific knowledge may result in changes to the existing regulatory definition," the House Committee stated that that definition "accurately reflects the meaning of the term optimum sustainable population and the intent of the Congress in passing the original Act." H.R. Rep. No. 228, 97th Cong., 1st Sess. 16 (1981).

[64]Recommended Decision, "In the Matter of the Request of the State of Alaska," MMPA Docket No. Wash. 76-1, June 30, 1977, at 37. For a discussion of the Alaska waiver request, see text accompanying notes 114–123 *infra*.

[65]44 Fed. Reg. 2457, 2550 (Jan. 11, 1979).

[66]44 Fed. Reg. 2450, 2541–2542, (Jan. 11, 1979).

[67]561 F.2d 1002 (D.C. Cir. 1977).

[68]*Id*. at 1014. Judge Wright's guarded holding may have been influenced by the finding of NMFS that the South African seal population under MSY-based management was "healthy and growing." *Id*.

[69]For a comparison of maximum net productivity, MSY, and other management

## Depletion

In addition to the OSP standard, the Act introduced the term "depleted" and applied strict protection to species or stocks determined to be depleted. For example, public display permits may not be issued for any depleted marine mammal, and otherwise exempt taking by Alaskan natives may be regulated when a determination of depletion is made. Most significantly, the moratorium against taking cannot be waived for a depleted marine mammal.

As originally enacted, there was no direct statutory linkage between OSP and depletion. However, by administrative practice, species, or stocks determined to be below OSP have been regarded as depleted. In 1981, Congress ratified this practice by expressly redefining depletion to refer to any species or stock determined to be below OSP.[70] Also considered depleted are those species or stocks listed as threatened or endangered under the Endangered Species Act.[71] For the latter category, no formal finding of depletion under the Marine Mammal Protection Act need be made; species or stocks listed under the Endangered Species Act are, by virtue of that fact, automatically considered depleted.

Somewhat unclear is how determinations of depletion are to be made for species or stocks not protected by the Endangered Species Act. Whereas elsewhere in the Act the Secretary is required to follow detailed procedures before taking actions affecting the status of marine mammals, the only thing that the Act expressly requires of his determination that a given species or stock is depleted is that it be done "after consultation with" the Marine Mammal Commission and the Committee of Scientific Advisors on Marine Mammals.[72] Moreover, if management of a species or stock has been transferred to a state, the Act simply provides that the state may make a determination of depletion without expressly incorporating any duty of

---

standards, see Nafziger, The Management of Marine Mammals After the Fisheries Conservation and Management Act, 14 Willamette L.J. 153 (1978).

[70] The original definition of depletion was riddled with ambiguities. However, with the revision of the definition in 1981, the discussion of those ambiguities at pages 342–347 of the first volume of this work is now of historic interest only. See Act of Oct. 9, 1981, Pub. L. No. 97-58, §1(b)(2)(A), 95 Stat. 979 (1981) (amending 16 U.S.C. §1362(1)(1976)).

[71] Id. In the case of any marine mammal protected by the Endangered Species Act, if there are conflicting provisions between the two statutes, the more restrictive of those provisions governs. See 16 U.S.C. §1543 (1976).

[72] Coggins, supra note 13 at 34, speculates that the failure to prescribe any specific procedures for determinations of depletion evidences a congressional intent to free protective measures from as much "red tape" as possible.

consultation. Finally, nothing in the Act compels either the Secretary or a state to make a determination of depletion.

## Waiver of the Moratorium

### Rulemaking

Technically, it is not proper to speak of a waiver of "the moratorium" for what in fact is waived is only that part of the moratorium applicable to a particular species or population stock of marine mammal, and then only to the extent provided in the waiver. In making such "partial waivers," the Secretary is obliged to act on the basis of the "best scientific evidence available and in consultation with the Marine Mammal Commission."[73] Further, he must give "due regard to the distribution, abundance, breeding habits, and times and lines of migratory movements of such marine mammals."[74] If satisfied that the proposed waiver will be "compatible with" the Act and if "assured that the taking of such marine mammals is in accord with sound principles of resource protection and conservation as provided in the purposes and policies" of the Act, the Secretary may waive the moratorium and permit the taking of such marine mammals pursuant to "suitable regulations."[75]

The net effect of the foregoing is to require, prior to any waiver of the moratorium, that the Secretary determine that the affected species or population be within the range of OSP and that the taking authorized by that waiver not reduce it below that level.[76] This conclusion is reinforced by the Act's requirements regarding the promulgation of regulations to implement the waiver.[77] Those regulations, like the waiver itself, must be promulgated "on the basis of the best scientific evidence available and in consultation with the Marine Mammal Commission."[78] Further, they must "insure" that the takings they authorize "will not be to the

---

[73]16 U.S.C. §1371(a)(3)(A)(1976).

[74]Id. The standard quoted is taken nearly verbatim from the language of the 1918 Migratory Bird Treaty Act, 16 U.S.C. §704 (1976). Significantly, however, in that earlier Act the list of factors to be considered includes the "economic value" of the migratory birds, a factor that is conspicuous by its omission in the Marine Mammal Protection Act.

[75]16 U.S.C. §1371(a)(3)(A)(1976).

[76]See Gaines & Schmidt, supra note 9 at 50009.

[77]Although the Act is not fully clear on the point, the waiver of the moratorium does not take effect until implementing regulations are finally promulgated. Otherwise, during the period between the Secretary's determination to waive the moratorium and the promulgation of final regulations, neither the Act nor any regulations would restrict the taking and importation of any mammal included in the waiver.

[78]16 U.S.C. §1373(a) (1976).

disadvantage of those species and population stocks and will be consistent with the purposes and policies" of the Act.[79]

Beyond these general directives, the Act requires that the Secretary give "full consideration" to at least five specific factors when promulgating regulations.[80] Two of these, requiring consideration of marine mammal population levels and marine ecosystem effects, are necessarily subsumed under the general duty to assure compliance with the policies of the Act. Two others, however, introduce considerations not clearly subsumed under those policies. One requires consideration of the effects of the proposed regulations on "the conservation, development, and utilization of fishery resources,"[81] and the other requires consideration of "the economic and technological feasibility of implementation."[82] The legislative history suggests that these latter two considerations are secondary to the former two.[83]

Once having decided to propose regulations to implement a tentative decision to waive the moratorium, the Secretary is subject to procedural requirements more stringent than those applicable to the promulgation of regulations under any other wildlife statute. That is, the Act requires that all such regulations "be made on the record after opportunity for an agency hearing."[84] The effect of that requirement is to bring into play the full

---

[79]*Id.* The Act does not define the term "disadvantage." The legislative history suggests that its use was intended as a shorthand way of incorporating the Act's prohibition against taking that would reduce a species or population stock below its OSP level. *See, e.g.,* note 53 *supra.*

[80]16 U.S.C. §1373(b) (1976).

[81]*Id.* §1373(b)(4).

[82]*Id.* §1373(b)(5).

[83]These various considerations were addressed in the following exchange in the House of Representatives:

> Mr. Biaggi. Mr. Chairman, the committee bill requires the Secretary in setting limitations to take into consideration the "conservation, development, and utilization of fishery resources" and "the economic and technological feasibility of implementation." Is not this the same as saying if the abalone fishing industry, for example, was allegedly being threatened by the sea otters, the Federal government could order a selective killing of the otters to protect the fishing industry?
>
> Mr. Dingell. No. The answer to that is the basic consideration to be kept in mind by the Secretary under 102(a) is that the taking must not be to the disadvantage of the species of marine mammals. The protection of fish and shell fish is secondary.

118 Cong. Rec. 7690 (1972). *See also* Judge Richey's discussion of the "technological feasibility" factor in Committee for Humane Legislation, Inc. v. Richardson, 414 F. Supp. 297, 308 (D.D.C.), *aff'd,* 540 F.2d 1141, (D.C. Cir. 1976).

[84]16 U.S.C. §1373(d) (1976). In fulfillment of its statutory obligation to "consult"

panoply of procedures applicable to an adversarial administrative hearing, the most important element of which is the right to cross-examine, rather than the more customary "notice and comment" procedures of informal rulemaking. Moreover, the scope of the hearing is not limited solely to the proposed regulations, but also extends to the antecedent decision to waive the moratorium.[85] Finally, when proposing regulations, the Secretary must publish and make available to the public statements describing the existing population levels of the affected marine mammal species or population stock, the anticipated impact of such regulations on the OSP of that species or stock, and the evidence on which he bases his proposed action.[86] He must also publish any relevant studies and recommendations made by or for him or the Marine Mammal Commission.

### Permits

Once promulgated, the regulations do not by themselves authorize any taking or importation of marine mammals. For that, the Secretary must issue permits, consistent with the regulations, specifying the number of animals to be taken, where they are to be taken, over what time period, and other similar conditions.[87] Where the permit is for importation, as distinct from taking, the Act imposes certain further requirements. That is, the Secretary may not permit the importation of marine mammals that were taken inhumanely, that were pregnant at the time of taking, or that were "nursing at the time of taking, or less than eight months old, whichever occurs later."[88]

---

with the Secretaries of Commerce and the Interior, the Marine Mammal Commission has actively participated in the formal public hearings concerning the promulgation of regulations under the Act. The Secretary of the Interior has sought to discourage this form of "consultation." *See* In re Waiver of Moratorium on Walrus, Dkt. No. MMPA Wash 75-1, Opening Brief on Behalf of United States Fish and Wildlife Service at 17. It remains to be resolved, however, whether the Commission can intervene in or even initiate litigation concerning implementation of the Act. To date, it has not attempted to do so.

[85]The requirement that the Secretary's regulations "insure" that the proposed taking not be disadvantageous to the species or stock involved presumably places on him the burden of proof at the required public hearing.

[86]16 U.S.C. §1373(d)(1976). It was the Secretary's failure to publish this required statement (or even to make the required underlying determinations) that was the narrow legal issue decided in Committee for Humane Legislation, Inc. v. Richardson, *supra* note 83.

[87]16 U.S.C. §1374(b)(1976). The Secretary may also issue so-called "general permits." *Id.* §1374(h). General permits have been utilized to authorize the taking of marine mammals incidental to commercial fishing operations.

[88]§1372(b).

Before issuing any permit the Secretary must publish a notice of application therefore in the Federal Register and allow 30 days for public comment thereon.[89] If during that period any person requests a hearing with regard to the permit application, the Secretary has the discretion to order one.[90] The applicant for a permit has the burden of demonstrating that the taking or importation he proposes is consistent with the terms of the regulations and with the policies of the Act.[91] Whether or not a hearing is held, the Secretary's decision to grant or deny the application is subject to judicial review at the behest of the applicant or any party opposed to the application.[92] This is the only express authorization of judicial review of any administrative action under the Marine Mammal Protection Act. While the Act fails to be very precise about the standard of review to be employed or even about the scope of that review, any alleged defect in the waiver of the moratorium or in the promulgation of implementing regulations should be considered in the review of any permit issuance.[93]

### Implementation

To date, apart from Alaska's request for return of management authority, discussed later, there has been only one moratorium waiver decision under the full administrative process required by the Act. That involved a request by the Fouke Company for a waiver of the moratorium to permit the importation of fur seals harvested in South Africa during 1975. Because the Act requires that before the Secretary may permit the importation of any marine mammal taken in another country he must certify that such country's management program is consistent with the purposes and policies of the Act,[94] he was in effect required to make the same findings regarding population size and OSP that would have been required were the taking to be done by persons subject to United States jurisdiction. In addition, he was required to make certain further determinations applicable solely to imported marine mammals.[95]

---

[89]§1374(d)(2).

[90]§1374(d)(4).

[91]*Id.* §1374(d)(3).

[92]*Id.* §1374(d)(6).

[93]Immediate review of a decision to waive the moratorium was apparently intended to be precluded on the grounds that it is not a "final action." *See* H.R. Rep. No. 1488 (Conf. Rep.), 92d Cong., 2d Sess. at 23. On the other hand, the Secretary's denial of a petition to waive the moratorium would certainly constitute final administrative action and would therefore be presumptively reviewable at the behest of any aggrieved person under general principles of administrative law.

[94]16 U.S.C. §1371(a)(3)(A)(1976).

[95]*See* text accompanying note 86 *supra*.

The Secretary made each of the required findings and waived the moratorium to the extent of an annual harvest, beginning in 1975, of not more than 70,000 seals. In so doing, however, he relied upon a number of interpretations of the Act that were initially subject to sharp criticism.[96] Principal among these was that, although the South African management policy expressly embraced the principle of maximum sustainable yield, the Secretary found that the population level that would produce that yield was within the Act's required OSP range.[97] Further, whereas the Act prohibits the importation of any marine mammal less than eight months old or nursing at the time of its taking, the Secretary brushed aside evidence that at least some of the seals to be imported were less than eight months old with the conclusion that the average seal taken exceeded that age. Then, relying upon a distinction between so-called "obligate" nursing necessary for "the physical health and survival of the animal" and mere "convenience" nursing, which may be done for "psychological purposes," the Secretary concluded that since the only evidence before him indicated that obligate nursing ceases prior to the attainment of eight months' age, none of the seals was taken while nursing.[98] By thus collapsing these two criteria, the Secretary was able to overlook the fact that those seals whose ages were in fact less than eight months might meet even his own questionable criterion of "obligate" nursing.[99]

Judicial review was initiated while the Fouke Company's application for a permit to import the seals was still pending. The district court, however, never reached the merits of the Secretary's action, initially because the South African harvest had exceeded the limit of 70,000 specified in the moratorium waiver. Thus the terms of the waiver having been violated for the 1975 season, the permit application was withdrawn and the case was temporarily dismissed. When Fouke subsequently applied for a permit to import seals killed in the 1976 harvest, the court vacated its earlier dismissal order to hear plaintiffs' arguments against importing those seals. This time, however, the court dismissed the suit on the grounds that the plaintiffs lacked standing to challenge the waiver regulations.[100] The court of appeals reversed.[101]

---

[96] See Gaines & Schmidt, supra note 9 at 50009–50010.

[97] See 41 Fed. Reg. 7537, 7538 (Feb. 19, 1976). The Secretary's interpretation of OSP as a range of population levels encompassing that which produces MSY is, of course, reflected in the current definition. See text accompanying notes 60–69 supra.

[98] See 41 Fed. Reg. 7537, 7538–7539 (Feb. 19, 1976) and 40 Fed. Reg. 17845–17846 (Apr. 23, 1975).

[99] The Marine Mammal Commission fought vigorously, but unsuccessfully, against the distinction between obligate and convenience nursing as lacking support either in law or scientific fact. See 40 Fed. Reg. 17845–17846 (Apr. 23, 1975).

[100] Animal Welfare Institute v. Richardson, Civil Action 76-0483 (D.D.C. Dec. 23, 1976).

[101] Animal Welfare Institute v. Kreps, 561 F.2d 1002 (D.C. Cir. 1977).

Acknowledging that the Act expressly grants judicial review only to parties regarding the "terms and conditions" of permits, the court of appeals nonetheless concluded that "Congress implicitly intended to confer standing to challenge waiver regulations on the same categories of people to whom it gave standing to challenge permits."[102] It rested this conclusion primarily upon the close relationship that ordinarily exists between waiver regulations and permits issued under them.[103] In the instant case, the terms and conditions of Fouke's permit *were* the regulations, incorporated expressly into the permit. In addition, the court determined that it would be both more efficient and more effective to grant judicial review of waiver regulations directly, rather than as part of challenges to individual permits, since "[t]here would rarely be enough time for full judicial review of any particular permit before the importation took place."[104] Although the court did not address whether the 60-day limit on challenges to permit denials or approvals should apply equally to challenges to waiver regulations, its opinion strongly suggests that such suits may be maintained throughout the period between promulgation of the waiver regulations and the first permit decision. Whether challenges to waiver regulations may be maintained thereafter only as part of a suit challenging a permit decision is unlikely but remains unresolved.

In finding that the challenged regulations violated the Act's prohibition against importation of animals killed while under eight months of age, the court acknowledged that it would be impractical to assure that every seal imported was older than eight months. Nonetheless, it held that the regulatory formula adopted, which allowed about half the seals imported to be under eight months, was "so far from meeting the statutory standard that it must be rejected."[105] Similarly, the regulations allowing importation of seals taken while engaged in "convenience" (as opposed to "obligate") nursing were also struck down. In the court's view, the statutory prohibition against importing seals taken while nursing admitted no such distinction.[106]

In making these determinations, the court appears to have treated these questions as questions of law, for which little, if any, deference was owed to the Secretary's expertise. In contrast, the claim that the waiver regulations permitted importation of animals killed in an inhumane manner was held to be one of fact, to be decided by the Secretary at the

---

[102]*Id.* at 1006. It should be noted that Judge Wright found that plaintiffs had standing both under the Marine Mammal Protection Act and under the traditional analysis of standing.

[103]*Id.*

[104]*Id.*

[105]561 F.2d at 1011.

[106]*Id.* at 1011-1012.

initial waiver hearing and not to be overturned if there were substantial evidence in the record supporting the Secretary's decision.[107] Similarly, the court deferred to the Secretary's determination that South Africa's MSY-based management regime satisfied the Act's OSP requirement because, in its view, these standards were not "definitely inconsistent."[108] Thus, in this respect, the court upheld the regulations.[109]

### Federalism: The Transfer of Management Authority to the States

An issue of considerable controversy concerns state and federal relations under the Marine Mammal Protection Act. Subject to certain exceptions to be discussed hereafter, section 109 of the Act provides that "[n]o State may enforce or attempt to enforce, any State law or regulation relating to the taking of any species...of marine mammal within the State."[110] Although this provision expressly refers only to "taking," the Act was also held implicitly to preempt any state law respecting the importation of marine mammals in *Fouke Company v. Mandel*,[111] a decision that has been severely criticized.[112]

Much like its moratorium, however, the Act's preemption of state regulatory authority need not be permanent. Rather, it provides the opportunity for states to regain the authority taken from them on certain specified conditions. The simplest and easiest form of state participation is contained in the Act's provision for "cooperative arrangements" between the Secretary and a state, under which the former delegates to the latter the "administration and enforcement" of the Act.[113] The Act does not define the term "administration," and it could arguably be deemed broad enough

---

[107]*Id.* at 1013.

[108]*Id.* at 1014.

[109]The statutory limitations placed upon importation of sealskins were challenged a year later in Globe Fur Dying Corp. v. United States, 12 Env't Rep. Cas. (BNA) 1926 (D.D.C. Nov. 16, 1978). Plaintiffs, commercial importers and dyers of foreign sealskins, alleged that these limitations violated their due process and equal protection rights. In holding for the Government, the district court found that protection of marine mammals for aesthetic purposes was a legitimate objective of congressional action and that, in any event, "a prohibition of the killing of young mammals is not an irrational means of conserving marine mammals." *Id.* at 1927.

[110]16 U.S.C. §1379(a)(Supp. V 1981).

[111]386 F. Supp. 1341 (D. Md. 1974).

[112]*See* Note, Federal Preemption: A New Method for Invalidating State Laws Designed to Protect Endangered Species, 47 U. Colo. Rev. 261 (1976).

[113]16 U.S.C. §1379(k)(Supp. V 1981). This was the only means of state participation provided by the House bill, which used the terms "protection and management" rather than "administration and enforcement." *See* H.R. Rep. No. 707, 92d Cong., 1st Sess. 8 (1971).

to include any duty that the Secretary otherwise must perform. However, it seems certain that a much narrower meaning was contemplated, primarily because elsewhere the Act imposes stringent procedural safeguards on the return of management authority to the states.

As originally enacted, section 109 of the Act provided a mechanism whereby the Secretary could waive the moratorium for any species or stock of marine mammal and return management authority for it to a state found by him to have laws and regulations consistent with the terms of the waiver and other requirements of the Act. Alaska sought almost immediately to regain management authority over 10 of its marine mammal species and in 1975 the Secretary of the Interior determined to return the management of the Pacific walrus to Alaska.[114] Subsequently, the Secretaries of the Interior and Commerce conditionally approved Alaska's request for a waiver and return of management with respect to the remaining species.[115] Before the conditions to effectuate the latter return were met, however, intervening events occurred that brought the Alaskan transfer request to an abrupt halt.

Shortly after Alaska resumed management of Pacific walrus, and while administrative proceedings continued regarding its request for return of management of nine other marine mammals, Alaskan natives filed a suit that ultimately had a major impact not only on these latter proceedings but on the Act as well. The question presented in *People of Togiak v. United States*[116] was whether the statutory exemption[117] from the moratorium for the taking of marine mammals for subsistence and handicraft purposes by Alaskan natives lapsed when Alaska resumed management. At the time management of walrus was returned to Alaska, the Interior Department decreed that the native exemption was thereby rescinded and superceded by Alaska's laws and regulations,[118] which significantly restricted native taking.[119] Interior reasoned that the provision in the Act exempting native taking from the moratorium also exempted native taking from the Act's provision preempting state management of marine mammals. Therefore, Alaska was free to regulate native taking *with or without* a return of management. The initial edition of this work expressed doubt that such reasoning would prevail.[120]

In an opinion denying its motion to dismiss, the court rejected

---

[114]40 Fed. Reg. 54959 (Dec. 24, 1975).

[115]44 Fed. Reg. 2540 and 2547 (Jan. 11, 1979).

[116]470 F. Supp. 423 (D.D.C. 1979).

[117]16 U.S.C. §1371(b) (1976) (amended 1981).

[118]41 Fed. Reg. 14372, 14373 (April 5, 1976).

[119]5 Alaska Administrative Code §81.340(4) (Reg. 59, Oct. 1976) (repealed July 4, 1980).

[120]First edition at 367.

Interior's statutory interpretation and found that the native exemption survived both the waiver and return of management to Alaska. Noting the native exemptions of the Endangered Species Act,[121] the Fur Seal Act,[122] and the Walrus Protection Act,[123] the court held that the native exemption within the Marine Mammal Protection Act represented a deliberate balance struck by Congress between two pervasive federal responsibilities: protection of wildlife and trust protection of Indians.[124] In a subsequent order, the court enjoined the federal government from approving any state laws that restrict native taking permitted under the Marine Mammal Protection Act.[125]

In the wake of *Togiak*, Alaska elected to return management authority over Pacific walrus to the federal government and stated its intention not to pursue further the return of management for the other nine species.[126] Alaska believed that the equal protection clause of its Constitution barred it from carrying out a management program containing a racially or ethnically based exemption. Accordingly, the Interior Department repealed its specific regulations conditionally approving Alaska's request and suspended the waiver for walrus.[127]

The *Togiak* decision and Alaska's response to it forced a legislative reconsideration of the Act's provisions relating to state and federal relations. The result was a major overhaul of section 109 and related provisions in 1981.[128] Though the controversy over Alaskan marine mammals precipitated that revision, the resulting changes apply to all states seeking return of marine mammal management authority.

The new provisions relating to resumption of state marine mammal management spell out in copious detail both the procedures and standards that govern such transfers of authority. There are now two major stages in that process. The first is the approval by the Secretary of a state program for conservation and management.[129] At that stage, the Secretary is not required, or even authorized, to determine the size or OSP range of

---

[121] 16 U.S.C. §1539(e) (1976).

[122] 16 U.S.C. §1152(a) (1976).

[123] Act of Aug. 18, 1941, ch. 368, 55 Stat. 632 (subsequently omitted from 16 U.S.C. as obsolete).

[124] 470 F. Supp. at 428.

[125] No. 77-0264 (D.D.C. Jan. 21, 1980).

[126] 44 Fed Reg. 45565 (Aug. 2, 1979).

[127] *Id.*

[128] Act of Oct. 9, 1981, Pub. L. No. 97-58, §4, 95 Stat. 982–986 (1981) (codified at 16 U.S.C. §§1379 (Supp. V 1981)).

[129] 16 U.S.C. §1379(b)(Supp. V 1981).

particular marine mammal species or stocks or to waive the moratorium against taking. He must, however, find that the state program includes an adequate process for making these determinations at the state level.[130] If he finds that such a process exists and the other requirements are met, the Secretary may transfer management authority to the state.[131] That transfer does not, of itself, authorize the state to permit the taking of the species or stock transferred.[132] Rather, the state must itself carry out what, in effect, is the second major stage in the overall transfer process.

In the second stage, the state must determine, prior to permitting the taking of any species or stock, that it is at its OSP and the maximum number of animals that may be taken without reducing it below its OSP.[133] The process by which these determinations must be made by the state is, in many respects, akin to the adjudicatory hearing process that the Secretary follows when promulgating regulations to implement a waiver of the moratorium. In particular, the state is obliged to present its evidence in support of its proposed determinations and to subject that evidence to cross-examination.[134] Judicial review comparable to that which would be available in federal courts to challenge federal agency action must also be available as part of the state process.[135] Once the determinations made pursuant to this state process are final, the state may resume regulating most forms of taking of the species or stocks that were the subject of that process.[136]

In addition to the requirements generally applicable to the management transfer process, the 1981 amendments impose a special requirement applicable only to the state of Alaska. Before management authority may be transferred to it, Alaska must adopt a statute and regulations under which subsistence uses of marine mammals are to be the priority consumptive uses.[137] Other uses, including sport and commercial hunting, may be

---

[130]*Id.* §1379(b)(1)(C)(i).

[131]The other requirements are set forth in 16 U.S.C. §1379(b)(1)(Supp. V 1981).

[132]*Id.* §1379(b)(2).

[133]*Id.* §1379(b)(3).

[134]*Id.* §1379(c)(2).

[135]*Id.* §1379(c)(4).

[136]The Secretary retains authority to regulate taking for scientific or public display purposes other than by or on behalf of the state. He also retains authority in the "fishery conservation zone" beyond the state's territorial waters for incidental taking authorized by section 101. *Id.* §1379(b)(3)(B). Because of this split authority, the Secretary and the state are required to enter into a "cooperative allocation agreement" with respect to any species or stock that is returned to state management authority and extends into the fishery conservation zone. *Id.* §1379(d).

[137]*Id.* §1379(f).

authorized only if the state determines that such uses "will have no significant adverse impact upon subsistence uses."[138] The definition of "subsistence uses" in this provision is taken nearly verbatim from the Alaska National Interest Lands Conservation Act.[139]

The 1981 amendments authorize the Secretary to make grants to the states to assist them in developing programs on which to base a return of management request.[140] Prior to these amendments, the Secretary could only make grants to assist the states in implementing programs. Although this change and the general revision of section 109 in 1981 were intended to provide a greater inducement for states to seek return of management authority, none has yet done so. In Alaska's case, its reticence to invoke the new procedures immediately was probably due to the pendency of a statewide referendum to repeal a state law making subsistence use the priority consumptive use of wildlife in the state. The failure of that referendum in November 1982 may now clear the way for the first application of the Act's novel procedures for the return of marine mammal management authority to the states.[141]

## The Problem of Incidental Taking

Whereas the waiver of the moratorium is the principal means whereby the directed harvest of marine mammals is to be regulated, other provisions of the Marine Mammal Protection Act are designed to provide some measure of control over other types of activities that, though they affect marine mammals only incidentally, may nonetheless have significant impact on efforts for their conservation. Originally, the focus of the Act in this regard was on the incidental taking of marine mammals in the course of commercial fishing operations, particularly the incidental taking of porpoises by the yellowfin tuna fishery of the eastern tropical Pacific Ocean. For that fishery, because the numbers of porpoises incidentally taken have been enormous, a comprehensive regulatory scheme has been necessary. Other commercial fisheries, however, encounter and take marine mammals in such small numbers and with such infrequency that a complex system of regulation may be inappropriate. In 1981, Congress authorized a more relaxed and flexible approach to these fisheries.

Commercial fisheries are by no means the only activity that results in

[138]*Id.* §1379(f)(1)(B)(i).

[139]*Compare,* §1379(f)(2) *with* 16 U.S.C.A. §3113 (Supp. V 1981).

[140]16 U.S.C. §1379(j)(Supp. V 1981).

[141]No regulations to implement the revisions to section 109 had been published as of January 1983. Proposed regulations were published by the Fish and Wildlife Service and the National Marine Fisheries Service at 47 Fed. Reg. 20508 and 20496 (May 12, 1982).

the incidental taking of marine mammals. Indeed, a plethora of other activities can and sometimes do result in such takings. Barges, speedboats, and other vessels have been known to strike and kill manatees, whales, or other marine mammals. Offshore oil and gas development activities have a similar potential to harass or otherwise take marine mammals. Prior to 1981, the Act simply prohibited such takings and presented violators with the threat of possible criminal or civil penalties. Although these theoretical prohibitions and penalties hung like the sword of Damocles over the heads of those engaged in such activities, both they and the government knew it was unlikely ever to be unsheathed. Thus, in 1981, Congress provided a more flexible and effective means of regulating the taking of marine mammals incidental to nonfishing activities.

The discussion that follows treats three aspects of the incidental taking problem separately. The first part concerns the well known tuna-porpoise controversy. The second part discusses the regulation of incidental taking of marine mammals in other fisheries. The final part focuses on nonfishing activities and the Act's new mechanism for regulating their impact on marine mammals.

## The Tuna-Porpoise Controversy

The one aspect of the Act that has been the subject of much litigation, as well as much public controversy, is its special exception from the moratorium for the taking of marine mammals incidental to commercial fishing operations. That exception was mainly directed at the practice of fishing for yellowfin tuna by means of "setting on" porpoise, a practice involving the encirclement of schools of porpoise and the tuna which, for reasons not fully known, are often found beneath them, with large nets known as purse seines. When the nets are hauled in, some of the porpoise are often unable to escape and become entangled in the net, causing them to drown or suffer serious injury. At the time of passage of the Act, Congress apparently thought that the tuna industry was near to finding a technological solution to this problem. To enable research aimed at finding that solution to continue, the Act created a special two-year exemption for the taking of marine mammals incidental to commercial fishing operations.[142] It also authorized a two-year program of research, for which $2 million was authorized to be appropriated, aimed at improving fishing methods and gear so as to reduce incidental taking "to the maximum extent practicable."[143]

---

[142] 16 U.S.C. §1371(a)(2)(repealed 1981).

[143] 16 U.S.C. §1381(a)(1976). This special research program was in addition to the authority conferred on the Secretary to make grants or give other forms of financial

Following the initial two-year grace period, incidental taking of marine mammals could continue, even without a waiver of the moratorium. However, such incidental taking could be permitted only after promulgation of the same sort of regulations and issuance of the same sort of permits that would normally follow a waiver of the moratorium.[144] In addition, after establishing that authority, the Act stated the following:

> In any event it shall be the immediate goal that the incidental kill or incidental serious injury of marine mammals permitted in the course of commercial fishing operations be reduced to insignificant levels approaching a zero mortality and serious injury rate.[145]

However, the Act failed to specify what level of take would be "insignificant" or over what period of time the goal was to be attained.

When the Secretary of Commerce promulgated regulations governing the taking of marine mammals incidental to tuna purse-seining operations and issued a general permit for such taking to the American Tunaboat Association in 1974 and 1975, several environmental organizations filed suit to have those regulations and permits invalidated. The plaintiffs' claims were upheld in a decision by Judge Charles Richey in May, 1976.[146]

Although Judge Richey's decision eloquently articulated the view that the "one basic purpose" of the Act was "to provide marine mammals, especially porpoise, with necessary and extensive protection against man's activities," the actual basis for his decision was very narrow.[147] That is, the regulations pursuant to which the general permits were issued had been promulgated without the required statement of estimated existing population levels and of expected impact on the optimum sustainable populations of the affected species and stocks.[148] The Secretary contended that the required information had not been provided because it was simply not known and that the Act's standard of "best scientific evidence available" was met where the only available information was insufficient to provide the required statements. Judge Richey refused to accept that interpretation, holding instead that the best scientific evidence standard required the Secretary to have affirmative scientific evidence that any proposed taking of marine mammals would not be to their disadvantage. [149] As an independ-

---

assistance to persons engaged in research "relevant to the protection and conservation of marine mammals." *Id.* §1380(a).

[144]*Id.* §1371(a)(2).

[145]*Id.*

[146]Committee for Humane Legislation, Inc. v. Richardson, 414 F. Supp. 297 (D.D.C. 1976).

[147]*Id.* at 306.

[148]*See* text accompanying note 86.

[149]414 F. Supp. at 311 n. 32.

dent, though obviously related ground for his decision, the Judge found that the American Tunaboat Association had failed to show in its permit application that the proposed taking would be "consistent with the purposes" of the Act.[150] Finally, because the general permit failed to state the "number and kind of animals" that it authorized to be taken, it was contrary to a further express requirement of the Act.[151]

The effect of Judge Richey's decision would have been to halt all tuna fishing by means of setting on porpoises if it had been made immediately effective. However, its effective date was postponed by some three weeks to provide adequate time for its implementation. During this period, the court of appeals stayed the effect of the lower court ruling until it had itself ruled on the case. At the same time, within days of Judge Richey's decision, proposed legislation had been introduced in Congress to overturn it, and hearings were promptly held.[152] As part of its effort to persuade the court of appeals to stay Judge Richey's ruling, the government agreed to amend the general permit to impose a ceiling of 78,000 porpoises, which could be taken in 1976. That quota was published officially on June 11, 1976.[153] In August, the court of appeals affirmed the Richey decision in all respects and directed the Secretary to promulgate lawful regulations prior to the 1977 fishing year; the decision allowed on-porpoise fishing to continue in 1976 subject, however, to the quota of 78,000.[154]

By late October, the 1976 quota had been reached and the Secretary announced that the industry's general permit was no longer valid. The tuna industry then filed suit in San Diego to restrain enforcement of the quota and secured a temporary restraining order. When that order expired, the industry was unsuccessful in obtaining a preliminary injunction.[155] The failure of the court of appeals to overturn that decision effectively terminated on-porpoise fishing for the brief remainder of 1976.[156]

New regulations and quotas were not yet in place when the 1977 fishing year began. When it became apparent that such regulations might not be forthcoming for several months, the industry went back to the district court in San Diego and again requested a preliminary injunction. This time, its request was granted, conditioned in such a way as to limit the

---

[150]*Id.* at 312–313.

[151]16 U.S.C. §1374(d)(3)(1976).

[152]An account of the prompt legislative response is found in Comment, Federal Courts and Congress Review Tuna-Porpoise Controversy, 6 Envtl. L. Rep. (Envtl. L. Inst.) 10147 (1976).

[153]See 41 Fed. Reg. 23680 (June 11, 1976).

[154]540 F.2d 1141 (D.C. Cir. 1976).

[155]Motor Vessel Theresa Ann v. Richardson, 7 Envtl. L. Rep. (Envtl. L. Inst.) 20065 (S.D. Cal. Nov. 2, 1976).

[156]American Tunaboat Association v. Richardson, No. 76-3309 (9th Cir. Nov. 11, 1976).

authorized taking to 10,000 porpoises, to be applied against the 1977 quota, when and if promulgated.[157] The Ninth Circuit then stayed the injunction pending disposition on appeal.[158] However, the Secretary, by regulation, extended the 1976 quota so as to permit the taking of nearly 10,000 additional porpoises in the first four months of 1977. Final regulations imposing an annual quota of 59,000 for 1977 were ultimately adopted by the Secretary and approved by the District of Columbia Court of Appeals.[159]

For much of the time in which the above was taking place, the American tuna fleet remained in port, protesting the regulatory actions and attempting to pressure Congress into amending the Marine Mammal Protection Act. The House of Representatives yielded to the pressure, passing a bill in June that would have legislatively fixed an annual quota of nearly 79,000 for 1977 and 1978.[160] The Senate, however, refused to budge, and the industry's boycott of the fishery ended.

Since the bitter battles of 1976 and 1977, the tuna-porpoise conflict largely abated for a period of years. Late in 1977 the Secretary promulgated new regulations, including annual mortality quotas that were to "ratchet down" over the next three years from nearly 52,000 in 1978 to only 31,510 in 1980.[161] In 1980, the Secretary replaced those with new regulations for the five-year period, 1981–85.[162] The annual mortality quota was again racheted down to 20,500, although that quota was to remain constant throughout the five-year period. The figure of 20,500 was determined to be both technologically and economically achievable by the American fleet; indeed, the fleet's estimated mortality was below 20,000 for each of years 1978 through 1981.

Despite its success since 1979 in living within the established quotas, the tuna industry remained fearful of the Act's ambiguous "immediate goal" that incidental taking "be reduced to insignificant levels approaching a zero mortality and serious injury rate."[163] The industry's fear was that at some point in the future either the Secretary or a court would conclude that this goal required the elimination of all incidental taking regardless of the technological feasibility or economic impact of so doing.[164] To allay

---

[157]Motor Vessel Theresa Ann v. Richardson, 9 Env't Rep. Cas. (BNA) 1726 (S.D. Cal. Jan. 21, 1977).

[158]Motor Vessel Theresa Ann v. Kreps, 548 F.2d 1382 (9th Cir. 1977).

[159]Fund for Animals v. Kreps, 9 Env't Rep. Cas. (BNA) 1880 (D.C. Cir. March 8, 1977).

[160]See 123 Cong. Rec. 17141-68 (1977) (House passage of H.R. 6970, 95th Cong., 1st Sess.).

[161]42 Fed. Reg. 65547 (Dec. 23, 1977).

[162]50 C.F.R. §216.24 (1981).

[163]See text accompanying note 145 supra.

[164]In the administrative proceedings that led to the promulgation of new regula-

that fear, Congress in 1981 clarified the Act's nebulous goal for the tuna fleet by providing that it would be satisfied "by a continuation of the application of the best marine mammal safety techniques and equipment that are economically and technologically practicable."[165] This clarification was consistent with the legislative history of the "immediate goal" provision of the Act and its subsequent administrative interpretation.[166]

The 1981 clarification was not intended to sanction in perpetuity either existing technology or existing incidental mortality levels. With respect to technology, the 1981 amendments directed the Secretary to finance and undertake "research into new methods of locating and catching yellowfin tuna without the incidental taking of marine mammals."[167] With respect to the kill levels, the legislative history of the 1981 clarification clearly reveals that it was not intended to affect the Secretary's authority to impose quotas,[168] an authority that is in any event required to be exercised elsewhere in the Act.[169] Conceptually, quotas now clearly function as a means of reinforcing the requirement that the fleet utilize the best technology and fishing practices available by requiring that incidental kill be reduced to the lowest level achievable with such technology and practices.

Unfortunately, the questions of what technology is best and what levels of incidental kill are achievable with that technology have recently been overshadowed by an industry initiated lawsuit that may strip the federal government of its ability to monitor compliance with the Act by the tuna fleet and punish violators in that fleet. In *Balelo v. Baldridge*, the Court of Appeals for the Ninth Circuit ruled that the Secretary had no authority to place warrantless observers aboard tuna vessels fishing on porpoise for the purpose of monitoring their compliance with the Act.[170] The court's decision expands the decision of the district court below, which only required that information gathered by warrantless observers not be made available for civil or criminal enforcement purposes.[171] Without

---

tions in 1980, the Committee for Humane Legislation contended that the Act required the industry to halt setting on porpoise altogether.

[165]16 U.S.C. §1371(a)(2)(Supp. V 1981).

[166]For a thorough analysis of the legislative origins and meaning of the Act's "immediate goal" requirement, *see* Erdheim, *supra* note 15.

[167]16 U.S.C. §1381(a)(Supp. V 1981).

[168]*See* H.R. Rep. No. 228, 97th Cong., 1st Sess. 17 (1981).

[169]Section 104(b)(2)(A) of the Act, 16 U.S.C. §1374(b)(2)(A)(1976), requires the Secretary to specify "the number and kind of animals which are authorized to be taken" under any permit.

[170]The Ninth Circuit's decision is unpublished. The court has agreed to rehear the case *en banc. See* 706 F.2d 937 (9th Cir. 1983).

[171]Balelo v. Klutznick, 519 F. Supp. 573 (S.D. Cal. 1981).

observers aboard, there are no practical means of monitoring the compliance either of individual vessels with the detailed requirements of the Secretary's regulations governing tuna fishing on porpoise or of the fleet as a whole with the mortality quotas. It may yet be possible for the Secretary to secure warrants for observers under section 107(d) of the Act.[172] Failing that, however, legislation overturning the *Balelo* result may be necessary if the Act's purposes are to be achieved.

The *Balelo* decision focuses attention on a critical aspect of the current regulatory regime for tuna fishing on porpoise. Current annual mortality estimates represent extrapolations from the mortality observed by federal observers assigned to approximately a third of the vessel trips. The critical assumption is that vessels without observers comply with applicable regulations and experience comparable mortality rates. The validity of that assumption has been called into serious question as a result of an unpublished study by a former crew member aboard a vessel without a federal observer.[173] Substantially higher mortality rates were reported for that vessel than the average rates for observed vessels that year. Moreover, there is even evidence to suggest that whether observers have enforcement powers may affect porpoise mortality rates. Prior to *Balelo*, when federal observer data could be used for law enforcement purposes, the mortality rates of vessels carrying such observers were lower than those of vessels carrying observers from the Inter-American Tropical Tuna Commission. Data from the latter observers is not available for law enforcement purposes. Subsequent to the district court's decision in *Balelo*, mortality rates for vessels carrying observers rose to the highest levels in many years.[174] Indeed, those rates were so high that the American fleet killed more porpoises than in any year since 1977 and apparently exceeded its quota for the first time since 1976.[175] Thus *Balelo* clearly may have a major adverse impact on the effectiveness of the Marine Mammal Protection Act in addressing the most serious marine mammal incidental taking problem in any commercial fishery.

---

[172] 16 U.S.C. §1377(d)(2)(1976).

[173] Croom, The Tuna Porpoise Problem: Management Aspects of a Fishery, *reprinted in* Marine Mammal Protection Act, Hearings Before the Subcomm. on Fisheries and Wildlife Conservation and the Environment of the House Comm. on Merchant Marine and Fisheries, 97th Cong., 1st Sess. 102–146 (1981).

[174] According to a preliminary report from the Department of Commerce, the American fleet in 1982 killed 4.83 porpoises per porpoise set and 0.40 porpoises per ton of yellowfin tuna caught while fishing on porpoise. These are the highest such rates for the fleet since 1976 and compare with rates of 2.95 porpoises killed per set and 0.25 porpoises killed per ton of yellowfin tuna caught in 1977. *See* Dept. of Commerce, Porpoise Mortality Status Report No. 82-19 (Jan. 12, 1983).

[175] The total estimated mortality for the American fleet in 1982 was 22,736. *Id.*

*Other Fisheries*

In 1981, Congress sought to provide an alternative means of regulating the incidental taking of marine mammals in certain fisheries. Basically, for any American fishery that the Secretary determines to take only "small numbers" of marine mammals and to have a "negligible impact" on any stock or species of marine mammal, the Secretary is to allow such taking free of the regulation and permit requirements applicable to other fisheries.[176] In lieu of regulations, the Secretary is to provide "guidelines" for a cooperative system to monitor incidental taking in any such fishery.[177] If, at any point, the Secretary determines that the allowed taking is having a greater than negligible impact, he must suspend or withdraw the permission previously granted.[178] To date, these new provisions have yet to be implemented administratively.[179]

The above provisions apply only to marine mammals that are not depleted. The congressional rationale for denying this authority with respect to depleted species was apparently that any taking of a depleted species is likely to have a greater than negligible impact upon it. A further limitation is that the new authority only applies to fishermen who are citizens of the United States. This limitation was adopted so as to exclude from it the Japanese high seas salmon gill net fishery, which is carried out in the United States fishery conservation zone off Alaska and which incidentally takes a thousand or more porpoises in such zone. The effect of limiting the Secretary's authority in this way was to insure that the Japanese fishery remained subject to the Act's permitting and regulatory requirements as described with respect to the tuna fishery. However, in 1982, Congress provided still a third variation on the incidental taking regulatory regime, this one applicable exclusively to the Japanese fishery.

By amendments to the North Pacific Fisheries Act of 1954,[180] Congress in 1982 effectively extended an incidental taking permit previously issued to the Japanese under the authority of the Marine Mammal Protection Act for a further period of three years until 1987.[181] However, the amendments also directed the Secretary of Commerce to take action to "reduce or eliminate" the incidental taking of marine mammals in this fishery by,

---

[176] 16 U.S.C. §1371(a)(4)(Supp. V 1981). The Secretary's determination is to be made with respect to the total anticipated taking over a five-year period.

[177] *Id.* §1371(a)(4)(A)(ii).

[178] *Id.* §1371(a)(4)(B).

[179] The Secretary of Commerce published an advance notice of proposed rulemaking to implement this new authority at 47 Fed. Reg. 40676 (Sept. 15, 1982).

[180] 16 U.S.C. §§1021-1035 (1976 & Supp. V 1981).

[181] Commercial Fisheries Research and Development Act of 1982, Pub. L. No. 97-389 §201, 96 Stat. 1949 (amending 16 U.S.C. §1034 (Supp. V 1981)).

among other things, requiring the use of "new fishing gear or techniques [to] reduce porpoise mortality to the greatest extent practicable."[182] That general directive is backed up by a specific timetable under which the Secretary is to require that gear and techniques determined by him to "offer the most practicable and effective opportunity for reducing porpoise mortality" be adopted by specified portions of the fleet within certain dates.[183] The Secretary may accelerate the statutory schedule if he determines "that faster implementation is technically and economically feasible."[184]

Although now set forth in a separate statute, the approach taken by Congress in 1982 toward the Japanese salmon fishery is fundamentally consistent with that previously taken toward the tuna fishery. In both cases the dominant objective of reducing or eliminating incidental mortality is qualified by considerations of economic and technological feasibility. In the case of the tuna fishery, this objective was obtained initially by ratcheting down annual porpoise mortality quotas to levels achievable with the use of the best gear and techniques available and maintained by requiring continued use of such gear and techniques and adherence to corresponding quotas. In the case of the Japanese fishery, the same result is to be obtained through a requirement of phased-in adoption of specified gear and techniques. Quotas have less value in the case of the Japanese fishery since a gill net fishery is a passive fishery in which incidental mammal mortality occurs as a result of entanglement with drifting nets. Once the nets are deployed, there is little or nothing that can be done by the fishermen themselves to influence the number of marine mammals incidentally taken. In the case of the tuna fishery, an active fishery in which porpoises are chased and purposely encircled with nets, it is the manner in which the gear is used far more than the inherent characteristics of the gear itself that determines how many porpoises are killed. Thus, in the tuna fishery, quotas will continue to be necessary to insure the most effective use of the safest gear available.

### Taking Incidental to Non-Fishery Activities

The 1981 amendments to the Marine Mammal Protection Act addressed yet another source of mortality to marine mammals, that incidental to activities other than commercial fishing.[185] The purpose of those amendments was to provide a more flexible means of regulating such incidental takings than the Act's simple prohibition previously provided. A unique

---

[182]*Id.* §201(a)(1).

[183]*Id.* §201(a)(2).

[184]*Id.*

[185]16 U.S.C. §1371(a)(5)(Supp. V 1981).

aspect of this new provision of the Act, however, is that it is not to be triggered by the Secretary's own initiative but by the formal request of one engaged in an activity likely to result in the incidental taking of marine mammals. Unless and until such a request is made, anyone engaging in an activity that may result in the incidental taking of marine mammal takes the risk that doing so will result in civil or criminal prosecution.

Like his new authority with respect to certain commercial fisheries, the Secretary may pursue the new alternative means of regulating nonfishing activities only if he determines that such activities will result in the incidental taking of "small numbers" of marine mammals and that such takings will have a "negligible impact" on any species or stock.[186] Unlike his authority with respect to fisheries, however, the Secretary must also find that any such takings will have a negligible impact on the habitat of the mammals taken and, in the case of activities in Alaska, on the availability of the species or stock for subsistence uses.[187] Once he has made these determinations, the Secretary must prescribe regulations (not "guidelines," as in the case of fisheries) that prescribe "means of effecting the least practicable adverse impact on such species or stock and its habitat, paying particular attention to rookeries, mating grounds, and areas of similar significance."[188] The Secretary's regulations are also to require the monitoring and reporting of any incidental takings.[189] If there is not substantial compliance with the Secretary's regulations or if the taking allowed has or may have a greater than negligible impact, he must withdraw or suspend the authority given.[190] To date, the Secretary of Commerce has promulgated general regulations implementing this new provision and specific regulations allowing the taking of ringed seals incidental to on-ice seismic exploratory activities in the Beaufort Sea during the period 1982–86.[191] The Secretary of the Interior has yet to implement the provision.[192]

## Penalties and Prohibited Acts

A wide array of civil, criminal, and other sanctions are available as the ultimate enforcement weapons under the Act. A civil penalty of up to

---

[186]*Id.* §1371(a)(5)(A). Both this authority and the similar authority with respect to fisheries are inapplicable to depleted marine mammals.

[187]*Id.* §1371(a)(5)(A)(i).

[188]*Id.* §1371(a)(5)(A)(ii)(I).

[189]*Id.* §1371(a)(5)(A)(ii)(II).

[190]*Id.* §1371(a)(5)(B).

[191]47 Fed. Reg. 21231 (May 18, 1982) (to be codified at 50 C.F.R. §228).

[192]The Secretary published an initial request for comments on how to implement this new authority at 47 Fed. Reg. 9869 (March 8, 1982).

$10,000 may be assessed against any person who violates the terms of any permit issued to him, any regulation issued under the Act or any provision of the Act.[193] Any person who "knowingly" commits any such violation is subject to a criminal fine of up to $20,000, or imprisonment for up to one year, or both.[194] Each unlawful taking or importation is treated as a separate offense for these purposes. Where a "vessel or other conveyance" is involved in the commission of any prohibited act, its entire cargo or the monetary value thereof is subject to seizure and forfeiture.[195] The vessel itself may be subject to a civil penalty of up to $25,000.[196] Finally, a "bounty" provision authorizes the Secretary of the Treasury to pay half of any fine, up to $2,500, to any person furnishing information that leads to conviction under the Act.[197]

While the Act's moratorium imposes a "complete cessation" on taking and importation of marine mammals, subject to various exceptions that have been discussed, the Act also contains a particularization of certain prohibited acts. These include a prohibition against the possession, transportation, sale, or importation of any marine mammal taken in violation of the Act;[198] a prohibition against persons or vessels subject to the jurisdiction of the United States taking marine mammals on the high seas;[199] and a prohibition against persons of any nationality taking marine mammals in waters or on lands under the jurisdiction of the United States, including its 200-mile fishery conservation zone.[200]

### International Program

The novel approach to federalism reflected in the Marine Mammal Protection Act has its counterpart in the equally novel aspects of the Act pertaining to international marine mammal protection. At its most basic level, the Act has obvious international ramifications simply as a result of its moratorium on the importation of marine mammals and the complex procedures required for waiver of that moratorium. Beyond that, however, the Act seeks to mandate the development of an affirmative international program for marine mammal protection. The principal features of that program are described in detail in Chapter 10.[201] To recapitulate them here

---

[193]16 U.S.C. §1375(a)(1976).

[194]*Id.* §1375(b).

[195]*Id.* §1376(a).

[196]*Id.* §1376(b).

[197]*Id.* §1376(c).

[198]*Id.* §§1372(a)(3), and 1372(c)(1)(A).

[199]*Id.* §1372(a)(1).

[200]*Id.* §1372(a)(2)(A).

[201]*See* Chapter 10 at text accompanying notes 22–26, 47–56, and 102–111.

briefly, they include a general directive to renegotiate existing international treaties and to initiate new treaties so as to embody the management principles contained in the Act. More specifically, they require a comprehensive study of the Interim Convention on Conservation of North Pacific Fur Seals and the immediate commencement of negotiations to bring that Convention into harmony with the Act if the study identified certain inconsistencies. Similarly, the Act directed the Secretary and the Secretary of State to commence negotiations within the Inter-American Tropical Tuna Commission to reduce the level of incidental taking of marine mammals in the tuna fishery. Finally, the Act contains authority to prohibit the importation of certain fishery products from countries using commercial fishing methods that result in the incidental kill or serious injury of marine mammals in excess of United States standards or that are proscribed for United States fishermen.[202]

---

[202] U.S.C. §1371(a)(2)(Supp. V 1981).

Chapter **12**

# THE CONSERVATION OF ENDANGERED SPECIES

The earliest federal efforts at wildlife regulation were motivated, at least in part, by a desire to prevent the extinction of wildlife as a result of man's activities. Thus the debates that preceded passage of the Lacey Act in 1900 show a great congressional concern with the virtual extermination of the recently abundant passenger pigeon and the drastic depletion of many other bird species.[1] The Lacey Act, however, like most of the federal legislation that followed it, was quite limited in terms of the range of wildlife it protected and the nature of the protection it afforded. Only within the last two decades has the need to confront the problem of endangerment more directly and more comprehensively become apparent.

Since 1966, three successive federal statutes, each building upon the preceding, and one major international treaty have attempted to establish a coordinated program to head off, or at least forestall, what had appeared to be the inevitable destruction of numerous wildlife species. Today that program utilizes each of the major wildlife regulatory tools available to accomplish its goal. Thus it restricts the taking of species currently in danger of extinction or likely to become so, regulates trade in them, provides authority for the acquisition of habitat needed for their survival, and mandates the consideration of impacts upon them resulting from various federal activities. In addition, it recognizes the international

[1] *See* remarks of Congressman Lacey at 33 Cong. Rec. 4871 (1900). The House report that accompanied the Lacey bill noted that "[in] many of the States the native birds have been well-nigh exterminated." H.R. Rep. No. 474, 56th Cong., 1st Sess. 1 (1900).

318

character of the problem of endangered wildlife and attempts to develop a variety of mechanisms to address that aspect of the problem.

This chapter examines the many facets of the federal program to conserve endangered species. It begins by tracing the development of that program from its inception in 1966. It concludes with a detailed examination of the many complex provisions of the Endangered Species Act of 1973,[2] the first federal statute to embody a truly comprehensive federal effort at wildlife preservation.

## BACKGROUND

### The Endangered Species Preservation Act of 1966

The federal effort to protect endangered species of wildlife was formally initiated by the Endangered Species Preservation Act of 1966.[3] That Act directed the Secretary of the Interior to "carry out a program in the United States of conserving, protecting, restoring and propagating selected species of native fish and wildlife."[4] Although Congress took note that a wide variety of causes, including loss of habitat, overexploitation, disease, and predation, contributed to the endangerment of many species of wildlife, the only clearly discernible element of the program it authorized was habitat protection. Thus the 1966 Act authorized the Secretary to use the land acquisition authority of existing laws to carry out the new program and in

---

[2] 16 U.S.C. §§1531–1543 (1976 & Supp. V 1981), as amended by The Endangered Species Act Amendments of 1982, Pub. L. No. 97-304, 96 Stat. 1411. (The Endangered Species Act Amendments of 1982 are hereinafter referred to as the 1982 Amendments).

[3] Pub. L. No. 89-669, §§1–3, 80 Stat. 926 (repealed 1973) (hereinafter referred to as the 1966 Act). Sections 4 and 5 of the 1966 Act, which consolidated various land units under the authority of the Department of the Interior into a single refuge system and established general standards for their administration, were subsequently designated as the National Wildlife Refuge System Administration Act of 1966. See Pub. L. No. 91-135, §12(f), 83 Stat. 275. That Act is discussed in Chapter 6.

[4] 1966 Act §2(a). Although the Department of the Interior was of the view that its authority under existing law was adequate to initiate an endangered species program, the House Committee on Appropriations refused to make any money available for that purpose until Interior's legislative authority was clarified. The principal purpose of the 1966 Act was to provide that needed clarification. See S. Rep. No. 1463, 89th Cong., 2d Sess. 3 (1966). For a useful discussion of some of the endangered species efforts of the Department of the Interior prior to the 1966 legislation, see S. Yaffee, Prohibitive Policy: Implementing the Federal Endangered Species Act 34–35, 190 n. 12, and 192 nn. 27–28 (1982).

addition created a new source of acquisition authority for which he could use up to $15 million from the Land and Water Conservation Fund.[5]

Beyond the land acquisition authority, the contents of the new endangered species program were vague and imprecise.[6] Thus the Secretary was directed to review other programs under his authority with a view to utilizing them "to the extent practicable" for furthering the purposes of the endangered species program and to "encourage other Federal agencies to utilize, where practicable, their authorities in furtherance of" that program.[7] Closely related to these directives to "review" and to "encourage" was the Act's declaration of congressional policy that the Secretaries of the Interior, Agriculture, and Defense and the heads of all agencies within their departments "shall seek to protect species of native fish and wildlife, including migratory birds, that are threatened with extinction, and, insofar as is practicable and consistent with the primary purposes of such bureaus, agencies, and services, shall preserve the habitats of such threatened species on lands under their jurisdiction."[8]

The wildlife for which the newly authorized program was to be carried out were those native wildlife "threatened with extinction." A species was to be determined as threatened with extinction upon a finding by the Secretary of the Interior

> after consultation with the affected States, that its existence is endangered because its habitat is threatened with destruction, drastic modification, or severe curtailment, or because of overexploitation, disease, predation, or because of other factors, and that its survival requires assistance.[9]

In making such determination, the Secretary was directed to "seek the advice and recommendations of interested persons," including wildlife scientists, and to publish in the Federal Register the names of all species found to be threatened with extinction.[10] The Act did not, however, specify any further procedures for the Secretary to follow in making such determinations. Finally, in addition to the obligation to consult with the states prior to listing particular endangered species, the Secretary was

---

[5] 1966 Act §2(b), (c). The Act provided that no more than $5 million could be appropriated annually from the Land and Water Conservation Fund for such purposes and that no more than $750,000 could be spent for the acquisition of any one area. For a discussion of the Land and Water Conservation Fund, see Chapter 8.

[6] *See* Palmer, Endangered Species Protection: A History of Congressional Action, 4 Envtl. Aff. 255, 259 (1975).

[7] Pub. L. No. 89-669, §2(d), 80 Stat. 926.

[8] *Id.* §1(b).

[9] *Id.* §1(c).

[10] *Id.*

directed to "cooperate to the maximum extent practicable with the several States" in carrying out the program.[11]

While the 1966 Act marked a significant first step in the effort to protect endangered species, it had a number of serious limitations, the most notable of which was that it placed no restriction whatever on their taking. That power remained solely with the states.[12] Nor did the Act restrict interstate commerce in endangered species. Further, very little was mandated in the way of habitat protection apart from the limited acquisition authority conferred on the Secretary, for the other major federal landholding agencies were directed to preserve habitats only "insofar as practicable and consistent with the primary purposes" of such agencies. Finally, the 1966 Act applied only to "native" wildlife, offering no protection for foreign wildlife in danger of extinction.

## The Endangered Species Conservation Act of 1969

Some of the deficiencies of the 1966 Act were remedied three years later when it was supplemented by the Endangered Species Conservation Act of 1969.[13] That Act expanded somewhat the acquisition authority conferred by the 1966 Act, defined the types of wildlife subject to protection under the 1966 Act, and amended the Lacey and Black Bass Acts so as to expand their respective scopes. Its major innovation, however, was its authorization to the Secretary to promulgate a list of wildlife "threatened with worldwide extinction" and to prohibit their importation into the United States, except for certain limited purposes.

For domestic wildlife, the changes introduced by the 1969 Act were relatively minor and, in one case, seemingly unnecessary if the earlier legislation it amended had been given a literal interpretation. Thus the 1969 Act amended the 1966 Act by adding to it a definition of "fish or wildlife" limited to "any wild mammal, fish, wild bird, amphibian, reptile, mollusk, or crustacean."[14] This definition was viewed as an

---

[11]*Id.* §3(a).

[12]Arguably, the declaration of policy that the Interior, Agriculture, and Defense Departments "seek to protect" endangered species obligated them to prohibit the taking of such species on lands under their jurisdiction. The legislative history seems to support such an interpretation. *See* Letter from the Office of the Secretary of the Interior to the Senate Commerce Comm., Sept. 7, 1965, quoted in Hearings on S.2117 Before the Subcomm. on Merchant Marine and Fisheries of the Senate Comm. on Commerce, 89th Cong., 1st Sess. 32 (1965). However, at that time the authority of the federal government to regulate the taking of wildlife on federal land in the absence of any threatened harm to the land was much in doubt. *See* Chapter 2 at text accompanying notes 60–75.

[13]Pub. L. No. 91-135, 83 Stat. 275 (hereinafter the 1969 Act).

[14]*Id.* §1(2).

expansion of the scope of the earlier Act only because the Department of the Interior had limited the undefined term "fish and wildlife" in that Act to vertebrate animals.[15] Similarly, the 1969 Act amended section 3 of the Lacey Act to expand its prohibition on interstate and foreign commerce in unlawfully taken wild birds and mammals to include reptiles, amphibians, mollusks, and crustaceans.[16] Finally, the 1969 Act expanded somewhat the acquisition authority conferred by the 1966 Act by authorizing the appropriation of up to $1 million annually for three years to acquire privately owned lands within the boundaries of areas already administered by the Secretary[17] and by increasing from $750,000 to $2.5 million the maximum amount that he could spend for acquisition of any one area with monies from the Land and Water Conservation Fund.[18]

Unlike the domestic aspects of the 1969 Act, its international aspects were major and far reaching. Most significantly, it authorized the Secretary of the Interior to promulgate a list of species or subspecies of fish or wildlife "threatened with worldwide extinction,"[19] and to prohibit their importation into the United States except for certain limited purposes.[20] The Secretary's determinations of what species or subspecies were threatened with worldwide extinction were to be based on essentially the same factors as the similar determinations for native species under the 1966 Act, and were subject to the further requirement that they be "based on the best scientific and commercial data available" to him.[21] Moreover, just as

---

[15]See letter of the Assistant Secretary of the Interior to the Speaker of the House of Representatives, dated January 17, 1969, in H.R. Rep. No. 382, 91st Cong., 1st Sess. 14 (1969).

[16]1969 Act §7(a). A major purpose behind this amendment was to achieve some measure of federal protection for the American alligator. See H.R. Rep. No. 382, 91st Cong., 1st Sess. 9 (1969).

[17]1969 Act §12(c).

[18]Id. §12(b). See note 5 supra.

[19]1969 Act §3(a).

[20]Id. §2. One of the few issues ever litigated under the 1969 Act concerned its effect on the authority of a state to restrict trade in wildlife determined by the state to be in danger of extinction. Two cases challenged New York laws that prohibited the sale of certain wildlife species and products derived from them, where the species protected were not among the list of federally protected species. In both cases, the claim that the 1969 act preempted the states from any regulatory authority over such matters was rejected. A.E. Nettleton Co. v. Diamond, 27 N.Y.2d 182, 264 N.E.2d 118, 315 N.Y.S.2d 625 app. den. sub nom. Reptile Prod. Ass'n v. Diamond, 401 U.S. 969 (1971); Palladio v. Diamond, 321 F. Supp. 630 (S.D.N.Y. 1970), aff'd 440 F.2d 1319 (2d Cir. 1971). For conflicting resolutions of this same question under the 1973 Act, see the two cases discussed at text accompanying notes 303–312 infra. For a related decision under the Marine Mammal Protection Act, see Fouke Company v. Mandel, 386 F. Supp. 1341 (D. Md. 1974).

[21]1969 Act §3(a). The standard of "best scientific and commercial data available"

determinations to list native species required consultation with affected states, so too determinations to list foreign threatened wildlife required "consultation, in cooperating with the Secretary of State, with the foreign country or countries, in which such fish or wildlife are normally found."[22] However, unlike the earlier Act, listing of endangered species under the 1969 Act was clearly required to be done pursuant to the rulemaking procedures of the Administrative Procedure Act.[23]

The 1969 Act carved out a limited number of exceptions to its general prohibition against the importation of endangered wildlife. Thus the Secretary was authorized to permit such importation "for zoological, educational, and scientific purposes, and for...propagation...in captivity

---

has been carried over into the Endangered Species Act of 1973, 16 U.S.C. §§1533(b)(1) and 1536(a)(2) (1976 and Supp. V 1981), and, in slightly modified forms, the Marine Mammal Protection Act ("best scientific evidence available"), 16 U.S.C. §1373(a) (1976), and the Fishery Conservation and Management Act ("best scientific information available"), 16 U.S.C. §1851(a)(2) (1976). When the standard was formulated in 1969, it was explained by the House Committee as follows:

> Many witnesses testifying at the hearings expressed concern that the legislation does not contain meaningful, objective standards to guide the Secretary when making a determination whether certain species are threatened with worldwide extinction. They feared that with the relative absence of standards, the Secretary could, at some stage, take arbitrary or frivolous action.
>
> Your committee does not believe specific standards can be written into the legislation without harming the effect of the legislation. Existing species are so varied that a standard to fit all appears incredibly complex and cumbersome. But your committee is cognizant of the fears expressed and is of the opinion that the bill, as reported, would prevent such arbitrary action. Nevertheless, to make it crystal clear of its intention, your committee hereby instructs the Secretary to consult with and work closely with the various persons, organizations, importers, businesses, and countries that may be affected by such a determination. Some of the witnesses at the hearings expressed great respect for the IUCN and its Red Data Book, which list rare and endangered species. Your committee also hereby instructs the Secretary to consult with and work closely with this knowledgeable and prestigious organization when making a determination of species that may be threatened with world-wide extinction.

H.R. Rep. No. 382, 91st Cong., 1st Sess. 6 (1969). It remains to be determined whether the standard of best scientific evidence implies an affirmative duty to undertake research designed to produce data not currently available before any action potentially harmful to the wildlife resource may be taken. See the discussion at text accompanying notes 244–247 infra.

[22]1969 Act §3(a).

[23]Id. Another innovation in the 1969 Act was its requirement that the Secretary review his list at least quinquennially and determine whether the species appearing thereon should continue to be treated as endangered. Id.

for preservation purposes."[24] In addition, "to minimize undue economic hardship," the Secretary could authorize any person who had entered into a contract for the importation of an endangered species prior to the time it was determined to be endangered to import such quantities of that species as the Secretary determined to be appropriate for a period of up to one year.[25]

In addition to the general prohibition against importation of endangered wildlife, the 1969 Act amended the Black Bass Act so as to prohibit the transportation in interstate or foreign commerce of any fish taken contrary to the law of a foreign country, thus bringing it into line with a similar amendment to the Lacey Act made in 1935.[26] A more noteworthy international aspect of the 1969 Act was its direction to the Secretary of the Interior to take several affirmative steps to achieve a coordinated international effort of wildlife preservation. Specifically, he was directed, in conjunction with the Secretary of State, to encourage foreign governments to provide protection to endangered wildlife and to take measures to prevent any fish or wildlife from becoming endangered, to provide technical assistance to foreign governments for the development and implementation of protection programs, and to encourage bilateral and multilateral treaties for the protection of endangered wildlife.[27] With respect to the last of these, the Act further directed the two Secretaries to "seek the convening of an international ministerial meeting...prior to June 30, 1971," at which would be concluded "a binding international convention on the conservation of endangered species."[28]

### The Convention on International Trade in Endangered Species of Wild Fauna and Flora

The international ministerial meeting for which the 1969 Act called finally took place, although more than a year and a half after the date specified in that Act. The agreement that it produced, the Convention on International Trade in Endangered Species of Wild Fauna and Flora, is, as its name implies, limited solely to matters of international trade and is not a truly comprehensive "convention on the conservation of endangered species" as the 1969 Act seemed to contemplate.[29] Nonetheless, the Convention is quite

---

[24]*Id.* §3(c).

[25]*Id.* §3(b). *Compare* the similar exemption in the Marine Mammal Protection Act, discussed in Chapter 11.

[26]1969 Act §9. *See* Chapter 5 *supra* at text accompanying notes 22–25.

[27]1969 Act §5(a).

[28]*Id.* §5(b).

[29]March 3, 1973, 27 U.S.T. 1087, T.I.A.S. No. 8249 (hereinafter referred to as the Convention). As its name likewise implies, the Convention is concerned not only with trade in endangered wildlife, but also with trade in endangered plants.

important, not only because of its substantive restrictions, but also because of the conceptual underpinnings that it provided for subsequent domestic legislation.

The most significant innovation of the Convention was its recognition of the varying degrees of vulnerability to endangerment and its provision for regulatory measures designed to reflect that recognition. Specifically, under the Convention, each protected species is assigned to one of three Appendices.[30] Those listed in Appendix I are the most vulnerable. They include "all species threatened with extinction which are or may be affected by trade" and are made subject to the most stringent protections.[31] The most significant restriction is that such species may not be traded for primarily commercial purposes.

Species listed in Appendix II are somewhat less vulnerable and include:

> (a) all species which although not necessarily now threatened with extinction may become so unless trade in specimens of such species is subject to strict regulation in order to avoid utilization incompatible with their survival; and
> (b) other species which must be subject to regulation in order that trade in specimens of certain species referred to in subparagraph (a) of this paragraph may be brought under effective control.[32]

The species referred to in (b) include any that are so similar in appearance to those referred to in (a) as to be nearly indistinguishable therefrom.[33] Appendix II species may be traded for commercial purposes, subject to a

---

[30]The Convention defines "species" to include "any species, subspecies, or geographically separate population thereof," thus recognizing that a particular species or subspecies not threatened with "worldwide" extinction, in the sense of the 1969 Act, might nonetheless be vulnerable to extinction in a given locale. Art. I(a). *See* the discussion of the protection of "population stocks" under the Marine Mammal Protection Act in Chapter 11 at note 11.

[31]Convention, art. II, §1. Trade is defined broadly in the Convention to mean "export, re-export, import, and introduction from the sea." *Id.* art. I(c). At the first Conference of the Parties in 1976, certain criteria were adopted pertaining to the addition of species to Appendix I. Under those criteria, if a particular species is, as a biological matter, "currently threatened with extinction," it should be included on Appendix I as long as it "might be expected to be traded for any purpose, scientific or otherwise." Since any species currently threatened with extinction would presumably be of potential interest to scientific investigators, it would seem that nothing more than the biological determination need be made. *See* Report of the U.S. Delegation to the Conference of the Parties, app. at 11 (hereinafter referred to as the U.S. Delegation Report).

[32]Convention, art. II, §2.

[33]*Compare* the "similarity of appearance" authority under section 4(e) of the Endangered Species Act of 1973, discussed at text accompanying notes 68–70 *infra*.

number of restrictions, the most important of which is that such trade not be detrimental to the survival of the species.

The lists of species in Appendices I and II were initially agreed upon at the time the Convention was adopted, and they may be amended from time to time as provided in the Convention.[34] Appendix III, on the other hand, consists of species unilaterally designated by any party "as being subject to regulation within its jurisdiction for the purpose of preventing or restricting exploitation, and as needing the cooperation of other parties in the control of trade."[35] Changes in Appendix III can come about only as a result of the withdrawal of a particular species by the party responsible for placing it there originally.

The major substantive provision of the Convention is its prohibition of trade in "specimens" of species included in any of the Appendices except in accordance with the terms of the Convention.[36] Trade in Appendix I species requires both an export permit (or a reexport permit if export is from a country other than the country of origin) and an import permit from the exporting and importing countries, respectively.[37] If an Appendix I species is taken in a marine environment not under the jurisdiction of any nation, only a certificate authorizing "introduction from the sea" is required.[38] The granting of permits and certificates is done by each nation's

---

[34]Appendices I and II may be amended by a two-thirds majority of parties voting at the biennial Conferences of the Parties, or between such Conferences by a two-thirds majority of those voting in a "postal vote" conducted under article XV. Any party making a timely reservation to a particular amendment will be treated as not a party to the Convention with respect to trade in the species concerned. Similarly, any nation may, upon ratifying or acceding to the Convention, enter a reservation as to any species on any of the Appendices or any parts or derivatives specified in relation to a species included in Appendix III. *See* Convention, art. XXIII, §2. *See also* notes 36 and 48 *infra*.

[35]Convention, art. II, §3.

[36]The term "specimen" has a different meaning in the Convention depending on whether the species concerned is a plant or an animal and on which appendix the species is listed. "Specimen" always includes the whole animal or plant, whether living or dead. It also includes "any recognizable part or derivative thereof," provided that such part or derivative is specified in Appendix III or, in the case of plants only, Appendix II. At the 1976 Conference of the Parties, it was decided, as a temporary measure, that any additions to Appendix III should specify that all readily recognizable parts and derivatives are also to be included. U.S. Delegation Report, app. at 1.

[37]Convention, art. III, §§2–4.

[38]*Id.* §5. Whether the 200-mile fishery conservation zone created by the Fishery Conservation and Management Act of 1976 or similar zones established by other countries will be deemed to be "under the jurisdiction" of such nations for purposes of the Convention is a question as to which the language of the Convention offers no clue. If it is answered affirmatively, a coastal nation claiming such a zone may

"Management Authority" on the advice of its "Scientific Authority."[39] Export permits for Appendix I species may be granted only if the Management Authority determines that the specimen has been lawfully obtained, that it will be "so prepared and shipped as to minimize the risk of injury, damage to health or cruel treatment," and that an import permit has been granted, and if the Scientific Authority determines "that such export will not be detrimental to the survival of that species."[40] Reexport permits require similar determinations by the Management Authority.[41] Import permits require determinations by the Management Authority "that the specimen is not to be used for primarily commercial purposes," and by the Scientific Authority "that the proposed recipient of a living specimen is suitably equipped to house and care for it" and "that the import will be for purposes which are not detrimental to the survival of the species involved."[42] With respect to certificates for introduction from the sea, the Management Authority has the same duties as it does with respect to import permits; the Scientific Authority must advise that introduction will not be detrimental to the species' survival.[43]

With respect to Appendix II species, the Convention operates in much the same way except that no import permits are required. Accordingly,

---

allow the introduction for commercial or other purposes of otherwise protected species taken in the zone without the need for any prior determination of the effect of that introduction on the survival of the species. *See* text at note 43 *infra.*

[39]Convention, art. IX. In 1979, the United States designated the Secretary of the Interior as both its Management and Scientific Authorities. 16 U.S.C. §1537A (Supp. V 1981). Earlier, the responsibilities of the Scientific Authority were vested in an independent "Endangered Species Scientific Authority." *See* 41 Fed. Reg. 15683 (April 13, 1976).

[40]Convention, art. III, §2.

[41]*Id.* §4.

[42]*Id.* §3. The function of this last required determination is not readily apparent. Presumably, if the Scientific Authority of the exporting nation is acting in good faith, its determination that export will not be detrimental to survival should make irrelevant any consideration of the purpose of importation. However, the requirement that the Management Authority of the importing nation determine that the specimen is not to be used for primarily commercial purposes seems to constitute a conclusive presumption that importation for commercial purposes is detrimental to the survival of any Appendix I species, notwithstanding the determination of the Scientific Authority of the exporting nation. The further required determination of the Scientific Authority of the importing nation that the importation be for purposes not detrimental to survival compounds the confusion inherent in these overlapping standards. A seemingly more sensible approach would be to require that the Scientific Authority of the importing nation determine that the purposes of the importation will affirmatively enhance the prospects for the species' survival, such as by artificial propagation or other similar mechanisms.

[43]*Id.* §5.

there is no requirement for a determination as to whether the purpose of the trade is commercial or noncommercial. However, the Scientific Authority of each nation is required to monitor the exportation of Appendix II species and to recommend to its Management Authority "suitable measures to be taken to limit the grant of export permits" for any such species whenever it "determines that the export of specimens of any such species should be limited in order to maintain that species throughout its range at a level consistent with its role in the ecosystems in which it occurs and well above the level at which that species might become eligible for inclusion in Appendix I."[44]

Finally, for Appendix III species, export from any nation responsible for its inclusion in that Appendix requires an export permit, which may be granted only upon a determination by that nation's Management Authority that the specimen was lawfully obtained and that it will be shipped in a humane manner.[45] An importing nation must require a certificate of origin and, if the state of origin is responsible for the species' inclusion in Appendix III, an export permit.[46]

The foregoing requirements are subject to a number of exceptions. The most important of these pertain to specimens acquired before the Convention applied to them, specimens that are "personal or household effects," and specimens loaned, donated, or exchanged by scientists or scientific institutions registered by the Management Authority of their nation.[47] The exceptions, however, are carefully qualified. Moreover, the

---

[44]Convention, art. IV, §3. *Compare* the language in the Marine Mammal Protection Act that marine mammal "species and population stocks should not be permitted to diminish beyond the point at which they cease to be a significant functioning element in the ecosystem of which they are a part." 16 U.S.C. §1361(2) (1976). It remains to be resolved whether this monitoring requirement of the Convention requires that the United States limit the export of any Appendix II species unless its numbers are such that the standards governing a waiver of the moratorium under the Marine Mammal Protection Act would be met. *See* Chapter 11 at text accompanying notes 48–69 and 74–76.

[45]Convention, art. V, §2. Appendix III is, in effect, an internationalized Lacey Act. For a discussion of its origins, see Comment, Commentary Upon the IUCN Draft Convention on the Export, Import and Transit of Certain Species of Wild Animals and Plants, 21 Cath. U. L. Rev. 665 (1972).

[46]Convention, art. V, §3.

[47]*Id.* art. VII. The first of these, the so-called "pre-Convention exemption," has been subject to varying interpretations by the Convention parties, particularly as it applies to parties that ratified or acceded after the effective date of a species' listing or that initially entered a reservation with respect to a species and subsequently withdrew it. Since the Convention applies to all specimens of a species as of the date of its listing, regardless of the location of such specimens, the relevant date should be that date rather than the subsequent date of a party's ratification or withdrawal of reservation. This view is not only compatible with the literal wording of the

Convention contains a means of gaining some leverage over nonparty countries by providing that "comparable documentation" may be required for import from, or export to, such countries.[48] Nonetheless, a potential threat to the success of the Convention is its omission of any effective enforcement mechanism against states that give it only perfunctory attention. At present, a substantial number of countries have joined the Convention, but the quality of their implementation of it varies markedly.[49] Even when it becomes fully operative, its value as a wildlife conservation device will be limited by the fact that the international trade that it seeks to control is but one of several causes of wildlife endangerment.

The Convention and its implementation in the United States occasionally generated significant controversy. A discussion of that controversy is included in the following analysis of the legislation that has, since 1973, implemented the Convention in the United States.

## THE ENDANGERED SPECIES ACT OF 1973

Even as the Convention was being signed in early 1973, it was already apparent to many in the United States that the task of conserving endangered wildlife would require a more comprehensive effort than the 1966 and 1969 Acts had authorized. In particular, it was widely felt that the protection those Acts afforded was often too little and too late. President Nixon had echoed that sentiment a year earlier in his Environmental Message of February 8, 1972, in which he said that existing law "simply does not provide the kind of management tools needed to act early enough to save a vanishing species."[50] Congress also had already accepted that principle when it provided in the Marine Mammal Protection Act that

---

Convention but also serves its purposes by discouraging hoarding in anticipation of ratification or withdrawal of a ratification and by promoting uniformity of implementation.

[48]Convention, art. X. At their 1976 Conference, the Parties decided that such documentation would be required of all nonparty countries, thus reducing the problem of "laundry" countries, which import from one country and reexport to another. *See* U.S. Delegation Report, app. at 1.

[49]The Convention entered into force on July 1, 1975, 90 days after deposit of the tenth nation's instrument of ratification. The United States, which was the first country to ratify the Convention, did not designate its Management and Scientific Authorities until April 1976, Exec. Order No. 11911, 41 Fed. Reg. 15683 (April 13, 1976), or propose regulations to implement the Convention until June 1976. *See* 41 Fed. Reg. 24367 (June 16, 1976). As of February 1983, more than 70 countries had ratified or acceded to the Convention.

[50]8 Weekly Comp. of Pres. Doc. 218, 223–224 (Feb. 8, 1972).

marine mammals might be considered "depleted," and therefore eligible for special protection, even before they became endangered.[51]

The failure of the protective provisions of the 1966 and 1969 Acts to come into play early enough was not their only recognized shortcoming. They also failed to give any measure of protection to endangered populations of otherwise healthy species. Again, however, the Marine Mammal Protection Act, through its provision for protection of individual population stocks, offered a model for change.[52]

The existing federal endangered species program was hobbled in three other critical respects. The first was that it included no prohibition on the taking of endangered species, preferring instead to leave the traditional authority of the states to regulate the taking of resident wildlife undisturbed. Here too, however, the Marine Mammal Protection Act, by providing for an indefinite federal preemption of that authority, was indicative of Congress's willingness to reconsider those traditional allocations of responsibility.[53] Second, to the extent that the 1966 and 1969 Acts contained an obligation to avoid adverse impacts of proposed federal activities on endangered species and their habitats, that obligation was limited to a few designated agencies and was hedged by considerations of what was "practicable and consistent with the primary purposes" of those agencies.[54] Finally, it was evident by 1973 that the problem of endangerment was not limited to vertebrates, mollusks, and crustaceans, but affected virtually all phyla of animals and plants.

To rectify these and other perceived inadequacies, Congress enacted the Endangered Species Act of 1973.[55] Its statement of congressional findings and purposes and its definitions reflect the truly comprehensive sweep intended for it. Recognizing that endangered species of wildlife and plants "are of esthetic, ecological, educational, historical, recreational, and scientific value to the Nation and its people,"[56] the Act declares the bold purpose of providing "a means whereby the ecosystems upon which [they] depend may be conserved."[57] To accomplish this, it further declares a policy "that *all* Federal departments and agencies shall seek to conserve

---

[51]For a discussion of the concept of "depletion" under the Marine Mammal Protection Act, see Chapter 11 at text accompanying notes 70–72.

[52]*See* Chapter 11 at note 11.

[53]For a discussion of the respective state and federal roles under the Marine Mammal Protection Act, see Chapter 11 at text accompanying notes 110–141.

[54]*See* text accompanying notes 7–8 *supra*.

[55]Pub. L. No. 93-205, 87 Stat. 884 (current version at 16 U.S.C. §§1531–1543 (1976 and Supp. V 1981), as amended by 1982 Amendments).

[56]16 U.S.C. §1531(a)(3) (1976).

[57]*Id.* §1531(b).

endangered species and threatened species and shall utilize their authorities in furtherance of the purposes of this Act."[58] The conservation measures it requires include "all methods and procedures which are necessary to bring any endangered species or threatened species to the point at which the measures provided pursuant to this Act are no longer necessary."[59] Finally, to eliminate any chance for a more restrictive interpretation, the Act defines the wildlife and plant species eligible for its protection as including any member of the animal or plant kingdoms.[60]

## The Act's Fundamental Units: Endangered Species, Threatened Species, and Critical Habitats

The 1973 Act builds its program of protection on three fundamental units. These include two classifications of species—those that are "endangered" and those that are "threatened"—and a third classification of geographic areas denominated "critical habitats." An understanding of these fundamental concepts is necessary to a proper appreciation of how the Act is intended to work.

The 1973 Act borrowed from the Convention and the Marine Mammal Protection Act the principle that the "species" to be protected include not only true species and subspecies, but also distinct populations thereof. For reasons not readily apparent, when the Act was originally passed it drew a distinction in this regard between plants and animals. Only for the latter did the term "species" encompass geographic populations.[61] By amendment in 1978, the authority to list and separately protect populations was further limited to vertebrate animals only.[62] Although the rationale for that amendment is not evident, it almost certainly had less to do with any biological distinction between vertebrates and other life forms than with a political desire to limit the number of listed taxa.

The authority to list and separately protect individual populations provides the flexibility to apply the Act's conservation measures selectively to those populations of a species that are currently in trouble while leaving unregulated other, healthy populations of the same species. Avoiding the local extirpation of a species is desirable not only because a series of such

---

[58]*Id.* §1531(c) (emphasis added). *Compare* the much more circumscribed statement of policy found in the 1966 Act at text accompanying note 7 *supra.*

[59]16 U.S.C. §1532(3) (Supp. V 1981).

[60]*Id.* §§1532(5), (9).

[61]16 U.S.C. §1532(11) (1976), amended by Act of Nov. 10, 1978, Pub. L. No. 95-632, §1, 92 Stat. 3751 (1978).

[62]Act of Nov. 10, 1978, Pub. L. No. 95-632, §1 (codified at 16 U.S.C. §1532(16) (Supp. V 1981)).

local extirpations frequently leads to endangerment of the species as a whole, but also because of the aesthetic, ecological, recreational, and other values such populations provide in their localities. The concern has sometimes been expressed, however, that the authority to list separate populations could be used to protect peripheral populations of otherwise abundant species. That is, since many quite common species are uncommon or rare at the extremities of their ranges, the Act could protect these peripheral populations even though the species as a whole needs no protection. Whatever the theoretical merits of that contention, it has not in fact characterized the implementation of the Act to date, with the exception of a few listings of the United States populations of species more common and unlisted in other countries. The protection of such populations is nonetheless sound policy because indifference to the loss of the United States populations of currently common species would leave the responsibility for insuring the ultimate survival of those species entirely with other nations.

Just as the 1973 Act borrowed from the Convention and the Marine Mammal Protection Act the principle of protecting geographic populations, so too did it borrow the concept of recognizing differing degrees of vulnerability and establishing protective measures appropriate to those differences. Thus the Act establishes two groups of protected species: those "endangered" and those "threatened." The former includes "any species which is in danger of extinction throughout all or a significant portion of its range;"[63] the latter includes "any species which is likely to become an endangered species within the foreseeable future throughout all or a significant portion of its range."[64] The category of "threatened" was intended to function not only as a means of giving some protection to species before they became endangered, but also as a means of gradually

---

[63] 16 U.S.C. §1532(6) (Supp. V 1981). For a discussion of some of the conceptual difficulties of determining what constitutes a "significant portion" of a species' range, see Lachenmeier, The Endangered Species Act of 1973: Preservation or Pandemonium, 5 Envtl. L. 29, 36–37 (1974). The Fish and Wildlife Service's implementing regulations give no guidance whatsoever. See 50 C.F.R. §17.3 (1981). The only species ineligible for protection as endangered species are insects "determined by the Secretary to constitute a pest whose protection under the provisions of this Act would present an overwhelming and overriding risk to man." 16 U.S.C. §1532(6) (Supp. V 1981). No occasion has yet arisen to test this limited exception, and it seems unlikely that it ever will, for the closer any insect pest approaches to the brink of extinction, the risk it poses to man will almost necessarily be reduced in significance.

[64] 16 U.S.C. §1532(20) (Supp. V 1981). When the Marine Mammal Protection Act was passed, its category of "depleted" species was, at least in part, the functional equivalent of the threatened status described in the text. When that Act was amended by the Endangered Species Act of 1973, however, the depleted category became, in effect, a category of marine mammals likely to become threatened.

reducing the level of protection for previously endangered species that had been successfully "restored" to the point at which the extreme protective measures provided for that category were no longer necessary.[65]

Endangered species are protected by a number of stringent prohibitions to be described later; threatened species are protected by "such regulations as...[are] necessary and advisable to provide for the conservation of such species," which may be as restrictive as the prohibitions applicable to endangered species.[66] Because the Act defines "species" to include distinct geographic populations (at least for vertebrate animals), it is possible to have a particular species subject to stringent protection as an endangered species in one area, less stringent protection as a threatened species in another, and no protection under the Act elsewhere.[67]

The Act's flexibility is increased still further as a result of the authority to designate any species as endangered or threatened if it is so similar in appearance to any other listed species that effective protection of the latter species requires listing of the former.[68] This provision, derived from a similar provision in the Convention,[69] is potentially of very broad scope, since it is frequently very difficult to distinguish the products of one species from those of related species. To date, however, this authority has been used very sparingly, and only to designate certain populations of a single species as threatened when other populations of the same species are in fact biologically threatened or endangered, as with the American alligator.[70]

The final building block of the Endangered Species Act is the concept of "critical habitat." As enacted in 1973, the Act neither defined this term nor specified a procedure for its designation, although it did impose a substantive duty, discussed later, that federal agency actions not modify or

---

[65] Assistant Secretary of the Interior Nathaniel P. Reed in 1972 likened the procedure of moving a given species from the endangered list to the then-proposed threatened list "to that of a hospital where the patient is transferred from the intensive care unit to the general ward until he is ready to be discharged." Endangered Species Conservation Act of 1972: Hearings on S.249, S.2199 and S.3818 Before the Subcomm. on the Environment of the Senate Comm. on Commerce, 92d Cong., 2d Sess. 70 (1972).

[66] 16 U.S.C. §1533(d)(1976). As a general rule, the Fish and Wildlife Service has, by regulation, made threatened species subject to the same restrictions as endangered species. See 50 C.F.R. §17.31(a)(1981).

[67] The bald eagle is an example.

[68] 16 U.S.C. §1533(e) (1976).

[69] See text accompanying notes 32–33 supra.

[70] See 40 Fed. Reg. 44412 (Sept. 26, 1975). When the Fish and Wildlife Service made its determination with respect to the American alligator, it announced that it would promptly propose listing several other crocodilian species pursuant to the same authority. Such a proposal would have constituted a substantially more far-reaching exercise of the similarity of appearance authority. To date, however, the promised regulation has not appeared.

destroy critical habitat. Prior to 1978, very few critical habitats had in fact been designated. Although the United States Fish and Wildlife Service and the National Marine Fisheries Service published an administrative definition of the term in January 1978, continuing controversy about the meaning of the term and the duties applicable to it resulted in a legislative definition 10 months later in the Endangered Species Act Amendments of 1978.[71]

As now defined, critical habitat can consist of a portion of the area occupied by a listed species, the entirety of such area, or even areas outside the currently occupied area. The key in each instance is whether such areas are "essential to the conservation of the species." Since the Act's broad definition of "conservation" encompasses measures to assure not only the survival of a listed species, but also its recovery,[72] critical habitats can include areas into which the future expansion of a listed species is essential to assure its survival or recovery. While preserving a broad authority to designate any area essential to the conservation of a listed species, the Act's definition was intended to discourage simply equating the existing range of a listed species with its critical habitat and to require instead a careful examination of the precise physical or biological features of most importance to the conservation of the species. Once designated, the principal functional significance of a critical habitat is to guide federal agencies in the fulfillment of their obligations under section 7 of the Act. Those important obligations will be analyzed later in this chapter.

### The Listing of Species and the Designation of Their Critical Habitats

The key determination from which all other consequences of the Endangered Species Act flow is the determination to list a species as endangered or threatened. Because of the pivotal significance of that determination, the procedures applicable to listing have been subject to increasingly detailed

---

[71] The administrative definition still appears at 50 C.F.R. §402.02 (1981) and has not been changed to reflect the subsequent legislative definition at 16 U.S.C. §1532(5) (Supp. V 1981).

[72] Section 3(3) of the Act, 16 U.S.C. §1532(3) (Supp. V 1981), provides as follows:

> The terms "conserve," "conserving," and "conservation" mean to use and the use of all methods and procedures which are necessary to bring any endangered species or threatened species to the point at which the measures provided pursuant to this Act are no longer necessary. Such methods and procedures include, but are not limited to, all activities associated with scientific resources management such as research, census, law enforcement, habitat acquisition and maintenance, propagation, live trapping, and transplantation, and, in the extraordinary case where population pressures within a given ecosystem cannot be otherwise relieved, may include regulated taking.

congressional prescription. The 1966 Act required only that the Secretary of Interior consult with affected states and seek the advice of other interested persons prior to determining that any species was threatened with extinction.[73] The 1969 Act added the requirement that listings be done in accordance with the notice and comment requirements of informal rulemaking under the Administrative Procedure Act.[74]

The 1973 Act embellished these procedural requirements still further, adding the requirement of consultation with affected foreign nations, amplifying the requirements with respect to consultation with states, and authorizing discretionary hearings. Though elaborated somewhat, the procedures applicable to the listing of species under the 1973 Act, as originally enacted, remained essentially the ordinary procedures of informal rulemaking. With respect to critical habitat designations, newly introduced by the 1973 Act, no procedures were specified.

When the Supreme Court's decision in *Tennessee Valley Authority v. Hill*[75] made evident what consequences could follow from the listing of a species, Congress undertook a wholesale revision of the procedures applicable to listing. That revision, embodied in the Endangered Species Act Amendments of 1978,[76] vastly complicated the listing process, adding numerous requirements for local notice and hearings, linking listing requirements to critical habitat designations, and, by requiring the consideration of economic factors in the latter determinations, subtly shifting the essential nature of the listing process from a purely biological inquiry to a more subjective "social balancing." Finally, all of these procedures had to be completed within two years of the date of proposal or the proposal had to be withdrawn.

The 1978 revisions to the listing process had a nearly crippling effect. Approximately 2,000 species listing proposals previously published were withdrawn because compliance with the new procedures within the prescribed deadlines proved impossible. More than eight months passed before the first new proposal was published. Proposals and actual listings of species sagged under the weight of the burdensome new procedures. In the first year of the Reagan Administration, the listing process halted completely as that Administration imposed still further economic review requirements beyond what the Act itself required. The collapse of the

---

[73] 1966 Act §1(c) (repealed 1973).

[74] Colorado River Water Conservation District v. Andrus, Civil Action 78-A-1191 (D. Colo. Dec. 28, 1981), held that informal rulemaking requirements also applied to listings under the 1966 Act but that republication under the 1969 Act of a species listed without compliance with those requirements pursuant to the 1966 Act cured the procedural defect of the original listing.

[75] 437 U.S. 153 (1978).

[76] Act of Nov. 10, 1978, Pub. L. No. 95-632, §1, 92 Stat. 3751 (1978) (hereinafter referred to as 1978 Amendments).

listing program in the Reagan Administration moved Congress to revise the listing procedures once again in the Endangered Species Act Amendments of 1982.[77] Those amendments repealed many of the burdensome requirements imposed only four years earlier. In other respects, they removed much of the administrative discretion to withhold action on species biologically qualified for listing. The remainder of this part analyzes the listing and critical habitat designation requirements embodied in the Act as a result of the 1982 amendments. Earlier requirements no longer applicable will be addressed only to the extent that they shed light on the meaning of the current requirements.

Authority to list species as endangered or threatened resides exclusively with the Secretary of the Interior, except as to those species over which the Secretary of Commerce was given authority by an executive reorganization in 1970.[78] For these, the Secretary of Commerce may determine to list a species initially or to change its status from threatened to endangered, and the Secretary of the Interior has the ministerial duty to effectuate such listing or change in status.[79] If, on the other hand, the Secretary of

---

[77]That the 1982 revision of listing procedures was intended as a direct slap at the performance of the Reagan Administration, and in particular its application to the listing process of "regulatory impact analyses" under Executive Order 12291, 46 Fed. Reg. 13193 (Feb. 19, 1981), is evident in both the House and Conference Committee reports. The House report stated:

> The Committee strongly believes that economic considerations have no relevance to determinations regarding the status of species and intends that the economic analysis requirements of Executive Order 12291, and such statutes as the Regulatory Flexibility Act and the Paperwork Reduction Act not apply. The Committee notes, and specifically rejects, the characterization of this language by the Department of the Interior as maintaining the status quo and continuing to allow the Secretary to apply Executive Order 12291 and other statutes in evaluating alternatives to listing. The only alternatives involved in the listing of species are whether the species should be listed as endangered or threatened or not listed at all. Applying economic criteria to the analysis of these alternatives and to any phase of the species listing process is applying economics to the determinations made under Section 4 of the Act and is specifically rejected by the inclusion of the word "solely" in this legislation.

H.R. Rep. No. 567, Pt.1., 97th Cong. 2d Sess. 20 (1982). The Conference Committee report endorsed the above conclusion. See H.R. Conf. Rep. No. 835, 97th Cong., 2d Sess. 20 (1982).

[78]See Reorg. Plan No. 4 of 1970, 35 Fed. Reg. 15627, 84 Stat. 2090. Although the Secretary of Agriculture has no authority with respect to the listing of plants, he is charged with the enforcement of the Act and the Convention insofar as they pertain to the importation and exportation of terrestrial plants. 16 U.S.C. §1532(15) (Supp. V 1981).

[79]Id. §1533(a)(2)(A).

Commerce recommends the removal of any such species from a protected status or the downgrading of such species from endangered to threatened, the Secretary of the Interior must concur in that determination before it becomes effective.[80] The functions of the Secretary of the Interior have been delegated to the United States Fish and Wildlife Service and those of the Secretary of Commerce to the National Marine Fisheries Service.

Listings, delistings, and changes in status may be initiated by the appropriate Secretary or pursuant to petition from any interested person.[81] In the event of a private petition, the Secretary is obliged, to the maximum extent practicable, to determine within 90 days whether the petition presents substantial information that the petitioned action may be warranted.[82] If he does so determine, then he is obliged to conduct a broader review of the status of the species concerned and to determine within 12 months of the receipt of the petition whether formally to propose the petitioned action.[83] He may decline to propose such action only if he publishes a written finding either that it is not warranted or that it is warranted but that he lacks the resources to proceed immediately with the proposal because of other pending proposals on which he is making expeditious progress.[84] A decision to decline proposing a petitioned action on either of these bases is expressly made subject to judicial review.[85] In addition, a decision to decline proposing a petitioned action because of other pending proposals must be reviewed at least annually thereafter to determine whether a formal proposal should then be made.[86]

Once the Secretary determines to propose a species for listing, he must publish notice thereof in the Federal Register, give actual notice to appropriate state and local governments, publish a summary of his proposal in a local newspaper, notify appropriate scientific organizations, and, if requested to do so, hold a public hearing.[87] If the species occurs in a

---

[80]*Id.* §1533(a)(2)(B).

[81]The 1973 Act's provision for the initiation of listing by private petition was one of several innovations designed to encourage public participation in its implementation. It was substantially revised by the 1982 Amendments to give citizen participation even greater influence.

[82]1982 Amendments §2(a)(2), (to be codified at 16 U.S.C. §1533(b)(3)(A)).

[83]*Id.* (to be codified at 16 U.S.C. §1533(b)(3)(B)). Prior to the 1982 Amendments, the Secretary could conduct a status review of indefinite duration following his determination that a petition presented substantial evidence. The 12-month deadline in the 1982 Amendments was intended to force the Secretary to conclude such reviews in an expeditious manner.

[84]*Id.*

[85]*Id.* (to be codified at 16 U.S.C. §1533(b)(3)(C)(ii)).

[86]*Id.* (to be codified at 16 U.S.C. §1533(b)(3)(C)(i)).

[87]*Id.* (to be codified at 16 U.S.C. §§1533(b)(5)(A), (C), (D), and (E)). State conservation agencies occupy a sort of "first among equals" position among those commenting on listing proposals in that, if the Secretary issues a final rulemaking

foreign nation or is taken on the high seas by citizens of a foreign nation, he must endeavor to notify such foreign nation and solicit its views.[88]

After proposing a listing action, the Secretary must make a final listing determination within one year. Although he can extend that deadline by an additional six months if there is need to do so to resolve substantial disagreements about the proposal, he must ultimately decide either that the species should be listed as threatened or endangered or that it should not be so listed.[89] That duty has special significance in light of the qualified duty elsewhere to designate critical habitat at the time of listing. The latter duty is imposed only to the extent that such designation is "prudent" and "determinable" when a species is found qualified for listing.[90] Thus, unlike the situation that prevailed as a result of the 1978 Amendments, the Secretary can no longer delay the listing of a species (or withdraw its proposed listing at the expiration of the applicable deadline) solely because he has been unable to determine its critical habitat or comply with the procedures applicable to such determination. Under the 1978 Amendments, the Secretary could fail to designate critical habitat at the time of listing only if such designation would be imprudent because it would expose a species to added risk, such as facilitating its location by unscrupulous collectors.[91] Now, however, he may list a species without simultaneously designating its critical habitat simply because the latter is not yet determinable at the time of listing.[92]

The foregoing changes worked by the 1982 Amendments represented a major relaxation of listing procedures that was intended to break the near stranglehold of the 1978 Amendments. The duty to designate critical habitats concurrently with listings, a duty introduced by the 1978 Amendments, posed a major barrier to further listings because of the related duty,

---

inconsistent with the recommendations of any such agency, he must furnish to it a written justification of his reason for doing so. *Id.* (to be codified at 16 U.S.C. §1533(h)). He is not, however, bound to follow the recommendations of such agencies, and the written justification can simply be a copy of the final rulemaking.

[88]*Id.* (to be codified at 16 U.S.C. §1533(b)(5)(B)).

[89]*Id.* (to be codified at 16 U.S.C. §1533(b)(6)).

[90]*Id.* (to be codified at 16 U.S.C. §1533(b)(6)(C)).

[91]16 U.S.C. §1533(a)(1) (Supp. V 1981) (amended 1982).

[92]1982 Amendments §2(a)(2), (to be codified at 16 U.S.C. §1533(b)(6)(C)(ii)). If a species is listed without concurrent designation of its critical habitat because the latter is not then determinable, the Secretary must nonetheless designate critical habitat for such species within a year, to the extent prudent. *Id.* Although section 4(b)(6)(C) of the Act uses the prudence standard as a limitation on the duty to designate critical habitat only for such previously listed species, section 4(a)(3) of the Act and the legislative history of the 1982 Amendments are clear that the prudence limitation applies both at the time of listing and subsequently. *See* H. Conf. Rep. No. 835, 97th Cong., 2d Sess. 24 (1982).

also introduced by the 1978 Amendments, to balance economic and biological considerations when designating critical habitats. The object of such balancing was to exclude from such designation any area for which the Secretary "determines that the benefits of such exclusion outweigh the benefits of specifying the area as part of the critical habitat."[93] In fact, this requirement was premised upon a fundamental misunderstanding of section 7 of the Act. The concept of "critical habitat" takes on operative significance only through section 7, which, as will be described in more detail later, prohibits federal actions likely to result in destruction or adverse modification of critical habitat. However, the adverse modification of any area that is in fact essential to the conservation of a listed species (whether it has been designated critical habitat or not) will also necessarily jeopardize the continued existence of that species.[94] Since federal actions resulting in such jeopardy are also prohibited by section 7, the exclusion of any area from a proposed critical habitat will never produce any "benefits" in the sense that federal actions otherwise prohibited would be permitted. Thus there will never be a proper occasion to exercise the discretionary authority to exclude areas from an otherwise appropriate critical habitat.[95] Although the 1982 Amendments retain this requirement to consider economic effects of critical habitat designation, it is unlikely to delay listings further because of the provisions previously discussed that distance the critical habitat designation process from the listing process.

The final listing decision that the Secretary makes after completing all the foregoing procedures must be "solely on the basis of the best scientific and commercial data available to him."[96] If that data supports the determination that a species is endangered or threatened because of any "natural or manmade factors affecting its continued existence," he must so

---

[93]16 U.S.C. §1533(b)(4) (Supp. V 1981) (to be recodified at §1533(b)(2)).

[94]The joint regulations of the Fish and Wildlife Service and the National Marine Fisheries Service define "jeopardize the continued existence of" as "an activity or program which reasonably would be expected to reduce the reproduction, numbers, or distribution of a listed species to such an extent as to appreciably reduce the likelihood of the survival and recovery of that species in the wild." 50 C.F.R. §402.02 (1981).

[95]Even if the analysis here is incorrect and there in fact are situations in which federal actions that adversely modify critical habitat do not jeopardize the continued existence of endangered species, then the provision can still be questioned from a policy point of view. The purpose of the elaborate exemption process constructed by Congress in 1978 and described later herein was to provide a system for the careful weighing of economic and endangered species conservation tradeoffs. If the Secretary, on his own, can make those tradeoffs at the very outset when a species is listed, then the purpose of the exemption process, with its detailed procedural requirements and substantive standards, is undercut.

[96]1982 Amendments, §2(a)(2) (to be codified at 16 U.S.C. §1533(b)(1)(A)).

list it.[97] The 1982 Amendments and their legislative history were emphatic that the listing process was to be an impartial and objective inquiry, free of economic or other extraneous considerations, particularly the "regulatory impact analyses" of the Reagan Administration.[98] Those other considerations, as will be shown later, come fully into play in other parts of the Act.

Nearly all of the procedural requirements applicable to listing can be bypassed, at least temporarily, in the case of an emergency posing a significant risk to the well being of any species.[99] Although originally limited to fish or other wildlife, this emergency listing authority was expanded in 1979 to encompass plants as well. Emergency regulations continue in effect for 240 days and expire automatically unless within that time they are promulgated pursuant to nonemergency procedures. Only two procedural requirements must be met with respect to emergency regulations. First, detailed reasons why such regulations are necessary must be published with the regulations. Second, if the regulation pertains to a resident species, the conservation agency of each state in which the species is known to occur must be given actual notice of the regulation.[100]

Although the provisions of the Act that pertain to citizen petitions restrict the Secretary's discretion somewhat, he still enjoys broad discretion in deciding when to consider the status of any unlisted species. The Act requires the Secretary to "give consideration" to species that have been identified as needing protection by state or foreign conservation agencies or international agreements,[101] but it establishes no priorities among potential candidates for addition to either list. Amendments adopted in 1979, however, were intended to require the Secretary to develop a system for assigning priorities to the review of species.[102] Although they required the Secretary to publish his system in the Federal Register and give the public

---

[97]*Id.* (to be codified at 16 U.S.C. §1533(a)(1)(E)).

[98]*See* note 77 *supra.*

[99]1982 Amendments §2(a)(2) (to be codified at 16 U.S.C. §1533(b)(7)).

[100]Although the Act does not define the term "resident species," implementing regulations interpret it, with respect to any given state, to include any "species which exists in the wild in that State during any part of its life." *See* 41 Fed. Reg. 47509 (Oct. 9, 1975) and 41 Fed. Reg. 24354 (June 16, 1976).

[101]1982 Amendments §2(a)(2) (to be codified at 16 U.S.C. §1533(b)(1)(B)). Although Appendix I of the Convention is comprised of species "threatened with extinction," the Fish and Wildlife Service has taken the view that the appearance of a species there does not *ipso facto* qualify it for listing as an endangered species under the Endangered Species Act. *See* 41 Fed. Reg. 24062 (June 14, 1976). Similarly, although section 12 of the Act required the Smithsonian Institution to report to Congress on plants needing federal protection, 16 U.S.C. §1541 (1976), the Service has treated the Smithsonian's report as an ordinary petition for listing of the species identified in it. *See* 41 Fed. Reg. 24524 (June 16, 1976).

[102]16 U.S.C. §1533(h) (Supp. V 1981) (slightly amended and redesignated as §1533(g) by §§2(a)(4)(C) and (E) of the 1982 Amendments).

an opportunity to comment upon it, he has yet to do either.[103] Once listed, the status of a species must be reviewed at least quinquenially to assure that listings continue to be based upon the best available information.[104]

## Judicial Review of the Listing Process

Three recent decisions have addressed various aspects of the listing process. Two concern the question whether, under the National Environmental Policy Act (NEPA),[105] the listing of a species is an action that requires the preparation of an environmental impact statement.[106] In *Pacific Legal Foundation v. Andrus*, the Court of Appeals for the Sixth Circuit concluded that it does not.[107] The principal rationale for the court's decision was the fact that the Secretary has no discretion to withhold listing of an otherwise eligible species because of environmental considerations. Beyond that, however, the court felt that listing species served the environmental purposes of NEPA, and thus "preparing an impact statement is a waste of time."[108] A directly contrary result was reached in an unreported decision by a district court in Oklahoma,[109] but the Court of Appeals for the Tenth Circuit later reversed on the ground that the plaintiff lacked standing to challenge the listing.[110]

A different listing question was presented in *Colorado River Water Conservation District v. Andrus*.[111] There the plaintiffs challenged, among

---

[103]In its report accompanying the bill that was to become the 1982 Amendments, the House Committee on Merchant Marine and Fisheries stated its intention "that the listing agencies...utilize a scientifically based priority list of species, subspecies and populations based on their degree of threat, and proceed through that list in an efficient and timely manner. Distinctions based on whether the species is a higher or lower life form are not to be considered." H.R. Rep. No. 567, Pt. 1, 97th Cong., 2d Sess. 21 (1982).

[104]16 U.S.C. §1533(c)(4) (Supp. V 1981) (redesignated as §1533(c)(2) by the 1982 Amendments). This requirement, which had previously been found in the 1969 Act, was added to the 1973 Act by §11(3) of the 1978 Amendments. *See* note 23 *supra*.

[105]42 U.S.C. §§4321–4347 (1976).

[106]With but one exception, it has been the consistent administrative practice not to prepare such statements in connection with species listings. For the exception, see Department of Commerce, National Marine Fisheries Service, EIS, Listing of the Green Sea Turtle *(Chelonia mydas)*, Loggerhead Sea Turtle *(Caretta caretta)*, and Pacific Ridley Sea Turtle *(Lepidochelys olivacea)* as Threatened Species Under the Endangered Species Act of 1973 (1978).

[107]657 F.2d 829 (6th Cir. 1981).

[108]*Id.* at 836.

[109]Glover River Org. v. Department of Interior, Civ. No. 78-202-C (E.D. Okla. Dec. 12, 1980).

[110]*Id.*, 675 F.2d 251 (10th Cir. 1982).

[111]Civ. No. 78-A-1191 (D. Colo. Dec. 28, 1981).

other things, the failure of the Secretary to designate critical habitat when he listed the totoaba, a marine fish that occurs only in Mexican waters. The Secretary argued that the Act's very limited requirements of consultation with foreign governments concerning the listing of species implied a congressional intent not to have critical habitat designated for (or, indeed, to have the requirements of section 7 applied to) foreign species. The court rather summarily rejected these arguments. Rather than invalidate the listing, however, the court ordered that the critical habitat be designated.

## Prohibitions and Penalties

When a fish or wildlife species is listed as endangered, it becomes automatically subject to certain very stringent protections. One of the most significant of these is that no person subject to the jurisdiction of the United States may "take" it anywhere in the United States, its territorial sea, or on the high seas.[112] The term "take" is defined in the following very broad terms:

> The term "take" means to harass, harm, pursue, hunt, shoot, wound, kill, trap, capture, or collect, or to attempt to engage in any such conduct.[113]

On its face, the definition is not necessarily limited to activities that are intentionally and directly aimed at the protected animal, but could also include activities that indirectly and unintentionally cause harassment, harm, or even death to it. The Senate Commerce Committee, in reporting on a bill that contained the same definition, except for the omission of the word "harm," emphasized that its definition was intended "in the broadest possible manner to include every conceivable way in which a person can 'take' or attempt to 'take' any fish or wildlife."[114]

From the above, it would seem that the Act's broad definition of "take" encompasses activities that destroy or have other substantial adverse effects on the habitat of an endangered species. The Fish and Wildlife Service, in its initial implementing regulations, adopted this interpretation by defining the term "harm" to mean:

---

[112]16 U.S.C. §1538(a)(1)(B), (C) (1976).

[113]*Id.* §1532(19) (Supp. V 1981). For a comparison of this definition with other definitions from earlier wildlife statutes, see Chapter 11 at text accompanying notes 20–22.

[114]S. Rep. No. 307, 93d Cong., 1st Sess. 7 (1973). Notwithstanding that declaration, the bill which the Senate Committee reported, when originally introduced, included "the destruction, modification, or curtailment of its habitat or range" in its definition of "take." S.1983, 93d Cong., 1st Sess. §3(6)(A).

> [A]n act or omission which actually injures or kills wildlife, including acts which annoy it to such an extent as to significantly disrupt essential behavioral patterns, which include, but are not limited to, breeding, feeding or sheltering; *significant environmental modification or degradation which has such effects is included within the meaning of "harm".*[115]

That interpretation was widely criticized by legal commentators.[116]

It was not until 1979, however, that an opportunity arose for a thorough judicial exploration of the scope of the taking prohibition. In *Palila v. Hawaii Department of Land and Natural Resources,* the Sierra Club and others charged that the state of Hawaii, by maintaining a population of feral sheep and goats in an area of native Hawaiian forest, was taking the palila, an endangered bird dependent upon the native forest for nesting sites.[117] The sheep and goats, which were maintained for sport hunting purposes, adversely affected the native forest through their grazing habits. The trial court found that the destruction of the native forest by the feral animals threatened the palila's very survival and that, under the Fish and Wildlife Service's definition of "harm," this constituted a prohibited taking.[118] The court of appeals affirmed on the basis that maintenance of the sheep and goats endangered the palila.

Subsequent to the *Palila* decision, the Fish and Wildlife Service sought to narrow its definition of harm, eliminating from it any reference to environmental modification or disruption of essential behavioral patterns.[119] This proposal, in effect an administrative attempt to overrule the decision in *Palila,* drew a storm of protest. Ultimately, the Service backed off its proposal and promulgated the following new definition of harm:

> "Harm" in the definition of "take" in the Act means an act which actually kills or injures wildlife. Such act may include significant habitat modification or degradation where it actually kills or injures wildlife by significantly impairing essential behavioral patterns, including breeding, feeding or sheltering.[120]

---

[115]50 C.F.R. §17.3 (1981) (emphasis added) (amended 1981).

[116]Several commentators concluded that the taking prohibition was not intended to encompass habitat modification. *See, e.g.,* Lachenmeier, *supra* note 63, at 39–41; Note, Obligations of Federal Agencies Under section 7 of the Endangered Species Act of 1973, 28 Stan. L. Rev. 1247, 1251 n. 31 (1976); Note, Endangered Species Act: Constitutional Tension and Regulatory Discord, 4 Colum. J. Envtl. L. 97, 100 n. 19 (1977). The original edition of this work acknowledged that there were forceful arguments in support of that view.

[117]471 F. Supp. 985 (D. Ha. 1979), *aff'd,* 639 F.2d 495 (9th Cir. 1981).

[118]471 F. Supp. at 991 and 995.

[119]46 Fed. Reg. 29490 (June 2, 1981).

[120]46 Fed. Reg. 54748, 54750 (Nov. 4, 1981).

The explanation accompanying this new definition makes clear that direct, physical injury to an individual member of a protected species is not required to constitute harm.[121] Rather, the significant impairment of essential behavioral patterns is sufficient to constitute actual injury to the species, whether or not any individual member of that species suffers direct, physical injury. To illustrate, if an activity results in the destruction of an area essential for nesting by an endangered migratory bird, that activity will be considered to "harm" the species by preventing it from nesting and reproducing even though the activity may have occurred while the birds were on their wintering grounds and thus may not have caused any immediate physical injury to any individual bird. This, it appears, is what the *Palila* court understood the Service's prior definition of harm to require.

Other restrictions pertaining to endangered species include prohibitions against importation,[122] exportation, sale or shipment in interstate commerce in the course of a commercial activity,[123] and possession of any species taken in violation of the Act.[124] The Act also prohibits the trade of any specimens contrary to the Convention or the possession of specimens so traded.[125] For plants, all the same restrictions apply, except those pertaining to taking. Originally, the Act contained no plant-taking prohibition. However, in 1982 a limited prohibition against the removal of endangered plants from federal lands was enacted.[126] In addition to being limited to federal lands, this prohibition is substantially narrower than the

---

[121]*Id.* at 54748, column 3.

[122]16 U.S.C. §1538(a)(1)(A) (1976). The Act defines "import" broadly to mean "to land on, bring into, or introduce into, or attempt to land on, bring into, or introduce into, any place subject to the jurisdiction of the United States, whether or not such landing, bringing, or introduction constitutes an importation within the meaning of the customs laws of the United States." *Id.* §1532(10) (Supp. V 1981).

[123]16 U.S.C. §1538(a)(1) (1976). The Act originally defined the term "commercial activity" very broadly to mean "all activities of industry and trade, including, but not limited to, the buying or selling of commodities and activities conducted for the purpose of facilitating such buying and selling." Act of Dec. 28, 1973, Pub. L. No. 93-205, §3(1), 87 Stat. 884. By amendment in 1976, the definition was revised so as expressly to exclude "exhibition of commodities by museums or similar cultural or historical organizations." Act of July 12, 1976, Pub. L. No. 94-359, §5, 90 Stat. 911, 913 (codified at 16 U.S.C. §1533(2) (Supp. V 1981)). In the interim, however, the Fish and Wildlife Service had by regulation interpreted the words "industry or trade" to include only those activities done for "gain or profit." 50 C.F.R. §17.3 (1981). The legislative history of the 1976 Amendment is clear that it was not intended to override that administrative interpretation. *See* 122 Cong. Rec. 3260 (1976) (Remarks of Rep. Leggett).

[124]16 U.S.C. §1538(a)(1) (1976).

[125]*Id.* §1538(c).

[126]1982 Amendments §9(b)(1) (to be codified at 16 U.S.C. §1538(a)(2)(B)).

taking prohibition applicable to animals, because it does not encompass the indirect sort of takings subsumed by the term "harm."[127]

Though all of the above prohibitions apply automatically to all endangered species, none applies automatically to threatened species. Rather, under section 4(d) of the Act, the Secretary must "issue such regulations as he deems necessary and advisable to provide for the conservation of" any threatened species.[128] These regulations may be as restrictive as if the species were protected as endangered, but they need not be. The few courts that have considered the scope of the Secretary's authority under section 4(d) have given him wide discretion in tailoring regulations necessary and advisable for the conservation of particular threatened species. In *Cayman Turtle Farm, Ltd. v. Andrus* the plaintiff contended that the Secretary's regulations for the threatened green sea turtle were too restrictive in that they prohibited importation of turtles raised by the plaintiff in captivity.[129] The plaintiff contended that the evidentiary basis in the rulemaking record for that restriction did not support the Secretary's determination that it was necessary. The court disagreed, reasoning that the Secretary's expert judgment was entitled to substantial deference.

Against a challenge that the Secretary has exercised his discretionary authority too leniently, there is some evidence that the courts may be less deferential. In *Defenders of Wildlife v. Watt*, the Secretary had eliminated essentially all restrictions with respect to three species of kangaroos while retaining them on the threatened list.[130] The plaintiff argued that permitting unlimited commercial trade in threatened species was inconsistent with the Secretary's duty to assure their conservation. The court disagreed because of what it perceived to be the unique circumstances of the case. Reasoning that the United States had "no control over the species or its natural habitat" the court accepted the lifting of the prior import ban as an appropriate *quid pro quo* in return for Australian management measures designed to conserve the kangaroo.[131] The court

---

[127]The Act makes it unlawful to "remove and reduce to possession" endangered plants on federal lands. Thus, not only environmental modifications but also acts which directly destroy a plant specimen are outside the scope of the prohibition. Because the common law has never treated plants as occupying the same conceptual status as wild animals, in terms of their susceptibility to private ownership, there may be a major constitutional impediment to prohibiting their taking on nonfederal lands. *See* Chapter 2.

[128]16 U.S.C. §1533(d) (1976).

[129]478 F. Supp. 125 (D.D.C. 1979), *aff'd without opinion* (D.C. Cir. Dec. 12, 1980).

[130]Civil Act. No. 81-1048 (D.D.C. May 28, 1981).

[131]Slip opinion at 7. The court did not address the question of whether the United States could exercise some influence over the species' habitat through section 7.

stated in dictum, however, that the plaintiff's arguments against allowing unrestricted commerce in a threatened species were appropriate with respect to domestic, *i.e.*, United States, species.[132] As to the retention of the species on the threatened list, the court apparently accepted the argument that doing so would facilitate immediate action if new information warranted it.[133]

A still different issue pertaining to threatened species was presented in *Fund for Animals v. Andrus*.[134] Although the special threatened species regulations there in issue were not challenged, the Fish and Wildlife Service's interpretation of them was. After looking very carefully at the circumstances leading up to the promulgation of the regulations, the court agreed with the plaintiffs and ordered the Service to comply with the regulations as the court interpreted them or amend them pursuant to the required procedures.

Penalties for violations of the Act's various prohibitions differ depending on whether the violation concerns a threatened or endangered species, the violator's state of knowledge, and, for some purposes, the violator's business. The stiffest penalties may be imposed against those who knowingly violate the Act's prohibitions with respect to endangered species. Such persons can be imprisoned for a year and fined $20,000.[135] Knowing violations of the Act's prohibitions pertaining to threatened species can be punished by six-months' imprisonment and a fine of up to $10,000.[136] In addition, the Secretary must suspend for up to a year or cancel any federal fishing or hunting permit of any person convicted of a criminal violation of the Act.[137] A broad range of discretionary administrative sanctions may also be imposed against those convicted of criminal violations, including the immediate revocation or suspension of any federal lease, permit, or license authorizing the import or export of wildlife

---

[132]*Id.* at 7. Although not addressed in this case, it would seem that the Secretary's discretion to allow the taking of threatened species is severely circumscribed by the Act's definition of "conservation." Under that definition, regulated taking is a permissible conservation measure only "in the extraordinary case where population pressures within a given ecosystem cannot be otherwise relieved." 16 U.S.C. §1532(3) (Supp. V 1981).

[133]*Id.* This argument does not withstand analysis. The addition of a species to the threatened list can be accomplished immediately through the emergency listing authority. *See* text accompanying notes 99–100 *supra*. (1979).

[134]11 Env't Rep. Cas. (BNA) 2189 (D. Minn. July 14 and Aug. 30, 1978).

[135]16 U.S.C. §1540(b)(1) (Supp. V 1981). The 1978 Amendments lowered the culpability standard for criminal violators from a "willful" to a "knowing" violation.

[136]*Id.*

[137]*Id.* §1540(b)(2).

or plants, the operation of a quarantine station, or the use of federal lands.[138]

Persons who knowingly violate the Act's prohibitions with respect to endangered species are also subject to the imposition by the Secretary of a civil penalty of up to $10,000 per violation.[139] Half that amount is the maximum civil penalty that may be imposed for threatened species violations.[140] The foregoing civil penalties may also be assessed against persons engaged in business as importers or exporters of wildlife or plants whether their violations are knowing or unknowing.[141] Apart from such persons, the maximum civil penalty that may be imposed on a strict liability basis against unknowing violators is $500.[142]

A third type of penalty authorized by the Act is of potentially even greater magnitude than the foregoing criminal and civil penalties. Not only the wildlife or plant specimens involved in any unlawful act, but the guns, equipment, vessels, aircraft, and vehicles used to aid such action are subject to forfeiture.[143] The Act's forfeiture provision was construed in an unusual factual context in *Carpenter v. Andrus*.[144] In that action the plaintiff had shot a leopard under authority of a Kenyan license. He instructed a shipper to ship the skull and skin to Haiti without shipping it through the United States. Contrary to his instructions, the skull and skin were shipped by common carrier into the United States where they were seized. Because section 11(e)(4)(A) subjects to forfeiture any wildlife imported contrary to the provisions of the Act, the court had to consider whether the products had been unlawfully imported. Despite the unqualified language of section 9(a)(1)(A) prohibiting any importation of any endangered species into the United States,[145] the court reasoned that the provision was not intended to impose on common carriers a "strict duty to inspect their freight to assure that it did not contain any endangered species."[146] Accordingly, if the common carrier had no duty to inspect, then

---

[138]*Id.* Section 9(d) of the Act requires importers and exporters of most wildlife and plants to be licensed by the Secretary. *Id.* §1538(d) (1976).

[139]*Id.* §1540(a)(1) (Supp. V 1981).

[140]*Id.*

[141]*Id.*

[142]*Id.*

[143]*Id.* §1540(e)(4) (1976). For a case upholding the authority to seize products derived in part from endangered species, see Delbay Pharmaceuticals, Inc. v. Department of Commerce, 409 F. Supp. 637 (D.D.C. 1976).

[144]485 F. Supp. 320 (D. Del. 1980).

[145]16 U.S.C. §1538(a)(1)(A) (1976).

[146]485 F. Supp. at 322.

the products were not imported contrary to the provisions of the Act and thus not subject to forfeiture. The extraordinary circumstances of the *Carpenter* case probably account for the court's strained result. The question whether a common carrier could be held to a standard of strict liability was not directly at issue because no action for recovery of civil penalties had been brought against it. Moreover, the maximum penalty that could be imposed against a common carrier for an unknowing violation is a modest, and presumably insurable, $500. Curiously, despite the court's holding that the products had not been unlawfully imported and were not subject to forfeiture, the court declared that the plaintiff "is not entitled to keep the property in the United States, for that would contravene the policy of the Endangered Species Act."[147] The holding of the *Carpenter* case was legislatively ratified in the 1982 Amendments, which except from the prohibition against importation the sort of inadvertent, noncommercial transshipments that occurred there.[148]

### Exceptions from the Act's Prohibitions

From the foregoing prohibitions, the Act creates a number of special exceptions. The list of these has expanded steadily since 1973 from an original four to at least a dozen today. The following analysis discusses each of them in roughly the order in which they were enacted.

### *The Original Exceptions*

Originally, the Act provided special exceptions for certain specimens already possessed at the time of its enactment, for specified cases of economic hardship, for certain Alaskan residents, and for scientific or propagation purposes. The first of these exempts certain activities with respect to "any fish or wildlife held in captivity or in a controlled environment" on the date of the Act's enactment or the species' listing, provided it was not then or subsequently held for commercial purposes.[149]

---

[147]*Id.* at 324.

[148]1982 Amendments §6(5) (to be codified at 16 U.S.C. §1539(i)).

[149]16 U.S.C. §1538(b)(1) (Supp. V 1981), as amended by 1982 Amendments §9(b)(2). This exemption originally applied to any action otherwise prohibited by section 9. The 1982 Amendments limited it, however, to import and export activities involving endangered species as well as any activity involving threatened species. This limitation makes sense in light of the clarification, also added by the 1982 Amendments, that the exemption is negated if the specimen was held for commercial purposes on the relevant date or anytime thereafter. That clarification was needed in light of the holding in United States v. Molt, 10 Envtl. L. Rep. (Envtl. L. Inst.) 20777 (3d Cir. July 17, 1980), that ambiguity as to the exemption rendered

However, the captive progeny of such exempt animals are not themselves exempt from the Act's proscriptions.[150] To provide a flexible means of regulating such progeny, as well as other captive endangered wildlife, the Fish and Wildlife Service, relying upon the Act's broad definition of "species" to include discrete populations of vertebrates, has listed as threatened certain captive populations of otherwise endangered species.

The 1973 Act also gave the Secretary a limited discretion to exempt otherwise prohibited activities to avoid "undue economic hardship" to persons who entered into contracts with respect to a species prior to the first published notice that it would be considered for listing.[151] This authority is of little practical significance since the exemption cannot extend beyond one year from the date of such notice, and, except in emergency situations, listings are seldom finalized within such one-year period.[152]

The third of the original exemptions applies to certain Alaskan natives and nonnative permanent residents of Alaskan native villages, who may take listed species "primarily for subsistence purposes" and may sell the nonedible byproducts thereof in interstate commerce "when made into authentic native articles of handicrafts and clothing."[153] If, however, the Secretary determines that such Alaskan native taking "materially and negatively affects the threatened or endangered species," he may prescribe regulations to restrict it for such period as is necessary.[154]

---

the Act's prohibition against importation unconstitutionally vague. The *Molt* decision was at odds with United States v. Kepler, 531 F.2d 796 (6th Cir. 1976), which interpreted the original commercial activity limitation on the exception to apply to a holding for commercial purposes after the Act's enactment.

[150] In Cayman Turtle Farm, Ltd. v. Andrus, *supra* note 129, the plaintiff alleged that the Act gave the Secretary no authority over animals raised in captivity. The court rejected that claim on the basis that the Act's limited exemption for captive animals implied that captive animals not encompassed by that exemption were subject to regulation.

[151] 16 U.S.C. §1539(b)(1976).

[152] A further curiosity of this exemption is that, although the Act defines "undue economic hardship" to include the curtailment of subsistence taking under certain circumstances, *id.* §1539(b)(2), such hardship does not qualify for the exemption unless the additional requirement of a contract is met. *Id.* §1539(b)(1). *Delbay Pharmaceuticals, supra* note 143, held that endangered species products lawfully imported pursuant to a hardship permit issued under the 1969 Act could not be sold in interstate commerce subsequent to passage of the 1973 Act if they were held for commercial purposes at the time of passage.

[153] 16 U.S.C. §1539(e)(1) (1976). This exemption should be compared closely with the Alaskan native provisions of the Marine Mammal Protection Act and the subsistence priority provisions of the Alaska National Interest Lands Conservation Act, discussed in Chapters 11 and 6, respectively.

[154] *Id.* §1539(e)(4).

Finally, the 1973 Act authorized the Secretary to permit any otherwise prohibited Act "for scientific purposes or to enhance the propagation or survival of the affected species."[155] Applications for such permits, as well as applications for hardship exemptions, must ordinarily be noticed in the Federal Register with the opportunity for public comment thereon. Although these provisions of the Act evidence an intent to promote scientific research and to avoid certain types of economic hardship, the Act is also clear that the conservation interests of listed species take priority over other concerns. The Secretary may grant such permits and exemptions only if they will "not operate to the disadvantage" of the affected species.[156]

### Subsequent Exceptions

The various exceptions set forth in the 1973 Act have all been retained and to them have been added numerous others by subsequent amendment. In 1976, Congress created a special exemption for certain sperm whale oil and scrimshaw products held within the United States on the effective date of the 1973 Act.[157] Originally, this exemption was to last for only three years, since Congress anticipated that the stocks on hand would be exhausted within that period. That expectation was not realized, however, and the Secretary was authorized in 1979 to extend the exemption for three more years.[158] A similar extension was authorized again in 1982 but with a significant limitation. In his administration of the original scrimshaw exemption, the Secretary of Commerce effectively exempted all such products held at the time of the 1973 Act, regardless of their ownership. Thus, not only those who held such products in December 1973, but all their subsequent purchasers were equally entitled to the exemption.[159] To limit the administrative and enforcement difficulties inherent in an exemption for an ever-increasing population of beneficiaries, Congress in 1982 prohibited, as of January 31, 1984, the sale of scrimshaw products, except by persons who had been the original beneficiaries of the 1976 exemption and only if they held the products sold on the date of the 1982 Amendments.[160]

---

[155]*Id.* §1539(a).

[156]*Id.* §1539(d)(2). The legislative history indicates that this requirement was intended "to limit substantially the number of exemptions that may be granted" and therefore applied only to endangered species. H. Rep. No. 412, 93d Cong. 1st Sess. 17 (1973).

[157]*Id.* §1539(f) (1976 & Supp. V 1981) (amended by 1982 Amendments §6(3)). Such products did not qualify for the "controlled environment" exemption discussed at text accompanying notes 149–150 *supra* since, at the time of the Act's enactment, they were held for commercial purposes.

[158]16 U.S.C. §1539(f)(8) (Supp. V 1981).

[159]50 C.F.R. §222.11-8 (1981).

[160]1982 Amendments §6(3) (to be codified at 16 U.S.C. §1539(f)(9)(B)).

Also exempted from most of the Act's restrictions are raptors held in captivity (whether for commercial or noncommercial purposes) as of the date of the 1978 Amendments and their captive progeny. [161] The Secretary of the Interior is, however, authorized to require the maintenance and production of records appropriate for administering the exemption.[162] Similarly, articles more than 100 years old and composed in whole or in part of listed species are exempted from certain requirements of the Act, subject to such documentation requirements as the Secretary of Treasury may impose.[163]

In the nature of an exemption is a "self-defense" provision also added in 1978. This provision makes it a defense in any criminal prosecution under the Act if the defendant's action was taken in defense of his own or anyone else's physical well being.[164] Civil penalties may still be assessed against such persons, however.

The 1982 Amendments added three new types of exemptions. The most novel of these was the authorization to list as "experimental populations" certain populations of otherwise endangered species and to apply more relaxed restrictions to those populations.[165] The impetus for this came from the recognition that the intentional establishment of populations of endangered species in new areas may be an important conservation measure, yet, because of the Act's stringent restrictions, the cooperation of private land owners or other government agencies in such conservation schemes may be impeded. To encourage that cooperation, Congress designed the new category of "experimental populations."

Although the rationale for the experimental population provision is easily understood, the provision itself is rather complicated. First, not every population purposely established through human effort qualifies as an "experimental population." Only populations established with the prior authorization of the Secretary outside the current range of the species are

---

[161] 16 U.S.C. §1538(b)(2) (Supp. V 1981) (amended by 1982 Amendments §9(b)(3)).

[162] *Id.* §1538(b)(2)(B).

[163] *Id.* §1539(h) (Supp. V 1981) (amended by 1982 Amendments §6(4)). Both the raptor and antique articles exemptions were added by the 1978 Amendments and, as originally added, provided exemptions from the requirements of both the Act and the Convention. The 1982 Amendments modified the raptor exemption so that the requirements of the Convention would remain applicable but made no comparable change in the antique articles exemption. The latter exemption is curiously structured. On its face, it provides an exemption for qualified antiques from both import and interstate commerce prohibitions. However, to be a qualified antique, an article must be entered into the United States through a specially designated customs port. Thus the exemption does not apply generally to all antiques, but only to those lawfully imported since 1978.

[164] 16 U.S.C. §1540(b)(3) (Supp. V 1981).

[165] 1982 Amendments §6(6) (to be codified at 16 U.S.C. §1539(j)).

"experimental populations" within the meaning of the Act.[166] Before authorizing the establishment of any such population, the Secretary must determine by regulation whether the population to be established is "essential to the continued existence" of the species.[167] Upon that determination hinges the applicability of section 7 to the new population. Experimental populations essential to the survival of a species are fully protected by section 7; those not essential are basically unprotected by section 7, except when they occur on units of the National Park or National Wildlife Refuge Systems.[168]

Whether essential to the survival of the species or not, any experimental population is to be separately listed as a threatened species.[169] Thus the Secretary can tailor as appropriate the particular prohibitions appli-

---

[166]*Id.* §1539(j)(1).

[167]*Id.* §1539(j)(2)(B). Populations established prior to the 1982 Amendments with the authorization of the Secretary may be declared experimental populations if the Secretary undertakes a comparable rulemaking. *Id.* §1539(j)(3). Unless and until the Secretary does so, however, the population remains fully subject to the other provisions of the Act. *See* H. Conf. Rep. No. 835, 97th Cong., 2d Sess. 34 (1982). Although new section 11(g)(1)(C) of the Act, added by the 1982 Amendments, authorizes citizen suits to compel the Secretary to undertake nondiscretionary listing actions mandated by section 4, no provision of the Act authorizes suits to compel the Secretary to determine whether previously established populations are "experimental populations."

[168]1982 Amendments §6(6) (to be codified at 16 U.S.C. §1539(j)(2)(C)). Such nonessential populations outside those areas are to be treated as species proposed to be listed, thus making them subject to the conferral requirements of section 7(a)(3). *See* text accompanying notes 235–236 *infra*. Even though an experimental population may not be essential to the continued existence of a species, it is not illogical to have section 7 apply to it in some fashion. An experimental population, once separately listed as such, becomes a "species" for purposes of the Act. Section 7(a)(3) thus applies directly to it and independently of other populations of the same biological species.

[169]*Id.* The language is inartful ("each member of an experimental population shall be treated as a threatened species"), but the legislative history is clear that it is the population itself, and not its individual members, that is to be treated as threatened. *See* H. Conf. Rep. No. 835, 97th Cong., 2d Sess. 34 (1982). Treating an experimental population as a separately listed species has an interesting consequence for the application of section 7 to other nonexperimental populations of the same species. When determining whether a federal action will jeopardize the continued existence of a listed species, the Secretary must evaluate the effects of the action solely on the nonexperimental populations since the experimental populations are treated as separately listed "species." This result seems intended since nothing in the legislative history of the 1982 Amendments suggests that the establishment of experimental populations was to serve as a mechanism for reducing section 7 obligations toward naturally occurring populations of a listed species. Of course, if the establishment of an experimental population brings about the recovery of a species, then it may be appropriate to delist all populations of the species.

cable to that population. This flexibility, together with the partial waiver of section 7 for nonessential populations, was intended to give the Secretary greater opportunity to gain the cooperation of landowners and other government agencies in establishing new populations of endangered species. That is not to say, however, that the threatened species regulations applicable to experimental populations are to be developed through direct bargaining. Like any other threatened species regulation, they must be developed through rulemaking and contain such measures as are necessary and advisable for the conservation of the species.

The remaining two exceptions added by the 1982 Amendments each pertain to the incidental taking of listed species. As the earlier discussion of the Act's taking prohibition revealed, neither direct physical injury nor the intention to cause any injury at all to a listed species is required by the Act's broad definition of "take." Thus an extremely wide range of activities, including forestry practices, land clearing, commercial fishing, and others, could result in the unintentional, incidental taking of listed species. Since all takings are prohibited and potentially punishable by significant civil and criminal penalties, the Act's potential for influencing activities that result in incidental taking depended, at least in part, on the public's perception of the government's willingness to prosecute such activities. Not surprisingly, such prosecutions were very rare, and the Act's theoretically absolute prohibition against any form of taking bore little resemblance to the reality of nonenforcement.

In 1982 Congress authorized the Secretary to permit otherwise prohibited takings of endangered species if they are "incidental to, and not the purpose of, the carrying out of an otherwise lawful activity."[170] On its face, this represents a relaxation of the Act's restrictions because it permits what has heretofore been prohibited. In fact, however, this provision is likely to increase the Secretary's leverage over activities that result in the incidental taking of endangered species because it substitutes a flexible regulatory authority for a threat of criminal prosecution which few found credible.[171] To receive an incidental taking permit, an applicant must submit to the Secretary a "conservation plan."[172] The Secretary must find that the plan includes measures to mitigate any incidental takings that occur and that adequate funding for the plan will be provided.[173] In

---

[170] 1982 Amendments §6(1) (to be codified at 16 U.S.C. §1539(a)(1)(B)).

[171] The Secretary's authority with respect to threatened species is sufficiently flexible to permit him to authorize some or all incidental takings by regulation. It is probably for this reason that the new permit authority added by the 1982 Amendments applies only to endangered, and not threatened, species.

[172] 1982 Amendments §6(1) (to be codified at 16 U.S.C. §1539(a)(2)(A)).

[173] *Id.* §§1539(a)(2)(B)(ii), (iii).

addition, the Secretary must find that any incidental takings will be kept to the minimal level practical,[174] but in no event may the incidental takings "appreciably reduce the likelihood of the survival and recovery of the species in the wild."[175] Since that is the administrative standard developed under section 7, the Secretary may not, under this new incidental taking authority, permit the continued existence of any endangered species to be jeopardized by such taking.

Adapting these requirements to the many varied activities that can result in incidental taking will require considerable administrative ingenuity. In cases in which the incidental takings occur in the course of habitat destruction, the mitigation element of the required conservation plan might be addressed by measures to protect or enhance other habitat areas.[176] In other cases, for example the incidental catch of endangered sea turtles in commercial fishing nets, measures such as the use of modified nets may be necessary to satisfy the requirement that incidental takings be minimized. In all cases, however, the opportunity to secure such permits should remove the reluctance of enforcement officials to seek sanctions against those who choose to go forward with activities causing incidental takings without ever applying for such permits.

The final new exception tries to harmonize the taking prohibition of section 9 with the federal agency duties of section 7. The provision is premised on the recognition that some agency actions that satisfy the requirement of section 7 that they not jeopardize the continued existence of a listed species may nonetheless cause the incidental taking of one or more individuals of that species. To insure that section 9 not prohibit federal actions that satisfy the standard of section 7, the 1982 Amendments effectively waived the taking prohibition for such actions, provided that the agency comply with measures specified by the Secretary to minimize incidental takings.[177] A proper understanding of this provision requires a fuller appreciation of the requirements of section 7, which are addressed in the next part.

---

[174]*Id.* §1539(a)(2)(B)(ii).

[175]*Id.* §1539(a)(2)(B)(iv).

[176]This is a feature of the so-called "San Bruno Mountain Conservation Plan," which is the first plan for which the new incidental taking permit was sought. *See* 47 Fed. Reg. 54366 (Dec. 2, 1982). Although the 1982 Conference Report describes the San Bruno plan as the "model" for the new incidental taking permit, that plan was largely developed in anticipation of seeking a "survival enhancement" permit under section 10(a)(1)(A) of the Act and was in any event not finalized until after the 1982 Amendments were enacted. *See* H. Conf. Rep. No. 835, 97th Cong., 2d Sess. 31 (1982).

[177]1982 Amendments §§4(a)(2) and (7) (to be codified at 16 U.S.C. §§1536(b)(4) and (o)).

## Special Duties of Federal Agencies Under Section 7

In addition to the various prohibitions that apply to all persons under section 9 of the Act, section 7 imposes additional duties on federal agencies. As originally enacted in 1973, section 7 was a mere two sentences long, attracted little attention during the course of legislative debate, and was almost entirely noncontroversial. However, because of the provision's command that federal agencies refrain from any action that would jeopardize the continued existence of a listed species, the original edition of this work predicted that section 7 would ultimately prove to be the Act's most potent weapon against the loss of species. That prediction has since proved correct; indeed, section 7 has been described as "the conscience of contemporary environmental law."[178]

One other prediction made in the original edition of this book was that if the appellate courts overruled the then-recent decision of a federal district court in Tennessee allowing the completion of Tellico Dam by the Tennessee Valley Authority despite its likely extirpation of the snail darter, an endangered fish, section 7 was likely to be amended by Congress. In retrospect, that prediction proved to be a remarkable understatement. When the Supreme Court in 1978 enjoined construction of Tellico Dam on the grounds that its completion would violate section 7,[179] the congressional response was swift and dramatic. In 1978, 1979, and again in 1982, section 7 was extensively amended. From an original two sentences, the provision has been expanded to occupy nearly 10 pages of statutory text and now includes detailed procedures for its implementation, new federal duties, and a complex procedure for exempting qualified activities from its commands. Remarkably, however, though the duties imposed by section 7 are no longer absolute, they remain stringent and highly protective of species threatened with extinction. Section 7 has been at the center of a storm of controversy for the past half decade, yet its essential command remains intact.

From its very beginning, section 7 has actually imposed both affirmative and prohibitory duties. The prohibitory duties have received the most attention, though the provision itself states the affirmative commands first. This analysis begins with the affirmative commands, turns to the important prohibitions of section 7, analyzes the procedures by which they are to be implemented, and then concludes with a discussion of the provision's unique exemption mechanism.

---

[178]Houck, The "Institutionalization of Caution" Under §7 of the Endangered Species Act: What Do You Do When You Don't Know?, 12 Envtl. L. Rep. (Envtl. L. Inst.) 15001 (1982).

[179]TVA v. Hill, 437 U.S. 153 (1978).

## The Affirmative Duties of Section 7

The first command of section 7 is directed to the Secretaries of the Interior and Commerce, the agency heads charged with immediate responsibility for the administration of the federal endangered species program. They are directed to review other programs administered by them and to "utilize such programs in furtherance of the purposes of this [Act]."[180] The second command, directed to all other agencies, requires them to "utilize their authorities in furtherance of the purposes of this [Act] by carrying out programs for the conservation of endangered species and threatened species."[181] Several cases have probed the nature of the former duty; none has yet done so for the latter. While it has been suggested that the latter duty "appears to create no enforceable obligations,"[182] it may at least establish the authority to carry out endangered species conservation programs in agencies that did not previously have such authority.

The few cases that have addressed the affirmative duties of section 7 all pertain to programs administered by the Secretary of the Interior. Both *Defenders of Wildlife v. Andrus*[183] and *Connor v. Andrus*[184] concerned hunting regulations promulgated by the Secretary pursuant to the Migratory Bird Treaty Act. In the former case, the plaintiff alleged that the challenged regulations, insofar as they permitted migratory bird hunting during twilight hours, failed to provide adequate assurance that endangered birds would not be mistakenly killed as a result of hunter misidentification. The court considered the duties of the Secretary in light of a finding that the administrative record upon which the regulations were based was "virtually barren of any information regarding the impact of the contested shooting hours on birds that should not be taken"[185] and a "substantial argument," presented through the plaintiff's affidavits, "that the destruction of protected species may be considerable."[186]

The *Defenders* court concluded that under the Endangered Species Act the Secretary must "do far more than merely avoid the elimination of protected species"; rather, he has "an affirmative duty to increase the population of protected species."[187] Since the rulemaking process had not adequately focused on this duty, the court found the resulting regulations to be arbitrary and unlawful.

---

[180] 16 U.S.C. §1536(a)(1) (Supp. V 1981).

[181] *Id.*

[182] Note, Obligations of Federal Agencies Under Section 7 of the Endangered Species Act of 1973, 28 Stan. L. Rev. 1247, 1253 n. 48.

[183] 428 F. Supp. 167 (D.D.C. 1977).

[184] 453 F. Supp. 1037 (W.D. Tex. 1978).

[185] 428 F. Supp. at 169.

[186] *Id.* at 170.

[187] *Id.*

In *Connor*, the Secretary had restricted duck hunting in parts of three states so as to insure that there would be no mistaken shooting of the endangered Mexican duck. That restriction was challenged as inadequately supported by the administrative record. Although the *Connor* court professed to agree with *Defenders* that the Secretary had an affirmative duty to restore endangered species, in its view the administrative record failed to show that the hunting ban would serve that duty.[188] Thus the *Connor* court, like that in *Defenders*, searched the administrative record for support of the challenged regulations, but found none. The superficial difference in the approach of the two courts was that one required affirmative record evidence to support the absence of restrictions while the other required such evidence to support restrictions. In fact, both courts seem to have been moved by extrarecord evidence produced by the plaintiffs showing possible harm to endangered species as a result of the challenged regulations.[189]

Two other cases, without directly discussing section 7, seem at least inferentially to explore the nature of its affirmative commands. In *Organized Fishermen of Florida v. Andrus*, the plaintiff challenged certain restrictions on fishing in Everglades National Park, including the placement of barriers against entry into a sanctuary for the endangered American crocodile.[190] Citing *Defenders* for the proposition that the Act imposes an affirmative duty to increase the populations of endangered species, the court rejected the challenge. Whether the administrative record revealed an adequate evidentiary basis that the challenged restrictions would serve that duty—the crucial issue in both *Defenders* and *Connor*—was not seriously disputed. The plaintiffs had apparently instead argued that the Fishery Conservation and Management Act of 1976 reflected a policy of promoting fisheries that was hindered by the restrictions at issue. The court, however, concluded that nothing in the later Act could "be said to have either expressly or impliedly repealed the high priority accorded protection of animal life under the Endangered Species Act."[191]

An implicit repeal of the Secretary's affirmative authority was found to have occurred in *Texaco v. Andrus*.[192] At issue there was the authority of the Secretary of the Interior to declare certain federal lands "unsuitable for all or certain types of surface coal mining operations" under section 522 of the Surface Mining Control and Reclamation Act.[193] Under that Act, the Secretary's authority to make such declarations is generally quite broad but

---

[188]453 F. Supp. at 1041.

[189]*See* 428 F. Supp. at 170 and 453 F. Supp. at 1041 n. 2.

[190]488 F. Supp. 1351 (S.D. Fla. 1980).

[191]*Id.* at 1356 n. 10.

[192]11 Envtl. L. Rep. (Envtl. L. Inst.) 20179 (D.D.C. Aug. 15, 1980).

[193]30 U.S.C. §1272 (Supp. V 1981).

specifically does not extend to lands on which a mining operator had made substantial legal and financial commitments before the Act's effective date.[194] Despite that statutory limitation, the Secretary's implementing regulations listed 20 criteria for assessing the suitability of areas for mining but failed to apply the limitation to each criterion. Among those to which it had not been applied were several criteria pertaining to the presence of endangered species. This, the court ruled, was unlawful, notwithstanding the authority conferred by the Endangered Species Act, since the Surface Mining Control and Reclamation Act, as a later expression of Congress, takes precedence over it.[195]

The language of the court's opinion in *Texaco* was far broader than necessary for the narrow issue actually before the court. Despite the court's assertion that "mining can ensue for those areas wherein substantial financial and legal commitments have been expended before the effective date of the [Surface Mining] Act,"[196] the opinion makes clear that no actual conflict between the needs of a particular species and mining plans for a particular area was at issue.[197] While the Secretary's authority to make advance determinations of unsuitability may be limited under such circumstances by the requirements of the Surface Mining Act, the *Texaco* decision does not hold, and should not be construed to imply, that the Secretary, when subsequently leasing land or regulating mining activities thereon, may escape the Endangered Species Act's prohibition against actions that jeopardize the continued existence of any listed species. That prohibition and the related duties of section 7 are taken up next.

### The Prohibitory Commands of Section 7

If section 7 is in fact the Endangered Species Act's most potent weapon against the loss of species, it is because of the important restraints it imposes on federal activities. The loss of natural habitats through the impoundment of rivers, the filling of wetlands, and the clearing of land for highways, airports, and a myriad of other activities, is the major cause of endangerment for virtually every species facing the threat of extinction. A great many of those diverse activities are either directly undertaken or indirectly authorized by federal agencies. Thus, to arrest the decline of species will require some effective way of influencing federal agency conduct. Section 7 seeks to do exactly that, by requiring each federal agency, in consultation with the Secretary of the Interior or Commerce to "insure that any action authorized, funded, or carried out by such

---

[194]*Id.* §1272(a)(6).
[195]11 Envtl. L. Rep. (Envtl. L. Rep.) at 20182 n. 3.
[196]*Id.* at 20182.
[197]*Id.* at 20182 n. 3.

agency...is not likely to jeopardize the continued existence of any endangered species or threatened species or result in the destruction or adverse modification of [critical] habitat of such species."[198]

The duties to avoid jeopardy to the species or adverse modification to its critical habitat are set forth in the statute as two separate duties. Other provisions of the statute appear premised on the assumption that these duties are separate and independent.[199] In the author's view, however, the former duty completely subsumes the latter, for any action that destroys or adversely modifies the critical habitat of a listed species must necessarily jeopardize its continued existence. This is so because any area of habitat can be designated as critical habitat only if it is essential to the survival and recovery (*i.e.*, "conservation") of a listed species, and any modification of such habitat should be considered "adverse" only if it diminishes the value of the habitat for the survival and recovery of that species. Any action that appreciably reduces the likelihood of survival or recovery of a listed species, however, must be considered to jeopardize its continued existence.[200] Thus any action that adversely modifies the critical habitat of any listed species must also jeopardize its continued existence.[201]

If the duty to avoid adverse modification of critical habitat is entirely redundant of the duty to avoid jeopardy to a listed species, then it can fairly be asked whether the designation of critical habitat serves any useful purpose. In the author's view, it clearly does because it gives advance notice of those areas in which federal activities will require especially close scrutiny to determine whether they meet the requirements of the jeopardy

---

[198]16 U.S.C. §1536(a)(2) (Supp. V 1981). Originally, the Act required federal agencies to insure that each of their actions "does not jeopardize" the continued existence of listed species. The change to the current "is not likely to jeopardize" standard was made as a result of the Endangered Species Act Amendments of 1979, Pub. L. No. 96-159, §4(1)(C), 93 Stat. 1225, 1226. The legislative history reveals that this change was not intended to alter the obligations of federal agencies. The most useful discussions of that legislative history are found in Erdheim, The Wake of the Snail Darter: Insuring the Effectiveness of Section 7 of the Endangered Species Act, 9 Ecol. L. Q. 629, 655 (1981), and Houck, *supra* note 178 at 15006-07. Although the court in Roosevelt Campobello International Park Comm'n v. EPA, 684 F.2d 1041, 1048 (1st Cir. 1982), stated that this change "softened the obligation" of federal agencies, it went on to impose duties more far reaching than any previously imposed by any court in an Endangered Species Act case. *See* text accompanying notes 244–247 *infra*.

[199]*See* text accompanying notes 93–95 *supra*.

[200]*See* the administrative definition of "jeopardize the continued existence of" at note 94 *supra*.

[201]If there are flaws in the logic of this argument, they are not yet evident in any reported decision, for no case has found a violation of the duty to avoid adverse modification of critical habitat absent a violation of the duty to avoid jeopardy to the species.

prohibition. The designation of critical habitat also typically entails the gathering of more detailed information about the specific conservation requirements of a species than is necessary to determine merely that the species is in fact endangered or threatened. As a result of that information gathering, the Secretary of the Interior or Commerce is better able to fulfill his consultative role in advising federal agencies as to their section 7 duties. The case law under section 7, both as it was originally enacted and as it has since been amended, underscores the importance of the consultative role played by the Secretary.

In *Sierra Club v. Froehlke*, for example, private citizens challenged the construction by the Corps of Engineers of Meramec Park Lake Dam near St. Louis.[202] Among other grounds the plaintiffs challenged the Corps' proposed action because it would allegedly jeopardize the continued existence of the endangered Indiana bat by flooding several caves in which the bats were known to dwell.[203] The district court found the evidence of adverse effects on the bat inconclusive and held that there was no violation of section 7.[204] The court of appeals affirmed and offered the following with regard to the meaning of section 7:

> Plaintiffs misread the requirements of the Act. Consultation under Section 7 does not require acquiescence. Should a difference of opinion arise as to a given project, the responsibility for decision after consultation is not vested in the Secretary [of the Interior] but in the agency involved....[205]

The decision in *Sierra Club* thus limited the role of the Secretary of the Interior to a purely consultative and advisory one. Moreover, it denied to the courts any power of review beyond the "narrow and limited one" of voiding "arbitrary and capricious action."[206] It seems significant, however, that the Secretary had never taken a firm position that construction of

---

[202]534 F.2d 1289 (8th Cir. 1976).

[203]Plaintiffs apparently contended that the proposed action would destroy the habitat of the bat, although at the time of trial no determination of critical habitat had yet been made. The Secretary of the Interior urged a moratorium on further construction pending a determination of critical habitat, which was finally proposed two months after the trial court's decision. *See* 40 Fed. Reg. 21499 (May 16, 1975). Neither the trial nor the appellate court seemed to attach much significance to the absence of a critical habitat determination, however.

[204]392 F. Supp. 130 (E.D. Mo. 1975).

[205]534 F.2d at 1303.

[206]*Id.* at 1304–1305. This standard has been generally accepted as the proper standard of review in section 7 cases. *See* Cabinet Mountains Wilderness v. Peterson, 685 F.2d 678, 686 (D.C. Cir. 1982) and cases cited therein.

Meramec Park Lake Dam would jeopardize the continued existence of the bat. Rather, he merely urged a moratorium on further construction pending additional studies. Moreover, in 1964, the Fish and Wildlife Service had submitted to the Corps of Engineers, pursuant to the Fish and Wildlife Coordination Act, a generally favorable report concerning the expected impacts of the dam on which the Corps and the Congress had relied. The district court attached considerable importance to the fact that, although the Department of the Interior subsequently attempted to withdraw the 1964 report from the Corps, it made no similar effort to withdraw it from congressional consideration.[207] With the Interior Department, as the expert agency, in this compromised and ambivalent posture, both the trial and the appellate courts seemed justified in granting the Corps wide discretion to decide whether to proceed.

The position of the Secretary of the Interior was measurably stronger in *National Wildlife Federation v. Coleman,* in which he had repeatedly expressed his opposition to the project there in issue, construction of a segment of Interstate Highway 10 in Mississippi, because of its adverse impact on the endangered Mississippi sandhill crane.[208] The Secretary had steadfastly insisted that, without the relocation of a proposed interchange and elimination of certain "borrow pits," construction of the segment in question could not be done in compliance with section 7.[209] The testimony of an Interior Department biologist at trial suggesting that construction of the highway was not the major threat to the cranes cast sufficient doubt on the credibility of that position to persuade the trial court to find no violation of section 7. The court of appeals, however, while recognizing that section 7 "does not give the Department of Interior a veto over the actions of other federal agencies"[210] and stating that its own power of review was limited to considering whether the agency had made a "clear error of judgment,"[211] held that the plaintiffs had sustained their burden of showing that actions necessary to insure the survival of the cranes and the nondestruction of their critical habitat had not been taken.

The relief that the court entered enjoined further work on certain aspects of the highway "until the Secretary of the Department of Interior determines that the necessary modifications are made in the highway

---

[207] 392 F. Supp. at 140–141.

[208] 529 F.2d 359 (5th Cir.), *cert. denied sub nom.* Boteler v. National Wildlife Federation, 429 U.S. 979 (1976).

[209] On the eve of the trial, the Secretary published an emergency determination of the cranes' critical habitat, which the proposed highway segment traversed. 40 Fed. Reg. 27501 (June 30, 1975).

[210] 529 F.2d at 371.

[211] *Id.* at 372.

project to insure that it will no longer jeopardize the continued existence...
or destroy or modify critical habitat of the Mississippi sandhill crane."[212]
The defendants filed a petition for rehearing or clarification, contending
that the relief was inconsistent with the court's statement that the Secretary
of the Interior could not exercise a veto power over the actions of other
agencies.[213] The court denied the petition.

In comparing these first two cases to arise under section 7, the key to
the difference in outcomes appears to be in the role played by the Secretary
as the recognized expert under the Act. Where the Secretary establishes a
firm and amply supported position that the proposed action will violate
section 7, and the agency statutorily required to consult with him is unable
to produce any overriding rebuttal evidence, the courts will give great
deference to the Secretary's judgment. That simple principle, that the firm
opinion of the expert wildlife agency is entitled to a presumption of
validity until overborne by contrary evidence, is the key to the effective
implementation of section 7.

The third case to arise under section 7 tested its applicability to federal
projects substantially completed at the time that the restrictions of the 1973
Act became operative. Although it presented a familiar transitional
problem like those that have accompanied other recent environmental
legislation,[214] the case ultimately proved to be a watershed for section 7. In
*TVA v. Hill,* plaintiffs challenged the completion of Tellico Dam, which
threatened to destroy virtually the entire habitat of a recently discovered
fish, the endangered snail darter.[215] Though the district court agreed that
the dam would surely jeopardize the continued existence of the endangered
fish, it refused to apply section 7 retroactively to prevent completion of a
project that was substantially constructed at the time the species was
discovered and that would entail the loss of several million dollars of
expenditures if halted.[216] Although the court acknowledged that balancing
the interests between wildlife conservation and development was a
legislative rather than a judicial function, it asserted that Congress had

---

[212]*Id.* at 375.

[213]At least one commentator took the same view. *See* Comment, Implementing §7 of
the Endangered Species Act of 1973. First Notices from the Courts, 6 Envtl. L. Rep.
(Envtl. L. Inst.) 10120 (1976).

[214]For a discussion of the many cases concerning the application of the National
Environmental Policy to substantially completed federal projects, see Anderson,
The National Environmental Policy Act, in Federal Environmental Law 396–410
(E. Dolgin & T. Guilbert, eds. 1974). Unlike other environmental legislation, the
1973 Act may be plagued with questions of its retroactive application indefinitely.
This is because the addition of new species to the lists of endangered and threatened
species will almost certainly create conflicts with projects initiated prior to the time
such listings occurred.

[215]437 U.S. 153 (1978).

[216]Hill v. TVA, 419 F. Supp. 753 (E.D. Tenn. 1976).

already done that balancing by appropriating funds for the dam's construction after the existence of the fish had become known.[217]

The court of appeals reversed the decision of the district court, holding that the lower court had no choice but to enjoin completion of the dam in light of its finding that completion would jeopardize the continued existence of the snail darter.[218] With the case in this posture, the Supreme Court agreed to review it. Attorney General Griffin Bell argued the case personally, a fact usually reflective of the great importance the United States attaches to an issue. In this remarkable case, however, the Attorney General's presence reflected instead bitter divisions within the federal government. The government's brief set forth the TVA position that the decision of the court of appeals was wrong and should be reversed. Appended to it, however, were the separate and diametrically opposite views of the Secretary of the Interior.

The Supreme Court, by a 6–3 majority, held that section 7 prohibited TVA from closing the gates on Tellico Dam, even though that action was but the culmination of a process that had begun years prior to passage of the Endangered Species Act.[219] Chief Justice Burger, who wrote for the majority, reasoned that "[o]ne would be hard pressed to find a statutory provision whose terms were any plainer than those in §7,"[220] in concluding that the final step of gate closure was a "federal action" subject to the prohibition against jeopardy. The literal wording of the provision was reinforced, in the Chief Justice's view, by the overall structure of the Act, which showed a "plain intent," reflected "in literally every section of the statute," to "halt and reverse the trend toward species extinction, whatever the cost."[221] Implicit in the Chief Justice's argument was the notion that, whenever a federal agency has any sort of choice affecting the well being of a listed species, the exercise of that authority constitutes an "action" subject to the requirements of section 7. Justice Powell, in a strong dissent, argued that section 7 applies only to "actions with respect to which the agency has reasonable decisionmaking alternatives still available" and that abandonment of the Tellico project was not a reasonable alternative.[222] Though the factual predicates of both Burger's and Powell's arguments were apparently erroneous, the Burger opinion became the law of the case.[223]

---

[217]*Id.* at 762.

[218]TVA v. Hill, 549 F.2d 1064 (6th Cir. 1977).

[219]TVA v. Hill, 437 U.S. 153 (1978).

[220]*Id.* at 173.

[221]*Id.* at 184.

[222]*Id.* at 205.

[223]Justice Powell's assumption that abandonment of the Tellico project was not a reasonable alternative (at least in economic terms) was subsequently rejected when the project and its alternatives were carefully reconsidered. *See* text accompanying

Before the year was out, Congress reconsidered by passing the Endangered Species Act Amendments of 1978. Despite extraordinary pressures simply to exempt Tellico Dam from the requirements of the Act, Congress elected instead to codify a formal process for considering the exemption of any project presenting an "irresolvable conflict" with section 7. Tellico Dam was required to be considered immediately for an exemption pursuant to an expedited and truncated procedure.[224] The determining factors were to be whether there were "no reasonable and prudent alternatives to the agency action" and whether the benefits of the action clearly outweighed the benefits of alternatives not jeopardizing endangered species.[225] By unanimous vote of the Endangered Species Committee, comprised of six federal officials and a representative recommended by the Governor of Tennessee,[226] Tellico failed on both counts.

---

notes 225–226 *infra*. The faulty premise of Chief Justice Burger's reasoning was that "by definition, any *prior* action of a federal agency which *would* have come under the scope of the Act must have already *resulted* in the destruction of an endangered species or its critical habitat" 437 U.S. at 186 n. 32 (emphasis in original). In fact, the adverse effects of many actions do not fully occur immediately. Where those adverse impacts have not yet been fully realized, the undoing of the action may avoid the jeopardy that is otherwise certain. That fact raises the question of the duty of federal agencies with respect to projects already completed, a question presented in Colorado River Water Conservation District v. Andrus, Civil Action 78-A-1191 (D. Colo. Dec. 28, 1981). There the plaintiffs somewhat disingenuously sought to compel the dismantling of every existing dam on the Colorado River because of the impacts of those dams on endangered fish in the river. The court refused to grant the plaintiffs' motion for summary judgment "because there is still a genuine issue of material fact as to which dams adversely affect the endangered fishes, and whether shutting down the dams will enhance or endanger the fishes population." (slip opinion at 23–24). Because of the erroneous factual premise of Chief Justice Burger's reasoning, TVA v. Hill offers little clear guidance as to how courts should handle such claims. In the author's view, Justice Powell's formulation is more instructive. Thus an agency with reasonable alternatives as to how to operate a completed project should be required to choose the mode of operation that avoids jeopardy to a listed species but should not be required to terminate the project or choose a mode of operation that negates its purpose.

[224]Grayrocks Dam and Reservoir, halted in Nebraska v. Rural Electrification Administration, 12 Env't Rep. Cas. (BNA) 1156 (D. Neb. Oct. 3, 1978), was also required to be considered immediately for an exemption. By virtue of 16 U.S.C. §1539(i)(1) (Supp. V 1981), the two projects were exempted from the threshold determinations described at text accompanying note 267 *infra* and from the requirement that the Endangered Species Committee make the third determination described in the text accompanying note 271 *infra*. Unless a final decision on an exemption were made within 90 days after the enactment of the 1978 amendments, the projects would be automatically exempted.

[225]16 U.S.C. §1536(h)(1)(A)(i) and (ii) (Supp. V 1981), as amended by 1982 Amendments §4(a)(6).

[226]Composition of the Committee is prescribed by 16 U.S.C. §1536(e)(3) (Supp. V 1981).

The decision to deny an exemption to Tellico killed the project—at least until Congress exempted it from all federal law by means of a rider attached to the Energy and Water Development Appropriation Act of 1980.[227] Thus Congress itself shouldered the burden of what apparently was the first conscious human decision to extirpate another species, notwithstanding the prior determination that the Tellico project was without economic merit. Subsequently, however, new and apparently naturally occurring populations of snail darters have been found elsewhere. Thus, for the moment at least, the endangered snail darter survives.·

The creation of an exemption process was the principal motivation for Congress's revision of section 7 in 1978, but far from the only result. The 1978 Amendments also formalized the process of consultation between the Secretary and the federal agencies whose actions are subject to section 7,[228] prescribed certain requirements for the "biological opinions" that result from that consultation process,[229] created a duty to conduct "biological assessments" prior to commencing new projects[230] and restricted the ability of federal agencies to commit resources to projects subsequent to the initiation of consultation.[231]

As a result of the Tellico experience, Congress sought through the 1978 Amendments to insure that the consultation process would be as effective as possible in identifying ways to avoid conflicts between proposed federal actions and listed species or their critical habitats. Key to that goal was insuring that the process was initiated at the earliest possible time in the planning of a proposed action. Thus section 7(c) requires, with respect to any federal action for which no actual construction had begun and no contract for construction had been entered into as of the time of the 1978 Amendments, that a "biological assessment" be conducted if the Secretary advises that any listed or proposed-to-be-listed species occurs in the area of the proposed action.[232] The purpose of a biological assessment is to

---

[227] Pub. L. 96-69, Title IV, 93 Stat. 449 (1979).

[228] 1978 Amendments §3 (codified at 16 U.S.C. §1536(a) (Supp. V 1981), as amended by 1982 Amendments §4(a)(1)).

[229] Id. (codified at 16 U.S.C. §1536(b) (Supp. V 1981), as amended by 1982 Amendments §4(a)(2)).

[230] Id. (codified at 16 U.S.C. §1536(c) (Supp. V 1981), as amended by 1982 Amendments §4(a)(3)).

[231] Id. (codified at 16 U.S.C. §1536(d) (Supp. V 1981)).

[232] 16 U.S.C. §1536(c)(1) (Supp. V 1981), as amended by 1982 Amendments §4(a)(3). The biological assessment may be carried out either by the federal agency involved or by any person eligible to apply for an exemption for the action under 16 U.S.C. §1536(g)(1) (Supp. V 1981), as amended by 1982 Amendments §4(a)(5). If done by the latter, it must be done in cooperation with the Secretary and under the supervision of the relevant federal agency. Id. §1536(c)(2) (Supp. V 1981).

determine whether any such species is "likely to be affected by such action."[233]

The only case thus far to construe the biological assessment requirement of section 7(c) is *No Oilport! v. Carter.*[234] In that action the plaintiffs challenged the failure of the Secretary of the Interior to have done a biological assessment prior to issuing a right of way permit for construction of a pipeline. The court, however, held that the permit did not constitute a "contract for construction" within the meaning of section 7(c) where the permittee required further authorization to proceed with construction and where the permit was expressly conditioned upon compliance with the Endangered Species Act.

If, through the biological assessment process or otherwise, a species that has been proposed to be listed as threatened or endangered is determined likely to be affected by a federal action in a way that would jeopardize its continued existence, the federal agency responsible for the action has a duty to "confer" with the Secretary regarding that action.[235] While the statute does not expressly describe what this conferral process is to produce, it is apparent that if the Secretary is not persuaded as a result of that process that the action will be modified to avoid jeopardy, he should invoke his powers to list the species pursuant to emergency rulemaking procedures.[236]

If a listed species is likely to be affected by a proposed federal action, the agency proposing that action must "consult" with the Secretary pursuant to section 7(a)(2).[237] The consultation process is normally to be completed within 90 days[238] and is to result in a "biological opinion" of the Secretary detailing how the proposed action will affect the species or its critical habitat.[239] If the action is likely to jeopardize the continued existence of the

---

[233]§1536(c)(1) (Supp. V 1981), as amended by 1982 Amendments §4(a)(3).

[234]520 F. Supp. 334 (W.D. Wash. 1981).

[235]16 U.S.C. §1536(a)(3) (Supp. V 1981) (redesignated as §1536(a)(4) by 1982 Amendments §4(a)(1)).

[236]*See* text accompanying notes 99–100 *supra.*

[237]16 U.S.C. §1536(a)(2) (Supp. V 1981).

[238]A longer period may be mutually agreed upon by the Secretary and the relevant federal agency. However, if the federal action concerned is the proposed issuance of a permit or license, the consent of the applicant must be secured for any extension beyond an additional 60 days. *Id.* §1536(b) (Supp. V 1981), as amended by 1982 Amendments §4(a)(2).

[239]*Id.* §1536(b)(3)(A). The 1982 Amendments authorize a sort of "advance consultation" for certain actions that will require a federal license or permit but for which no permit application has yet been filed. The purpose of this provision is to allow prospective permit applicants to learn at the earliest possible time whether their proposed actions will encounter section 7 difficulties. If the result of this advance consultation is an opinion from the Secretary that no such difficulties are likely,

species or result in the destruction or adverse modification of its critical habitat, the biological opinion must also suggest reasonable and prudent alternatives, if any, to avoid those effects.[240]

The detailed requirements of the statute with respect to the consultation process and the necessary elements of a biological opinion largely codify administrative practice prior to the 1978 Amendments. Similarly, case law since those amendments has continued to emphasize the importance of the Secretary's expert views reflected in the biological opinion and to give considerable deference to them. Thus, in *Romero-Barcelo v. Brown*, the court of appeals vacated a decision of the district court, rendered without benefit of a prior biological opinion, that certain Navy practices on and near the Puerto Rican island of Vieques satisfied the requirements of section 7.[241] The court reasoned that, by failing to obtain a biological opinion from the Secretary, the Navy "sidestepped the administrative process that Congress expected would resolve many of the conflicts between agency action and the requirements of §7."[242] Thus, even though "the district court apparently found that the refuge effect created by the Navy's activities satisfied [section 7], a biological opinion could alter this conclusion."[243]

In *Roosevelt Campobello International Park Commission v. EPA*, both the Fish and Wildlife Service and the National Marine Fisheries Service had issued biological opinions concluding that the Environmental Protection Agency could not issue a permit authorizing construction of an oil refinery in Maine without violating its duty to insure no jeopardy to the survival of endangered bald eagles and whales.[244] Despite those opinions, EPA issued the permit following an adjudicatory hearing in which an EPA administrative law judge concluded that the refinery would not jeopardize those species. Plaintiffs challenged the issuance of the permit.

A critical factual issue in the case was the likelihood of an oil spill as a result of tanker traffic servicing the refinery. The administrative law judge concluded that the risk of such a spill was extremely small. The court of

---

formal consultation need not be undertaken when the permit application is later filed, provided that both the action and the information available about its impacts have not changed in the interim. If, on the other hand, advance consultation results in an opinion that the action is likely to jeopardize a listed species or adversely modify its critical habitat, the prospective permit applicant must apply for the permit and secure final agency action thereon before he may seek an exemption.

[240]16 U.S.C. §1536(b) (Supp. V 1981).

[241]643 F.2d 835 (1st Cir. 1981), *rev'd on other grounds sub nom.* Weinberger v. Romero-Barcelo, 456 U.S. 305.

[242]643 F.2d at 857.

[243]*Id.*

[244]684 F.2d 1041 (1st Cir. 1982).

appeals did not directly dispute the reasonableness of this conclusion in light of the evidence presented at the adjudicatory hearing. Indeed, the court acknowledged that "[w]ere the issue whether, by a preponderance of the evidence, it had been established that [tankers] could make the transit through Head Harbor Passage to Eastport with reasonable safety, the ALJ's decision might be accepted."[245] The court, however, fixed upon the requirement of section 7(a)(2) that "each agency shall use the best scientific and commercial data available" in fulfilling its duty to insure no jeopardy to listed species.[246] That requirement, scarcely noticed when it was added by the 1979 Amendments, obliged EPA to develop other information that was not in the hearing record but that the record revealed "would contribute a more precise appreciation of risks of collision and grounding"; such information, in the court's view, "obviously represent[s] as yet untapped sources of 'best scientific and commercial data.'"[247]

*Roosevelt Campobello*, while affirming the principle that the federal action agency, and not the Secretary, has the ultimate authority to determine whether to go forward with a proposed action, erects a major hurdle for an agency that chooses to do so in the face of an adverse biological opinion. Not only must that agency rely upon convincing evidence to rebut the Secretary's opinion, but it must also affirmatively seek out the best evidence available (in the sense of capability of being acquired) that is relevant to the issue of jeopardy. This requirement obviously gives a strong incentive for agencies to pursue the reasonable and prudent alternatives specified in biological opinions.

The desire to identify reasonable and prudent alternatives as a means of avoiding conflicts between endangered species and federal actions pervades section 7. To insure that the consultation process serves as an effective tool for that purpose, Congress in 1978 added subsection (d), which prohibits federal agencies, subsequent to the initiation of consultation, from making "any irreversible or irretrievable commitment of resources...which has the effect of foreclosing the formulation or implementation of any reasonable and prudent alternative measures" that would not conflict with endangered species preservation.[248] Section 7(d) effectively codified preexisting regulations of the Fish and Wildlife Service and National Marine Fisheries Service[249] that were central to the decision in *Nebraska v. Rural Electrification Administration*.[250] There the court held

---

[245]*Id.* at 1054–1055.

[246]*Id.* at 1052–1053.

[247]*Id.* at 1055.

[248]16 U.S.C. §1536(d) (Supp. V 1981).

[249]50 C.F.R. §402.04(f) (1981).

[250]12 Env't Rep. Cas. (BNA) 1156 (D. Neb. Oct. 3, 1978).

that the issuance by the Corps of Engineers of a permit authorizing the private construction of Grayrocks Dam and the making by REA of a loan guarantee to the sponsors of the project prior to the completion of section 7 consultation constituted "the kind of commitment which, as a practical matter, forecloses consideration of the kinds of modifications or alternatives...that would avoid endangering the whooping crane and its habitat."[251] The court emphasized that the determination whether alternatives were foreclosed should focus not on narrow legalisms but rather on the practical effect of resource commitments.

The emphasis on the practical effects of resource commitments has not, however, characterized the courts' treatment of section 7(d). The most expansive discussion of the duties imposed by section 7(d) is contained in two cases challenging outer continental shelf lease sales, *North Slope Borough v. Andrus*[252] and *Conservation Law Foundation v. Andrus*.[253] These cases actually considered the interrelationship between the duties to consult under section 7(a), to secure a biological opinion under section 7(b) and to refrain from irreversible or irretrievable commitments of resources subsequent to the initiation of consultation, as provided in section 7(d).

Outer continental shelf leasing is, by statute, segmented into three distinct phases: (1) lease sale and preexploration activities, (2) exploration activities, and (3) production activities. Federal approval is required prior to each phase. The district court in *North Slope Borough* rejected the government's argument that each discrete phase should be treated as a separate federal "action" to which the duty of consultation applies.[254] Rather, it concluded that the "action" to which that duty applies was the lease sale and all resulting activities.[255] "Otherwise," in the court's view, "any statute providing an agency with maximum flexibility and planning ability...would also tacitly relieve that agency from much of the scrutiny required by the [Endangered Species Act]."[256] The Court of Appeals stated that it was "in qualified agreement" with this aspect of the district court's ruling.[257]

In *North Slope Borough* the Secretary of Commerce was unable to say, because of insufficient information, whether the total action, inclusive of all three stages, was likely to jeopardize the continued existence of the endangered bowhead whale. The Secretary could conclude, however, that

---

[251]*Id.* at 1172.

[252]642 F.2d 589 (D.C. Cir. 1980).

[253]623 F.2d 712 (1st Cir. 1979).

[254]486 F. Supp. 332, 350 (D.D.C. 1979).

[255]*Id.* at 351.

[256]*Id.* at 350.

[257]642 F.2d at 608.

the initial stage of lease sale and preexploration activities would not have that effect, provided certain conditions were met. Accordingly, the district court reasoned, despite its holding on the scope of the action to be considered in a biological opinion, that, "[w]hen no definitive biological opinion can be issued because of inadequate information, the [Endangered Species Act] does not require that the government halt all activities, unless the intermediate activities violate §7(a)(2)."[258] The court of appeals apparently concurred.[259] The effect of that reasoning is thus to allow the action to proceed incrementally through its various phases toward completion. The plaintiffs in both *North Slope Borough* and *Conservation Law Foundation* argued that the prohibition against irreversible commitments of resources in section 7(d) would be violated by such an approach. Both courts disagreed, emphasizing the legal authority of the Secretary of the Interior to modify or cancel leases at any stage of the process if evidence of prohibited jeopardy to endangered species were developed.[260] Without extended discussion, that same result was reached in yet a third oil-leasing case.[261]

The outer continental shelf leasing cases provide limited guidance for the application of section 7(d) in other contexts. Few federal actions are required by statute to be undertaken in discrete, separable phases. For those that are not, these cases should not authorize a segmented approach that encourages a momentum toward completion of the action before the Secretary can with reasonable certainty ascertain the likely effect of the completed action on endangered species.[262]

### The Exemption Process

When the Supreme Court in *TVA v. Hill* held that section 7 barred the completion of federal projects in conflict with endangered species "whatever the cost," Congress quickly responded with amendments designed to allow some balancing of the economic, social, and ecological values at stake. The congressional response took the form of an elaborate and stringent process for exempting qualified federal actions from the prohibitions of section 7. To date, that process has been rarely used. Indeed, apart from Tellico Dam itself and one other project halted by section 7 prior to the 1978 Amendments, no federal action has yet been considered for an

---

[258]486 F. Supp. at 357.

[259]*Cf.* 642 F.2d at 611.

[260]*Id.* at 610–611 and 623 F.2d at 714–715.

[261]California v. Watt, 520 F. Supp. 1359, 1387 (C.D. Cal. 1981).

[262]For excellent discussions of the outer continental shelf leasing cases and of the interpretational difficulties of section 7(d), see Erdheim, *supra* note 198 and Houck, *supra* note 178.

exemption.[263] The reasons for this may include the tough, substantive standards and complex procedures of the exemption process itself. A likely additional factor, however, is that most institutions, whether public or private, recognize that merely by seeking an exemption they risk being perceived as hostile to endangered species preservation. As long as public support for that goal is believed to be high, the incentive for compromise that avoids the need for an exemption will be great.

The exemption process was intended to be a recourse of last resort, available only after all other avenues for avoiding conflicts have been exhausted. It may be initiated only after the consultation process has been completed and a final biological opinion issued.[264] If the action involves the issuance of a federal license or permit, however, the exemption process may not be initiated until after final agency action is taken on the permit or license application, and then only if the permit is denied "primarily because of the application of section 7(a) to such agency action."[265]

Those entitled to seek an exemption include the federal agency proposing the action, the governor of the state in which the action will occur, if any, and, in the case of actions involving the proposed issuance of federal licenses or permits, the permit or license applicant.[266] The exemption application is submitted initially to the Secretary who must within 20 days make certain threshold determinations whether the Act's requirements with respect to biological assessments, good faith consultation, and the irreversible commitment of resources have been met.[267] If he determines that they have not been met, he is to deny the application immediately.[268]

---

[263] An exemption application was filed on behalf of the same oil refinery at issue in *Roosevelt Campobello International Park Commission v. EPA, supra* note 244. However, that application was dismissed on the grounds that it was prematurely filed in light of the pendency of EPA review proceedings. *See* Pittston Co. v. Endangered Species Committee, 14 Env't Rep. Cas. (BNA) 1257 (D.D.C. March 21, 1980).

[264] 16 U.S.C. §1536(g)(2) (Supp. V 1981), as amended by 1982 Amendments §4(a)(5)(C).

[265] *Id.* and 16 U.S.C. §1532(12) (Supp. V 1981).

[266] 16 U.S.C. §1536(g)(1) (Supp. V 1981). The qualifying language "if any" in reference to the state in which the action occurs appears premised on the congressional belief that section 7 applies extraterritorially. For a useful discussion of this question, see Erdheim, *supra* note 198 at 668–673.

[267] 16 U.S.C. §1536(g)(5) (Supp. V 1981), amended and recodified as §1536(g)(3) by 1982 Amendments §4(a)(5)(E). Prior to the 1982 Amendments, the functions of the Secretary described here were to be undertaken by a three-member "Endangered Species Review Board."

[268] *Id.* A decision to deny is considered a final agency action subject to judicial review.

If the Secretary determines that the threshold requirements have been met, he must hold a formal hearing and, on the basis of that hearing, prepare a report summarizing the evidence with respect to each of the factors that must be addressed in any final exemption decision.[269] The Secretary's report is submitted to a seven-member "Endangered Species Committee."[270] That Committee has the ultimate responsibility for granting or denying an exemption. It may grant an exemption only if at least five of its members determine that:

> (1) there are no reasonable and prudent alternatives to the agency action;
> (2) the benefits of such action clearly outweigh the benefits of alternative courses of action consistent with conserving the species or its critical habitat, and such action is in the public interest;
> (3) the action is of regional or national significance; and
> (4) neither the Federal agency concerned nor the exemption applicant made any irreversible or irretrievable commitment of resources prohibited by subsection (d).[271]

The Committee must also establish "reasonable mitigation and enhancement measures" as conditions to any exemption it grants.[272] Judicial review of any decision granting or denying that an exemption may be had in any appropriate United States Court of Appeals.[273]

There are three special circumstances in which the normal procedures of the exemption process may be bypassed. First, the Secretary of State may review applications for exemption and, if he certifies in writing that carrying out the action for which an exemption is sought would violate an international treaty or other international obligation of the United States, the Endangered Species Committee may not grant the exemption.[274] Conversely, if the Secretary of Defense determines that any action must be exempted "for reasons of national security," then the Committee must

---

[269] 16 U.S.C. §1536(g)(6) (Supp. V 1981), amended and recodified as §1536(g)(4) by 1982 Amendments §4(a)(5)(F).

[270] The Committee is composed of the Secretaries of the Interior, Agriculture, and Army; the Administrators of the Environmental Protection Agency and the National Oceanic and Atmospheric Administration; the Chairman of the Council of Economic Advisors; and a presidentially appointed representative from any affected state. 16 U.S.C. §1536(e)(3) (Supp. V 1981).

[271] 16 U.S.C. §1536(h)(1)(A) (Supp. V 1981), as amended by 1982 Amendments §4(a)(6).

[272] *Id.* §1536(h)(1)(B) (Supp. V 1981).

[273] *Id.* §1536(n).

[274] *Id.* §1536(i).

exempt it.[275] Finally, in emergency situations involving a presidentially declared disaster area, the President may make the threshold and final determinations otherwise required of the Secretary and Committee.[276] To date, none of these special provisions has yet been utilized.

## Enforcement

The Act authorizes two types of enforcement, public and private. Public enforcement, through which criminal or civil penalties are imposed against violators, is the responsibility of the Secretaries and the Department of Justice. The 1982 Amendments also authorize the Attorney General to seek injunctive relief against the Act's violators.[277]

The power to enjoin violations of the Act may also be exercised by private citizens under the Act's liberal citizen suit provision. That provision authorizes any person to enjoin any other person, including any agency of the United States, from violating any provision of the Act.[278] It also authorizes suits in the nature of mandamus to compel the Secretary to carry out any nondiscretionary duty with respect to the listing of species under section 4 of the Act.[279] The citizen suit provision has served as the basis for all of the litigation to compel federal agencies to carry out their obligations under section 7.

Although the citizen suit provision authorizes "any person" to commence an action to enjoin a violation of the Act, not all courts have construed this provision to confer automatic standing on any plaintiff alleging a violation of the Act. Indeed, three cases have denied standing to certain plaintiffs who had failed to demonstrate any actual injury as a result of the actions they challenged.[280] Each of those cases involved a challenge to the listing of species and together they may suggest a judicial reluctance to entertain suits that are brought to negate the Act's purposes. In the ordinary case, however, the Act's express citizen suit provision should confer automatic standing on plaintiffs who invoke it.

Before anyone may commence a citizen suit under the Act, he must give written notice of his intention to do so to the Secretary and to any alleged

---

[275]*Id.* §1536(j).

[276]*Id.* §1536(p).

[277]1982 Amendments §7(1) (to be codified at 16 U.S.C. §1540(e)(6)).

[278]16 U.S.C. §1540(g) (1976), as amended by 1982 Amendments §7(2).

[279]1982 Amendments §7(2) (to be codified at 16 U.S.C. §1540(g)(1)(C)).

[280]Glover River Organization v. Department of the Interior, 675 F.2d 251 (10th Cir. 1982); Pacific Legal Foundation v. Andrus, 13 Env't Rep. Cas. (BNA) 1266 (May 23, 1979), *aff'd on other grounds,* 657 F.2d 829 (6th Cir. 1981); Colorado River Water Conservation Dist. v. Andrus, Civ. No. 78-A-1191 (D. Colo. Dec. 28, 1981).

violator of the Act.[281] The purpose of requiring such notice to the Secretary is to enable him to initiate appropriate action against the alleged violator or, if he himself is the alleged violator, to correct the alleged violation. Although the statute specifies that such notice must be given at least 60 days in advance of commencing suit, many courts have not insisted on strict compliance with that requirement. Various justifications have been offered for disregarding this requirement. They include the newness of the statute,[282] compliance "with the spirit of the notice requirement,"[283] waiver by the defendants,[284] and the assertion that the citizen suit provision does not provide the exclusive remedy for violations of the Act.[285] The only case to hold that failure to comply with the notice requirement bars the suit was implicitly overruled by the court of appeals.[286] Thus, in practice, it appears that courts are willing to take a pragmatic approach to the notice requirement that balances such considerations as the likelihood that the violation may be voluntarily halted, the economy of judicial resources, and the urgency of the threat that the violation poses to a listed species.[287]

The final point about the Act's citizen suit provision is that it authorizes the award of attorneys' fees and other costs of litigation to any party whenever a court determines such award to be appropriate.[288] Thus successful plaintiffs are not automatically entitled to such awards, but neither are unsuccessful plaintiffs barred from them. In the *North Slope Borough* case, unsuccessful plaintiffs were initially awarded their costs and fees on the rationale that their suit, even though unsuccessful, was a "prudent and desirable effort to achieve an unfulfilled objective of the Act."[289] The court of appeals, however, denied the award on the grounds that the suit "was not so 'exceptional' and such a 'substantial contribution

---

[281] 16 U.S.C. §1540(g)(2) (Supp. V 1981), amended by 1982 Amendments §7(2).

[282] Sierra Club v. Froehlke, *supra* note 202.

[283] Village of Kaktovik v. Corps of Engineers, 12 Env't Rep. Cas. (BNA) 1740, 1744 (D. Alas. Dec. 29, 1978) (suit filed 42 days after notice).

[284] Fund for Animals v. Andrus, 11 Env't Rep. Cas. (BNA) 2189, 2199 (D. Minn. July 14 and Aug. 30, 1978).

[285] Libby Rod & Gun Club v. Poteat, 457 F. Supp. 1177, 1185 (D. Mont. 1978).

[286] Romero-Barcelo v. Brown, 478 F. Supp. 647, 691 (D.P.R. 1979), *vacated and remanded*, 643 F. 2d 835 (1st Cir. 1981), *rev'd sub nom.* Weinberger v. Romero-Barcelo, 456 U.S. 305 (1982).

[287] The 1982 Amendments waive the notice requirement altogether with respect to mandamus actions to compel a listing decision in the case of "an emergency posing a significant risk to the well-being of any species." 1982 Amendments §7(2)(B) (to be codified at 16 U.S.C. §1540(g)(2)(c)).

[288] 16 U.S.C. §1540(g)(4)(1976).

[289] North Slope Borough v. Andrus, 16 Env't Rep. Cas. (BNA) 2101, 2104 (D.C.C. May 5, 1981).

[] to the statutory goals' of the underlying acts that an award is appropriate."[290]

### Federalism Under the Endangered Species Act

When Congress passed the Marine Mammal Protection Act of 1972 and the Endangered Species Act of 1973, thus prohibiting the taking of all marine mammals and endangered species, it gave to the federal government a power that, with the few exceptions discussed in Chapter 4, had previously been exercised only by the states. In each Act, however, Congress intended to avoid ousting the states altogether from their established jurisdiction by creating a cooperative program in which both the states and the federal government would play important roles. Though only a little more than a year separated the two Acts, both the content and the manner of implementation of the cooperative programs they established differed quite markedly. In the preceding chapter, the state and federal relationship under the Marine Mammal Protection Act was described in detail.[291] Here the object will be to compare that relationship with the counterpart relationship established by the Endangered Species Act.

The first major difference between the two Acts was that the Endangered Species Act's preemption of state authority over taking was neither immediate nor total. Rather, the 1973 Act established a transition period of up to 15 months during which federal restrictions on taking of resident endangered and threatened species would be inapplicable.[292] In addition, it expressly permits the states to enforce laws or regulations pertaining to taking that are more restrictive than the exemptions or permits provided for in the Act.[293]

---

[290]Village of Kaktovik v. Watt, 17 Env't Rep. Cas. (BNA) 2097, 2098 (D.C. Cir. Oct. 1, 1982).

[291]See Chapter 11 at text accompanying notes 110–141.

[292]16 U.S.C. §1535(g) (1976). The statement in the text was made subject to three exceptions. The first of these, an exception so large as nearly to swallow the rule, provided that federal restrictions on taking were applicable, even during the transition period, to those species listed on Appendix I of the Convention or otherwise protected by international agreement. Although the Convention does not restrict the taking of any species on its various appendices, this exception was apparently designed to facilitate enforcement of the Convention's restrictions on exportation. A second exception allowed the federal restrictions on taking to become operative upon the request of a state. Id. §1535(g)(2)(B)(i). A final exception permitted the Secretary to impose them unilaterally for a limited period in emergency situations. Id. §1535(g)(2)(B)(ii).

[293]Id. §1535(f). This provision was intended to allow the state of Alaska to restrict the taking of endangered and threatened species by Alaskan natives who would otherwise be exempt from federal regulation. See H.R. Rep. No. 740, 93d Cong., 1st Sess. 27–28 (1973) and text accompanying notes 153–154 supra.

At the expiration of the transition period, the Act's restriction on taking become fully applicable to all listed species. However, like the Marine Mammal Protection Act, the 1973 Act offered the states an opportunity to continue to play a role in the management and conservation of resident endangered and threatened species and to receive federal financial assistance in carrying out that role. The mechanism for doing this is the signing of a "cooperative agreement."[294]

Cooperative agreements under the 1973 Act are unlike "cooperative arrangements" under the Marine Mammal Protection Act. The latter simply provide for delegation to the states of administration and enforcement of the federal act without entitling the states to receive federal matching grants.[295] Yet cooperative agreements are also unlike the more complex mechanism provided by the Marine Mammal Protection Act for approval of state laws relating to the taking of marine mammals. Under that mechanism, such state laws can be approved only after a lengthy and detailed administrative process involving a formal public hearing.[296] Cooperative agreements, on the other hand, are *required* to be signed whenever the Secretary determines, without any public hearing, informal rulemaking procedure, or even public notice, that a state's proposed program for conservation of endangered species meets certain criteria specified in section 6(c). The Act contemplates separate cooperative agreements with respect to plants and animals. The criteria for each are identical except that the authority to acquire habitat is a necessary element of a state program only with respect to animals.[297]

What the states receive in return for meeting the criteria specified in the Act is eligibility for federal financial assistance of up to three-fourths of the costs of approved programs.[298] That assistance is allocated among eligible states at the Secretary's discretion based upon certain criteria specified in the Act.[299] The states also receive a very limited exemption from the

---

[294] 16 U.S.C. §1535(c) (Supp. V 1981).

[295] *See* Chapter 11 at text accompanying note 113.

[296] *Id.* at text accompanying notes 129–139.

[297] *Compare* 16 U.S.C. §§1535(c)(1) and (2) (Supp. V 1981). Prior to the 1978 Amendments, section 6(c) appeared to contemplate cooperative agreements only with respect to animals.

[298] 16 U.S.C. §1535(d)(2) (1976), as amended by 1982 Amendments §3(1). Where two or more states have a common interest in one or more endangered or threatened species, they may jointly enter into an agreement with the Secretary for which the federal share of funding may be as high as 90 percent. *Id.* §3(2).

[299] The following factors are required to be taken into consideration by the Secretary:

(A) the international commitments of the United States to protect endangered species or threatened species;

otherwise applicable requirement that they obtain a federal permit before taking any protected species pursuant to their conservation programs.[300] Thus, while the procedures for gaining a state role under the Endangered Species Act are substantially simpler than under the Marine Mammal Protection Act, the substance of that role is much narrower.[301]

One of the more complex aspects of the relationship between the states and the federal government under the Act is the question of preemption of state authority over trade in listed species. Generally, section 6(f) prohibits the states from permitting what is prohibited by the Act or from prohibiting what is permitted by the Act.[302] Two decisions by two judges of the Eastern District Court of California have considered the validity under section 6(f) of a California law prohibiting the importation for commercial purposes, the possession with intent to sell, and the sale within the state of certain species, among them alligators, pythons, kangaroos, and elephants.[303] In *Fouke Co. v. Brown*, Judge Wilkens held that the California law had been preempted by section 6(f) insofar as it applied to the American alligator.[304] Two years later, however, Judge Ramirez, without citing the *Fouke* decision, upheld the California law as applied to the other three above-named species in *H.J. Justin & Sons, Inc. v. Brown*.[305] Of the two decisions, the latter is clearly the more carefully reasoned. In the author's view, however, neither is entirely correct.

The plaintiffs in *Fouke* were a non-California company engaged in the processing, tanning, and sale of alligator hides for which it held a federal permit issued under special threatened species regulations[306] and a

---

    (B) the readiness of a State to proceed with a conservation program consistent with the objectives and purposes of this Act;

    (C) the number of endangered species and threatened species within a State;

    (D) the potential for restoring endangered species and threatened species within a State; and

    (E) the relative urgency to initiate a program to restore and protect an endangered species or threatened species in terms of survival of the species.

16 U.S.C. §1535(d)(1) (1976).

[300]*See* 50 C.F.R. §§17.21(c)(5) and 17.31(b) (1981).

[301]In addition to cooperative agreements, the Act provides that the Secretary may enter into agreements with the states for the administration and management of areas established for the conservation of endangered and threatened species. 16 U.S.C. §1535(b) (1976).

[302]*Id.* §1535(f).

[303]Cal. Penal Code, §§653o and 653r (West).

[304]463 F. Supp. 1142 (E.D. Cal. 1979).

[305]Civ. S-80-941 RAR (E.D. Cal. Aug. 21, 1981).

[306]50 C.F.R. §17.42(a) (1980).

California company desirous of purchasing the former's products for subsequent fabrication and sale. Without any detailed analysis of the regulations or permit, Judge Wilkens concluded that the California law prohibited what had been permitted pursuant to the federal law and was therefore void under section 6(f).

In *Justin & Sons* the plaintiff was a boot fabricator who sought to make boots from the hides of African elephants, Indonesian pythons, and wallaby kangaroos. Since the last two of these are neither threatened nor endangered, the court was presented at the outset with the question of whether section 6(f) limits the authority of the states to restrict trade in such species. The plaintiff argued that under section 6(f) the only regulatory authority of the states that had not been preempted was with respect to indigenous species and that such authority had been altogether preempted with respect to nonindigenous species. Judge Ramirez took the first premise of this argument a step further, reasoning that section 6(f) worked *no* preemption of state authority over indigenous species.[307] As to nonindigenous species, he held that state authority was preempted only to the extent that it conflicted with the federal Act's provisions respecting threatened or endangered species. Since neither the Indonesian python nor the wallaby kangaroo is listed as threatened or endangered, he found no conflict with the federal Act and therefore no preemption of the state law.

The African elephant is listed, however, as a threatened species, and the plaintiff held a federal permit, issued under special threatened species regulations, authorizing him to sell its products in interstate commerce. Rather than follow the *Fouke* rationale and strike down the California law on that basis, however, Judge Ramirez chose instead to scrutinize the terms of the permit. One term conditioned the validity of the permit upon "strict observance of all applicable foreign, state, local, or other federal law."[308] Judge Ramirez reasoned that, although the Secretary of the Interior clearly had the legal authority to preempt state regulation by issuance of a permit, he had refrained from doing so, as evidenced by the condition quoted. Thus the California law was valid even with respect to the African elephant.

If Judge Ramirez was correct with respect to the African elephant, then the validity of Judge Wilkens's decision in *Fouke* concerning alligators is highly dubious. The special threatened species regulations applicable to alligators include a provision that prohibits permittees from violating "any State, Federal, or foreign laws concerning any hide, part, or product of

---

[307]This reasoning is implicit in the judge's concurrence with the defendant's interpretation of section 6(f), which effectively divided it into two parts: a first sentence applicable only to nonindigenous species and a final two sentences applicable only to indigenous species. *Justin & Sons,* slip opinion at 6.

[308]*Id.* at 14.

any species of the Order Crocodilia."[309] By parity of reasoning, this provision could be read to evidence a failure to preempt state regulation of alligators.

However dubious it may be that the interpretation placed upon the elephant permit condition by Judge Ramirez comports with the actual intent of the Department of the Interior, it at least enables the Department to correct the result administratively and obliges it to be quite specific about its intent when doing so. In the author's view, however, neither Judge Ramirez nor Judge Wilkins has properly understood section 6(f).

The distinction Judge Ramirez drew between indigenous and nonindigenous species was unconvincing and ultimately led him to the erroneous conclusion that state law can be preempted only with respect to nonindigenous species.[310] In fact, it is not the nature of the species but rather the nature of the activity regulated that determines whether federal preemption can occur. Thus, for *any* threatened or endangered species, the Secretary can preempt state regulatory authority over importation, exportation, and interstate or foreign commerce. He cannot, however, preempt state regulation of other activities, including, most notably, sales within the state. The legislative history clearly evidences an intent to preserve the authority of California and other states with similar laws to prohibit sales within their jurisdictions but not in interstate commerce.[311] Thus Judge Wilkens should have ruled in *Fouke* that California was without the authority to prohibit the importation of alligators or the sale thereof in interstate commerce but that it could continue to prohibit intrastate sales of alligators. The same rules should apply as well to elephant products if the Department of the Interior subsequently eliminates the permit condition to which Judge Ramirez attached so much significance.

The interpretation suggested here allows each part of section 6(f) to operate without resort to extrastatutory distinctions like that used by Judge Ramirez and appears consistent with the provision's legislative history. The only remaining inquiry in future cases like *Fouke* and *Justin & Sons*

---

[309]50 C.F.R. §17.42(a)(3)(iii)(C)(3) (1980).

[310]The statute itself does not refer to "indigenous" species. The second sentence of section 6(f) disclaims any intention to void state laws intended to conserve, or prohibiting the sale of, "migratory, resident, or introduced fish or wildlife," except as otherwise provided in the first sentence. The term "otherwise" clearly means that such "migratory, resident, or introduced" species, apparently equated by Judge Ramirez with "indigenous species," are subject to the preemptions specified by the first sentence. The second sentence thus serves the purpose of giving the states the express reassurance that they have not been preempted of *all* authority over listed wildlife within their borders. It does not, however, imply a broader preemption with respect to other wildlife than what is expressly defined in the first sentence.

[311]H.R. Rep. No. 412, 93d Cong., 1st Sess. 14 (1973).

will be whether the authority to preempt the operation of state law with respect to those activities subject to preemption has in fact been exercised.[312]

### The International Component

The final feature of the 1973 Act deserving mention is its international component. Besides implementing the Convention on International Trade in Endangered Species of Wild Fauna and Flora, it also directs the President to begin to implement, some three decades after its signing, the Convention on Nature Protection and Wildlife Preservation in the Western Hemisphere.[313] In addition, it directs the Secretary to encourage foreign nations to establish and carry out endangered species programs of their own and authorizes both financial assistance and the loan of federal wildlife personnel for such purposes.[314] Finally, it authorizes the Secretary to conduct law enforcement investigations and research abroad.[315]

Apart from these specific directives, the 1973 Act has an obvious impact on international wildlife protection through its prohibition of the importation of endangered and threatened species. Finally, although the Secretary of the Interior has proclaimed his lack of authority to designate critical habitat in foreign countries, section 7 requires that federal actions not jeopardize the continued existence of endangered or threatened species in foreign countries.[316]

The principal source of controversy was the 1977 decision by the Convention parties to add all unprotected species of cats to Appendix II. While an Appendix II listing does not preclude international commercial trade, it does require that the scientific authority of the country of export

---

[312]The recent decision to remove all trade restrictions on three threatened species of kangaroos, challenged unsuccessfully in Defenders of Wildlife v. Watt, *supra* at text accompanying notes 130–133, may present an interesting fact situation in which the California law will again be tested. The three species have apparently been retained on the threatened list because of the mistaken notion that doing so will facilitate prompt action if new information warrants the imposition of currently absent regulatory restrictions. See note 133, *supra*. If, as Judge Ramirez correctly held in *Justin & Sons*, the Act does not preempt state laws relating to unlisted species, it seems hard to justify the preemption of state laws relating to species retained on the threatened list for such minimal reasons. Yet that may be the result unless a court is willing to say that trade has not been "authorized" by such regulations in any affirmative sense and such affirmative authorization is necessary under section 6(f) to preempt the operation of state law.

[313]16 U.S.C. §1537(A)(e)(Supp. V 1981), as amended by 1982 Amendments §5(3). *See* the discussion in Chapter 10 at text accompanying notes 80–98.

[314]16 U.S.C. §1537(a), (c) (1976).

[315]*Id.* §1537(d).

[316]*See* note 266 and text accompanying note 111 *supra*.

determine that the export of an Appendix II specimen "will not be detrimental to the survival of that species."[317] The application of that standard to the export of bobcats from the United States was the focus of a 1981 decision of the United States Court of Appeals for the District of Columbia, *Defenders of Wildlife v. Endangered Species Scientific Authority*.[318]

The Endangered Species Scientific Authority was, until 1979, the designated "scientific authority" of the United States under the Convention.[319] In 1978 it published certain guidelines governing how it would make the "no detriment" determination required of it.[320] The guidelines identified population trend, total harvest, harvest distribution, and habitat evaluation information as the principal information bases upon which such determinations would be made. Applying those guidelines, the scientific authority approved the export in 1979 of bobcats taken in 34 states and the Navajo Nation.[321]

Defenders of Wildlife challenged both the guidelines and the decision to authorize export. The district court rejected most of the plaintiff's claims, enjoining export only from part or all of seven states. The court of appeals, in a decision reached after the export for the season in question was over, struck down the guidelines but remanded to the district court for a determination whether the administrative record, considered in light of the appellate court's decision, supported no detriment findings for any of the states in question.[322]

In the course of its decision, the court of appeals addressed a number of important questions. It rejected the plaintiff's claim that the listing of a species on Appendix II obligated no detriment findings with respect to each subspecies thereof prior to authorizing export.[323] The court also rejected the claim that state-by-state determinations were unlawful.[324] With respect to the challenged guidelines, however, the court determined, after first holding that the Convention provides a source of rights enforceable by private parties in court,[325] that they were unlawful because they did not require "(1) a reliable estimate of the number of bobcats and (2) informa-

---

[317]Convention, art. IV, §2.

[318]659 F.2d 168, (D.C. Cir.), *cert. denied*, 454 U.S. 963 (1981).

[319]*See* Exec. Order No. 11,911, 3 C.F.R. 112 (1976 Compilation), *reprinted in* 16 U.S.C. §1537 (1976).

[320]43 Fed. Reg. 15098 (April 10, 1978).

[321]44 Fed. Reg. 55540 (Sept. 26, 1979).

[322]659 F.2d at 183.

[323]*Id.* at 179–180.

[324]*Id.* at 180.

[325]*Id.* at 175. Interestingly, the court did not rely upon the express citizen suit provision of the Act in reaching this holding.

tion concerning the number of animals to be killed in the particular season."[326]

The court's bobcat decision led to an immediate major controversy. Critics of the decision charged that it placed impossibly onerous duties on state and federal decision makers and that such duties were likely to be imposed pursuant to other wildlife statutes as well. Neither fear appeared justified. First, the court of appeals expressly disavowed the need to have "some kind of head count," insisting instead only on "a reasonably accurate estimate."[327] Second, the requirement of reasonably accurate estimates has in fact not imposed insuperable burdens in other statutory contexts. For example, the Marine Mammal Protection Act mandates population estimates of overlapping and often very similar porpoise stocks distributed over several million square miles of the Pacific Ocean, and the administratively developed estimates have not been set aside by the courts.[328] Nonetheless, Congress in the 1982 Amendments nullified the court's decision by specifying that, in carrying out his responsibilities with respect to Appendix II species, the Secretary is neither required to make, nor may he require the states to make, population estimates.[329]

Thus far, the only other reported decision to address any aspect of the Convention was *Cayman Turtle Farm, Ltd. v. Andrus*.[330] There the court upheld certain threatened species regulations against a challenge that the regulations should have provided an exception for the plaintiff's captive-reared specimens. The court considered the narrow exception in the Convention for specimens of Appendix I species "bred in captivity"[331] and the restrictive definition of that term agreed upon by the Convention parties[332] in concluding that the challenged regulations were consistent with the limited exception and therefore lawful.[333]

A final development directly related to the Convention was the expansion by Congress in 1978 of the so-called "Pelly Amendment" to the Fishermen's Protective Act of 1967.[334] As described in the initial text, the

---

[326]*Id.* at 178.

[327]659 F.2d at 178.

[328]See the discussion of the tuna-porpoise controversy in Chapter 11.

[329]1982 Amendments §5(1) (to be codified at 16 U.S.C. §1537A(c)(2)).

[330]478 F. Supp. 125 (D.D.C. 1979), *aff'd without opinion* (D.C. Cir. Dec. 12, 1980).

[331]Convention, art. VII, §4.

[332]Proceedings of the Second Meeting of the Conference of the Parties, Conf. Doc. 2.12 (1979).

[333]478 F. Supp. at 131 n. 2. Even had the challenged regulations been more restrictive than required by the Convention, such "stricter domestic measures" are expressly authorized by Article XIV thereof. 478 F. Supp. at 131–132.

[334]22 U.S.C. §1978 (Supp. V 1981).

Pelly Amendment was originally enacted to reinforce whale conservation through the International Convention for the Regulation of Whaling[335] by authorizing the embargo of fish products from nations diminishing the effectiveness of that agreement or other international fishery conservation programs.[336] As amended in 1978, the provision was expanded to confer similar authority to embargo wildlife products from any country whose nationals are found by the Secretary of Commerce or the Interior to be "directly or indirectly... engaging in trade or taking which diminishes the effectiveness of any international program for endangered or threatened species."[337]

It is significant to note that, although the endangered species Convention itself only authorizes the regulation of international trade in wildlife, the broadened language of the Pelly Amendment requires the two Secretaries to consider whether trade *or taking* by foreign nationals diminishes the effectiveness of the Convention.[338] Thus excessive taking of a Convention-protected species could be a basis for sanctions under the Pelly Amendment even if the specimens taken do not subsequently enter international trade. If the taking or trade diminishes the effectiveness of the international program, the legislative history of the 1978 Amendments is clear that the Secretaries have a mandatory duty to certify that fact to the President, who then has the discretion to order a trade embargo.[339] To insure that the secretarial duty is not ignored or treated lightly, Congress reamended the provision in 1979 to require that the Secretaries "periodically monitor the activities of foreign nationals that may affect" relevant international programs, "promptly investigate" such activities as may be cause for certification to the President, and "promptly conclude; and reach a decision with respect to; any investigation."[340] Though the Pelly Amendment elsewhere authorizes the two Secretaries to promulgate regulations for the carrying out of their various functions,[341] they have yet to do so.

---

[335] December 2, 1946, 62 Stat. 1716, T.I.A.S. 1849.

[336] The term "international fishery conservation program" is defined broadly in the statute to encompass any multilateral agreement that applies to the United States and that has as its purpose the conservation or protection of the "living resources of the sea." 22 U.S.C. §1978(h)(3) (Supp. V 1981).

[337] *Id.* §1978(a)(2) (Supp. V 1981).

[338] The term "taking" is defined in the Pelly Amendment in the same broad way as the term "take" is defined in the Endangered Species Act. *See* 22 U.S.C. §1978(h)(7) (Supp. V 1981) and 16 U.S.C. §1532(19) (Supp. V 1981).

[339] H.R. Rep. No. 1029, 95th Cong., 2d Sess. 11 (1978), *reprinted in* 1978 U.S. Code Cong. & Ad. News 1768, 1775.

[340] 22 U.S.C. §1978(a)(3) (Supp. V 1981).

[341] *Id.* §1978(g).

Chapter **13**

# NEW DIRECTIONS IN THE CONSERVATION OF OCEAN FISHERIES

The most recent comprehensive federal wildlife statute is the Fishery Conservation and Management Act of 1976.[1] That Act, which became fully operational on March 1, 1977, attempts to establish a comprehensive regime of fisheries conservation in a 197-mile-wide zone contiguous to the United States. In the degree of planning it requires and in the mechanisms it establishes for the accomplishment of its goals, the Act introduces wholly new ideas not found elsewhere in the body of federal wildlife law. This chapter first describes the background of the Act and then analyzes its many complex provisions.

## BACKGROUND

By the beginning of the seventeenth century, the right of all nations to fish on the high seas had come to be recognized as a fundamental principle of international law.[2] Notwithstanding agreement on that general principle, there were often disputes as to whether specific areas constituted the "high seas" or the "territorial sea" of a particular coastal nation.[3] Until the

---

[1] 16 U.S.C. §§1801–1882 (1976 & Supp. V 1981), as amended by Act of June 1, 1982, Pub. L. No. 97-191, 96 Stat. 107.

[2] *See* S. Rep. No. 416, 94th Cong., 1st Sess. 5 (1976) (hereinafter referred to as Senate Report).

[3] Chapman, The Theory and Practice of International Fishery Development-Management, 7 San Diego L. Rev. 408 (1970).

present century, however, those disputes were generally localized matters involving neighboring states. With the development of modern fishing vessels capable of traveling great distances and capturing enormous quantities of fish, the problem became of greater international significance.

Adding to complexity of this problem was President Truman's declaration in 1945 that the United States would regard it as proper

> to establish conservation zones in those areas of the high seas contiguous to the coast of the United States wherein fishing activities have been or in the future may be developed and maintained on a substantial scale...and all fishing activities in such zones shall be subject to regulations and control.[4]

While Truman apparently intended only to proclaim a policy of seeking negotiated international agreements with other nations fishing in nearby waters, his remarks were interpreted by at least some to mean that the United States recognized the validity of a coastal nation unilaterally establishing a special "conservation zone" between its territorial waters and the high seas, in which it alone would regulate all fishing. Thus Chile promptly responded by declaring for itself a conservation zone extending out 200 miles from its coast.[5]

By 1958, the Truman proclamation had become an accepted tenet of international law. In that year, the International Conference on the Law of the Sea concluded a Convention on Fishing and Conservation of the Living Resources of the High Seas, which proclaimed that coastal nations have a "special interest in the maintenance of the productivity of the living resources in any area of the high seas adjacent to [their] territorial sea[s]."[6] The Convention further provided that, if efforts to reach a negotiated agreement with nations fishing in such adjacent areas are unsuccessful, the coastal nation may "adopt unilateral measures of conservation appropriate to any stock of fish or other marine resources."[7] The Convention did not, however, specify the size of the adjacent area in which such unilateral actions could be taken, nor did the simultaneously concluded Convention on the Territorial Sea and Contiguous Zone specify the limits of the territorial sea.[8]

---

[4]Presidential Proclamation No. 2667, 59 Stat. 884, 10 Fed. Reg. 12303 (Sept. 28, 1945).

[5]Senate Report at 6.

[6]April 29, 1958, [1966] 17 U.S.T. 138, T.I.A.S. No. 5969, art. 6, §1.

[7]Id. art. 7, §1.

[8]April 29, 1958, [1964] 15 U.S.T. 1606, T.I.A.S. No. 5639.

Notwithstanding the failure of the 1958 Conventions to establish precise boundaries, most nations claimed territorial seas of three miles and conservation zones of twelve miles. The United States did so with passage of the Bartlett Act, which prohibited any foreign vessel from fishing in the territorial sea or the contiguous fisheries zone of the United States or from taking any sedentary living resources from the continental shelf unless specifically so permitted by the Secretary of the Treasury or pursuant to international agreement.[9]

Reliance upon international agreements to prevent the overexploitation of the oceans' living resources had already been established as a basic tenet of United States policy since well before the Truman proclamation. The 1911 agreement pertaining to north Pacific fur seals and the 1931 convention on whaling, previously considered in Chapter 10, were among the earliest expressions of this policy.[10] Bilateral agreements with Canada pertaining to the Pacific halibut fishery and the sockeye salmon of the Fraser River system were concluded in 1923 and 1930 respectively.[11] The principal regulatory measure of the former is the establishment of an overall quota on the annual take of halibut. The latter attempts to allocate the quota it establishes equally between the two nations.

Since the Truman proclamation, however, the number of international fishing agreements to which the United States is a party has proliferated greatly. By 1974, some 20 such agreements were in existence.[12] These varied greatly in terms of the regulatory measures they authorized. Some, like the Convention for the Establishment of an Inter-American Tropical Tuna Commission, merely authorized an international commission to make nonbinding recommendations to member governments.[13] Others, like the International Convention for the High Seas Fisheries of the North Pacific Ocean, obligated particular nations to abstain from taking certain types of fish in particular areas.[14] Still others, like the International Convention for the Northwest Atlantic Fisheries, attempted to allocate the

---

[9]16 U.S.C. §§1081–1086 and 1091–1094 (1976) (repealed as of March 1, 1977).

[10]See Chapter 10 at text accompanying notes 9–30 and 36–58.

[11]The current version of the halibut agreement is known as the Convention for the Preservation of the Halibut Fishery of the North Pacific Ocean and Bering Sea, March 2, 1953, United States–Canada, 5 U.S.T. 5, T.I.A.S. No. 2900. It is implemented through the North Pacific Halibut Act, 16 U.S.C. §§772–772j (1976 & Supp. V 1981). The agreement pertaining to salmon of the Fraser River is known as the Convention for the Protection, Preservation, and Extension of the Sockeye Salmon Fishery of the Fraser River System, May 26, 1930, United States–Canada, 50 Stat. 1355, T.S. No. 918. It is implemented by the Sockeye Salmon or Pink Salmon Fishing Act of 1947, 16 U.S.C. §§776–776f (1976 & Supp. V 1981).

[12]For a listing, see Senate Report, app. I.

[13]May 31, 1949, 1 U.S.T. 230, T.I.A.S. No. 2044. The Convention is implemented by the Tuna Convention Act of 1950, 16 U.S.C. §§951–961 (1976).

[14]May 9, 1952, United States–Canada–Japan, 4 U.S.T. 380, T.I.A.S. No. 2786.

aggregate annual take of multiple species among more than a dozen participating nations.[15]

By the 1960s, it was evident that at least some of the international fishery agreements were failing in their principal aim of conserving fish. A variety of factors contributed to this failure. Enforcement of compliance with the terms of an agreement by the nationals of a signatory nation was generally left to that nation alone. Moreover, there was no means of enforcement whatever against nations who chose not to join the agreement. Few international agreements provided a mechanism for limiting entry into the fishery, thus encouraging overcapitalization and consequent political pressure for larger harvests than could be scientifically justified. Finally, sometimes the scientific data base was inadequate to assure that a given level of taking would not deplete the resource. This last problem was particularly acute when the fishery involved several interrelated stocks or species of fish.[16]

Because of the perceived failure of international agreements to conserve fish, a growing number of nations, particularly those with valuable fishing areas in nearby waters, began to assert ever broader claims to exclusive fishery zones. This trend, together with other emerging disputes concerning development of the ocean's resources, stimulated the United Nations to convene the Law of the Sea Conference in 1974 in an effort to resolve the many issues left unsettled by the 1958 Conventions. At that Conference and its subsequent session in 1975, a consensus appeared to emerge in favor of a uniform 12-mile territorial sea and 200-mile resource conservation zone for all coastal nations. The United States somewhat reluctantly joined in this view, provided that it be coupled with agreement on a number of other vigorously disputed issues.[17] As the Conference headed for its third session in 1976, it appeared doubtful that such overall agreement could be reached. Moreover, by that time some 36 coastal nations had declared exclusive fishing zones beyond 12 miles.[18] Meanwhile, the foreign fishing fleets just outside the 12-mile fisheries zone of the United States grew larger, and so did their harvest of fish.[19]

## THE ACT

Weary of the slow pace of international negotiation and alarmed at the impact on the domestic fishing industry of the growing foreign fleets,

---

[15]Feb. 8, 1949, [1950] 1 U.S.T. 477, T.I.A.S. No. 2089.

[16]Each of these problems is discussed in Chapman, *supra* note 3.

[17]*See* Senate Report at 8–9.

[18]Senate Report, app. II.

[19]*See* H.R. Rep. No. 445, 93d Cong., 1st Sess. 34–41 (1975) (hereinafter referred to as House Report).

Congress passed the Fishery Conservation and Management Act in the spring of 1976, just as the third session of the United Nations Law of the Sea Conference was opening. Its principal feature is the establishment of a 197-mile-wide exclusive fishery conservation zone contiguous to the territorial sea of the United States.[20] Within that zone, the Act asserts for the United States the exclusive management authority, not merely over all fish, but also over "all other forms of marine animal and plant life other than marine mammals, birds, and highly migratory species."[21] In addition, at all places outside the zone, except the recognized territorial sea or fishery conservation zone of a foreign nation, the Act claims for the United States the same exclusive authority over anadromous species of fish that spawn in its fresh or estuarine waters.[22] Finally, wherever the continental shelf extends beyond the conservation zone, the Act claims for the United States exclusive management authority over certain sedentary species found there.[23]

Probably more significant than the fact of claiming exclusive management authority over the various species within and beyond the zone is the Act's requirement that they be managed in accordance with comprehensive plans to be drawn up by newly created "Regional Fishery Management Councils," composed of both state and federal officials. In prescribing the mechanisms for the development of those plans and the

---

[20]16 U.S.C. §1811 (1976).

[21]*Id.* §§1802(6), 1812(1). The term "highly migratory species" is defined to mean those "species of tuna which, in the course of their life cycle, spawn and migrate over great distances in waters of the ocean." *Id.* §1802(14). This important exception was carved out for the domestic tuna industry, which is dependent upon access to waters within 200 miles of several Latin American nations. *See* House Report 42-43. *See also* Comment, The 200-Mile Exclusive Economic Zone: Death Knell for the American Tuna Industry, 13 San Diego L. Rev. 707 (1976).

[22]16 U.S.C. §1812(2)(1976). Literally, since the Act asserts exclusive United States jurisdiction over an anadromous "species" that spawns in the waters of the United States, this authority could be interpreted to extend to all stocks of any species that has at least one stock that spawns in the United States waters. The rationale that supports special treatment for anadromous fish is that the "host state" in which they spawn expends substantial sums to enhance their populations, thus giving it paramount rights to the fish wherever they may be found. *See* Senate Report at 23. Since the rationale clearly does not support a claim to jurisdiction over those stocks originating in the waters of other nations, it is unlikely that the literal interpretation suggested above will be adopted. One must ask why the Act requires respect for the fisheries zones of foreign nations when anadromous species spawned in United States waters enter those zones, yet refuses to acknowledge such zones for highly migratory tuna, which may never have been in United States waters.

[23]16 U.S.C. §§1802(4), 1812(3)(1976). The Act expressly identifies certain corals, crabs, mollusks, and sponges as "Continental Shelf fishery resources" and authorizes the Secretary of Commerce to add other species to that list if they are sedentary at their harvestable stage. *Id.* 1802(4).

substantive standards that they must meet, the Act breaks significant new ground in federal wildlife law.

## Procedures for the Development of Management Plans

Primary responsibility for the development of management plans rests with eight Regional Fishery Management Councils.[24] Each Council has authority over the fisheries seaward of the states comprising it.[25] The voting members of each Council include the principal official with marine fishery management responsibility from each state in the region, the regional director of the National Marine Fisheries Service for the geographic area concerned, and from four to twelve persons appointed by the Secretary of Commerce from lists of qualified individuals submitted to him by the governors of the states in the region.[26]

Each Council is charged with the responsibility of preparing and submitting to the Secretary a fishery management plan with respect to each fishery within its geographical area of authority.[27] If any fishery overlaps the geographical areas of authority of two or more Councils, the Secretary may designate one Council to prepare the plan or require that it be prepared jointly.[28] In the preparation of the plans, the Councils are required to conduct public hearings in the area concerned "so as to allow all interested persons an opportunity to be heard."[29]

---

[24]*Id.* §1852 (1976 & Supp. V 1981).

[25]Certain coastal states are represented on more than one Council. For example, Florida is included in both the South Atlantic and the Gulf Councils, which have jurisdiction over fisheries in the Atlantic Ocean and the gulf of Mexico, respectively. *Id.* §1852(a)(3), and (5). The "states" represented include the Virgin Islands, Puerto Rico, Guam, and American Samoa.

[26]The Act defines a "qualified individual" as one "who is knowledgeable or experienced with regard to the management, conservation, or recreational or commercial harvest, of the fishery resources of the geographic area concerned." *Id.* §1852(b)(1)(C)(ii). Each Council also includes, as nonvoting members, one representative each from the Fish and Wildlife Service, the Coast Guard, the Department of State, and the appropriate Marine Fisheries Commission, if any. *Id.* §1852(c)(1). The Pacific Council has an additional nonvoting member appointed by the Governor of Alaska. *Id.* §1852(c)(2).

[27]*Id.* §1852(h). The Act defines a "fishery" as "one or more stocks of fish which can be treated as a unit for purposes of conservation and management and which are identified on the basis of geographical, scientific, technical, recreational, and economic characteristics." *Id.* §1802(7)(1976). Applying that general definition in a particular fact situation may sometimes be difficult. For example, are one or several "fisheries" involved in the taking of salmon in the Pacific Northwest? Those salmon are taken for commercial, recreational, and subsistence purposes by commercial trolling, gill nets, reef nets, and purse seines.

[28]16 U.S.C. §1854(f)(1)(1976).

[29]*Id.* §1852(h)(3).

Upon receipt of any plan prepared by a Council, the Secretary must review it for conformity with the requirements of the Act and notify the Council within 60 days of his decision to approve, disapprove, or partially disapprove the plan.[30] If he approves the plan, he may proceed to implement it.[31] If he disapproves it in whole or in part, he must explain his reasons for doing so, make suggestions for improvement, and request that the Council submit a modified plan within 45 days.[32] If the Council fails to modify the plan in an appropriate fashion, the Secretary may himself prepare a plan.[33]

When the Secretary prepares a plan, he must transmit it to the appropriate Council for consideration and comment. The Council may recommend changes within 45 days, but after that period the Secretary may proceed to implement the plan.[34]

As a transition measure, the Act also provided that, if the Secretary of State notified the Secretary of Commerce that a foreign nation had submitted an application to participate in any fishery subject to the exclusive management jurisdiction of the United States, and if the Secretary of Commerce determined that no management plan would be prepared and implemented for that fishery before March 1, 1977, he could prepare a "preliminary fishery management plan."[35] The Act specifies no procedures for the development of such preliminary plans other than to require that any "interim regulations" that implement it must be

---

[30]*Id.* §1854(a). In carrying out his review, the Secretary is obligated to consult the Secretary of State with respect to foreign fishing and the Secretary of the department in which the Coast Guard is operating (*i.e.,* the Department of Transportation during peacetime or the Department of Defense during wartime) with respect to enforcement. *Id.* §1854(b).

[31]The implementation of management plans is discussed *infra* at text accompanying notes 56–63.

[32]16 U.S.C. §1854(a)(1976).

[33]*Id.* §1854(c)(1)(B). The Secretary may also prepare a plan if the Council fails altogether to submit a plan "after a reasonable period of time" for any fishery that "requires conservation and management." *Id.* §1854(c)(1)(A). Presumably, if the fishery does not "require" conservation and management, or if the Secretary chooses not to prepare a plan in such a situation, there will be no plan for that fishery, notwithstanding the Act's directive to the Councils to prepare a plan for "each fishery" in the areas of their authority. *See* text accompanying note 27 *supra.*

[34]*Id.* §1854(c)(2).

[35]*Id.* §1821(h)(1976 & Supp. V 1981). The Secretary of Commerce did not wait for notification from the Secretary of State to begin preparation of preliminary fishery management plans. Instead, in October 1976, he began preparation of preliminary plans for those fisheries "for which foreign nations may be expected to apply for permits to fish" and for which the Councils "may not be able to prepare and implement fishery management plans before March 1977." 41 Fed. Reg. 47570 (Oct. 29, 1976).

promulgated pursuant to the informal rulemaking procedures of the Administrative Procedure Act.[36] Once prepared, preliminary plans remain in effect until replaced by a management plan prepared in accordance with the procedures previously described.[37]

## The Content of Management Plans

All management plans, whether prepared by the Secretary or a Council, must incorporate "conservation and management" measures that comply with seven national standards set forth in the Act.[38] Paraphrased, those standards require that such measures: (1) prevent overfishing and assure an optimum yield from each fishery, (2) be based on the best scientific information available, (3) provide for the management of individual or interrelated stocks as a unit, (4) not discriminate between residents of different states, (5) promote efficiency, (6) allow for contingencies, and (7) minimize costs.[39] The Act directs the Secretary to establish guidelines based on these standards to assist in the development of the plans.[40]

The most important of these standards is the first.[41] To comply with it, each management plan must, in addition to describing the fishery involved and specifying certain data to be reported periodically, "assess and specify... the maximum sustainable yield and optimum yield" from the fishery and "the capacity and the extent to which fishing vessels of the United States, on an annual basis, will harvest the optimum yield."[42] Only that portion of the optimum yield which will not be harvested by fishing vessels of the United States can be made available to foreign fishermen.[43]

---

[36] 16 U.S.C. §1821(h)(1976 & Supp. V 1981).

[37] *Id.*

[38] 16 U.S.C. §1853(a)(1)(C)(1976). The Act defines "conservation and management" to include all measures "which are required to rebuild, restore, or maintain, and which are useful in rebuilding, restoring, or maintaining, any fishery resource *and the marine environment." Id.* §1802(2) (emphasis added). It remains to be resolved whether the italicized language authorizes the Councils or the Secretary to include in management plans conservation measures not directly related to the taking of fish. The guidelines issued by the Secretary to assist in the development of management plans encourage the Councils to "propose recommendations that the Secretary will convey" to appropriate authorities concerning problems of pollution and habitat degradation. 48 Fed. Reg. 7402, 7413 (Feb. 18, 1983) (to be codified at 50 C.F.R. §602.16(c)(2)(iv)).

[39] 16 U.S.C. §1851(a)(1976).

[40] *Id.* §1851(b). The current guidelines are published at 50 C.F.R. §§602.3–602.6 (1981) and at 48 Fed. Reg. 7402 (Feb. 18, 1983).

[41] The Senate Report at 31 describes the overfishing prohibition as "the most basic objective of fishery management."

[42] 16 U.S.C. §1853(a)(3), (4)(A)(1976).

[43] *Id.* §1853(a)(4)(B).

The determination of the "optimum yield" of a given fishery not only establishes the permissible level of foreign participation in that fishery, but it may also limit the participation of United States fishermen. That is, the Act allows any management plan to include "a system for limiting access to the fishery in order to achieve optimum yield."[44] In the development of such a system, the Act requires that the following factors be taken into account:

> (A) present participation in the fishery;
> (B) historical fishing practices in, and dependence on the fishery;
> (C) the economics of the fishery;
> (D) the capability of fishing vessels used in the fishery to engage in other fisheries;
> (E) the cultural and social framework relevant to the fishery; and
> (F) any other relevant consideration.[45]

In addition, under the national standards, any allocation of fishing privileges among United States fishermen must be:

> (A) fair and equitable to all such fishermen;
> (B) reasonably calculated to promote conservation; and
> (C) carried out in such manner that no particular individual, corporation, or other entity acquires an excessive share of such privileges.[46]

Since so very much hinges upon the determination of what will constitute the "optimum yield" of a given fishery, one might expect the Act to define that term with narrow particularity. Instead, one finds the following broad and general definition:

> The term "optimum", with respect to the yield from a fishery, means the amount of fish—
> (A) which will provide the greatest overall benefit to the Nation,

---

[44]*Id.* §1853(b)(6). If a plan is prepared by the Secretary, it may include a system for limiting access only if first approved by a majority of the voting members of the appropriate Council. *Id.* §1854(c)(3).

[45]*Id.* §1853(b)(6). By requiring consideration of these diverse factors, the Act illuminates the meaning of the national standard, which, while requiring "efficiency in the utilization of fishery resources," specifies that no conservation and management measure "shall have economic allocation as its sole purpose." *Id.* §1851(a)(5). Yet how can this standard be reconciled with the standard requiring all conservation and management measures to be "based upon the best scientific information available"? Note that the Secretary's guidelines define "scientific information" to include "information of a biological, ecological, economic, and sociological nature." 48 Fed. Reg. 7402, 7411 (to be codified at 50 C.F.R. §602.12(b)(1)).

[46]16 U.S.C. §1851(a)(4)(1976).

with particular reference to food production and recreational opportunities; and

(B) which is prescribed as such on the basis of the maximum sustainable yield from such fishery, as modified by any relevant economic, social or ecological factor.[47]

The use of concepts like "greatest overall benefit" and "relevant" social factors obviously vests the Councils and the Secretary with a great deal of discretion in making this crucial determination. The only element of the definition that is more or less capable of precise quantification is that of "maximum sustainable yield."[48] That element, however, is clearly intended to serve only as the point of departure for a determination of optimum yield.[49] How far the Councils or the Secretary choose to depart from that standard is probably beyond any effective judicial review.[50]

---

[47]*Id.* §1802(18).

[48]For a definition of maximum sustainable yield, see Chapter 10 at note 44.

[49]The House Report, at 47–48, contains the following useful discussion of "optimum sustainable yield," a term that was defined in essentially the same manner as the term "optimum yield" in the Act:

> Once the MSY of the fisheries or stock has been determined with reasonable scientific accuracy, and the same determination made with respect to the total biomass of an ocean area where many different, but inter-related fisheries occur, the developer of a management plan can begin to think in terms of the optimum sustainable yield (OSY). Thus while biologists in the past have tended to regard any unused surplus of a fishery as a waste, the resource manager may well determine that a surplus harvest below MSY will ultimately enhance not only the specific stock under management, but also the entire biomass. Conversely, the fisheries manager may determine that the surplus harvest of the entire biomass must be reduced substantially below MSY, in order to restore a valuable depleted stock which is taken incidentally to the harvesting of other species in this biomass....
>
> The preceding concepts relate to the biological well-being of the fishery. The concept of optimum sustainable yield is, however, broader than the consideration of the fish stocks and takes into account the economic well-being of the commercial fishermen, the interests of recreational fishermen, and the welfare of the nation and its consumers. The optimum sustainable yield of any given fishery or region will be a carefully defined deviation from MSY in order to respond to the unique problems of that fishery or region. It cannot be defined absolutely for all stocks of fish or groups of fishermen, and will require careful monitoring by the Regional Marine Fisheries Councils and the Secretary of Commerce. While optimum sustainable yield may have many complex components, their quantification should not be beyond the capability of the broad range of individuals who will serve on the Councils, supported by trained economists and marine biologists.

[50]*See* Maine v. Kreps, 563 F.2d 1043 (1st Cir. 1977), discussed at text accompanying notes 74–88 *infra*.

In addition to the various required provisions of management plans, the Act permits the inclusion of certain discretionary provisions in such plans. These include gear restrictions, area closures, size limitations, limitations on incidental catch, and other similar restrictions.[51] In addition, a plan may require United States fishing vessels to obtain a permit to participate in a particular fishery.[52] The fees that may be charged for such permits must be established by the Secretary and may not exceed the administrative costs incurred by him in their issuance.[53]

Because preliminary management plans were to be prepared on an abbreviated time schedule and were to serve only as interim measures pending promulgation of final management plans, the Act prescribed minimal substantive requirements for them. That is, they were required to contain preliminary descriptions of the fisheries involved and preliminary determinations of the optimum yields from those fisheries. They had also to provide for the periodic submission of certain data pertaining to the fishery and to require permits for foreign vessels engaged in the fishery. All these provisions, however, were required only "[t]o the extent practicable."[54] Finally, "to the extent necessary to prevent irreversible effects from overfishing," preliminary management plans may include conservation and management measures similar to those that may be included in final plans, but applicable solely to foreign fishing.[55]

## Promulgation of Regulations to Implement Management Plans

When a management plan containing the required substantive provisions has been prepared in accordance with the procedures previously described, the Secretary must publish it in the Federal Register together with any regulations that he proposes to promulgate in order to implement it.[56] He must allow at least 45 days for submission of written comments from interested persons, and he may also, at his discretion, hold a public hearing.[57] If, after consideration of those written comments and the views expressed at the hearing, the Secretary finds that the plan is consistent with the national standards and the other provisions of the Act, he may implement it by promulgating final regulations.[58]

---

[51] 16 U.S.C. §1853(b)(1976).
[52] Id. §1853(b)(1).
[53] Id. §1854(d).
[54] Id. §1821(h)(1976 & Supp. V 1981).
[55] Id. §1821(h)(4).
[56] Id. §1855(a)(Supp. V 1981).
[57] Id. §1855(b)(1976).
[58] Id. §1855(c).

Within 30 days after the Secretary's final regulations are promulgated, any person may file a petition for judicial review in any federal district court. Although a reviewing court may not enjoin implementation of challenged regulations pending completion of its review, it may declare them invalid if they are found to be "arbitrary and capricious" or if they were otherwise unlawfully promulgated.[59] The courts have split as to whether judicial review of implementing regulations can be obtained more than 30 days after their promulgation.[60] At least one court has interpreted the Act's prohibition of preliminary relief against challenged regulations as barring an expedited trial on the merits.[61]

In the event of an emergency, the Secretary may promulgate emergency regulations to implement a fishery management plan or amend regulations pertaining to an already implemented plan. Emergency regulations may be promulgated without observance of the procedures required for ordinary regulations but may remain in effect for no more than two successive periods of 45 days each.[62] Emergency regulations are subject to judicial review on the same basis as other regulations.[63]

## Fishery Management Planning and Judicial Review

Although the Act explicitly authorizes review only of implementing regulations, several courts have addressed the question whether review of the plans themselves is available. In *Washington Trollers Association v. Kreps,* the plaintiffs attacked the adequacy of the 1978 Pacific Salmon Fishery Management Plan.[64] They did not attack any specific provision of the implementing regulations, but rather the adequacy of the plan's summary of information used for its development. The district court reasoned that the express statutory provision for review of implementing regulations did "not necessarily preclude review of other actions by the Secretary."[65] Although the promulgation of regulations, and not the approval of the plan they implement, constitutes final agency action, "the

---

[59]*Id.* §1855(d).

[60]*Compare* United States v. Seafoam II, 528 F. Supp. 1133, 1138 (D. Alas. 1982) (30-day limitation inapplicable to a collateral attack on regulations as a defense in an enforcement proceeding) *with* Hanson v. Klutznick, 506 F. Supp. 582, 585–586 (D. Alas. 1981) (30-day limitation bars later direct challenge to regulations).

[61]Pacific Coast Federation of Fishermen's Ass'n v. Secretary of Commerce, 494 F. Supp. 626, 627 (N.D. Cal. 1980). *Contra,* Louisiana v. Baldridge, 538 F. Supp. 625, 628 (E.D. La. 1982).

[62]16 U.S.C. §1855(e)(1976).

[63]*See* S. Rep. No. 711, 94th Cong., 2d Sess. 55 (1976).

[64]466 F. Supp. 309 (W.D. Wash. 1979), *rev'd,* 645 F.2d 684 (9th Cir. 1981).

[65]466 F. Supp. at 312.

existence of a plan conforming to the statutory prerequisites is a condition to the Secretary's authority to promulgate regulations."[66] Accordingly, "the Court, in passing on the validity of the regulations, must review the plan to the extent necessary to determine whether the Secretary abused her discretion" in finding that the plan complies with the statute.[67] The correctness of this analysis was endorsed in *Pacific Coast Federation of Fishermen's Association v. Secretary of Commerce*, and in *Louisiana v. Baldridge*.[68]

On the merits of the claim in *Washington Trollers*, the district court upheld the adequacy of the challenged plan, reasoning that, "[s]o long as a good faith effort appears to have been made to supply available information, and no information material to the choices of management options made by the Secretary has been withheld, the Secretary's finding should be upheld."[69] A divided court of appeals reversed the decision of the district court, holding that, although the Act requires only that a summary of the information relied upon appear in the plan, the provisions of the Act encouraging public participation in the development of plans and regulations require that documents containing such information "must be reasonably available to the interested public."[70] Since there was disagreement as to the availability of such documents, the court of appeals concluded that there was an issue of fact to be resolved at trial, rendering the district court's award of summary judgment inappropriate.

The decision of the court of appeals in *Washington Trollers*, because it was limited to the availability of information relied upon in a plan, probably will not diminish the force of the decision in *Pacific Coast Federation*, which concerned the extent of economic analysis required in a plan. The plaintiffs in the latter case argued that "the Plan must include a detailed analysis of the fishing industry before any regulations can be adopted."[71] The court concluded that, if it could have appeared to the Secretary that the Regional Council "considered the economic impact of its Plan on the salmon fishing industry," the court would not disturb the Secretary's finding of plan adequacy.[72] Neither "in-depth forecasting" nor "a rigorous exercise in microeconomic analysis" is required, in the court's

---

[66]*Id.*

[67]*Id.*

[68]Both cases are cited in note 61 *supra.* Louisiana v. Baldridge stated in dictum that deviation from the Secretary's guidelines interpreting the national standards "is not actionable absent affirmative proof that the deviation makes the Secretary's approval arbitrary and capricious." 538 F. Supp. at 630 n. 1.

[69]466 F. Supp. at 313.

[70]645 F.2d at 686.

[71]494 F. Supp. at 629.

[72]*Id.* at 631.

view, because such tasks are "not fitted for an agency whose job is to weigh broad environmental and economic elements."[73]

The only major case thus far to have considered the conformity of a plan with the Act's national standards for fishery conservation and management is *Maine v. Kreps,* involving a challenge to the preliminary fishery management plan prepared by the Secretary of Commerce for the herring fishery of the Georges Bank area.[74] That fishery had been governed by the International Commission for the Northwest Atlantic Fisheries (ICNAF) prior to enactment of the FCMA.[75] The United States withdrew from ICNAF in late 1976, after ICNAF had set a herring quota of 33,000 metric tons for 1977, of which 12,000 tons was to be allocated to United States fishermen. In her preliminary plan, the Secretary of Commerce fixed 33,000 metric tons as the optimum yield of the fishery and allocated 21,000 metric tons to foreign fishermen, the precise allocation developed by ICNAF.

The plaintiffs alleged that the figure of 33,000 metric tons was an impermissibly high optimum yield in view of the status of the herring stock. Under the statute, the optimum yield of a fishery is to be based on the fishery's maximum sustainable yield (MSY), "as modified by any relevant economic, social, or ecological factor."[76] The evidence before the Secretary was that the stock size at which an MSY of 150,000 metric tons could be realized was 500,000 metric tons, whereas actual stock size was slightly below 225,000 metric tons, the level at which recruitment failure was feared.[77] The plaintiffs argued that under such circumstances the Secretary had a duty to fix the optimum yield at a level that would assure the quickest recovery of the stock by excluding all foreign fishing.[78]

The court rejected the plaintiffs' contention, noting that a harvest of 33,000 metric tons was expected to allow a 10 percent increase in the size of the stock. The court concluded that there was "nothing in the Act which

---

[73]*Id.*

[74]563 F.2d 1043 (1st Cir. 1977). The development of preliminary fishery management plans is discussed at text accompanying notes 35–37 *supra.*

[75]ICNAF was created by the International Convention for the Northwest Atlantic Fisheries, Feb. 8, 1949, 1 U.S.T. 477, T.I.A.S. No. 2089.

[76]16 U.S.C. §1802(18) (1976). *See* text accompanying notes 42–50 *supra.*

[77]Evidence introduced at trial indicated that actual stock size was slightly above the 225,000-metric-ton threshold level and that MSY might be realized at a stock size as low as 350,000 metric tons. *See* 563 F.2d at 1048 nn. 7 and 8.

[78]The plaintiffs clearly did not think that the duty to assure prompt stock recovery should be met at the expense of United States fishermen. They challenged the allocation of 12,000 metric tons for United States fishermen as too low, even though such fishermen had never taken more than 4,000 tons in any year since 1960. *Id.* at 1048.

prescribes a particular annual rate at which a below-par stock need be rebuilt."[79] Rather, the rate of stock growth was to reflect the Secretary's judgment of what would "provide the greatest overall benefit to the Nation."[80] The only limitation on that judgment that the court acknowledged was the proscription of the Act's first national standard against "overfishing."[81] Without any effort to explore the meaning of that standard, the court quickly dismissed it by noting that the proposed harvest could allow 10-percent stock growth.[82]

Though the court's cryptic discussion of "overfishing" makes analysis speculative, the opinion does allow the reader to draw some inferences about the scope of discretion allowed the Secretary. There were two benchmark population levels to which the court attached importance. One is the level at which MSY can be realized; the other is the level at which "recruitment failure" occurs. The former is explicitly tied to the statute; the latter is not. When a stock is below the level at which MSY can be realized, which the court characterized as "depleted,"[83] the court seemed to suggest that the overfishing standard requires that harvest levels be set as to allow at least some growth toward the MSY level. Though the court never said so explicitly, the required rate of stock growth will probably be greater (or, if not, it will at least require a greater justification) the closer the stock size is to the level of potential recruitment failure. Finally, the overfishing standard probably would prohibit setting a harvest level that kept or drove a stock below the latter level.

Although the court was unpersuaded that anything in the Act prohibits the Secretary from fixing an optimum yield figure for a depleted stock at a level that allows foreign fishing, the Act does require that the record of the Secretary's decision clearly "reflect a rational weighing" of the considerations that led to the decision.[84] Because the record before it did not do so, the court remanded the case to the district court and ordered the Secretary to supplement the record so as to explain the basis for her optimum yield decision.[85]

---

[79]*Id.* at 1048–1049.

[80]16 U.S.C. §1802(18)(A) (1976).

[81]*Id.* at §1851(a)(1).

[82]563 F.2d at 1049.

[83]*Id.* at 1052. Though the Act nowhere uses the term "depleted," the National Marine Fisheries Service has used it in the same sense as the court did. *See* H.R. Rep. No. 445, 94th Cong., 1st Sess. 95 (1975). For an alternative definition, see Beaver, Herring, Sardines, and Foreign Affairs: Determination of Optimum Yield Under the Fishery Conservation and Management Act of 1976, 53 Wash. L. Rev. 729, 747 n. 101 (1978).

[84]563 F.2d at 1049.

[85]*Id.* at 1051–1052.

Following remand, the Secretary supplemented the record with affidavits emphasizing the adverse impact that an abrupt termination of foreign fishing would have on international fisheries relations. The district court held that the affidavits demonstrated an adequate basis for the 33,000-metric-ton optimum yield figure, and the court of appeals affirmed.[86] The latter court concluded that, although historic fishing patterns and past scientific cooperation were factors explicitly required by the statute to be considered in allocating permissible foreign harvest among nations, they could also be taken into account in the initial setting of the optimum yield figure.[87] The potential significance of that decision, however, was diminished by the emphasis the court gave to the fact that "[t]his is a transitional year. What is reasonable now may be less so later."[88]

*Louisiana v. Baldridge*[89] involved a challenge to the Gulf of Mexico Fishery Management Council's shrimp management plan on the ground that one of its measures violated the Act's second national standard, requiring that management measures be based upon the best scientific information available.[90] The court rejected that contention on the basis that the scientific information proffered by the plaintiffs had previously been submitted to the Council and thus was part of the administrative record before the Secretary.[91] In effect, the court treated the requirement that management measures be "based upon" the best scientific information as requiring only that the Council and the Secretary "consider" such information. The court's decision effectively requires plaintiffs challenging plans on the basis of the second national standard to find new and better scientific information outside the administrative record. In the author's view, that is a dubious reading of the second standard.

## State and Federal Relations Under the Act

Among the most significant provisions of the Fishery Conservation and Management Act are those pertaining to state and federal relations. As has already been described, the principal responsibility for the development of comprehensive fishery management plans rests with the Act's unique Regional Councils. These hybrid state-federal agencies represent a signif-

---

[86]Maine v. Kreps, 563 F.2d 1052 (1st Cir. 1977).

[87]*Id.* at 1056.

[88]*Id.* For a discussion of foreign policy considerations as factors in the determination of optimum yield, see Beaver, *supra*, note 83, at 741–748.

[89]538 F. Supp. 625 (E.D. La. 1982).

[90]16 U.S.C. §1851(a)(2)(1976).

[91]538 F. Supp. at 629.

icant innovation having no clear counterpart elsewhere in federal wildlife law.[92]

Beyond the creation of wholly new planning institutions, the Act represents yet a third variation, among the three most recent major federal wildlife statutes, on the accommodation of respective state and federal roles. Unlike the Marine Mammal Protection Act and the Endangered Species Act of 1973, the Fisheries Management and Conservation Act does not include any automatic preemption of state regulatory authority over fishing. Rather, with the one exception discussed below, the Act preserves the right of the states to regulate all fishing within their boundaries.[93] It even provides that management plans established for fisheries within the conservation zone may incorporate "the relevant fishery conservation and management measures of the coastal States nearest to the fishery."[94]

The only time that a state may be preempted of its authority to regulate fishing within its boundaries is when the Secretary of Commerce, after notice and an opportunity for a full adversarial hearing, makes two findings: (1) that the fishing in a fishery covered by a fishery management plan "is engaged in predominantly within the fishery conservation zone and beyond such zone," and (2) that a state has taken or omitted to take any action, "the results of which will substantially and adversely affect the carrying out of such fishery management plan."[95] Thus the Secretary has the burden of establishing the legitimacy of federal authority. State authority is protected by what is in effect a presumption of validity. That presumption can be overcome, but only pursuant to rigorous adversarial procedures. If the Secretary makes the necessary findings, he must notify the state and the appropriate Council of his intention to regulate the fishery within the boundaries of the state pursuant to the plan and implementing regulations in effect.[96] At any time thereafter, the state may apply for reinstatement of its authority over the fishery, and, if the Secretary finds that the reasons for which he assumed that authority no longer prevail, he shall promptly terminate it.[97]

---

[92]The hybrid character of the Regional Councils creates uncertainties as to whether they should be regarded as "federal agencies" for purposes of the National Environmental Policy Act, section 7 of the Endangered Species Act, and other statutes. The Secretary's guidelines apparently conclude that they should be so regarded. *See* 50 C.F.R. §602.5(a)(6)(1981).

[93]16 U.S.C. §1856(a)(1976).

[94]*Id.* §1853(b)(5).

[95]*Id.* §1856(b)(1).

[96]The Secretary's regulatory authority does not extend to the internal waters of any state. *Id.*

[97]*Id.* §1856(b)(2).

Prior to the Act, a growing body of decisional law recognized the jurisdiction of coastal states to regulate fishing activities occurring beyond their traditional three-mile seaward boundaries.[98] By negative implication, section 306(a) of the Act preserves that state authority, concurrent with the exercise of federal authority, at least with respect to vessels "registered" under the laws of the state.[99] Because the Act fails to define the term "registered," however, the precise effects of the Act on state extraterritorial jurisdiction remain in doubt.[100]

In *People v. Weeren*, a California court enjoined state prosecution of a violation of state fishing law by owners of a federally documented vessel outside California's territorial waters.[101] The court held that the Act's provision prohibiting states from "directly or indirectly" regulating fishing in the fishery conservation zone precluded extraterritorial enforcement of state fishing laws despite the fact that defendants were California residents and had committed "preparatory acts" within the state. The court also held that the boating license that defendants had been issued by California did not constitute "registration" under California law. Similarly, in *United States v. Seafoam II*,[102] the federal district court for Alaska held that boats to which the state of Alaska had issued various fishing licenses were not "registered" under the laws of the state for purposes of making those boats "vessels of the United States" within the meaning of section 3(27) of the Act.[103] These cases leave fishermen and the states in considerable confusion as to the scope of state extraterritorial jurisdiction.[104]

---

[98]Skiriotes v. Florida, 313 U.S. 69 (1941) (state may assert jurisdiction over extraterritorial conduct of state citizens); Bayside Fish Flour Co. v. Gentry, 297 U.S. 422 (1936) (state may regulate fishing beyond its borders if the fish caught is later "landed" within the state); State v. Bundrant, 546 P.2d 530 (Alas.), *appeal dismissed sub nom.* Uri v. Alaska, 429 U.S. 806 (1976) (state may assert jurisdiction over fishery directly associated with the state).

[99]16 U.S.C. §1856(a) (1976) provides in part: "No State may directly or indirectly regulate any fishing which is engaged in by any fishing vessel outside its boundaries unless such vessel is registered under the laws of such State."

[100]For a discussion of congressional intent regarding abrogation of preexisting sources of state extraterritorial authority, see Comment, The Fishery Conservation and Management Act of 1976: State Regulation of Fishing Beyond the Territorial Sea, 31 Maine L. Rev. 303 (1980).

[101]93 Cal. App. 3d 541, 155 Cal. Rptr. 789 (1977).

[102]528 F. Supp. 1133 (D. Alas. 1982).

[103]16 U.S.C. §1802(27)(Supp. V 1981).

[104]Since the Act does not define registration, many states have sought to provide their own expansive definitions. Subsequent to enactment of the Act, Maine redefined registration to include any vessel "which is used to bring a marine organism into the State or its coastal waters." Me. Rev. Stat. Ann. Tit. 12 §6001 (36)

## The Regulation of Foreign Fishing

Even more important than the provisions of the Act pertaining to state and federal relations are its international ramifications. As of March 1, 1977, no foreign fishing was permitted in any fishery over which the United States had exclusive management authority unless conducted pursuant to an international agreement in effect on April 13, 1976, or pursuant to a "governing international fishery agreement" negotiated under the Act. In addition, all foreign fishing is required to be conducted in accordance with permits issued under the Act.[105]

The major significance of the above requirements is in the degree to which they interject the Congress into the realm of international fisheries negotiations. The "governing international fishery agreements" that the Act requires are not intended to be "treaties" in the constitutional sense, which are negotiated by the President and ratified by two-thirds of the Senate, but are instead "binding commitments" which become effective 60 days after being transmitted to Congress, provided that in that period neither house passes a resolution prohibiting their coming into force.[106]

The central feature of a governing international fishery agreement is its acknowledgment of the exclusive fishery management authority of the United States proclaimed in the Act. In addition, it obligates the foreign nation with which it is signed, and the owners and operators of the fishing vessels of that nation, to abide by all regulations issued by the Secretary under the Act, to cooperate in the enforcement of the Act, to permit authorized United States observers on board such vessels and to reimburse the United States for the cost of such observers, to pay all applicable permit fees, and to take no more than the share of the total allowable level of foreign fishing allocated to such nation.[107] The total allowable foreign catch for any fishery, which is that part of the optimum yield not harvested by United States vessels, is to be allocated by the Secretary of State, in

---

(Cum. Supp. 1978-1979). Similarly, Oregon redefined registration to include the licensing of boats for fishing. Or. Rev. Stat. §508.26. It is questionable whether Congress anticipated such broad concepts of registration. *See* note 100 *supra*. The laws relating to federal documentation of vessels were revised by the Vessel Documentation Act of 1980, Pub. L. No. 96-594, 94 Stat. 3453. That revision does not elucidate the ambiguity in the Act.

[105]16 U.S.C. §1821(a)(1976 & Supp. V 1981).

[106]*Id.* §§1821(c), 1823. When President Ford signed the Act into law, he expressed his concern about certain aspects of it, one of which was that it "purport[ed] to encroach upon the exclusive province of the Executive relative to matters under international negotiations." Statement by the President Upon Signing H.R. 200 into Law, *reprinted in* Senate Comm. on Commerce, 94th Cong., 2d Sess., A Legislative History of the Fishery Conservation and Management Act of 1976, at 35 (1976).

[107]16 U.S.C. §1821(c)(1976 & Supp. V 1981).

cooperation with the Secretary of Commerce, among foreign nations according to certain criteria specified in the Act.[108]

The Act has been amended on several different occasions in recent years to place additional restrictions on foreign fishing operations in the fishery conservation zone. For example, as a result of amendments in 1978, foreign vessels may receive at sea from United States vessels only that portion of the optimum yield of a particular fishery that exceeds the capacity of United States fish processors.[109] Amendments in 1979 required the Secretary of State to reduce, by at least 50 percent, the allocation of fish to any nation whose nationals, "directly or indirectly, are conducting fishing operations or engaging in trade or taking which diminishes the effectiveness of the International Convention for the Regulation of Whaling."[110] A package of 1980 amendments struck even more directly at foreign fishing in the fishery conservation zone.

The 1980 amendments were embodied in the American Fisheries Promotion Act.[111] As its name implies, the purpose of the 1980 Act was to promote the American fishing industry, principally at the expense of the foreign industry. Indeed, as it originated in the House, the legislation was designed to phase out foreign fishing in the fishery conservation zone altogether.[112] As finally passed, it provides a mechanism whereby the total allowable level of foreign fishing in a particular fishery may be reduced below that which would otherwise be available to foreigners by subtracting the anticipated harvest by United States vessels from the optimum yield.[113] It also requires substantially increased foreign fishing permit fees so that the aggregate of such fees represents that portion of the total cost of administering the Act that is equal to the portion of the total fish harvest in the fishery conservation zone taken by foreign vessels.[114] The 1980 Act also requires, subject to limited exceptions, that "a United States observer... be stationed aboard each foreign fishing vessel while that vessel is engaged in fishing within the fishery conservation zone."[115] The full cost of this

[108]*Id.* §1821(e).

[109]16 U.S.C. §§1824(b)(6), 1857(3)(Supp. V 1981).

[110]*Id.* §1821(e)(2)(i). This sanction is in addition to the discretionary sanctions that may be imposed under the Pelly Amendment to the Fishermen's Protective Act, discussed in Chapter 10.

[111]The Act is Part C of Title II of Pub. L. No. 96-561, 94 Stat. 3296.

[112]H.R. Rep. No. 1138, 96th Cong., 2d Sess. 45, *reprinted in* 1980 U.S. Code Cong. & Ad. News 6869, 6901.

[113]The complex formula by which the allowable foreign catch may be calculated under this alternative is set forth in 16 U.S.C. §1821(d) (Supp. V 1981).

[114]*Id.* §1824(b)(10).

[115]*Id.* §1821(i)(1). This requirement applies to all foreign fishing activities, whether carried out pursuant to a "Governing International Fishing Agreement" under section 201(c) of the Act, 16 U.S.C. §1821(c) (1976 & Supp. V 1981), or pursuant to a

observer coverage is to be borne by the foreign fishermen and is in addition to the permit fee previously described.[116]

When a governing international fishery agreement has been entered into with any foreign nation, that nation must submit to the Secretary of State an application for a permit for each of its fishing vessels that wishes to engage in any fishery under United States management authority.[117] The Secretary of State must publish the application in the Federal Register and promptly transmit copies of the same to the Secretary of Commerce, each appropriate Council, the Secretary of the department in which the Coast Guard is operating, and appropriate committees of Congress. Interested persons may submit comments to any Council to which the application has been transmitted. That Council in turn must consider those comments and submit its own comments to the Secretary of Commerce within 45 days.[118]

After considering the views of the Councils and consulting the Secretary of State and the Secretary of the department in which the Coast Guard is operating, the Secretary of Commerce may approve an application if it meets the requirements of the Act.[119] With respect to any approved application, he must establish conditions and restrictions that include the requirements of any applicable fishery management plan or preliminary fishery management plan.[120] If the foreign nation notifies the Secretary of State of its acceptance of such conditions and restrictions, it shall be issued permits for the vessels for which it had applied. The Secretary may charge "reasonable fees" for such permits.[121]

Although the Act permits foreign fishing to continue pursuant to any international agreement in effect on the date of enactment of the Act, it prohibits any such agreement (other than a treaty) from being renewed,

---

treaty such as the International Convention for the High Seas Fisheries of the North Pacific Ocean, May 9, 1952, United States–Canada–Japan, 4 U.S.T. 380, T.I.A.S. No. 2786.

[116] 16 U.S.C. §1821(i)(4) (Supp. V 1981). Full observer coverage of foreign vessels whose operations might result in the incidental taking of billfish was required by an earlier amendment in 1980. *Id.* §1827.

[117] *Id.* §1824(b)(1)(1976). Foreign "scientific research vessels" conducting "scientific research activity" do not require permits because they are not engaged in "fishing" under the Act. *See id.* §1802(10). However, any vessel "aiding or assisting one or more vessels at sea in the performance of any activity relating to fishing, including, but not limited to, preparation, supply, storage, refrigeration, transportation, or processing," is required to have a permit because it is deemed a "fishing vessel." *Id.* §1802(11).

[118] *Id.* §1824(b)(5).

[119] *Id.* §1824(b)(6)(Supp. V 1981).

[120] *Id.* §1824(b)(7).

[121] *Id.* §1824(10). Such fees are to total not less than seven percent of the ex vessel value of the total foreign harvest in the fishery zone during 1979. *Compare* the much

extended, or amended after June 1, 1976, unless it is in conformance with the requirements applicable to governing international fishing agreements.[122] As to treaties in effect on the date of enactment, the Act directs that they be renegotiated so as to make them consistent with the provisions of the Act. If they are not so renegotiated "within a reasonable period of time," the Act expresses the "sense of Congress" that the United States should withdraw from them.[123] Any fishing done by foreign vessels pursuant to existing international agreements after March 1, 1977, must be done pursuant to "registration permits."[124]

One other international aspect of the Act concerns the rights of United States fishermen to fish in fishery conservation zones of foreign nations. The Act directs the Secretary of State, upon the request of the Secretary of Commerce, to initiate negotiations for the purpose of securing for United States fishermen "equitable access" to the fisheries in such zones.[125] If the Secretary of State is unable to conclude such agreements "within a reasonable period of time," because of the refusal of the foreign nation to negotiate in good faith or to commence negotiations, he must certify that fact to the Secretary of the Treasury.[126] The Secretary of the Treasury is directed to take "necessary and appropriate" action immediately to prohibit the importation into the United States of all fish and fish products from the fishery involved.[127] The same restrictions on importation may be imposed if a United States vessel is seized by a foreign nation as a result of a claim of jurisdiction not recognized by the United States.[128]

While the Act reflects what Congress thought was the emerging international consensus of the Law of the Sea Conference, it recognizes that a comprehensive treaty may emerge from the Conference that differs from that apparent consensus. If that contingency occurs, the Act authorizes the Secretary, in consultation with the Secretary of State, to promulgate amendments to any regulations promulgated under the Act so as to conform those regulations to the terms of the treaty.[129]

---

more limited fees that may be charged United States fishermen. *See* text accompanying note 53 *supra*.

[122] 16 U.S.C. §1822(c)(1976).

[123] *Id.* §1822(b).

[124] *Id.* §1824(c).

[125] *Id.* §1822(a)(4).

[126] *Id.* §1825(a).

[127] *Id.* §1825(b)(1). If the Secretary of State so recommends, the Secretary of the Treasury shall also prohibit the importation of fish or fish products from other fisheries of the foreign nation.

[128] *Id.* §1825(a)(4)(C). For the criteria according to which the United States will refuse to recognize the claim of a foreign nation to a fishery conservation zone beyond its territorial sea, see *id.* §1822(e).

[129] *Id.* §1881.

## Prohibitions and Penalties

A formidable array of both civil and criminal penalties may be imposed for violations of the Act, of the regulations and permits issued under it, and of any applicable governing international fishery agreement. A civil penalty of $25,000 per day may be assessed for any such violation.[130] The same civil penalty may be assessed against anyone who ships, transports, offers for sale, sells, purchases, imports, exports, or has custody, control, or possession of any fish taken or retained in violation of the Act, the regulations and permits issued under it, and any applicable governing international agreement.[131]

Criminal penalties may be imposed against United States fishermen only if they refuse to permit an authorized enforcement officer on board their vessels, interfere with such officer's search and inspection activities, resist a lawful arrest, or interfere with the apprehension or arrest of another. Such offenses are punishable by a fine of not more than $50,000, or imprisonment for not more than six months, or both.[132] The maximum penalties are $100,000 and ten years imprisonment when such offenses are committed with the use of a dangerous weapon or in such a manner so as to place the enforcement officer in fear of imminent bodily injury.[133]

Criminal penalties of the same amounts may be imposed against foreign fishermen for the same offenses. In addition, it is a criminal offense for any foreign fisherman to engage in any fishery under the exclusive management authority of the United States, except in accordance with an applicable permit.[134] The maximum fines and prison terms for that offense are likewise $50,000 and six months, respectively.

In addition to the foregoing, any fishing vessel, including all of its gear and cargo, is subject to forfeiture for any of the above described violations.[135] Also subject to forfeiture are all fish taken or retained in connection with or as a result of any violation of the Act. The Act establishes a rebuttable presumption that all fish found on board a seized vessel were taken or retained in violation of the Act.[136]

Two cases in the United States district court for Alaska have decided several important issues pertaining to the enforcement of the Act. The first,

---

[130]*Id.* §1858(a).
[131]*Id.* §1857(1)(G).
[132]*Id.* §1859(a)(1), (b).
[133]*Id.* §1859(b).
[134]*Id.* §1859(a)(2).
[135]*Id.* §1860(a).
[136]*Id.* §1860(e).

*United States v. Tsuda Maru*,[137] held that section 311(b)(1)[138] authorizes warrantless inspections or searches of vessels fishing in the fishery conservation zone even without any probable cause to believe that the vessel had violated the Act and that such authorization was constitutionally permissible because the fishing industry was a "pervasively regulated" industry. The court emphasized the long history of regulation of the industry,[139] extending back to the first federal licensing laws of 1793. The second case, *United States v. Kaiyo Maru No. 53*, reached the same result, although it emphasized the comprehensive nature of federal regulation rather than the length of time that such regulation had been exercised.[140]

The *Kaiyo Maru* decision also answered several other enforcement questions. Section 204(b)(12) provides that a permit issued to a foreign vessel may be revoked or suspended if a civil penalty or criminal fine is unpaid and overdue for any violation of the FCMA by the vessel *or* if the vessel "has been used in the commission of any act prohibited by" it.[141] Although no civil or criminal penalties had been assessed against the vessel involved in that case, the United States promptly secured a forfeiture of its catch and then revoked its permit.[142] The court invalidated the permit revocation because it had not been preceded by a hearing to determine whether the vessel had been used to commit a prohibited act, a procedural requirement that the court concluded was mandated by the Act. In so holding, the court relied upon an unpersuasive fragment of legislative history and ignored the fact that a court hearing had been held in connection with the prior forfeiture.[143]

---

[137]470 F. Supp. 1223 (D. Alas. 1979).

[138]16 U.S.C. §1861(b)(1) (1976).

[139]470 F. Supp. at 1229.

[140]503 F. Supp. 1075 (D. Alas. 1980). The result in these two cases should be compared with the contrary holding under the Marine Mammal Protection Act in Balelo v. Klutznick, 519 F. Supp. 573 (S.D. Cal. 1981) *aff'd, without published opinion* (9th Cir., Jan. 5, 1983), *rehearing granted sub nom.* Balelo v. Baldridge, 706 F.2d 937 (9th Cir. 1983). *See* Chapter 11 at text accompanying notes 170–175.

[141]16 U.S.C. §1824(b)(12)(1976).

[142]503 F. Supp. at 1077.

[143]The court concluded that a hearing *was* required because a statement in the Conference Report said a hearing in connection with a permit revocation would *not* be required "since a hearing will already have been held to determine whether the vessel was in fact used in the commission of a prohibited act (or in the assessment of a civil penalty under section 308(a) or the imposition of a criminal penalty under section 309)." S. Conf. Rep. No. 711, 94th Cong., 2d Sess. 49, *reprinted in* 1976 U.S. Code Cong. & Ad. News 660, 672–673. The most plausible interpretation of this language is that the conferees were of the view that a hearing on civil or criminal penalties must precede *any* permit sanction. Such an interpretation, however, renders the word "or" in the above parenthetical meaning-

Other enforcement issues decided in *Kaiyo Maru* included the holding that under section 310(a)[144] the courts have discretion as to the extent of forfeiture to be applied against an offending vessel but are required to order total forfeiture of its unlawful catch.[145] The court also rejected the constitutional claims that the arrest of the vessel without prior notice and hearing was unlawful[146] and that the Act unlawfully discriminated against aliens.[147]

---

less and, more importantly, effectively changes the first "or" in section 204(b)(12), 16 U.S.C. §1824(b)(12)(1976), to "and." The court may, nonetheless, have felt compelled to reach its strained conclusion as a way of avoiding the issue of whether a hearing in such circumstances was constitutionally required.

[144]16 U.S.C. §1860(a) (1976).

[145]503 F. Supp. at 1088–1089.

[146]*Id.* at 1087–1088.

[147]*Id.* at 1086. The court relied upon the reasoning of United States v. Tsuda Maru, 479 F. Supp. 519 (D. Alas. 1979).

# Chapter **14**

# CONCLUSION

When the Supreme Court in the nineteenth century enunciated the principle that wildlife was not the private property of any individual or group of individuals, but rather the collective property of all the people, it established the paramount role of the government as public trustee in the task of wildlife conservation. Until the dawn of the present century, that role was filled almost exclusively by the states. Beginning in 1900, however, the federal government assumed an increasingly significant share of that role.

The expansion of the federal role in wildlife regulation occurred largely by a process of accretion. Federal wildlife regulation was initially limited to filling in the lacunae of state regulation, as with the Lacey Act,[1] or addressing narrowly defined wildlife exigencies as they arose. The result was a patchwork of federal laws having little apparent unity of purpose or method. As such, those laws were not immediately viewed by legal commentators as a coherent body of law worthy of analysis.

Over the course of this century, the nature of the federal role in wildlife regulation has changed significantly. The federal effort has shifted from prescribing narrowly circumscribed remedies for particularly acute problems to attempting to provide comprehensive programs that address more broadly based wildlife conservation needs. Notwithstanding that change in purpose, the basic regulatory tools of recent federal wildlife legislation are the same as those utilized in the earliest federal statutes. Restrictions on taking and commerce, acquisition of habitat, and mandatory consideration of wildlife impacts are all regulatory tools developed by the 1930s. The major innovation of recent legislation is in the effort to coordinate the use

---

[1]*See* Chapter 5.

of these various regulatory tools to achieve comprehensive programs of wildlife conservation and to establish a relationship between the states and the federal government capable of carrying out those programs.

There are more subtle changes that can be perceived in the evolution of federal wildlife law, changes that may in fact represent the most significant aspects of that evolution because they give tangible content to the nineteenth-century conception of wildlife as a public trust resource. The first of these changes is the steady expansion of the range of wildlife subject to legal protection. Initially, the exclusive focus of federal wildlife law was on game and other commercially valuable wildlife. The Lacey Act, although it applied literally to all "wild animals and birds," was understood to apply only to "game birds and fur bearing mammals."[2] In time, however, the need to expand the scope of its application became apparent, and it was amended to include all vertebrates, mollusks, and crustaceans. The Black Bass Act of 1926 underwent a similar process of expansion from an initial application to only two species of game fish, then to all game fish, and finally to all fish of any kind.[3] The culmination of this steady process of expansion of the range of wildlife subject to federal protection came with enactment of the Endangered Species Act of 1973, which defined the term "fish or wildlife" to include "any member of the animal kingdom,"[4] and which embraced the goal of preserving plant life as well. For the first time, the public trust responsibility of the government encompassed all forms of wild animal and plant life.

The expansion of the range of wildlife subject to federal protection is inextricably tied to a parallel expansion of the legally recognized values served by wildlife. If the term "wild animals and birds" meant only game birds and fur-bearing mammals at the time of the Lacey Act, it was precisely because the only value of wildlife that the law was prepared to recognize at that time was its value as a source of food or other commercial products. The nineteenth-century decisions of the Supreme Court upholding state wildlife regulation emphasize the importance of wildlife as a food resource, even suggesting at times that such regulation was proper only because wildlife had that importance.[5]

The Lacey Act provision authorizing the Secretary of Agriculture to prohibit the importation of animals injurious to agriculture or horticulture reflected the same limited understanding of the value of wildlife. The 1916 Convention with Great Britain for the Protection of Migratory Birds was likewise aimed primarily at protecting the nation's food resources.[6] Its

---

[2]See Chapter 5 at text accompanying note 19.

[3]16 U.S.C. §§851–856 (1976) (repealed 1981). See Chapter 5 at text note 23.

[4]16 U.S.C. §1532(8)(1976). See Chapter 12.

[5]See the cases discussed in Chapter 2 at text accompanying notes 8–34.

[6]See Chapter 4 at text accompanying notes 4–9.

preamble recites that the birds it seeks to protect "are of great value as a source of food or in destroying insects which are injurious to forests and forage plants...as well as to agricultural crops." Even the close seasons established by the Convention were made subject to an express exception whenever any of the otherwise protected birds "become[s] seriously injurious to agricultural or other interests in any particular community." The 1930s and 1940s witnessed the growing internalization of this fundamental objective as the United States entered into numerous bilateral and multilateral agreements designed to assure the sustained harvest of a commercially valuable wildlife resource.[7]

Gradually, however, new values came to be expressed through federal wildlife law. As wildlife became less significant as a food resource, and hunting and fishing became primarily recreational activities, acts like the Migratory Bird Treaty Act shifted their focus from preserving a food supply to regulating a recreational activity, even without the need for legislative amendment.[8] Moreover, new legislation expressly embraced wholly new purposes. The Bald Eagle Protection Act of 1940, for example, was a direct recognition of the need to preserve an animal as a symbol of the nation.[9] The symbolic value of wildlife was further affirmed in the Wild Free-Roaming Horses and Burros Act.[10] In 1960, the Lacey Act was amended so as to prohibit the importation into the United States of not only those animals determined to be injurious to agriculture and horticulture, but also those determined to be injurious "to wildlife or the wildlife resources of the United States," thus recognizing the protection of native wildlife as a worthy end in and of itself.[11]

The culmination of this process of expanding wildlife value can also be seen in the Endangered Species Act of 1973. Its statement of congressional findings declares that endangered wildlife "are of esthetic, ecological, educational, historical, recreational, and scientific value to the Nation and its people."[12] This articulation is significant because it represents the most comprehensive statement of the diverse values that wildlife represents, and because it encompasses those values within the purposes to be served by federal wildlife law. Most importantly, it recognizes the obligation of the government, as a public trustee of the nation's wildlife resources, to protect its many diverse values.

---

[7]See Chapter 10.

[8]16 U.S.C. §§703-711 (1976 & Supp. V 1981). See Chapter 4 at text accompanying notes 44-115.

[9]16 U.S.C. §§668-668d (1976 & Supp. V 1981). See Chapter 4 at text accompanying notes 116-166.

[10]16 U.S.C. §§1331-1340 (1976 & Supp. V 1981). See Chapter 4 at text accompanying notes 167-198 and Chapter 6 at text accompanying notes 233-267.

[11]18 U.S.C. §42(a)(1)(1976). See Chapter 5 at text accompanying notes 63-64.

[12]16 U.S.C. §1531(a)(3)(1976).

Yet another trend evident in the evolution of federal wildlife law is the mandating of new goals for the management of wildlife. Nowhere is this more forcefully presented than in the Marine Mammal Protection Act, which signals a turning away from species-oriented and harvest-oriented management toward ecosystem management.[13] This wholly new mandate of federal wildlife law, by implicitly positing that a well-balanced ecosystem offers the greatest potential for good to the greatest variety of wildlife, furthers the trend of expanding the scope of wildlife within the protection of law. Moreover, it necessarily assumes that a healthy ecosystem offers the best chance of achieving the maximum satisfaction of the diverse interests now recognized as being properly served by wildlife law. Whether the new management concept introduced in the Marine Mammal Protection Act, that of "optimum sustainable population," will prove to be a lasting formulation is as yet uncertain.[14] What is not uncertain, however, is that the purposes it was designed to serve will continue to shape federal wildlife law.

The expansion of the various wildlife values recognized by federal wildlife law, and of the meaning of the very term "wildlife," is also both a cause and a result of yet another clearly discernible trend, the opening up of that body of law to the interested citizenry. If the concept of wildlife as a public trust resource has any meaning at all, it is that the views of the public must be fully taken into account in all decisions affecting the use of that resource.[15] The Marine Mammal Protection Act, the Endangered Species Act of 1973, and the Fishery Conservation and Management Act of 1976[16] permit and encourage the active participation of the public in their implementation in a host of ways, including public hearings, informal rulemaking proceedings, and express provision for judicial review. The result has been to bring wildlife law squarely into the domain of administrative law, thus leading ultimately to an expanded role for the judiciary in overseeing it.

While the courts have had a long history of adjudicating disputes between the states and the federal government over the constitutional limits of their respective wildlife authorities, frequent judicial oversight of the actual implementation of wildlife policies has been much more recent. As federal legislation has imposed increasingly detailed standards for wildlife

---

[13]16 U.S.C. §§1361–1362, 1371–1384, and 1401–1407 (1976 & Supp. V 1981). *See* Chapter 11.

[14]*See* Chapter 11 at text accompanying notes 48–69.

[15]*See* Sax, The Public Trust Doctrine in Natural Resource Law: Effective Judicial Intervention, 68 Mich. L. Rev. 471, 558–559 (1970).

[16]16 U.S.C. §§1801–1882 (1976 & Supp. V 1981).

administrators and federal agencies to heed[17] and conferred ever greater opportunity for citizens to participate in their implementation, the judiciary has assumed a new and important role. The courts have not been reluctant to enforce actively the substantive and procedural duties that recent federal wildlife legislation imposes.

The active intervention of the courts in the administration of wildlife laws has in turn thrown back to Congress the task of fine tuning the broad regulatory standards that heretofore have been the exclusive province of federal wildlife agencies. Nowhere is this better illustrated than in recent amendments to the Endangered Species Act and the Marine Mammal Protection Act. Court decisions addressing problems unforeseen or inadequately considered in Congress's initial delegation of broad authority under those statutes have necessitated closer congressional scrutiny not only of the ends that they are to serve but also of the means by which they are to attain them.

Ultimately, the ability of federal wildlife law to achieve the goal of wildlife conservation will be limited by the fact that the well being of wildlife is vitally affected by a host of activities, the regulation of which has not traditionally been thought to be included within the compass of wildlife law. Efforts to extend the boundaries of wildlife law to encompass regulation of those activities, such as by way of the Fish and Wildlife Coordination Act[18] and section 7 of the Endangered Species Act of 1973,[19] have had only limited applicability and have met with only mixed success. Yet, unless those and similar measures are extended and made more effective, the ultimate well being of wildlife will be decided by factors other than wildlife law.

---

[17] One of the standards common to all recent comprehensive federal wildlife statutes is the requirement that management decisions be based on the "best scientific evidence available." Judicial enforcement of that standard may require that courts be the ultimate arbiters of issues of scientific controversy. Courts are, of course, already required to do this in many other environmental areas. Some observers have called for a specialized "science court" to resolve such controversies. *See* Task Force of the Presidential Advisory Group on Anticipated Advances in Science and Technology, The Science Court Experiment: An Interim Report, 193 Science 653 (Aug. 20, 1976).

[18] 16 U.S.C. §§661–667e (1976). *See* Chapter 7.

[19] 16 U.S.C. §1536 (1976 & Supp. V 1981). *See* Chapter 12.

# TABLE OF CASES

Bayside Fish Flour Co. v. Gentry, 297 U.S. 422 (1936).

Biderman v. Secretary of Interior, 7 Env't Rep. Cas. (BNA) 1279 (E.D.N.Y.) *aff'd sub nom.* Biderman v. Morton, 5 Envtl. L. Rep. (Envtl. L. Inst.) 20027 (2d Cir. 1974).

Bishop v. United States, 126 F. Supp. 449 (Ct. Cl. 1954).

Bogle v. White, 61 F.2d 930 (5th Cir. 1932).

Brown v. Anderson, 202 F. Supp. 96 (D. Alas. 1962).

California v. Bergland, 483 F. Supp. 465 (E.D. Cal. 1980), *aff'd in part, rev'd in part sub nom.* California v. Block, 690 F.2d 753 (9th Cir. 1982).

California v. S.S. Bournemouth, 307 F. Supp. 922 (C.D. Cal. 1969), *judgment granted* 318 F. Supp. 389 (C.D. Cal. 1970).

California v. Sierra Club, 451 U.S. 287 (1981).

California v. Watt, 683 F.2d 1253 (9th Cir. 1982).

Calvert Cliffs Coordinating Committee v. AEC, 449 F.2d 1109 (D.C. Cir. 1971).

Cameron Parish Police Jury v. Hickel, 302 F. Supp. 689 (W.D. La. 1969).

Cape Henry Bird Club v. Laird, 359 F. Supp. 404 (W.D. Va.), *aff'd,* 484 F.2d 453 (4th Cir. 1973).

Cappaert v. United States, 426 U.S. 128 (1976).

Carpenter v. Andrus, 485 F. Supp. 320 (D. Del. 1980).

Cayman Turtle Farm, Ltd. v. Andrus, 478 F. Supp. 125 (D.D.C. 1979), *aff'd without opinion* (D.C. Cir. Dec. 12, 1980).

Cerritos Gun Club v. Hall, 96 F.2d 620 (9th Cir. 1938).

Chalk v. United States, 114 F.2d 207 (4th Cir. 1940).

Choctaw Nation v. United States, 119 U.S. 1 (1886).

Chrysler Corp. v. Brown, 441 U.S. 281 (1979).

Citizens Committee for the Columbia River v. Callaway, 494 F.2d 124 (9th Cir. 1974).

City of Milwaukee v. Illinois, 451 U.S. 304 (1981).

City of Murray v. Kentucky, 13 Env't Rep. Cas. (BNA) 1558 (Ct. App. Ky. 1979).

Clemons v. United States, 245 F.2d 298 (6th Cir. 1957).

Colorado River Water Conservation District v. Andrus, 476 F. Supp. 966 (D. Colo. 1979).

Colorado River Water Conservation District v. Andrus, Civ. No. 78-A-1191 (D. Colo. Dec. 28, 1981).

Committee for Humane Legislation v. Kreps, No. 77-0564 (D.D.C. June 30, 1977).

Committee for Humane Legislation v. Richardson, 540 F.2d 1141 (D.C. Cir. 1976), *aff'g* 414 F. Supp. 297 (D.D.C.).

Commonwealth Edison Co. v. Montana, 453 U.S. 609 (1981).

Commonwealth of Puerto Rico v. SS Zoe Colocotroni, 658 F.2d 652 (1st Cir. 1980), *cert. denied,* 450 U.S. 912 (1981).

Commonwealth v. Agway, Inc., 210 Pa. Super. 150, 232 A.2d 69 (1967).

Connor v. Andrus, 453 F. Supp. 1037 (W.D. Tex. 1978).

Conservation Law Foundation v. Andrus, 623 F.2d 712 (1st Cir. 1979).

Cook v. State, 192 Wash. 602, 74 P.2d 199 (1937).

County of Trinity v. Andrus, 438 F. Supp. 1368 (E.D. Cal. 1977).

Coupland v. Morton, 5 Envtl. L. Rep. (Envtl. L. Inst.) 20507 (4th Cir. July 7, 1975).

Environmental Defense Fund v. Ruckelshaus, 439 F.2d 584 (D.C. Cir. 1971).

Environmental Defense Fund v. Watt, 18 Env't Rep. Cas. (BNA) 1336 (E.D.N.Y. Oct. 22, 1982).

Flood v. Kuhn, 407 U.S. 258 (1972).

Foster-Fountain Packing Company v. Haydel, 278 U.S. 1 (1928).

Fouke Co. v. Brown, 463 F. Supp. 1142 (E.D. Cal. 1979).

Fouke Co. v. Mandel, 386 F. Supp. 1341 (D. Md. 1974).

Fund for Animals v. Andrus, 11 Env't Rep. Cas. (BNA) 2189 (D. Minn. July 14 and Aug. 30, 1978).

Fund for Animals v. Kreps, 9 Env't Rep. Cas. (BNA) 1880 (D.C. Cir. March 8, 1977).

Fund for Animals v. Frizzell, 530 F.2d 982 (D.C. Cir. 1976).

Fund for Animals v. Morton, Civil No. 74-1581 (D.N.J. 1974).

Gandt v. Hardin, Civil No. 1334 (W.D. Mich., Dec. 11, 1969).

Geer v. Connecticut, 161 U.S. 519 (1896).

Globe Fur Dying Corp. v. United States, 12 Env't Rep. Cas. (BNA) 1926 (D.D.C. Nov. 16, 1978).

Glover River Organization v. Department of Interior, 675 F.2d 251 (10th Cir. 1982).

Grindstone Butte Project v. Kleppe, 638 F.2d 100 (9th Cir. 1981), cert. denied, 454 U.S. 965 (1982).

Gulf Oil Corp. v. Morton, 493 F.2d 141 (9th Cir. 1973), modified on rehearing, 4 Envtl. L. Rep. (Envtl. L. Inst.) 20377 (9th Cir. 1974).

H.J. Justin & Sons, Inc. v. Brown, Civ. S-80-941 RAR (E.D. Cal. Aug. 21, 1981).

Haavik v. Alaska Packers Association, 263 U.S. 510 (1924).

Hanson v. Klutznick, 506 F. Supp. 582 (D. Alas. 1981).

Hill v. TVA, 419 F. Supp. 753 (E.D. Tenn. 1976).

Hopson v. Kreps, 622 F.2d 1375 (9th Cir. 1980).

Hughes v. Oklahoma, 441 U.S. 322 (1979).

Humane Society of the United States v. Morton, Civil No. 73-1566, (D.C. Cir., July 31, 1974).

Humane Society of the United States v. Udall, Civil No. 2158-68 (D.D.C. 1968).

Humane Society of the United States v. Watt, 551 F. Supp. 1310 (D.D.C. 1982).

Hunt v. United States, 278 U.S. 96 (1928).

In re Steuart Transportation Co., 495 F. Supp. 38 (E.D. Va. 1980).

Izaak Walton League of America v. St. Clair, 353 F. Supp. 698 (D. Minn. 1973), rev'd, 497 F.2d 849 (8th Cir. 1974).

Just v. Marinette County, 56 Wis. 2d 7, 201 N.W.2d 761 (1972).

Kisner v. Butz, 350 F. Supp. 310 (N.D.W. Va. 1972).

Kittitas Reclamation District v. Sunnyside Irrigation District, Civ. No. 21 (E.D. Wash. Nov. 28, 1980).

Kleppe v. New Mexico, 426 U.S. 529 (1976).

Lansden v. Hart, 168 F.2d 409 (7th Cir.), cert. denied, 335 U.S. 858 (1948).

Lansden v. Hart, 180 F.2d 679, (7th Cir.), cert. denied, 340 U.S. 824 (1951).

Leo Sheep Co. v. United States, 440 U.S. 668 (1979).

Libby Rod & Gun Club v. Poteat, 457 F. Supp. 1177 (D. Mont. 1978).

Lone Wolf v. Hitchcock, 187 U.S. 553 (1903).

Louisiana v. Baldridge, 538 F. Supp. 625 (E.D. La. 1982).

Lynden Transport, Inc. v. Alaska, 532 P.2d 700 (Alas. 1975).

State v. Jersey Central Power & Light Co., 69 N.J. 102, 351 A.2d 337 (1976).
State v. Dickinson Cheese Co., 200 N.W.2d 59 (N.D. 1972).
State v. McKinnon, 153 Me. 15, 133 A.2d 885 (1957).
State v. Shattuck, 96 Minn. 45, 104 N.W. 719 (1905).
Stryker's Bay Neighborhood Council, Inc. v. Karlen, 444 U.S. 223 (1980).
Sun Enterprises, Ltd. v. Train, 532 F.2d 280 (1st Cir. 1976).
Swan Lake Hunting Club v. United States, 381 F.2d 238 (5th Cir. 1967).
Takahashi v. Fish and Game Commission, 334 U.S. 410 (1948).
TVA v. Hill, 437 U.S. 153 (1978).
TVA v. Hill, 549 F.2d 1064 (6th Cir. 1977).
Tennessee *ex rel.* Goodrich v. Riggan, Tenn. Ct. of App. Western Section (Aug. 31, 1976).
Texaco v. Andrus, 11 Envtl. L. Rep. (Envtl. L. Inst.) 20179 (D.D.C. Aug. 15, 1980).
Texas Committee on Natural Resources v. Alexander, 12 Env't Rep. Cas. (BNA) 1676 (E.D. Tex. Dec. 8, 1978).
Texas Committee on Natural Resources v. Butz, 433 F. Supp. 1235 (E.D. Tex. 1976), *rev'd sub nom.* Texas Committee on Natural Resources v. Bergland, 573 F.2d 201 (5th Cir. 1978).
The Abby Dodge, 223 U.S. 166 (1912).
Thornton v. United States, 271 U.S. 414 (1926).
Toomer v. Witsell, 334 U.S. 385 (1948).
Train v. Natural Resources Defense Council, 421 U.S. 60 (1975).
Trustees for Alaska v. Watt, 524 F. Supp. 1303 (D. Alas. 1981), *aff'd*, 690 F.2d 1279 (9th Cir. 1982).
Tulee v. Washington, 315 U.S. 681 (1942).
Udall v. FPC, 387 U.S. 428 (1967).
Udall v. Wisconsin, 306 F.2d 790 (D.C. Cir. 1962), *cert. denied*, 371 U.S. 969 (1963).
United States v. Adair, 478 F. Supp. 336 (D. Ore. 1979).
United States v. Albrecht, 496 F.2d 906 (8th Cir. 1974).
United States v. Allard, 397 F. Supp. 429 (D. Mont. 1975).
United States v. Anderson, No. 3643 (E.D. Wash. July 23, 1979).
United States v. Brown, 552 F.2d 817 (8th Cir. 1977).
United States v. Bryson, 414 F. Supp. 1068 (D. Del. 1976).
United States v. Bullock, 579 F.2d 116 (8th Cir. 1978).
United States v. Byrnes, 644 F.2d 107 (2nd Cir. 1981).
United States v. Cain, 454 F.2d 1285 (7th Cir. 1972).
United States v. Christiansen, 504 F. Supp. 364 (D. Nev. 1980).
United States v. Conners, 606 F.2d 269 (10th Cir. 1979).
United States v. Corbin Farm Service, 444 F. Supp. 510 (E.D. Cal.), *aff'd*, 578 F.2d 259 (9th Cir. 1978).
United States v. Cutler, 37 F. Supp. 724 (D. Idaho 1941).
United States v. Decker, 600 F.2d 733 (9th Cir.), *cert. denied*, 444 U.S. 855 (1979).
United States v. Delahoussaye, 573 F.2d 910 (5th Cir. 1978).
United States v. FMC Corp., 572 F.2d 902 (2nd Cir. 1978).
United States v. Fifty-three (53) Eclectus Parrots, 685 F.2d 1131 (9th Cir. 1982).
United States v. Fryberg, 622 F.2d 1010 (9th Cir. 1980).

Vermont Yankee Nuclear Power Corp. v. NRDC, 435 U.S. 519 (1978).

Village of Kaktovik v. Corps of Engineers, 12 Env't Rep. Cas. (BNA) 1740 (D. Alas. Dec. 29, 1978).

Village of Kaktovik v. Watt, 17 Env't Rep. Cas. (BNA) 2097 (D.C. Cir. Oct. 1, 1982).

Ward v. Race Horse, 163 U.S. 504 (1896).

Washington State Commercial Passenger Fishing Vessel Association v. Tollefson, 89 Wash. 2d 276 571 P.2d 1373 (1977).

Washington Trollers Association v. Kreps, 466 F. Supp. 309 (W.D. Wash. 1979), rev'd, 645 F.2d 684 (9th Cir. 1981).

Washington v. Washington State Commercial Passenger Fishing Vessel Association, 443 U.S. 658 (1979).

Watt v. Alaska, 451 U.S. 259 (1981).

West Virginia Division of Izaak Walton League of America Inc. v. Butz, 522 F.2d 945 (4th Cir. 1975).

White Earth Band of Chippewa Indians v. Alexander, 518 F. Supp. 527 (D. Minn. 1981).

Wilderness Society v. Hathaway, Civil No. 75-1004 (D.D.C. Jan. 26, 1976).

Winters v. United States, 207 U.S. 564 (1908).

Worcester v. Georgia, 31 U.S. (6 Pet.) 515 (1832).

Wyoming v. Hathaway, 525 F.2d 66 (10th Cir. 1975).

Wyoming Outdoor Coordinating Council v. Butz, 484 F.2d 1244 (10th Cir. 1973).

Zabel v. Tabb, 430 F.2d 199 (5th Cir. 1970), cert. denied, 401 U.S. 910 (1971).

Zieske v. Butz, 406 F. Supp. 258 (D. Alas. 1975).

# TABLE OF FEDERAL STATUTES

Act for the Preservation of American Antiquities, 16 U.S.C. §§431–443 (1976).
Administrative Procedure Act, 5 U.S.C. §§551–559 and 701–706 (1976).
Agriculture Appropriation Act of 1907, 34 Stat. 1269.
Airborne Hunting Act, 16 U.S.C. §742j–742l (1976).
Alaska National Interest Lands Conservation Act, Pub. L. No. 96-487, 94 Stat. 2371 (1980) (codified in scattered sections of 16, 43 U.S.C.).
American Fisheries Promotion Act, Pub. L. No. 96-561, Tit. II, pt. C, 94 Stat. 3296 (1980).
Anadromous Fish Conservation Act of 1965, 16 U.S.C. §757b (1976).
Animal Welfare Act, 7 U.S.C. §§2131–2155 (1976).
Bald Eagle Protection Act, 16 U.S.C. §§668–668d (1976 & Supp. V 1981).
Black Bass Act, 16 U.S.C. §§851–856 (1976) (repealed 1981).
Classification and Multiple Use Act of 1964, 43 U.S.C. §§1411–1418 (1976).
Clean Air Act of 1970, 42 U.S.C. §§7401–7642 (Supp. IV 1980).
Clean Water Act, 33 U.S.C. §§1251–1376 (Supp. V 1981).
Clean Water Restoration Act of 1966, Pub. L. No. 89-753, 80 Stat. 1246 (amended 1972).
Coastal Zone Management Act, 16 U.S.C. §§1451–1464 (1976 & Supp. V 1981).
Commercial Fisheries Research and Development Act, Pub. L. No. 97-389, 96 Stat. 1949.
Comprehensive Environmental Response, Compensation and Liability Act of 1980, 42 U.S.C. §§9601–9657 (Supp. IV 1980).
Endangered Species Act, 16 U.S.C. §§1531–1543 (1976 & Supp. V 1981).
Endangered Species Act Amendments of 1978, Pub. L. No. 95-632, 92 Stat. 3751.
Endangered Species Conservation Act of 1969, Pub. L. No. 91-135, 83 Stat. 275 (repealed 1973).
Endangered Species Preservation Act of 1966, Pub. L. No. 89-669, §§1–3, 80 Stat. 926 (repealed 1973).
Energy and Water Development Appropriation Act of 1980, Pub. L. No. 96-69, 93 Stat. 449 (1980).
Estuarine Areas Act, 16 U.S.C. §§1221–1226 (1976).
Federal Advisory Committee Act, 5 U.S.C. App. I (1976).
Federal Aid in Fish Restoration Act, 16 U.S.C. §§777–777k (1976 & Supp. V 1981).

Federal Aid in Wildlife Restoration Act, 16 U.S.C. §§669–669i (1976 & Supp. V 1981).

Federal Environmental Pesticide Control Act, 7 U.S.C. §§136–136y (Supp. V 1981).

Federal Insecticide, Fungicide, and Rodenticide Act, June 25, 1947, ch. 125, 61 Stat. 163.

Federal Land Policy and Management Act, 43 U.S.C. §§1701–1782 (1976 & Supp. V 1981).

Federal Noxious Weed Act of 1974, 7 U.S.C. §§2801–2813 (1976).

Fish and Wildlife Act of 1956, 16 U.S.C. §§742a–754 (1976 & Supp. V 1981).

Fish and Wildlife Conservation Act of 1980, 16 U.S.C. §§2901–2911 (Supp. V 1981).

Fish and Wildlife Coordination Act, 16 U.S.C. §§661–667e (1976).

Fish and Wildlife Improvement Act of 1978, Pub. L. No. 95-616, 92 Stat. 310.

Fishermen's Protective Act of 1967, 22 U.S.C. §1978 (Supp. V 1981).

Fishery Conservation and Management Act of 1976, 16 U.S.C. §§1801–1882 (1976 & Supp. V 1981).

Forest Reserve Act of 1891, ch. 561, §24, 26 Stat. 1103 (repealed 1976).

Forest Reserve Transfer Act of 1905, 16 U.S.C. §472 (1970).

Forest Service Organic Administration Act of 1897, 16 U.S.C. §475 (1976).

Fur Seal Act, 16 U.S.C. §§1151–1187 (1976).

Insecticide Act of 1910, ch. 191, 36 Stat. 331.

Intervention on the High Seas Act, 33 U.S.C. §§1371–1387 (1976).

Knutson-Vandenburg Act, 16 U.S.C. §576b (1976).

Lacey Act, 16 U.S.C. §§701, 3371–3378, and 18 U.S.C. §42 (1976 & Supp. V 1981).

Land and Water Conservation Fund Act, 16 U.S.C. §§4601-4604 through 4601-4611 (1976 & Supp. V 1981).

Marine Mammal Protection Act, 16 U.S.C. §§1361–1407 (1976 & Supp. V 1981).

Marine Protection Research and Sanctuaries Act, 33 U.S.C. §§1401–1444 and 16 U.S.C. §§1431–1434 (1976 & Supp. V 1981).

Migratory Bird Act of 1913, ch. 145, 37 Stat. 878 (repealed 1981).

Migratory Bird Conservation Act, 16 U.S.C. §§715–715d, 715e, 715f–715k, 715n-715r (1976).

Migratory Bird Hunting Stamp Act, 16 U.S.C. §§718–718h (1976 & Supp. V 1981).

Migratory Bird Treaty Act, 16 U.S.C. §§703–711 (1976 & Supp. V 1981).

Mineral Leasing Act, 30 U.S.C. §§181–287 (1976 & Supp. V 1981).

Mineral Leasing Act for Acquired Lands, 30 U.S.C. §§351–359 (1976).

Multiple Use–Sustained Yield Act of 1960, 16 U.S.C. §§528–531 (1976).

National Environmental Policy Act, 42 U.S.C. §§4321–4361 (1976).

National Forest Management Act, 16 U.S.C. §§1601–1614 (1976 & Supp. V 1981).

National Park Service Act, 16 U.S.C. §1 (1976).

National Wildlife Refuge System Administration Act, 16 U.S.C. §§668dd–668ee (1976 & Supp. V 1981).

North Pacific Halibut Act, 16 U.S.C. §§772–772j (1976).

Outer Continental Shelf Lands Act of 1953, 43 U.S.C. §§1331–1343 (1976 & Supp. V 1981).

Pacific Northwest Electric Power Planning and Conservation Act of 1980, 16 U.S.C. §§839–839h (Supp. V 1981).

Plant Patent Act, 35 U.S.C. §§161–164 (1976).

# TABLE OF TREATIES AND INTERNATIONAL AGREEMENTS

Agreement on the Conservation of Polar Bears, Nov. 15, 1973, T.I.A.S. No. 8409.
Antarctic Treaty, Dec. 1, 1959, 12 U.S.T. 794, T.I.A.S. No. 4780.
Convention Concerning the Conservation of Migratory Birds and Their Environment, Nov. 19, 1976, United States–U.S.S.R., 29 U.S.T. 4647, T.I.A.S. No. 9073.
Convention Concerning the Protection of the World Cultural and Natural Heritage, Nov. 23, 1972, T.I.A.S. No. 8226.
Convention for the Conservation of Antarctic Seals, June 1, 1972, 29 U.S.T. 441, T.I.A.S. No. 826.
Convention for the Establishment of an Inter-American Tropical Tuna Commission, May 13, 1949, 1 U.S.T. 230. T.I.A.S. No. 2044.
Convention for the Preservation of the Halibut Fishery of the North Pacific Ocean and the Bering Sea, March 2, 1953, United States–Canada, 5 U.S.T. 5, T.I.A.S. No. 2900.
Convention for the Protection of Migratory Birds, Aug. 16, 1916, United States–Great Britain (on behalf of Canada), 39 Stat. 1702, T.S. No. 628.
Convention for the Protection of Migratory Birds and Birds in Danger of Extinction, and Their Environment, March 4, 1972, United States–Japan, 25 U.S.T. 3329, T.I.A.S. No. 7990.
Convention for the Protection of Migratory Birds and Game Mammals, Feb. 7, 1936, United States–Mexico, 50 Stat. 1311, T.S. No. 913.
Convention for the Protection, Preservation and Extension of the Sockeye Salmon of the Fraser River System, May 26, 1930, United States–Canada, 50 1355, T.S. No. 918.
Convention for the Regulation of Whaling, Sept. 24, 1931, 49 Stat. 3079, T.S. No. 880.
Convention on Fishing and Conservation of the Living Resources of the High Seas, Apr. 29, 1958 [1966] U.S.T. 138, T.I.A.S. No. 5969, 559 U.N.T.S. 285.
Convention on International Trade in Endangered Species of Wild Fauna and Flora, March 3, 1973, 27 U.S.T. 1087, T.I.A.S. No. 8249.
Convention on Nature Protection and Wildlife Preservation in the Western Hemisphere, Oct. 12, 1940, 56 Stat. 1354, T.S. No. 981, U.N.T.S. No. 193.

# TABLE OF SECONDARY SOURCES

F. Anderson, NEPA in the Courts: A Legal Analysis of the National Environmental Policy Act (1973).

Anderson, The National Environmental Policy Act, in Federal Environmental Law 238–419 (E. Dolgin & T. Guilbert eds. 1974).

Andrews, Agency Response to NEPA: A Comparison and Implications, 16 Nat. Res. J. 301 (1976).

Arnold, The Substantive Right to Environmental Quality Under the National Environmental Policy Act, 3 Envtl. L. Rep. (Envtl. L. Inst.) 50028 (1973).

Baum, Negative NEPA: The Decision Not to File, 6 Envtl. L. 309 (1976).

Beaver, Herring, Sardines, and Foreign Affairs: Determination of Optimum Yield Under the Fishery Conservation and Management Act of 1976, 53 Wash. L. Rev. 729 (1978).

W. Blackstone, Commentaries.

Bleicher, The Impact of Superfund on Government Claims for Damages to Natural Resources, Envtl. Protection Rep. (Aug. 1981).

Blumm & Noble, The Promise of Federal Consistency Under §307 of the Coastal Zone Management Act, 6 Envtl. L. Rep. (Envtl. L. Inst.) 50047 (1976).

Blumm, Hydropower vs. Salmon: The Struggle of the Pacific Northwest's Fish Resources for a Peaceful Coexistence with the Federal Columbia River Power System, 11 Envt'l L. 211 (1981).

Brewer, Federal Consistency and State Expectations, 2 Coastal Zone Mgm't J. 315 (1976).

Butler, Federal Pesticide Law, in Federal Environmental Law 1232–1288 (E. Dolgin & T. Guilbert eds. 1974).

R. Carson, Silent Spring.

Chapman, The Theory and Practice of International Fishery Development-Management, 7 San Diego L. Rev. 408 (1970).

Christol, Schmidhauser & Totten, Law and the Whale: Current Developments in the International Whaling Controversy (work paper presented at the Seventh Conference on the Law of the World, 1975).

F. Christy, Alternative Arrangements for Marine Fisheries: An Overview (1973).

430

M. Clawson, America's Land and Its Uses (1972).

Coggins, Legal Protection for Marine Mammals: An Overview of Innovative Resource Conservation Legislation, 6 Envtl. L. 1 (1975).

Coggins, Wildlife and the Constitution: The Walls Come Tumbling Down, 55 Wash. L. Rev. 295 (1980).

Coggins & Hensley, Constitutional Limits on Federal Power to Protect and Manage Wildlife: Is the Endangered Species Act Endangered?, 61 Iowa L. Rev. 1099 (1976).

Coggins & Patti, The Resurrection and Expansion of the Migratory Bird Treaty Act, 50 U. Colo. L. Rev. 165 (1979).

Comment, Accommodation of Indian Treaty Rights in an International Fishery: An International Problem Begging for an International Solution, 54 Wash. L. Rev. 403 (1979).

Comment, Animals Ferae Naturae—Commonwealth Not Permitted to Recover Damages in Trespass for Negligent Killing of Fish by Pollution, 72 Dick. L. Rev. 200 (1967).

Comment, Closing the Mining Loophole in the 1964 Wilderness Act, 6 Envtl. L. 469 (1976).

Comment, Commentary Upon the IUCN Draft Convention on the Export, Import and Transit of Certain Species of Wild Animals and Plants, 21 Cath. U. L. Rev. 665 (1972).

Comment, Congressional Reaction to TVA v. Hill: The 1978 Amendments to the Endangered Species Act, 13 U. Richmond L. Rev. 557 (1979).

Comment, Criteria for Self-Executing Treaties, 1968 U. Ill. L. F. 49 (1968).

Comment, Endangered Species Act Amendments of 1978: A Congressional Response to TVA v. Hill, 5 Colum. J. Envt'l L. 283 (1979).

Comment, Federal Courts and Congress Review Tuna-Porpoise Controversy, 6 Envtl. L. Rep. (Envtl. L. Inst.) 10147 (1976).

Comment, Geothermal Energy Exploitation in Wilderness Areas: The Courts Face a Hot Issue, 4 Envtl. L. Rep. (Envtl. L. Inst.) 10119 (1974).

Comment, Geothermal Leasing in Wilderness Areas, 6 Envtl. L. 489 (1976).

Comment, Implementing §7 of the Endangered Species Act of 1973: First Notices from the Courts, 6 Envtl. L. Rep. (Envtl. L. Inst.) 10120 (1976).

Comment, Marine Mammal Protection Act and U.S. v. Mitchell: Disregarding the Moratorium?, 16 Urban L. Ann. 375 (1979).

Comment National Game Ranges: The Orphans of the National Wildlife Refuge System, 6 Envtl. L. 515 (1976).

Comment, NOAA's Marine Sanctuary Program, 2 Coastal Zone Mgm't J. 177 (1975).

Comment, Not Saving Whales: President Ford Refuses to Ban Fish Imports from Nations Which Have Violated International Whaling Quotas, 5 Envtl. L. Rep. (Envtl. L. Inst.) 10044 (1975).

Comment, State Regulation of Indian Treaty Fishing Rights: Putting Puyallup III Into Perspective, 13 Gonzaga L. Rev. 140 (1977).

Comment, The 200-Mile Exclusive Economic Zone: Death Knell for the American Tuna Industry, 13 San Diego L. Rev. 707 (1976).

Comment, The Back Bay Wildlife Refuge "Sand Freeway" Case: A Legal Victory in Danger of Political Emasculation, 5 Envtl. L. Rep. (Envtl. L. Inst.) 10148 (1975).

Comment, The Courts Take Flight: Scienter and the Migratory Bird Treaty Act, 36 Wash. & Lee L. Rev. 241 (1979).

Comment, The Fishery Conservation and Management Act of 1976: State Regulation of Fishing Beyond the Territorial Sea, 31 Maine L. Rev. 303 (1980).

Comment, The Migratory Bird Treaty: Another Feather in the Environmentalist's Cap, 19 S.D.L. Rev. 307 (1974).

Comment, Treaty-Making Power as Support for Federal Legislation, 29 Yale L. J. 445 (1920).

Commentary, Oil and Oysters Don't Mix: Private Remedies for Pollution Damage to Shellfish, 23 Ala. L. Rev. 100 (1970).

Council on Environmental Quality, Environmental Impact Statements: An Analysis of Six Years' Experience by Seventy Federal Agencies (March 1976).

Croom, The Tuna-Porpoise Problem: Management Aspects of a Fishery, reprinted in Marine Mammal Protection Act, Hearings before the Subcommittee on Fisheries and Wildlife Conservation and the Environment of the House Committee on Merchant Marine and Fisheries, 97th Cong., 1st Sess., ser. 97–98, at 102–146 (1981).

Dein, State Jurisdiction and On-Reservation Affairs: Puyallup Tribe v. Dept. of Game, 6 Envtl. Aff. 535 (1978).

Department of Commerce, National Marine Fisheries Service, Administration of the Marine Mammal Protection Act of 1972, 41 Fed. Reg. 30152 (July 22, 1976).

Department of Commerce, National Marine Fisheries Service, Final Environmental Impact Statement, Renegotiation of Interim Convention on Conservation of Fur Seals (1976).

Department of Commerce, National Oceanic and Atmospheric Administration, International Whaling Commission and Related Activities (July 1976).

Department of the Interior, Bureau of Land Management, Draft Environmental Impact Statement, Livestock Grazing Management On National Resources Lands (March 1974).

Department of the Interior, Bureau of Land Management, Second Report to Congress: Administration of the Wild Free-Roaming Horses and Burros Act (1976).

Department of the Interior, Bureau of Outdoor Recreation, Final Environmental Impact Statement, Nationwide Outdoor Recreation Plans (FES 73-69, 1973).

Department of the Interior, Fish and Wildlife Service, Conserving Our Fish and Wildlife Heritage, Annual Report—FY 1975.

Department of the Interior, Fish and Wildlife Service, Draft Environmental Statement on Proposed Injurious Wildlife Regulations (DES 75-6, Feb. 1975).

Department of the Interior, Fish and Wildlife Service, Environmental Assessment: Ratification of the Agreement on Conservation of Polar Bears (April 1975).

Department of the Interior, Fish and Wildlife Service, Federal Aid Manual (1973).

Department of the Interior, Fish and Wildlife Service, Final Environmental Statement, Operation of the National Wildlife Refuge System (Nov. 1976).

Department of the Interior, Fish and Wildlife Service, Final Environmental Statement for the Issuance of Annual Regulations Permitting Sport Hunting of Migratory Birds (FES 75-54, June 1975).

Department of the Interior, Fish and Wildlife Service, Environmental Statement: Operation of the Federal Aid in Sport Fish and Wildlife Restoration Program (1978).

Department of the Interior, Fish and Wildlife Service, Final Environmental Statement, Proposed Use of Steel Shot for Hunting Waterfowl, in the United States (Jan. 1976).

Department of the Interior, Fish and Wildlife Service, Fishery Rehabilitation of the Rock River (FES 75-42, 1975).

Department of the Interior, Fish and Wildlife Service, Final Environmental Statement, The Use of Compound PA-14 Avian Stressing Agent for Control of Blackbirds and Starlings at Winter Roosts (FES 76-39, 1976).

Durchslag & Junger, HUD and the Human Environment: A Preliminary Analysis of the Impact of the National Environmental Policy Act of 1969 Upon the Department of Housing and Urban Development, 59 Iowa L. Rev. 805 (1973).

Elliott, Federal Law and Population Control, in Federal Environmental Law 1518–1600 (E. Dolgin & T. Guilbert eds. 1974).

Erdheim, The Immediate Goal Test of the Marine Mammal Protection Act and the Tuna/Porpoise Controversy, 9 Envtl. L. 283 (1979).

Erdheim, The Wake of the Snail Darter, Insuring the Effectiveness of Section 7 of the Endangered Species Act, 9 Ecol. L. Q. 629 (1981).

Federal Water Pollution Control Administration, The National Estuarine Pollution Study (1969).

Ferenbaugh, Acid Rain: Biological Effects and Implications, 4 Envtl. Aff. 745 (1975).

Fish and Wildlife Service, Final Environmental Assessment, Subsistence Hunting of Migratory Birds in Alaska and Canada (1980).

Fish and Wildlife Service, Final Environmental Impact Statement, U.S. Fish and Wildlife Service's Mammalian Predator Damage Management for Livestock Protection in the Western States (1979).

Fish and Wildlife Service, Predator Damage in the West: A Study of Coyote Management Alternatives (Dec. 1978).

Friesma & Culhane, Social Impacts, Politics, and the Environmental Impact Process, 16 Nat. Res. J. 339 (1976).

Gaines & Schmidt, Wildlife Population Management Under the Marine Mammal Protection Act of 1972, 6 Envtl. L. Rep. (Envtl. L. Inst.) 50096 (1976).

General Accounting Office, Improved Federal Efforts Needed to Equally Consider Wildlife Conservation with Other Features of Water Resource Development (1974).

Gottschalk, A Sovereign Union of Sovereign States, in Council on Environmental Quality, Wildlife and America (1978).

Greenberg, Federal Consistency Under the Costal Zone Management Act: An Emerging Focus of Environmental Controversy in the 1980's, 11 Envtl. L. Rep. (Envtl. L. Inst.) 50001 (1981).

Guilbert, Wilderness Preservation I: A Recent Case and a Not-so-Recent Treaty, 3 Envtl. L. Rep. (Envtl. L. Inst.) 50023 (1973).

Guilbert, Wilderness Preservation II: Bringing the Convention into Court, 3 Envtl. L. Rep. (Envtl. L. Inst.) 50044 (1973).

Guilbert, Wildlife Preservation Under Federal Law, in Federal Environmental Law 550-94 (E. Dolgin & T. Guilbert eds. 1974).

Hagenstein, One Third of the Nation's Land—Evolution of a Policy Recommendation, 12 Nat. Res. J. 56 (1972).

Halter & Thomas, Recovery of Damages by States for Fish and Wildlife Losses Caused by Pollution, 10 Ecol. L. Q. 5 (1982).

Hardin, The Tragedy of the Commons, 162 Science 1243 (1968).

Hayes et al., State Recovery for Wildlife Destruction: New Life for an Old Doctrine, 2 ISL L. Rev. 13 (1977).

Hobbs, Indian Hunting and Fishing Rights II, 37 Geo. Wash. L. Rev. 1251 (1968).

Houck, The "Institutionalization of Caution" Under §7 of the Endangered Species Act: What Do You Do When You Don't Know? 12 Envtl. L. Rep. (Envtl. L. Inst.) 15001 (1982).

House Committee on Government Operations, Our Waters and Wetlands: How the Corps of Engineers Can Help Prevent Their Destruction and Pollution, H.R. Rep. No. 917, 91st Cong., 2d Sess. (1970).

Isherwood, Indian Fishing Rights in the Pacific Northwest: Impact of the Fishery Conservation and Management Act, 8 Envt'l L. 101 (1977).

Kumin, Substantive Review Under the National Environmental Policy Act: EDF v. Corps of Engineers, 3 Ecology L. Q. 173 (1973).

Lachenmeier, The Endangered Species Act of 1973: Preservation or Pandemonium, 5 Envtl. L. 29 (1974).

R. Liroff, A National Policy for the Environment: NEPA and its Aftermath (1976).

Lund, British Wildlife Law Before the American Revolution: Lessons from the Past, 74 Mich. L. Rev. 49 (1975).

T. Lund, American Wildlife Law (1980).

MacGrady, The Navigability Concept in the Civil and Common Law: Historical Development, Current Importance, and Some Doctrines that Don't Hold Water, 3 Fla. St. U. L. Rev. 513 (1975).

Margolin, Liability Under the Migratory Bird Treaty Act, 7 Ecol. L.Q. 989 (1979).

Marine Mammal Commission, The Concept of Optimum Sustainable Populations (undated).

McCloskey, The Wilderness Act of 1964: Its Background and Meaning, 45 Ore. L. Rev. 228 (1966).

McMahan, Legal Protection for Rare Plants, 29 Am. U.L. Rev. 515 (1980).

Megysey, Governmental Authority to Regulate the Use and Application of Pesticides: State vs. Federal, 21 S.D.L. Rev. 652 (1976).

Meyer, Travaux Préparatoires for the UNESCO World Heritage Convention, 2 Earth L. J. 45 (1976).

Miller, Anderson, & Liroff, The National Environmental Policy Act and Agency Policy Making: Neither Paper Tiger nor Straitjacket, 6 Envtl. L. Rep. (Envtl. L. Inst.) 50020 (1976).

Nafziger, The Management of Marine Mammals After the Fisheries Conservation and Management Act, 14 Willamette L.J. 153 (1978).

National Academy of Science, An Evaluation of Antarctic Marine Ecosystem Research (1981).

National Academy of Sciences, Pest Control: An Assessment of Present and Alternative Technologies (1975).

W. Nelson, The Laws Concerning Game (1962), in W. Sigler, Wildlife Law Enforcement (3d ed. 1980).

Note, Bureau of Land Management Primitive Areas—Are They Counterfeit Wilderness? 16 Nat. Res. J. 621 (1976).

Note, Endangered Species Act: Constitutional Tension and Regulatory Discord, 4 Colum. J. Envtl. L. 97 (1977).

Note, Federal Preemption: A New Method for Invalidating State Laws Designed to Protect Endangered Species, 47 U. Col. L. Rev. 261 (1976).

Note, Managing Federal Lands: Replacing the Multiple Use System, 82 Yale L. J. 787 (1973).

Note, Massey v. Appollonio: Is Residency an Impermissible Conservation Device?, 6 Envtl. L. 543 (1976).

Note, Obligations of Federal Agencies Under Section 7 of the Endangered Species Act of 1973, 28 Stat. L. Rev. 1247 (1976).

Note, State Control of Natural Resources, 66 Va. L. Rev. 1145 (1980).

Note, The Least Adverse Alternative Approach to Substantive Review Under NEPA, 88 Harv. L. Rev. 735 (1975).

Note, The Multiple Use–Sustained Yield Act of 1960, 41 Ore. L. Rev. 49 (1971).

Palmer, Endangered Species Protection: A History of Congressional Action, 4 Envtl. Aff. 255 (1975).

Parenteau, Unfulfilled Mitigation Requirements of the Fish and Wildlife Coordination Act, 42 N. Am. Wildlife Conf. Proc. 179 (1977).

Plimpton, Power of State to Designate Game Preserves, 6 Nat. Res. J. 361 (1966).

Power, The Federal Role in Coastal Development, in Federal Environmental Law 792–843 (E. Dolgin & T. Guilbert eds. 1974).

Predator Control—1971, Report to the Council on Environmental Quality and the Department of the Interior by the Advisory Committee on Predator Control (1972).

Prosser, Law of Torts (4th ed. 1971).

Public Land Law Review Commission, One Third of the Nation's Land (Government Printing Office, 1970).

Reed, Should Rivers Have Running? Toward Extension of the Reserved Rights Doctrine to Include Minimum Stream Flows, 12 Idaho L. Rev. 153 (1976).

Reiger, Song of the Seal, 7 Audubon 6 (Sept. 1975).

Restatement of Torts.

Review of the Animal Damage Control Program, U.S. Department of the Interior, Office of Audit and Investigation (No. E-FW-FWS-1-78, Nov. 1978).

Risebrough, The Effects of Pesticides and Other Toxicants, in Council on Environmental Quality, Wildlife and America (1978).

G. Robinson, The Forest Service: A Study in Public Land Management (1975).

Rosenberg, Regulation of Off-Road Vehicles, 5 Envtl. Aff. 175 (1976).

Savini, Report on International and National Legislation for the Conservation of Marine Mammals, Part I: International Legislation (Food and Agriculture Organization Fisheries Circular No. 326, 1974).

Sax, The Public Trust Doctrine in Natural Resource Law: Effective Judicial Intervention, 63 Mich. L. Rev. 471 (1970).

C. Schoenfeld & J. Hendee, Wildlife Management in Wilderness (1978).

Shipley, The Fish and Wildlife Coordination Act's Application to Wetlands, in A. Reitze, Environmental Planning: Law of Land and Resources (1974).

W. Sigler, Wildlife Law Enforcement (3d ed. 1980).

Sohn, The Stockholm Declaration on Human Environment, 14 Harv. Int'l L. J. 523 (1973).

Stone, Should Trees Have Standing—Toward Legal Rights for Natural Objects, 45 S. Cal. L. Rev. 450 (1972).

Swanson, Wildlife Conservation on Public Lands, in Council on Environmental Quality, Wildlife and America (1978).

Task Force of the Presidential Advisory Group on Anticipated Advances in Science and Technology, The Science Court Experiment: An Interim Report, 193 Science 653 (Aug. 20, 1976).

The Whale Problem: A Status Report (W. Schevill ed. 1974).

L. Tribe, American Constitutional Law (Supp. 1979).

U.S. Army Corps of Engineers, Draft Impact Analysis of the Corps Regulatory Program (1982).

U.S. Department of the Interior, Final Recommendations on the Management of the National Wildlife Refuge System (1979).

Wichelman, Administrative Agency Implementation of the National Environmental Policy Act of 1969: A Conceptual Framework for Explaining Differential Response, 16 Nat. Res. J. 264 (1976).

Wildlife Management Institute, Current Investments, Projected Needs & Potential New Sources of Income for Nongame Fish & Wildlife Programs in the United States (1975).

S. Yaffee, Prohibitive Policy: Implementing the Federal Endangered Species Act (1982).

Yarrington, Judicial Review of Substantive Agency Decisions: A Second Generation of Cases Under the National Environmental Policy Act, 19 S.D.L. Rev. 279 (1974).

Zener, The Federal Law of Water Pollution Control in Federal Environmental Law 682–791 (E. Dolgin & T. Guilbert eds. 1974).

# INDEX

437

# ABOUT THE AUTHOR

MICHAEL J. BEAN is chairman of the Environmental Defense Fund's Wildlife Program. From 1973 to 1976 he was associated with the Washington, D.C. law firm of Covington & Burling, and from 1976 to 1977 he served on the staff of the Environmental Law Institute.

Mr. Bean has published widely in the area of wildlife conservation. His articles and reviews have appeared in *Natural History,* the *Quarterly Review of Biology, Defenders, National Parks and Conservation Journal,* and the *Harvard Law Review.*

Mr. Bean holds a J.D. from Yale Law School and a B.S. from the University of Iowa.